INTRODUCTION
TO LABOR
ECONOMICS

INTRODUCTION TO LABOR ECONOMICS

FOURTH EDITION

ORME W. PHELPS

Senior Professor of Economics

Claremont Men's College

MC GRAW-HILL BOOK COMPANY

New York ● St. Louis

San Francisco ● Toronto

London ● Sydney

African Resting Place.

One man show.

Real Estate Exam.

ken.

6/23/72

Bayo. Oshinnaiye.

Bayo

INTRODUCTION TO LABOR ECONOMICS

ISBN 07-049777-X

567890 MP 74321

TO MY MOTHER AND SISTER

PREFACE

This is an introductory textbook in labor economics, intended for upper-division students (juniors or seniors) in liberal arts colleges or in professional schools of business administration, social service, or applied economics. It assumes that the student has had a course in economic principles. Ideally, the student of labor problems should have had training in a number of the formal social disciplines, such as economic analysis, law, government, statistics, and sociology. On the other hand, labor questions receive such wide publicity and are the subject of so much discussion and controversy that the problem of vocabulary is minimized and many of the important issues are common knowledge. In addition, a considerable portion of labor economics (as of all economics) is necessarily concerned with descriptive institutional material, for which only limited technical analysis is necessary. As a result, it is possible for students with slight backgrounds in the social studies to do good work, epecially if their interest and application are strong.

The distinguishing feature of labor economics is its heavy emphasis on policy. Since policy choices are related to issues, the major emphasis in this book will be to describe the principal labor issues and explain the methods of analysis which have been developed to handle them. It is well established that the study of labor, especially in its early stages, should be on a problem basis, since the questions raised will not in most cases yield to any single discipline (economics, law, sociology). To find reasonable answers to labor questions, it is necessary to use a variety of analytical methods and to weigh the outcomes—frequently in terms of highly subjective value preferences.

The difficulty with the problem method, in turn, is formlessness. Labor problems tend to shade off into population problems, welfare problems, management problems, or legal problems. It is one assumption of this book that the beginning student of the subject will be helped by a conscious attempt to "fence off" labor problems from other social-problem areas and to outline the particular conflicts of interest which create them. Consequently, the chapters which follow will concentrate on issues, principles, and trends. Factual data will be limited to those necessary to illustrate the problems and will be taken mainly from standard sources. The book is not intended as either a research treatise or an encyclopedia. Instead, the objective is a concise statement of the main problems growing out of the employer-employe relationship. The stress will be upon controversy, argument, and joinder of issues at all levels of analysis.

Facts and circumstances change rapidly, especially in economic matters. Short-term adjustments and proposed "solutions" to current labor difficulties are numberless. But the basic issues, with their moral, political, and economic implications, their theoretical propositions, and their fundamental conflicts of interest, shift much more slowly. An understanding of these issues and the methods developed for dealing with them is the best basis for evaluation of proposals in the constantly changing society of today.

I have the customary obligations to colleagues, associates, and students that go with any attempt to understand a subject matter well enough to teach it to others.

Orme W. Phelps

CONTENTS

Part Three. Full Employment

No Theory ? Labour Econs.

Part Four. Wages and Earnings

labor. The shorter-hours movement. The economics of minimum-wage laws. *Minimum-wage Enforcement.* Recent child labor violations. *Readings.*

PART ONE
LABOR
MARKET

ONE

THE
ART OF
CONTROVERSY

TO THE STUDENT

A job is a way of life, whether it be that of a United States senator or a janitor of an office building. It dictates where one spends his working hours (the mine, the shop, the courtroom, the office, the classroom), the hours to be worked, and the kind of people dealt with: customers, bosses, colleagues, subordinates, students, etc. In large part it settles the kind of clothes that can be worn, the language to be used, and the types of problems to be solved. The routines of a bus driver are not those of a salesman, a laboratory technician, a schoolteacher, or a corporation executive. More important, every job has a career factor; it represents security or insecurity, opportunity or the lack of it. There are many "dead-end" jobs, with little or no chance of movement up the scale—the only way to advance is to break out into a completely different line of work, a difficult decision and one that is harder to make with every passing year. On the other hand, many other jobs are simply stepping-stones in a promotional sequence. They have automatic progression built into them: the management trainee, the college instructor, the junior law clerk, and the second lieutenant.

When you get out of college, the way you live will probably be determined by the job you have.[1] Your job will be the main factor in such decisions as the kind of house you live in, the kind of car you drive, the way you entertain and spend your vacations, how you educate your children, how your budget is divided, and whether you spend all you make or save some. (Not entirely—some people make a budget go further than others, and it can be split up in different ways—but practically, a given level of income permits a given standard of living.) Most jobs have very definite, specific levels of earnings—the wage or the salary; other jobs,

[1] Or that your husband has.

3

however, have variable incomes, as a result of sales or profit-sharing bonuses, opportunities for extra earnings by writing or consultation (college professors), or work done on a fee basis, like that of doctors, lawyers, and accountants. Executives and supervisors in general have steady, regular work the year round. On the other hand, actors and entertainers work intermittently, as do cotton and grain buyers, building construction specialists, resort managers, and many others.

Your job will also affect importantly the kind of people you associate with. Many of your social contacts will be friends from the office, the company, the industry, or the profession. Lawyers tend to associate with lawyers, business executives with other business executives, junior executives with the younger management crowd, and trade unionists with other trade unionists. It will also set the pattern of life you lead: hours worked, time at and away from home, movement from one territory or section of the country to another. Outside salesmen travel a great deal as do many executives with broad territorial responsibilities. Junior (and sometimes senior) management personnel are often moved from one territory or branch to another; they can decline a transfer only at risk to their career. Plant production and maintenance supervisors may have to "work shift" and sleep in the daytime. Certain industries—shipping, railroading, trucking, newspaper publishing—force a special pattern of hours of work or travel upon large numbers of employes.

These are just a few of the ways that working for a living may affect you and your family; there are many others. If you are a supervisor or an executive—and the chances are that you will be—you will have the responsibility for making decisions that influence other people's lives: hiring, pay raises, promotions, transfers, disciplinary action, contract negotiation, and grievance bargaining. In this capacity you will discover just how complicated the labor market is—how many "interests" are involved in each decision and how strong are the feelings of those affected: the employe, management, other employes, the union, and now and then the government. At times, the decision will be clean-cut and easy: the best employe available for promotion, the transfer to which there is no objection, the shift assignment which the worker prefers and for which there are no competitors, etc. Very often, however, it will be clear that you cannot satisfy everyone (perhaps anyone), and you will have to do the best you can in a controversial situation.

This feature—controversy (dispute, disagreement, contention)—is the prime characteristic of labor relations and one of the reasons why it merits study, both as a preparation for practical affairs and as an intellectual exercise in its own right.[2]

---

[2] This is true of the social disciplines generally, especially economics and politics. However, of all the social disciplines, labor relations is the one most charged with tension, both in theoretical arguments and in practice.

CONTROVERSY

Controversy, rather than competition, is the true spice of life. The essence of controversy is dispute or disagreement, and the subject of the dispute is usually the right to ownership or control of something desirable, which may be anything from the presidency of a corporation [3] to a parking space. Controversy grows out of *competing interests* of great importance to the persons involved: their rank, income, status, security, wealth, or convenience.

The practical value of studying controversial material is the preparation it gives for dealing with the competitive aspects of life. To get a job, hold it, earn a promotion, operate a business, negotiate or administer a labor agreement, run for office, win at golf or tennis, or just keep up with the Joneses, often means beating out a number of competitors who have their eyes on the same goal. In a competitive society, with everyone "on the make," so to speak, the advancement and the reconciliation of competing interests have become a fine art, a day-by-day practical necessity, and one of the major keys to success. The usual solution is some form of compromise and the principal methods by which it is reached are competition under rules, bargaining, argument, persuasion (appeal to emotions, loyalties, prejudices), or submission to third parties (judge and jury) for settlement. If none of these works, force may be resorted to. Kept within bounds, a forced settlement may be a form of competition under rules; however, extralegal methods are often used by desperate persons faced with a possible loss of income, security, or repute. In the world of practical affairs, controversy cannot be avoided; it can only be adjusted to. The ways and means of adjusting are techniques of survival; they must be learned if one is to take part.

As an intellectual discipline, the study of controversial material is equally valuable. Just as students are trained in rigor of logical analysis in the natural sciences and in discrimination among values and tastes in the humanities, so in the social sciences they must learn to pick their way through disputed matters of fact, method, principle, purpose, and result to the conclusion which seems to offer the greatest probability of correctness. In labor economics, for example, it is not only possible, it is common, for two authorities to agree closely on a set of facts but reach quite different conclusions as to the meaning of the facts, as a result of preferences for alternative theories of explanation. If they agree upon the meaning of the facts, they may still differ in their judgments—whether good or bad, harmful or beneficial—if, as is often the case, they start from different

[3] Read, for example, Cameron Hawley's novel, *Executive Suite* (Boston: Houghton Mifflin Company, 1952); John P. Marquand, *Point of No Return* (Boston: Little, Brown and Company, 1949).

A life or committee without } pp. 9
controversy is very dormant. }

premises. If they agree in their judgments, they may still disagree violently in their policy recommendations. And to complete the cycle, in the great majority of the cases, there is dispute about the facts to begin with.

The reason for this is the wide range of choice open at every step of social analysis. The facts of the case are elusive, constantly changing, varying in degree of objective proof, and often debatable as to their relevancy. The theoretical systems available for analysis of the facts are fragmentary, disputed, and often logically unsatisfactory; the more precise and elegant their formulation, the further removed they seem to be from the occurrences of the market place or the political campaign. The basic premises (or value judgments) of liberals and conservatives or management and labor are often conflicting and at times seem irreconcilable. Any student might well be pardoned for concluding that if controversy is what gives life its seasoning, a steady diet of seasoning is nevertheless very wearing.

How then, in the face of such difficulties, is anything settled, and how does anything get done? The answer, on the practical level, is the techniques of adjustment developed in an open, free-contract society: competition, persuasion, bargaining, and compromise. The *formal* study of social problems makes a great contribution to this process by defining terms and analyzing issues, thus narrowing the areas of dispute. In labor relations, for instance, an agency like the Bureau of Labor Statistics of the U.S. Department of Labor gathers a tremendous number of facts each month, analyzes them statistically, and publishes the results in the *Monthly Labor Review*, either in the statistical tables at the back of the journal or in articles such as "Effects of Minimum Wage on Employment and Business," and "The Trade Union as an Organization." [4] The BLS (standard abbreviation for Bureau of Labor Statistics) also publishes a large number of special studies, in numbered bulletins and reports, such as *Prices: 1964*,[5] *Employment and Earnings Statistics for the United States, 1909–64*,[6] and many others. In another monthly journal, *Employment and Earnings*, the Bureau carries forward scores of monthly and yearly statistical series on the labor force, by age, sex, occupational and industrial classification, hours of work, hourly and weekly earnings, etc. These are primary, authoritative, official sources of information on the labor market in this country. The Consumer Price Index, for example, which is kept up to date in the *Monthly Labor Review*, is incorporated into union contracts covering millions of employes. Changes in the index affect the pay rates and earnings of a great many people.

The Bureau of Labor Statistics is the number one fact-gathering agency for labor-market data in this country, but it is just the beginning. There are scores of state and local agencies which gather and analyze and

[4] Issue of May, 1965, pp. 541, 497.
[5] BLS Report 291, 1965.
[6] Bulletin 1312-2, 1964.

publish labor-market information, as well as other Federal boards and commissions of great importance in labor matters: the National Labor Relations Board, the Federal Mediation and Conciliation Service, the National Railroad Adjustment Board, and so on. All of them collect employment data and publish various kinds of reports. (This kind of work, in fact, is a farily important career field for college graduates in economics, business administration, and statistics.) And in scholarly journals of business, economics, political science, psychology, and sociology, may be found labor articles of all sorts: arguments over wage and employment theory, field surveys and investigations, analyses of proposed policies, and evaluation of the results of those in effect.

Three major journals—*Industrial Relations, Industrial and Labor Relations Review*, and the *Labor Law Journal* [7]—and one annual volume, the *Proceedings of the Industrial Relations Research Association*, are devoted entirely to this kind of material. One of the first jobs of the serious student of labor economics is to become familiar with the major sources of the treatise literature as well as the current basic data of the labor market. He can do no better than to start with the above and the publications of the major institutes and centers for the study of industrial relations at the University of California (both Berkeley and Los Angeles), the University of Chicago, Harvard University, the University of Illinois, Massachusetts Institute of Technology, the University of Minnesota, Princeton University, Yale University, and others.

The employment relationship. The employment relationship is fundamentally controversial or contentious, since it brings a number of powerful competing interests into such direct and obvious conflict with one another. To begin with, it calls for a valuation of the services of human beings on a comparative basis. Now, just as very few students care to admit that they are poor scholars and overgraded, so very few employes judge themselves to be poor workmen or overpaid; the overwhelming majority have just the opposite opinion. The money they receive and the other perquisites of their jobs set the standard of living for them and their families. Either in a general way or sometimes very specifically—down to the last cent—they know how they are rated in comparison with other people doing the same job and other people doing different but related jobs. Almost without exception they expect to progress each year in rank, prestige, earning power, and security. A promotion for someone else, a merit increase passed over, or a reprimand on a service rating is a blow to these expectations. Either publicly or privately, they may question its fairness. To the individual employe—staff or line, management or rank-

[7] Published respectively by the Institute of Industrial Relations of the University of California (Berkeley); the New York State School of Industrial and Labor Relations, Cornell University, Ithaca, N.Y.; and Commerce Clearing House, Chicago 30, Ill.

and-file—his job and all that goes with it are intensely personal things, and he usually looks at them from a limited point of view.

If you are a manager, on the other hand, you represent the company and you must try for equity among the many different classes of jobs as well as among the people holding them. If you are typical, you will consider yourself both fair and generous. Your judgment of the value of one job relative to other jobs in the department or the company may differ from that of the worker doing the job, just as your judgment of his performance may depart widely from his own evaluation of his effort and efficiency.[8] No employer can pay all his employes all they want or even all they think they are worth—which may be the same thing. In every case, there is a limit to what can be done individually; yet it is a part of the necessity of maintaining an organization as well as a mark of fair play to reward superior effort. The only possible outcome of the conflict of interests between the employer (to whom wages are costs) and the employe (to whom wages are income) is a compromise, and many elements besides pay go into the framing of personnel policies that are acceptable: decent treatment, job security, opportunities for advancement, regularity of employment, handling of grievances, fringe benefits, and so on.[9]

Where employes are represented by unions, the struggle to resolve the controversy is often public and may become quite bitter. This is one type of situation where the techniques of compromise are put to the strongest test. If the union demands too much, it is refused and the union and its members face the choice of modifying their demands or going out on strike. Both the union and the employer may try to bluff, threaten, cajole, or persuade the other, or they may bargain—by either adjusting the wage demand or trading on some other point to make the total "package" acceptable. There may be (will be, in most cases) governmental intervention in the form of mediators trying to find a formula which will bring the union and the employer into agreement. In rare cases (in contract negotiations), to avoid a work stoppage, the two parties will turn the disputed matters—or some of them—over to a third party, an arbitrator, for final and binding settlement. Before this is done or before a new agreement is signed otherwise, the terms of the proposed contract will be put up to the union membership for ratification by majority vote.

In a sense, the whole process, including a strike if one occurs, is an

---

[8] You and the employe may in fact be in dispute as to just what job he has. There are many formal disagreements of this nature, known as "classification" disputes, which go into the grievance procedure and are resolved there or in subsequent arbitration.

[9] However, individual rulings on any of these matters affect other jobs and other employes. These decisions can seldom be handled in isolation any more. It is like moving one marble in a bowl; every other marble shifts position.

example of "competition under rules." At every stage of the proceeding there are formal regulations setting limits to the tactics which either party may use. The union may not call a "quickie" strike. Both the employer and the union must bargain in good faith. The union may not demand certain things prohibited by law (*e.g.,* "hot cargo" clauses). The employer may not discriminate against the union or its members in any way to influence the outcome. The union may not use secondary or hot-goods boycotts to bring pressure on third parties. If the dispute threatens the national health or welfare, the President of the United States is empowered to delay or halt a walkout while a public board investigates the issues.

These are some of the rules of competition in labor-management relations, just as there are rules limiting the price policies, product quality, and monopoly combinations of corporations under the interstate commerce, food-and-drug, and antitrust laws. There are a great many such rules in labor relations, some of them simple and easy to understand, others highly technical; they are constantly changing and are vigorously debated by the persons affected by them. One of the important things for the student to learn is the general outline of the "code of good conduct" in Federal and state law for the governing of industrial relations, how it has worked, and the principles underlying it.

Controversy is one of the main facts of life—not just in labor relations, but in family matters, business competition, domestic politics, and international affairs. However, there are few areas in which it affects as many people as directly, as pervasively, and as importantly as in employment. This is because the overwhelming majority of the population is supported by wages and salaries and not by self-employment on family farms or in family businesses as was true half a century ago. Today, five people out of six get their living by selling their services in the labor market; what that living is depends on the job, the industry, and the "structure" of the market wherein they work.

Market structure. There are many different jobs in many different industries in the United States. The *Dictionary of Occupational Titles* of the U.S. Employment Service lists more than 20,000 different occupations, and the standard industrial classification of the Bureau of Labor Statistics in its monthly report on the labor force [10] contains 36 major industrial groups, with 168 subclassifications, many of them very large industries in themselves. This coverage is not complete, as it omits the widespread area of employment by private individuals (not businesses): domestic servants in private homes, farm labor, staff members of private nonprofit institutions, and employes in the offices of self-employed professional men.

[10] In *Employment and Earnings.*

Neither does it include the several million persons in the armed services. Nevertheless, around sixty million people earn their living in one of these occupations and one of these industries.

Unfortunately, it cannot be said of the labor markets in the United States (or anywhere else, for that matter) that a job is a job is a job. Jobs differ, even when called by the same name and even when involving exactly the same duties. A clerical worker, for example, will find the market he works in quite different if he is employed by a railroad, a government agency, or an industrial corporation. To put it technically, the markets are "structured" differently. Market structure is the set of formal rules which determines how people qualify for jobs, get jobs, hold their jobs or advance in them, and what their rights are while employed. Market structure affects their base pay, overtime, job security, rights of transfer and promotion, leaves and other fringe benefits, their right to organize and bargain collectively, and their protection against discipline and discharge. The clerical worker used as an example above would enter the government civil service by competitive examination, be a union member on the railroad, and have very different pay and benefits patterns as well as promotional opportunities in the three different employments.

There are many different sets of labor-market rules. Professional employes qualify for jobs by meeting degree and certification requirements. A number of skilled occupations are open only to bona fide union members, who get their journeyman status by early and long apprenticeship. Entrance to the officer corps of the armed services is through the service academies, the ROTC, and officer candidate schools. Civil servants and employes on the seniority list in unionized industrial plants have tenure; that is, they may not be fired except for cause. All large corporations have a network of personnel policies which are standard practice throughout the company. The Federal and state and local governments have many important employment regulations which are represented by extensive labor codes administered by regulatory agencies. The key to understanding the labor market is a knowledge of market structures and the reasons for their existence. To help you reach such an understanding is one of the primary purposes of this book.

PRESSURES ON THE LABOR MARKET

The most important influences on the labor market in this country are private employers, unions, and the government. *Private employers* number 10 to 12 million and range from the shopkeeper employing one person part-time (on whose wages he must pay social security taxes) to the General Motors Corporation, with more than half a million people on its payroll. Most employers are very small, but a large proportion of all employes work for quite large firms. The personnel practices of these

large firms by now have a standard pattern and are the employers' contribution to labor-market structure. For many years, *employes* in this
country had little or no influence on the labor market; they could take
what they found or leave it alone, and if they did not like the employment
arrangement their sole recourse was to quit and find another job. This
situation changed quite abruptly, with the extension of labor organization
and collective bargaining during the 1930s and the first half of the 1940s.
Today, organized employes influence the labor market directly; their ideas
and wishes are embodied in union contracts which cover some 18 million
workers and influence directly or indirectly the wages and working conditions of several million others. The government is the third important
institution in the labor market, both as employer itself and as the regulatory agency which sets many of the rules for private employment. In both
capacities, public agencies have been extremely influential in the direction
of more formal employment contracts and the recognition of employe
rights.

The employment policies of private employers and of unions and the
governmental regulations affecting both are matters of much controversy.
The first two represent the interests of highly organized and articulate
groups, while the last is an attempt to referee the dispute—by legislation
and administrative control—in the interest of the general public. Since
both employers and employes are also members of the general public, the
issues are very involved and the compromises reached are seldom uniformly satisfactory. It is at this point—public policy in labor relations—
that the complexity of fact, issue, and result reaches a climax. No type of
legislation generates more heat in Congress than the proposal of a new
labor law or amendments to existing acts. It often takes years merely
to find out if the provisions of new labor legislation are constitutional or
what they mean in practice when applied to employers, employes, and
unions.

Private employers. Private employers influence the labor market
by setting the terms of employment. Except as limited by union contract
or by government regulation, they have a very free hand. Theoretically,
the private employer is restricted by the competition of other employers.
That is, he must pay the "going rate," meet the standard of working hours,
and provide reasonably similar working conditions and benefits, or he will
not be able to get people to work for him. This proposition, however, is
in itself highly controversial. If the theory is correct, it can be argued, the
exceptions are so numerous as to bring the rule into question. There are
low-wage and high-wage employers, employers with short and those with
long working hours, and employers who provide excellent working conditions while others leave much to be desired. All find people who are
willing to work for them, and it is yet to be proved that a significantly

different quality of personnel go to the more favored places of employment.

The result is great diversity. A laborer going to work on a farm may be paid $8 a day; [11] if he takes a factory job he will probably get at least $12 for 8 hours; while if he is employed in contract construction his rate will be $18 to $25 a day, depending upon the region and type of construction project. In most small firms and in practically all nonbusiness employment (domestic service, farm labor, etc.) the employer sets the rate and the pattern of the job. These are markets with very little structure in the sense of specific, enforceable rules for hiring, transfer, promotion, tenure, etc. What rules there are set by law (social security, minimum-wage) or found in the customary practices of employers; the latter may be varied at will without notice to or consultation with the employe.

In large firms, on the other hand, personnel practices of necessity become standardized. Handling large numbers of employes presents problems just as handling a large volume of merchandise or raw material does. The company must set specifications regarding ability, training, and experience, and it must apply tests of conduct and of adequate performance.[12] To a degree the large firms (1,000 or more employes each) may become self-contained individual labor markets, with very complete job and wage structures and formal policies which supervisors are to follow in all personnel matters.[13] If nonunion, the pattern will be set by the employer, but it is of necessity more stable than in the smaller organizations and less subject to modification by individual bargaining. If the company is organized (unionized), however, as most large industrial concerns are, the pattern will be jointly negotiated for employes covered by the labor agreement and the effects of the agreement will extend to employes outside the bargaining units.

Labor unions.   Unions are private (nongovernmental) organizations of employes set up for the express purpose of regulating the labor market. They exercise their control through written agreements with employers covering the terms of employment, through union work rules, and through restriction of the labor supply in certain occupations via the closed shop and limitations upon union membership. Unions have done more to formalize (structure) the employment relationship than any other kind of organization. The union contract has become the symbol of job security for millions of employes, and its influence extends far beyond the

[11] The United States average per hour without room or board in 1964 was $1.08. It ranged from $.75 in the South to $1.36 on the Pacific Coast. *Statistical Abstract of the U.S., 1965*, p. 244.

[12] See any standard textbook on personnel management for a review of the techniques of hiring, transfer, promotion, wage payment, etc.

[13] Around 17 million employes work in firms of this size.

actual contract coverage to a great many nonunion employes in the same firms or the same labor markets.

The labor movement in this country has a long and checkered history, running back to revolutionary days. Unions have had a hard fight to become legally acceptable (that is, to overcome such obstacles as the conspiracy doctrine and the labor injunction and to gain protection of the right to organize and bargain collectively), to convince the general public that employes have the same moral right to combine as employers, and to prove that collective bargaining will work in practice without detriment to the efficiency and profitability of private enterprise. Collective bargaining has had less than 30 years to mature in the United States and much of the controversy still to be found in union-management relations has its roots in the past. It is incumbent on the student to be aware of the principal issues and crisis points in labor history during the past hundred years. In the light of this background, the present-day pattern of industrial relations is more easily understood and has more meaning.

Among the many direct and indirect effects of unionism on the labor market, three may be singled out as of primary importance: *First*, it has given the employes a voice (and a vote) on matters affecting their jobs. Stated technically, it has put the organized employes on an "equal bargaining" basis with employers so that wages, hours, and working conditions are genuinely "negotiated" and not laid down unilaterally by management. *Second*, the employment contract has been expanded to cover many nonwage or "noneconomic" factors which are highly important to employes but which in the absence of a written agreement are administered freely and sometimes arbitrarily by the employer. Two examples are seniority rights in layoff and recall, promotion, etc., and job tenure—the protection against discharge except for just cause. *Third*, the negotiation of union contracts and their distribution to employes has brought about publicity where before there was much secrecy. The result has been a close scrutiny of relative wage rates for inequities, and comparisons of one agreement with another in regard to pay, security provisions, fringe benefits, etc. This has had a marked standardizing effect, both within firms and industries and between regions of the country. As the major institution representing the interests of the worker in a nation of employes, organized labor deserves careful study: its history, philosophy, methods of internal organization and operation, and its relations with employers, government, and the public in general.

Nevertheless, trade unionism as such still raises many controversial issues. Although it has been the policy of the United States since 1935 to protect the right to organize and to encourage collective bargaining and although almost a third of the employed labor force are union members, there remains strong opposition in many quarters to the extension of labor organization, and the purposes, methods, and results of collective bargaining are frequently called into question. Thus, while the legal basis of unionism seems relatively secure, its philosophical groundwork and practical effects are by no means fully accepted. A primary concern of those studying labor relations must be to sort out the issues involved, discover the implications of policy and practice, and reach the conclusions that their own system of value judgments dictates.

This will not be easy, and if the reader is honest with himself, he may be surprised to find that his conclusions in specific cases are inconsistent with more fundamental views which he holds (or thinks he holds) quite strongly. Almost no one is exempt from this kind of experience, and the exercise of reconciling logically conflicting steps in an analytical scheme is often fruitful and revealing. The one basic rule is not to mislead one's self. In labor relations, as in many other affairs of life, "advocacy," or loyalty on policy issues, is often a necessity. Nevertheless, the advocate should always start with the most clear-cut resolution of conflicting issues in his own mind, to find out where he stands and what are the strengths or weaknesses of opposing interests.

Another rule of almost equal importance is thoroughness. Labor issues arise in the context of the whole society. Few societies are as large, as complex, and as fluid as the United States in the last half of the twentieth century. The volume of data bearing on major issues such as wage policy, the impact of collective bargaining, full employment, and inflation is extremely large; the number of "interests" involved is manifold and various; and the manner in which they are affected is difficult to isolate and measure. Careful, systematic coverage of the pertinent data and points of view will not in itself guarantee correct answers, but without such thorough study it is almost certain that the conclusions reached will be one-sided and indefensible. This is especially true of questions of public policy.

Public policy. There is a Federal "code" of labor relations, consisting in the main of four laws—the Landrum-Griffin Act of 1959, the Taft-Hartley Act of 1947, the Norris–La Guardia Act of 1932, and the Railway Labor Act of 1926—plus the administrative regulations and court decisions resulting from them. In addition, the Federal government has adopted even broader policies governing employment in such legislation as the Employment Act of 1946, the Fair Labor Standards Act, and the Social Security Act.[14] Some of these—for example, the Taft-Hartley Act and the Landrum-Griffin Act—are so important and have such a direct bearing on labor relations that the student cannot escape responsibility for knowledge of the reasons for their passage, their major provisions, and results. They are therefore discussed extensively in the chapters which

[14] This is not intended as a complete list, and of course it omits entirely the extensive network of state legislation governing industrial relations and employment.

follow and the full texts of the laws are reproduced in the Appendices to Chaps. 8 and 9. 266 — 309

Labor law is a field of study in its own right, so extensive in terms of legislation, administrative regulation, and judicial review that even the specialists have trouble keeping up with developments. The beginning student should be aware of the major outlines of the Federal code, including the activities of the principal regulatory agencies (National Labor Relations Board, Federal Mediation and Conciliation Service, Wage and Hour and Public Contracts Administration, etc.), and the arguments and conclusions of the Supreme Court of the United States in some of its more influential labor decisions. Beyond this, he should let his curiosity be his guide.[15]

This is where labor-market controversy comes to a climax, with competing special-interest groups (the National Association of Manufacturers, the AFL-CIO, the Chamber of Commerce of the United States) pressing their views on legislators, courts, and board members. The presumed test is the general welfare, but there is seldom agreement on what promotes or advances the good of all. Higher minimum wages are opposed by employers and right-to-work laws are opposed by labor leaders, both on the grounds of the welfare of employes generally. Testimony based on wage theory is met with data collected in labor-market surveys. Facts are disputed, theories upheld and discredited, value terms such as "freedom," "security," "justice," and "opportunity" applied indiscriminately. In counterarguments, it may be asked: Freedom for what? Security and justice for whom? and Whose opportunity and what kind? Who is to say what is right, which arguments good, which specious? There are data enough and to spare to buttress any sort of proposition, and a theory to fit almost any set of facts. Yet choices must be made and policies decided on and administered.

The problem of choice.   Like the legislator, the jury, or the judge, the reader must learn to make choices among facts, principles, and reasoning. For example, his job is not just to learn a given set of facts—which will soon be outdated anyway—but to learn how to deal with the different classes and kinds of facts that appear regularly in labor-market analysis. There are a great many of these: statistical facts in all their ranges of variation—averages, samples, coefficients of correlation—descriptive facts,

[15] There are few areas of controversy that exceed in fascination the awards of labor arbitrators, the decisions and awards of the National Labor Relations Board, hearings on labor bills before Congress, and the reasoning of the courts in labor cases. For a taste of this kind of material, the student might sample the advance sheets of one of the big labor services published by the Bureau of National Affairs, Inc., Prentice-Hall, Inc., Commerce Clearing House, etc.

facts of choice based on subjective tastes and attitudes, facts on the record and facts not available in published form, historical facts, current facts, and statements based on predictions of the future. All economic writing is full of statements of fact, which may or may not be true or relevant and which must be judged by the appropriate standards of accuracy or cogency befitting the case.

Are they genuine enough?!

Theories are facts, as are value judgments. The reader's job is not to learn which theory is "so," but to learn to evaluate any systematic explanation of relationship on the basis of its presuppositions, its logical consistency, and its appropriateness to the data of the situation. In a similar manner, there is a wide range of value judgments to choose from, and the only imperative is that the student have some knowledge of the available alternatives and be aware of his own position and its bearing on his conclusions.

My Duty =

In actual practice, the problem of choice may not be as complicated nor as difficult as it sounds. Many people are at work on problems of labor-market analysis and as a result there is much agreement on the value and relevancy of many kinds of information and the explanations to which they lend themselves. In scholarly and official sources, particularly, the limitations of the data and the tentativeness of the conclusions are carefully emphasized for the reader. Debate and controversy have narrowed many issues and pointed up the alternative conclusions which may be reached. Last, most people have spent a lifetime dealing with somewhat similar problems of choice and have well-developed attitudes of skepticism toward pat answers and ready-made conclusions.

weigh

" Partiality

The study of labor economics is further training in the great game of weighing and measuring before deciding. The subject matter is important and the issues current and exciting—often too immediate in time and too closely related to actual experience for impartiality. However, there is nothing intrinsically wrong with partiality. Very few of us are free from bias or prejudice, since we all have vested interests growing out of our social background, our sources of income, or our investment in the training and experience necessary to hold a job or practice a profession. We expect a banker to think like a banker and his son to be influenced by his father's reasoning and experience; it is taken for granted that a union member will be prejudiced in favor of his union and that his son will be sympathetic toward collective bargaining. Farmers, lawyers, salesmen, and teachers have their own points of view, dictated by their occupational environment and needs, just as lathe operators, longshoremen, locomotive engineers, and assemblers have economic philosophies which grow out of the problems of work and job security.

It is nothing uncommon for people to equate the general welfare with the welfare of their own portion of the community. However, it may be slightly uncommon for a person to examine his own position on a disputed

"Controversy is the stimulant to livelihood."

issue in the light of his own special interests and then to try to decide if a policy in line with it will lead to the "greatest good of the greatest number." It is probable that the exercise alone, regardless of outcome, will be both thought-provoking and beneficial. It is recorded of Socrates that he said "the unexamined life is not worth living." Statistically, a great deal of the national life is spent in the labor market, and individually, the same is true for each of the 75 million members of the labor force. Since you will probably be deeply involved in the labor market before long, if you are not already, there is nothing to lose and much to gain from an investigation of how it works and why.

TWO

THE
UNITED STATES
LABOR FORCE

The United States is a nation of employes, with that part of the population which "has a job" growing steadily larger, both in absolute numbers and in proportion to the whole. These are the wage and salary workers, and there are about 65 million to 70 million of them, depending on the season. They are not the total labor force, nor even the entire civilian labor force. The civilian labor force includes self-employed persons (farmers, businessmen, doctors, etc.) plus the unpaid family workers who do not receive a wage or a salary; the total labor force takes in also the 3 million or more members of the armed services. However, for many years, employes have been becoming a larger fraction of the total. Today, at least five out of six people who are gainfully employed work for a wage or a salary on a farm, in a private home, or in a business firm, a government agency, or a nonprofit corporation.

The "labor force" concept is not a simple one, either to measure or to understand. It does not stand still, even from day to day, and it has a number of other dimensions besides those noted above: the "potential" versus the "actual" labor force, for example, or the transient versus the permanent, the agricultural versus the nonagricultural, those at work and those unemployed, and so on. These groupings are a part of the basic pattern of the labor market.[1] The differing interests they represent give rise to many issues and controversies—over pay, hours of work, regularity of employment, government regulation, and the effects of policies pursued by employers and labor unions.

The labor force, however, is not something apart; it is a product of the population of the country, and some labor problems are related directly to the population issue, to wit: (1) Population is the place the labor

[1] This pattern is most completely outlined each month in the BLS journal, *Employment and Earnings and Monthly Report on the Labor Force*. This is the bible of labor-force statistics, and every student of the subject should be familiar with it.

supply comes from, and it therefore determines the quantity and quality of personnel available for the work force. (2) The size and composition of the population are important factors in setting the average standard of living, which is the employe's real wage. (3) The most celebrated theory of population, that of Malthus, was made the basis of an equally celebrated (or notorious) theory of wages, Ricardo's subsistence theory, or the "iron law" of wages, as it was styled by critics.

THE POPULATION EXPLOSION

Resources versus population. If any single problem can be said to be *the* labor problem, inclusive of all others, it is the question of the average standard of living. Certainly, that is the major concern from an economic point of view. The per capita standard of living, by definition, is the output of goods and services divided by the number of people in the area. The output of goods and services is, in turn, limited by the resources available for processing and distribution. This brings us to the basic economic ratio, which fundamentally determines the level of prosperity of any people, whether they be a tribe, nation, continent, or world. This ratio is simply the ratio of resources to population, which may be expressed as *resources/population.* If resources are large but the population also large, the standard of living may still be very low, as in China. If resources are very low, even a small population may have to live close to the subsistence level, as in the Sahara Desert.

Resources are of various kinds. Since food and clothing are the primary necessities of life and since most human food and clothing comes from agricultural sources, either directly or indirectly, the number one world resource is arable land. It is a very instructive exercise to compare the ratios of acres of arable land per person in a few of the leading nations of the world, such as the United States, the U.S.S.R., Great Britain, China, and the Argentine. However, an industrial civilization does not rely on agriculture entirely, or even primarily, for its wealth and income. In the United States, for example, one of the leading agricultural producers of the world, farm employment and income account for less than 20 per cent of the national total. Much of the remainder comes from the extraction and processing of metals, fuels, stone, sand, and timber, particularly the minerals. Arable land, timber, water power, and mineral deposits are the principal natural resources of an industrial society. A number of modern nations have built up and kept a relatively high standard of living in spite of a shortage of land, since they had large supplies of a few important minerals. An example is Great Britain, with her iron ore and coal.

Natural resources are those laid down by nature without the aid of man. Some, like arable land, are not used up in the process of production, and their quantity and productivity may even be increased by measures

like irrigation, fertilization, etc. Others, like timber deposits, are re-
placeable—but slowly—and require careful conservation. Still others, the
minerals especially, are exhaustible and in some cases appear to be approaching the scarcity level. Exploration and discovery which produce
new deposits or new uses for old deposits are the only means of extending
the supply. By and large, it is these natural resources, relatively fixed in
quantity, which people have in mind when they refer to the "numbers/
resources" or "man to land" ratio as essentially determining the standard
of living.

It is a fact, however, that the output of the "means of subsistence,"
which is derived from the natural resources referred to above, has risen
and continues to rise from year to year. This increase comes about because
of the accumulation of certain "artificial" resources, of which there are two
main kinds. The first consists of invested capital of all kinds: factories,
office buildings, railroad systems, equipment, tools, power plants, and the
like. The second is the technical and scientific knowledge of the population itself. Both of these must be entered on the "resources" side of the
ratio, since they directly increase the production of goods and services
from a given quantity of natural resources. It is a moot question, but one
which enters into all sorts of arguments over population theory and policy,
as to what rate of increase of the means of subsistence is possible in the
face of fixed quantities of land and declining mineral resources.

People, people, people.   Whether basic natural resources are increasing (as a result of new discoveries), decreasing, or holding their own
is a point open to argument. There is no argument, on the other hand,
with respect to population. The population of the world, of each of the
continents, and even that of most countries, has been mushrooming during
the twentieth century. In the 250 years, 1650 to 1900, the world's population multiplied three times, from 465 million to 1,551 million; however,
between 1900 and 1964 it doubled again, from 1,551 million to 3,220 million. The actual numerical increase in those 64 years—of 1,670 million
—was one and one-half times as much as for the preceding 250 years:
1,086 million. The population of the North American continent increased
from 106 million to 286 million, South America from 38 million to 162
million. The Asian continent, already in 1900 the home of more than half
the world's people, again more than doubled in size from 859 million to
1,783 million. Africa, the most underdeveloped of areas, more than doubled in number of inhabitants. Table 2-1 shows the changes for selected
periods by continental divisions, from the middle of the seventeenth century to the middle of the twentieth.

The most significant feature of world population growth has been
the rise in the *rate* of increase. For each of the four 50-year periods from
1750 to 1950, there was an absolute increase in numbers, and the rate of

**Table 2-1.   Estimated population of the earth by continents, 1650–1964
(In millions)**

Continent	1650	1750	1800	1850	1900	1950	1964
Europe	100	140	187	266	401	396*	440
Asia	250	406	522	671	859	1,272*	1,783
Africa	100	100	100	100	141	198	304
North America	7	6	15	39	106	216	286
South America	6	6	9	20	38	110	162
Oceania	2	2	2	2	6	13	17
U.S.S.R.						193	228
Total	465	660	835	1,098	1,551	2,398	3,220

* Excluding the U.S.S.R.

Source: *Demographic Yearbook, 1951,* cited in *The World Almanac, 1953,* p. 387 (New York: New York World-Telegram and Sun, 1953). Figures for 1964 estimated by Statistical Office of the United Nations; in *The World Almanac, 1966,* p. 379.

increase also went up. For example, from 1750 to 1800, the population increase was 175 million and the rate of increase 27 per cent. Between 1800 and 1850, population rose 263 million, which was at a rate of 31 per cent. In the next half century, with the Industrial Revolution under way, the absolute increase was 453 million, a 41 per cent rise from the preceding base. And in the first half of the twentieth century, the rise in numbers was 847 million, the rate of increase 55 per cent. During the 14 years from 1950 to 1964, there was another increment of 822 million (about equal to the combined populations of *all* of Europe, *all* of North America, plus Argentina and Brazil), which was at the rate of *140 per cent* increase per half century. If continued until the year 2000, this would mean doubling of the 1964 population to a world total of around 6.5 billion.

At one time or another the rapid increase of world population or the population of a certain country has agitated both scholars and public officials, with the result of stirring up lively controversy over theories and policy proposals. The main concern has been over standards of living, and several of the theories have been incorporated directly into explanations of wages or economic inequality.

✝ *The Malthusian dogma.*   The most celebrated theory of population and the starting point of all discussions of population theory is that contained in *An Essay on Population,* by Thomas Robert Malthus.[2] In essence, Malthus maintained that there was a natural law of population

---

[2] Malthus rewrote his *Essay* several times, with each edition getting longer and more tedious. The best edition for the beginner to read is the first, entitled *An Essay on the Principle of Population, as It Affects the Future Improvement of Society, with Remarks on the Speculations of Mr. Godwin, M. Condorcet, and Other Writers* (London: Macmillan & Co., Ltd., 1926).

which doomed the great majority of the people of the world to an existence at the bare level of subsistence. The two principal elements in his population law were (1) a growth factor, consisting of the urge to reproduce; and (2) a limitation factor, resulting from the slower rate of increase of the means of subsistence. He expressed these ideas dramatically in mathematical form, saying that population tended to increase by geometrical progression, while the means of subsistence grew by arithmetical progression. Starting from unity, population would thus rise 1, 2, 4, 8, 16, 32, 64, while the means of subsistence would increase at the slower rate of 1, 2, 3, 4, 5, 6, 7. As the two rates of increase are fundamentally incompatible, Malthus came to the conclusions (1) that population is necessarily limited by the means of subsistence, (2) that it invariably increases when the means of subsistence increase, unless (3) it is prevented by the checks of moral restraint, vice, or misery.

Malthus did not state how he arrived at his rates of progression or why some members of the population, the upper classes, were exempt from the operation of the law. A major, unstated premise upon which his argument rested was the assumption that the urge to marry, have children, and bring up families was a nonrational factor of such overpowering force that it could never or only seldom be modified on rational (economic) grounds. The policy conclusions that Malthus arrived at were: (1) Communism is unworkable, since private property and its accompanying responsibility is the only humanitarian check which will keep families within limits. (2) The working classes can improve their conditions only by reducing their numbers. (3) Poor relief defeats its own purpose, since it removes the principal check (of want) from those guilty of producing more children than they can support.

This was a very depressing view and was immediately and vigorously criticized, as well as defended, from all sides. Critics concentrated on the assumption of a "natural law," the lack of proof of the rates of progression cited, and Malthus's relative indifference to the possible effects of a rise in the standard of living on family size, all of them very vulnerable points in the presentation. On the other hand, very few persons have questioned the main point in the argument, that population tends to encroach upon the means of subsistence and that the latter sets a final limit to the growth of the former. A number of very able thinkers have pointed out that in the long run—and a population theory can be only a long-run theory—the propositions contained in Malthus's essay are hard to explain away.[3]

---

[3] Consult, for example, the quotations from J. M. Keynes and Dean Inge in Harold Wright, *Population* (New York: Harcourt, Brace & World, Inc., 1923), pp. 55–57. The gloomy views of Keynes and Inge were expressed in 1919, at the end of the First World War; they are even more appropriate to the situation today, with a world population explosion accompanying the "revolution of anticipations" in underdeveloped countries.

Two Englishmen were impressed by Malthus's reasoning—Francis Place, the reformer, and David Ricardo, the economist. The former accepted the warning without the principle (that it was a "natural law" and that nothing could be done about it) and immediately instituted a campaign for birth control, which has come to be known as "neo-Malthusianism." The latter adopted the theory whole, simply reexpressing it in the form of wages, to the effect that in the long run wages tend to the level which barely supplies working people with the means of subsistence and that temporary departures therefrom on the up side will be compensated for by an increase in births, which will force the wage down again, while short-run reductions below the subsistence level will have the obvious effect of eliminating the surplus population, thereby bringing the population and the means of subsistence once more into agreement.

No wage theory has ever been more bitterly attacked or more completely rejected by its opponents than Ricardo's "iron law," notwithstanding the fact that the overwhelming majority of the world's population has always lived at or near the starvation level, that even in the Western civilized world probably a majority of working-class families have no savings or surplus of any kind, and that, as national incomes have increased, the most noticeable effect has been the increase in numbers of people rather than the rise in individual living standards. The facts are admitted, but the theory is denied. Rather, the blame is placed on the existing social, political, and economic institutions.

The optimum theory of population.   Malthus's theory was not the only "natural" theory of population growth, but it was far and away the most influential. It has been countered by theories based on the social or institutional environment, in which the prevailing note is a determined optimism that man's future numbers are controllable and that a favorable solution may be expected, either from conscious manipulation of the institutional environment (Karl Marx, Henry George, and others) or from an unconscious choice of smaller families and a consequent higher standard of living (Carr-Saunders and Dumont).

Probably the most carefully formulated such theory is the "optimum" theory of A. M. Carr-Saunders. According to this hypothesis, man always endeavors to reach the optimum economic balance within his environment, "the number which—taking into consideration the nature of the environment, the degree of skill employed, the habits and customs of the people concerned, and all other relevant facts—gives the highest average return per head."[4] Carr-Saunders finds the evidence for his conclusions in the voluntary adoption of the "small family system" in Europe, the British dominions, and the United States, through the medium of birth

[4] *The Population Problem* (Fair Lawn, N.J.: Oxford University Press, 1922), p. 476.

control, mainly by contraceptive practices. In fact, the "optimum" theory is substantially an affirmation of the triumph of the neo-Malthusianism of Francis Place, plus some elements of Dumont's theory of "social capillarity." [5] The author's explanation of the small family system is as follows:

Birth control can be held to explain sufficiently the facts of the decline of the birth-rate within the sphere of European civilization. . . .

That contraception, having once become established, should have spread, requires no explanation. There has been unceasing propaganda in its favour; it became associated with the powerful movement for women's rights, and was taken up with religious fervour by some advocates with a gift for publicity. . . . The small family fits in, not only with the enduring wishes of the mother, but also with the new mode of life. The last sixty years have seen an immense increase in leisure time, and a still greater increase in facilities for employing that leisure; and children are impediments to those who want to avail themselves of these facilities. In relation to making a living children are now seldom a help and are often an encumbrance. Finally, the effort to rise in the social scale may well be frustrated by a large family.

The evidence is that, once the small family system has gained a hold, it continues to spread. [6]

Somewhat surprisingly, Carr-Saunders finds that the spread of birth control has been uninfluenced by density of population, industrialization, or variation in economic conditions. "There is in general," he observes, "no association between the decline [of the birthrate] and material welfare." How then does he explain the spread of the small family system? By imitation:

The countries to which the habit first came were . . . associated in sharing a similar mode of life, a fact sometimes expressed by saying that they had reached a fairly similar level of civilization. They used the same mechanisms and contrivances, they adopted very similar clothes and ate very similar foods. Moreover, they observed similar social conventions and fashions. . . . There can be little doubt that the practice of family limitations spread over this group of closely associated countries much as so many other novel habits and new ideas spread. The small family habit came later to southern Europe, and still later to eastern Europe, because the countries in these regions stood, in respect of general level of civilization, rather apart from the group of countries in northwest Europe and in Europe overseas. But they are European also, and just as the more trivial habits and conventions of western Europe were taken up by them in course of time, so the more important novel habits, and among them the small family system, were also adopted by them, although later than in the west.

[5] The Dumont theory rests on the premise that all people try to rise to higher social levels and, as they succeed, are less and less likely to reproduce themselves. In countries where there are few obstacles to movement from one social class to another, social capillarity is greater and the birth rate suffers most (*e.g.*, France). In caste countries, such as India, where capillarity is low, there is no tendency for the birth rate to decline or for the population to die out.

[6] A. M. Carr-Saunders, *World Population: Past Growth and Present Trends* (Fair Lawn, N.J.: Oxford University Press, 1936), pp. 105, 111, 113, 326.

These conclusions were expressed in England in 1936. It is doubtful that the same easy optimism prevails—for the world at large—after another generation of war, depletion of resources, and population growth. Malthus has recently been restated in very emphatic terms by several scientists, who find little evidence that the human race is effectively limiting its numbers.[7]

Whatever else it may have accomplished, Carr-Saunders's theory raised the question of the "optimum" (best, most favorable) population in economic terms, which means a population total in balance at the point of "maximum economic welfare." If the optimum is to be attained anywhere in the world, it will probably be up to the United States to set the example.

POPULATION GROWTH IN THE UNITED STATES

The population of any country is the source from which its work force is drawn. As such it is a major economic resource. The social organization required by a large industrial output makes severe demands upon the labor force in terms of energy, self-discipline, and cooperation. The gross national product will be significantly influenced by the size of the population, its age distribution, the level of its education and technical training, and its geographical location.

The population upsurge in the United States. In matters of population growth, as in other departments of activity, the United States has been the wonder of the world. In the 170 years between the First Census in 1790 and the Eighteenth in 1960, total inhabitants multiplied 46 times, from 3,929,000 to 178.5 million, while the gross area (land and water) increased four times. There was a steady rise in population every decade, with a constantly growing absolute increment until interrupted by the First World War and the depression decade of the 1930s. In 1940, the incremental rise was resumed. The percentage increase of the 1950s was the greatest since the 10 years 1900 to 1910, and the absolute growth of 27,766,875 gave a hint of what the future might hold. The total population by census periods, the absolute and percentage increases by decades, and the rising man-land ratio are shown in Table 2-2.

No other official agency in the United States has been more fantastically wrong in its estimates of future growth than the Census Bureau, nor has any been more reluctant to adjust to new trends. In 1947, the official Census Bureau estimate, based on medium fertility, medium mortality, and no net immigration, showed a *maximum* population of 164,585,000,

[7] See, for example, Robert L. Heilbroner, *The Great Ascent* (New York: Harper & Row, Publishers, Incorporated, 1963—Harper Torchbooks, TB 3030), pp. 54–57, 85, 88–94.

Table 2-2.   Population increase in continental United States, 1790–1965

Census date	Population	Increase over the preceding census		Population per sq. mi. of land
		Number	Per cent	
1790	3,929,214			5
1800	5,308,483	1,379,269	35	6
1810	7,293,881	1,931,398	36	4
1820	9,638,453	2,398,572	33	6
1830	12,866,020	3,227,567	34	7
1840	17,069,453	4,203,433	33	10
1850	23,191,876	6,122,423	36	8
1860	31,443,321	8,251,445	36	11
1870	39,818,449	8,375,128	27	13
1880	50,155,783	10,337,334	26	17
1890	62,947,714	12,791,931	26	21
1900	75,994,575	13,046,861	21	26
1910	91,972,266	15,977,691	21	31
1920	105,710,620	13,738,354	15	36
1930	122,775,046	17,064,426	16	41
1940	131,669,275	8,894,229	7	44
1950	150,697,361	19,028,086	14	51
1960	178,464,236	27,766,875	18	50.5*
1965	194,032,000	15,568,000	9	54*

* Alaska and Hawaii added.
Source: U.S. Bureau of the Census, *Statistical Abstract of the U.S., 1965*, p. 5.

to be reached by the year 1990.[8] This estimate proved to be in error by 35 years or 75 million population, depending on the date used for comparison. The population reached and passed 165 million in 1955; by 1990, current forecasts by the Census Bureau indicate a population in excess of 240 million. Hence, the protests of statisticians like Joseph S. Davis, of the Food Research Institute, Stanford University, began to sound realistic.[9] There was a hasty reshuffling of trend lines, and a new set of projections came forth. The latest guess, extending to 1980, gives the reader his choice of two series, depending upon his optimism about the continuance of the high postwar birthrates. The more reliable of the projections, in terms of current fit (Series III), gives the result shown in Table 2-3.

The Census Bureau's readjustment did not come easily, however. Consider the year 1970. In 1947, total population for 1970 was forecast

[8] *Forecasts of the Population of the United States, 1945–1975*, U.S. Bureau of the Census, p. 39 (1947).

[9] Joseph S. Davis, *The Population Upsurge in the United States*, War-Peace Pamphlet 12 (Stanford: Stanford University Food Research Institute, December, 1949).

Table 2-3.   Forecasts of total population of the United States, 1960-1980

Year (July 1)	Population
1960	180,677,000
1965	194,454,000*
1970	208,931,000
1975	225,963,000
1980	245,736,000

* Almost precisely what the preliminary releases for early 1965 showed.
Source: *Statistical Abstract of the U.S., 1963*, p. 6.

at 159,847,000; six years later (1953), the estimate was revised upward to 196,269,000, an increase of 36 million.[10] By 1958, only 5 years further on, the comparable estimate was 208,199,000, a further jump of 12 million. Since it is now a certainty that total United States population will pass 200 million several years *before* 1970, what the next 30 years will produce becomes a matter of speculation. One highly qualified guesser whose predictions are becoming more pertinent every year is Joseph S. Davis, cited previously. Davis said, 15 years ago:

Considering that our population passed 156 million early in 1952, in the year 2000 it is likely to be between 200 and 300 million, and an excess over 300 million seems to me as conceivable as a falling short of 200 million. . . . This revised prospect may seem pleasing to some, appalling to others. For better or worse our economic, political, and social problems will be radically different from what the former outlook had led us to expect.[11]

A population policy for the United States?   The figures and estimates given above show the trend. The reader might try his hand at extrapolation (meaning hypothetical extension of a statistical series) and see where he comes out. For example, during the twentieth century the United States population seems to be doubling every 50 years: 1900—75 million, 1950—150 million, 2000—(300 million-plus?). If this keeps up, the figure for 2050 will be something over 600 million.[12] Is this good, bad, or indifferent? And if it seems, as Davis said, "appalling," what can or should be done about it?

In June, 1965, the newspapers announced that 78 Nobel Prize winners had signed two letters to Pope Paul VI asking that the Roman Catholic Church carefully reconsider its ban on artificial birth control. In the same issue it was reported that the United States Senate "broke historic

[10] Population Estimates, Series P-25, No. 78, Aug. 21, 1953.
[11] In *American Economic Review*, June, 1952, pp. 314–315.
[12] There are other formulas for extrapolation, of course, some of which produce larger and some, smaller, totals.

ground . . . by opening the first congressional inquiry into the politically touchy issue of whether the Federal government should supply birth control information." However, "the biggest push toward involving the government in efforts to curb the world's population explosion came from former President Dwight D. Eisenhower. In an admitted reversal of the views he held while President, Gen. Eisenhower said if the government ignores the problem of population growth 'then history will rightly condemn us.' " [13]

Should the United States have a population policy? And if so, what should it be? Is there an optimum (best) size for the population of this country? Is it 200 million (about where we are now)? 300 million (where we are likely to be by the beginning of the twenty-first century)? 400 million? 500 million? No question could be more controversial, and perhaps none is more important. The policy issue is in part theoretical; a Malthusian is likely to have a very different view of the policy question than a follower of Carr-Saunders. (Incidentally, what would be the difference in policy positions, and why?) In part, the decision would rest on value judgments: the desirability of different national and world population totals, the moral issue of interference with life processes (the religious view), attitudes toward government intervention in intimate family decisions, etc. Then, as Davis pointed out, there are major economic, social, and political problems as well.

To date, the United States is the classic example disproving Malthus: an exploding population with steadily rising per capita income and standards of living. Between 1941 (when the present population boom began) and 1965, per capita income rose from $870 to $2,655. Per capita *real* income (in 1954 prices) went from $1,645 to $2,200, a rise of $555, or almost exactly one-third. The economic question is: Will the rise continue as population moves to 300 million? 400 million? 600 million?

Our immigration policy. It may come as a surprise to some to realize that the United States already has a population policy, and a restrictive one at that. A considerable portion of the fall in the rate of increase of population in the 1930s was due to the choking off of immigration, one of the few positive population policies adopted in the United States and remarkable for the fact that it was restrictive in nature. In general, a national population policy has meant only one thing: a program of expansion. This has been equally true of aggressive nations—Italy, Germany, and Japan prior to the Second World War—and those of more peaceful inclination, *e.g.*, France, Belgium, Sweden, and Great Britain. Restriction of immigration was both a population and a labor policy. It was first urged and finally adopted on the primary grounds of support of

[13] *Los Angeles Times,* June 23, 1965, pp. 1, 7.

Table 2-4.   Population growth in the United States by sources of new arrivals, 1900–1960
(In thousands, figures rounded)

Census period	Population increase	Source		Per cent increase	
		Birth	Immigra-tion	Birth	Immigra-tion
1900–1910	15,980	7,180	8,800	45	55
1910–1920	13,740	8,000	5,740	58	42
1920–1930	17,060	12,950	4,110	76	24
1930–1940	8,890	8,360	530	94	6
1940–1950	19,028	18,149	879	95	5
1950–1960	28,297	25,832	2,465	91	9

Source: *Statistical Abstract of the United States, 1963*, p. 12.

the domestic labor market through protection against the influx of cheap foreign labor. No group was more vigorous in lobbying for the restrictions than the American Federation of Labor. The influence of immigration restriction upon population increase is illustrated in Table 2-4.

The rising age level.   However, restriction of immigration was not the only downward influence on population growth from 1930. Beginning with the late 1920s there was a sharp downturn of the birthrate which would have accounted for an even greater decline had it not been for an over-all reduction in deaths throughout the population. The most impor-tant effect of these combined forces was a change in the age composition of the population, shifting more and more people into the older age groups. This was merely an acceleration of a trend already under way. For example, the median age of the total population rose from 25 in 1920 to 27 in 1930, to 29 in 1940, and to 30 in 1950 and 1960. What this fact implies for the major age group is shown in Table 2-5.

Table 2-5.   Age composition of the population of the United States, 1920–1970

Age group	1920		1940		1950		1960		1970 (est.)	
	Number (000's)	%	Number (000's)	%	Number (000's)	%	Number (000's)	%	Number (000's)	%
Under 20	43,143	41	45,306	34	51,099	35	69,005	39	75,165	37
20–59	54,652	51	72,615	56	81,269	53	86,615	48	99,132	49
60 and over	7,916	8	13,748	10	18,329	12	23,702	13	28,244	14
Total	105,711		131,669		150,697		179,323		202,541	

Source: *Statistical Abstract of the United States, 1963*, p. 26; U.S. Bureau of the Census, Population Reports, Population Estimates, Series P-25, No. 187.

Thus, the forecasts indicate that by 1970, about one person in seven will have passed his sixtieth birthday; in spite of the continuing "baby boom," the older group is still increasing more rapidly than those in the middle brackets—which is where most of the effective labor force is located. Every step of medical advance—particularly in diseases of the elderly—raises the median age of the population. For a mechanical society which has already sensed the problems of industrial old age, this prospect poses a number of issues in the areas of employment, productivity, retirement, pensions, and medical care. For the decade of the 1960s, the 20 to 59 age group is at its lowest point, less than half the total population. With rising college attendance at the bottom end of the scale, and with pressure for retirement at the other, there seems little likelihood that this group will be reinforced any time soon in its drive to increase the gross national product and the standard of living.

Education.   The United States is once more in a class by itself among large nations in the high level of literacy and general education of its population. The median year of school completed by members of the labor force (18 to 64 years of age) in 1965 was 12, or high school graduation. One out of five had had some college work and one out of ten was a college graduate. The technical versatility and superiority of the American workman is explained in large part by these figures on schooling, especially when it is remembered that the data do not include reports from private trade and vocational schools or private correspondence schools.

The population of the United States, then, is large, still growing rapidly, getting older (at a gradually slowing rate), more and more derived from native stock without benefit of immigration, and composed predominantly of urban (or at least suburban) people. The average person 18 to 64 years old has completed high school; one out of five has been to college. This is the group from which the world's largest free labor force is drawn. The next step is to find out precisely what the term "labor force" means, who is included and who is left out, and how it is distributed by occupation and by industry.

LABOR–FORCE MEASUREMENT AND CLASSIFICATION

The labor force consists of the gainfully employed, those people who have a job or are looking for one. In the words of the Census Bureau it is all persons 16 years of age or over who (1) "work for pay or profit, or work without pay for 15 hours a week or more on a family farm or business"; (2) have a job but are "temporarily absent because of vacation, illness, industrial dispute, bad weather, or layoff with definite instructions to return to work within 30 days"; or (3) do not have a job but are looking for work. The civilian labor force consists of these people minus the members of the armed services.[14]

Although it is considerably less than the total population, the United States labor force runs into the tens of millions, and keeping track of its size and condition is a big statistical job. It is also an important job, since it is probably our most important index of prosperity. The figures on employment and unemployment are followed closely by economists, government officials, and businessmen as measures of national health. If the country has a single economic pulse, it is the unemployment ratio. Two agencies of the Federal government measure the labor force month by month, using entirely different methods: the Bureau of the Census of the Department of Commerce and the Bureau of Labor Statistics of the Department of Labor. The former uses the "population approach," while the latter relies on the "establishment" survey. Both have their advantages and disadvantages.[15]

The "population approach."   All official reports on the size and composition of the labor force, except those contained in the decennial censuses, are based on statistical "samples" made regularly by one agency or another. The 10-year census figures, the most reliable of all, are the result of a full count of every household in the country. The Census Bureau's monthly reports on the labor force, which are to be found in the Bureau of Labor Statistics' journal, *Employment and Earnings,* keep these totals up to date by means of regular monthly surveys—made by trained interviewers—of approximately 35,000 households in 330 areas throughout the United States. This is what is meant by the "population approach," to wit, a head count of representative homes and readjustment of labor-force totals in line with the changes in the sample. The principal advantage of this method is the inclusive nature of the information received.

The labor force is a function of the general population. If the Census Bureau's sample is representative, changes in the 35,000 households will reflect accurately changes in the labor force as a whole, giving personal characteristics (sex, age, color, etc.), the numbers employed and unemployed, the number reporting themselves in each occupation and in each industry, and the like. The sample includes farm workers, self-employed people, the armed services, new entrants into the labor force by reason of age or change of interest, and nonworkers. It counts each person only once. Statistically, it is the correct approach. Its only weakness is the size of the sample, which touches less than 1 out of every 1,000 families in the country. In this respect the Bureau of Labor Statistics' measurements are superior, but they are inadequate in other ways.

[14] "Labor Force Data," *Employment and Earnings,* December, 1966, p. 6.

[15] And both are explained in the "Technical Note," found at the back of each issue of *Employment and Earnings.*

↖ The "establishment" method.   The "establishment" method is a form of survey based on regular reports (by questionnaire) from employing establishments, mostly private business firms and government agencies. The BLS gets more than 100,000 reports a month from business firms in many different industries, and the coverage is broad, as many as 10 million employes being included.

In view of the large size of the sample, the information is very precise for the industries and occupations covered. Nonetheless, there are gaps in the data which must be filled in from other sources. For example, some of the reports cover production workers only, others both production workers and salaried personnel, and all exclude executives and officials. The totals are dominated by large firms. Farmers and farm workers, small proprietors, self-employed persons, domestic servants, and personnel of the Armed Forces are excluded entirely.

These are serious omissions from a picture of the total labor force and must be filled in by data from the Department of Agriculture on agricultural employment, and by additional material from other governmental agencies. Another weakness is that when employees of reporting firms change jobs within the month, they may be counted twice. Nonetheless, for analytical data on the nonagricultural civilian labor force (which includes the bulk of all workers and is the source of practically all labor problems), the BLS reports are the most reliable. (They are found in a series of tables in each issue of the *Monthly Labor Review*.) For many special kinds of labor information, such as payrolls, labor turnover, earnings and hours of work, prices and cost of living, and work stoppages, the BLS figures are the official guide.

How the labor force is derived from population figures.   The labor force is by no means all the population; it is not even half of it. Before the Second World War, about 40 per cent of all men, women, and children in this country were either working or looking for work. Since 1945, the proportion has been slightly higher, ranging usually from 40 to 43 per cent, with the higher ratio coming in summer when students and others move into the labor force temporarily. The size of the labor force is found by taking the total population and progressively eliminating those persons who are not in the labor market; that is, those who are neither at work nor looking for a job. The four main groups to be eliminated are children under 14, those 14 and over but going to school, housewives, and the elderly. Table 2-6 shows how the final figure is arrived at.

Of a total population, then, of 194,030,000, in April, 1966, there were 78,914,000 (40.2 per cent) in the labor force (total). Subtracting the 3,008,000 persons in the Armed Forces left 75,906,000 in the civilian labor force, of whom 73,104,000 were employed and 2,802,000 (3.7 per cent) were out of work and looking for a job. This was regarded as a very

Table 2-6.   Deriving the labor force of the United States, April, 1966
(In thousands, figures rounded)

Total population (all ages), April, 1966	194,030
Less 1. Persons under 14 years of age, and inmates of penal and mental institutions and homes for the aged, infirm, etc., none of whom are considered eligible for the labor force. (Age 14, an arbitrary cutoff date, should probably be raised to 18, or high school graduation, when most people enter the labor market full time)	59,420
Potential labor force (total noninstitutional population)	137,908
Less 2. Persons keeping house. Since they do not work for pay or profit, they are excluded from the labor-force count	35,514
	102,394
Less 3. Full-time students, with no job (either part- or full-time) and not looking for one	14,158
	88,236
Less 4. Other persons not in the labor force, mostly people too old to work	9,322
Total labor force—40.2% of the total population	78,914
Less 5. Members of the armed services: Army, Navy, Air Force, etc.	3,008
Civilian labor force—the basis of unemployment estimates and the key figure in the labor-force model	75,906
Less 6. The unemployed—anyone over 14 and outside of institutions who does not have a job but is looking for one—3.7% of civilian labor force	2,802
Employed labor force—those at work and those with jobs but temporarily idle because of illness, bad weather, etc.	73,104

Source: *Employment and Earnings*, May, 1966, p. 25; *Statistical Abstract of the U.S., 1965*, p. 216.

satisfactory (low) rate of unemployment, the lowest in 9 years, and 1.1 per cent lower than a year earlier.

It is clear that the American economy has large reserves of man-power—in the student group (which is growing rapidly in the age group over 14), the housewives, and in cases of emergency, in the younger age levels, from 10 to 13 and even below. This is illustrated by the range of expansion and contraction in the civilian labor force within the year. Employment is customarily lowest in winter and highest in summer as a result of bad weather conditions around the year's end and the concentration of farm work in the summertime. In January, 1964, for example, the civilian labor force was 71,793,000; by June, it had risen to 76,645,000 (an increase of 4,852,000 or almost 7 per cent); however, by January, 1965, it had dropped back again to 72,992,000.

The disappearing entrepreneurs.   It is not enough to know the size of the labor force and how it is arrived at; it is even more important to

Table 2-7. The self-employed in the labor force, 1940–1965

Class	1940		1953		1965	
	Number (000's)	%	Number (000's)	%	Number (000's)	%
Employed labor force	52,020	100	60,764	100	71,070	100
Self-employed and family help						
Self-employed	9,980		9,093		8,815	
Unpaid family workers	1,470		1,035		1,425	
	11,450	22	10,128	17	10,240	14
Wage and salary workers	40,570	78	50,636	83	60,830	86

Source: *Employment and Earnings*, May, 1965, p. 7; *Monthly Report on the Labor Force*, December, 1953; *Statistical Abstract of the U.S., 1947*, p. 170.

know something about its composition and the significance of the various classes that make it up. The most basic division is that between wage and salary workers, on the one hand, and the self-employed-plus-family-help on the other.

The latter are the true "entrepreneurs" of the economics textbooks, who risk their own time and capital, set up a business or professional office, and run it for a profit. They are mainly (1) farmers (30 per cent of the total); (2) shopkeepers, such as the owners of drugstores and "mamma-and-papa" grocery stores; proprietors of service establishments: beauty parlors, service stations, laundries, restaurants, motels, cleaning and dyeing shops, etc.; and (3) professional people: doctors, lawyers, accountants, real estate brokers, income tax advisers, etc. These are the people whose business firms are still organized as "sole proprietorships" and "partnerships." Most of them are "shoestring" operators; in 1960, for example, out of 9,090,000 sole proprietorships, 8,350,000 (or 92 per cent) had total sales for the year of less than $50,000.[16] And they are a disappearing class. Table 2-7 records the decline of the self-employed as a percentage of the employed labor force during the quarter of a century from 1940 to 1965.

It is an instructive exercise to speculate on the policies, programs, or circumstances which are bringing about the disappearance of the self-employed farmer and businessman from the American scene, and of its significance for the future. Before doing so, the reader should go to the statistics themselves, in the latest *Statistical Abstract of the U.S.* and other sources, for a detailed breakdown by classes and trends—the collapse of independent farming, the rise of the service industries, the doubling in number of corporations between 1947 and 1960, the impact of business taxes, etc. Of the facts there can be little doubt; of their sig-

[16] *Statistical Abstract of the U.S., 1963*, p. 489.

nificance there is much dispute, and of the desirability of the trend there will be vigorous controversy. For better or for worse, the United States is each year closer to being a nation of employes, with all the problems of pay, rank, status, mobility, and security that jobholding brings, from the shop floor to the executive suite.

The job aristocracy.   Most of us are now or will be employes all our lives. As was pointed out in Chap. 1, the job we hold will probably be the most important single factor affecting the way we and our families live and think. It will be the principal determinant of our social and financial position in the community in which we live. What these are for a business executive [17] or a junior law clerk is quite different from what they are for a truck driver, a congressman, a garage mechanic, a sales-clerk, or an engineer. It is therefore correct to call the basic job structure of the labor force the "socioeconomic" classification of the population.

We have no peerage in this country comparable to the British orders of knight, baronet (Bart.), baron, viscount, earl, marquis, and duke.[18] The American aristocracy is an aristocracy of jobs, and therefore, to a very considerable degree, of ability. Neither birth nor inherited wealth, for instance, is a bar (or apparently much of a help) to the top spots of President and Vice-President of the United States (witness the back-grounds of the present incumbent and his predecessors of the past 25 years). The chances are 100 to 1 that the social and economic position of your family, as well as of the other 50 million families in the United States, will be settled by the occupation of the head of the house.[19]

Just for fun, the reader might try setting up a job aristocracy for this country, by both classes and individual positions, starting with the Presidency and Vice-Presidency of the United States, and going on to Chief Justice and the associate justices of the Supreme Court, senators, congress-men, members of the Cabinet, chairmen of important agencies such as the Joint Chiefs of Staff, the Federal Reserve Board, governors of the 50 states, mayors of the biggest cities. Where would you slot in the presi-

[17] See, for example, *The Executive Life,* by the editors of *Fortune* (Garden City, N.Y.: Doubleday & Company, Inc., 1956).

[18] Or even the annual "honours list," with such grants as Order of the British Empire (OBE), Commander, St. Michael and St. George (abbreviated CMG—"Call me God"), Knight Commander, St. Michael and St. George (KCMG—"Kindly call me God"), and Grand Commander, St. Michael and St. George (GCMG—"God calls me God"). Taken from Anthony Sampson, *Anatomy of Britain* (New York: Harper & Row, Publishers, Incorporated, 1962), pp. 292–297. This admirable book is indispensable reading for anyone interested in the British "Establishment."

[19] There were 46,341,000 families in the United States in March, 1962, and they were increasing at a rate of about 600,000 per year, which would bring the total to 50,000,000 sometime in 1968. *Statistical Abstract of the U.S., 1963,* p. 42. Besides the above, there were 8,311,000 "individuals" living alone, bringing total "households" to 54,652,000.

dents or chairmen of the boards of U.S. Steel, General Motors, Ford, AT&T, IBM, etc.? the presidents of Harvard, Yale, Princeton, Stanford, MIT, Caltech, and the Universities of Chicago, California, and Michigan? publishers such as the Sulzbergers (*New York Times*) and the Chandlers (*Los Angeles Times*)? columnists and commentators like Walter Lippmann, Eric Sevareid, Joseph Alsop, Drew Pearson, and Raymond Moley? actors, entertainers, athletes, artists, and architects: Katharine Cornell, Helen Hayes, Martha Graham, John Wayne, Cary Grant, Gregory Peck, Bob Hope, Mickey Mantle, Willie Mays, Jim Brown, Horowitz, Rubinstein, DeKooning, Neutra, Stone? scientists and scholars: Pauling, Rabi, Oppenheimer, Viner, Samuelson, Morrison, Commager, Edmund Wilson? labor leaders: George Meany, Walter Reuther, John L. Lewis? churchmen: Martin Luther King, Bishop Kennedy, Carson Blake, Cardinal Spellman? poets and novelists: Robert Lowell, William Carlos Williams, Archibald MacLeish, Steinbeck, Cozzens, Salinger? Note that the overwhelming majority of the above, including those in the public offices, made it on their own—an aristocracy of merit.

There are a number of ways of classifying the labor force on a job basis, but the standard one is that worked out by the Bureau of the Census for the decennial census reports and kept up to date in its monthly reports. The 10 main groups, with subclasses, totals, and percentages, are shown in Table 2-8.

There are several reasons why the occupational classification of the labor force in the United States is of interest. The relative positions of different classes of jobs provide one of the main sources of motivation in a free, competitive, materialistic society. (This is Dumont's "social capillarity" in action but without any necessary agreement with his conclusions as to the effect on population growth.) People constantly try to improve their positions by moving from one class to another higher in the scale.

A prime objective of parents is to see their children better off in life than they were, and "better off" usually means in a different (higher) occupation. The usual methods by which this change is brought about are education, apprenticeship training, or investment, leading to professional or skilled employment, management opportunities, or the ownership of one's own business. One symbol of a free society is freedom of movement between occupational classes, without discrimination on grounds of birth, politics, race, or religion. While the United States cannot claim to be 100 per cent successful in this respect, few countries can show as large or as rapid migration upward from unprivileged beginnings.

One proof of the upward pull of better jobs is the high proportion of the labor force in the skilled classes. If clerical workers and salespeople are included in the skilled groups, over 60 per cent of the experienced labor force is in this category, with more than one out of every four

Table 2-8. Socioeconomic classification of the labor force, April, 1965 (In thousands)

Class		Persons	Per cent
Employed labor force (total)		71,070	100.0
Managerial and professional classes		18,864	26.4
Managerial:			
Managers, officials (government), and proprietors (nonfarm)	7,483		
Farmers and farm managers	2,325		
		9,808	13.9
Professional, technical, and kindred workers (includes doctors, lawyers, accountants, engineers, teachers, scientists, nurses, draftsmen, etc.)		8,876	12.5
Sales and clerical employes		15,731	22.1
Sales workers (inside and outside—traveling)		4,637	6.5
Clerical and kindred workers (stenographic, secretarial, general office work)		11,094	15.6
Blue-collar workers		27,593	38.8
Craftsmen, foremen, and kindred workers (skilled)		8,918	12.5
Operatives and similar workers (semiskilled)		13,196	18.6
Laborers, nonfarm (unskilled factory hands, mostly)		3,668	5.2
Farm laborers and foremen		1,811	2.5
Service workers		9,063	12.7
Service workers, in business and industry (barbers, waiters, bartenders, bellhops, ushers, etc., and custodial employes: janitors, charwomen, guards)		6,986	9.8
Private household workers (domestic servants: maids, cooks, cleaning women, butlers, etc.)		2,077	2.9

Source: *Employment and Earnings*, May, 1965, p. 7.

persons to be found in the professional or proprietor-official-managerial ranks.

Over the years there has been a persistent increase in the number of professional and technical people and just as consistent a decline in the number and proportion of unskilled. With time out for the wartime decade of the 1940s, service employes also multiplied in the 1930s and the 1950s. The ratio of proprietors-managers-officials dropped off 50 per cent from 1930 (most of the decline being in the proprietor or self-employed sector), while the ratio of skilled workers—foremen and craftsmen—held steady. Clerical employment proliferated slightly but steadily year by year—the blizzard of paperwork and record keeping associated with the increase in size of organizations. The trends are shown in Table 2-9.

This table also gives a clue to an important source of labor problems. Job changes by individuals do not always occur smoothly and easily in an

Table 2-9.   Trends in occupational distribution, 1930–1966

Job class	Per cent of the labor force					Change, per cent, 1930–1966
	1930	1940	1950	1960	1966	
Professional, technical, etc.	6	7	9	12	13	Up 117
Proprietors, managers, officials	20	18	16	15	10	Down 50
Clerks and salespeople	16	17	19	21	22	Up 38
Skilled workers and foremen	13	12	14	13	16	Up 23
Semiskilled (operatives)	17	18	20	19	19	Up 12
Unskilled workers	21	18	12	8	7	Down 67
Farm laborers	8	7	4	3	2	Down 75
Nonfarm laborers	13	11	8	5	5	Down 62
Service workers—all types	7	10	10	12	13	Up 86

Sources: *Statistical Abstract of the U.S., 1947*, p. 144; *1955*, p. 199; *Employment and Earnings*, May, 1966, p. 32.

atmosphere of unruffled calm and tranquillity. It is customarily more of a strain to change one's occupation than to shift from one industry to another or to go back to work after being unemployed. Changing occupations calls for the abandonment of habits, skills, and customary routines which may have taken years to acquire. New positions imply different working environments, and if the direction of change is advancement, there is frequently a heavier load of responsibility.

Where occupational change has been so marked and so divergent, it may be assumed that competition has been strong, rivalry keen, and disappointments numerous. No large community can absorb in a generation a proportionate increase of 117 per cent in its professional class and of 86 per cent in its "service" occupations, while at the same time experiencing a loss of 50 per cent of its managerial and proprietary group [20] along with two-thirds of its unskilled labor, without some tension and discord. All this occurred against a background of flux, disorder, and rapid social change: the desperation of the depression years and the union-management conflict of the 1930s; the strain of mobilization for the Second World War, accompanied by the forced migrations from job to job, industry to industry, and region to region during the war and reconversion; the violent dispute, controversy, and realignment within the or-

[20] The decline is almost entirely—perhaps entirely—in the proprietary (self-employed) class. Part of it is merely a "bookkeeping" change. When a business is incorporated, the former proprietor, who may hold all the stock, then becomes an "employe" of the corporation. However, there is little doubt about the decline of the self-employed entrepreneurial class—especially on farms; this has been a persistent trend in labor-market statistics for decades. The small employer has succumbed to absorption (being bought out by a chain or a larger firm), to merger, and to just plain bankruptcy in the face of strong competition. The ex-proprietor then becomes an employe with new duties, responsibilities, and working environment.

ganized labor movement itself; the armaments race in missiles and space exploration since the Korean conflict; and the threat of unlimited technological displacement (automation) of the nuclear age.

INDUSTRIAL DISTRIBUTION OF THE LABOR FORCE

In this country, community standing depends on occupation. However, a major determinant of the occupations available and their importance is the industry in which they are located. Some industries are small, some large; some are contracting in terms of manpower while others expand, and so on. Some industries offer very few opportunities for certain kinds of work, e.g., professional or technical employment in retail trade, clerical work in agriculture, sales work in the utilities; some industries are heavily unionized while others are practically open shop. The distribution of the labor force by industry and the characteristics peculiar to different industries are therefore worth examining.

The decline of agriculture. The primary division in labor-market statistics is between agricultural and nonagricultural employment. The former has been declining relatively (as a percentage of the labor force) for as long as there are records and absolutely since 1910, while the latter has been moving in the opposite direction. In recent years, the drop has been extreme. In 1940, for instance, there were 9,540,000 persons (20 per cent of an employed labor force of 47,520,000) engaged in tilling the soil; 25 years later, there were less than half as many—4,473,000 (6 per cent of an employed labor force which had grown to 71,070,000). Agriculture is *the* self-employed industry; most of the 4,473,000 were self-employed farmers (2,410,000) and unpaid family workers (782,000); just 1,280,000 persons worked on farms for wages or a salary.[21] All told—farmers, family help, and hired hands—they constituted only 1 out of every 17 members of the civilian labor force.[22]

The long-run shift from a rural (farm) to an urban (industrial) society is probably nowhere more clearly outlined than in the comparative statistics of agricultural and nonagricultural employment, given in Table 2-10.

The surprising feature of the table is the accelerated rate of decline in the 2 decades, 1940 to 1950 and 1950 to 1960. In the 1940s, agricultural employment fell 35 per cent—by far the largest decrease registered up to that time. However, during the next 10 years, even this was exceeded, with a drop of 46 per cent. Between 1940 and 1960, the agricultural labor force was more than cut in half, with the decline continuing to 1965.

[21] The figures for 1965 are for the month of April.
[22] And still were able to feed the nation and pile up huge crop surpluses in government warehouses. Agriculture is one of the triumphs of postwar technology and demonstrates dramatically the possibilities of mechanical displacement of workers.

Table 2-10.   Agricultural and nonagricultural employment, 1820–1965

Year	Employed labor force	Farm employment		Nonfarm employment	
		Number	%	Number	%
1820	2,881,000	2,068,958	72	812,042	28
1840	5,420,000	3,719,951	69	1,700,049	31
1860	10,532,750	6,207,634	59	4,325,116	41
1880	17,392,099	8,584,810	49	8,807,289	51
1900	29,073,233	10,911,998	38	18,161,235	62
1910	37,370,794	11,591,767	31	25,779,027	69
1920	42,433,535	11,448,770	27	30,984,765	73
1930*	45,480,000	10,340,000	23	35,140,000	77
1940*	47,520,000	9,540,000	20	37,980,000	80
1950*	59,748,000	7,497,000	13	52,251,000	87
1960*	64,267,000	4,565,000	7	59,702,000	93
1965*	71,070,000	4,473,000	6	66,597,000	94

* Figures from 1930 onward based on a labor force 14 years old or over; earlier figures are for a labor force of persons 10 years old and over.
Sources: Years 1820–1920 from *Historical Statistics of the United States, 1789–1945.* U.S. Bureau of the Census, p. 63; from 1930 onward from *Employment and Earnings,* May, 1965, p. 1.

This was technological displacement; farm production continued at a rate to embarrass the Agricultural Administration with recurring crop surpluses. (For many years, the farm problem in the United States has been overproduction.) The decline of the farm labor force reflects the application of "scientific management" and machine technology to the growing and harvesting of crops. It was also speeded up by high wages and strong demand in industrial employment, so that the transfer of 5 million workers out of agriculture and into a mushrooming (up 29 million) nonfarm labor force during the 25 years 1940 to 1965 was accomplished with no serious unemployment and a minimum of disorder. The transferees were absorbed smoothly into nonagricultural pursuits and city life. The answer, above all others, to technological displacement of workers (automation)—as to so many other labor problems—is full employment: a strong labor market at high wages, short hours, and good working conditions.

Employment in commerce, industry, government.   The bulk of employment and the bulk of labor problems are found in the nonagricultural industries. In April, 1965, there were 66,599,000 people at work in these pursuits, 7,050,000 (10.5 per cent) of them self-employed or unpaid family workers and the remaining 59,500,000 (89.5 per cent), wage and salary workers. The latter were spread among the eight major industrial groupings as shown in Table 2-11.

Table 2-11.   Civilian employment in commerce, industry, government, 1965

Industrial group	Employment	Per cent
Mining	627,000	1
Contract construction	3,027,000	5
Manufacturing	17,724,000	30
Transportation and public utilities	4,001,000	7
Wholesale and retail trade	12,512,000	21
Finance, insurance, and real estate	2,985,000	5
Service and miscellaneous (hotels, restaurants, movies, garages, service stations, etc.)	8,750,000	15
Government	9,924,000	16
Total	59,550,000	100

Source: *Employment and Earnings*, May, 1965, p. 13.

The leaders, from the standpoint of employment, are manufacturing and trade, with government third. If the 3 million members of the armed services were included—raising the government total to 12,920,000—then governmental employment moves into second place, a position it seems likely to occupy for some time to come.

Table 2-12 shows the retreat of the traditional "heavy" industries (mining-construction-manufacturing-utilities) from their commanding situation in the employment picture after the First World War, to equality in 1940, and by 1960 to a position subordinate to the rapidly rising "service" industries.[23] The trends are too obvious to be ignored: the consistent "Down's" in the upper half of the table (with the single exception of building construction) and the uniform "Up's" in the lower half. In the future, more and more high school and college graduates will be employed in trade, finance, one of the service industries, or in government, either as a civilian or a member of the armed services. Since the government's share of professional employment is high, the chances are better than one out of five that any college graduate will end up teaching, serving as a commissioned officer in one of the armed services, or in a government bureau somewhere.

Women in the labor force.   Every year, there are more women, both absolutely and proportionately, working for a living and therefore in the labor force. By April, 1965, they were just over one-third of the total: 26,139,000 out of 77,307,000, or 34 per cent. This was a considerable in-

[23] If agriculture, the most "traditional" industry of all, is included, the contrast is even more dramatic. In 1920, some 27 per cent of all gainful workers were in agriculture, the heavy industries employed 45 per cent, and the service industries only 28 per cent. By 1965, the comparative figures were agriculture—6 per cent, heavy industries —37 per cent, and service industries—57 per cent. In other words, the exodus from agriculture was to the services in its entirety. *Historical Statistics of the U.S., Colonial Times to 1957*, p. 74, *Employment and Earnings*, May, 1965, p. 13.

Table 2-12.   Distribution of employment in commerce, industry, government, 1920–1965

Industry group	Per cent of wage and salary workers				Change, per cent, 1920–1965
	1920	1940	1960	1965	
The heavy industries					
Mining	5	3	1	1	Down 80
Contract construction	3	4	4	5	Up 67
Manufacturing	39	34	32	30	Down 23
Transportation, public utilities	14	9	7	7	Down 50
	61	50	44	43	Down 30
The service industries					
Trade: wholesale and retail	16	22	22	21	Up 30
Finance, insurance, real estate	4	4	5	5	Up 25
Service and miscellaneous	9	11	12	15	Up 67
Government—civilian	10	13	17	16	Up 60
(including armed services)	(11)	(14)		(20)	(Up 82)
(armed services excluded)	39	50	56	57	Up 46

Sources: *Employment and Earnings*, May, 1965, p. 13; *Historical Statistics of the U.S. . . . to 1957*, p. 736. Note that if the armed services are included, in 1965 one out of five wage and salary workers in the United States received their paychecks from some governmental unit—Federal, state, or local.

crease from prewar 1940, when there were only 14,160,000 females in a labor force of 56,180,000, or 25 per cent. Women have more than their share of the domestic service, clerical, nursing, and teaching jobs, and considerably less than their share of the managerial and professional positions. They work mostly in nonagricultural industries (in April, 1965 they were less than one-sixth of the agricultural labor force) and predominantly in the service group of trade-finance-service-government. They are often discriminated against in both pay and advancement and have an unemployment rate that is consistently higher than that for men.

There are many other ways of classifying the labor force: by age, color, marital status, labor-force participation rate (per cent of the potential labor force—by age, sex, etc.—that is working or looking for a job), hours worked, full- or part-time status, etc. All of them may be found analyzed in detail in each month's copy of *Employment and Earnings*. The reader is advised to consult the statistics available in this journal for many interesting trends and relationships of too special a nature to be listed here.

Population and the labor force.   The source of the labor force is the general population, but its character and composition are also functions of the social environment. The goods and services produced by the labor force constitute the national product, which, divided among the population, comprises the standard of living. The standard of living cannot escape the limitations of the basic economic ratio of resources to population, but a given quantity of resources can be made immensely more productive if the labor force is strong, healthy, intelligent, resourceful, and well trained, both technically and in procedures of organization. Few populations in the world's history have had more favorable opportunities to realize their maximum productiveness than the inhabitants of the United States.

This country has the people, the technical skills, and the natural resources in quantities and in combination almost beyond belief. The rate of increase of scientific knowledge and technical application of new discoveries is far ahead of the most optimistic guesses of even a decade or two ago. The country's industrial plant alone of the major powers of the world is as yet untouched by war damage and is without a rival in the world in capacity, equipment, and staff. It remains to be seen whether the most complicated, efficient, and interdependent productive mechanism yet brought forth by man can be kept functioning at a high level of capacity and its product distributed among the members of the population in a fashion which will call forth their best efforts and satisfy their sense of justice.

READINGS

Every student should read Malthus's *Essay on Population*, preferably the first edition (1798) which is the shortest and most lucid statement of his theory. They might also read A. M. Carr-Saunders, either *Population* (London: Oxford University Press, 1925) or *World Population* (Oxford: Clarendon Press, 1936), the former a brief treatise of about 100 pages. For more recent comments, see Harrison S. Brown, James Bonner, and John Weir (all of California Institute of Technology), in *The Next Hundred Years* (New York: The Viking Press, Inc., 1957).

The definitive measurement of the United States labor force is found in John D. Durand, *The Labor Force in the United States 1890–1960* (New York: Social Science Research Council, 1948). Clarence D. Long's *The Labor Force under Changing Income and Employment* (Princeton, N.J.: Princeton University Press, 1958), though complicated and technical, is carefully summarized as to conclusions and well worth examining.

The best short summary of the issues raised by the world population explosion is to be found in "The Economist and the Population Question," presidential address of Joseph J. Spengler to the American Economic Association at the 78th Annual Meeting, found in *American Economic Review*, March, 1966, pp. 1–24.

THREE

THE
UNITED STATES
LABOR MARKET

The preceding chapter gave an introductory survey of the United States labor *force:* its relationship to the general population, how it is defined and measured, its classification by occupation and industry, etc. Each member of the labor force sells "personal services" (labor) in a labor *market*, whether the services are those of the board chairman of U.S. Steel, with his annual salary and bonus in the hundreds of thousands of dollars, or those of a farm laborer earning $8 to $10 a day. The purpose of this chapter is to try to give some sort of coherent picture of the general labor-market structure in America, with a few illustrations of the controversial issues which are raised.

Labor-market structure. The United States is often described as the world's largest free labor market. However, it is by no means a single market, but a great many different markets, which display almost infinite variations in size, composition, and character. Most of them are limited geographically to a single area: town, city, district, or region. (Not all, though; see the Sunday edition of any big metropolitan newspaper for page after page of block advertisements, many of them trying to get scientists and engineers to move West or come back East and work.) However, within each geographical labor market, there are a limited number of major types, the primary distinction between one type and another being the way the market is "structured." [1]

Labor-market structure is simply the set of formal rules (devices, mechanisms) which are observed regularly by employers and workers in their dealings with one another. These rules may be created by law, con-

[1] Portions of this chapter are adapted from O. W. Phelps, "A Structural Model of the U.S. Labor Market," *Industrial and Labor Relations Review*, April, 1957, pp. 402–423.

tract, local or industry custom, or by managerial policy. The basic function of the rules is to regulate hiring and the conditions of employment: wages, hours, shifts, job assignments, etc. Their main effect—an effect usually intended—is to limit the employer's discretion in dealing with his employes. However, they also introduce certainty and regularity into the handling of personnel, especially in casual-labor markets (by union work rules) and in large firms, by providing standard practices for carrying out the complicated procedures of hiring and maintaining a work force.

The importance of any particular set of rules is directly related to the certainty with which they will be applied and to the recourse of employes (or employers) in case of violation. Some rules are very rigid—for example, regulatory legislation. The minimum-wage and child labor restrictions of the Fair Labor Standards Act set precise limits to wage payment and choice of personnel by employers and carry severe penalties for violation; civil service rules dictate exactly how employes are to be recruited, selected, paid, and fired; the National Labor Relations Act outlaws employer and union practices which interfere with employe rights of self-organization and collective bargaining, and so on. In each case, there is a government agency to which the aggrieved employes or employers may appeal if the rules are violated.

Union work rules and the provisions of labor agreements are just as precise as, but more detailed and more closely supervised than administrative regulations. Custom is also a very powerful regulator at times; for example, the segregation of Negro and white labor and other forms of discrimination. In large firms, personnel policies are carefully adopted and enforced to standardize the handling of large numbers of employes. There is a difference, however, between law and contract on the one side and custom and employer policy on the other. The former always provide specific, formal channels of appeal for aggrieved employes; the latter seldom do and in any case the final decision lies with the employer.

Labor markets range all the way from the heavily structured to the unstructured, with every possible gradation in between. Nevertheless, there is a limited number of distinct types (or classes) of markets, each characteristic of large numbers of employers and employes, which may be quite clearly distinguished. The principal differences are between (1) large and small employers, (2) public and private employers, and (3) employment under union-management contract as compared with employment on terms set and administered unilaterally by the employer.

LABOR–MARKET TYPES: BY STRUCTURE

Employment problems are a function of size. That is to say, the larger the employing firm (or government agency), the more problems *per employe* it will have to deal with.[2] The small organization has the tremendous advantage of the "personal approach," which has been described as:

a combination of an informal "family" plant atmosphere, human relations, and personal services, which may include anything from posting bail for an employe to counseling on marital problems. In each plant it is different and to each worker and each employer it is something different. Yet where it exists, it is invaluable.[3]

The personal approach is simply not available to the large employer, no matter how good his intentions. It is impossible for a plant manager to know the names and personal interests and circumstances of each of a thousand employes, even if he is willing to work at it full time, which he cannot.

The breaking point which separates the small from the medium-sized firm comes when the head of the organization can no longer know all his employes as individuals. When the organization expands beyond this point, personal contacts must be delegated to supervisors. This is the first, the longest, and the most irrevocable step in the process of formalizing (structuring) the employment process.[4]

The actual breaking point will depend on a number of things: turnover, management attitudes, physical proximity of the work force, residence location of employes, and other factors. In most cases, it will not occur with less than 200 employes, and it will seldom be delayed until employment passes 400. For practical purposes, therefore, it may be said to come at the level of 300 employes. The distribution of business firms by size and total employment in each size class, as of 1965, is shown in Table 3-1.

The striking fact is that almost two of every five employes of business firms (19 million workers) are employed in 3,700 companies with 1,000 or more workers each. Half of these are on the payrolls of 250 giant corporations, each with a minimum of 10,000 employes and some employing hundreds of thousands of persons. Another 6 million workers are in firms ranging in size from 300 to 1,000, bringing the total of medium-sized and

---

[2] It is well known that the ratio of personnel department staff to plant workers increases with the size of the firm.

[3] Sherrill Cleland, *The Influence of Plant Size on Industrial Relations* (Princeton, N.J.: Institute of Industrial Relations, Princeton University, 1955), p. 36.

[4] "The difference in industrial relations in a two-man shop as against a mass-production industry is one of kind rather than merely of degree. Size is an important determining condition. . . . (It) affects the nearness of managers and of union leaders to workers; the identity of interest or lack of it among the three groups; and the amount of knowledge held in common. It usually establishes who is the boss—the owner, the manager, the superintendent, or the foreman. It decides the extent to which formal substitutes are required to replace informal and more spontaneous relationships." Clark Kerr, "The Collective Bargaining Environment," in Clinton S. Golden and Virginia D. Parker (eds.), *Causes of Industrial Peace* (New York: Harper & Row, Publishers, Incorporated, 1955), p. 11.

Table 3-1. Estimated employment by size of firm in the United States, 1965

Size class	Firms		Employment	
	Number	%	Number	%
Total	4,904,000	100	49,625,000	100
99 or less employes	4,860,300	99	20,346,000	41
100 or more employes	43,700	1	29,279,000	59
300 or more employes	19,600	0.4	25,310,000	51
500 or more employes	7,400	0.15	21,840,000	44
1,000 or more employes	3,430	0.07	18,860,000	38
10,000 or more employes	250	0.005	8,930,000	18

Sources: Ratios from Betty C. Churchill, "Size of Business Firms," *Survey of Current Business*, September, 1959, p. 15; adjusted for changes in employment data and business population. *Employment and Earnings*, May, 1965, p. 13; *Statistical Abstract of the U.S., 1963*, p. 488.

large firms up to about 20,000 and their total employes to 25 million, or more than half of all commercial and industrial employment. For these millions of employes, the personal approach on a casual, informal basis is out of the question. The solution of their employment problems must be a matter of policy and administration rather than the casual flexibility of individual face-to-face relations between two persons who happen to be employer and employe.

The personnel department versus the union. There are two basic methods of approach to policy and administration in the labor market: management's and the worker's. The management solution is a specialized personnel department, with formal hiring practices, a wage and salary division, industrial engineering (time-and-motion studies), and a wide variety of special services. The worker's preference is organization into unions and collective bargaining. Since 1935, collective bargaining has prevailed in some of the most important industrial labor markets, thereby superseding managerial personnel practices governing wages, hours, and conditions of work.

Speaking generally, the unionized industries are the big industries, the big-firm industries, the manual-labor industries.[5] They are also the industries where formal managerial personnel policies are most prevalent.

[5] *E.g.:* mining, with 53 per cent of all employes in the top 1 per cent of firms—average size 1,000; manufacturing with 59 per cent of employment in the top 1 per cent of firms—average size 3,200; transportation and public utilities, with 80 per cent of employment in 1 per cent of firms—average size 1,600 employes. In 1965, these three industrial groups accounted for 22,351,000 out of 49,625,000 wage and salary workers in business firms. The only heavily organized industrial groups where employment is usually small scale are contract construction and the maritime trades.

To a considerable degree, the union and the personnel department appeared as answers to the same set of problems, and in every large corporation their jurisdictions continually overlap.[6] However, just as they differed in point of origin, so the two have differed as to objectives and methods. They have seldom been amalgamated into a single, unified attack upon the problems of employer-employe relations.[7]

Labor-market types. A labor market may be fully structured, or partly structured, or unstructured. The *fully structured* markets fall into two main classes: (1) the market for public employes, hedged in from entry to exit by legislation and administrative rules; and (2) the "organized" labor market, bounded by the labor agreement and union work rules. In the latter, there are several important subtypes, some of which merit discussion in detail. The *partly structured* markets are mainly the nonunion sectors of large firms, where the regulatory mechanisms are the employer's personnel policies supplemented by Federal and state statutes. *Unstructured* markets are made up of small, nonunion employers—both business firms and private individuals outside the business community. In these markets, there are few or no rules limiting employers, other than local custom, the minimum protection of the common law (an employe's right to any pay he has earned and to a reasonably safe workplace), and whatever protective statutes may apply. Unstructured labor markets have almost no formal mechanisms by means of which workers obtain information, move into and out of jobs, qualify for advances in rank or pay, or identify themselves with any type of organization for purposes of security or self-support.

The general labor market in the United States and its division into eight basic types is shown in Table 3-2.

THE UNSTRUCTURED LABOR MARKETS

Private (nonbusiness) employment. The unstructured labor markets in the United States are large, diverse, and confusing. They have one characteristic in common, however; most of them are strictly *local*, that is, confined to a single and usually a quite small geographic area.[8] A great

[6] A great many industrial firms have both a personnel department and a division of labor relations, thus emphasizing the two methods of approach described here.

[7] However, there are exceptions. See Clinton S. Golden and V. D. Parker (eds.), *Causes of Industrial Peace* (Washington: National Planning Association, 1948). This is a series of case studies of selected examples of successful union-management adjustment.

[8] The exception here (and there are exceptions to practically any generalization with respect to labor markets) is the case of scientific, technical, and professional people hired by teaching and research institutions: universities, clinics, libraries, and the like.

Table 3-2.   The United States labor market by main structural types, 1965
(Figures rounded)

Total civilian labor force		74,600,000	
Less proprietors, self-employed, unpaid family labor		10,200,000	
Wage and salary workers (civilian only)		64,400,000	
Unstructured labor markets:			
Nonunion employes outside business firms	8,000,000		
Nonunion employes of small business firms	15,000,000		
Employes in the unstructured labor markets		23,000,000	(36%)
Partly structured labor markets: *			
Employes of large unorganized firms	6,000,000		
Employes outside the bargaining units in large organized firms	6,000,000		
Employes in the partly structured labor markets		12,000,000	(19%)
Fully structured labor markets:			
Public employes: Federal, state, local		10,000,000	(15%)
Union members in small firms, usually organized by craft †	8,000,000		
Union members privately employed outside of business firms—mostly craft †	300,000		
Union members in large firms, typically under an industrial agreement †	10,000,000		
Nonunion employes under union contract (industrial agreement) †	1,100,000		
Employes working under union contract terms		19,400,000	(30%)

* Governed by management personnel policies and legal requirements.
† Employed under union contract.
Sources: Ratios from Betty C. Churchill, "Size of Business Firms," *Survey of Current Business,* September, 1959; *Employment and Earnings,* May, 1965, p. 13 and *passim; Directory of National and International Labor Unions in the United States, 1963,* BLS Bulletin 1395; Table 3-1 above. See also O. W. Phelps, "A Structural Model of the U.S. Labor Market," *Industrial and Labor Relations Review,* April, 1957, pp. 402–423.

many employes—an estimated 8 million—in this kind of market do not work for any regular business firm at all. They are hired by private individuals as domestic servants, farm laborers, odd-job service and repairmen, and receptionists and clerks in the offices of self-employed professional men: doctors, lawyers, accountants, etc. Or they are on the staffs of private, nonprofit organizations such as universities, colleges, preparatory schools, hospitals, museums, churches, etc. They are distributed about as shown in Table 3-3.

Private, nonbusiness employment is an area of great flux. Large numbers of people move into and out of the labor market, with long layoffs for school attendance, housework, and other personal reasons. There is a marked seasonal variation of demand in agriculture, schoolwork, and home service and repair. Apart from the larger institutions, where profes-

Table 3-3.   Estimated private employment outside business firms, 1965

Class of employment	Number of employes
Farm labor	1,280,000
Domestic service in private households	2,080,000
Institutional work: universities, hospitals, museums, etc.	2,500,000
Office and laboratory work for self-employed professionals	1,400,000
Odd-job service and repair work	740,000
Total	8,000,000

Sources: *Statistical Abstract of the U.S., 1963*, p. 82; *Employment and Earnings*, May, 1965, pp. 7, 13, and *passim*.

sional, technical, and custodial employment predominates, the market as a whole is almost completely without structure.

Employment in this type of market is long-hour, low-pay, insecure, and under the poorest working conditions.[9] The fast-growing field of fringe benefits is relatively unknown to such employes, except as forced on their employers by law through OASDI (old-age, survivors', and disability insurance), minimum-wage, maximum-hour, and child labor legislation. Organization into unions is for the most part impracticable. The workers are widely scattered; most of them are unskilled; employment is transient and fluctuating; and the industries and occupations involved are often exempt from the protection of the Federal statutes regulating employment, either by specification in the law itself (for example, farm labor in the Fair Labor Standards Act) or as being in intrastate (local) commerce and so outside the scope of congressional regulation. With the exception of the minority in the larger nonprofit institutions, these employes are strangers to either formal personnel management or the protection of a union contract. About one worker out of eight in this country earns his living in a market of this type.

Small-firm employment.   Working for a small business firm differs only in degree from employment by a private person (farmer, doctor, housewife) or a nonprofit corporation. Much of it is in *very* small firms,[10] and much of it (probably at least two-thirds) is nonunion. The distribution of the 20 million wage and salary workers in businesses with less than 100 employes each is shown in Table 3-4.

[9] There are exceptions to this, of course, mainly in the nonprofit institutional group, where security is above average and working conditions often satisfactory. For the group of markets as a whole, however, the statement is not misleading.

[10] In 1959, 20 per cent of all business firms in the United States (this would be around 1 million companies today!) had no employes at all; they were run by self-employed people either alone or with the aid of unpaid family labor. Betty C. Churchill, "Size of Business Firms," *Survey of Current Business*, September, 1959.

Not many employers with a work force of less than 100 will find it necessary to have even one full-time personnel officer—and even fewer of the 4.7 million with staffs ranging from 0 to 49. Few, in fact, will have any formal personnel policies, unless such have been forced on them by union contract. The overwhelming majority of small employers, as a practical matter, have no employment policies as such, in the sense of regular procedures; they rely instead on individual recruitment, private negotiation, the personal approach, and *ad hoc* treatment of problems as they arise. Small employers are typically shopkeepers, restaurateurs, laundry operators, barbers, cleaners and dyers, service station operators. They do not report to or come under the jurisdiction of the National Labor Relations Board, the Federal wage and hour administrator, or other national labor bureaus. They seldom contract with the Federal government. This leaves them subject only to state and local labor regulations, and both are notoriously spotty, in coverage as well as administration.

There is one type of employment regulation, however, from which the small employer is not exempt—the labor union with its contract and work rules. Employment in the unionized small firm (notably building construction, longshoring, printing) is very highly structured, with wage schedules and work rules administered by the union members (employes) themselves and union business agents. It is usually craft unionism, often closed shop and frequently closed union. It must therefore be clearly distinguished from nonunion employment in the small shop, grocery store, and beauty parlor, where rates, hours, jobs, and hiring are handled loosely on a catch-as-catch-can basis, with great individual variation be-

Table 3-4.   Estimated employment in small firms, classified by size, 1965

Size class	Firms		Employment		Average number of employes per firm
	Number	%	Number	%	
Total firms (all sizes)	4,904,000	100	49,625,000	100	10
50–99 employes	49,000	1	3,482,000	7	74
20–49 employes	147,000	3	4,963,000	10	34
8–19 employes	394,000	8	5,459,000	11	14
4– 7 employes	589,000	12	3,464,000	7	6
3 or less employes	3,681,000	75	2,978,000	6	0.8
All firms 99 or fewer employes	4,860,000	99	20,346,000	41	4

Source: Ratios from Betty C. Churchill, "Size of Business Firms," *Survey of Current Business,* September, 1959, with adjustment for changes in business population and civilian labor force.

tween one employer and another, one job and another, and between different firms in the same industry in the same labor market.[11]

THE PARTLY STRUCTURED LABOR MARKETS

Just over half the employes of business firms in the United States work for companies large enough to make formal personnel management a necessity. Something less than a majority of these work under union contracts (how many nobody knows exactly). The remainder are in unorganized firms or outside the bargaining unit—as office workers or supervisors—in companies which are parties to one or more labor agreements. The market in which they work is often very heavily structured in terms of policies, mechanisms, devices, etc., but the regulations are those of management, for the benefit of the firm, and are subject to change without notice or to varying interpretations by supervisors and personnel representatives.

There are many such companies, some of them industrial, but most of them in the white-collar industries of retail and wholesale trade, finance, and the service industries—hotels, restaurants, movies, etc. Some of them are quite large, as:

Company	Employes
Merchandising chains:	
Sears	249,272
A & P Stores	135,000
Woolworth's	80,020
J. C. Penney	51,000
Montgomery Ward	82,890
Safeway	66,605
Insurance companies:	
Metropolitan	59,841
Prudential	55,909
Travelers	21,694
Banks:	
Bank of America	28,872
First National City (N.Y.)	20,800
Chase Manhattan	15,340
Hotels:	
Hilton	29,600

Source: Figures on employment from *Moody's Industrial Manual, 1964; Moody's Bank and Finance Manual, 1965.*

[11] The special characteristics of craft-union employment are treated in detail in various parts of this volume: later in this chapter and in the section on "Organized Labor."

Personnel management in these firms and others like them is typically white-collar personnel administration. Apart from a minority of custodial and stock-handling workers, it is the management of clerical, sales, supervisory, and semiprofessional employes. Although there are exceptions, most of it is nonunion.[12] The market structure is therefore set by the firm's personnel policies, usually worked out and often enforced by a personnel department. This is a recognized staff function of management, a field of specialization in college and university work, and a career choice of many students.

In its most complete form, personnel administration includes standard procedures for:

1. Recruitment, through employment agencies, by advertising, and by visits to college campuses
2. Selection, by tests, interviews, and studies of applicants' training and experience records
3. Induction, or orientation of new employes
4. Training programs, for the upgrading of employes and improvement of efficiency
5. Job analysis—for wage-setting, employe assignment, etc.
6. Wage and salary administration
7. Advice to supervisors on transfer, promotion, demotion, and layoff
8. Administration of discipline, especially discharge
9. Employe services: research, counseling, grievance handling, publication of house organs, credit unions, and others

Employes outside the bargaining unit in unionized firms.   These consist mainly of the office (clerical) and supervisory employes in the big, solidly organized industrial firms. In most cases, they are excluded from the bargaining unit, as in the following:

It is mutually agreed that for the duration of this Agreement the term "employee" shall *not include* office workers, employees of the engineering department, employees of the industrial security department, officials who have the right to hire and discharge and all other supervisors including and above the rank of Assistant Foreman, unless such exclusions be changed by reason of future certifications by the National Labor Relations Board.[13]

These workers are in a special category in terms of personnel management. They are not union members nor covered by any agreement between management and a union; nevertheless, they often find themselves the beneficiaries of the union's negotiations with management just as

---

[12] The principal exceptions are in the hotels, restaurants, and bars where the Hotel and Restaurant Employees and Bartenders International Union has its membership of 445,000.

[13] From the "Recognition" provisions of a United Auto Workers agreement, italics added.

though the contract applied to them directly. This occurs because of the obvious inequities which would arise if negotiated improvements in wages, hours, and working conditions were withheld from the salaried payroll. A pay raise, shorter working hours, additional holidays for plant workers receive wide publicity when negotiated by union representatives. They are commented on, discussed, and envied. Few managements care to yield such gains to the union and incur the dissatisfaction of the office workers and plant foremen by withholding them from the latter.[14] It is therefore common practice to match the negotiated union "package" cent for cent, hour for hour, and holiday for holiday, with similar improvements for supervisory and clerical workers who are without benefit of union representation.

Employes of the unionized firm who are outside the bargaining unit thus occupy a sort of "twilight zone" in terms of market structure. They cannot themselves affect the terms and conditions of their employment. At the same time, management does not have a free hand either. To a considerable extent, their wages and working conditions are settled in union-management negotiations—not their union, but a union. Just enough of them are now organized to constitute a warning against managerial negligence. They do not have the job security of the organized production and maintenance employes in the bargaining unit, and only in rare and unusual circumstances do they have access to a formal grievance procedure. Nevertheless, it is undeniable that they benefit from the union's presence, and it is certain that they receive more systematic and careful consideration in matters of transfer, discipline, etc., than would be the case otherwise.

Employes of the large unorganized industrial firm, especially the exceptional nonunion firm in an otherwise heavily organized industry, are a similar case. The company is always under heavy pressure to conform to the pattern of wages, hours, and working conditions laid down in union-management agreements in other sections of the industry or in related industries. The standard rule is to meet or exceed the union pattern as the price of avoiding union organizers.

Company personnel policy.   The nonunion employes of large firms work in a labor market framed by the personnel policies of management. These policies bind the employe, but not the employer. Their terms are subject to change without notice by management and such changes do not infringe any legal or contractual right of the employe, so long as no specific statute is violated. In the decision as to appropriate policy, the opinions of employes are seldom invited and final decision on policy and its application is reserved exclusively to the management. The employe

[14] For one thing, it would be a direct invitation to the discriminated employes to vote for union representation for themselves.

receives his information about the job and his position vis-à-vis the company from a handbook prepared by the personnel department: *You and Your Job* (Marshall Field & Co.), *Setting Your Course* (Ford Motor Company), *The Prudential Way, You and Sears.* The message contained is variable as to content and style; it may be specific and detailed or it may be vague and general. If specific, it will probably feature "Rules of Conduct" and the accompanying penalties for violation; it rarely contains advice on how to present a grievance or make a complaint.

THE FULLY STRUCTURED LABOR MARKETS—PUBLIC EMPLOYMENT

Governmental employment in the United States offers the most extreme examples of labor markets structured by law.[15]

The formal personnel rules of public (civilian) employment are at times avoided ("got around") by political interference—political patronage—and they may be influenced by employe organizations (unions or employe associations), but the steady growth of the civil service, or "merit system," has been a feature of the last half century and seems unlikely to be reversed. The main characteristics of the public service are its impersonality and technicality; civil service procedure is the special province of the expert, the "personnel technician." (It is also at times the despair of operating line officers in public agencies, who find that the simplest kind of transfer or promotion or pay raise involves masses of red tape, the reasons for which are either obscure or unacceptable. Suggestion to the reader: check with any government administrator.) About one wage or salary worker in six in the United States—one in five if the uniformed members of the armed services are included—earns his living working for a public agency. About a quarter of the total of such workers are on the Federal payroll; the rest work for state or local agencies, half of them in education. See Table 3-5.

The market for public personnel is widely distributed geographically, it is secure and growing steadily, and it offers medium pay. Over half the total are municipal employes and more than half of these are in

[15] The armed services are a special and by no means insignificant branch of the public labor market. Together they employ in uniform 4.6 per cent of all wage and salary workers of the country: 3,008,000 out of 65,462,000 in April, 1966. Each of the services—Army, Navy, Air Force, Marines—is a career world of its own, with complicated systems of recruitment, promotion, pay, perquisites, and retirement, and each should be at least considered as a career option by every young man of college age. They are differentiated of course from the civilian labor market by the aspect of compulsion which pervades them from entry to discharge.

No adequate description is available in personnel terms to describe the peculiar and often arbitrary system of service academies, ROTC, Officer Candidate Schools, the noncommissioned ranks, the status of enlistees and draftees, etc. This is an area of personnel research which badly needs attention.

Table 3-5.   Public employment in the United States, March, 1965

Level and branch of government		Employment
Federal government		2,326,000
Executive branch	2,295,300	
Department of Defense	920,900	
Post office	592,100	
Other depts. and agencies	781,800	
Legislative branch (Congress)	24,900	
Judicial branch	5,800	
State government		1,942,000
Local (municipal) government		5,606,000
Education: the public schools	3,167,000	
Other local agencies	2,439,000	
Total public employment		9,874,000

Source: *Employment and Earnings,* May, 1965, p. 20.

the public school systems of the country, as teachers, administrators, and custodial personnel. In 1965, out of a total of 9,900,000 (civilian) government workers, there were 3,167,000 local public school employes and 682,000 employes (faculty, administrators, custodians) in state colleges and universities and departments of education, for a total of 3,849,000 in education: 39 per cent (two-fifths) of all public employment. Even the Federal work force is spread around the country and not—as is often thought—concentrated in Washington, D.C. (There are more Federal employes in California than in the District of Columbia.)

Pay levels in public employment, formerly very modest, have risen markedly in recent years. Average pay in the Federal government (full-time civilian employes) in 1962 was $114 per week ($5,921 per year) and in state and local agencies, $102 per week ($5,316 per year), with professional and supervisory personnel included in the totals. They may be compared with the average weekly earnings in 1962 of production workers *only* in contract construction—$122; metals mining—$118; petroleum refining—$131; basic steel and automobile manufacturing—$127; and so on. However, the lower-paid industries, such as banks and trust companies ($72), retail trade ($66), and hotels and laundries ($47 and $51) suffered by comparison.[16] The public service is a rapidly growing area of employment in this country: up from 11 per cent of all nonagricultural workers in 1930, 13 per cent in 1950, to 15 per cent in 1960 and 17 per cent in 1965. Since education is the largest single department of activity and it is now and for some years to come under the pressure of rapidly expanding school enrollments, the likelihood of an early change in the trend seems remote.

[16] *Statistical Abstract of the U.S., 1963,* pp. 410, 436, 239–241; *1964,* p. 408.

Public personnel administration.   Public employment is regulated
by statute and administrative agency. The terms and conditions of work
are either set forth in a law, or the policies governing them are so stated
and the responsibility for management is assigned to a staff agency such as
a civil service commission, a wage board, or a personnel board. This
agency in turn issues rules and regulations which have the force of law.
It may also administer directly some phases of employment—recruitment
and selection, for example—and usually has enforcement powers over the
rest. Either the legislature or the personnel board may consult with
employe representatives, but the government as such rarely commits itself
to a union agreement. (This general rule may be undergoing change at
present, with some executive departments of the Federal government
bargaining collectively, and with the collective bargaining rights won by
the American Federation of Teachers in some large cities, *e.g.*, New York,
Detroit, Philadelphia, but the proposition still holds in 90 per cent of all
public employment.) It retains the right to revise or change the terms of
employment at any time; as a matter of fact, however, wage schedules
and other terms of employment are quite stable over long periods—
mainly due to budgetary necessities and the slowness of legislatures to
act.

There are unions of public employes, some of them long-established
and with very respectable memberships, like the National Association of
Letter Carriers of the U.S.A.—AFL–CIO (168,000 members); the United
Federation of Postal Clerks—AFL–CIO (139,000 members); and the
American Federation of State, County and Municipal Employees—AFL–
CIO (235,000 members).[17] However, most public employment is nonunion, and where employes are organized, they are under the handicap
(for a union) of not being permitted to strike [18] or bargain, as that term
is commonly understood. Government agencies are always exempted from
Federal or state labor relations acts that require employers to recognize
unions or deal collectively with their employes. The customary explanation is the importance of the public service and its uninterrupted operation, plus the security features of public employment not usually offered
by private firms.

The civil service.   A high proportion of all regular, permanent public employes—Federal, state, and local—are eligible for civil service status.
In the Federal government, for example, about 85 per cent of all civilian
employes are subject to the competitive requirements of the Civil Service

---

[17] *Directory of National and International Labor Unions in the U.S., 1965.* BLS
Bulletin 1493.

[18] Forbidden by law for Federal employes (in Sec. 305 of the Taft-Hartley Act)
and in many state laws and by the constitutions or bylaws of most unions of public
employes.

Act. The ratio is smaller in state and local jurisdictions, but still high. Once attained, civil service rank carries with it a number of definite advantages: rights to tenure (job security), increases in pay, and opportunities for promotion. "Merit system" employment is classified, short-hour, moderate-pay, secure. While the theory and the practice may differ, especially in strongly political jurisdictions—where party affiliation is a prerequisite for many appointments—nevertheless, civil service procedures are now widely used. The principal steps in the process are:

1. *Selection* by the personnel agency on the basis of performance on written and oral tests, followed by precise numerical ranking of the successful candidates on "eligible lists" set up for specific occupations or for related "job families."

2. *Certification* of the top three or five names from the appropriate list to administrative officials in need of personnel, who make the final choice, usually after a series of interviews.

3. A *probationary period* of from 90 days to a year, at the end of which the appointee acquires civil service status if still employed.

4. *Rate of pay* determined by classification and grade assignments, with salary progress in-grade based on a supervisor's "service ratings."

5. *Promotion* either by examination or by transfer approved by the personnel agency.

6. Numerous *fringe benefits* (extensive leaves, generous retirement pay at low ages, paid holidays and vacations, etc.).

7. *Discharge* for cause only, after a hearing, and with the right of appeal not only to the supervisor but also to the personnel agency, which can and does reverse the supervisor on occasion.

The main advantage of civil service status is the same as that of union membership—job security. Both civil service rules and labor agreements are designed to protect the employe from arbitrary decisions by management, whether based on political preference, judgments of the employe's competence as a worker, or more personal reasons. In its over-all effects, merit system employment falls somewhere between nonunion private employment and the fully unionized situation. The market is fully structured, probably overstructured, in places—for example, in hiring and at separation. All jobs are classified and movement from one class to another or one grade to another is wrapped up in cumbersome red tape. The employe is protected from discrimination, in theory at least, and an agency exists with the responsibility to hear his case and defend him. (In many cases, this protection is neither as complete nor as selective as that exercised by the stronger unions.) There is a formal grievance procedure in most systems, but its use is customarily confined to discharge cases. The terms and conditions of employment are on record but not always available to the employe and often subject to wide variations of interpretation. The employe has no one to bargain for him—unless he is a member of a union or an association of public service employes—and his pay, hours, and other perquisites are subject to the often uninformed views of city councils, state legislatures, and the United States Congress.

The significant factor in civil service employment is the emphasis on job security and employe rights. Where employment is a matter of public policy, the pattern has moved farther and farther in the direction of a fully structured labor market. In this respect, the public labor market parallels the unionized sector of the private economy. In both cases, the trend has been toward limitation of management's free administration of the employment contract and the substitution therefor of formal limits, written rules, and appeals.

WORKING UNDER A UNION CONTRACT

The market structure in the unionized firm is founded on a written agreement negotiated by two independent agencies: the employer (or an employer association) and the union. No term of the contract may be changed without notice, consultation, and a meeting of the minds of the two parties. If such a change is made without these formalities, it is a simple matter for the employe to "grieve" to his steward (or his business agent, in the case of the craft unionist) and the grievance procedure is brought into action to settle the issue.[19] The employe knows his rights. They are printed in his copy of the agreement and will be explained to him by the steward or some other union official if he does not understand the wording.

Interchange and discussion between union officials in the plant and company personnel representatives or supervisors go on constantly. The reason is the inherent complexity of any operating situation and the difficulty of applying general rules covering many aspects of wages, hours of work, and working conditions, to specific cases. The number of rules is large, the list is growing, and disputes over interpretation (grievances) run into the millions every year. It is a rare agreement that does not provide for the handling of grievances. In the absence of a union, on the other hand, it is equally rare for an employer to designate a channel of appeal for employe complaints other than through the immediate supervisor—whose decision is usually the cause of the dispute. In the unionized plant, the grievance procedure is a fundamental of good industrial relations, as the employe's guarantee of "due process of law"; it is the feature of the labor agreement most difficult to duplicate in nonunion personnel

---

[19] The employer has the right to grieve, too, but seldom needs to exercise the privilege. Management is in charge and makes the original decisions as to the meaning of the agreement; most grievances arise over questions of managerial interpretation.

management. In the typical case, it is a formal, carefully timed, multiple-step, joint bargaining process, ending in arbitration if the dispute is not settled by the parties themselves.

The key factors in the unionized market structure are certainty, publicity, and security. They are obtained by means of written contracts, formal methods of dispute settlement, established work rules, definite and measurable standards (such as seniority for the determination of job rights), and compulsory union membership to assure equal treatment of the work force. However, unionized markets are anything but standardized. There are significant differences in the way contract terms and work rules affect the members of different bargaining units. The primary distinction is between *craft* and *industrial* unionism.[20] In the former, union membership is based on occupation—as in the Plumbers, Bricklayers, Locomotive Engineers. In the latter, the basis of organization is the industry —the Mine Workers, Auto Workers, Steelworkers, etc. Some unions have both types of organization (in separate locals)—the Carpenters, Machinists, Electricians. In fact, the characteristics of craft and industrial organization may shade off by degrees to a point where they much resemble each other. Also, in many business firms there are clear examples of the two systems side by side, each operating within the framework of its own agreement and set of rules.

The craft-union labor market.   There is very extensive union membership among the employes of some small-firm industries (construction, longshoring, shipping, entertainment, the garment trades) and in a variety of occupations ordinarily found in small firms: chauffeurs, musicians, printers. In some regions—*e.g.*, the San Francisco Bay Area—large numbers of other small-scale business operators are under union contract; examples are hotels, restaurants, bars, newspapers, garages, service stations, laundries. Labor organization may be partial or complete, but typically in the small firm it is by craft.

Treatment of the labor market in such cases is just the reverse of the casual, variable treatment found in the small nonunion firm. Once organized, the small employer is more than likely to yield practically full control of the employment relationship to the union. The union may and often does tell him whom he may hire, what he will pay them, what hours they will work, and what rules govern job assignment, eligibility for overtime work, or any other condition or privilege of the trade. There are two main reasons for this. One is the tight organization and strict control of the local labor market exercised by craft unions. The other is the inherently

[20] Or "factory" and "nonfactory" unionism, as the two are called by Van Dusen Kennedy in *Nonfactory Unionism and Labor Relations* (Berkeley, Calif.: Institute of Industrial Relations, University of California, 1955). This is an excellent brief discussion of the closed-shop, (often) closed-union, craft-organized labor market.

unequal bargaining power of the small employer in dealing with a large and powerful craft union.[21]

Union control of the organized small-firm labor market is based on the closed shop and strict regulation of admission of new members into the local union. The worker's identification is with his occupation and his union, not his employer. This identification (as a Brakeman or a Long-shoreman or a Painter) is complete and exclusive. There is no movement from one type of job to another (a carpenter does not become a lather, even if he is out of work and there is a shortage of lathers) but movement from one employer to another is frequent, in some occupations constant. Movement is therefore horizontal—from firm to firm—and always at the same level and within the framework of the same set of work rules, those of the local union and its job territory. If employers need the skills which the union controls, they must hire union members or take the consequences. Entrance to the labor market is through the union via apprenticeship systems which often require the worker to decide on a specific occupation when he is young and to make some sacrifice to get his journeyman's card.

As described succinctly by Clark Kerr:

Once fully in the market, the craft worker can move anywhere within it. . . . Inside the market, wages, working conditions, and job requirements are equalized, and the worker has an unusual knowledge of conditions and job opportunities. Sometimes worker performance is standardized also, so that no employer need prefer any worker any more than any worker need prefer any employer. . . . Ejection from the market is controlled by the union. An employer can discharge a man from a specific job but not from the market. Few discharge grievances are filed in craft markets because the man gets his security from union control of the market and not from the employer.[22]

About 8 million employes—one out of eight of all wage and salary workers—earn their living in markets predominantly of this type.

Craft unionists in private, nonbusiness employment. There are union members who work for private individuals and nonprofit institutions, but the number is small. They consist principally of miscellaneous building tradesmen (carpenters, plumbers, painters) who are not working on contract construction projects but are engaged in odd-job home service and maintenance work; a few thousand farm laborers in the National Agricultural Workers' Union; and organized custodial and semiprofessional employes who work for private hospitals, universities, and such. A

[21] As Kennedy puts it: "The small employer has little hope of prevailing against the union on an issue which affects him alone. In a showdown the union can regard the few jobs he provides as expendable." *Op. cit.,* p. 31.

[22] Clark Kerr, "Balkanization of Labor Markets" in *Labor Mobility and Economic Opportunity* (New York: John Wiley & Sons, Inc., 1954), p. 99.

numerical estimate is only a guess, but it seems unlikely that the total exceeds 300,000.

Craft unionists in this category are often very independent with regard to the terms and conditions of employment. Their dealings with private individuals (homeowners, farmers) make it almost impossible for union business agents to police the rates charged, the hours worked, or any other conditions of employment. Working arrangements are usually oral understandings, with few of the formal trappings of supervised employment. Trade unionists in the institutional group are probably the largest and most important of the three classes mentioned above, but they are still insignificant relative to anything in the business world. Unions have never had much success with nonprofit institutions. One reason is the exemption of such enterprises from most Federal regulation and the absence of covering state laws giving protection to the right to organize and bargain collectively. Others are relatively high employment security, strictly classified work in the professional and semiprofessional classification with large numbers of employes who are normally cool to unionism, and some very conservative management attitudes among institutional administrators.

The industrial-union labor market.   In the typical case, a large or even a medium-sized industrial firm will have a labor relations department handling personnel matters and also be a party to a detailed labor agreement covering its production and maintenance employes in the plant.[23] The contract will usually be with an industrial union (Steelworkers, Auto Workers) or a craft union that has expanded into industrial unionism— Machinists, Teamsters, Electricians. The chief feature of this type of labor market is joint management of the work force, which means not only that there is some reasonable equality of bargaining power at the time the agreement is negotiated but also that there is close association and joint review by management and the union during the life of the contract. Contract "administration" is carried on by the firm's labor relations office and a carefully organized hierarchy of union representatives (stewards, committeemen, and grievance chairmen) in the plant. The union's authority in personnel matters is reflected in the standard practice of the employer's agreement to pay for time spent by union representatives in the investigation and handling of grievances. This is the most effectively structured type of labor market in the United States, taking in about 11 million employes, or one out of six of all wage and salary workers.

The industrial-union labor market differs sharply from that inhabited by craft unionists. The essential fact is that the employe's security is not associated with his occupation or skill but with long service and promo-

---

[23] Now and then the agreement will also cover office employes, but this is rare.

tion within the firm. Movement is therefore vertical, from grade to grade, and lower-rated job to higher-rated job, instead of horizontal, from employer to employer. The worker's basic security is his position on the seniority roster. Specific skills are of minor importance and can be acquired on the job; the employe advances as he acquires a long service record and greater competence. Union work rules are few in industrial employment, their place being taken by specific provisions of the agreement covering wage progression, seniority, promotional opportunities, layoff and recall rights, fringe benefits, welfare and pension plans, etc. Discharge is a major blow and is fought to a finish through the grievance procedure and arbitration, since it means a break in seniority and starting over again at the foot of the seniority roster somewhere else. Horizontal transfer across departmental lines is carefully limited and defined in the agreements, as it too may mean going to the foot of the departmental seniority list.[24]

The labor-market structure in the big industrial firm under union contract is very complicated. Employment is subject to all Federal, state, and local regulations—Federal labor laws, state factory and FEPC acts, and applicable local ordinances. If the employer contracts with the Federal government, there are additional regulations covering security, nondiscrimination, hours, and pay rates. Personnel policies other than those imposed by law have two sources, the labor agreement and decisions of management. The former is in writing; some, but seldom all, of the latter may be found in the employe handbook or posted in the form of plant rules here and there about the plant. Management claims jurisdiction over all employment prerogatives not specifically limited or modified in the agreement, but what is in the contract and what is excluded from it are themselves matters of dispute. Contract interpretations pile up in the form of oral understandings, customary practices, grievance settlements, and arbitrators' decisions. The trend in recent times is clearly in the direction of more detailed agreements, more complex terms, more rigid restrictions upon both management and the union, and less chance for the employe to leave the bargaining unit without giving up valuable vested interests in seniority, job rights, and accrued fringe benefits.

This is the country's most important labor market, not only by virtue of size, but also by reason of the interplay between large and powerful unions and large and powerful employers and employer associations, resulting in notable innovations in employment practice: long-term contracts, guaranteed wages, escalator (cost-of-living) clauses, pension systems, supplementary unemployment benefits, medical welfare plans, job-security programs, nondiscrimination policies, and community wel-

[24] See Kerr, *op. cit.*, p. 105.

fare projects. The employers involved are the country's largest and most influential firms, *e.g.*:

Company	No. of employes
American Telephone and Telegraph (Bell System)	733,138
General Motors Corporation	640,073
Ford Motor Company	316,568
General Electric Company	282,029
United States Steel Corporation	187,721
Standard Oil Company of New Jersey	147,000
Bethlehem Steel Corporation	117,489
Westinghouse	115,170
International Harvester Company	106,230
North American Aviation, Inc.	103,505
Goodyear Tire and Rubber Company	98,729

Source: Figures on employment from *Moody's Industrial Manual, 1964,* and *Public Utility Manual, 1964.*

The policies adopted in this labor market color employment practices in adjacent markets, even though the legal or contractual basis is absent or different. Craft unionism in large plants tends to take on the characteristics of the industrial big brother and to emphasize security, seniority, rate ranges, and promotional ladders. Nonunion white-collar employes are awarded pensions, welfare plans, and rate increases coordinate with those gained in negotiations by the union for production and maintenance employes in the plant. Cost-of-living increases are handed out to supervisory, technical, and professional personnel after they are publicized by union negotiators or framed in escalator clauses. The grievance procedure becomes synonymous with industrial citizenship, and management finds it necessary to establish guarantees of impartial review of disciplinary action against nonunion workers.

Nonunion employes under union contract.   There are nonunion workers inside many bargaining units, eligible for all the benefits and protections of the agreement. These are the "free riders" [25] under sole-bargaining certifications of the National Labor Relations Board and under agreements with maintenance-of-membership union security clauses. In both, the union is committed by law to bargaining for everyone in the unit, but membership is not compulsory.

[25] A derogatory term used by union members to designate employes who "ride free" by accepting the benefits of the contract without paying dues or assuming the other responsibilities of union membership.

For these employes, a fully structured labor market is a fact, just as it is for the union member. The difference is that the nonunion employe gives no support to the union either financially or otherwise and is regarded by his union coworkers at best as a parasite. The union bargains for him and he is entitled, under the agreement, to full union support of all his contract rights, including the grievance procedure. In practice, of course, it is unlikely that he can expect any energetic assistance at union expense. The nonunion man within the bargaining unit is almost by definition "antiunion." Although their number is probably decreasing, as indicated by the growth of union-shop coverage in recent years, various estimates set the total at around a million workers.

EXECUTIVE, PROFESSIONAL, AND OFFICIAL LABOR MARKETS

There remains for discussion the most important group of labor markets of all—that in which the managers and policy setters of the country sell their services.[26] These range all the way from the fully structured markets for elected public officials to the nonstructured, competitive selection of managerial and supervisory personnel in large business firms and big unions. They include, for example, tens of thousands of elected public officers on Federal, state, and local levels, some on a full-time and some on a part-time basis: President of the United States, governors, mayors, congressmen, state legislators, city councilmen, county sheriffs and judges, prosecuting attorneys, and so on.

Elected public officials. This is a very special type of labor market, much too complex to be treated fully, but also much too large and important to be passed over without mention. It has several prime characteristics: (1) It is dominated by lawyers, who enter the competition for office for a wide variety of reasons: public service, career advancement, representation of special-interest groups, enjoyment of the game of politics. (2) It is the market where maximum emphasis is put on candidacy—getting the job and holding it—and often minor emphasis on performing the duties of office; in no other labor market is the basis of selection so widely separated from actual job performance. (3) It is preeminently the market of part-time service, even though the assumption may be that the job is a full-time one. For example, a great many attorneys continue their private practice of the law while also serving as legislators, judges, prose-

[26] This classification cuts across all the markets analyzed previously and so is not separated in the statistics of Table 3-2. Numerically, it will conform roughly to the "professional" and "proprietor-manager-official" categories in Table 2-8, or about 18 to 19 million persons—a little more than a quarter of all wage and salary workers. This assumes that the self-employed included in the "professional" and "managerial" category are balanced off by supervisors listed as "sales" and "foremen."

cuting attorneys, or on elective boards and commissions; elected businessmen do likewise, as do candidates from other types of occupations. (4) As
a market, it offers the widest range of security and insecurity. Some types
of elected officials—judges, for example—either have tenure or are almost
automatically returned to office for life; other officials must face the certainty of keen competition and the possibility of return to private life
after a single period of service or even a portion of one. Election, however, is always for a term, and during that term job security is high; the
number of impeachments and recalls is negligible. (5) Few kinds of jobs
are more demanding or less remunerative financially per hour put in.
Success is practically always preceded by a long apprenticeship at no pay
or very low pay, either in the political party or as representative of a
special-interest group or both. There is little doubt that the prime return
of public officeholding is psychic income: excitement, prestige, and service.

Appointive public officials. This is an even larger group than the
elective officers, and perhaps just as important. These are the men who
run the government—the administrators. They include, for example, on
the national level (1) Cabinet officers, their deputies and assistants on
down to bureau chiefs; (2) the members of the "independent agencies"
(boards and commissions—the General Services Administration, the Veterans Administration, the Federal Reserve System, the National Labor
Relations Board, the FPC, the FAA, the CAB) and a large number of
principals on their staffs such as legal counsel and other professionals;
(3) congressional employes; and many others. Their counterparts are
found at all levels in state and municipal government. As policy-making
officials, they are uniformly exempt from civil service requirements. Practically all of them are sharply identified politically, by party, faction, and
candidate. As a result, this is the area of maximum turnover in government employment.

Recruitment of appointive public officials is usually through political
party channels and the people involved (a large proportion of whom are
full-time political workers) shift back and forth from Federal to state
and local levels of governmental work or from public to private life, as
the exigencies of political success dictate. While publicly employed, they
have two jobs: one is to perform the duties of their appointive office, the
other and often the more important function is to maintain and strengthen
that section of the Democratic or Republican party organization for which
they are responsible. These are the craft unionists of politics. Job security
for them depends upon party affiliation and service; it ebbs and flows
with the success of the party or that portion of it with which the office-
holder is identified. The pay is low, especially in the top jobs ($35,000
per year for a United States Cabinet officer), the hours long, the work
demanding. Here also the principal return appears to be the psychic in-

come of prestige, the excitement of organization and campaigning, and
the opportunities for public service.

*Managerial, professional, and technical personnel in private employ-
ment.*   This is the main career field for college and university graduates
in the United States. As a market, it is practically unstructured, except
for a minority of occupations which fall in professional or technical categories, for which the candidates must meet formal certification or degree
requirements: certified public accountant, college or university professor,
lawyer, or other. Managerial employes in general are exempt from practically all labor legislation.[27] Professional employes must be segregated
from other workers in plant "bargaining units" unless a majority of them
vote to be included.[28] The Fair Labor Standards (Wages and Hours) Act
excludes executive, administrative, and professional employes and "outside salesmen"; if they receive overtime pay, it is by special agreement,
not legal right. The unemployment insurance and pension provisions of
the Social Security Act apply to everyone on the payroll up to the president of the corporation, but applications for job insurance by laid-off
managerial employes are few. Most are salaried people and not subject
to layoff when business is slack.

There are two main sources of supervisory and managerial personnel:
by promotion from the ranks and by recruitment from colleges and universities. As the technical and educational requirements of industry
increase, the second source becomes more and more important. Most
upper-level management people today have college degrees, and a growing number of jobs in middle management and staff divisions (personnel,
controllership, research, public relations) are being filled with college-
graduate trainees. As time goes on, it will be increasingly difficult for the
bright employe with ambition and experience but limited educational
background to fight his way to the top.

Part of the reason is the increasing complexity of all social organization, including especially commerce and industry, for the understanding
of which a college education or its equivalent is now almost a prerequisite. An even stronger reason, however, is the simple fact of corporate
emphasis upon the hiring of college graduates, on grounds not only of
special training but also of natural selection. College graduates are the
survivors of a long-range competitive process which at a minimum is a test
of ambition, sustained effort, and long-range vision, and at a maximum (in

---

[27] Supervisory personnel (foremen, etc.) are not "employees" as defined in the
Taft-Hartley Act, and they are therefore not protected by the National Labor Relations
Board. They can still organize if they wish, but employers are not required by law to
recognize them or bargain collectively with them. Sec. 14a of the National Labor Relations Act, Title I of the Taft-Hartley Act.

[28] Sec. 9b of the National Labor Relations Act.

the strongest colleges and universities) admits and graduates only the representatives of the top 1 to 5 per cent in ability among the general population. The door to high-level achievement is not closed to the employe without college training, but the competition gets tougher every year.

Professional and technical (subprofessional) employes are even less likely to be trained on the job than managerial timber. The Taft-Hartley Act defines a professional employe as:

any employee engaged in work (i) predominantly intellectual and varied in character as opposed to routine mental, manual, mechanical, or physical work; (ii) involving the consistent exercise of discretion and judgment in its performance; (iii) of such a character that the output produced or the result accomplished cannot be standardized in relation to a given period of time; (iv) requiring knowledge of an advanced type in a field of science or learning customarily acquired by a prolonged course of specialized intellectual instruction and study in an institution of higher learning or a hospital, as distinguished from a general academic education or from an apprenticeship or from training in the performance of routine mental, manual, or physical processes; or

any employee, who (i) has completed the courses of specialized intellectual instruction and study described . . . [above] . . . and (ii) is performing related work under the supervision of a professional person to qualify himself to become a professional employee. . . .[29]

Professional education is very highly structured nowadays in university schools of law, medicine, business, social service, journalism. Every year the requirements are made stiffer (higher standards, longer periods of instruction) and every year more occupations are moved into the professional and technical groups. No general job classification has increased more rapidly than that of "professional, technical, and kindred workers," which has doubled in the last 30 years as a percentage of the work force. This is both cause and effect of the increase in college and university enrollments. Professional skills are sharpened in practice, but they are acquired in institutions of higher learning. As a consequence, the prime source of recruits is college graduates.

First-line production supervision—assistant foremen, foremen, general foremen—and some staff jobs, especially in labor relations, are the principal career opportunities for rank-and-file employes, whether from the bargaining unit or outside it. Here the prime qualification is day-by-day knowledge of the specific operating problems of the individual department or plant, acquaintance with the work force, and knowledge both of job requirements and specific abilities of workers and leadmen. The move across the line, however, from bargaining unit to supervision, is an important step for the union member and some are deterred by the loss of job security and other vested interests under the union contract. The precise limits of the bargaining unit and the sharp line of demarcation drawn

[29] Sec. 2(12).

Table 3-6. Average salaries and salary ranges: Selected professional and administrative jobs

Occupation and class	Mean annual salary	Monthly salary range—2d and 3d quartiles
Auditors and accountants		
Auditors I	$ 5,832	$ 441–524
Auditors IV	10,284	755–948
Accountants I	6,240	481–563
Accountants III	7,908	603–711
Accountants V	11,568	855–1,054
Chief accountants II	12,576	918–1,188
Chief accountants IV	15,948	1,139–1,479
Attorneys		
Attorneys I	7,248	551–662
Attorneys III	10,464	751–992
Attorneys V	16,032	1,153–1,487
Attorneys VII	24,288	1,693–2,314
Office managers		
Managers, office services I	7,500	563–699
Managers, office services IV	12,948	1,014–1,170
Personnel management		
Job analysts I	6,576	473–622
Job analysts IV	10,154	764–924
Directors of personnel I	9,660	693–903
Directors of personnel III	13,896	984–1,311
Directors of personnel IV	16,512	1,195–1,547
Chemists and engineers		
Chemists I	6,456	501–588
Chemists IV	10,632	789–976
Chemists VI	14,748	1,087–1,348
Chemists VIII	21,084	1,567–1,847
Engineers I	7,344	584–643
Engineers IV	11,016	829–1,001
Engineers VI	14,820	1,095–1,370
Engineers VIII	20,484	1,524–1,887
Engineering technicians I	4,872	366–446
Engineering technicians III	6,672	510–609
Engineering technicians V	8,556	655–766
Draftsmen, junior	5,400	389–506
Draftsmen, senior	7,020	511–650

Source: *Monthly Labor Review,* December, 1964, p. 1427.

by the Taft-Hartley Act between the protected status of employes and the unprotected status of supervisors often makes the transition seem a matter of "changing sides." [30] There are still plenty of candidates, but there would be more if the line drawn between the two levels of organization were not so explicit.

The labor market for managerial and professional personnel in general is lightly structured, competitive, high-pay, long-hour, and relatively secure. In the main, it is a series of markets limited to the individual business firm. Top executives, middle management, and supervisors are "moved up" on the basis of long service, demonstrated ability, strict and uncompromising loyalty, and identification with successful superiors or the performance of a strategic function. What structure there is is usually traditional—"the way it is done here." Employes have few enforceable rights; those in effect are usually related to compensation and for a definite term. With no contractual or legal basis of employment, there is no formal grievance procedure or other appeals machinery. Grievances are individually bargained out with immediate supervisors or simply absorbed into the total calculation of gains and losses from the job. Discharge is infrequent, although it occurs, and some companies and some managements acquire a reputation for arbitrary treatment of even senior executives.[31] A wide variety of special pay arrangements (bonuses, stock options, profit sharing, etc.) and liberal fringe benefits—expense allowances, noncontributory pensions, cars for personal use, company-paid vacation trips—supplement stated salary figures.

The salaries themselves are the highest to be found in any labor market in the world, with top-level executive compensation running into the hundreds of thousands of dollars a year. Most of the 4,600,000 "consumer units" (families and individuals) with incomes of more than $15,000 per year are headed by persons in this labor market.[32] They are 8 per cent of all income receivers in the United States. The salary ranges in selected professions and administrative jobs are shown in Table 3-6.

READINGS

For a general sociological approach to the labor market, see William F. Whyte, *Men at Work* (Homewood, Ill.: Richard D. Irwin, Inc., 1961), and Elton Mayo's classic, *The Human Problems of an Industrial Civilization* (New York:

[30] Some labor agreements permit the supervisor to continue to accumulate seniority in the bargaining unit, either indefinitely or for a term of years, which has the effect of maintaining his job security and is a form of encouragement to candidates for supervisory jobs.

[31] The student might look into the recent history of Montgomery Ward and Co., under the management of Mr. Sewell Avery.

[32] *Survey of Current Business*, April, 1964, p. 4.

The Macmillan Company, 1933). A good collection of essays on the various phases of unionized market structure is Jack Barbash, *Unions and Union Leadership* (New York: Harper & Row, Publishers, Incorporated, 1959). Anthony Sampson's *The Anatomy of Britain Today* (New York: Harper & Row, Publishers, Incorporated, 1965) is the definitive statement of the British "Establishment"—the managerial, professional, and governmental classes that constitute the "ruling group" of that country. Unfortunately, there is no comparable survey of American institutions.

PART TWO

ORGANIZED
LABOR

FOUR

LABOR AT THE CROSSROADS: THE 1960s

The 1960s have been a baffling period for organized labor in the United States. Prosperity, high wages, shortening hours, liberal fringe benefits, and a friendly administration in Washington should spell a growing labor movement with a strong unified leadership. Between 1960 and 1965, organized labor endorsed and helped elect two Presidents in a row: Kennedy and Johnson; it also helped produce a more and more liberal Congress, and it watched one of its own—Arthur Goldberg, formerly general counsel to the United Steelworkers and the CIO—take his place in the Cabinet, on the Supreme Court, and then succeed Adlai Stevenson as delegate to the United Nations. During the same period, prices were relatively stable, the gross national product swung upward through the longest period of sustained prosperity in history, and unemployment dropped to around 4 per cent. Yet within this encouraging environment, trade unionism backed and filled: membership fell, organizing efforts hit a new low, clumsy and arbitrary bargaining on the railroads, in automobiles, and in the newspaper industry gave labor leadership a black eye, while prominent union leaders were indicted for crimes and were voted out of office.

At the December, 1964, meeting of the Industrial Relations Research Association, a panel of experts considered the question: "Is the American collective bargaining system obsolete?" [1] Though the answers were generally no, the statements were brief, qualified, and defensive. At the same meeting, Professor Joel Seidman of the University of Chicago analyzed "The Sources for Future Growth and Decline in American Trade Unions." [2]

[1] The panel members were Nathan Feinsinger (University of Wisconsin), B. C. Roberts (British), George Shultz (University of Chicago), and Frederick Harbison (Princeton University). *Proceedings,* 17th Annual Meeting, pp. 156–169.

[2] *Ibid.,* pp. 98–108. See also, *e.g.,* Paul Jacobs, *Old before Its Time: Collective Bargaining at 28* (Santa Barbara, Calif.: Center for the Study of Democratic Institutions, 1963), and Solomon Barkin, *The Decline of the Labor Movement and What Can Be Done About It* (Santa Barbara, Calif.: Center for the Study of Democratic Institutions, 1961).

Looking ahead 10 years, he found that the chances of further decline were at least equal to the prospects for growth. Discussing his paper, a panel member said:

It is my conviction that the most urgent needs of workers have already been satisfied by unions themselves, and the remaining needs will increasingly be fulfilled by the government and management. It sounds paradoxical, but the success of unions appears to be self-defeating. . . . This suggests that the law of diminishing return is valid in industrial relations too.[3]

THE QUESTIONS

Whether on the rise or on the decline, organized labor in the United States is today a fact, and a very big fact. Both economically and politically it is a powerful force; few people escape its influence entirely. The 150,000 contracts under which union members work affect the livelihood of more than 60 million people directly and at least half as many again indirectly. Labor disputes (strikes, lockouts, picketing) add many more to the number. For management, these agreements must be negotiated and administered; they set limits to operating procedures, affect costs, and through them, prices and sales. No session of Congress rolls around without its quota of bills for the regulation or de-regulation of labor relations; every term of the Supreme Court has its precedent-setting labor decisions. To understand how the United States economy works, some grasp of the institution of organized labor is indispensable.

Then what questions should the student of the labor movement try to find the answers to? Certainly they should include the following:

1. Description: The anatomy of organized labor today—size, organization, leadership, public support, etc.
2. History: How did it get where it is and what have been the major influences on its growth and development?
3. Theory: Why do workers organize?
4. Goals and strategies: What are unions after and how do they try to get what they want?
5. Law: What are labor's legal rights, privileges, limitations?

Warning.   Trade unions are news; they are "good copy" for newspapers, magazines, and books. As a result, many people feel, by the time they have reached college at least, that they know what a union is, how it operates, how an employer will react to it, what "strike," "picket," "lockout," "collective bargaining," and other labor terms mean, and they have heard of the main labor laws which protect or limit union actions. They are often right; they do know these things. They may even have had firsthand knowledge of union membership and operation, either through a

---

[3] Julius Rezler, *Proceedings* (above), p. 118.

father or relative or through a job of their own. The only trouble with this knowledge is that, while correct as far as it goes, it is frequently sketchy, one-sided, and based on limited experience.

It is almost never safe to assume that one union has exactly the same problem as another, that one strike is for the same ends or will be equally as successful or as much of a failure as another, or that management re-action in one firm or industry will match that of another firm or industry. At the same time, there are many similarities. One of the big problems of the serious student of labor relations is to try to get the over-all picture, the features which are common to all or most unions and the principles on which unions or management agree, as well as those over which they argue, in order to have a basis for judging the variations.

There is probably more opinion, prejudice, bias, and partiality per capita in union-management affairs than in any other kind of human activity, not even excluding family or domestic relations. It is that kind of problem. Most people are either "for" organized labor or "against" it; there are very few who find it natural to take a middle position. Nevertheless, this is the position that the student should try to reach, and it is much harder to do than to learn the facts and theories. It may be stated categorically that no one has become mature about labor relations so long as he thinks that every strike should be won or that every strike should be lost, or that the union leader is naturally right or naturally wrong, or that management's side is the right side, come what may, or that it is just as certainly the wrong one. Withholding judgment until all the facts are in is the fundamental rule in labor-management analysis. At the same time, it is about the hardest thing to do.

The questions listed above indicate the subjects covered in the rest of this part of the book. The discussion will be in outline form, with the idea of raising the issues and showing how the land lies in the world of organized labor, rather than of listing every detail of organization and method. There is plenty to learn about organized labor and plenty to study; the volume of merely *current* union activity—contract negotiations, strikes, organization campaigns, lawsuits, representation elections, conventions, publications, lobbying, political activity—is stupendous. All of it (or at least, most of it) makes sense and falls into a pattern, but the pattern is sometimes not too clear. The purpose of the chapters which follow is to make a general survey of the trade-union universe in the United States, its current position, its historical background, authoritative opinions as to what caused it, its policies and tactics, and its legal situation.

THE KEY MEASURES: SIZE, STRATEGIC FUNCTION

There are two principal measures of union power and influence. One is *size*—membership. The other is the strategic importance of *the industry* in which the union is located or of *the occupation* which it controls.

Size. A large membership means strong locals, saturation of the industry or (for craft unions) the local labor markets, high morale, and a strong treasury. In unions, just as in other organizations, numbers mean prestige—they are evidence of leadership, loyalty, and popularity. At the relatively low ebb of 1964, the major unions still dwarfed the corporations they dealt with, even in such big-firm industries as steel, automobiles, aerospace, and the railroads. The "Big Six" of trade unionism, with individual rosters of 600,000 or more each, and with more than one-third of the total membership, are shown in Table 4-1, for 1956 and 1964.[4]

The "Big Six" are the Goliaths of organized labor in this country, in a size class of their own.[5] The least of them, the Electricians, has over 300,000 more members than the next in line, the Hotel and Restaurant

[4] Union membership figures should always be taken with a dash of salt. There are great difficulties in determining just how many members a union, especially a big industrial union, has at any given time. Craft-union membership is relatively stable. The journeyman carpenter or painter rarely shifts out of his occupation; if he moves, it is to another local of his union, and he keeps up his dues as a matter of course between jobs. Nevertheless, many craft workers become self-employed businessmen (the painting or plumbing contractor) and owner-operators (trucking) and so on. They usually keep their cards but often do not pay dues. The industrial unionist, on the other hand, may change unions or go nonunion at any time as he moves from a plant organized by the Auto Workers to one with a Steelworkers bargaining unit or to a job in an unorganized shop. When unemployed, his dues are often excused or reduced and some unions continue to count him while some do not. There are many marginal cases: the member promoted or transferred temporarily (?) out of the bargaining unit, the member in bad standing for nonpayment of dues, the retired "old boy," etc. Some unions do not publish membership figures; others raise or lower the totals for financial or political reasons.

Another difficulty is the time factor. Membership figures are collected biennially by the Bureau of Labor Statistics and published in the *Directory of National and International Labor Unions in the United States.* They are always from 12 to 18 months out of date by the time of publication. For example, the *1965 Directory,* with survey figures for the year 1964, was published April, 1966, as BLS Bulletin 1493. A more frequent (annual) survey of union memberships for organizations with 23,000 or more members is to be found in the *World Almanac,* and the biennial *Proceedings* of the AFL–CIO give the reported memberships of affiliated unions for odd-numbered years, based on payment of per capita dues. The BLS figures and totals have been sharply criticized by Leo Troy in a survey of union membership from 1897 to 1962. (Leo Troy, "Trade Union Membership, 1897–1962," *The Review of Economics and Statistics,* February, 1965, p. 98.) All in all, trade-union census data leave much to be desired.

[5] The Teamsters Union is the largest labor organization in the world, the biggest bona fide union in existence. It is challenged only by the Transport and General Workers Union of Great Britain, which in 1961 had 1,302,000 members. Anthony Sampson, *Anatomy of Britain* (New York: Harper & Row, Publishers, Incorporated, 1962), p. 557.

Table 4-1. The "Big Six" of American unions: 600,000 or more members each, 1956 and 1964

Union and affiliation	Membership		
	1956	1964	Change
Teamsters (International Brotherhood of Teamsters, Chauffeurs, Warehousemen and Helpers of America)—independent	1,368,000	1,507,000	Up 10%
Auto Workers (International Union, United Automobile, Aerospace and Agricultural Implement Workers of America)—AFL–CIO	1,321,000	1,168,000	Down 12%
Steelworkers (United Steelworkers of America)—AFL–CIO	1,250,000	965,000	Down 23%
Carpenters (United Brotherhood of Carpenters and Joiners of America)—AFL–CIO	850,000	760,000	Down 11%
Machinists (International Association of Machinists and Aerospace Workers)—AFL–CIO	950,000	808,000	Down 15%
Electricians (International Brotherhood of Electrical Workers)—AFL–CIO	675,000	806,000	Up 19%
Total	6,414,000	6,014,000	Down 6%

Sources: *Directory of National and International Labor Unions in the United States, 1957, 1965, passim.*

Employees, with a membership of 445,000. Together the "Big Six" are 3 per cent of all unions but register a third (33.5 per cent) of all union members. Each is solidly grounded in one or more major industries, to wit:

Teamsters: trucking, local delivery, warehousing

Auto Workers: automobile, aerospace, agricultural machinery

Steelworkers: steel, aluminum, and their products

Carpenters: building construction, lumbering, wood products

Machinists: aerospace (with the UAW) and metals manufacturing in general

Electricians: building construction and electronics

Somewhat less influential than the unions in the "Big Six" are a group of 15 labor organizations ranging in scale from 200,000 to 500,000 members each. They are listed in Table 4-2. The concentration of manpower in unions is thus much greater than that in corporations. The 21 unions in Tables 4-1 and 4-2, with 10.9 million members, contain 64 per cent of all trade unionists but constitute only 11 per cent of the unions. Their combined membership is about one-sixth of all employes in the country, organized and unorganized.

The big unions reflect—sometimes in aggravated form—the trends and problems of the labor movement as a whole. From a total of 17,383,000 in 1956, union membership slipped in 8 years to 17,187,000, a decline of 1 per cent. (Over the same interval, the six biggest unions fell 6 per cent—from 6,414,000 to 6,014,000.) The decline was far from uniform, however; in general, membership in the service trades (transportation, communications, retailing, building service) held steady or increased, while in most branches of manufacturing, in building construction, and on the railroads there were losses. Mechanization and automation took their toll; while the Teamsters expanded from 1,368,000 to 1,505,000, and the Electricians were up almost a fifth, the Steelworkers lost 23 per cent of their membership. In the same period, the Building Service Employees International Union gained 40 per cent (230,000 to 320,000), and the Auto Workers fell off by 153,000 members. The railway unions slumped under the impact of competing transport and automation: the Clerks, 350,000 to 270,000; the Trainmen, 217,000 to 185,000; and the Telegraphers, 65,000 to 49,000. (The last-named changed its title to Transportation-Communication Employees Union.) Labor unity, a chronic and perplexing issue, was highlighted by the Teamsters, still outside the "House of Labor."

The 15 unions in Table 4-2 had a combined membership in 1956 of

Table 4-2.   American unions with 200,000 to 500,000 members, 1964

Union and affiliation—all AFL–CIO but the UMWA (short name capitalized)	Membership
HOTEL AND RESTAURANT Employees and Bartenders International Union	445,000
International LADIES' GARMENT WORKERS' Union	442,000
LABORERS' International Union of North America*	432,000
RETAIL CLERKS International Association	428,000
Amalgamated CLOTHING WORKERS of America	377,000
Amalgamated MEAT CUTTERS and Butcher Workmen of North America	341,000
BUILDING SERVICE Employees International Union	320,000
International Union of OPERATING ENGINEERS	311,000
COMMUNICATIONS WORKERS of America	294,000
American Federation of MUSICIANS	275,000
International Union of Electrical, Radio and Machine Workers (IUE)	271,000
Brotherhood of Railway and Steamship CLERKS, Freight Handlers, Express and Station Employees	270,000
United Association of Journeymen and Apprentices of the Plumbing and Pipe Fitting Industry of the United States and Canada (PLUMBERS)	256,000
American Federation of STATE, COUNTY and MUNICIPAL EMPLOYEES	235,000
International Union of DISTRICT 50, United Mine Workers of America	210,000
Total	4,907,000

* Formerly the Hod Carriers, Building and Common Laborers Union of America.
Source: BLS Bulletin 1493 (1965).

Table 4-3.   Concentration of union membership, 1964

Unions with membership of	Number of unions	Union membership	% of unions	%, cumulative	% of members	%, cumulative
600,000 to 1,600,000	6	6,014,000	3.3	3	33.5	34
200,000 to 500,000	15	4,907,000	7.9	12	27.4	61
100,000 to 200,000	26	3,790,000	13.8	25	21.2	83
50,000 to 100,000	26	1,696,000	13.8	39	9.5	92
25,000 to 50,000	25	885,000	13.2	51	4.9	97
Under 25,000	91	628,000	48.2	100	3.4	100
Total	189	17,919,000*	100.0		100.0	

* This total includes something over a million union members in Canada, and excludes unaffiliated (company) union members in the United States, as well as members in locals directly affiliated with the AFL–CIO. The United States total, with the corrections as noted above, is given by the BLS as 17,187,000.
Source: BLS Bulletin 1493 (1965), pp. 50, 53.

4,890,000; thus, in 8 years, they just managed to hold their ground. As is the case with business firms, the great majority of unions are of modest size: three out of four have less than 100,000 members; six out of ten (116 out of 189) have less than 50,000 each. But the great majority of the members are in the big unions. The six biggest, for example, with a third of the total American membership, outweigh the 142 smallest, with less than a fifth. Table 4-3 shows the general distribution of membership by size of union.

Concentration as an issue.   Table 4-3 illustrates a highly controversial issue currently agitating both the labor movement and the scholars who study it. Very simply, it is centralization versus decentralization. The American labor movement has always been a prime example of the latter; the principle of "exclusive jurisdiction" by a single union over a given trade or job territory has been a fundamental tenet of organized labor since the days of Samuel Gompers. The American Federation of Labor was organized for the specific purpose of *protecting* the autonomy of its members, not to act as a central directing group or governing body. Individual unions have moved into or stayed out of the Federation without loss of membership, status, or prestige. Examples are the Teamsters, the Mineworkers, and the Locomotive Engineers today, the Carpenters and the Machinists in the past. The big question is: Does this autonomy of the nationals and internationals weaken the labor movement in its struggle to organize the unorganized and bargain with employers? (Or, in fact, is there a labor movement as such or just a series of fractional labor movements, each of which is looking out for Number 1?)

Many think so and recommend merger and amalgamation to reduce the number of smaller, less effective organizations. It has also been proposed many times that the Federation should be strengthened so as to give it real power to coordinate and direct organizing campaigns with authority to penalize noncooperating unions.[6] The case of Great Britain is cited, where there are about the same number of unions as in the United States (182 in 1961), but the concentration is much greater and the proportion of the labor force that is organized is far higher. The six biggest unions in Britain have just under half the total membership, and about 90 per cent of the members are in unions affiliated with the Trades Union Congress (TUC), the British counterpart to the AFL–CIO.[7]

The merger of the AFL and the CIO in December, 1955, was for the exact purpose of strengthening the "House of Labor" by eliminating competition between unions of the two federations, eliminating "dual unionism" (two unions claiming the same job territory), reducing the number of unions by merger (fairly successful: from 215 unions in 1953 to 189 in 1964), and concentrating on the battle with employers. Unhappily, the stagnation of the labor movement has coincided almost exactly with the life of the merged federation, and the Teamsters, outside the AFL–CIO since 1957, have been the biggest union success story in the country.

Which is best for the labor movement: concentration or competition? The answer is by no means clear to all and the argument will probably continue for some time.

Strategic function. Union power depends on things other than size. Leadership is a big factor. Money in the bank also helps, as does an indoctrinated, disciplined membership. As significant as either of these in some cases, however, is the union's strategic location in an occupation or an industry of vital importance. Unions considerably smaller than any mentioned above may be in a position to shut down a complete industry as a result of tight control of a few crucial jobs. An example is the International Longshoremen's Association, with 50,000 members, which can and does immobilize the entire East Coast and Gulf shipping industry through its control of the ship-to-shore transfer of freight. Where strategic location is buttressed by size, a strong financial position, shrewd management, and a rugged, disciplined membership, the union may be in a position to challenge the largest corporations in the country or even an entire industry, as the Auto Workers do regularly.

As the national economy becomes more tightly integrated, more mechanized, and moves at higher speed, the number of strategic industries and occupations increases. It is not necessary to get all or even a majority

---

[6] See discussions in *Proceedings* of the 17th Annual Meeting of the Industrial Relations Research Association, Chicago, Dec. 28–29, 1964, pp. 109–125.

[7] Sampson, *op. cit.*, pp. 554, 557.

of the 221,000 employes of the airlines to strike to shut down service. A work stoppage by less than 10 per cent—the 13,470 members of the International Air Line Pilots Association—will accomplish the same result just as effectively. Likewise, a steel strike soon starves the automobile and construction industry, the shutdown of an automobile manufacturer cuts off orders to suppliers, subcontractors, and dealers, and a local-lines trucking strike will soon close down most of the wholesale and retail outlets in the area. A coastwise strike by a few thousand members of the International Organization of Masters, Mates and Pilots or of the National Marine Engineers' Beneficial Association would immediately tie up 90 per cent of the shipping in the area.

A considerable number of major industrial groups are quite solidly organized. Some examples are listed in Table 4-4.

In most of the above industries, there is union representation of 75 to 100 per cent of all production and maintenance employes. In some of them—*e.g.*, coal mining, basic steel, women's clothing—control is in the hands of a single union. In others, it is divided among several employe

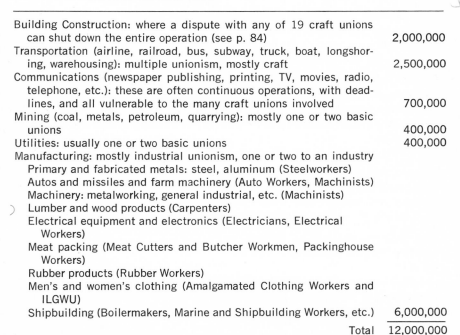

Table 4-4.   **Estimated nonsupervisory employment in strongly organized sectors of industry, 1965**

Building Construction: where a dispute with any of 19 craft unions can shut down the entire operation (see p. 84)	2,000,000
Transportation (airline, railroad, bus, subway, truck, boat, longshoring, warehousing): multiple unionism, mostly craft	2,500,000
Communications (newspaper publishing, printing, TV, movies, radio, telephone, etc.): these are often continuous operations, with deadlines, and all vulnerable to the many craft unions involved	700,000
Mining (coal, metals, petroleum, quarrying): mostly one or two basic unions	400,000
Utilities: usually one or two basic unions	400,000

Manufacturing: mostly industrial unionism, one or two to an industry
  Primary and fabricated metals: steel, aluminum (Steelworkers)
  Autos and missiles and farm machinery (Auto Workers, Machinists)
  Machinery: metalworking, general industrial, etc. (Machinists)
  Lumber and wood products (Carpenters)
  Electrical equipment and electronics (Electricians, Electrical Workers)
  Meat packing (Meat Cutters and Butcher Workmen, Packinghouse Workers)
  Rubber products (Rubber Workers)
  Men's and women's clothing (Amalgamated Clothing Workers and ILGWU)
  Shipbuilding (Boilermakers, Marine and Shipbuilding Workers, etc.)
	6,000,000

Total	12,000,000

Source: *Employment and Earnings,* May, 1965, pp. 14–19.

combinations, by craft. Possibly the most extreme example of the latter is the building construction industry, with the work divided among 19 different trades, as given in Table 4-5. Other industries with multiple-union control are the railroads, newspaper printing and publishing, the maritime trades.

In building construction, the power associated with *strategic function* is at its maximum. Foundations cannot be dug without the use of equip-

Table 4-5. Unions in the building construction industry, 1964

Union (short name capitalized)	Membership
International Association of Heat and Frost Insulators and ASBESTOS WORKERS	14,000
International Brotherhood of BOILERMAKERS, Iron Ship Builders, Blacksmiths, Forgers and Helpers	. . . . . .*
BRICKLAYERS, Masons and Plasterers International Union of America	135,000
United Brotherhood of CARPENTERS and Joiners of America	760,000
International Brotherhood of Electrical Workers (ELECTRICIANS)	806,000
International Union of ELEVATOR CONSTRUCTORS	13,000
International Union of OPERATING ENGINEERS	311,000
GRANITE CUTTERS' International Association of America	3,000
LABORERS' International Union of North America	432,000
International Association of Bridge, Structural and Ornamental IRON WORKERS	143,000
The Wood, Wire and Metal LATHERS International Union	16,000
International Association of Marble, Slate and Stone Polishers, Rubbers and Sawyers, Tile and MARBLE SETTERS' Helpers and Marble Mozaic and Terrazzo Workers' Helpers	10,000†
Brotherhood of PAINTERS, Decorators, and Paperhangers of America	199,000
Operative PLASTERERS' and Cement Masons' International Association of the United States and Canada	68,000
United Association of Journeymen and Apprentices of the Plumbing and Pipe Fitting Industry of the United States and Canada (PLUMBERS)	256,000
United Slate, Tile and Composition ROOFERS, Damp and Waterproof Workers Association	22,000
SHEET METAL WORKERS' International Association	100,000
Journeymen STONE CUTTERS' Association of North America	1,000
International Brotherhood of TEAMSTERS, Chauffeurs, Warehousemen and Helpers of America	. . . . . .‡
Total	3,289,000

* Only a few Boilermakers are engaged in building construction; most of them work in factories, foundries, shipyards, and railroad shops.
† The longest name in American trade unionism.
‡ Like the Boilermakers, only a small percentage of the Teamsters is in building construction.
Source: BLS Bulletin 1493, *passim.*

ment run by Operating Engineers; they cannot be poured without Labor-ers, Teamsters and Cement Masons; pipes cannot be laid without Plumb-ers, nor wiring installations be made without Electricians; beams and joists require Carpenters, and so on. Each craft is skilled, each is tightly organized, and a picket line for one is a picket line for all. The leverage exerted by each group in turn is terrific; hence, the employers organize into associations (Associated General Contractors) to bargain with several crafts at once and delegate broad powers to the associations to administer and interpret the agreements (grievance procedure and arbitration).

The skilled crafts have always been the aristocrats of organized labor: highly paid, independent, exclusive. Strategic function explains why. As minority groups providing indispensable skills, they can and do exact higher rates per hour, shorter work weeks, more overtime at higher premium pay, than their industrial-union counterparts. For this they pay a price, sometimes a high one: restricted entry (in many unions, the appli-cant must be sponsored before being admitted to apprenticeship), long apprenticeships (three to five years), and intermittent work schedules with a higher rate of unemployment. They are specialists,[8] and their wages, more than most, are quasi-rents.[9] If the industry they are in is prosperous, their earnings run very high; if the industry declines, they suffer more than proportionately due to their immobility as a result of specialization. They are the professional men of the blue-collar world, with status, author-ity, and variable earnings.

Trade Unionism in the Twentieth Century.   Getting under way around the turn of the century, the American labor movement peaked in 1920 at 5 million members, following the First World War, then slid gently downward to less than 3 million by 1933. The rise of organized labor to a position of real national influence started two years later and took about a dozen years—from 1935 to 1948. During this period:

1.   Trade-union membership multiplied four times over from 3.75 million to 15 million.

2.   Governmental protection of the right to organize and bargain collec-tively was firmly established by statute (the Wagner Act), by administra-tive action (the National Labor Relations Board), and by court decision (*NLRB v. Jones & Laughlin Steel Corp.*, and subsequent rulings).

3.   The CIO got under way and grew from eight unions with something over a million members to more than 30 unions with 6 million members, while the AFL expanded in size from 2 million to more than 7 million.

4. In 1947, Congress set about regulating the colossus it had created by imposing a set of stiff controls in the Taft-Hartley (Labor Management Relations) Act of 1947.

[8] Recommended reading: Chic Sale's wonderful book, *The Specialist*.
[9] See Alfred Marshall, *Principles of Economics*, 8th ed., pp. 577–579.

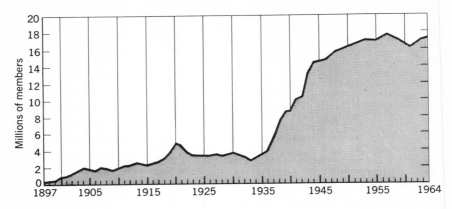

Fig. 4-1.   Sixty-seven years of growth in the American labor movement.

After a short breathing spell, from 1948 to 1950, union membership took another quantum jump during the Korean conflict to 17.3 million in 1953. The 11 years beginning with 1953 were really a long plateau: the high point was reached in 1957 at 17.7 million; by 1964, the membership figure was back below what it had been at the beginning: 17,187,000.

Since the AFL–CIO merger went into effect in 1956 (ratification date —December, 1955), the trend has been downward. The loss of ground is greater than the membership drop indicates, since both the labor force as a whole and the number of nonagricultural wage and salary employes in particular have increased steadily. In 1956, organized labor was 33 per cent of the nonfarm workers in the United States; by 1964, its share had dropped to 29 per cent.

The reasons? You name them; many have tried: automation, adverse legislation (the Taft-Hartley Act, Landrum-Griffin Act), employer opposition, an unfriendly government (the Eisenhower administration), union corruption (McClellan committee), prosperity and full employment (a seller's market for labor), elimination of competition between the AFL and the CIO, better personnel management by big corporations, poor labor leadership.

The fluctuations of trade-union membership from 1897 to 1964 are shown in Figure 4-1.

THE "HOUSE OF LABOR"

Merging of the AFL and the CIO.   For 20 years, organized labor in America was a divided movement, split three ways—among the two major federations, the American Federation of Labor (AFL) and the Congress of Industrial Organizations (CIO), and a number of unaffiliated unions described as "independents." This state of affairs was changed in 1955, when the two federations merged into a single body, with the mouth-filling title of "American Federation of Labor and Congress of Industrial Organizations." The title is seldom used; the Federation is usually referred to as the AFL–CIO.

The independents. The merger of 1955 cemented the major split in the American labor movement, but, as in the past (and probably in the future), a number of unions remain unaffiliated, or independent. There are various reasons for this. Expulsion is one; the union is thrown out and refused readmission until it meets standards set by the Federation. Examples are the Teamsters, in 1957, for corruption disclosed by the McClellan committee; the West Coast Longshoremen (ILWU), in 1949, for Communist domination. In each case, the target was the president of the union, Jimmy Hoffa of the Teamsters and Harry Bridges of the ILWU.

For some unions, independence is a long-time choice. The four railway operating brotherhoods—Conductors, Engineers, Firemen, and Trainmen—refused for 75 years to affiliate with either the AFL or the CIO, but this united front of individualism was broken after the merger by the Firemen and the Trainmen, who have now joined up. Independence may represent a sort of transient status, due to disagreement with the policies of the Federation, as was the case with the Miners, Machinists, and Carpenters at times in the past. Usually it is followed in a short time by re-affiliation.

Independence is more noticeable, more questionable, and possibly more precarious now than formerly. It is one thing to stand apart from two competing "Houses of Labor," and another to refuse to join or to be expelled from the organization that represents 84 per cent of American trade unionists. Independent unions are typically small (57 out of 60 have less than 100,000 members each) and many of them are of a rather nondescript character. They include such organizations as the Writers Guild, the International Mailers Union, the National Industrial Workers Union, and a number of lesser unions of government employes. On the other hand, they also include a number of very large and powerful labor organizations: the Teamsters, the Mine Workers, the International Longshoremen's and Warehousemen's Union, the Order of Railway Conductors and Brakemen, the Brotherhood of Locomotive Engineers, and so on. It is nevertheless a conglomerate group, with no common element to bind it together. Being unaffiliated, even among themselves, their influence is less than would be indicated by their combined memberships.

The AFL–CIO. The AFL–CIO is *not* a union. It is a *federation* (league, association, coalition) of national and international unions which have joined together voluntarily on a mutual-assistance basis to help one another, work out their common problems, advance the cause of the workingman, and promote the general welfare. The AFL–CIO has 68 per cent of the unions (129 out of 189) with 84 per cent of the membership: 15.1 million out of 17.9 million. Its organization blankets the United States and laps over into Canada, while its executive council is a "Who's Who" of trade-union officialdom. On paper, at least, the AFL–CIO is an impressive aggregation of political and economic power. Its main outlines are shown in Table 4-6.

The AFL–CIO is the primary organization in the world of organized employes. It serves four main purposes: (1) as a symbol of the unity of labor, (2) as an important channel for communication and policy determination among unions representing employes with many diverse and sometimes conflicting interests, (3) as a national forum for the expression of labor's opinions on important questions, and (4) as a very powerful and effective pressure group for the presentation of organized labor's views to Congress and the President of the United States. (There are 51 local counterparts of the AFL–CIO serving the various states and territories.) Situated conveniently in Washington, D.C., the AFL–CIO heads up the labor lobby, competing with, for example, the National Association of Manufacturers and the United States Chamber of Commerce, who lobby for business interests; the Farm Bureau Federation, which lobbies for the farmers; and the American Legion and Veterans of Foreign Wars, who lobby for the veteran.

The officers of the AFL–CIO are the only persons who can speak authoritatively for organized labor—and hence for all labor, since unorganized workmen, by the nature of things, have no spokesmen. When the AFL–CIO takes a position in matters of public policy, it speaks with a powerful voice. The voice is listened to by Presidents, congressmen, governors, mayors, employer associations, and business executives.

As direct political objectives (both candidates and programs) become more important to organized labor, the power and influence of the AFL–CIO in the labor world may be expected to increase. The Federation's main functions have always been political functions (policy formation, campaigns, publicity, lobbying) and its main tools, political tools (conventions, committees, research departments, public speakers, publications). As trade unions concern themselves more and more with public-policy matters, their action must necessarily be collective in nature. Such action can emanate, on a national scale, only from the "House of Labor." The AFL–CIO has an established political department—the Committee on Political Education—as a matter of course and expects to keep up a continuous round of political organization and campaigning in the indefinite future.[10]

[10] See below, Chap. 11, for a more detailed account of the AFL–CIO's organization and functions.

Table 4-6. The American Federation of Labor and Congress of Industrial Organizations (AFL–CIO)

President George Meany (Salary: $70,000)	815 Sixteenth Street NW Washington 6, D.C.	Secretary-Treasurer William F. Schnitzler (Salary: $45,000)

Executive Council

George Meany—AFL–CIO
Wm. F. Schnitzler—AFL–CIO
I. W. Abel—Steelworkers
Harry C. Bates—Bricklayers
Jos. A. Beirne—Communications Workers
Geo. Burdon—Rubber Workers
Jos. Curran—National Maritime Union
A. J. DeAndrade—Printing Pressmen
David Dubinsky—Ladies' Garment Workers
Karl F. Feller—Brewery Workers
Jno. J. Grogan—Marine and Shipbuilding
Paul Hall—Seafarers' International Union
Geo. M. Harrison—Railway Clerks
Ralph Helstein—Packinghouse Workers
M. A. Hutcheson—Carpenters

Paul Jennings—Electrical Workers (IUE)
Jos. D. Keenan—Electricians (IBEW)
Herman D. Kenin—Musicians
Lee W. Minton—Glass Bottle Blowers
Paul L. Phillips—Papermakers
Jacob S. Potofsky—Amalgamated Clothing Workers
A. Philip Randolph—Sleeping Car Porters
Walter P. Reuther—Auto Workers
Peter T. Schoemann—Plumbers
P. L. Siemiller—Machinists
James A. Suffridge—Retail Clerks
David Sullivan—Building Service Employees
Richard F. Walsh—Theatrical Stage Employees
Hunter P. Wharton—Operating Engineers

Structure

Members: 129 national and international unions, with total membership of 15,100,000

State and territorial branches: 51—all states and Puerto Rico

Standing committees: 15—civil rights, community services, economic policy, education, ethical practices, housing, international affairs, legislation, organization, political education, public relations, research, safety and health, social security, veterans

Major (jurisdictional) departments and councils: 7

Building and Construction Trades	Railway Employes
Industrial Union	Union Label and Service Trades
Maritime Trades	Government Employes
Metal Trades	

Department of Organization—Wm. L. Kircher, director: 23 regions in the United States and Puerto Rico

Staff departments: 15—accounting, civil rights, community services, education, international affairs, investments, legal, legislation, library, political education, publications, public relations, purchasing and supplies, research, social security

Functions

Conventions: biennially, in the fall of odd-numbered years
Publications: Weekly: *The AFL–CIO News*
  Monthly: *The American Federationist, Education News and Views, Free Trade Union News, Labor's Economic Review, Collective Bargaining Report*

Sources: *Proceedings, 6th Constitutional Convention, AFL–CIO, December 9–15, 1965; Directory of Natl. and Intl. Labor Unions in the U.S., 1965* (BLS Bulletin 1493); *Monthly Labor Review,* February, 1966, p. 145.

THE LABOR LEADERS

Trade unionism is a going concern and big business. This calls for management, and the need for skilled and dedicated management was never greater than it is today. Whether trade unions grew because of expert leadership or whether capable leaders appeared in response to the growth of unions is a fruitless inquiry. Just like businessmen and politicians, union leaders enjoy power and influence as a result of growth on the part of the organizations they head. This is as true of the modern crop of Meanys, Reuthers, and Hoffas as of the old-timers like John Mitchell, Samuel Gompers, and others who came to power during adversity and are remembered as much for their struggles as for their successes.

Organized labor is now a career field, with many young men and women preparing for service in the labor movement, just as others get themselves ready for business or the professions. There is a difference, however; in the great majority of cases, the true managerial jobs in labor unions are restricted to men or women who come up through the ranks. This rather effectively excludes college graduates from being promoted to the presidencies, the secretaryships, and the jobs of business agent or district representative. There are exceptions but they are few. The distinction arises from the fact that union officials, especially at the lower levels, are almost always elected by their fellow workers, and a period of apprenticeship on the job (at the bench, in the shop) is prerequisite for consideration. This, combined with a lower scale of pay, has the unfortunate result of discouraging large numbers of able and well-trained young men and women from going into union work. Nevertheless, at the top the salaries are good and the influence of an officer of a large international union or the AFL–CIO may equal that of an executive of the largest corporation.

The challenge to labor leadership.   Union leaders started the 1960s under a cloud—with a "bad image" as a result of the McClellan committee investigations of fraud and corruption in the late 1950s, and as the beneficiaries of one of the most stringent pieces of regulatory legislation ever passed by Congress: the Labor-Management Reporting and Disclosure Act of 1959, usually referred to as the "Landrum-Griffin Act." [11]

By the middle of the decade, the situation had improved very little, if at all. Union membership had dropped a quarter of a million. The head of the biggest union in the country, James R. Hoffa of the Teamsters, stood convicted of crime and was under indictment for more violations of law.

[11] See below, Chap. 11 and Appendix.

the AFL – CIO *dispute* of *their constructive effort*
Pres: the to work with management, intentionally – an political
motive & as a cover-up for the defence of
their employee prolonging most strikes by
refusing to compromise on the
91 *bargaining*
table. If
The result
could be
destructive.

Two of the most prominent labor leaders in the country—James B. Carey
of the IUE and David J. McDonald of the Steelworkers—had been voted
out of office, one of them (Carey) after a protest to the Secretary of Labor
and an investigation which showed that the union trustees had mis-
counted the ballots and declared the incumbent Carey the winner by
2,193 votes, whereas he had really lost by 23,316 votes.[12] Management was
taking a "hard line" in bargaining,[13] and it was clear that there was increasing public sensitivity to the inconvenience caused by strikes and
lockouts.

Speaking to the National Academy of Arbitrators in 1963, the U.S. Secretary of Labor made the point: "It is more frequently true now than it
used to be that a shutdown will hurt the public badly before it hurts one
party or the other enough that someone has to cry uncle." [14] He summarized some of the recent causes of public unrest:

Seven airlines closed suddenly by a wildcat strike in 1961.

All shipping stopped on the East Coast for 18 days the same year.

All West Coast ports closed three times during 1961 and 1962.

Most building construction stopped for substantial periods in New York
City, Northern California and the Pacific Northwest.

A 38-day shutdown of all East Coast and Gulf ports by the longshoremen.

Newspaper blackouts in two major cities: New York and Cleveland.

Production of Polaris and Minute Man missiles put under the last-ditch
protection of 80-day injunctions.

The long-drawn-out railway firemen's dispute.

"A decision has been made," he said, "and that decision is that if collective bargaining can't produce peaceable settlements of these controversies,
the public will." [15] In August, 1963, Congress imposed the first peacetime
compulsory arbitration of a labor dispute in the 1963 Railroad Arbitration
Act.[16]

[12] See "Interim Report on the IUE Election," *Monthly Labor Review*, May, 1965,
pp. 562–565. McDonald had been president of the Steelworkers for 12 years, since the
death of Philip Murray in 1952; Carey had headed the IUE since it was chartered in
1949 and had never before been opposed for re-election.

[13] See "A Symposium: The Employer Challenge and the Union Response," in *Industrial Relations*, October, 1961, pp. 9–55, especially Jack Barbash, "Union Response
to the 'Hard Line.' "

[14] U.S. Labor Department release, Feb. 1, 1963, p. 5. As an example he pointed
out that in the New York newspaper strike, where all the city papers were closed off
for four months, during the first month of the walkout the Printers (ITU) were receiving up to $90 a week in strike benefits and the publishers were sharing in a sub-
stantial strike insurance program.

[15] *Ibid.*, pp. 3, 6.

[16] *Monthly Labor Review*, October, 1963, pp. 1187–1188; Public Law 88–108.

For union officials, the Landrum-Griffin Act of 1959 was proving to be more than just a paper threat. The removal of presidents McDonald and Carey is an example. Both contests were close (Carey lost, 55,159 to 78,475; McDonald, 298,768 to 308,910); without the ironclad restrictions of the law upon the conduct of union elections, the impounding of the ballots for at least a year, with criminal penalties for violation, and the authority of the Secretary of Labor to investigate irregularities, it is doubtful that either incumbent would have been unseated. At almost a single step, this law transformed unions from their previous status as "voluntary private associations" (with some exceptions) to quasi-public organizations whose operations must conform to rigid rules laid down in the act and whose every transaction must be reported regularly in detail. It is a very stiff law. Criminal penalties (fines and imprisonment) are provided for a dozen different types of violation on the part of union officials, employers, and their agents; and the enforcement provisions permit union members to sue their officers—with full legal protection against any union disciplinary action, coercion, or even "influence"—or to call upon the Secretary of Labor to investigate and prosecute. The "good old days" of freewheeling action in union meetings, elections, trusteeships, and financial management are gone.

The act also tightened down on union organizational activity and collective bargaining. The final section of the statute amended the Taft-Hartley Act to cut back hard on secondary and hot-goods boycotts, especially by the Teamsters—"the refusal to pick up, deliver or transport any goods"—and either prohibited or severely limited two kinds of picketing: extortionate picketing (prohibited: $10,000 fine and/or 20 years in jail) and "organizational" or "recognition" picketing (restricted). The "no man's land" in labor relations law was removed by putting labor disputes which are turned down by the National Labor Relations Board under state or territorial law (which in general is more restrictive of unions than Federal legislation). The net effect of the amendments was to make cooperative action among unions during labor disputes more difficult, and the amendments were therefore strongly opposed by labor representatives.

What has been the effect on management-union relations? Some profess to see a worsening of collective-bargaining relationships and a stiffening of management attitudes toward extension of organization and in negotiations. The final outcome, of course, will depend to a considerable extent on the capabilities of the leaders of labor and their opposite numbers in management. Working within the much more complicated framework of rules and regulations is not easy and can produce unexpected frictions; it calls for a type of labor leadership different from that of recent years and appears to demand qualities of imagination and resourcefulness which may be very dissimilar to those that have produced the "power play" of the past. The number one question is: Will the labor leaders now in office and those coming up be able to produce the adjustments and compromises necessary to successful operation under the changed conditions?

Another problem for labor leaders in the years to come will be politics and public opinion. There is little doubt that unions will be active in politics continuously from now on. To be effective, labor must not only win the elections but also find ways of bringing its influence to bear on Congress and state legislatures afterward. To a considerable degree, these two results have seemed to diverge up to now. In 1948, the unions helped to retire over a hundred congressmen who voted for the Taft-Hartley Act, and it was widely and confidently predicted that the law would be promptly repealed. Not so; its restrictions are still in effect, some of them in aggravated form. On the surface, organized labor won the congressional election of 1958; it helped elect a large number of its favored candidates and retired several prominent antilabor congressmen and senators. The labor movement also defeated five out of six proposed state right-to-work laws. Then, in 1959, Congress passed the Labor Reform Act, over the solid opposition of the labor lobby.

Why?

One explanation is the ineptness of some union officials in dealing with Congress.[17] Much more important, however, has been the failure of labor leaders to assess properly the strength of public support for the proposed legislation and their unwillingness to cooperate in working out compromises. The Taft-Hartley Act of 1947 was passed over the veto of President Truman after the President had vetoed a much milder bill the year before. In 1959, the major influence on Congress was the U.S. Senate Select Committee on Improper Activities in the Labor or Management Field, better known as the McClellan committee. This committee's report was a shocking catalog of fraud, corruption, and abuse within unions. The labor organizations that were investigated were few in number and the most serious criticisms applied to less than half a dozen unions, but the most prominent offender among these was the largest and most powerful union in the country, the Teamsters. The committee underlined several categories of "improper activities" by unions and management, and gave a number of specific examples of each: undemocratic procedures, abuse of trusteeships, management-union collusion, misuse of union funds, violence, labor spies, extortionate picketing, gangsters and criminals in union office, etc.[18]

Unfortunately, organized labor has not yet completely lived down the "image" produced by the McClellan committee of the union leader as

[17] See Sar A. Levitan, "Union Lobbyists' Contributions to Tough Labor Legislation," *Labor Law Journal,* October, 1959, p. 675.

[18] See *Monthly Labor Review,* September, 1959, pp. 981–991, for details of the findings.

a domineering, dictatorial, self-serving individual, hiding behind the Fifth Amendment, careless of the rights of his own members as well as of employers and the public.[19] Incidents such as the Hoffa convictions and the Carey election tend to perpetuate it. The fact that the stereotype is quite inaccurate and not in the least typical of union officers generally seems to have less effect on public opinion than the drama of the disclosure in the press and on television. Nor was anything like the same publicity given to the prompt expulsion of the Teamsters, Bakery Workers, and Laundry Workers by the AFL–CIO for "improper activities." One of the major objectives of labor leadership must be to recreate a public image of the union official as he is in fact, in order to gain support for favorable legislation and for union demands in contract negotiation.[20]

Finally, and perhaps most important of all, ever since the Second World War labor leaders have been contending with an important change in the structure of industry that affects their membership and influence. The popular name for this is "automation," the current form of technological change. The basic fact for the labor movement is that the number of white-collar workers in industry (clerical, supervisory, technical) is growing at a much faster rate than the number of production and maintenance employes, from whom the unions have traditionally got their members. Manufacturing is an example: in the 17 years from 1947 to 1964, the employment of production workers in manufacturing in this country hardly increased at all—from 12,795,000 to 12,808,000, a total of 13,000, or about one-tenth of one per cent. At the same time, the employment of nonproduction workers rose 2,028,000—from 2,495,000 to 4,513,000, or 81 per cent. Put another way, 99.9 per cent of the increase in manufacturing employment during the 17 years was accounted for by

[19] The McClellan committee was still active in 1965. An AP dispatch reported that "Eight New York labor leaders invoked the Fifth Amendment against self-incrimination 157 times Wednesday when asked by Senate probers about their unions' welfare funds. The Senate investigations subcommittee has charged that the union leaders (executive board members of either the Allied Trades Council or Teamsters local 815) manipulated $3.6 million in money outside the country into research and education foundations in Liberia and Puerto Rico." *Los Angeles Times,* July 22, 1965.

[20] The labor movement's public relations problem has not been helped by the fact that Hoffa, the most publicized labor leader in the country, with the longest and dreariest record of union chicanery, the direct target of the Landrum-Griffin Act, is also one of the most vigorous and astute practitioners of collective bargaining to be found anywhere. At a time when union memberships generally were declining, the Teamsters expanded in size, improved their contracts, and consolidated their hold over the crucially strategic trucking industry. Most of these gains are traceable directly to Hoffa's personal skill in negotiations and choice of strategy. See the remarkable series of articles on Hoffa and his various moves to build a nationwide power organization, in *Industrial Relations,* May, 1963, pp. 67–95; October, 1963, pp. 73–93; October, 1964, pp. 60–76; and May, 1965, pp. 46–60, by Ralph and Estelle James. Now available in book form: *Hoffa and the Teamsters* (Princeton, N.J.: D. Van Nostrand Company, Inc., 1965).

employes who would normally be outside the bargaining units in the plants.[21] Up to now, the American labor movement has had only indifferent success in organizing the white-collar, nonproduction worker, or "salaried" employe. Unless some device is invented to make unionism more attractive to the new class of technical, professional, and related workers, the influence of organized labor will decline. The problem is not simple, as the United Auto Workers, a major victim of automation to date, can testify.[22]

automation is a threat to the O.L.

WHO'S WHO IN ORGANIZED LABOR [23]

Who are the men available to meet the challenges outlined above and how are they equipped to deal with the problems? No single person dominates the labor movement as Samuel Gompers did from 1886 through the First World War or John L. Lewis did in the 1930s. Labor leadership is distributed among a small group of experienced men who head the AFL–CIO and some of the more powerful national and international unions. There are several new names—men as yet not really tested by the rigors of high office, but necessarily included due to the standing of the unions they head: Abel of the Steelworkers, Siemiller of the Machinists, etc. However, the top three in power and influence are men well known both to the labor movement and the general public. They are:

George Meany, president of the AFL–CIO since its formation in 1955

Walter P. Reuther, president of the United Auto Workers and of the Industrial Union Department of the AFL–CIO

James R. (Jimmy) Hoffa, president of the International Brotherhood of Teamsters, Chauffeurs, Warehousemen & Helpers of America

---

[21] See S. E. Hill and F. W. Harbison, *Manpower and Innovation in American Industry* (Princeton, N.J.: Princeton University Press, 1959), p. 4; *Monthly Labor Review*, June, 1965, pp. 713, 717.

[22] In 1955 (a 7-million-car year), the motor vehicle industry employed 746,400 production workers and 157,400 nonproduction workers, for a total of 903,800. In 1964 (another 7-million-plus year), the industry used 593,200 production workers and 177,900 nonproduction employes: total, 771,100. Thus the production worker total fell 153,200, or 20.5 per cent, while the nonproduction total rose 20,500, or 13 per cent. In 1956, the UAW reported a membership of 1,320,513; in 1964, this had declined to 1,104,000. The connection is obvious.

[23] With apologies to Marquis—*Who's Who*. The data below are from a variety of sources, of which *Who's Who in America* is only a minor one. Labor leadership has never been a popular category with the editors of *Who's Who*, and union officials are still only sparsely represented. Trade unions are not a category in the listings of "those included on account of position—civil, military, religious, educational, corporate or organizational." See *Who's Who in America*, 1964–1965, vol. 33, p. 2; also O. W. Phelps, "Community Recognition of Union Leaders," *Industrial and Labor Relations Review*, April, 1954, pp. 421–422.

After them come a number of prominent labor leaders, some better known than others, most of them experienced and frequently in the public eye. They are:

I. W. Abel, president of the United Steelworkers of America

Harry Bridges, president of the International Longshoremen's and Ware-housemen's Union

Joseph Curran, president of the National Maritime Union of America

David Dubinsky, of the International Ladies' Garment Workers' Union

George M. Harrison, chief executive of the Railway and Steamship Clerks, Freight Handlers, Express and Station Employes

Joseph D. Keenan, secretary of the International Brotherhood of Electrical Workers

P. L. Siemiller, president of the International Association of Machinists and Aerospace Workers

William F. Schnitzler, secretary-treasurer of the AFL–CIO

THE "BIG THREE"

George Meany.   Meany is the number one man in organized labor today, both by virtue of his job as president of the AFL–CIO and by virtue of his talents: energy, drive, courage, and integrity. Meany is a big, powerful, domineering man, with a stentorian voice and a genuine talent for intraorganizational politics. In committee and other small group meetings, where the basic decisions of a bureaucracy like the AFL–CIO are reached, he dominates without effort. He was the prime mover in the merger of the American Federation of Labor with the Congress of Industrial Organizations in 1955, has been a leader in insisting that member unions meet a minimum set of "ethical standards" or be expelled from the Federation (for years he has almost personally blocked the return of the Teamsters to the AFL–CIO so long as Hoffa held the union's presidency), heads the labor lobby in Washington, and is solidly entrenched in his job. No one questions his integrity or his sincerity. These are great virtues, especially for the man who more than any other represents organized labor as a whole.

However, Meany also has serious weaknesses, which his genuine and increasing influence render more serious still. On August 16, 1967, Meany was 73 years old. Labor leadership is a demanding occupation; not many trade unionists have made an outstanding contribution after passing 65, and a number of unions have made that the constitutional mandatory retirement age: the Machinists, Rubber Workers, Building Service Employees, and so on. Unless forced to, labor leaders seldom retire; they

[handwritten annotation at top: Mgmt of the AFL-CIO deserves dynamic & powerful individual who understands the modern-day theory of Computerization. How is Meany? & co.?]

tend to die in office.[24] Meany himself fretted noticeably when his predecessor as president of the AFL, William Green, put off retirement year after year and finally died in office at the age of 79. Green had not approved of Meany's obvious eagerness to succeed him. Meany has the same problem; he has had his strongest disagreements within the AFL–CIO with Walter P. Reuther, who is a likely candidate for his job when he leaves it. If anything will keep him from retiring, it will be the prospect of turning over the office to someone who is openly critical of the way the Federation is currently being run and who is by temperament, intellect, and background almost the antithesis of the former plumber.

Meany comes from a background of craft unionism and is most at home with other representatives of the "aristocrats of labor," the solid, old-line crafts which have avoided or only reluctantly joined the trend to industrial unionism: carpenters, bricklayers, barbers, plumbers, electricians, painters, and paperhangers. This is not where the problems are located in the age of computers; they are technological (automation) and industrial; the new breed of employes to be recruited is technical, professional, white-collar. Meany knows little about union management, having never headed up a national union or had any operating union job bigger than business agent of a plumbers local in New York City, and that a long time ago. No one has ever accused him of an excess of imagination. One critic, more outspoken than most, reported bleakly on the 1963 AFL–CIO Constitutional Convention, run by Meany and an Executive Council with a majority of members over 65 (ten of them over 70):

Lacking are new leaders and new ideas. The delegates are just older and more tired. Unionism-as-usual dominates, and labor projects a poor image as a force seeking to preserve the *status quo*, rather than vividly attracting a new generation with new ideas.[25]

[handwritten annotation: It does.]

If, as seems likely, the issues ahead require a new approach, new techniques, or anything resembling a fundamental change—like the swing to industrial unionism of the 1930s—it will be out of character for Meany to initiate them.

Walter P. Reuther. If Meany should retire, it is probable that Reuther will be a candidate to succeed him. The latter is not in the direct line of succession, which by tradition runs to the secretary-treasurer, the second man in most labor organizations, but tradition has never hampered

[24] There are exceptions, of course, John L. Lewis, being different as usual, retired in 1960 (at the age of 79) in favor of his vice-president, Thomas Kennedy, a youngster of 72, who turned over the reins in 1963 to W. A. Boyle, a stripling of 58. It might be noted that the United Mine Workers slid steadily downhill in membership and influence during the decade 1953–1963 while led by septuagenarians.

[25] B. J. Widick, "Labor Ducks the Future," *Nation*, Dec. 7, 1963, p. 390.

the boss of the UAW up to now and probably will not in the future. He came to the presidency of the Auto Workers in 1946 and that of the CIO in 1952 from similar out-of-line positions, following a vigorous campaign and a free-for-all vote fight on the convention floor. Reuther's career has demonstrated ambition, ability, energy, intelligence, and imagination. For a while there was some question of his stability; he was too clearly a "young man in a hurry" for many unionists, with their esteem for experience and seniority. However, the part he played in bringing about the merger of 1955, particularly his own willingness to step down from the presidency of the CIO to a vice-presidency of the merged Federation, was reassuring and the years since then have strengthened the impression of a man willing to wait his turn. How he stands with the labor movement as a whole will be a question mark until put to the test.

Reuther, once the boy wonder of the union world (at 39, he became president of the million-member UAW), is now the senior man among the leaders of really big and influential labor organizations. His 20-year presidency of the Auto Workers is unmatched among the other members of the "Big Six"—the Carpenters, Electricians, Machinists, Steelworkers, and Teamsters—and is equaled only by a few holdovers such as Bridges of the ILWU, Moreschi of the Laborers, and Potofsky of the Amalgamated Clothing Workers. He has taken a front-line, active part in 3 decades of (1) bloody organizing struggle (the "battle of the over-pass," in which Reuther and Frankensteen were savagely beaten by Ford guards is a union *cause célèbre* of the 1930s); (2) violent internal union strife, during which Communists and conservatives fought for control of the union; (3) the tensions of the growth and stabilization of the CIO, culminating in 1949 with the expulsion of several unions for Communist domination; and (4) the readjustment since the merger of 1955.

Reuther is one of the handful of union leaders with some college education, having attended Wayne University in Detroit for 3 years.[26] A tool and die maker by trade, he was fired by the Ford Motor Company for union activity in 1932, took a 3-year trip around the world, and jumped into the middle of the organizing drive in the auto industry upon his return in 1935. He was highly successful as an organizer, becoming successively president, Local 174, UAW–CIO; vice-president, UAW–CIO; director, General Motors Division, UAW–CIO; and member of the War Manpower Commission and the War Production Board during the Second World War. In 1946, he became president of the United Auto Workers, and upon the death of Philip Murray in 1952, he succeeded to the presidency of the CIO. The way has not been smooth and easy; in both presidential elections he was vigorously opposed, and he has survived one outright attempt at assassination, a shotgun blast at close quarters that struck him in the left shoulder.

---

[26] The university gave him an honorary LL.D. in 1953.

In his negotiations with the automobile manufacturers, Reuther has introduced such innovations as the long-term contract (starting with a 5-year agreement with General Motors in 1950), the escalator clause (wage rates rising with increases in the cost of living), the productivity factor (deferred annual wage increases in line with assumed increases in productivity in the industry), supplementary unemployment benefits (at times inaccurately referred to as "the guaranteed annual wage"), and retirement incentives (higher pensions for early retirement) in 1964. A shrewd, tough, and flexible bargainer, Reuther enjoys needling the opposition with dramatic comparisons. For example, he pointed out in 1962 that the $15,700,000 in salaries and bonuses paid to General Motors' 56 executive officers exceeded by almost $2 million the total salary bill of the 606 top public officials in the United States: the President, the Vice-President, 10 Cabinet members, 9 Supreme Court justices, 100 senators, 435 congressmen, and the governors of the 50 states.[27] Under his leadership, the UAW has surmounted the shrinkage brought on by automation and flourishes as an example of honesty, democratic procedure (the Public Review Board for appeals of members against the union), and support for civil rights.

Reuther is vigorously active in politics, both in his home state of Michigan and on the national level. He is regarded with respect and some apprehension by the business community and some of his fellow labor leaders, for his liberal views, his direct-action political approach (he believes in taking sides, not just "rewarding friends and punishing enemies"), his freewheeling, nontraditional solutions to labor problems, and his over-all energy and effectiveness. If there are answers to the unique political, social, and organizational problems of organized labor in the years ahead, they are as likely to be supplied by the president of the UAW and the Industrial Union Department of the AFL–CIO as by anyone else currently on the scene.

James Riddle Hoffa. Although Hoffa is customarily referred to as "Jimmy," the emphasis should be put on his middle name. He and the huge Teamsters union, which he dominates to a degree unmatched by any other head of a big international union, are a riddle wrapped in an enigma. They have confounded their critics, pushed aside opposition, extended their membership, and perfected their agreements, to the accompaniment of congressional investigations, lawsuits, expulsion from the AFL–CIO, and a rising chorus of dismay and reproof from the press and other news sources. As one experienced observer has put it:

The International Brotherhood of Teamsters, the nation's biggest, strongest, and most investigated union, is a monument to the sweet uses of adversity, a testimonial to the proposition that nothing succeeds like bad publicity. For nearly seven

[27] A. H. Raskin, "Walter Reuther's Great Big Union," *Atlantic Monthly*, October, 1963, p. 90.

years all the awesome powers of the federal government, reinforced by every instrument of mass communication, have been focused on the destruction of the union's
iron-fisted president, James R. Hoffa. Yet both Hoffa and the Teamsters have prospered, while the AFL–CIO, which cast them out as a disgrace to organized labor,
is sunk in bureaucratic torpor.[28]

On October 4, 1957, Hoffa was elected president of the Teamsters by a comfortable majority (1,208 votes out of 1,671), only 2 weeks after the AFL–CIO Ethical Practices Committee had issued a 64-page report con-cluding that the union was dominated by corrupt influences, chief among which was Hoffa: using union money for personal purposes, profiting from conflict-of-interest deals with employers, and associating with, sponsoring, and promoting the interests of notorious labor racketeers. On the basis of the report, the Teamsters were suspended and then expelled by the AFL–CIO in December. Much of the information in the report came from the McClellan committee (United States Senate Select Com-mittee on Improper Activities in the Labor or Management Field), which uncovered 82 specific improper practices ranging from "sweetheart con-tracts" (low-wage agreements with favored employers) to bribery and intimidation. According to the committee, Hoffa had: [29]

1.   Betrayed his own union members with contracts at substandard wages.
2.   Cooperated with gangsters and racketeers: John Dioguardi, "Tony Ducks" Corallo, "Shorty" Feldman, Paul "the Waiter" Ricca.
3.   Taken payoffs from employers to settle strikes.
4.   Loaned union funds to friends for business deals.
5.   Granted lavish expense accounts to Teamster organizers.
6.   Manipulated the union's health and welfare funds to favor one broker, Allen Dorfman, while benefits were reduced.
7.   Regularly condoned violence and intimidation of members of various Teamster locals.

The committee's final report was issued early in August, 1959. Six weeks later, Congress passed and sent to the President the Labor-Management Reporting and Disclosure Act of 1959, with its itemized controls over every facet of internal union activity and its numerous criminal penalties for violation. To a very considerable extent, Hoffa bears the responsibility for this legislation.

Who is Jimmy Hoffa and where did he come from?

Born February 14, 1913, son of a coal miner who died when Jimmy was 4 years old, Hoffa grew up in Detroit. Needless to say, the family was poor and in 1931, at the age of 18, the boy went to work for the Kroger grocery chain at 32 cents an hour unloading boxcars. While there, he

[28] A. H. Raskin, "The Power of James R. Hoffa," *Atlantic Monthly,* January, 1964, pp. 39–45.

[29] For a brief rundown on the Hoffa case, check the *Monthly Labor Review,* Oc-tober, 1957, p. 1254; November, 1957, pp. 1335–1338 and 1381–1382; February, 1958, pp. 146–147; and September, 1959, pp. 981–988.

organized his first strike and showed his instinct for the jugular by choosing a shipment of fresh strawberries. It was successful, and in 1932 he
went into Local 299 of the Teamsters, where he demonstrated a talent
for organizing. He went through the Depression as head of the local
(becoming president in 1935), met his wife-to-be on a picket line and
was married in 1937. In 1940 he was negotiating chairman of the Central
States Drivers Council, the Teamsters union's potentially most powerful
division, with jurisdiction of over-the-road drivers (intercity truckers) in
12 Midwestern states bunched around the Great Lakes. He was then 27
years old.

For 12 years he concerned himself primarily with the problems of
the Central States Drivers Council, organizing, negotiating, and always
pressing for the key to power in the trucking industry: "centralized area-
wide bargaining designed to establish uniform wages, hours, and working
conditions." [30] He proved to be a negotiating genius: tough, aggressive,
persistent, fully informed about the trucking business, and in general
well liked by the businessmen he dealt with. He neither smoked nor
drank, had amazing energy (upon occasion he bargained continuously
for as long as 36 hours without noticeably running down), was considered
hard-boiled but fair, and always kept his word.

In union politics, Hoffa demonstrated ability to match his negotiating
skill. By 1952, now a vice-president of the union, he joined up with Dave
Beck, executive vice-president and chairman of the Western Conference
of Teamsters, to move the aging (77) Dan Tobin out of the presidency
and put Beck in Tobin's place. For this, Hoffa apparently got a free hand
to do as he pleased as chairman of the Central States Conference. It was
about this time that he began to compile the record unearthed by the
McClellan committee, using every means at hand to extend and consoli-
date his personal control of the union within his jurisdiction. By 1957,
with Beck under heavy fire from the McClellan committee for misap-
propriation of more than $300,000 of union funds and also under investi-
gation for income tax evasion,[31] Hoffa was ready to move into the president's chair.

If the events of 1957 to 1959 were to be regarded as censure, Hoffa
gave no sign. He took them all in stride: the McClellan committee, expulsion from the AFL–CIO, the Landrum-Griffin Act, and a set of court-
appointed monitors to supervise local elections and check on procedures
within the international. In July, 1961, the monitors having been brushed

[30] Ralph and Estelle James, "Hoffa's Acquisition of Industrial Power," *Industrial
Relations*, May, 1963, p. 73. See this article for a fascinating account of Hoffa's early
struggle for control of the Central States Drivers Council and his debt to Farrell
Dobbs, the strategic genius of the Teamsters, who showed him the way.

[31] Beck was eventually convicted of the latter offense and served several years in
Federal prison.

aside, Hoffa presided over the eighteenth constitutional convention of the Teamsters at Miami Beach, Florida. He was reelected president by acclamation, had his salary increased from $50,000 to $75,000 a year and supervised revision of the union's constitution to maximize the president's (his) control over policy and administration. A pension plan for union officers was authorized. Dues were raised a minimum of $1 a month, with 60 cents of the increase going to international headquarters: a revenue increase of around $11 million per year. The union's net worth was revealed as $38 million, and membership was reported to be 1,700,000 the preceding November, an all-time peak.[32]

Two and one-half years after the victory convention of 1961, Hoffa reached the major bargaining goal of his career: a national trucking agreement with Trucking Employers, Inc., an employers association representing approximately 1,000 large trucking firms from all sections of the United States. The new master contract with its area supplements covered both over-the-road drivers and "local cartage" (industry term for intracity trucking—carts are now as rare as teamsters on city streets) and set the terms of employment of more than 400,000 drivers. However, its key provision was a common termination date: March 31, 1967. By that time, Teamster negotiators would be in a position to call a legal nationwide strike and thus bring the trucking industry of virtually the entire country to a halt simultaneously.[33]

It was the top of the mountain for the union, but Hoffa was already on the way down. Since 1957, he had been under almost constant indictment for alleged violations of law based on evidence produced by the McClellan committee. The tempo of prosecution rose noticeably when Robert F. Kennedy, former chief investigator for Senator McClellan and his committee, became Attorney General of the United States in January, 1961.[34] Although Hoffa beat rap after rap, with the country's leading crimi-

---

[32] With the still new Landrum-Griffin Act in effect and with the still newer Attorney General, Mr. Robert F. Kennedy, just beginning his campaign to "get" the allegedly corrupt union chief he had pursued for 4 years as chief investigator for the McClellan committee, every precaution was taken to stay legal. There were over 40 Teamster attorneys in attendance (due to its numerical size the union's legal staff is often referred to as the "Teamster Bar Association"), and every word and much of the action of the convention was recorded on tape and film. See the report on the convention in *Monthly Labor Review*, August, 1961, pp. 829–834.

[33] "Underlying Hoffa's collective bargaining policy has been a vision of power aggrandizement for himself and the union, the building of an industry-wide contractual structure under a single unified command—his own." Ralph James and Estelle James, "Hoffa's Impact on Teamster Wages," *Industrial Relations*, October, 1964, p. 75.

[34] In Kennedy's first 33 months as Attorney General, the Justice Department got 168 indictments against Teamster officials or persons involved with them; out of the first 115 settled, there were 93 convictions, 14 dismissals, and 8 acquittals. Raskin, "The Power of James R. Hoffa," *loc. cit.*, p. 44.

nal lawyer, Edward Bennett Williams, as counsel,[35] his luck could not
hold indefinitely. On Mar. 12, 1964, he was found guilty of tampering with
a Federal jury during a trial in Nashville for violation of the Taft-Hartley
Act, and was sentenced to 8 years in prison and a $10,000 fine. Five
months later, in Chicago, he was again found guilty of fraud in the misuse
of Teamster union pension funds. For this he was sentenced to 5 years
in prison and another $10,000 fine.[36]

Penalties.

And the result?

The Teamsters' 1966 convention in Miami Beach, Florida, made the
victory celebration of 1961 look like a county fair.[37] The meeting was one
long unanimous vote of approval of Hoffa, his policies, and everything he
stood for. Hoffa and his entire slate of incumbent officers were reelected
by acclamation. The president's salary was increased from $75,000 to
$100,000 a year and the other officers were voted substantial raises. To
provide for a possible vacancy in the president's office (*i.e.*, Hoffa going
to jail on one or the other of his current convictions, both of which were
under appeal), the delegates created the new post of general vice-president, with the incumbent automatically succeeding the president for the
balance of his current term, should the latter be disabled from serving
by death, resignation, or "removal" (*i.e.*, imprisonment). The general vice-
president's duties, salary, and expenses were to be set by the president.
Hoffa's oldest and closest friend in the Teamsters, Frank E. Fitzsimmons,
of Hoffa's home local 299, in Detroit, was elected without opposition to
the new job.

Re-elected again.

Any effort to suspend or expel Hoffa either as a member or officer of
the union was eliminated by two constitutional changes: (1) prohibition
of trials of members or officers on the same set of facts which they might
be facing in criminal or civil trial, pending final verdict in court, including
appeal; and (2) a statute of limitations providing that elective officers can
only be brought before the union on charges arising during the current
term of office. The latter provision, of course, wiped the slate clean for
Hoffa up to July, 1966. The union reported a membership of 1,600,000
and net worth of $50 million. Per capita payments to the international
were raised from $1 to $1.50 per month and members' monthly dues were
set at a minimum of $6, with a mandatory raise of at least $1.

Horrible!

Which is the real Hoffa? The Spartan, energetic, hard-driving, skilled
negotiator, who has raised wages, shortened hours, and improved the

[35] Williams's most adroit performance, perhaps, was to get Hoffa acquitted of a
charge of attempting to bribe a McClellan committee staff aide, one J. C. Cheasty,
who was to deliver confidential documents and information to Jimmy. Hoffa was arrested by the FBI, with three of the incriminating papers on his person, moments
after they had been delivered in the lobby of the Dupont Plaza Hotel, but Williams
procured an acquittal. *New York Times,* March 14, p. 1; July 20, p. 1.

[36] *New York Times,* Mar. 13, 1964, p. 1; Aug. 18, 1964, p. 1.

[37] See the *Monthly Labor Review,* July, 1966, pp. iii–iv.

working conditions of truckers the country over? Or is it the cynical, arrogant associate of thugs and gangsters, who has made himself wealthy at the expense of the union he heads? The question may be academic, with Hoffa on his way to prison (apparently), but something is out of line when two Teamster presidents in succession are convicted of crime and both remain popular with the rank and file.[38]

The "Big Three" of organized labor reflect the current disorganization and chaos of labor leadership in the United States. Two of the three must be practically counted out as leaders in any revival of influence or prestige: Meany on grounds of age and background and resistance to change, Hoffa as indelibly tarnished by the McClellan committee investigations and conviction for crime. In the group below, the pattern is repeated: disqualification by age, Communist sympathies, and inexperience. Little more is needed to explain the decline of the labor movement than the shortage of young, vigorous, outstanding leaders of major unions. Until the unions learn the lesson and apply the techniques of "executive recruitment and development," for the past 25 years so heavily stressed by corporations, they are probably doomed to a steady decline in relative importance among the pressure groups in American life. So long as they shut themselves away from the brightest and best-trained minds coming out of the colleges and universities, just so long will they trail behind their competitors, who offer the inducements of pay, promotion, and responsibility to these graduates.

LABOR LEADERSHIP: AGE, TURNOVER, INEXPERIENCE

Harry Bridges.   As founder and president (since 1934) of the International Longshoremen's and Warehousemen's Union, Harry Bridges has long been one of the most controversial figures of the American labor movement. In 1950, the ILWU was expelled by the CIO on grounds that it was Communist-dominated, with everyone knowing that the reference was to the head man. There is little doubt that Bridges himself was for many years a follower of the "Party line"; there is some doubt that he was ever a full-fledged member of the Communist party, since few people have been as exhaustively scrutinized for evidence of such membership as he; and there is great doubt that any "Communist" influence exercised by the president has "dominated" the ILWU at the working level. The ILWU is a strong candidate for the title of most democratically run union in the United States. The union's hiring hall is a model of equal-opportunity assignment of jobs. Local union candidates and policies are freely

[38] Dave Beck, former president of the Teamsters, drew a $50,000 per year pension from the union all the time he was in jail at McNeil Island Federal penitentiary, from June, 1962 to December, 1964.

voted on after open debate, and as often as not the candidate or policy backed by Bridges—frequently in person at local meetings—is turned down by the membership. No union relies on the referendum more, and a union that uses the referendum is hard to dominate from above.

Bridges himself is now past 65 (he was born in 1900 in Melbourne, Australia). Due to his political views and the long-continued efforts of the government to deport him, he is probably in no position to exercise a major influence on the future of the American labor movement. This is unfortunate, since his record as a labor leader is excellent.[39] As the chief influence in organizing the West Coast docks in the 1930s and the plantations of the "Big Five" sugar agencies in Hawaii in the 1940s,[40] Bridges is one of the labor leaders who has done his full share to improve working conditions and raise the standard of living of some really submerged groups. In return for this service, he was "due processed."[41]

Bridges's most recent contribution is on a par with his past record as an innovator of workable solutions to major labor problems. In 1960, he negotiated a precedent-setting long-term agreement with the Pacific Maritime Association (the Pacific Coast waterfront employers association) as the ILWU's solution to the twin problems of low labor productivity and high worker insecurity. In return for abandonment of practically all restrictive work rules (featherbedding) such as limitations on sling loads, required work crews larger than necessary to do a job, the Pacific Maritime Association agreed to set up a full-employment fund financed by payments of $5 million per year for 5½ years, the term of the contract. From this fund were to come (1) guaranteed wages (35 hours a week) to all fully registered longshoremen and clerks whether or not work was available, (2) lump-sum retirement payments of $7,920 to any longshoreman reaching age 65 with 25 years of service (in addition to regular pension), (3) higher pension rates for early retirement, (4) "vesting" after 15 years of service, etc.[42] It was a bold attack upon the two evils of high labor cost, on the one hand, and worker insecurity (from mechanization)

[39] Try comparing it, for example, with that of his opposite number, Joseph P. Ryan, long-time president of the International Longshoremen's Association, the East Coast longshore union.

[40] See Curtis Aller's excellent monograph, *Labor Relations in the Hawaiian Sugar Industry* (Berkeley, Calif.: Institute of Industrial Relations, University of California, 1957), for a review of the Hawaiian campaign and industry's adjustment to it.

[41] The term is taken from Paul Jacob's article, "The Due Processing of Harry Bridges," in *The Reporter*, March 8, 1956; it refers to deportation proceedings (Bridges was an alien until 1945) involving innumerable investigations by the FBI and other Federal agencies; two congressional hearings and bills aimed at his deportation; two hearings before special examiners; one criminal trial; one civil trial; eleven court decisions, including two by the Supreme Court of the United States; and so on.

[42] The deal was referred to as "selling the jobs back to the employers."

on the other; what is more, it has worked and apparently better than anticipated.[43]

Young out *old story* (handwritten margin note)

Carey out, Jennings in.   In today's complicated labor leadership pattern, the younger men seem to get voted out of office, retire, or go to jail, while some of the older ones go on forever. On April 6, 1965, James B. Carey resigned as president of the 265,000-member International Union of Electrical, Radio and Machine Workers (IUE), the day after the United States Secretary of Labor announced a miscount of the ballots by the union trustees and loss of the election of the previous October by 23,316 votes.[44] His opponent, Paul Jennings, up to then secretary of District 3 of the union, was installed in the presidency April 7th.

The outcome was something of a shock; as founder and president of the union since 1950, Carey had never before even been opposed for office. When voted out, at the age of 53, the loser had 29 years of concentrated experience in organized labor, as president of the United Electrical Workers (Ind.) for 5 years, secretary and secretary-treasurer of the CIO, 1938 to 1955, secretary-treasurer of the Industrial Union Department and vice-president of the AFL–CIO since the merger in 1955, and president of the IUE for 14 years. An old friend and colleague of Walter Reuther's, he had been a delegate to numerous labor conferences in the United States and abroad, was an outspoken opponent of discrimination, a champion of civil liberties, a political activist, and a good staff man but a poor line officer. As a two-time loser (he was voted out of the UE in 1941 by a Communist faction in the union), he is probably through as a labor leader of influence.

Carey's loss, like that of McDonald of the Steelworkers at almost the same time, stands as a warning to labor leaders not to disregard the rank and file. The Carey replacement was a victory for union democracy, for the Landrum-Griffin Act, and for "Boulwarism." A poor strategist and internal politician, he aroused factionalism, led the union into strikes which the membership would not support, and was an easy victim of the General Electric Company's antiunion campaign, led by its vice-president, Lemuel Boulware. The election of late 1964 was a vote of no-confidence in Carey, not a vote of confidence in his successor. However, as was made clear by the subsequent Labor Department inquiry, the protest vote would have got nowhere without the strict regulations of the Labor Reform Act, with its requirement that all ballots be impounded for one year.

[43] See Max D. Kossoris's detailed appraisal of the remarkable results from the agreement in his account of the "1966 West Coast Longshore Negotiations," in *Monthly Labor Review*, October, 1966, pp. 1067–1075.

[44] On Dec. 29, 1964 (the balloting was by mail), Carey had been declared winner by a margin of 2,193. See *Monthly Labor Review*, May, 1965, pp. 562–565, for excerpts from the Secretary's interim report.

Carey's successor, Paul Jennings, is a relative unknown. He will inherit both a divided union and the union's continuing struggle with "Boulwarism," the unique collective bargaining strategy developed by the former vice-president for industrial relations of General Electric, with its fixed company position on all issues, full publicity during bargaining conferences, public relations campaign to members and their families, and general disregard of the union's function of representation. It will be no easy job and how he fares will be watched with interest.

David Dubinsky.   Dubinsky is one of the "grand old men" of the American labor movement. He has been an active trade unionist for well over 50 years—since 1911, when he joined Local 10 of the International Ladies' Garment Workers' Union. He was a vice-president by 1922, president by 1932, and in 20 years had brought the union out of the red and into the black to the tune of assets in excess of $160 million and a yearly income of $70 million. The ILGWU is an outstanding example of "welfare unionism," with its educational, cultural, and recreational activities, which include vacation resorts, health centers, and one of the first training institutes for union officials. Dubinsky was also among the first to apply strict business methods to union operations, with public audits of union accounts and the additional function of giving business advice and assistance to employers in the garment industry. A colleague of John L. Lewis and Sidney Hillman in the CIO rebellion of the middle 1930s, Dubinsky withdrew shortly afterward and returned to the AFL on grounds of labor unity but was unable to heal the breach between the veterans of the AFL and the industrial unionists of the Committee for Industrial Organization.

Now in his seventies (he was born in 1892), Dubinsky has lived an active life with a background of experience ranging from banishment to Siberia at the age of 16 for union activities in Poland, to labor consultant to the United Nations Economic and Social Council almost 50 years later. His list of memberships, appointments, honors, and public services, too long to repeat, may be consulted in *Who's Who in America.* In line with a developing trend, Dubinsky announced his retirement from the presidency of the ILGWU in 1966, in favor of the secretary-treasurer, Louis Stulberg, who was then 65 years old. However, Dubinsky retained his place on the Executive Council of the AFL–CIO, and his wisdom and counsel will be available in the years ahead.

George M. Harrison.   Another elder statesman of the labor movement in the United States is George Harrison, who will be 72 in 1967. He is "chief executive" of the Railway Clerks (the president is C. L. Dennis), formerly the largest union in the industry, and one that has taken a heavy beating in membership decline, being cut from 361,000 to 270,000 in 7 years. Harrison is an example of labor's "public man," his specialty being liaison work with other unions and the government. He has been chairman of the Railway Labor Executives' Association, member of the Draft Committee of the Social Security Act, member of the Joint Railroad Labor-Management Committee on the War Effort, member of the National Defense Mediation Board and of the Executive Committee of the President's Management-Labor Commission, assistant to the Director of the Economic Stabilization Administration, and so on. Harrison is known as an intelligent, forceful labor executive, with an excellent grasp of public issues. He has been prominent in an industry in which labor relations have been strictly regulated by Congress for 40 years. Since public supervision of labor-management relations appears to be a permanent issue, this may make his advice especially useful in the years ahead.

Steelworkers: McDonald out, Abel in.   In February, 1965, the United Steelworkers of America voted out of office their 62-year-old president of the past 12 years (and secretary-treasurer 11 years before that), David J. McDonald. The winner was not an unknown. Inside the union, he was as familiar as McDonald. He was I. W. ("Abe") Abel, secretary-treasurer of the international during the years of McDonald's presidency. It was a clean sweep; Abel carried into office with him a new vice-president and his own candidate for secretary-treasurer. His vote margin was 10,142 out of 607,678, or 1.67 per cent.[45]

Abel is 6 years younger than McDonald but looks older. The personal contrast was dramatic: the former "working stiff" versus the "big executive." McDonald, a graduate of Carnegie Tech (in drama, not engineering), never held an industrial job in his life; he went to work as secretary to Philip Murray, then vice-president of the United Mine Workers, in 1923 and rose with his chief through the executive suites of the Steel Workers Organizing Committee and the United Steelworkers. Abel, on the other hand, was a molder in a foundry for 14 years, was in and out of jobs during the Great Depression (working part of the time for 16¢ an hour), and became a Steel Workers Organizing Committee organizer in 1937. McDonald, never really popular with the members, was always the perfect "front man"—handsome, smartly dressed, a clubman and golfer, the owner of a winter retreat in Palm Springs, California. Abel, most at home at local union meetings, probably knows more rank-and-file union members than any other international officer. Abel's announced intention, before and after the election, was to give the United Steelworkers once more the image of the working man.

[45] *Monthly Labor Review,* June, 1965, p. 692. Once again, the Labor-Management Reporting and Disclosure Act may be credited with ensuring a fair test between the challenger and an incumbent.

There is more to the job than that, of course. The United Steelworkers lies across the basic steel industry, and every so often the dispute with "Big Steel" and the other major firms of the industry is sure to get nationwide attention. Until recently, the union has been the foremost exponent left of the "power play" type of labor relations, handled so expertly by Philip Murray as a legacy from his longtime superior, John L. Lewis. The results—and McDonald must be credited with his full share—are certainly nothing to be ashamed of. Steelworkers' wages and fringes are at the top of the list,[46] far above the average for all manufacturing and challenged only by the aristocrats of the union world: bituminous coal mining and the building trades crafts.[47] Abel will also be faced with all the problems brought on by rapid technological change in an industry where work stoppages have loud repercussions throughout the economy. (One example: Steelworkers' membership dropped from a reported 1,250,000 in 1957 to 965,000 in 1964.) This will certainly test his statesmanship in the days to come, as will the Federal government's steady and increasing concern with prices and wages in the industry.

Machinists: Hayes out, Siemiller in.   On July 1, 1965, Al J. Hayes retired after 41 years as an officer (16 of them as president) of the International Association of Machinists and Aerospace Workers. He was 65 and had reached the union's mandatory retirement age for officials. A quiet, able, effective labor leader, Hayes had guided the union through the industrial expansion following the Second World War to a top membership of 993,000 in 1959, then watched automation and the decline of the aircraft industry cut the total by a fifth—to 808,000 in 1964. His successor, installed without opposition, is P. L. Siemiller, chairman of the union's Aerospace Committee and Atomic Energy Council. Sixty years old when he took office, Siemiller had only 5 years to go in the top job. This will not be much time to cope with technological change, which is wiping out several thousand jobs per week in the machinery and aerospace industries, and with the problems raised by sharing jurisdictions with the United Auto Workers (in aerospace) and the Oil, Chemical, and Atomic Workers (in atomic energy installations).[48] The transfer from Hayes to Siemiller was notable mainly for its smoothness, simplicity, and unanimity.

[46] For example, in basic steel, half the workers get 13-week vacations (sabbaticals) every 5 years.

[47] In January, 1965, gross weekly earnings of production workers were as follows: blast furnace and basic steel products (the United Steelworkers' main preserve)—$142.46, bituminous coal mining—$138.80, specialty building construction—$139.20, all manufacturing—$105.93. See *Monthly Labor Review*, May, 1965, pp. 602–604.

[48] The Oil, Chemical, and Atomic Workers got a new chief in 1965, too, with its 25-year president, O. A. Knight, deciding on *early* retirement (at age 62), a move with few precedents in the labor field.

The importance of union leadership. It is possible that not enough attention has been paid to the importance of leadership in the union movement. Trade unionism is an organic development, with many standard practices and considerable uniformity all along the line. However, it is also full of variations, contradictions, divergences, and paradoxes. Much of this variation may be traced to the environment: employment conditions are infinitely varied and call for wholly different treatment and approach. However, it can be argued that an equally significant factor is the character and capacity of the men who, by chance or design, come to positions of power in the unions. A Samuel Gompers at the head means one kind of labor movement; a Eugene V. Debs, a John L. Lewis, or a George Meany, another. The personal power of important labor leaders is very great, their opportunities to make vitally important decisions ever present. There are a number of reasons for this fact.

In the first place, internal discipline in unions is traditionally very strict, approximating that of military organizations, so that a policy, once decided upon, is rarely questioned afterward. An announced policy therefore becomes a *fait accompli*, making it easy for the official group in charge to control the decision making. In fact, it is difficult for them to avoid it. In the second place, union leaders are typically the heads of very large groups of workers who are geographically scattered and represented only through local and district officials, who have inadequate opportunities both to sound out the membership and to get the ear of their superiors. The annual convention may make legislative action possible, but the interim decisions are left to the top officials without benefit of referendum. In the third place, union members are for the most part inadequately trained and educated and must rely to a much greater extent than other groups upon their leaders for advice. Very few workers are in a position to evaluate the wisdom of a set of bargaining proposals containing policy implications, as well as many technical rules. They must rely upon the recommendations of a few top officials whom they trust.

Fourth, and finally, is the element of trust. Trade unionism is a doctrine, a creed. Union leaders are not just business representatives or even legislators for their membership. They are semiheroes, often bearing scars of long-forgotten strikes and jail sentences. The typical member's reliance upon Walter Reuther or Joe Curran or Harry Bridges is supported by his knowledge that they have been martyrs in the "Battle of the Overpass" or the "Great Strike of 1934," have served on the picket line, or have otherwise proved the depth of their convictions. To question their decisions would be almost to question the member's own faith in trade unionism. He therefore delegates to his leaders an initiative and authority which are far-reaching in their implications, especially when a vital industry is at stake or when union membership runs into the hundreds of thousands.

THE FRIENDS OF ORGANIZED LABOR

The labor movement does not consist entirely of members of trade unions and their families. They have influential friends, many of whom are entirely outside the labor movement as such. Organized labor is a minority group in the United States, although one of the largest and most powerful of such. It would never have reached its present size and influence without the help of an assortment of sympathetic well-wishers in politics, education, religion, and the professions.

Political.   In politics, at the national level at least, organized labor and its program are the property of the Democratic party. This proprietorship has been honestly come by, with a consistent record throughout the twentieth century of Democratic administrations friendly to trade unionism and with no competing record of cordiality on the part of the Republicans. It was Woodrow Wilson's administration which brought about the passage of the Clayton Act (incorrectly hailed by Samuel Gompers as "Labor's Magna Charta," although intended as that by Congress), the prolabor Adamson Act, and which gave organized labor its first big taste of wartime encouragement in 1917 to 1918 by treating labor leaders as worthy of equal standing with business leaders. The tradition was both maintained and improved upon by Franklin D. Roosevelt during his three terms in office and by Harry S. Truman in the two that followed. The increase of union fortunes between 1933 and 1953 may be traced on the membership charts, in the assets columns, and in the terms of dispute settlements, many of which were signed in the White House. The solid support given by organized labor to Presidents Kennedy and Johnson and their reciprocal assistance in the form of prolabor appointments and favorable legislation is current history.

On the Republican side, Presidents Taft, Harding, Coolidge, and Hoover were decidedly neutral, if not cool, to organized labor. Only Theodore Roosevelt had a program which might have enlisted union enthusiasm, but the "progressive" spirit in the party was soon overwhelmed by the conservative wing. Coolidge first attracted national attention when he broke a policemen's strike in Boston, and the historical sympathy of Republican politicians for big business, sound money, low taxes, and limited government has done little to endear the Republican party to union officials or the men they represent.

The Eisenhower administration extended the traditional Republican pattern another 8 years (1953 to 1961) without noticeable change. After an abortive effort to give organized labor representation in the Cabinet (through the appointment of a trade unionist, Martin Durkin, as Secretary of Labor), relations between labor leaders and the White House deteriorated steadily, culminating in passage of the Labor-Management Reporting and Disclosure Act in 1959—the labor movement's "most severe setback in more than a decade," according to the AFL–CIO executive council.

Religious.   In its contest for public support, organized labor can usually count upon the churches. A feature of the Depression and post-Second World War years was the shift of religious influence to the side of organized workmen and the criticisms of managerial labor relations which have been aired in church conferences and pulpits. The Catholic Church is a leader in this respect, its representatives having demonstrated great sympathy with union labor upon many occasions. They have been strongly seconded, however, by leaders of the major Protestant faiths, who have sided with employe organizations both as to general objectives and in specific disputes with employers.

Educational.   Trade unionism was first made "respectable" in the United States by a small group of college professors who insisted upon studying the institution of organized labor as a social phenomenon and who eventually got "labor economics" accepted as a branch of general economics, a proper field for teaching and research. Among the earliest of these were Richard T. Ely at Johns Hopkins and John R. Commons at the University of Wisconsin, from whose classes came a number of scholars and administrators of labor agencies, with an important influence upon early union growth and acceptance. The study of trade unionism was continued at Johns Hopkins by D. A. McCabe and his associates, at Wisconsin by Commons and Selig Perlman and E. E. Witte, and was carried on extensively at the University of Chicago by Robert F. Hoxie, Harry A. Millis, and Paul H. Douglas.

These pioneers have a large following today, including such well-known scholars as: Professors Benjamin Aaron and Irving Bernstein (UCLA), John Dunlop (Harvard), William Haber (Michigan), George Hildebrand (Cornell), Clark Kerr (California), Richard Lester (Princeton), Jean McKelvey (Cornell), Lloyd G. Reynolds (Yale), Joel Seidman (Chicago), among many others. The industrial relations profession has its own professional association—the Industrial Relations Research Association—and operates not only through college and university classes but also through industrial relations "institutes" and "centers," staffed in part by faculty and in part by research specialists.

The fellowship of the study of industrial relations goes far beyond the campus, to include professional labor arbitrators like David L. Cole, government administrators (Arthur Ross, Commissioner of Labor Statistics), and union officials such as Nathaniel Goldfinger, director of research for the AFL–CIO. In colleges and universities, classes are offered in union history, policies, and techniques; collective bargaining; labor law; mediation and arbitration, and so on, while the institutes offer training programs for trade-union officers and management representatives with responsibility for labor relations. All the major universities offer graduate work in industrial relations leading to the Ph.D. degree, drawing students from a number of the social disciplines—economics, sociology, political science, history, etc. It is undeniable that most scholars working in industrial relations are strongly sympathetic with the philosophy and aims of organized labor and that in their teaching and research they have contributed to a widespread understanding and acceptance of the institution of trade unionism.

READINGS

The basic data on the current labor movement—officers, membership, organization, and statistical analysis—are reported regularly at 2-year intervals by the Bureau of Labor Statistics in its *Directory of National and International Labor Unions in the United States.* The 1965 issue was Bulletin 1493, price 55 cents, obtainable from the Superintendent of Documents, U.S. Government Printing Office, Washington 25, D.C. This would be money well spent by any student.

Comparisons can at times be quite dramatic. It is suggested that students refer to H. A. Millis and R. E. Montgomery's exhaustive treatise on *Organized Labor* (New York: McGraw-Hill Book Company, 1945). This book brings the development of unionism up to the middle of the Second World War, emphasizing the rapid increase in size and influence of the labor movement after 1933.

For biographies of labor leaders, the student might try Charles A. Madison, *American Labor Leaders* (New York: Harper & Row, Publishers, Incorporated, 1950), which may be supplemented by the first four chapters of J. B. S. Hardman and Maurice F. Neufeld (eds.), *The House of Labor* (Englewood Cliffs, N.J.: Prentice-Hall, Inc., 1951). For the seamier side of the picture, the hearings and reports of the McClellan committee are voluminous and revealing.

Two books based on a critical analysis of union strategy and tactics are Sidney Lens, *The Crisis of American Labor* (New York: Sagamore Press, 1959) and Sylvester Petro, *Power Unlimited: The Corruption of Union Leadership* (New York: The Ronald Press Company, 1960). The first is a troubled view by a professional trade unionist, which attempts to point out the road which organized labor must take to regain its leadership and momentum. The second, by a professor of law, also a former professional trade unionist, is drawn almost entirely from the record of the McClellan committee hearings, and shows how the committee's investigations piled up evidence to support a labor reform bill such as the Labor-Management Reporting and Disclosure Act of 1959.

Ralph James and Estelle James's remarkable study of *Hoffa and the Teamsters* (Princeton, N.J.: D. Van Nostrand Company, Inc., 1965) is almost required reading for a current understanding of the world's largest and most powerful labor organization and its controversial head.

FIVE

THE
FIRST
HUNDRED
YEARS: 1786-1886

It's a tough life and the first hundred years are the hardest.
WILSON MIZNER

History is an attempt to interpret the effect of the time factor in human affairs; it is therefore a matter of events, dates, and periods. The principal historical issues are issues of interpretation; there is often considerable agreement on the facts. Interpretation means deciding what events, dates, and periods have been important in the given case. In this book, the history of the labor movement in the United States will be divided into three principal periods:

1786–1886: the first hundred years, during most of which there was no real labor movement, although there were several events of the utmost importance to the future of organized labor;

1886–1936: the fifty years of American Federation of Labor domination, during which the labor movement took root, established itself, worked out its philosophy and methodology, and became an accepted part of American life; and

1936– : the rise of industrial unionism (and the CIO), with its accompanying rapid expansion of union membership and resultant growth of organized labor's power and influence.

WHAT TO LOOK FOR

To understand the growth of organized labor in America, one should be familiar with the pattern of events which significantly influenced the rise or decline of trade unionism over the years. But which events and what kind? There are so many of them! This is where interpretation (selection) comes in, and no two historians will agree precisely, although in broad outline there is often a great deal of overlapping. One way of reducing the problem is to identify a limited number of historical "factors" (influences

114

or institutions) which have been of consequence to organized labor. Some of these were (and are still) of great importance—for example, the government.

The government.   Trade unions have always felt the stern hand of public regulation, whether it was administered by judges under the name of the common law or by agencies like the National Labor Relations Board administering a specific statute. The attitude of the government— and often of specific agencies or even persons occupying important positions in the government—has been crucial a number of times for the growth (or lack of it) of the labor movement. However, the "government" is a very large and amorphous and, in this country, decentralized institution. It operates at three main levels: Federal, state, and local, and is always (nominally, at least) divided among three branches—the legislative, executive, and judicial. The attitudes of different branches of the government toward labor organization at a given time may be anything but uniform.[1] The emphasis here will be almost exclusively on the Federal level of government,[2] but even with this restriction it will be necessary to keep in mind, not just "the government," but at a minimum, Congress, the Presidency, the courts, and the major labor agencies: the National Labor Relations Board, the National Mediation Board, the Federal Mediation and Conciliation Service, etc.

Politics and political parties.   An extra dimension of government in this country is the political party system. The periods of greatest growth in union membership in the United States have coincided with Democratic administrations in Washington; periods of arrested growth or decline have occurred while Republican Presidents occupied the White House. Is the connection as obvious as it appears to be, and does it carry through at state and local levels as well? A major policy question emanating from the facts of the record is: Should the organized labor movement abandon its traditional nonpartisan policy of "rewarding friends and punishing enemies" in favor of a formal alignment with the Democratic Party? It did so briefly in the presidential elections of 1952 and 1956 and its candidate was badly beaten. It did so again in 1960 and 1964 and its candidates were successful. How should the past be interpreted and what does the future hold?

[1] Compare the attitudes of Congress and the Supreme Court toward organized labor during President Franklin D. Roosevelt's first term, 1933 to 1937.

[2] Thereby omitting some large and highly important areas of labor regulation—the local (municipal) level especially, much of whose story remains to be written. For students who wish to try their hands at field research, the City Hall is always there, with its record of municipal ordinances, policing of strikes, and the general network of regulation of industrial activity.

Labor leadership.   Another factor the influence of which can hardly be denied is labor leadership. Whether or not one accepts the "hero" or "great man" theory of history generally, the labor movement has clearly at times benefited from outstanding leadership and, at other times, been the victim of weak, misguided, or corrupt officials. Without Gompers, would American trade unionism have been on the solid footing it had reached by the time of the First World War? If John L. Lewis had been elected president of the AFL in 1924 (he was more than willing to be a candidate) instead of William Green, would the swing to industrial unionism which occurred in the 1930s have been as long overdue and as violently disruptive as it turned out to be? Without Meany and Reuther, would the AFL and the CIO have merged in 1955? What was the effect upon the labor movement in the 1950s of the election by the Teamsters of two presidents in succession who were shown by congressional investigation to be dictatorial, corrupt, and irresponsible?

Employer associations.   Balanced off against labor leadership is the factor of organized employer opposition. The key agencies have been for years the National Association of Manufacturers and the United States Chamber of Commerce, both headquartered in Washington, D.C. They are supplemented by local and regional associations such as the Merchants and Manufacturers Association of Los Angeles, industrial employer associations like the National Metal Trades Association and the Pacific Maritime Association, and less formal, *ad hoc* bargaining groups such as The Steel Companies Coordinating Committee of 1959. At times—as in the 1920s—the organized employer opposition has been overwhelmingly powerful; at other times—as in the mid-1930s—it has been scattered and ineffective.[3] Like union officials, the big associations and management generally try to judge the temper of the times, tie their campaigns to favorable issues—inflation, featherbedding, union corruption, etc.—and strengthen the position of employers in their contest with their organized employes.

Business conditions.   Another major influence bearing upon the growth of organized labor is the business cycle. One very widely accepted theory of labor history has been based in part on the presumed rise in union fortunes during prosperity and the subsequent falling away of membership during recession periods.[4] (Unless explained away by counter-

---

[3] How effective do you think it is today? Try writing a short (1,000-word) memo in answer to the question.

[4] See Mary Beard, *A Short History of the American Labor Movement* (New York: Harcourt, Brace & World, Inc., 1936). The analysis, however, is derived from J. R. Commons and Associates, *History of Labor in the United States* (New York: The Macmillan Company, 1918–1934).

balancing influences, this theory received a heavy jolt in the Depression of the 1930s.) Whether or not the theory is correct, the level of economic activity is of primary concern to organized labor. No one keeps a closer watch on unemployment figures or is more fertile with suggestions for correcting local "soft spots" in the labor market than labor leaders. *automate?*

Miscellaneous.   Finally, there are several miscellaneous groups which have at times strongly influenced the position of organized labor in America. Some are formally and very powerfully organized, while others are without organization but held together by a common set of ideas. Among the latter is the "intelligentsia" or "intellectuals," a conglomerate collection of "liberal" college professors, professional writers, clergymen, and reformers. Although generally favorable and often helpful, they cannot be counted on to follow the union "line" at all times and are often a trial to operating trade unionists. On the other side of the fence, generally speaking, are the press, movies, and TV (newspapers, for example, are published by owners and managers), the organized farmers, professional groups such as the American Medical Association and the American Bar Association, and the military.

The military—officers and ex-officers of the armed services—are relative newcomers as a pressure group, but very influential newcomers, and rapidly becoming entrenched in high government and industrial jobs. It may be said almost categorically that professional military men are antiunion, the whole notion of industrial democracy and collective bargaining being contrary to their training and their belief in the virtues of discipline and authority. The probability of a continuance or even of an intensification of military influence in governmental and business decisions during the foreseeable future raises another major problem for labor statesmanship to deal with in the years to come.

BACKGROUND AND BEGINNINGS

The first century of trade unionism in the United States starts with the earliest recorded strike (of some Philadelphia printers for a minimum wage of $6 a week) and ends with the formation of the American Federation of Labor in Columbus, Ohio. In between were 100 years of national growth, during which the country fought two foreign wars and one civil war, national boundaries spread westward to the Pacific Ocean and southward to the Rio Grande, population grew from 4 million to 58 million, and the center of population moved westward from 23 miles east of Baltimore, Maryland, to 20 miles east of Columbus, Indiana. It was a period dominated by the frontier, expansion, free land, and movement westward. Two years before the founding convention of the AFL in 1886, Grover Cleveland, the first Democratic President in 24 years, was elected to his first term. The period ended in a blaze of economic expansion between the great depressions of the 1870s and the 1890s.

What happened to trade unionism in this 100 years? The answer is: There was not much of it, at least until the very end of the period, and what there was had its ups and downs. It is perhaps equally important to keep in mind that some of the things that happened to the labor movement in the United States in the nineteenth century were to a considerable degree a reflection of what had occurred in Great Britain during a period running back almost 500 years. The law as applied to American trade unions in the early days was British law and the lawyers and judges were British-trained professional men. There was already a long record of legal restriction upon employe "combinations" in Britain, when the first strike took place on this side of the Atlantic, and the standing of labor organizations in society was considered fairly well settled, since it had not changed much since the fourteenth century.

1351: The British Statute of Labourers.   The history of labor legislation in the English-speaking world starts with the aftermath of the Black Death (bubonic plague) which spread across Europe in the Middle Ages and about the middle of the fourteenth century cut the population of Britain to a half or a third of its previous number. The immediate result was a serious labor shortage which produced a seller's market in personal services and threatened to disrupt existing economic arrangements to the disadvantage of the titled landowners. An Ordinance of Labourers, issued in 1349 by King Edward III, acted as a temporary protection, and in 1351, Parliament passed the Statute of Labourers, a broad and inclusive law whose terms sound today something like a Fair Labor Standards Act in reverse.[5]

The Statute of Labourers made it the duty of everyone (without land, position, or a title) to work, and established the terms of employment as to hours and rates of pay. And what were the terms? They were those in effect prior to the plague. Instead of minimum wages and maximum hours of work, the statute set *wage maximums* and *minimum hours of work*. Heavy penalties were established for accepting wages above those already in effect, and all hiring was required to be done openly (in public) and for long terms, to avoid the possibility of competition among employers for the services of laborers. Getting an employe to leave his master (inducing breach of a contract of employment) was made a punishable offense. It is the classic example of class legislation, and it stood as the law of the land for 200 years.[6] It also influenced British and American thinking

[5] 25 Edw. 3, st. 1 (1351).

[6] See J. M. Landis and M. Manoff, "Historical Introduction," *Cases on Labor Law* (Brooklyn, N.Y.: Foundation Press, Inc., 1942), for an excellent brief summary of early English labor legislation and its enforcement.

on the law of labor contracts for more than 500 years; there are vestiges today in the American common law of employment (still called, from the British, the law of "master and servant") of doctrine carried over from the great statute of the fourteenth century.

The Elizabethan Statute of Labourers and the "century of combination acts."   Most of the prosecutions for violation of the Statute of Labourers were to stop collective action by workingmen who insisted on combining to force wages upward. Approximately two centuries after its enactment, Parliament (in 1548) again took steps to protect the masters by passing the Bill of Conspiracies of Victuallers and Craftsmen,[7] which was purely and simply an anticombination law. What it did was to prohibit under pain of heavy penalty any combined action by employes to raise wages, limit output, or reduce hours of work. This act was supplemented 14 years later (1562) by the comprehensive Elizabethan Statute of Labourers, which (1) reaffirmed the duty of all to work, either in industry or agriculture, (2) established official rates of pay, hours of work, and terms of service, (3) placed restrictions on the movement of laborers from country to town and vice versa, (4) made paying or receiving excessive wages punishable by fine and imprisonment, (5) made breach of a labor contract a penal offense, and (6) authorized the jailing of laborers until they were willing to work upon the prescribed terms.[8] There were few liberalizing features in the law and several additions to the rigor of the labor code. For another 150 years the Bill of Conspiracies and the Elizabethan Statute set the dimensions of the labor contract, with no space left open for combined action.

But combined action there was, nonetheless, especially with the improvement of economic conditions at the beginning of the eighteenth century. These "worker rebellions" were put down with the help of a series of acts of Parliament throughout the 1700s which made any form of collective action illegal. The century of (anti) combination acts was capped by the Combination Acts of 1799 and 1800, which imposed criminal penalties for any form of joint action by employes to improve their pay, hours, or working conditions, and the next 20 years saw prosecution after prosecution based on the statutes. What this meant for American trade unionism was brought out in the Philadelphia Cordwainers case.

1806: The Philadelphia Cordwainers case.   This is one of the most celebrated court cases in American trade-union history. A cordwainer is a shoemaker. The full name of the case reveals the purpose of the prosecution. It was "The Trial of the Boot and Shoemakers of Philadelphia on an Indictment for a Combination and Conspiracy to Raise Their Wages."

[7] 2 & 3 Edw. 6, c. 15 (1548).
[8] Eliz., c. 4 (1562).

The attitude of the Court was made clear in one brief, pointed passage: "A combination of workmen to raise their wages may be considered from a twofold point of view; one is to benefit themselves, the other to injure those who do not join their society. The rule of law condemns both." This was the so-called "conspiracy doctrine," which meant that the activities of trade unions were in themselves illegal conspiracies, punishable by fine and imprisonment. Until it was reversed, there was obviously little scope for trade-union operations, except as secret societies outside the law.

1810 to 1830: Extension of the suffrage.   During these 20 years Maryland, South Carolina, New York, Massachusetts, and Virginia removed practically all property restrictions from the right to vote, thus making it possible for propertyless workingmen to have a voice in the selection of political leaders and the formation of basic policies. The lead of these important states was subsequently followed throughout the country, and the "rise of the common man" and the "era of reform" were under way. In view of subsequent developments there were few occurrences in the history of the country more favorable to the cause of organized labor. Trade unionism is a workingman's movement. Even with the vote there have been long periods when hostile courts and administrative officers have defeated the clear will of the electorate on labor issues. Without the ballot, trade unionism would have been powerless to influence, much less initiate and force through, the many social reforms associated with its support.

It may or may not be a coincidence that there was a resurgence of union activity during the decade 1827 to 1837, which included the organization of a Workingmen's party in Philadelphia and New York, followed in 1833 by a General Trades' Union, which brought all the trade societies of New York City into one organization. A year later this body called a convention and established the National Trades' Union, the first attempt at nationwide trade-union federation. By 1836, Philadelphia had 58 local unions; New York, 52; Newark, 16; Pittsburgh, 13; Cincinnati, 14; and Louisville, 7.[9] None of them were on very solid foundations, though. A financial panic arrived in 1837, and in a year or two every form of labor organization, from the local trade societies to the National Trades' Union, had disappeared. From 1837 to 1850 the labor movement wallowed in a sea of "isms": associationism, agrarianism, socialism, Owenism, etc. It did not return to "safe and sane" unionism until the middle of the 1850s, when a number of national unions were started, some of which are still in existence, *e.g.*, the typographers, locomotive engineers, cigar makers, machinists, and blacksmiths.

[9] Selig Perlman, *History of Trade Unionism in the United States* (New York: The Macmillan Company, 1922), p. 19.

1824: Turn of the tide in Britain.   In 1824, Parliament repealed all existing combination acts and replaced them with a law permitting full freedom of collective action. It was legal to strike, picket, or boycott; to negotiate collective agreements; and to get others to quit work in support of union objectives. For none of these things could workers be prosecuted for conspiracy under either common or statute law. The act, sponsored by Francis Place, the reformer, and Joseph Hume, a liberal M.P., was a great victory for organized labor—and it lasted exactly one year. A series of strikes enraged the public, and the Combination Act of 1825 took away most of the gains that had been made. However, the 1825 law still permitted employes to meet together to agree upon common action in regard to wages and hours (banned prior to 1824), and officially approved labor agreements. Actually, from 1825 onward, the position of organized labor in Britain improved steadily, both in membership and before the courts. The Era of Reform (1830 to 1846) saw the formation (by Robert Owen and associates) of the short-lived Grand National Consolidated Trades Union, which acquired over 500,000 members before collapsing, and it included the rise of the Chartist Movement. The end of the period was marked in America by a far-reaching court decision, *Commonwealth v. Hunt.*

1842: Commonwealth v. Hunt.[10]   This case is even more celebrated than that of the Philadelphia cordwainers (at least, by trade unionists) because it reversed the latter. In *Commonwealth v. Hunt* the conspiracy doctrine as applied to trade unions was specifically, carefully, and authoritatively reversed. The opinion was rendered by Chief Justice Shaw of the Supreme Judicial Court of Massachusetts, and the prestige of this jurist was so great that the precedent he set was seldom disregarded afterward, even in other states whose judicial systems were supposed to be independent of the Massachusetts court.

It was another cordwainers' (shoemakers') case. The issue was the right of the Boston Journeymen Bootmakers' Society (the union) to enforce a closed-shop agreement upon one Isaac B. Wait, a master cordwainer (the employer), by compelling him to discharge one Jeremiah Horne, a member of the union, who had refused to pay a union fine and thus fell into bad standing. The lower court found the society guilty of a criminal conspiracy, and the verdict was appealed. Chief Justice Shaw's ruling was as follows:

The averment is this; that the defendants and others formed themselves into a society, and agreed not to work for any person who should employ any journeyman or other person, not a member of such society, after notice given him to discharge such workman. The manifest intent of the association is, to induce all those en-

[10] 4 Metc. (Mass.) 45.

gaged in the same occupation to become members of it. *Such a purpose is not unlawful.* It would give them a power which might be exerted for useful and honorable purposes, or for dangerous and pernicious ones. If the latter were the real and actual object, and susceptible of proof, it should have been specially charged. Such an association might be used to afford each other assistance in times of poverty, sickness and distress; or to raise their intellectual, moral and social condition; or to make improvement in their art; or for other proper purposes. Or the association might be designed for purposes of oppression and injustice. . . .

Nor can we perceive that the objects of this association, whatever they may have been, were to be attained by criminal means. The means which they proposed to employ, as averred in this court, and which, as we are now to presume, were established by the proof, were, that they would not work for a person, who after due notice, should employ a journeyman not a member of their society. Supposing the object of the association to be laudable and lawful, or at least not unlawful, are these means criminal? The case supposes that these persons are not bound by contract, but free to work for whom they please, or not to work, if they so prefer. In this state of things, we cannot perceive, that it is criminal for men to agree together to exercise their own acknowledged rights, in such a manner as best to subserve their own interests. . . .

We think, therefore, that associations may be entered into, the object of which is to adopt measures that may have a tendency to impoverish another, that is, to diminish his gains and profits, and yet so far from being criminal or unlawful, the object may be highly meritorious and public spirited. The legality of such an association will therefore depend upon the means to be used for its accomplishment.[11]

The importance of the *Hunt* case was that it made trade unionism legal; it removed the same disabilities from organized labor in America that had been cleared away in Britain by repeal of the old combination acts in 1824. That it was a major turning point in the rise of the labor movement is undeniable. Some years ago, John R. Commons and his colleague, John B. Andrews, described a historical trend in the development of governmental attitudes towards organized labor in this country and Great Britain. The steps in the sequence were, from: [12]

1. Repression, to
2. Toleration, to
3. Encouragement, to
4. Intervention

For the United States, the step from repression to toleration came with the decision of Chief Justice Shaw in 1842. Trade unions still had to meet legislative and judicial restrictions of varying intensity, but they were never again declared illegal *per se* at common law.

1848: Revolt of the European workingman. The year 1848 marked the climax of a series of radical reform movements throughout Europe,

---

[11] Italics supplied.

[12] J. R. Commons and J. B. Andrews, *Principles of Labor Legislation*, 4th rev. ed. (New York: Harper & Row, Publishers, Incorporated, 1936), pp. 374–376.

all of them based on worker discontent. In France, Germany, and Austria, there were revolutions. Bloody street fighting in Paris, the most severe yet seen in Europe, was led by officers of the "national workshops" (trade unions). It brought prompt reprisals. French conservatives, alarmed by the "spectre of Communism," supported a military regime under General Cavaignac, which was succeeded by the virtual dictatorship of Prince Louis Napoleon, and the radical movement was crushed.

What was the "spectre of Communism" which so appalled the property owners?

It was a reference to the first line of the *Manifesto of the Communist Party*, by Karl Marx and Friedrich Engels, a French translation of which was distributed in Paris shortly before the insurrection of June, 1948. The first line is far more accurate today than it was in January, 1848, when it was written. It goes: "A spectre is haunting Europe—the spectre of Communism. All the powers of old Europe have entered into a holy alliance to exorcise this spectre. . . ."

The *Communist Manifesto* is important as the symbol of an idea and a movement. The idea is the class struggle; the movement, the rise to power of workingmen through organization and political action (to the "dictatorship of the proletariat"). According to the authors:

The history of all hitherto existing society is the history of class struggles. . . . Freeman and slave, patrician and plebeian, lord and serf, guild-master and journeyman, in a word, oppressor and oppressed, stood in constant opposition to one another, carried on an uninterrupted, now hidden, now open fight, a fight that each time ended either in a revolutionary reconstitution of society at large, or in the common ruin of the contending classes. . . .

The modern bourgeois society that has sprouted from the ruins of feudal society, has not done away with class antagonisms. It has but established new classes, new conditions of oppression, new forms of struggle in place of the old ones.

Marx and Engels were by no means the sole proprietors of the notion that the lot of the workingman should be improved. They and their manifesto were simply the most notable in an era of reform which included the work of Saint-Simon, Fourier, Blanc, and Proudhon in France, Bakunin in Russia, Rodbertus and Lasalle in Germany, and Robert Owen in England. Everywhere the reasons were the same—the Industrial Revolution, misery and destitution among workers and their families, and insecurity born of alternating periods of employment and unemployment, prosperity and depression. In America the same influences were at work, but they were overshadowed by the slavery issue and the war that grew out of it. They reappeared, following the war, in a form of abortive mass unionism and political action, which reached its high point in the explosive growth of the Knights of Labor.

The importance of Marxian ideology to the growth of organized labor is debatable, but its relationship is not. For 70 years, the preamble to the constitution of the American Federation of Labor read:

Whereas, A struggle is going on in all the nations of the civilized world between the oppressors and the oppressed of all countries, a struggle between the capitalist and the laborer, which grows in intensity from year to year, and will work diastrous results to the toiling millions if they are not combined for mutual protection and benefit. It, therefore, behooves the representatives of the Trade and Labor Unions of America, in convention assembled, to adopt such measures and disseminate such principles among the mechanics and laborers of our country as will permanently unite them to secure the recognition of rights to which they are justly entitled.

In 1864, Marx formed the First International Workingmen's Association (the First International), with headquarters first in London and then in New York. Its purpose was the spread of Marxian socialism, and it was aimed at the organization of workers in various countries. The American branches of the International were termed "sections." Three graduates of these training schools for Socialists were Samuel Gompers, founder and long-time president of the AFL, Adolph Strasser, founder of the Cigar Makers' Union and cofounder with Gompers of the AFL; and P. J. McGuire, founder of the Brotherhood of Carpenters & Joiners.

Whether or not it is true, the Marxian dogma is a fundamental of the labor movement. Briefly stated, that dogma is the existence of a proletarian class of wage laborers whose fundamental interests are everywhere the same and in the main opposed to the interests of their employers. In the United States, which is today of all the great powers the furthest from the modern communist ideology, it is only necessary to read any current issue of the *AFL–CIO News, Labor,* or the *American Federationist,* to find this basic idea expressed again and again.[13]

The importance of Marx lies not so much in his economic analysis, which is thoroughly faulty, but in the remarkable appeal of his social philosophy, the vitality of which, among the mass populations of today, is the modern wonder of the world.

1861 to 1865: The war between the states. The United States Civil War was the central event in the slavery issue, the influence of which dominated the country from the Compromise of 1850 to 1877—and is still with us 100 years later. The immediate effect of the war was highly disruptive of the labor movement. Coming on the heels of the depression of 1857, the dislocation of men and industry occasioned by military mobilization eliminated most unions which had revived during the preceding decade. They began to reappear during the latter part of the conflict, as

[13] This of course does not imply that organized labor must support the policies of any particular government (like that of the U.S.S.R.) which calls itself Communist.

the pressure for industrial production brought on a labor shortage and price increases forced workers to combine in order to raise wages. For the future of organized labor the most important result of the war was the diversion of political and economic power to the industrial states of the North and East, where a conservative business philosophy characterized all major decisions. The changing character of labor organization and activity during the 20 years immediately following 1865 are undoubtedly in part attributable to "the triumph of business enterprise," as Charles A. Beard called it, and the accompanying rapid industrialization of the country. One illustration of this rapid change was the prevalence of the "one big union" idea, of which the most prominent examples were the National Labor Union and the Knights of Labor.

1866: The National Labor Union.   This was an attempt, for a while apparently successful, to federate all the common people of the country, especially labor and the farmers, into one big organization for the improvement of working conditions and for political action. Its principal members were miscellaneous local and national unions, city centrals (combinations of local craft unions on a municipal basis), and a variety of reform organizations of a socialistic type, which had their own special purposes but were also interested in the brotherhood of man and the improvement of his condition. It had a big program: the 8-hour day, exclusion of Orientals, protection of women workers, extension of collective bargaining through trade agreements, easy money for the farmers, producers' cooperatives, limitation of interest rates and profits, the use of strikes but only as a last resort, a cooperative industrial system, etc. It is given credit for achieving the 8-hour day for employes of the Federal government in 1868, but for little else. After a short existence the National Labor Union disappeared in 1872.

1882: The Chinese Exclusion Act.   The Chinese Exclusion Act was labor's first political victory of major size, just as the strikes against the Gould railways 3 years later were its first economic victory against big-league opposition. Oriental immigration into California had been a problem since the Gold Rush days, culminating in a race riot in 1871. By 1877 the formation of a Workingmen's party in the state was the means of bringing the matter to the attention of Congress, which 5 years later barred Chinese laborers from entrance into the United States for a period of 10 years. (In 1902 the exclusion was made permanent and extended to cover Chinese in Hawaii and the Philippines, which were American possessions.) Three years afterward, in 1885, Congress prohibited the importation of contract labor. These measures were forerunners of organized labor's attitude on immigration in general, which coalesced into active opposition following the First World War and helped produce the Immigration Laws of 1921 and 1924, and the exclusion of *braceros* (Mexican nationals admitted to the United States for a term of work) in 1965.

1869 to 1886: The Knights of Labor. The Noble Order of the Knights of Labor is the most complete expression of the "one big union" movement yet seen in the United States. In a number of ways it was remarkable. For one thing, during its relatively short lifetime it was successful beyond the hopes of its founders or the expectations of its critics. At its peak in 1886 it claimed 700,000 members, more than double the total enrollment of the entire organized labor movement at any time prior to that date. Its 1886 membership record was not surpassed by any single union in the United States until the CIO Autoworkers went over the 750,000 mark more than 50 years later. Its rise was meteoric, and its decline almost as rapid. In 1881, the reported membership was 19,400, a good, round figure by nineteenth-century standards but nothing to startle the world with. By 1883 it had more than doubled to 52,000, to make it far and away the largest single labor organization on record. But this was only the beginning, and a modest one at that, considering what was to come. Two years later, in 1885, the reported membership had doubled again to 104,000. Then, within 12 months or so, it shot up to *more than 700,000.*[14] This was increase at an increasing rate, starting from a fair-sized base, and obviously could not continue. It did not. In 1886 several factors combined to stop the boom. By 1888 the figures were down to 222,000 and by 1890, to 100,000. Ten years later the Knights had disappeared.

One distinctive feature of the Knights was the "mixed assembly," wherein a local union included both skilled and unskilled workmen, without distinctions of craft or rank. This was anticipating the industrial basis of organization by a good many years. After 1881 women were admitted, and, after 1883, Negroes. Eventually room was made for farmers, shopkeepers, small tradesmen, and some professional men, although non-wage earners were limited to one-fourth the membership of any local. There were a number of positive exclusions. The minimum age limit was 16. One regulation stated: "No person who either sells or makes a living, or any part of it, by the sale of intoxicating drink, either as manufacturer, dealer or agent, or through any member of the family, can be admitted to membership in this order, and no lawyer, banker, professional gambler or stock broker can be admitted." After 1881 physicians were allowed to join. Without the miscellaneous membership provisions, particularly those admitting unskilled and semiskilled working people, the massive enrollments of 1885 and 1886 would have been impossible.

Another remarkable characteristic of the Order was its pacific nature

[14] Terence V. Powderly, who was Grand Master Workman at the time, says the top figure was 600,000. The discrepancy is of little consequence. Either figure was astronomical for a labor organization in those days.

and aims. It professed not to believe in strikes, maintaining that they
should be avoided whenever possible. (It is a paradox that the great recruiting drive of 1886 was apparently a result of a series of successful
strikes against the railway systems of Jay Gould.) The theory was that
strikes afforded only temporary relief and that the members should rely
instead upon organization, cooperation, and political action. The favored
weapon of the Knights was the boycott, which was more effective in the
hands of an organization with the general membership of the Order than
when applied by the ordinary craft union. It also recommended publicly
the compulsory arbitration of industrial disputes and enforcement of the
decisions.

A third unique feature of the Order was its major purpose—abolition
of the wage-earning class. This aim was not as revolutionary as it sounded,
however, since the method by which it was to be accomplished was not
the dictatorship of the proletariat but the creation instead of a class of
independent, self-employed producers, or proprietors. Its principal targets
were the trusts and corporations, the concentration of wealth and industrial power. In their place it proposed producers' cooperation. The
Knights, in fact, experimented extensively with cooperative enterprises
along the lines of the Rochdale (England) plan and that of the Owenites,
but without marked success. Theirs was a long-run program. "Our mission cannot be accomplished in a day or a generation," read the constitution. "Agitation, education, and organization are all necessary."

Finally, the reform program of the Order was more inclusive even
than that of the National Labor Union (including many features now
common in the governmental landscape): establishment of bureaus of
labor statistics in the Federal and state governments, taxation of unearned
increment in land, industrial health legislation, weekly pay laws, prohibition of child labor, compulsory schooling and free textbooks, income and
inheritance taxes, restrictions on the contract system with respect to
convict labor, Greenbackism, free coinage of silver at a ratio of 16 to 1,
government ownership of railroads and telegraph systems, the merit system in government service, the 8-hour day, and equal rights (including
equal pay for equal work) for both sexes. For these proposals it lobbied
in Washington and the state capitals and participated actively in the political campaigns from 1884 to 1900.

RISE AND COLLAPSE OF THE KNIGHTS OF LABOR

The secret society of Uriah Stevens.   It all began in 1868 with a
meeting of seven tailors in the home of Uriah Stevens in Philadelphia.
Their own union, the Garment Cutters, was a war casualty. It had gone
to pieces as a result of cheap labor competition on government war contracts, and the survivors wanted to replace it. Stevens was a Baptist

minister, full of evangelistic zeal and highly critical of what seemed to him the narrow, selfish purposes of craft unionism. He conceived a secret society which would have the eventual aim of improving the lot of all the underprivileged, regardless of craft, industry, faith, creed, color, or national origin. However, he and his followers were shrewd enough to start with tailors, a trade they understood and whose members were without affiliation, and expand slowly and carefully through the device of "associate members" into other trades. As these "associates" grew familiar with the Order and demonstrated conviction, they were permitted to organize their own "assemblies," as the local bodies were called. In 1871 the name of the Noble Order of the Knights of Labor was adopted.

The local assemblies eventually formed district assemblies, which were given numerical designation. District Assembly 1, with Master Workman Stevens at its head, was the center of influence and authority. In 1878, on the organization's tenth anniversary, a general assembly was formed, with Grand Master Workman Stevens as chief officer. By this time there were delegates from seven states representing 15 trades. A year later, 13 states were represented. Annual conventions became the rule, and under Grand Master Workman Terence V. Powderly, who had succeeded Stevens, the membership drive went forward rapidly.

The upswing. In 1878, when Powderly took over, secrecy was abolished, and the Order's aims, activities, and organization became common knowledge. (Secrecy had been an asset during the severe depression of the 1870s as a means of avoiding antilabor retaliation by employers and police.) The new leadership, abolition of secrecy, and adoption of a number of new policies coincided with the end of the depression of the 1870s, and the business upswing which followed. Trade unionism in general prospered, the Knights along with the rest. Most of all, however, the Knights appear to have capitalized on the breadth of their political program and the reformist character of the purposes stated in their charter. These seem to have appealed strongly to many otherwise simon-pure unionists who were permanently affiliated in local craft unions on the railways and in industry generally but whose membership in the Knights of Labor was made possible by the latter's inclusive policy. This dual organization in a number of crafts was the eventual cause of the Order's downfall, but not before it had demonstrated a drawing power that is one of the trade-union wonders of the world to this day.

The boom. The two main factors in the Knights' phenomenal rise in 1886 were (1) aggressiveness to the point of militancy (in spite of the pacific ideology of the Order's constitution) and (2) the admission of unskilled workmen. In spite of the no-strike policy adopted by the general assembly in 1883, a number of the local and district assemblies became increasingly combative. Early in 1885 the shopmen, engineers, firemen, brakemen, and conductors on two of the Jay Gould railways, the Wabash and the Missouri, Kansas & Texas, struck in protest against wage reductions. All were members of the Knights of Labor. They were joined in sympathy by members of the Order on the Missouri Pacific (another Gould road) at all points where the struck lines touched the latter. The strike was won, wage rates were restored, and strikers were put back in their jobs.

Six months later there was a layoff on the Wabash, by this time in receivership, which appeared to violate the terms of the earlier settlement. The Knights' general assembly declared a boycott of all Wabash rolling stock, which might have had the effect of slowing down operations on 20,000 miles of railway lines. Gould was engaged in stock manipulation, and a fall in the price of Wabash securities would have embarrassed him. He therefore threw his influence in favor of a strike settlement on the terms demanded by the Knights. The capitulation was complete: strike replacements in the Wabash shops were discharged, the victorious Knights were reinstated, and a promise of no further discrimination was given. Gould himself assured the leaders of the Order that he believed in labor organization and arbitration.

It was a great victory, or rather series of victories, over the most prominent industrial capitalist of the time, the first time, in fact, that a trade union in the United States had beaten a major corporation in open economic warfare. (The fact of Gould's shaky financial position was not disclosed, so it did not detract from the brilliance of the triumph.) These strikes were in 1885, and as word of their successful conclusion got around, there was a rush to climb aboard the Knights' band wagon. Upon settlement of the second contest, late in the year, the rush became a stampede, especially among the class which up to then had found no place reserved for it in the labor movement—the unskilled.

Common laborers flocked to assemblies all across the country, clamored for admission to locals reserved for members of special crafts, overwhelmed the skilled workmen in local, district, and national meetings by sheer force of numbers, and throughly alarmed old-line trade unionists who had been drawn to the Order by its reform program. Above all else they demonstrated the conflict of principle between the Knights and traditional labor organization, *viz.*, trade autonomy. It was industrial unionism 50 years too soon. Trade autonomy was the rock on which the Knights' ship foundered.

Downfall.   In the year of the Knights' greatest triumph, the principle of trade autonomy was reaffirmed in a modest meeting at Columbus, Ohio. It convened on Dec. 8, 1886, called together by a trade-union committee of five, of which Samuel Gompers was a leading member. The purpose of the meeting was to form a federation to oppose the Knights, to reestablish the principle of trade autonomy, to eliminate dual unionism, and to promote collective bargaining on business principles to take the place of the hodgepodge of political and social reform that the labor movement had become. The meeting was successful, and the new organization took the name of the American Federation of Labor. A similar federation had been set up in 1881 under the name of the Federation of Organized Trades and Labor Unions of the United States and Canada, but it had languished. Gompers was determined to get closer and more vigorous cooperation in order to fight off the mass unionism of the Knights.

The Columbus meeting marked the beginning of powerful opposition to the Knights of Labor within trade-union ranks. The Order had already had a number of brushes with the earlier Federation (of Organized Trades and Labor Unions), wherein the latter had practically invited the Knights to commit suicide by breaking up its mixed locals, refraining from organization activity in trades where bona fide unions already had jurisdiction, and restricting its operations to benevolent, educational, and humanitarian enterprises. This it had refused to do, suggesting instead *mutual* recognition of working cards and union labels and mutual exclusion of suspended or expelled members by itself and the unions in the Federation. The very thought of such an indecisive brand of dual unionism horrified the members of the Federation, and the proposal was summarily rejected.

In 1886, with the swamping of the Knights by unskilled laborers and with the growing public suspicion of any labor union with a reform program, an aftermath of the Haymarket affair, skilled craftsmen were more ready to consider countermeasures. They withdrew from the Knights and aligned themselves with the new AFL so rapidly that by 1890 the latter organization outweighed the former in membership, 150,000 to 100,000. The Knights of Labor was never again an important factor in organized labor in America.

1886: The Haymarket affair.   It is possible that the decline of the Knights of Labor might not have been so abrupt if the Haymarket riot had not tended to be identified with it in the public mind. The meeting at which the riot occurred was a gathering called for May 4, 1886, in Haymarket Square, Chicago. The organizers were some radical leaders of the International Working People's Association (the "Black International," as it was called). The purpose of the meeting was to protest police brutality of the day before, when a struggle between strikers and nonstrikers at the McCormick Harvester Company's plant had been broken up and one man had been killed. The May 4 meeting was small in size and deceptively peaceful throughout until police appeared and ordered the crowd to disperse. A bomb thrown at the police killed one outright, injured six more fatally, and wounded scores of onlookers. Eight members of the Black International were convicted of participation in the crime. Four were hanged, one committed suicide in his cell, and the other three were later pardoned by Governor Altgeld of Illinois on grounds of lack of evidence and judicial partiality. The Governor was reviled for the act as few people in public life in this country have ever been. Subsequent review of the evidence by impartial analysts has reinforced the conclusion that innocent men were convicted and executed.

There was no direct link between the Knights of Labor and the Haymarket meeting. The general assembly of the Knights, in fact, was on record as being opposed to the demonstration. On the other hand, the date was 1886, at a time when the Order was receiving the greatest membership landslide in trade-union history. The Knights' program was political and reformist; it was aimed at elimination of the "system of wage slavery." The popular support which had enabled the union to win its strikes in 1885 was replaced in many quarters by suspicion, which was not diminished by the withdrawal of large numbers of conservative union men who decided to return to "safe and sane" business unionism. Many writers interpret the Haymarket affair as the beginning of the end for Powderly and his followers.

SUMMARY

During most of the century 1786 to 1886, there was no real labor movement in the United States and no good reason why there should have been. The frontier and free land removed economic pressure, kept the population on the move, and offered such rewards to the enterprising as had seldom been seen anywhere. The laborer of one decade was often the master of the next, simply by virtue of expansion of population and the demand for goods and services. Large-scale organization of production was still in the future. Few shops or stores employed more than a hundred men, and the modern industrial plant with thousands and tens of thousands of employes was not even dreamed of. Employer-employe relations were mostly face to face, personal, and friendly. Not until the Civil War did even medium-scale industrial production appear (to supply the Northern troops), and at just about that time the first stable unionism began to develop. The growth of the labor movement was handicapped, however, by upset conditions in the Reconstruction period; by an influx from Europe of various philosophies of socialism, communism, and utopianism; and by the constant lure of the West, where railroad building, the discovery of gold and silver, and Indian fighting continued to draw off the more adventurous spirits and make the struggle over wages and hours seem prosaic and uninspiring.

The philosophers and statesmen of the century, with one exception,

offered little encouragement to an organized labor movement. The Tory-
ism of the early Bostonians was about on a par with New York Federalism
in its recognition of the working class, and there was little gain for the
urban proletarian in Jefferson's brand of agrarian *laissez faire*. Clay's
"American plan," Calhoun's defense of the plantation aristocracy, and the
Republicanism of Lincoln's successors, Grant, Hayes, and Garfield, were
similar in their respect for property rights and their lack of concern for the
workingman. Only the Democracy of Andrew Jackson could be interpreted
as a political philosophy which rested on the "common man" and therefore made room for an organized labor movement. The two really basic
developments of significance to organized labor during the century—reversal of the conspiracy doctrine and extension of the suffrage—occurred
during the Jacksonian era.

Throughout most of the century, none of the ordinary trappings of a
labor movement were present. There were few national unions, no federated organizations on a national basis, no labor intelligentsia, no program
of governmental assistance. There were a few local unions, some strikes,
and sporadic political action. The upsurge of the Knights of Labor, the
formation of the AFL, and congressional recognition of the labor vote in
the form of the Chinese Exclusion Act came at the very end of the period
and were distinctly transitional features, in fact more characteristic of the
labor movement which took form in the 1880s and has had a steady growth
to the present day.

READINGS

The standard condensed history of the American labor movement is Mary Beard,
Short History of the American Labor Movement (New York: Harcourt, Brace
& World, Inc., 1936), which carries the development of trade unionism in this
country to 1935. The Beard interpretation has been widely adopted by subsequent writers. Mrs. Beard's book is a condensation of the authoritative four-
volume *History of Labor in the United States* (New York: The Macmillan
Company, 1918–1934), by John R. Commons and associates. A still shorter,
official report is the *Brief History of the American Labor Movement*, Bulletin
1000, Bureau of Labor Statistics, U.S. Department of Labor (1950). This pamphlet, available from the Superintendent of Documents for 25 cents, brings the
labor movement up past the Second World War in 66 succinct pages. Practically
all textbooks on labor economics contain some sort of historical review as a preliminary to taking up the problem of organized labor. See, for example, Melvin
W. Reder, *Labor in a Growing Economy*, Chaps. 3, 4 (New York: John Wiley
& Sons, Inc., 1957) for a summary of the historical changes in organization,
purpose, philosophy, and politics of the trade-union movement.

SIX

THE AFL ERA:
1886-1936

During the 50 years from 1886 to 1936, the labor movement in America was dominated by the American Federation of Labor. Organized labor grew, in much the form that it takes today, from a handful of national unions with perhaps a quarter of a million members to an army of 5 million by the end of the First World War. After 1920 the Federation— and with it trade unionism—went into an eclipse from which it did not emerge until rescued by Franklin D. Roosevelt's New Deal of 1933. In labor's case it is accurate to say that "the institution was the lengthened shadow of a man." The man was Samuel Gompers, founder and for 37 years, president of the American Federation of Labor. After Gompers's death in 1924, the Federation withered on the vine, declining steadily during the prosperity of the 1920s and the early depression years which followed.

The fortunes of trade unionism, following the First World War, thus reversed the pattern established in the nineteenth century, when prosperity for business meant union growth and expansion, while depression was synonymous with union decline and disintegration.

1886: Birth of the American Federation of Labor.   The AFL had an understandably quiet beginning. For one thing, it was completely over-shadowed by the extraordinary Knights of Labor, fresh from their victories over Jay Gould and boasting more than 700,000 members. For another, it was an obvious outgrowth of the Federation of Organized Trades and Labor Unions of the United States and Canada, which had been conspicuously unsuccessful since its formation in 1881. There seemed little reason at the time to suppose that the revised Federation would fare any better than the old; on the surface it looked more like a change of name and a game of musical chairs. In fact, about the only assets the delegates had were unity and an idea. The idea was "strict autonomy of the trade,"

133

the principle of "exclusive jurisdiction." The AFL was essentially a defensive alliance, formed to protect the sovereignty of individual craft unions and to fight the "dual unionism" of the Knights of Labor.

It was a ragged group that showed up at the founding meeting in Columbus, Ohio, on Dec. 8, 1886. The convention was called together by a trade-union "committee of five," consisting of P. J. McGuire, Adolph Strasser, Josiah Dyer, P. J. Fitzpatrick, and John S. Kirchner. There were 42 delegates representing a miscellaneous group of 25 labor organizations, which included 13 national unions (iron molders, typographers, granite cutters, stereotypers, miners, tailors, bakers, furniture workers, metal workers, carpenters, and cigar makers); the city central bodies of New York, Chicago, Philadelphia, St. Louis, and Baltimore; and some locals of barbers, waiters, and bricklayers. The delegates adopted a constitution, arranged for financing (through charter fees and a per capita membership tax of 6 cents a year), and elected Samuel Gompers full-time president at a salary of $1,000 a year plus his traveling expenses.

As it turned out later, the selection of a chief officer was the most important act of all. Although his name had not appeared on the "call," Gompers was one of the most determined advocates of a new federation. Upon his election to the presidency, he set out to make the AFL the American labor movement in fact, a task to which he dedicated every waking moment of his life from then on. Gompers held the presidency uninterruptedly until his death in 1924, except for a single year (1894 to 1895). The Federation was his food, drink, and religion. It was also, in most important respects, his creation, the product of his work and imagination. Under his dogged leadership it weathered the depression of the 1890s and by the last year of the century contained 53 unions with a total membership of 350,000.

Samuel Gompers, 1850–1924.   Samuel Gompers was born Jan. 27, 1850, in a London tenement, the son of a cigar maker who had emigrated from Holland. He attended a Jewish free school from the age of 6 until he was 10, when he became a cigar maker's apprentice. In 1863, the family crossed the Atlantic and settled in New York. The following year, already a journeyman at the age of 14, Sam joined the Cigar Makers' Union. As a youth and as a man he was short, thickset, with a strong voice, a powerful constitution, an extroverted, gregarious personality, and a consuming ambition to be someone of importance.

The end of Gompers's formal education did not mean the end of his actual education. He was a wide reader, a careful student of matters that interested him, and a tenacious seeker after important principles. He attended Cooper Union and took part in some of the debates and forums there, but his true intellectual development he himself attributed to the political and economic discussions which went on endlessly in the cigar shops, and his association with a group of refugee Socialists from Europe, who were instrumental in forming the ideas which eventually produced the AFL. Gompers himself skirted around the fringes of the Socialist movement, but on the advice of his most influential tutor he did not join or commit himself in any way. That tutor was Ferdinand Laurrell, a Swedish Marxist cigar maker, whose interpretation of the *Communist Manifesto*, word by word, sentence by sentence, and paragraph by paragraph, Gompers says, revealed a "hidden world of thought," the true Marxism of trade unionism and labor's struggle for betterment. To Laurrell, Gompers dedicated his autobiography, *Seventy Years of Life and Labor*.

By the time the AFL was organized in 1886, Gompers was a seasoned trade unionist, a member of the Cigar Makers' International since 1864, holding union card No. 1. With Adolph Strasser, he helped to reorganize the union in 1877, after its practical disappearance during the depression of 1873. The two men agreed on four principal policies: (1) International officers were to be supreme over the local unions. (2) Membership dues should be raised to an unheard-of figure in order to build up a treasury which could withstand the assaults of employers and hard times. (3) Control of the union funds should be in the hands of the national officers. (4) The union should undertake a program of sickness, accident, and unemployment benefits. According to John R. Commons, this was "the beginning of militant, persistent unionism in America."

Gompers was a dedicated, energetic believer in the idea of federation —"group cooperation without loss of individual sovereignty." As president of the AFL, he was, according to Commons, "the official head of the American labor movement," with his influence resting not alone on his official position but on his "moral authority" and his knowledge of labor fundamentals. The success of the Federation and its member unions during his 37 years of leadership is sufficient testimony to the effectiveness of the principles he espoused. Under Gompers, organized labor became a major institution in the United States. Much of the subsequent growth of trade unionism may be attributed to the solid foundation which he did most to build during the last decade of the nineteenth and the first quarter of the twentieth century.

In the process of representing the American labor movement Gompers became a well-known public figure. He was a voluminous speaker and writer, publishing scores of articles in the *American Federationist* (journal of the AFL) and authoring the following books: *Labor in Europe and America* (1910), *American Labor and the War* (1919), *Labor and the Common Welfare* (1919), *Labor and the Employer* (1920), and his two-volume autobiography, which appeared in 1925, a year after his death. Gompers was appointed by President Wilson to the Council of National Defense in 1917; organized the War Committee of Labor, composed of labor leaders and employers, for assistance to the war effort; and was a

Quest. Political participation of Labour Unionism
help fulfil most of the aims of Unions
= (Congress — Pension
*   social welfare)*
*   laws*

member of the Committee on International Labor Legislation at the Peace Conference in Paris. In public affairs, as in other matters, he set the standard of the modern labor leader in the United States. He died Dec. 13, 1924, in the midst of a fight to save the gains which organized labor had realized during the First World War. Samuel Gompers is rightfully regarded as the father of the American labor movement.

Bed-rock

The labor philosophy of Samuel Gompers.   Gompers's philosophy of labor organization became the bedrock foundation of trade unionism during the rise of the AFL, and much of it is today regarded as gospel. It consisted of the following fundamentals:

1. *"Safe and sane" business unionism:* to raise wages, shorten hours, and improve working conditions; no radicalism or utopianism.
2. *Exclusive jurisdiction:* one union to each trade for one labor movement.
3. *Nonpartisanship in politics:* reward labor's friends and punish labor's enemies, but no mixing in political parties.   *Not   nowadays*
4. *Preference for direct action (against employers):* suspicion of governmental interference, especially the courts.
5. *Belief in capitalism and free enterprise:* uncompromising rejection of "producers' cooperation" in any form.
6. *Practicality:* opposition to "theorizers" and "intellectuals" as leaders of the labor movement.
7. *Discussion and debate:* education and the discussion of issues, particularly for the rank and file.
8. *Cooperation in action:* the achievement of labor unity through the use of persuasion rather than dictation or force.

1890: The Sherman Act and the courts.   Organized labor in the United States feels that it has had few crosses to bear more grievous than the Federal antitrust laws. The Sherman Act was a brief, loosely worded statute of eight paragraphs, containing the following significant declarations.

Sec. 1. Every contract, combination in the form of trust or otherwise, or conspiracy, in restraint of trade or commerce among the several States, or with foreign nations, is hereby declared to be illegal. Every person who shall make any such contract or engage in any such combination or conspiracy, shall be deemed guilty of a misdemeanor. . . .
     Sec. 8. That the word "person," or "persons," wherever used in this act shall be deemed to include corporations and associations existing under or authorized by the laws of either the United States, the laws of any of the Territories, the laws of any State, or the laws of any foreign country.

Did "person" mean labor unions? Fifty years of argument and research have not disclosed what was in the minds of the legislators, but the courts answered loudly yes. During the 50 years from 1890 to 1940, trade unions were regularly and consistently hailed before the bar of justice on charges of conspiracy to restrain trade. Thus the conspiracy doctrine, which in common-law form had been laid to rest by Chief Justice Shaw in 1842, was resurrected by statute as a limitation upon organized labor's purposes and activities during a crucial half century of union growth.

The Sherman Act contained three kinds of sanctions: (1) criminal penalties of fines and imprisonment, (2) equity proceedings for restraining orders and injunctions, and (3) civil suits for triple damages. In a series of major cases before the United States Supreme Court, all three were applied impartially to union tactics, and the precedents established thereby were effective limitations upon the activities of organized labor.

If any fact is clearly established, it is that for roughly the first 150 years of American history public regulation of trade unions was court regulation. The principal instruments of the judges were the conspiracy doctrine, the injunction, judicial interpretation of statutes, and the declaration of unconstitutionality. During this period Congress and the state legislatures either avoided the subject or treated it gingerly, and the laws they passed were promptly rewritten in line with the economic and social sentiments of the judges. The period was long enough, and the record is clear enough, to justify fully the deep-seated union distrust of courts and court-made justice in this country.

1892: The Homestead strike: Preview of industrial violence.　　The coming depression of 1893 cast its shadow in the summer of the year before, when the Carnegie Steel Company of Homestead, Pennsylvania, in the face of falling prices for pig iron, asked the Amalgamated Association of Iron and Steel Workers to accept a 10 per cent reduction in wages. The union refused. On June 30, 1892, the men went out on strike. Using tactics that were subsequently to be expanded into the "Mohawk Valley formula," the company imported armed strikebreakers who were protected by Pinkerton detectives.[1] A pitched battle between the workers and the armed guards was the result, with several killed on both sides. In this skirmish, the employes were victorious, but state militia were called in to restore order, and the strike was eventually lost. At the same time, large sections of the steel industry went open-shop and were never effectively recaptured by organized labor until the United States Steel Corporation recognized the Steel Workers Organizing Committee (CIO) in 1937.

The significance of the dispute is found in its disclosure of the defense tactics of large corporations against union penetration. Nonrecognition, labor spies, armed strikebreakers, and violence became standard elements of labor disputes in the mill and factory towns of the industrial Northeast

[1] For a description of the "Mohawk Valley formula" in classic form, see the Remington Rand decision of the NLRB: 2 NLRB 626 (1937).

and the mining communities of Pennsylvania, West Virginia, Ohio, Kentucky, and Illinois.

1894: The Pullman strike and the labor injunction.   The Pullman strike of May 11, 1894, one of the great industrial disputes in American history, was the work of Eugene V. Debs. Debs was a believer in industrial unionism and his organization, the American Railway Union, enlisted members from all the crafts and trades among the train-operating employes and the shop workers in the industry.

In March, 1894, employes of the Pullman Palace Car Company, located on the south side of Chicago, voted to join the union and 2 months later struck for a restoration of pay levels of the year before. The depression of the 1890s was on, and the company refused the demands. The strike was endorsed by the American Railway Union in June and was soon supported by a wide following, including the Knights of Labor, the Farmers' Alliance, and many individual members of the railroad operating brotherhoods (trainmen, firemen, engineers, and conductors). It has been estimated that 750,000 men were on strike at the height of the work stoppage. Since strikers refused to handle or service Pullman cars, train service was interfered with and the mails were held up. On these grounds, an injunction was issued by the Attorney General of the United States, Federal troops were sent to Chicago by President Cleveland (over the protest of Governor Altgeld of Illinois), and the strike collapsed. Debs refused to obey the injunction and was jailed for contempt of court.

There were several elements of importance to the Pullman dispute. It was the first big labor dispute in which the Sherman Act was invoked. It was the most extensive work stoppage in the experience of the country in terms of number of workers involved. Most important of all, it was a walkout planned on the European model of the "general strike," and its short-run success alarmed the general public as well as many labor leaders who were afraid that it would disrupt their unions and draw off the members into another mass organization like the recently punctured Knights of Labor.

There was, nevertheless, strong sentiment within the AFL for official support of the walkout, and a conference was called in the summer of 1894 to consider the question. The conference appointed a committee of five, with Gompers as chairman, to bring in a recommendation. Gompers, fearing for the Federation and the principle of exclusive jurisdiction, persuaded the committee and the conference to advise member unions *to refrain from taking part in either the general strike or any local disputes emanating from it.*

For his part in this decision the Socialists in the Federation punished Gompers by defeating him for the presidency in the convention of 1894,

electing in his place John McBride of the United Mine Workers.[2] The
Federation, however, emerged from the Pullman affair with its conservative reputation enhanced and the position of its members strengthened in
the eyes of the public. The policy which Gompers advocated successfully
in the disturbed summer of 1894 was never abandoned. The AFL has
always stood for conservative, safe-and-sane business unionism. It has had
no truck with radical leadership, new theories, or innovations in organization or bargaining. At times the policy has seemed costly, but at others
it has paid off handsomely, and it remains the fundamental rule of many
labor leaders today.

1893 to 1896: Unions ride out depression.   During the depression
of the 1890s, trade unionism in the United States recorded a significant
achievement. It survived. For the first time, a group of national unions
pulled through a major depression without disintegrating into utopianism,
political action, or the espousal of radical reforms. The conservative craft
unions in the AFL and a few independents equally committed to the
principle of craft solidarity—the railway operating brotherhoods especially
—resisted the appeals of the Socialists, the Populists, and the mass organizers like Debs, and tended strictly to their knitting, to wit, the maintenance and strengthening of their unions. This was not easy to do in the
face of aggressive employer tactics (as in the Homestead, Coeur d'Alene,
Buffalo, and Tennessee miners' strikes) and militant government opposition (as in the Pullman walkout). The situation was also aggravated by
unemployment and a general worsening of pay scales and working conditions. But when the panic which originated with the failure of the
Baring Brothers in London had subsided, there were still 400,000 American workingmen holding union cards, and more than 250,000 of them
were in unions affiliated with the AFL.

The federated craft form of organization had passed its first big test.
Conservative business unionism had proved that it could "take it" in hard
times as well as good and come back for more.

1897 to 1904: Trade-union boom.   In 1897 Gompers moved the
headquarters of the AFL from New York City to Washington, D.C. The
next 7 years were big ones for the Federation and for organized labor.
Total union membership multiplied over four times, AFL membership
more than six times (as shown in Table 6-1). The latter improved its
position steadily until it represented four out of every five trade unionists
in the country.

By 1904, the AFL consisted of 114 national and international unions,

---

[2] Gompers was reelected easily in 1895. He referred to his year out of office as
"my sabbatical."

Table 6-1. American trade-union membership, 1897–1904

Year	Total	AFL	AFL % of total
1897	440,000	265,000	60
1898	467,000	278,000	59
1899	550,000	349,000	60
1900	791,000	548,000	69
1901	1,058,000	788,000	74
1902	1,335,000	1,024,000	77
1903	1,824,000	1,466,000	80
1904	2,067,000	1,676,000	81

Source: BLS, *Handbook of Labor Statistics, 1947*, p. 130.

828 directly affiliated locals, 549 city central bodies, and 29 state federations of labor. Revenues climbed with membership. Income was $18,639 in 1898, $115,220 in 1901, $247,800 in 1903, and $220,995 in 1904. In the latter year, the Federation had a field force of 99 paid organizers, working with member unions or independently.[3] (An interesting comparison: in 1963, with a membership of $14\frac{1}{2}$ million and an income of $9,690,897, the AFL–CIO had a field staff of 154: 23 regional directors, 16 assistant regional directors, and 115 field representatives [organizers].) [4]

What caused the boom of 1897 to 1904?

Three things: sound organization, prosperity, and war.

The war-induced prosperity of 1898 and beyond set things off. At the first sign of an upturn in 1897, a number of strikes were won, drawing in recruits to the miners and typographers and stimulating wage demands in other trades. Union positions in bargaining negotiations were strengthened, with a corresponding improvement in pay scales, hours, and working conditions. The approach was safe-and-sane, conservative business unionism, and it prospered beyond the expectations of anyone, including Gompers himself. The upward rush of the labor movement was not as precipitous as that of the Knights of Labor a decade earlier or as large in absolute numbers as the growth during the First World War, but it was a permanent, definitive accomplishment. It put the AFL on a paying basis and settled the questions of union structure (craft), method (collective bargaining), and philosophy (business) for many years to come. They were not reopened seriously until the Committee for Industrial Organization was formed at a rump meeting following the 1935 AFL convention.

Another significant tradition was inaugurated in 1898. With talk of

[3] Lewis L. Lorwin, *The American Federation of Labor* (Washington, D.C.: The Brookings Institution, 1933), pp. 59–60.

[4] *Proceedings,* 1963 Convention, vol. II, pp. 20, 275, 10.

*[handwritten margin notes: Gompers On\
Precedent est.]*

war everywhere and war itself soon to become a fact, President McKinley
received the executive council of the AFL and invited Gompers and his
assistants to suggest recommendations for labor legislation to be included
in his message to Congress. He also suggested to Congress that an industrial commission be established to study the relations between labor and
capital. It was the first time any President had given such friendly recognition to a labor organization. This precedent of exceptional treatment of
organized labor in wartime was later copied by Woodrow Wilson in 1917, *[handwritten: Copied]*
Franklin Delano Roosevelt in 1941, and Harry S. Truman in 1950. As a
result, some of trade unionism's greatest gains have been registered while
the country was under arms. In 1898, Congress also tried to outlaw the
yellow-dog contract on the railroads.

[handwritten margin note: Congress attempted regulating labour Relations]

    1898: The Erdman Act.   This law was the second attempt by Con-
gress to regulate labor relations on the railways.[5] It provided for mediation and for voluntary arbitration if agreed to by both parties. However,
its most significant provision was an anti-yellow-dog-contract clause, which
was the first instance of legislation friendly to organized labor to come
from the Congress of the United States. Section 10 of the law read as
follows:

Any employer . . . who shall require any employee, or any person seeking employment, as a condition of such employment, to enter into an agreement . . . not to
become or remain a member of any labor . . . organization . . . or shall threaten
any employee with loss of employment, or shall unjustly discriminate against any
employee because of his membership in such a labor organization . . . is hereby
declared to be guilty of a misdemeanor, and, upon conviction . . . shall be punished for each offense by a fine of not less than one hundred dollars and not more
than one thousand dollars.

It was hardly to be expected that anything so radical would be permitted
to stand, and 10 years later, in *Adair v. United States,*[6] the Supreme Court
held the section an unconstitutional limitation upon the right to enter into
contracts. The mediation and arbitration provisions, meanwhile, became
rather popular. Between 1906 and 1913 more than 60 disputes between
the railroads and their train-operating employes were settled with the
law's assistance.

    It was in trying to regulate industrial relations on the railways that
Congress learned its union-management ABC's. The 1934 amendments to
the Railway Labor Act of 1926 were the eighth major statute in direct line
from the law of 1888. In the railway labor legislation there were worked
out practically all the principles and mechanisms which were used later in

    [5] 30 Stat. 424 (1898). The first was the Railroad Arbitration Act of 1888 (25
Stat. 501), which was ineffective and used only once: a commission set up under its
authority investigated the Pullman strike and reported to the President.
    [6] 208 U.S. 161 (1908). See below, pp. 142–143.

labor laws of more general application, such as the Norris–La Guardia Act, the National Industrial Recovery Act, the National Labor Relations Act, and the Labor Management Relations Act, 1947 (Taft-Hartley Act). Looking backward, it is easy to see that the railroads were an indispensable proving ground for congressional regulation of industrial relations.

1905: The IWW.   In 1905, the radical fringe of the American labor movement was organized as the Industrial Workers of the World, holding its first convention in Chicago. The founders included such extremists as William D. (Big Bill) Haywood, Daniel DeLeon (militant Socialist), and Eugene V. Debs. The union's program was syndicalist and revolutionary, as indicated in its preamble, part of which read as follows:

> The working class and the employing class have nothing in common. There can be no peace so long as hunger and want are found among millions of working people and the few, who make up the employing class, have all the good things of life. Between these two classes a struggle must go on until the workers of the world organize as a class, take possession of the earth and the machinery of production and abolish the wage system. . . .[7]

The IWW advocated the general strike, sabotage, and violence. It is doubtful that its membership ever exceeded 50,000, but its influence was greater than the numbers indicate, because of the apprehension caused by its inflammatory program. After a few strikes, concentrated mainly in the textile region of the East, and some desultory wartime sabotage in the wheat fields and other agricultural areas of the West, the organization dwindled away to a shadow during the 1920s.

1908 to 1909: The Supreme Court and organized labor.   In two important decisions and a statement of principle, the United States Supreme Court and a President who was later to be Chief Justice of the United States made clear their views regarding the legal position of organized labor. The decisions were *Adair v. United States* and *Loewe v. Lawlor;* the statement occurred in President William Howard Taft's inaugural address of Mar. 4, 1909. The views reflected in them turned out to be controlling for many years.

In *Adair v. United States,* the Court vetoed the prohibition of yellow-dog contracts which Congress had inserted in the Erdman Act. The reasons? Interference with freedom of contract and lack of regulatory jurisdiction. Said the majority: "There is no such connection between interstate commerce and membership in a labor organization as to authorize Congress to make it a crime . . . for an agent of an interstate carrier to discharge an employe because of such membership on his part." [8]

[7] H. S. Commager, *Documents of American History,* Sec. 2 (New York: Appleton-Century-Crofts, Inc., 1944), p. 338.
[8] 208 U.S. 161 (1908).

[handwritten annotations: against yellow dog contract as regards Congress.]

Justice Holmes dissented, and his minority opinion has received more attention than that of the majority. He observed that:

The section is, in substance, a very limited interference with freedom of contract, no more. It does not require the carriers to employ anyone. It does not forbid them to refuse to employ anyone, for any reason they deem good, even where the notion of a choice of persons is a fiction and wholesale employment is necessary upon general principles that it might be proper to control. The section simply prohibits the more powerful party to exact certain undertakings, or to threaten dismissal or unjustly discriminate on certain grounds against those already employed. I hardly can suppose that the grounds on which a contract lawfully may be made to end are less open to regulation than other terms. . . . I confess that I think that the right to make contracts at will that has been derived from the word "liberty" in the Amendments, has been stretched to its extreme by the decisions.

In *Loewe v. Lawlor* (the Danbury Hatters' Case),[9] the Supreme Court applied the Sherman Act to the secondary boycott. In an attempt to organize a hat manufacturing company in Danbury, Connecticut, the United Hatters of North America instituted a nationwide boycott against hat stores which patronized the struck firm. The company asked for an injunction, which was granted, and sued for $80,000 damages. The Court found that the boycott was in effect "a combination in restraint of trade or commerce" and in line with the act awarded triple damages. With court costs, the total bill ran over $250,000. Payment was finally made, with the help of the AFL, but the union was wrecked, and many of its members lost their savings and property through court judgments and execution. It was a disastrous affair and one which trade unionists still remember with resentment. Few legal decisions have done more than *Loewe v. Lawlor* to strengthen organized labor's resentment of the courts.

[handwritten annotation: The Hatters' Strike]

[handwritten annotation: Labour Union payed dearly!!]

With the right of Congress to protect trade unions denied and with labor's use of the boycott severely circumscribed, union officials listened with apprehension to President Taft's inaugural remarks on the secondary boycott and the labor injunction. Taft, a former circuit judge, was not regarded as prolabor. On the injunction he had this to say:

Another labor question has arisen which has awakened the most excited discussion. That is in respect to the power of the federal courts to issue injunctions in industrial disputes. As to that, my convictions are fixed. Take away from the courts, if it could be taken away, the power to issue injunctions in labor disputes, and it would create a privileged class among the laborers and save the lawless among their number from a most needful remedy available to all men for the protection of their business against lawless invasion. . . . The proposition is usually linked with one to make the secondary boycott lawful. . . . The secondary boycott is an instrument of tyranny, and ought not to be made legitimate.

On the legal side, it was a dismal year. The outlook would have been blacker still, had it been foreseen that the speaker was destined to end his

[9] 208 U.S. 274 (1908).

Table 6-2. American trade-union membership, 1905–1911

Year	Total	AFL	AFL % of total
1905	1,918,000	1,494,000	78
1906	1,892,000	1,454,000	77
1907	2,077,000	1,539,000	74
1908	2,092,000	1,587,000	76
1909	1,965,000	1,483,000	75
1910	2,116,000	1,562,000	74
1911	2,318,000	1,762,000	76

Source: BLS, *Handbook of Labor Statistics, 1947*, p. 130.

term of public service as Chief Justice of the United States from 1921 to 1930.

From 1905 to 1911, the labor movement marked time, consolidated gains, perfected organization, and matured relations with employers. The membership record is shown in Table 6-2.

WOODROW WILSON, FRIEND OF LABOR

Woodrow Wilson was the second Democratic President since Lincoln, a liberal, a political unknown. Gompers said of him: "Woodrow Wilson was not my choice for the presidential candidate for the Democratic Party. I had never met him, but what I had heard of him was not calculated to predispose me in his favor. . . . Upon the issues which were of fundamental interest to organized labor I did not know what was the personal opinion of Mr. Wilson." [10] However, this suspicious attitude changed rapidly into a "feeling of well-nigh reverential admiration," and well it might. Before Wilson left office, he had appointed a trade unionist Secretary of Labor, supported the Clayton Act which was supposed to halt the use of the labor injunction, upheld the 8-hour day for railway workers, made organized labor an official partner in the war effort of 1917 to 1918, and directly encouraged union growth and collective bargaining on the railroads while they were under Federal control.

When Wilson was elected in 1912, trade-union membership in the United States was just short of 2,500,000; at the end of his administration in 1920, it had risen to the impressive total of double that figure. The rise is shown in Table 6-3.

1913: Trade unionist in the Cabinet.   The last official act of President William Howard Taft in March, 1913, was to sign the bill creating

[10] Gompers, *Seventy Years of Life and Labor* (New York: E. P. Dutton & Co., Inc., 1925), pp. 543–544.

Table 6-3.   American trade-union membership, 1912–1920

Year	Total	AFL	AFL % of total
1912	2,405,000	1,770,000	74
1913	2,661,000	1,996,000	75
1914	2,647,000	2,021,000	76
1915	2,560,000	1,946,000	76
1916	2,722,000	2,073,000	76
1917	2,976,000	2,371,000	80
1918	3,368,000	2,726,000	81
1919	4,046,000	3,260,000	81
1920	5,034,000	4,079,000	81

Source: BLS, *Handbook of Labor Statistics, 1947*, p. 130.

the U.S. Department of Labor. As Secretary of the new department, incoming President Woodrow Wilson appointed William B. Wilson, a Scottish immigrant miner, a lifetime trade unionist and union official who had ended up as secretary-treasurer of the United Mine Workers of America before going to Congress in 1907. Secretary Wilson served 8 years. This set a precedent, after a fashion, the next two Secretaries (under Presidents Harding, Coolidge, and Hoover) also being card-carrying trade unionists: James J. Davis (1921 to 1930) and William N. Doak (1930 to 1933). The tradition was broken, strangely enough, by Franklin D. Roosevelt and Harry S. Truman, both highly sympathetic to organized labor, who appointed three Secretaries in a row—Frances Perkins, Lewis B. Schwellenbach, and Maurice J. Tobin—none of whom had any union background. President Eisenhower revived the practice, with an abortive appointment of Martin Durkin, a plumber, but Durkin lasted only a few months; Eisenhower then named James J. Mitchell, a department store executive. President Kennedy made an oblique gesture toward organized labor, appointing Arthur J. Goldberg, general counsel of the United Steelworkers and of the AFL–CIO. President Johnson's Secretary is Willard Wirtz, a labor lawyer and arbitrator of national reputation, who moved up from Undersecretary when Goldberg went to the Supreme Court.

1914: The Clayton Act and the labor injunction.   No chapter in American legal history is more repugnant to trade unionists than the section dealing with the labor injunction.[11] The first important use of the

[11] There is an extensive literature on the use of injunctions in labor disputes. See, among others, Felix Frankfurter and Nathan Greene, *The Labor Injunction* (New York: The Macmillan Company, 1930); John P. Frey, *The Labor Injunction* (Cincinnati: Equity Publishing Co., 1923); E. E. Witte, *The Government in Labor Disputes* (New York: McGraw-Hill Book Company, 1932); and J. F. Christ, "The Federal Courts and Organized Labor," *Journal of Business*, vol. 5 (1932), pp. 283–300.

restraining order by the Federal government seems to have been in the railroad strike of 1877, after which a number of injunctions were granted by state courts in the labor disputes of the 1880s. However, the plug was finally pulled, perhaps unwittingly, with the passage of the Sherman Act in 1890, which applied the conspiracy doctrine in connection with restraint of trade and provided for injunctive relief along with civil and criminal penalties. Widely publicized by the Pullman strike in 1894 and the subsequent trial and imprisonment of Eugene V. Debs for disobedience of the Court's order, the injunction became the standard reliance of Federal and state officials for the control of aggressive union action. Its effectiveness probably reached an all-time high in the sweeping order of Judge Wilkerson ending the Railway Shopmen's strike of 1922, which forbade conversation, assembly, distribution of funds, or any other activity in connection with the strike and included within its restraints, not only the strikers themselves, but also "all of their attorneys, servants, agents, associates, members, employers and all persons acting in aid of or in conjunction with them."

In the Clayton Act, Congress tried to limit the use of injunctions in labor disputes and to move trade unions per se out from under the antitrust laws. The act said, very plainly in fact, that trade unions were not "combinations or conspiracies in restraint of trade" as the courts had found in some of the Sherman Act decisions and that the law was not to be construed so as to forbid either their existence or their activities. The precise wording was as follows:

Sec. 6. Nothing contained in the anti-trust laws shall be construed to forbid the existence and operation of labor . . . organizations . . . or to forbid or restrain individual members of such organizations from lawfully carrying out the legitimate objects thereof; nor shall such organizations, or the members thereof, be held or construed to be illegal combinations or conspiracies in restraint of trade, under the anti-trust laws.

In Sec. 20, the law took up the labor injunction, and directed:

That no restraining order or injunction shall be granted by any court of the U.S. . . . in any case . . . involving or growing out of a dispute concerning terms or conditions of employment, unless necessary to prevent irreparable injury to property, or to a property right, of the party making the application, for which injury there is no adequate remedy at law. . . .

And no such restraining order or injunction shall prohibit any person or persons, whether singly or in concert, from terminating any relation of employment, or from ceasing to perform any work or labor, or from recommending, advising, or persuading others by peaceful means so to do . . . or from ceasing to patronize or to employ any party to such dispute . . . or from paying or giving . . . any strike benefits or other moneys or things of value; or from peaceably assembling in a lawful manner . . . or from doing any act or thing which might lawfully be done in the absence of such dispute . . . nor shall any of the acts specified in this paragraph be considered or held to be violations of any law of the U.S.[12]

To gullible trade unionists this was plain English. Gompers was so elated that he publicly declared the act to be "labor's Magna Charta." But he and they had reckoned without the judges. In a series of decisions, the United States Supreme Court repealed the act by interpretation, holding that it amounted to nothing more than a restatement of existing law on the subject and upholding the application of Sherman Act penalties to organized labor.

It was not until 1940 that a changed Supreme Court admitted its error. In *United States v. Hutcheson,*[13] Justice Frankfurter said: "It was widely believed that into the Clayton Act courts read the very beliefs which that Act was designed to remove. . . . The underlying aim of the Norris–La Guardia Act was to restore the broad purpose which Congress thought it had formulated in the Clayton Act but which was frustrated, so Congress believed, by unduly restrictive judicial construction." With this conclusion no one has seriously disagreed. The Hutcheson decision emancipated organized labor from the control of the judiciary under the Sherman Act, just as the Clayton amendment had intended a quarter of a century earlier.

1915: Coppage v. Kansas, and the antilabor policies of big business. *Coppage v. Kansas*[14] is the "little Adair case." The Adair decision involved a Federal statute, the Erdman Act; the Coppage case was over a state law which prohibited employers from using the yellow-dog contract. An employe of the Frisco Railroad refused to sign the agreement or to leave the union. He was discharged and brought suit against the company, which appealed the decision of the local court on grounds that the act was unconstitutional. The United States Supreme Court agreed: "In *Adair v. United States* . . . this Court had to deal with a question not distinguishable in principle from the one now presented." Relying in this case on the Fourteenth Amendment to the Federal Constitution, the Court held that such a law violated the guarantee of "due process." Justices Holmes, Day, and Hughes dissented. The Holmes dissent, a classic, is now the law of the land:

I think the judgment should be affirmed. In present conditions a workman not unnaturally may believe that only by belonging to a union can he secure a contract that shall be fair to him. . . . If that belief, whether right or wrong, may be held by a reasonable man, it seems to me that it may be enforced by law in order to establish the equality of position between parties in which liberty of contract be-

[12] 38 Stat. 370 (1914).
[13] 312 U.S. 219.
[14] 236 U.S. 1 (1915).

gins. Whether in the long run it is wise for the workingmen to enact legislation of this sort is not my concern, but I am strongly of opinion that there is nothing in the Constitution of the U.S. to prevent it, and that Adair v. U.S. . . . should be over-ruled.

It is possible that Justice Holmes had looked into the final report of the United States Commission on Industrial Relations, published early in 1915. If he had, he would have found his own tentative conclusions well documented. The title of the report was "The Concentration of Wealth and Influence." Its findings were a powerful indictment of the labor policies of big business.[15] After observing that the concentration of corporate ownership and control was greatest in the basic industries, the report found that (1) almost without exception the employes of the large corporations were unorganized; (2) in order to prevent the organization of their employes, corporation managements had set up "elaborate systems of espionage," had refused to deal with labor unions, and discharged workers suspected of union affiliation; and (3) the "industrial dictators" who ran the companies were totally unconcerned with regard to the working and living conditions of employes and their families.

1916: The Adamson Act, an 8-hour day on the railways. In an election year, with all Europe at war, the train-operating brotherhoods (unions of conductors, engineers, firemen, and trainmen) demanded an 8-hour day without reduction of pay and threatened to strike if they did not get it. With their extensive organization they were in a position to tie up railroad transportation from one end of the country to the other. Such a walkout, bad enough in normal times, would have been catastrophic in the middle of the country's effort to supply the Western Allies. In the crisis, Wilson appeared personally before Congress and asked that the union demands be granted by law. Congress agreed ("with a pistol at its head," according to critics) and passed the Adamson Act on the day set for the strike.[16] The law was immediately attacked as unconstitutional but was upheld by the Supreme Court in *Wilson v. New* the following year.[17]

1917: The yellow-dog contract and the labor injunction. In *Hitchman Coal & Coke Co. v. Mitchell*, the United States Supreme Court legalized the nefarious combination of the yellow-dog contract and the labor injunction. The Hitchman Co., a mining corporation operating in Marshall County, West Virginia, went open-shop (nonunion) in 1906. Beginning in 1908, it required all employes to sign individual bargaining (yellow-dog) contracts in which they stated (1) that they were not members of

[15] Commager, *op. cit.*, pp. 287–288.
[16] 39 Stat. 721 (1916).
[17] 243 U.S. 332 (1917).

Meaning of Yellow dog — signing of individual on contract as belonging to no union - e.g. U.M.W.

the United Mine Workers of America or (2) that they would resign their membership, and (3) that they would not join in the future while employes of the company. A union organizer tried to persuade some of the employes to join, and the company obtained an injunction against his efforts on the grounds that he was inducing a breach of contract, the "contract" being the nonunion commitment. The case went to the United States Supreme Court, where the injunction was upheld, Justices Brandeis, Holmes, and Clark dissenting.[18]

Court Case

The decision gave employers a potent weapon against trade unionism. It was relatively easy to get employes and applicants for work to sign the nonunion agreements. The decision had been based on the common-law rule of sanctity of contract, so it stood as a precedent for state as well as Federal courts. With the example set by the top court of the land and with the Clayton Act subsequently repealed by a series of judicial decisions, it was easy to find judges who would grant restraining orders when "contractual" rights were threatened. The open-shop drive of employers, which began in 1921, would have had much less chance of success without the basic legal foundation laid down in the Hitchman case. The Norris–La Guardia Act of 1932 was a legislative broadside aimed squarely at the combination of the yellow-dog contract and the injunction.

Potent

1918: The National War Labor Board. In the United States trade unionism thrives on war. War brings prosperity, demands for unlimited production, work for everybody, and disregard of costs. War often produces an outright labor shortage, which greatly strengthens organized labor's bargaining position. The First World War saw the governmental adoption and wide extension of the "cost-plus" contract. This is a contract in which the price to be paid is not set in advance but is fixed afterward on the basis of costs, with a flat percentage fee going to the contractor as his "profit." The cost-plus contract made haggling over wage rates and hours ridiculous. Wage increases merely meant higher costs and higher costs in turn meant a larger fee. This highly strategic situation enabled unions to get immediate and dramatic improvements in terms, which attracted new members in large numbers. Many employers, faced with organizing drives and possible trouble, shrugged their shoulders and recognized the unions.

cost - plus contract — & the recognition of unions

Nevertheless, there were disputes, erupting now and then into work stoppages, and to handle these the National War Labor Board was created in April, 1918. It was a tripartite agency, with members representing employers, labor, and the public. President Wilson had already appointed Gompers a member of the Advisory Commission to the Council of National Defense. One effect of Gompers's influence was to see that organized

[18] 245 U.S. 229 (1917).

tripartite

labor (which meant the AFL) was given equal representation with management in the staffing of the NWLB.

The policies of the National War Labor Board, which had jurisdiction over disputes between employers and employes in war-production industries, were extremely influential. The Board was an agency of the national government; during the emergency the rules it laid down had the force of law. These rules marked a tremendous advance for organized labor over anything previously granted by a public agency. The most important ones were (1) no strikes or lockouts for the duration of the war; (2) the right of workers to organize in trade unions and bargain collectively through representatives of their own choosing; (3) no discharge of workers for union membership or legitimate union activities; and (4) no coercive action by organized labor to force employes to join or employers to recognize the unions.

The record of the War Labor Board in the 490 cases it settled sounds like a preview of the work of the National Labor Relations Board 20 years later.

In all cases where the issue of organization was involved, the Board insisted upon reinstatement of workers discharged for union activity and forbade blacklisting and individual (yellow-dog) contracts. Where the Board could not secure for employes the right to bargain collectively through trade unions, it provided some form of joint dealing if the employes demanded it. Frequently the Board took the initiative in setting up shop committees for handling local grievances, and sometimes local mediation boards were added. It looked upon such arrangements as preparatory steps towards trade unionism. That was the reason employers feared these committees and boards.[19]

This was strong medicine, and, while employers feared it, organized labor loved it. Principle 2, "the right of workers to organize and bargain collectively through representatives of their own choosing," was successively embodied in the Railway Labor Act, the National Industrial Recovery Act (Sec. 7a), and the National Labor Relations Act. It is now the basic rule in union-management relations in this country.

On the railroads, which were being run by Secretary of the Treasury William G. McAdoo, the same policy was followed. The United States Railroad Administration proved to be a sympathetic employer. It recognized the unions, bargained with them in an atmosphere of friendliness and generosity, established nationwide boards of arbitration to handle grievances, and agreed to numerous changes in the working rules which were advantageous to the workers. For this it was severely criticized, especially by the railroad managements, but it did succeed in untangling the transportation system, and it returned the roads to their owners in 1920 in relatively good shape.

The wartime trade-union boom did not end with the armistice of

[19] Lorwin, op. cit., p. 166.

November, 1918, but continued through the brief postwar prosperity which
followed. It reached its high point in 1920, with more than 5 million
workmen carrying union cards, 4 million of which were in unions affiliated
with the AFL. It was the high point of Sam Gompers's career, but there
were already signs of change. A strike late in 1919 against the 12-hour day
in the steel mills was defeated. In the fall of 1920 the country "returned to
normalcy" with the election of Warren G. Harding to the Presidency. At
about the same time the depression of 1920 to 1922 got under way.

THE 1920s: DECLINE OF THE LABOR MOVEMENT

One of the amazing chapters in the history of trade unionism in the
United States is the steady decline in membership, power, and influence
during the prosperous 1920s. It was contrary to precedent and to logic.
The pattern of union growth from colonial times up to the First World
War, as pointed out by Commons, Beard, and many others, had been (1)
rapid expansion of organized labor during prosperous periods and (2)
disintegration during periods of depression, with widespread loss of faith
in trade-union tactics and frequent political sorties of more or less radical
design. The historical record was reinforced by the common sense of the
situation. In prosperous times employers are busy making money and look
with misgiving upon the possibility of a shutdown. They are more able to
afford concessions in the form of wage increases, shorter hours, and improved working conditions and are therefore more amenable to compromise. With improvement in their bargaining position unions make gains,
and these gains attract new members. Organization is extended, recognition forced from hesitant managements, and the momentum thus gained
makes new recruiting drives feasible.

In depression all this is reversed. Management regards the chance of
a shutdown calmly. Business is bad anyway, and there may be a question
of the wisdom of continuing operations. Union men are unemployed or on
short time, union treasuries are low, and there is no great heart for militant action which seems unlikely of success. Marginal union members drop
away, nonmembers are uninspired by recruiting talk, and many unions
close their books against newcomers in order to reduce competition for
those jobs which the union may control.

What went wrong from 1921 to 1929, so that the usual depression
pattern was superimposed upon the most prosperous period of the
country's history? A number of things have been pointed to by the historians, of which the most influential seem to be the following:

1. Stable wages, and full employment.   Prosperity was not a myth.
Prices fell hard from 1920 to 1923 (from 118 to 100 on the Consumer
Price Index) and thereafter fluctuated within a range of 4 points, ending

up in 1929 unchanged from 1923. Between 1923 and 1929, unemployment rose as high as 5 per cent only once, and factory earnings (by the hour or the week) went up slightly each year. The net effect was that real earnings held their own or rose slightly. The beneficial effect was enhanced by some very real fringe benefits that were being introduced in personnel programs across the country.

2. Improved personnel administration.   This was a carry-over from the slightly discredited "scientific management" of Frederick W. Taylor around the turn of the century and also from the highly successful use in the First World War of the Army Alpha and Beta tests for the classification of draftees. During the 1920s, industrial psychologists had a field day, testing, rating, selecting; evaluating jobs; setting rates; and carrying on time-and-motion studies. The idea was to match men with jobs appropriate to their abilities, reward the deserving, weed out the unfit, raise production and profits, and divide the gains on a rational basis between the owners and the employes. It was an enticing vision and much of it proved true. Along with it came many employe benefits: better tools; improved lighting, heating, and ventilation; canteens, rest periods, and cafeterias; bonuses, credit unions, and savings plans; music rooms and ball clubs. Employes saw little reason to protest, and the warnings of professional trade unionists concerning the paternalism of the programs were disregarded. Labor leaders, on the other hand, were faced with a genuine peril, a planned, concentrated, and powerful open-shop drive.

3. Open-shop drive.   The "American plan" was a carefully coordinated campaign originated by a group of employer associations, whose objective was the nonunion open shop. Sponsored by the United States Chamber of Commerce, the National Association of Manufacturers, the National Metal Trades Association, and many smaller local organizations, the plan called for propaganda, employe-representation plans (company unions), yellow-dog contracts, assistance to struck fellow employers, and the black-listing of union organizers. It was well financed, carefully organized, perfectly timed, and it worked to perfection. Part of the plan's success was unquestionably due to its conformity to the political philosophy of the times and the attitude of the courts.

4. Tired labor leaders.   The obstacles of the 1920s would have been a challenge to young and vigorous labor leadership; they were too much for the elderly gentlemen running the AFL after Gompers's death in 1924. The labor movement badly needed new blood and a new point of view—toward industrial unionism, toward organization of the mass-production industries. The men were there (for example, John L. Lewis of the UMWA and Sidney Hillman of the ACW) but they lacked seniority.

Table 6-4.   American trade-union membership, 1921–1933

Year	Total	AFL	AFL % of total
1921	4,722,000	3,907,000	83
1922	3,950,000	3,196,000	81
1923	3,629,000	2,926,000	81
1924	3,549,000	2,866,000	81
1925	3,566,000	2,877,000	81
1926	3,592,000	2,804,000	78
1927	3,600,000	2,813,000	78
1928	3,567,000	2,896,000	81
1929	3,625,000	2,934,000	81
1930	3,632,000	2,961,000	81
1931	3,526,000	2,890,000	82
1932	3,226,000	2,532,000	79
1933	2,857,000	2,127,000	74

Source: BLS, *Handbook of Labor Statistics, 1947*, p. 130.

They were by-passed, the Federation elected William Green as president, and the labor movement ran on downhill. At the bottom, in 1933, total union membership in the United States was below 3 million for the first time in 15 years, and the AFL's share had dropped from 83 per cent in 1921 to 74 per cent. The record is shown in Table 6-4.

   5. Chief Justice Taft and the return to normalcy.   The dominant political philosophy of the Harding-Coolidge-Hoover era was the "return to normalcy." To many, normalcy meant release from the tensions of war, industrial strife, and reform—which, translated, appeared to mean a return to peace, Republicanism, and "business as usual." If business as usual meant no government intervention on the side of the workingman, then the courts were also on the side of "normalcy." From 1921 to 1930, former President William Howard Taft was Chief Justice of the United States. During these 10 years, the Court held that Congress could not (or should not) regulate either the minimum wages of women or the work of children; it restated Secs. 6 and 20 of the Clayton Act, ruling that strikes, picketing, and boycotts were still conspiracies under the antitrust laws, and it found again—as in *Coppage v. Kansas* earlier—that the states (Arizona, this time) could not constitutionally limit the use of the labor injunction. The Chief Justice himself wrote five of the leading labor decisions and concurred in all the others. With some reason, labor liberals regard this as the period of sublime reaction in American constitutional jurisprudence.

1921 to 1927: Antilabor decisions of the 1920s.   From 1921 to 1927, there were seven major antilabor decisions by the United States Supreme Court, five of them bearing directly on organized labor and its activities.

The cases, with dates, citations, and the justice responsible for the opinion, are:

1921:   *Duplex Printing Press Co. v. Deering* (254 U.S. 443). Pitney: the Clayton Act "gives to private parties a right to relief by injunction in any court of the United States against threatened loss or damage by a violation of the anti-trust laws"; injunction against a hot-goods boycott upheld. Brandeis, Holmes, and Clark dissent.

1921:   *American Steel Foundries v. Tri-City Central Trades Council* (257 U.S. 184). Taft: the Clayton Act permits the issuance of a labor injunction to restrain picketing in large numbers.

1921:   *Truax v. Corrigan* (257 U.S. 312). Taft: an Arizona state law identical in wording with Sec. 20 of the Clayton Act (limiting the use of the labor injunction) held unconstitutional. Holmes, Brandeis, and Pitney dissent.

1922:   *Bailey v. Drexel Furniture Co.* (259 U.S. 20). Taft: a Federal law regulating child labor via taxation is held unconstitutional.

1923:   *Adkins v. Children's Hospital* (261 U.S. 525). Taft: a Federal law setting minimum wages for women workers in the District of Columbia is held unconstitutional, thereby making several similar state laws invalid. Holmes and Brandeis dissent.

1925:   *Coronado Coal Co. v. United Mine Workers of America* (268 U.S. 295). Taft: a strike in an Arkansas coal mine held to be a part of a conspiracy to restrain interstate commerce in coal.

1927:   *Bedford Cut Stone Co. v. Journeymen Stone Cutters' Assn. of North America* (274 U.S. 37). Sutherland: a Sherman Act decision authorizing a suit for damages against a union engaging in a hot-goods boycott. Brandeis and Holmes dissent.

Within 15 years, every labor decision of the decade of the 1920s had been overruled by the same court but with a different membership.

1922: Railway shopmen's strike.   The Transportation Act of 1920, which returned the railroads to their private owners, set up a Railway Labor Board to settle disputes between the carriers and their employes. The Board had nine members, three each representing the carriers, the unions, and the public. It was the first full-time administrative agency created by Congress to regulate labor-management relations in time of peace. In 1922, the railway shopmen struck against one of the Board's wage decisions. The strike was broken by an injunction granted by Judge Wilkerson of the Federal district court in Chicago, but not before it had

re - pp. 146

showed that the Board was without power to enforce its rulings. This led to a reexamination of the problem of dispute regulation on the railways and eventually to the Railway Labor Act of 1926.

1926: The Railway Labor Act. The Railway Labor Act of 1926 [20] marks the beginning of the modern era in Federal labor legislation in the United States. The law can lay claim to a notable number of *firsts* in congressional regulation of labor relations. (1) It was the *first* Federal law to guarantee to employes the right to organize and bargain collectively through representatives of their own choosing without interference by employers, a principle which has become the basis of all subsequent labor legislation by Congress and most state legislatures. This principle is now a fundamental rule of law in the United States. (2) It was the *first* impor- tant example of congressional protection of unions to be approved by the Supreme Court. In *Texas & New Orleans Ry. v. Brotherhood of Clerks,* the Court not only upheld the Railway Labor Act, it provided an impor- tant precedent for supporting the National Labor Relations Act 7 years later. (3) It was the *first* of the big laws regulating labor relations in interstate commerce to stand the test of time. During more than 40 years of operation under the statute, there has been only one important walkout (in 1946) and that collapsed within 48 hours. (4) It was the *first* labor law on the Federal level which union officials helped to write; the act was the outcome of a joint effort by management and union representatives to find a substitute for strikes and lockouts as a way of settling disputes. (5) Largely as a result of point 4 above, it was the *first* example of Federal regulation of labor relations to disclose any grasp of the technical prob- lems of dispute settlement. The Railway Labor Act is still technically the best labor law in the Federal code, and most Federal legislation on union- management relations since it was passed has drawn on it for principles or methods or both.

1926 to 1927: Setback in Britain. In contrast to the more amiable spirit displayed in the United States, relations between the government and organized labor in Britain became badly strained in 1926. For 20 years, the British labor movement had enjoyed the freedom provided by the Trade Disputes Act of 1906. This law strictly limited the doctrine of civil conspiracy as applied to unions, exempted unions as organizations from legal action, and approved any form of peaceful picketing. An amendment in 1913 permitted unions to use their funds for political purposes if the members authorized it. This was going about as far as the government could go; British trade unionism was free, legal, unen- cumbered. Then, in May, 1926, a labor dispute in the coal fields mush- roomed into a general strike, involving $2\frac{1}{2}$ million of the 6 million trade

[20] 44 Stat. 577.

unionists in the country, and including some unions of government employes. The reaction in government and throughout the country was extremely adverse. In June, 1927, Parliament passed the Trade Disputes and
Trade Unions Act prohibiting sympathetic strikes, strikes designed to
coerce the government, mass and residential picketing, and the political
use of union funds without individual authorization of members. Violations were punishable by fine and imprisonment. The law stood for 20
years. In 1946, a Labor government repealed it.

1930: Chief Justice Hughes and the T&NO case.   In 1930, the
Railway Labor Act came before the United States Supreme Court in the
case of *Texas & New Orleans Ry. v. Brotherhood of Clerks.*[21] The T&NO
had been employing the customary method of open-shop organization on
the railways—firing union men, especially the active leaders and organizers, replacing them with nonmembers, and at the same time forming a
"system association" (company union) of clerks to take the place of the
brotherhood. The case was remarkable in one respect. It turned on the
union's request for an injunction *against the employer,* on grounds that
the employer was violating the guarantee in the Railway Labor Act of
the right to select bargaining representatives "without interference, influence, or coercion." The T&NO's contention was that the act was unconstitutional, like the anti-yellow-dog provisions of the Erdman Act in *Adair
v. United States,* and that, even if constitutional, it provided no sanctions
or penalties for violation and so was advisory only.

The Court had changed. Chief Justice Taft was dead, and his place
had been taken by Charles Evans Hughes, former associate justice of the
same Court, former Governor of New York, and at one time Republican
candidate (against Wilson) for President of the United States. The change
in personnel carried with it a change in viewpoint. In a unanimous decision read by the Chief Justice, the Court upheld the constitutionality of
the act and rejected the view that a law of the United States prohibiting
a form of conduct (coercion) could be disregarded with impunity. The
company was permanently enjoined from continuing its interference and
required to take constructive action in the form of rehiring the discharged
men and dissolving the system association. It was a great legal victory
for organized labor, made still greater 7 years later when the fundamental
dogma of the decision, that "this act does not interfere with the employer's
normal right to hire and fire," was repeated in upholding the Wagner Act.

1929 to 1933: Beginning of the Great Depression.   The stock-
market crash of October, 1929, is generally accepted as marking the end
of the prosperity of the 1920s and the beginning of the Great Depression
of the next decade. In depth and duration, nothing like it had ever been
[21] 281 U.S. 548.

seen before. The collapse of economic activity took 4 years, and full recovery did not come for another 8. In those years, depression became almost a way of life. The policies and events of the decade—in government, business, labor, agriculture—can be understood only by remembering that they occurred within a constant setting of bankrupt businesses, farm mortgage foreclosures, and an average of 10 million unemployed wage earners, with thousands of families enduring for years on end not only inadequate clothing and shelter but also the constant possibility of not having enough to eat. Literally millions of previously self-supporting and self-respecting people were saved from starvation by government relief programs.

The statistics of the decline from 1929 to 1933 indicate its catastrophic nature:[22]

Gross national product was cut almost in half, from $104 billion in 1929 to $56 billion in 1933.

Unemployment multiplied eight times—from 1,550,000 (3 per cent of the labor force) to 12,830,000 (25 per cent).

Farm mortgage foreclosures almost tripled, from a rate of 15 per 1,000 farms in 1929 to 39 per 1,000 farms 4 years later, while emergency crop and feed loans outstanding jumped from $8 million to $90 million.

Bank closings skyrocketed from 659 in 1929 to 4,004 in 1933, with losses by depositors rising still faster—from $77 million to $540 million.

It was a ghastly 4 years, made even worse by the 8 which followed with little or no sign of recovery. The memory seems like a nightmare to many who lived through it, and the atmosphere of the period can hardly be comprehended by those who did not. The Depression of the 1930s brought down a government, destroyed confidence in big business, ended the policy of *laissez-faire*, produced the welfare state, and created the labor movement of today.[23] In 1930, one good omen for organized labor had already appeared in the form of the T&NO decision; by 1932, a major shift in public policy was in the making.

FDR AND THE NEW DEAL

In 1932, there occurred two events of importance to the labor movement in the United States, one of them legislative and the other political. In March, Congress passed and the President approved the Norris–La Guardia Federal Anti-injunction Act,[24] a law so binding and definite in its provisions as to preclude the kind of misinterpretation which had neutral-

[22] *Statistical Abstract of the United States, 1959, passim.*

[23] See A. J. Schlesinger, Jr., *The Crisis of the Old Order*, vol. I, "The Age of Roosevelt" (Boston: Houghton Mifflin Company, 1957), for a graphic picture of the period.

[24] 47 Stat. 70.

Horris-La-Guardia Act

latest friend
of Unions ever

ized the Clayton Act. Then in November the voters turned against the Republican party and elected Franklin Delano Roosevelt as President, thereby bringing into office the greatest friend of organized labor yet to occupy the Presidency.

Norris-La Guardia Act

The Federal Anti-injunction Act was sponsored by two great liberals, Senator Norris of Nebraska and Representative Fiorello La Guardia of New York. It prohibited outright the yellow-dog contract as "contrary to ① the public policy" of the United States, unenforceable, and providing no basis for any form of legal or equitable relief. It also barred the use of ② injunctions to restrict any form of peaceful union activity and placed severe limitations upon their issuance to prevent violence or other unlawful acts. The law put an end to the use of the labor injunction in disputes in interstate commerce, and it was also adopted in identical or similar ③ form by the legislatures of a number of the more important industrial states. Since the injunction had been the principal means of combating mass and violent picketing, its elimination was a tremendous addition to strike efficiency. From the time the act was upheld in 1937 until the passage 10 years later of the Taft-Hartley Act, which relaxed its provisions somewhat, no major employer was successful in continuing operations during a strike.

The election of 1932 was not on its face such an auspicious event for organized labor. It was more of a repudiation of the "Hoover depression" than anything else. The Democratic platform of 1932 did not mention organized labor other than in a vague promise to revise the antitrust laws "for the better protection of labor and the small producer and distributor." The AFL was only lukewarm toward the campaign promises of old-age and unemployment insurance. The new President had a good record as a liberal governor of New York, where he had continued in the Al Smith tradition, but his position on national domestic issues was largely unknown. The overwhelming problems of the day were depression, bankruptcy, and unemployment. The trade unions were trying to survive; aggressive organizing activity was out of the question. Like many other groups, trade unionists were ready for a change, but they had no idea it was to be so advantageous to them. They first discovered their good fortune when President Roosevelt authorized the inclusion of Section 7a in the National Industrial Recovery Act.

Existing Problem

1933 to 1935: Section 7a and the labor boards.

The National Industrial Recovery Act [25] (NIRA) was the Roosevelt administration's main effort to whip the Depression. It provided for Federal control of the entire industrial structure of the country through the mechanism of codes of fair competition, industry agreements, and governmental supervision (the "Blue Eagle" and General Hugh Johnson), plus a program of public

[25] 48 Stat. 195 (1933).

works. The purpose was the increase of production, consumption, purchasing power, and employment. An important part of each code was a set of labor standards: minimum wages, maximum hours of work, limitation of child labor, and the now famous (or notorious) Sec. 7a:

(1) That employees shall have the right to organize and bargain collectively through representatives of their own choosing, and shall be free from the interference, restraint, or coercion of employers of labor, or their agents, in the designation of such representatives or in self-organization or in other concerted activities for the purpose of collective bargaining or other mutual aid or protection; (2) that no employee and no one seeking employment shall be required as a condition of employment to join any company union or to refrain from joining, organizing, or assisting a labor organization of his own choosing.

It was soon apparent that employers *were* interfering with their employes' rights of self-organization and selection of bargaining representatives, and two successive boards were set up to handle disputes and say what was and what was not "interference, restraint, or coercion" by employers. The first was the *National Labor Board,* an unpaid, part-time public body, organized on the traditional basis of three-way representation: three public members, two industry members, and two labor members. It had no directions, no clear idea of what it was to do, no power to enforce its decisions, and it did not last. Nevertheless, in the 11 months of its existence, it did a lot of work (handling 3,532 cases involving 1.8 million employes, holding 183 employe representation elections) [26] and began the difficult process of defining and classifying the unfair labor practices of employers. Both jobs were continued by its successor, the (first) [27] National Labor Relations Board.

The (*first*) *National Labor Relations Board* was appointed June 29, 1934, by President Roosevelt under authority of Public Resolution 44 of the Seventy-third Congress. It was quite different from the National Labor Board. It had only three members, all of them impartial, full-time, salaried employes of the government. The Board had the power to subpoena witnesses, hold elections, and enforce its orders through the Federal district courts. It also lasted 11 months (to May 27, 1935, when the NIRA was held unconstitutional in *Schechter Poultry Corp. v. United States*) [28] and did a lot of work (9,364 cases involving 2,154,000 workers; 154 representation elections, and the like).[29] Most important of all, it found out what the main types of employer interference consisted of and what powers an administrative labor board needed to put a stop to them. Its experience

[26] Harry A. Millis and Royal E. Montgomery, *The Economics of Labor,* vol. III, "Organized Labor" (New York: McGraw-Hill Book Company, 1945), p. 758.

[27] So designated to distinguish it from the National Labor Relations Board set up under the Wagner Act in 1935.

[28] 295 U.S. 495. The so-called "sick chicken" case.

[29] Millis and Montgomery, *op. cit.,* p. 760.

provided the basis for the Wagner Act, which took the place of Sec. 7a
after the NIRA was struck down.

1934: The National Railroad Adjustment Board.   One of the things
which the union representatives wanted in the Railway Labor Act of 1926
but which the carriers would not agree to were national adjustment boards
for the settlement of "grievances," which are disputes over the interpretation of contracts. In 1934 the unions got their boards. Congress amended
the Railway Labor Act to establish a National Railroad Adjustment Board
with offices in Chicago to handle disputes "growing out of grievances or
out of interpretation or application of agreements concerning rates of pay,
rules or working conditions." Any dispute not settled within the system's
grievance machinery could be appealed to the appropriate division of the
National Railroad Adjustment Board, where it would eventually be arbi-
trated and the decision enforced, by a court award if necessary.

THE NEW DEAL LABOR POLICY

Commons and Andrews found the historical trend of governmental attitudes toward collective bargaining to be: repression—toleration—encouragement—intervention.[30] They placed the date of change from repression
to toleration at 1842 (elimination of the conspiracy doctrine via *Commonwealth v. Hunt*), and from toleration to encouragement at 1933, with the
inauguration of the Roosevelt administration. The shift had in fact begun
several years before and was not completed until 1937, with the "reorganization" of the Supreme Court. The real issue was the basic one of the
authority of Congress and the President to decide and administer the
economic policies of the country. This controversy came to a climax with
the passage of the National Labor Relations Act, popularly known as the
Wagner Act.[31] The policy of "protecting the exercise by workers of full
freedom of association, self-organization, and designation of representatives of their own choosing," begun as far back as 1898 in the anti-yellow-
dog provisions of the Erdman Act and continued in the Clayton Act, the
Railway Labor Act, and the National Industrial Recovery Act, here received its ultimate expression.

1935: The National Labor Relations Act.   The Wagner Act was a
model law in several respects. It did what it was designed to do with great
efficiency, it stood up in the courts, and for more than 10 years it resisted
repeal or modification, in spite of constant criticism from business, government, and trade-union sources.

[30] See above, p. 122.
[31] 49 Stat. 449 (1935). Named for its sponsor, Senator Wagner of New York.

   The Wagner Act was a labor law of general application (covering industry generally, except the railroads) but with a limited purpose, which
was carefully spelled out in its provisions. That purpose was to stop employer interference with the attempts of unions to organize American
employes. The law's terms were simple and well defined, as follows:
1.   One general and four specific "unfair labor practices" by employers
were prohibited. They were outlined in Sec. 8, which said: "It shall be an
unfair labor practice for an employer . . ."
   a.   To interfere with, restrain, or coerce employes in the exercise of
   their rights of self-organization and collective bargaining through representatives of their own choosing.
   b.   To dominate, or interfere with, the formation or administration of
   any labor organization or to contribute financial or other support to it
   (the "company union" provision).
   c.   By discrimination in regard to hire or tenure of employment or any
   term or condition of employment to encourage or discourage membership in any labor organization (the only exception being bona fide
   closed-shop agreements, which were permitted).
   d.   To discharge or otherwise discriminate against an employe because
   he has filed charges or given testimony under the act.
   e.   To refuse to bargain collectively with the representatives of his employes, subject to the provisions of Sec. 9 (which provided for certification of unions representing a majority of the employes).
2.   A three-man National Labor Relations Board was set up to administer
the act, with power to investigate, hold hearings, subpoena witnesses and
papers, render decisions, issue cease-and-desist orders, and require constructive action of employers.
3.   The NLRB was authorized to investigate questions of representation
(arguments over a union's right to recognition) and to certify unions as
the official representatives of groups of employes if they were found to
have signed up a majority of the employes in the "appropriate bargaining
unit." When a union was so certified, the employer could not refuse to
"bargain collectively" without violating the fifth unfair labor practice.
   The Wagner Act was a superb example of policy making and execution, a fact which is all the more surprising since its subject matter was so
controversial. Probably nothing contributed more to its success than the
circumstance that two boards had tried for 2 years to find the formula for
stopping employer interference with unions, and the members were permitted to write the results of their experience into a statute. The law was
drafted principally by men who knew what employers did to stop unions
from organizing, who knew what powers an administrative board would
need to stop them from stopping unions, and who wrote the necessary
powers and prohibitions into the act.

1935: The Committee for Industrial Organization (CIO).   By
1935, the times had changed and the structure of industry had long since
changed, but the leaders of the AFL were still under the spell of Gompers's principle of exclusive jurisdiction—"one union to each trade." The
difficulty was that in the great mass-production industries of steel, autos,
rubber, glass, lumber, electrical appliances, etc., a "trade" had little meaning; men moved from job to job as they qualified by training and experience. Few took the time or trouble to go through the apprenticeships
necessary to membership in a craft union. At successive conventions of
the American Federation of Labor, the executive council of the Federation
brushed off the demands of a little group of leaders of industrial unions,
that a new basis of organization be adopted. A minority report of the
committee on resolutions of the convention of 1935 stated this group's
belief that "in the great mass-production industries, and in those in which
the workers are composite mechanics, specialized and engaged upon
classes of work which do not qualify them for craft-union membership,
industrial organization is the only solution. . . ." [32]

The report was voted down, and industrial unionism rejected. In a
rump meeting after the close of the convention the leaders of eight unions
formed the Committee for Industrial Organization. The key men were
John L. Lewis (United Mine Workers), Sidney Hillman (Amalgamated
Clothing Workers), and David Dubinsky (International Ladies' Garment
Workers). The historic eight unions represented were the United Mine
Workers, the Amalgamated Clothing Workers, the International Typo-
graphical Union,[33] the United Textile Workers, the United Hatters, Cap
& Millinery Workers, the International Union of Mine, Mill, & Smelter
Workers, the International Ladies' Garment Workers, and the Oil Field,
Gas Well, & Refinery Workers. They were joined shortly afterward by
four others: the Federation of Flat Glass Workers, the Amalgamated
Association of Iron, Steel, & Tin Workers, the United Automobile Work-
ers, and the United Rubber Workers. All told, these unions represented
between a million and a million and a half members.

The committee had no intention of seceding. It stated its purpose to
be "encouragement and promotion of organization of the unorganized
workers in the mass production and other industries upon an industrial
basis . . . to bring them under the banner and in affiliation with the
American Federation of Labor." But to diehards in the AFL it was dual
unionism and treason. In a series of actions throughout 1936 to 1938 the
offending unions were first suspended and then expelled. The CIO was on

[32] *Proceedings* of the 1935 Convention, AFL, p. 524.
[33] The ITU never actually joined the CIO; its president, Howard, was present at
the original meeting but could never get the union to leave the AFL and join the
other group. The same is true of Max Zaritsky of the United Hatters.

Criomes! John L. Lewis's
3. David Dubinsky

Table 6-5.   American trade-union membership, 1933–1937 2. Sidney Hillman

Year	Total	AFL	AFL % of total
1933	2,857,000	2,127,000	74
1934	3,249,000	2,608,000	80
1935	3,728,000	3,045,000	82
1936	4,164,000	3,422,000	82
1937	7,218,000	2,861,000	40 — AFL = CIO

Source: BLS, *Handbook of Labor Statistics, 1947*, p. 130.

its way, and the American labor movement was split into two great federated groups.

   1936: The upswing and the CIO.   It was the second year of the
Roosevelt administration before American trade unionism began to respond to the series of stimulants administered to it, and even then the
recovery was slow and halting. Membership figures crawled upward, from
the 2,857,000 of 1933 to 3,249,000 in 1934 and 3,728,000 in 1935. By 1936,
after 3½ years of solid government support, the organized labor movement in this country was still far smaller than it had been in 1920. It had
4,164,000 members as compared to 5,048,000 a decade and a half earlier.
It was this dawdling pace of increase that had exasperated John L. Lewis
and his industrial-union allies, Sidney Hillman and David Dubinsky. Paus-
ing only long enough to set up their Committee for Industrial Organization, they pitched into the job of showing how it was to be done.
   Throughout 1936, while the AFL was solemnly issuing orders to dis-
band, stand trial, suspend or be expelled, the CIO was hard at work, trying, with some success, to organize the supposedly impregnable steel and
auto industries. With a war chest of $500,000 furnished by John L. Lewis's
United Mine Workers, the Steel Workers Organizing Committee (SWOC)
was plowing head on into Big Steel and the even tougher smaller-scale
independents. On Mar. 2, 1937, U.S. Steel recognized the SWOC, as earlier
in the same year General Motors Corporation had recognized the United
Automobile Workers. The dam had burst. By the end of 1937 total trade-
union membership had jumped more than 3 million, and the CIO was
bigger than the AFL. The turn of the tide is shown in Table 6-5.

SUMMARY

The 50 years of AFL leadership illustrate the rise and decline of the craft
principle in organization. The doctrine of "exclusive jurisdiction" was ap-

propriate to the times, a sound and efficient theory up to the First World War. Then, like many another useful concept, the facts upon which it was based changed, and it became an outworn shibboleth, a principle which its adherents often disregarded in practice and which had a hampering effect upon the extension of union organization to millions of potential members. In the rebirth of the AFL during the late 1930s and the Second World War the successful unions were those which expanded their jurisdiction, by amalgamation and extension, with complete disregard of craft lines. The fluidity of industrial society during a mass-production epoch made organization by industry as much a necessity as organization by craft had been 30 years earlier.

The half century from 1886 to 1936 also demonstrated the fundamental necessity of political action for union welfare. A friendly government means union growth, official antagonism means union stagnation and decline. The periods of greatest union development came without exception in times of governmental encouragement, during the administrations of McKinley, Wilson, and the two Roosevelts. Even the opposition of the judges could not overcome the effect of a friend in the White House. But to realize its full potential, organized labor had to be accepted by the courts, an objective which it did not achieve until 1937.

Finally, the first 50 years of an established trade-union movement in the United States saw the practical disappearance of radical, revolutionary mass organization and the full acceptance of safe and sane business unionism. The public disapproval of left-wing labor organizations and the prompt reprisals visited upon Debs, the Progressive Miners, and the IWW taught union leaders conservatism and limited objectives. Instead of "elimination of wage slavery" and abolition of the industrial system, they demanded higher wages, shorter hours, and better working conditions. They learned to work with and influence Congress and the President. They avoided tying political commitments and third-party adventures and advised members to "reward friends and punish enemies." They became, in fact, too conservative, but they established the principle of collective bargaining as an American institution and put trade unions among the leaders of the accepted special-interest groups in American political and economic life.

READINGS

For the full flavor of this remarkable period of struggle and growth on the part of organized labor in America, the student should start with selections from Samuel Gompers, *Seventy Years of Life and Labor*, 2 vols. (New York: E. P. Dutton & Co., Inc., 1925), and Lewis Lorwin, *The American Federation of Labor* (Washington, D.C.: The Brookings Institution, 1933). The first is the autobiography of the man who built the AFL; the second is the official story as told by a sympathetic outsider.

However, from 1886 to 1936, the courts set the labor policy of the United States. A sampling of the decisions handed down in the cases listed below will round out the picture. (Incidentally, there is no real substitute for a reading of the full opinion in its official form, with concurring opinions and dissents. *Read at least one decision complete!*)

1.   Compare *Adair v. United States* (1908) with *Texas & New Orleans Ry. v. Brotherhood of Clerks* (1930), wherein the doctrine of the earlier decision was overruled.

2.   Compare the following three cases: *Hitchman Coal & Coke Co. v. Mitchell* (1917), the common-law authorization of the yellow-dog contract as a basis for the labor injunction, and *Duplex Printing Press Co. v. Deering* (1921), in which the Clayton Act was misinterpreted and an injunction granted, with *U.S. v. Hutcheson* (1940), which finally took organized labor out from under the Sherman Act, via the Norris–La Guardia Act.

3.   Compare *Adkins v. Children's Hospital* (1923), giving Chief Justice Taft's views of the constitutionality of minimum-wage laws, with the case that settled the issue: *West Coast Hotel v. Parrish* (1937).

4.   Just for fun compare *T&NO Ry. v. Brotherhood of Clerks* (1930) and *NLRB v. Jones & Laughlin Steel Corp.* (1937), both decisions by Chief Justice Hughes, Taft's successor, and both upholding the constitutionality of Federal labor laws still on the books today.

SEVEN

GROWTH AND
MATURITY:
1936 TO DATE

The story of the labor movement in the United States since 1936 is one of a steady 20-year rise to a position of major influence in national affairs, followed by a decade of stagnant membership and declining prestige. From 1957 on, union officials have matured bargaining relationships with employers, worked to surmount the scandals unearthed by the McClellan committee, and struggled with problems of job security brought on by automation and other forms of mechanized work handling. The period began with the rise of industrial unionism and the CIO—whose formation, expulsion, reorganization into a separate federation, and mushroom growth provided the impetus and the philosophy of a labor movement in tune with the times. Competition, however, brought about the rebirth of the AFL. The older Federation, jarred by what it considered the defection of some of its most powerful members, shook itself loose from the handicap of the principle of exclusive jurisdiction and went after new recruits. In doing so, it practically abandoned the ancient dogma of "one union to one trade," and its most successful members proselytized with abandon among miscellaneous groups of employes.

1936: Reelection of President Roosevelt.   The overwhelming re-election of President Franklin Delano Roosevelt in 1936 set the stage for organized labor's explosive advance the following year. Roosevelt won the electoral and popular votes of all states except Maine and Vermont. His first 4 years in office had shown him to be vigorous and aggressive, and his policies were on the record for all to see. Friendship for and assistance to organized labor were high on the list. He had supported Sec. 7a of the National Industrial Recovery Act, had appointed the National Labor Board and the (first) National Labor Relations Board, and had sponsored the Wagner Act as an administration "must" bill. He was strongly opposed to the "judicial obstructionism" of the United States

Supreme Court, which he felt was handicapping Congress and the Executive. The size of his popular and electoral majority could only be interpreted as a powerful mandate to continue in the direction he had started. He made clear that he regarded it as such with his bill for the reorganization of the Federal judiciary (the United States Supreme Court was his real target), which was introduced into Congress early in 1937.

1937: TURNING POINT FOR ORGANIZED LABOR

If any one year can be said to mark the date when the United States as a nation was committed to the principle of collective bargaining, that year is 1937. In 1937 the United States Supreme Court was "reformed" and by a slim margin of 5 to 4 began to uphold Federal labor legislation which it had been expected to reverse and some of which it had previously declared unconstitutional. The Wagner Act and the Norris–La Guardia Act were thus judicially established along with minimum-wage legislation. Some of the most powerful antiunion fortifications in American business began to crumble. Organized labor, in the shape of two CIO subsidiaries, the Steel Workers Organizing Committee and the United Automobile Workers of America, split open the twin Gibraltars of the open shop: the steel and automobile manufacturing industries. The AFL, unable to divert the unions in the Committee for Industrial Organization from their unorthodox but highly successful recruiting drives in the mass-production industries, rushed back into the field with a series of organizing campaigns. Trade-union membership increased by 3 million—more, in absolute numbers, than in any other year before or since.

FDR versus the Supreme Court. The reorganization of the United States Supreme Court came in the spring of 1937. In 1936 the Court had held invalid a minimum-wage law of the state of New York in the case of *Morehead v. People ex rel. Tipaldo.*[1] Since there was growing support of minimum-wage legislation after the wide use of wage standards in the industry codes of the NIRA, there was a violent public protest against the decision.

It was an election year. Both presidential candidates expressed disapproval of the decision, and promises of support for minimum wages and maximum hours were inserted in the 1936 campaign platforms of the two parties. Roosevelt won the election and submitted a bill for the reorganization of the Federal judiciary to the Seventy-fifth Congress.[2]

The bill proposed, in substance, to permit the President to appoint one additional justice, up to a total of six, for every justice of the Supreme

[1] 298 U.S. 597.
[2] This was popularly known as the "court-packing bill."

Court who failed to retire after serving 10 years and was past the age of 70. Since the Court was splitting 5 to 4 on most liberal-conservative issues and since there were a number of the justices who were past 70 and had served 10 years, the new rule would permit the President to add enough liberal members to ensure a majority. It was the most controversial measure of Roosevelt's career. Arguments over it shook the country, and the debate continued at a high pitch into the summer of 1937. On June 7 the Senate Committee on the Judiciary returned an adverse report, which recommended "the rejection of this bill as a needless, futile, and utterly dangerous abandonment of constitutional principle." The bill was lost. In its stead there was passed an innocuous reform measure with a provision for the retirement at full salary of any Supreme Court justice who had reached the age of 70.

The failure of the Court reorganization plan is regarded by many as President Roosevelt's greatest defeat. However, in this case as in others, the battle was lost, but the campaign was won. During the height of the controversy over the proposed "court-packing" reform some of the New Deal's most important legislation came before the Court for review, to wit: the Social Security Act, the National Labor Relations Act, and a state copy of the Norris–La Guardia Act. And with them came another state minimum-wage law, this time from the Commonwealth of Washington. In a series of startling opinions, several of them by a 5 to 4 division, the laws were upheld, even to the minimum-wage decision, which required a humiliating shift from the position taken a year earlier.

Since the introduction of President Roosevelt's "court-packing" bill early in 1937, no major piece of Federal legislation has been declared unconstitutional by the United States Supreme Court, and the judicial freedom allowed administrative agencies, such as the National Labor Relations Board, to interpret their grants of power has steadily increased.

THE BIG LABOR DECISIONS OF 1937

The spring term of the 1936 to 1937 session of the Supreme Court was a decisive one for both the Court and organized labor. The National Labor Relations (Wagner) Act was up for review after an adverse decision (that it was unconstitutional) in the circuit court of appeals; a Wisconsin state law which contained the substance of the anti-injunction provisions of the Norris–La Guardia Act was being challenged; and the constitutionality of a Washington state minimum-wage law was being defended in spite of the *Morehead* decision of the previous year. Important provisions of the Social Security Act, which carried benefits for labor in the form of unemployment compensation and old-age assistance, were also on the docket. The tip-off came in the minimum-wage case, which was tried first.

West Coast Hotel v. Parrish.[3]   The Washington state minimum-wage decision was emphatic proof that the Supreme Court had changed its mind. In the Morehead case of the year before, the Court had had an opportunity to uphold a state minimum-wage law without specifically overruling the Adkins decision of 1923, since the New York law was carefully drafted to meet the objections of Chief Justice Taft and his associates. The Washington law was not. It was practically the D.C. law over again, and, to uphold it, the Court had to brush aside the Adkins decision. This it did without delay. Chief Justice Hughes read the majority opinion and, after comparing the reasoning of Taft and Holmes (who dissented) in 1923, concluded with the flat statement: "Our conclusion is that the case of *Adkins v. Children's Hospital* . . . should be, and it is, overruled."

NLRB v. Jones and Laughlin Steel Corp.   On Apr. 12, 1937, in five decisions,[4] the Supreme Court upheld the Wagner Act as a constitutional exercise of the power of Congress to regulate interstate commerce. At the same time it decided that the manufacture of steel, as practiced by the Jones and Laughlin Corporation, was interstate commerce, thereby opening the manufacturing and processing industries to congressional regulation, from which they had been rigorously excluded since the time of John Marshall. It was a 5 to 4 decision, read by Chief Justice Hughes.

At issue was the company's right to discriminate against members of the Beaver Valley Lodge 200 of the Amalgamated Association of Iron, Steel & Tin Workers of America, by coercing and intimidating employes to stop their organizing activities and by discharging the most active union members. The National Labor Relations Board had ordered the company to cease and desist from such action, to reinstate with back pay 10 of the fired employes, and to post notices of its change of policy. The company refused, and the Board went to the circuit court of appeals for an enforcement order, which was denied on grounds that the order was beyond the range of Federal power, *i.e.*, the company was not engaged in interstate commerce. Before the Supreme Court, the company argued that the act regulated labor relations and not interstate commerce, that its production employes were not subject to regulation by the Federal government as they were not engaged in commerce, and that the law was unconstitutional in that it was an invalid exercise of the judicial power by an administrative agency and denied "due process of law."

[3] 300 U.S. 379 (1937).

[4] The other four were: *National Labor Relations Board v. Friedman-Harry Marks Clothing Co.*, 301 U.S. 58; *Washington, Virginia, and Maryland Coach Co. v. National Labor Relations Board*, 301 U.S. 142; *National Labor Relations Board v. Fruehauf Trailer Co.*, 301 U.S. 49; and *Associated Press v. National Labor Relations Board*, 301 U.S. 103. The Jones and Laughlin citation is 301 U.S. 1 (1937).

As for the company's being in interstate commerce, the Chief Justice pointed to the facts: 19 subsidiaries, wholly owned or controlled; mines in Michigan, Minnesota, Pennsylvania, West Virginia; ownership and operation of steamships, towboats, barges, and railroads; warehouses in Chicago, Detroit, Cincinnati, and Memphis; steel fabricating shops in Long Island City and New Orleans; sales offices in 20 cities in the United States; 75 per cent of the company's product shipped out of Pennsylvania, where the home plant was located. Said the judge:

The stoppage of those operations by industrial strife would have a most serious effect upon interstate commerce. . . . It is obvious that it would be immediate and might be catastrophic. We are asked to shut our eyes to the plainest facts of our national life and to deal with the question of direct and indirect effects in an intellectual vacuum. . . . The facts of respondent's enterprise . . . present in a most striking way the close and intimate relation which a manufacturing industry may have to interstate commerce. . . .

On the question of the constitutionality of the congressional guarantee of the right to organize and bargain collectively the Court was equally definite. "That is a fundamental right. Employees have as clear a right to organize and select their representatives for lawful purposes as the respondent has to organize its business and select its own offices and agents. Discrimination and coercion . . . is a proper subject for condemnation by competent legislative authority." The procedure of the National Labor Relations Board was approved, the question of improper use of judicial power brushed aside, and the case was remanded to the circuit court of appeals for disposal in line with the opinion. It was a great decision, the forerunner of a long and consistent series of opinions supporting the right to organize and the administrative protection of that right.

The labor injunction annulled.   The Norris–La Guardia Federal Anti-injunction Act came before the Supreme Court by proxy in May. The case, *Senn v. Tile Layers' Protective Union,*[5] involved a part of the Wisconsin state labor code which declared peaceful picketing and patrolling lawful and prohibited the granting of an injunction against such conduct. It was an odd case. Senn was a tile-laying contractor on a small scale, employing only one or two journeymen and their helpers at best, and he often did work that was within the jurisdiction of the members of the tile layers' union. He was not a member of the union and could not become one, since he could not afford to spend 3 years in the apprenticeship required for membership (a requirement rigorously applied whether the applicant was qualified or not). He agreed to hire only union men, but the union still objected to his working on his own jobs, and when he persisted, they picketed him as unfair. Senn asked for an injunction against

[5] 301 U.S. 468 (1937).

the picketing, which was refused by the trial court and the supreme court of the state. He then appealed to the United States Supreme Court on grounds that the Wisconsin labor code violated the Fourteenth Amendment by denying him equal protection of the laws and due process. Justice Brandeis read the decision of the majority, upholding the law as constitutional and denying the injunction. It was another 5 to 4 decision, Butler, Van Devanter, McReynolds, and Sutherland dissenting. The following year the Norris–La Guardia Act itself appeared before the Court in *Lauf v. E. G. Shinner & Co.,*[6] and was upheld. With this decision the labor injunction became practically extinct until revived in limited form in the Taft-Hartley Act 10 years later.

Social security upheld. On the same day that the Senn decision was rendered the Supreme Court upheld the unemployment-compensation (job insurance) and old-age assistance provisions of the Social Security Act. In *Steward Machine Co. v. Davis,*[7] the Federal unemployment tax was declared constitutional; in *Helvering v. Davis,*[8] the old-age benefit tax was found to be within the general welfare clause; and in *Carmichael v. Southern Coal & Coke Co.,*[9] the Alabama unemployment insurance law was approved. These decisions (on May 24, 1937) brought to a close the Supreme Court's most widely publicized session in history. On June 1, Mr. Justice Van Devanter retired, and in his place President Roosevelt appointed Senator Hugo Black of Alabama. Other retirements came soon afterward. The "reorganization" of the Supreme Court was complete.

THE LABOR–MANAGEMENT SCENE: 1937

Strikebreaking and industrial espionage. Late in 1937, the La Follette committee of the United States Senate reported on some of the methods by which big corporations conducted their industrial relations; its findings got wide publicity. For example, there was a total of $9,440,132 spent on "industrial espionage (labor spies), munitioning, and strikebreaking, 1933–37." Sample outlays for the period were: Baldwin Locomotive Works, $159,078; Chrysler Corporation, $275,534; General Motors Corporation, $1,019,056; Radio Corporation of America, $1,007,350.

The committee revealed that merely a partial count of the labor spies in operation from January, 1933, to July, 1936, ran into the thousands.[10]

[6] 303 U.S. 323 (1938).
[7] 301 U.S. 548.
[8] 301 U.S. 619.
[9] 301 U.S. 495.
[10] "Industrial Espionage," *Violations of Free Speech and Rights of Labor,* Report of the Committee on Education and Labor pursuant to S. Res. 266 (74th Cong.), S. Rept. 46, 75th Cong., 2d sess., part 3, p. 21.

Organization	Spies
Agencies replying to questionnaires	658
Railway Audit and Inspection Co., Inc., and affiliates	313
National Corporation Service and affiliates	437
National Metal Trades Association	104
Corporations Auxiliary Companies	677
Wm. J. Burns International Detective Agency, Inc.	440
Pinkerton's National Detective Agency, Inc.	1,228
Total	3,857

The Pinkerton agency alone had spies planted in 93 labor organizations, many of them holding important union offices. The disclosures of the La Follette committee had much to do with eliminating organized anti-union and strikebreaking techniques from the labor scene.

The La Follette committee's investigation had been carried out against a backdrop of reviving business activity, intensive union recruiting drives, violence and bloodshed on the picket lines, and the exchange of taunts and recrimination between the AFL and its suspended Committee for Industrial Organization. It was a recovery year, the first time in almost a decade for business activity to appear really to be on the upgrade, and the CIO was riding the boom. Under the leadership of John L. Lewis, two CIO affiliates, the Steel Workers Organizing Committee (SWOC) and the United Automobile Workers of America (UAW), had invaded the mills and factories of the leading producers of steel and automobiles.

Sit-down at General Motors.   It was the year of the sit-down strike. The campaign started in Flint, Michigan, with the simultaneous closing of seven General Motors Corporation plants by sit-downs in the last day of December, 1936. A little over 30,000 employes were involved, but they were so strategically placed as to eventually bring about the layoff of more than 200,000. The shutdown lasted 6 weeks, ending by agreement between Lewis and President William S. Knudsen of General Motors, on Feb. 11, 1937. The terms were immediate recognition of the union; prompt reopening of the plants without discrimination against strikers, whether sit-down or not; and a bargaining conference on specific union demands regarding wages, hours, and working conditions. It was a momentous victory, soon to be followed by another of equal magnitude.

Big steel signs.   On Mar. 2, less than 3 weeks after the General Motors dispute was settled and almost without warning, the United States Steel Corporation signed a contract with the SWOC, recognizing it as the bargaining agency for its own members in the corporation's largest subsidiary, the Carnegie-Illinois Company. The agreement also raised wages 10 per cent and established the 40-hour week with time and a half for overtime. This settlement occurred after numerous conferences between Myron C. Taylor, president of the corporation, and John L. Lewis, and between Taylor and President Roosevelt. Within less than 6 months, the Steel Workers Organizing Committee had signed agreements with more than 100 additional steel companies, including a dozen large U.S. Steel subsidiaries. Recognition was achieved practically without the use of strikes.

Chrysler.   The Chrysler Corporation agreed to start negotiations with the United Auto Workers on Mar. 3, the day following the signing of the U.S. Steel agreement. Here the path to agreement was less smooth, and before there was a meeting of minds between Lewis and the Chrysler officials, sit-down strikes occurred in all the main Chrysler plants. The main issue was exclusive bargaining rights for the union. These were not yielded by the company, and the strike was settled in the first week of April with the customary company recognition of the union as representative of its members only and a bargaining conference on the union's demands. President Martin of the UAW (CIO) stated that the union now had over 300,000 members, making it in all probability the largest labor organization in the country.

Ford and Little Steel.   The CIO had obtained solid footholds in both the steel and automobile industries, but the vote was not unanimous. Five of the larger independent steel producers (Republic, Youngstown Sheet and Tube, Inland, Weirton, and Bethlehem) rejected the policy of the United States Steel Corporation and, with the help of friendly state and local officials, succeeded in breaking the strikes at their plants and continuing operations on a nonunion basis. On the automobile front the Ford Motor Company took the same position. All were able to hold out against general union recognition until 1941. In each case there was extensive picket-line violence and bloodshed. The Ford dispute came to a head in the celebrated "battle of the overpass," in which a number of UAW organizers (including Walter Reuther, now president of the union) who were distributing literature at one of the exits from the River Rouge plant were attacked and beaten by company guards. The "Little Steel" struggle culminated in a Memorial Day riot at the South Chicago plant of the Republic Steel Company.

Memorial Day at Republic Steel.   The 1937 Memorial Day affair grew out of the tension resulting from attempts to unionize three of the "Little Steel" companies in the South Chicago–Gary Harbor steel district at the southern end of Lake Michigan: Republic, Inland Steel Company, and the Youngstown Sheet and Tube Company. The struggle between Republic and the union had assumed almost the character of a military campaign, with armed guards in the plant, interference by union pickets with the delivery of supplies, the dropping of food and other essentials by parachute from planes flying overhead. In order to mobilize opposition to the company's resistance, the SWOC organized a mass demonstration for Memorial Day of several thousand demonstrators in front of the closed plant. A large detail of Chicago police was sent to the spot to maintain order.

The demonstrators assembled and faced the police, who stood with their backs to the plant. Some shots were fired, whether by demonstrators or (as claimed by the SWOC) by company guards from the plant windows no one knows. The police thereupon fired into the crowd and then attacked the demonstrators with clubs. Four people were killed outright, and more than eighty wounded. At least six more of the wounded eventually died. The general impression was of police irresponsibility and poor handling, not an unusual conclusion with respect to the policing of industrial disputes. The strike collapsed soon afterward.

The Republic Steel affair is the last of the great picket-line killings which are associated with the dispute over recognition in American labor history. It came several weeks after the judicial validation of the Wagner Act in the Jones and Laughlin decision, but the dispute from which it emerged arose while the law's constitutionality and its application to a manufacturing firm were still in question. It was one of the main purposes of the statute to eliminate arguments over recognition, and in this it has been conspicuously successful. Since its final acceptance there have been no further examples in this country of mass murder to force or deny the right of workers to organize and bargain collectively through representatives of their own choosing.

1937: The AFL expels the CIO.   The split between the AFL and CIO, which opened late in 1935, grew and widened in 1936 and began to solidify in 1937. It had become a matter of personalities, as well as union rivalries. Lewis's capacity for vigorous expression and his disinclination to restrain himself when commenting upon the character and capacities of his former colleagues in the AFL were one obstacle to reconciliation. His acerbity had not been diminished by the prompt labeling of the committee as "dual unionism," "insurrection," and "rebellion" or the direction that its officers stand trial before the executive council of the AFL. CIO leaders had offered to provide one-third of a $1.5 million war chest to finance a campaign in the steel industry. The offer was rejected, of course, and with the organizing successes of 1937 in steel and automobiles the assurance of the younger group increased.

Early in 1937 the AFL expelled all CIO unions from city central

bodies and the state and municipal federations. It was expulsion, not
suspension—an acknowledgment that the differences between the two were
irreconcilable. The CIO retaliated by organizing state and local industrial
councils, similar in structure and function to the ones they were expelled
from. This *was* dual unionism in fact. Both groups intensified their organizing campaigns, and raiding and recrimination increased. In the 1937
convention of the AFL the executive council was authorized to revoke the
charters of the unions affiliated with the CIO. A last-minute attempt to
compromise the differences between the two failed, and early in 1938, the
CIO unions were summarily expelled from the AFL.

Partly because of the rapid expansion of union membership in the
basic and mass-production industries, where the CIO was recruiting with
great energy and success, and partly because of AFL competition with its
junior rival, 1937 is the banner year of union growth in the United States.
Total trade-union membership rose more than 3,000,000 to 7,218,000
(from 4,164,000 in 1936). This was a new high, more than 2,000,000
above the previous peak of 5,034,000 in 1920. It was divided as follows:
AFL, 2,861,000 (40 per cent); CIO, 3,718,000 (52 per cent); and independent, 639,000 (8 per cent).

1938: RECESSION AND CONSOLIDATION

The depression of 1937 to 1938 reversed the swing toward business recovery. There was a withering away of demand, an almost simultaneous
fall in output, and the industrial economy collapsed in a downward spiral
of deflation that moved faster than any previously on record. Unemployment, which had declined to 7,700,000 in 1937, jumped back to 10,390,000,
approximately 19 per cent of the labor force. The effects of the deflation
lasted 3 years; for the labor movement this meant 3 years of marking time,
reorganization, and assimilation of gains already achieved. Nevertheless,
there was progress here and there.

"Bloody Harlan" organized.   In August, 1938, the Coal Operators
Association of Harlan County, Kentucky, signed its first agreement with
the United Mine Workers of America, recognizing the union as bargaining representative of the employes and authorizing the checkoff of union
dues. This recognition brought to a close one of the longest and most lurid
stories of violence, bloodshed, and intimidation in American trade-union
history. It followed closely a court decree upholding NLRB intervention,
in which the Board had ordered the reinstatement with back pay of 60
miners discharged for union activity. The taming of Harlan County was
as big a thing, in its way, as the conquest of General Motors or Big Steel
in their respective industries. It was a milestone in the upward progress
of the workers in coal mining.

The busy NLRB. After the *Jones and Laughlin* decision of April, 1937 broke the logjam of noncompliance by business firms, the National Labor Relations Board had become a very busy agency. Approval by the courts however had not relieved it of criticism, a steady stream of which came from two main sources: Congress and the AFL. In Congress, it was variously charged that (1) the law was one-sided, disruptive of good employer-employe relations, and coercive of individual workers; (2) it permitted unions to violate contracts with impunity; and (3) its interpretation and administration were biased and unfair. The AFL agreed with Number 3 above, arguing that the Board had shown gross favoritism and bias in the handling of cases, favoring one form of union organization (industrial) over another (craft) in its decisions with respect to the "appropriate bargaining unit," and complaining that the Board had set aside legally valid and binding agreements between AFL unions and employers. (It *had* done this, but most of them were "sweetheart" closed-shop contracts in which the union did not represent a majority of the employes.)

To counter its critics, the NLRB presented in its 1938 *Annual Report* a careful analysis of its workload and disposition of cases.[11] The volume alone was impressive. Pointing out that the fiscal year, July 1, 1937, to June 30, 1938, was its first real year of operation, because of constitutional uncertainties which were not resolved until the spring of 1937, the Board summarized its operations as follows:

	Cases	Employes involved
Carried over, July 1, 1937	2,202	1,000,000
Received during the year	10,419	2,000,000
Total on the docket for year	12,621	3,000,000
Disposed of during the year	8,851	1,846,000
Carried over, June 30, 1938	3,770	1,154,000

The disposals consisted of:

	Cases	Per cent
Settlements agreed to by the parties (the great majority of which came before a formal complaint was issued)	4,621	52
Cases withdrawn (settled by the parties themselves)	2,345	27
Cases dismissed during hearings by regional directors or trial examiners (lack of evidence, etc.)	1,439	16
Board decisions or orders (certifications, cease-and-desist rulings, dismissals, etc.)	446	5
Total	8,851	100

[11] The NLRB's *Third Annual Report,* for the fiscal year ended June 30, 1938, is an important historical document, well worth careful reading by anyone seriously interested in the growth of the labor movement in this country.

There were two notable features of the "disposals." First, only 5 per cent of the cases, or 1 out of 20, went to a final decision after hearing, and the great majority of these (342 out of 446) were certifications of unions as the legal representatives of the employes involved. Second, more than half of all cases were disposed of before any formal complaint was issued, by the parties either agreeing to a settlement proposed by NLRB representatives, or by a withdrawal of the charges due to the parties working out an agreement on their own, or by dismissal or transfer to some other government agency. This feature of the report gave rise to another criticism, that the NLRB was "mediating" disputes, when it was supposed to act as a quasi-judicial agency of arbitration. When the National Labor Relations Act was amended in the Taft-Hartley Act of 1947, it contained a provision forbidding "conciliation or mediation" (Sec. 4a).

To meet the AFL's charge of bias, the Board carefully compared its treatment of unions affiliated with the AFL and the CIO. During the year, it closed 1,128 cases received from AFL unions and 1,655 from CIO labor organizations. In the principal categories of "disposals" the percentage results were almost identical. CIO unions withdrew a few more complaints than AFL unions; AFL unions carried a few more cases to formal action. In the largest single class—settlement before formal complaint was issued—the AFL total was 603 cases (54 per cent) and the CIO total 893 (54 per cent). It was a standoff.

Finally, the Board turned to its record before the courts. The picture was more than encouraging; it was remarkable. Out of nine cases before the United States Supreme Court the NLRB was successful in eight. Only once did the Court decide against the agency. Four of the favorable decisions were after retrial before the upper bench, and four were denials of petitions of appeal from circuit court decisions upholding Board awards. Before the circuit courts of appeal, the NLRB was successful in getting its orders enforced without modification in 15 cases; it was upheld with modifications in two others; and there were six decisions denying enforcement of its orders. The NLRB obtained 11 consent decrees, and eight cases were withdrawn for settlement. Altogether, it was a record of judicial approval of an administrative agency almost without precedent in the American courts. When the controversial nature of the subject matter and the inflammatory character of the disagreements between the parties are considered, the Board's consistent record of court victories is all the more unusual.

The Congress of Industrial Organizations.   Expulsion of nine CIO unions from the AFL during the first half of 1938 was the climax of the labor drama which had been splitting the American trade-union movement for 3 years. The permanent organization of the CIO into the Congress of Industrial Organizations (to keep the distinctive initials, which had become the trademark of industrial unionism) was almost an anticlimax.

The CIO met in constitutional convention at Pittsburgh, Nov. 14 to 18, 1938. The major structural details had already been worked out. The CIO was a practical copy at all levels of the AFL. Delegates were present from 35 affiliated national or international unions, 675 local industrial unions, 9 organizing committees, 23 state industrial councils, and 115 city industrial councils. They represented a claimed membership of 3,787,877 workers. In a closely controlled meeting, with little or no discussion of issues, they adopted a constitution, arranged their finances, and elected officers. The management structure of the federation consisted of an unpaid president (John L. Lewis), two vice-presidents (Philip Murray and Sidney Hillman), a secretary (James E. Carey, president of the United Electrical Workers), and an executive board composed of representatives of each affiliated national or international union. The federation was to be supported by a tax of 5 cents a month per member of each affiliated national union and 50 cents per month per member of each directly affiliated industrial local.

The long-run objectives of the Congress of Industrial Organizations were declared to be:

1. To bring about the effective organization of the workingmen and working women of America regardless of race, creed, color, or nationality and to unite them for common action into labor unions for their mutual aid and protection.

2. To extend the benefits of collective bargaining and to secure for the workers means to establish peaceful relations with their employers by forming labor unions capable of dealing with modern aggregates of industry and finance.

3. To maintain determined adherence to obligations and responsibilities under collective bargaining and wage agreements.

4. To secure legislation safeguarding the economic security and social welfare of the workers of America, to protect and extend our democratic institutions and civil rights and liberties, and thus to perpetuate the cherished traditions of our democracy.

Minimum wages, maximum hours, and child labor.   The recession of 1938 was a disheartening aftermath of the 1937 recovery. There were renewed demands for legislation, many of which took the form of minimum-wage and share-the-work proposals. The Fair Labor Standards Act of 1938 (popularly known as the Wages and Hours Act) was the legislative answer to the crisis.[12] It established a progressive schedule of gradually rising minimum wages and gradually shortening maximum hours of work to be observed by employers in interstate commerce, and it abolished child labor below the age of 16 in any form and below the age of 18 in dangerous occupations. The main ideas were to raise purchasing power

[12] 52 Stat. 1060.

by requiring an increase in pay rates in the lowest-income brackets and to spread the existing employment by shortening working hours and removing children from the labor market. The act was primarily a *wage* law. Long working hours were not prohibited; they were simply made more costly by requiring that employers pay workingmen time and a half for any work done beyond the statutory maximum.

The unions' stake in the new law was their position as watchdog over its administration. Complaints of violation could be made by individuals *or their representatives,* and the new legal standards for wage payment were a strong inducement for unions to bring charges against low-wage employers as a publicity move in organizing campaigns among under-privileged employes.

1940: Murray heads the CIO.   In 1940, President Roosevelt ran for a third term. The event was significant for labor, since it ensured a friendly administration during the war which was already under way in Europe. In the short run, however, it precipitated a flurry of opposition on the part of Lewis which resulted in his resignation from the presidency of the CIO and his replacement by Philip Murray. The opposition to Roosevelt, it soon became clear, was limited to the personal antagonism of Lewis and had little support among other labor leaders or the rank and file. In an extreme statement of his position shortly before Election Day, Lewis threatened to resign if Roosevelt won. Roosevelt did win, and on Nov. 18, 1940, Lewis announced his retirement from the presidency of the federation. Four days later Philip Murray was elected to succeed him.

It was the beginning of a period of maverick independence on the part of Lewis and the Mine Workers. In 1942 the United Mine Workers of America left the CIO and the next year petitioned for readmission to the AFL. The petition was not granted until 1945, after which the reconciliation lasted a short 2 years. In 1947, Lewis again stalked out of the AFL and resumed his more natural role of thorn in the side of both labor federations and the Federal government as well.

1940: United States v. Hutcheson.[13]   This case marked the emancipation of American trade unionism from the Sherman Act. Justice Frankfurter, the former Harvard law professor, read the majority opinion. Using the Norris–La Guardia Act as a prop, the learned justice proceeded to rehabilitate Sec. 20 of the Clayton Act and to argue that its interpretation by the Supreme Court between 1914 and 1932 was incorrect:

The Norris–La Guardia Act reasserted the original purpose of the Clayton Act by infusing into it the immunized trade union activities as redefined by the later Act. In this light section 20 removes all such allowable conduct from the taint of being "violations of any law of the United States," including the Sherman law.

[13] 312 U.S. 219 (1940).

Table 7-1.   American trade-union membership, 1937–1940

Year	Total	AFL		CIO		Independent	
		Members	%	Members	%	Members	%
1937	7,218,000	2,861,000	40	3,718,000	52	639,000	8
1938	8,265,000	3,623,000	44	4,038,000	49	604,000	7
1939	8,980,000	4,006,000	45	4,000,000	44	974,000	11
1940	8,944,000	4,247,000	47	3,625,000	41	1,072,000	12

Source: BLS, *Handbook of Labor Statistics, 1947*, p. 130.

There has been no attempt to prosecute a trade union under the antitrust laws of the United States since the Hutcheson decision.

The recession which began in the fall of 1937 slowed down the membership boom, and the fight between the AFL and the CIO used up energies which might otherwise have been put to use in recruiting among the unorganized. Through 1938 to 1940, there was only a modest increase, while the gains of 1937 were digested and the labor movement regrouped into competing sections. The distribution of membership during this prewar "period of consolidation" is shown in Table 7-1.

1941 TO 1945: WAR AND UNION GROWTH

Once again, war proved to be the great catalyst of union expansion. The United States became involved economically before it did militarily. In 1941, defense production and military conscription cut the number of unemployed to a little over 5 million, the lowest figure since 1930. From there it dropped to 2.5 million in 1942 and 1 million in 1943. At the same time there was a rapid shift of the working population from agriculture, trade, and service establishments, which are typically small in size and hard to unionize, into mines and factories, which are typically large in size and the common target of union organizers. Several key manufacturing industries (munitions, aircraft, shipbuilding) rose from almost nothing to positions of top significance in the economy, and a number of others (automobiles, heavy machinery, railroad equipment) expanded steadily under the impact of war orders. The situation was made to order for a labor movement which had temporarily composed its differences, clarified its organization, and had governmental backing.

There was no question of the government's stand on the matter of labor organization and collective bargaining. In agency after agency set up for purposes of defense, the President included organized labor on an equality with management representatives. In a number of special cases the President, going over the heads of the administrative agencies which were responsible, showed his determination to strengthen the union position. All suggestions that the operations of the National Labor Relations Board and the limitations of the Wages and Hours Act be suspended for the duration of the war were vigorously and successfully resisted. The only important piece of legislation intended to limit union activities which was passed during the war period—the Smith-Connally War Labor Disputes Act—was enacted by Congress over the President's veto. As organized labor well knows, there is no friend like a friend in the White House. It had one, in both war and peace, in Franklin Delano Roosevelt.

1941: Cleanup in autos and steel.   The CIO went into the lend-lease and rearmament period of 1941 with some unfinished business on its hands: the Ford Motor Company and the Little Steel group of Bethlehem, Republic, Youngstown, Inland, and Weirton. In these plants strikes were resisted, company unions flourished, and managements refused to deal with the United Automobile Workers and the Steel Workers Organizing Committee. A series of prosecutions by the NLRB dragged interminably through the long schedule of investigation, hearings, award, refusal to comply, appeal to the circuit courts, and appeal to the Supreme Court. In the spring of 1941 these final bastions of militant antiunionism gave way. On Feb. 10 the United States Supreme Court upheld the NLRB in a judgment it had made in 1937 that the Ford Company had been guilty of coercion and intimidation of its employes in trying to prevent their organization and selection of representatives for purposes of collective bargaining.

It was the end of the trail for Ford. A National Labor Relations Board representation election was held at the River Rouge plant, with its 85,000 employes. The UAW (CIO) won by a clear majority, and the company was immediately directed by the NLRB to disestablish its company union and reinstate a number of men previously discharged at various plants throughout the country. On June 20 the company signed an agreement with the UAW which amounted to complete surrender. The firm agreed to the union shop, the checkoff of union dues, wages equal to the highest in the industry, and abolition of its private detective unit, called euphoniously the "service department." In return it received the right to put the union label on its cars. The agreement covered 130,000 employes in all parts of the country.

The progress with Ford was duplicated by the steady advance among the hard-boiled independent steel producers. The first to give in was Youngstown Sheet and Tube. On Mar. 30 the company reached a settlement with the SWOC in which it agreed to pay strike claims running back to 1937. Bethlehem came next, with a circuit court of appeals ruling upholding an NLRB order to oust a company union. In rapid succession, master agreements were signed with the SWOC at the Bethlehem and

Buffalo plants, following representation elections which were won by wide margins. In May the Republic Steel Company was found guilty by the NLRB of unfair labor practices at its South Chicago plant and was ordered to reinstate 610 employes fired for union activity. Six weeks later the company signed a Wagner Act compliance agreement with the SWOC and rehired the discharged employes with full pay for time lost, some of it running back 4 years. In August an NLRB check showed SWOC majorities at 17 Republic plants.

1942: The National War Labor Board. Following Pearl Harbor, organized labor and management had voluntarily presented the government with no-strike and no-lockout pledges, assurances of maximum production, and promises to bury the hatchet for the duration. However, all agreed that there would still be disputes—plenty of them—over wages, hours, organizing campaigns, grievances, etc. And all agreed that there should be some sort of agency to settle the disputes, which might otherwise interfere with war production. The pattern had already been set in the First World War, and it was renewed without delay by President Roosevelt. On Jan. 12, 1942, by Executive order, he established a 12-man National War Labor Board (4 representatives each, of industry, labor, and the public) with final power to settle all disputes certified to it by the Secretary of Labor.

The NWLB was only one of a succession of public defense agencies on which organized labor was given full representation, *e.g.,* the Advisory Council for National Defense, the National Defense Mediation Board, the Office of Production Management, and the War Production Board. The NWLB, however, was the most important of the wartime mediation and arbitration bodies. It lasted out the war and was responsible for a number of important decisions which became national policy and strongly influenced wartime and postwar labor relations. Two of the most notable of these were the wage-stabilization rule known as the "Little Steel formula" and the union-security award called "maintenance of membership."

THE LITTLE STEEL FORMULA. War means a shortage of consumers' goods, an increase in employment, incomes, and spending, and inflation if there are no controls placed on prices. The United States' answer to this danger in 1942 was price control, rationing, and wage stabilization. In April, 1942, President Roosevelt announced a stabilization policy. Price control and rationing were the job of the Office of Price Administration (OPA). Demands for increases in wages would come up to the National War Labor Board. In July, 1942, the NWLB handed down a historic decision in a wage case involving the same four steel companies that had come to terms with the SWOC the year before: Bethlehem, Republic, Youngstown, and Inland. The rule, which came to be known as the "Little Steel formula," was that a maximum wage increase of 15 per cent was permissible between Jan. 1, 1941, and May 1, 1942, to match a 15 per cent rise shown by the Bureau of Labor Statistics' cost-of-living index. The plan was to hold the line at that point, relying upon the Office of Price Administration (OPA) to keep prices at a constant level, thereby stabilizing the civilian economy.

The Little Steel formula was restated by President Roosevelt in a "hold the line" order of April, 1943, and it became the wartime wage policy of the country. By the end of the war the original rule had been invalidated by price rises (in spite of OPA) and shortages of many kinds of consumers' goods, and its application had been twisted beyond recognition through "correction of inequities," authorization of "fringe" wage items, and exceptional rulings. It was the country's first taste of full-scale compulsory arbitration of wages and after it was over no one was willing to admit that he liked it.

The arbitration feature came about as a result of action by Congress in October, 1942, giving the NWLB official responsibility for passing on all wage (or salary) increases—individual or general, union or nonunion. It was a huge administrative job. In the 3 years between October, 1942, and August, 1945, more than 450,000 voluntary wage-adjustment cases ("voluntary" meaning that the employers were willing) were submitted to the Board. The staff of the agency rose from less than 200 to over 4,000 by the end of the war.[14]

MAINTENANCE OF MEMBERSHIP.   The NWLB also had to pass on the kind of "union security" appropriate to wartime. Should unions be permitted to recruit actively in war industries and what kind of contract should they be permitted to demand of employers? The central problem was expansion. For example, if a shipyard (or an airplane plant) expanded from 500 employes to 5,000 within a year or two, it made a great difference to the union having jurisdiction over the original group if it had a closed- or a union-shop contract. If it had a closed-shop agreement, all the new employes had to pass through the union hiring hall first. If it had a union-shop contract, all the new employes had to join the union within a specified period (usually a month) after being hired. In either case the union expanded with employment. Unions were aware of this, and they rushed to get such "union security" agreements with employers in the mushrooming defense plants.

But the employers balked. The fair thing, they said, was to maintain the *status quo* for the duration of the war—no strikes, no lockouts, no recruiting, and no management interference with unions in existence. In short, a quick freeze of the labor-management situation, to be thawed out and the traditional warfare resumed when the crisis was over.

[14] George W. Taylor, *Governmental Regulation of Industrial Relations* (Englewood Cliffs, N.J.: Prentice-Hall, Inc., 1948), p. 178.

But what was the *status quo* in an expanding plant and how was it maintained? If 300 of 500 original employes were union members, would 300 of 5,000 employes a year later represent a continuation of the *status quo*? Was it a question of absolute numbers or of proportionality? And suppose the new employes *wanted* to join the union on their own and with no coercion whatsoever—what then? Should they be denied the right to take out membership? And if a union had a good solid majority (say, 75 per cent) of the employes in its membership and in normal times would demand and would have a good chance of getting a closed- or union-shop agreement, should such a demand be ruled out because of the no-strike, no-lockout rule?

These were the kinds of questions that the NWLB faced every time it turned around, and it had no national policy to help it reach a decision. So it worked out a compromise. The compromise was the famed "maintenance of membership" award. In terms of union security, the award was a modified union-shop arrangement. The employer could hire when and where he pleased, union or nonunion men. The union, in turn, could recruit among the new workers without limitation, but no one was obliged to join. Those who did join, however, were required to remain members for the life of the agreement, usually 1 year. This was also true of men who were members of the union at the time of hiring. After a 2- or 3-week "escape period," they were required to keep up their union membership in good standing while the agreement was in effect. Thus, under a maintenance-of-membership agreement, union membership was not compulsory, but it was a one-way street. Once entered into, it was a prerequisite to continued employment, for a period at least.

1943: The Smith-Connally War Labor Disputes Act.[15]   The War Labor Disputes Act of 1943 was aimed at John L. Lewis, who had just conducted the first of a series of successful wartime coal strikes. It had two main features: (1) it gave the President power to seize establishments (mines, plants, or firms) in which strikes or labor disputes threatened to interrupt production essential to prosecution of the war; and (2) it required advance notice of disputes which might threaten production, called for maintenance of the *status quo* for 30 days, and made a strike at the end of the 30-day period lawful only if it was approved by a majority of the employes affected in an election conducted by the National Labor Relations Board.

The law was an example of the kind of brainstorm Congress can produce when it is working without the cooperation of the executive branch of the government or the parties involved. Clause 2 (above) in effect provided for the *legalization* of wartime work stoppages, after they had already been ruled out by the no-strike, no-lockout agreement. Clause

[15] Public 89, 78th Cong., 1st sess., Chap. 144.

1 gave the President a power which he had already as Commander in Chief in time of war and which he had already used several times to put an end to strikes and lockouts. To seize a plant *after* an election would put the government in the anomalous position of appearing to deny a privilege granted by statute after the parties had taken the legally required steps to exercise it.

The act was passed over President Roosevelt's veto on June 25, 1943. Its provisions were subsequently exercised a number of times, but there is little evidence that they reduced strikes, either in numbers or effect. The general conclusion is that as a labor relations measure the law was a mistake. It expired at the end of "hostilities," on Dec. 31, 1946, with no expression of regret from labor, management, or the public.

1944: The CIO's Political Action Committee.

The Political Action Committee (or PAC, as it came to be referred to) was the brain child of Sidney Hillman, president of the Amalgamated Clothing Workers. Hillman was a socially conscious labor leader in the socially conscious needle trades (garment industry), but he was no visionary. He was an astute, practical, hard-hitting organizer, negotiator, strike leader, and politician. Hillman's faith in President Roosevelt was demonstrated on numerous occasions. The President, in turn, had reciprocated the confidence by giving Hillman the top-ranking labor position in every major government defense agency created between 1940 and 1943. It was obvious to Hillman and others that policies adopted and pursued during postwar reconversion might have a lasting effect on the long-run interests of organized labor. Hillman remembered 1920, with its political overturn, 1921 and the "American plan," and the disastrous years that followed. He therefore turned to Murray and the executive board of the CIO with a plan for a new kind of trade-union political organization. They named it the Political Action Committee (PAC).

The PAC was a modern type of union political weapon, patterned directly on tested, old-line political party methodology. It called for organization, by state, county, city, ward, precinct, block, and cell. It called for work: doorbell ringing, solicitation, vote counting, distribution of literature by the ton, and delivery service to the polls on Election Day. It called for mobilization of relatives, associates, and friends, and their education in the issues of the campaign. It used every modern device of publicity: radio, sound truck, platform speakers, debates, forums, motion pictures, handbills, newspapers, magazine articles, and pamphlets. Above all, it called for cooperation with friends, especially the political organizations which were already lined up in support of the candidates which the PAC was for. In big city after big city the PAC merged its efforts with the local Democratic managers in an all-out combined effort to reelect President Roosevelt and others on the ticket that had labor's endorsement. The

Table 7-2.   American trade-union membership, 1941–1945

Year	Total	AFL		CIO		Independent	
		Members	%	Members	%	Members	%
1941	10,489,000	4,569,000	43	5,000,000	48	920,000	9
1942	10,762,000	5,483,000	51	4,195,000	39	1,084,000	10
1943	13,642,000	6,564,000	48	5,285,000	39	1,793,000	13
1944	14,621,000	6,807,000	47	5,935,000	40	1,879,000	13
1945	14,796,000	6,931,000	47	6,000,000	40	1,865,000	13

Source: BLS, *Handbook of Labor Statistics, 1947*, p. 130.

PAC stopped just short of endorsing an entire party, but its active efforts in favor of Roosevelt constituted the most vigorous application so far of the rule of "rewarding friends and punishing enemies." The PAC put unions into politics on a scale unknown prior to 1944; its methodology is now standard for the labor movement in campaign years.

1941 to 1945: Union growth.   The combination of a friendly government and a favorable economic situation had proved irresistible. In 5 years of war the organized labor movement registered a gain of almost 6 million members, from 8,944,000 in 1940 to 14,796,000 in 1945. In doing so, it raised its proportionate representation of the nonagricultural labor force from 27 per cent (more than 1 out of 4) to 36 per cent (more than 1 out of 3). The largest gains came in 1941 and 1943. In the former year there was a general tightening of the labor market from war spending and conscription, with consequent gains for organized labor, but the year is most notable for the final capitulation of the Ford Motor Company and "Little Steel" to the CIO. In 1943 there was a rapid increase in union membership, resulting from the adoption of the National War Labor Board's policy of "maintenance of membership" awards in union-management disputes. As the war progressed, the three-way split in union affiliation became more pronounced. The increase by years and its distribution are shown in Table 7-2.

RECONVERSION: STRIKE WAVE

1945: End of the war.   In 1945, Franklin D. Roosevelt died (April), and the war ended—first in Europe (June) and then in Japan (August). The problems of peace—demobilization, disarmament, reconversion of industry to nonmilitary production, and readjustment to the new world of the atomic bomb and the rise of the U.S.S.R.—all fell into the lap of the new President, Harry S. Truman. Along with them there was a labor problem.

When the fighting stopped, the voluntary no-strike, no-lockout agreement of labor and management expired. However, the wartime program of economic stabilization (wage freeze, price limitations, rationing, etc.) was still in effect; by law, it did not expire until the "emergency" was declared at an end. Unions could strike and employers could lock out, but wage increases were not legal unless they could be absorbed by profits without a rise in prices. There was violent disagreement as usual between the parties as to the effects of any increase in costs on profits. In an effort to avoid extensive work stoppages during reconversion, President Truman called a Labor-Management Conference to formulate a national industrial relations policy. The conference, composed of representatives of the AFL, the CIO, the United States Chamber of Commerce, the National Association of Manufacturers, and a number of other business and labor groups, fell flat. No common ground could be found with respect to wage increases or methods of dispute settlement and after a week or so of bickering it broke up. The stage was set for the series of massive strikes in 1946.

1946: Record strike year.   The 1946 strike year began in November, 1945, with a walkout by the United Automobile Workers (CIO) at the General Motors Corporation plants. More than 150,000 production employes took part and the dispute lasted 4 months—until the following March. In January, a strike by 750,000 Steelworkers shut down the industry and cut steel production from 85 per cent of capacity to about 6 per cent. Agreement was reached in February, the main provision being an 18-cent-per-hour wage increase, which became the pattern for 1946.

The General Motors and steel strikes were merely the lead-off actions. In January, 200,000 members of the United Electrical, Radio & Machine Workers of America walked out of 75 plants of the General Electric Company, Westinghouse, and the electrical division of General Motors Corporation. They were followed the same month by 125,000 packing-house employes. On Apr. 2, some 350,000 members of the United Mine Workers of America stopped work in the bituminous coalpits and stayed out until the Federal government seized the mines and a new contract was negotiated between Lewis and the Secretary of the Interior. On May 23 the Brotherhood of Locomotive Engineers and the Brotherhood of Railroad Trainmen stopped work in the first nationwide railway strike since passage of the Railway Labor Act in 1926. They brought all principal rail traffic to a standstill for 2 days. During the first week of June, 75,000 anthracite coal miners stayed away from the job while a new contract was being negotiated with the operators. In September a strike of maritime workers paralyzed all shipping on the East, West, and Gulf Coasts. The same month, electric light and power were cut off in the Pittsburgh area by a strike of an independent employes' association, and 30,000 truck drivers walked off the job in New York City. In November, Lewis called another strike of 300,000 miners in the bituminous coal fields.

All told, there were 31 large strikes involving 10,000 or more workers which began in 1946. They involved 2,925,000 employes and produced most of the 116 million man-days of idleness resulting from work stoppages during the year, the highest total since records have been kept.

1947: John L. Lewis versus the United States.   The last of the big strikes of 1946 was a walkout of 300,000 soft-coal miners. The shutdown was not only a threat to the national welfare (winter was coming on, stocks of coal were low, and fuel was badly needed for steel and other basic industries); it was also a strike against the government. The soft-coal mines had been under the direction of a Federal Coal Mines Administrator since May, when President Truman took them over to put a stop to a strike over new contract terms. After a series of charges and counter-charges by Lewis and Administrator Krug (Secretary of Interior), the miners stayed away from work on Nov. 21. There was no formal strike call, merely the published statement of Lewis that no contract existed between the union and the government. That was enough; in coal mining the rule was "no contract, no work." The notice was the signal for industry-wide shutdown.

However, Lewis's move had been anticipated; 3 days before the walk-out (or "stayaway"), the government had obtained an injunction restraining the United Mine Workers of America or its president from issuing any such notice. On Dec. 3, Lewis and the union were found guilty of both civil and criminal contempt. The union was fined $3.5 million ($250,000 a day for the 14 days of the work stoppage) and Lewis was fined $10,000. The injunction was extended indefinitely. Lewis then directed the miners to go back to work while the Supreme Court reviewed the decision. In March, 1947, the Court upheld the contempt conviction and ruled that the Norris–La Guardia Act was inapplicable to the Federal government acting as employer. Lewis backed down and the strike appeared to be broken. Three weeks later, the mines were shut again.

Late in March, 1947, an explosion at the Centralia (Illinois) Coal Company No. 5 mine killed 111 men. Three days later, Lewis wrote the officers and members of the union that a memorial period (which was in accordance with their contract) should be observed from Mar. 31 to Apr. 6. On Apr. 3, the Federal Administrator shut down 518 soft-coal mines indefinitely, pending review of safety conditions, while Lewis argued that all but two mines in the country (which met the full requirements of the Safety Code) should be closed. By Apr. 10, the shutdown was still in effect and the government questioned the union's good faith. Lewis then authorized the district presidents to permit reopening of individual mines which they believed to be safe, and production slowly returned to normal. There is little doubt that Lewis's intransigence during 1947 was a major factor in producing the Taft-Hartley Act of 1947, with its strict regulation of all phases of collective bargaining, just as the chicanery of Jimmy Hoffa 10 years later was a prime cause of the Landrum-Griffin Act of 1959.

POSTWAR UNITED STATES LABOR POLICY: REGULATION

The issue: Voluntarism versus intervention.   The Second World War added a great deal to American experience in labor regulation, but its applicability to peacetime industrial relations was a subject of vigorous debate. The principal comparisons were of results obtained by the National War Labor Board as contrasted with experience under the War Labor Disputes Act. The work of the NWLB was a combination of mediation and arbitration, and in its most successful department—the settlement of disputes between employers and employes—it had no statutory authority to compel either the submission of disputes or the acceptance of its decisions. The whole thing was voluntary. Employers and unions brought in their problems, argued them before the Board, and accepted the rulings which came forth—often with protest and grumbling—as personal mandates. There were some refusals by both unions and employers to accept Board orders, but on the whole, the rate of compliance was exceptionally high.

responsibility of the N.W.L.B.

The (Smith-Connally) War Labor Disputes Act of 1943, on the other hand, was quite different. There was nothing voluntary about the law; it was a return to the tried and true principles of definition, requirement, governmental intervention, and penalties for violation. And the almost unanimous verdict is that it missed fire, whereas the War Labor Board, resting on voluntary compliance by employers and unions, was successful. The obvious conclusion, said some, was that the road to good industrial relations is less government intervention and more reliance on "free collective bargaining" between employers and employes, with no public agencies taking part to cloud the issues.

Real industrial Relations.

There were others, however, who accepted this argument only with important reservations. Their point was that a wartime experience, with its compulsions of patriotism, coupled with a real national emergency, was a poor basis for predicting what would happen in peacetime. These reservations came quickly to the surface during the strike-bound year of 1946. Within 2 years of the end of the war, intervention won a sweeping victory with the passage of the Taft-Hartley Act, and there seemed little likelihood of a return to the "good old days" when labor disputes were regarded as private fights between employers and unions.

1943 to 1947: Restrictive state labor laws.   Between 1943 and 1947, the change in public sentiment and the flood of restrictive labor laws which accompanied it had already amounted to a practical revolution. In addition to Federal statutes, more than 30 states had amended their constitutions or passed laws restricting union activity. In content, the state laws had everything to be found in the War Labor Disputes Act or the Taft-Hartley Act, plus many details never yet framed in a Federal statute. Among other things, the states:

1.   Regulated and prohibited strikes
2.   Called for secret-ballot elections prior to walkouts, picketing, and boycotts
3.   Demanded incorporation, annual reports, and financial statements
4.   Made unions suable and their agreements legally enforceable in the courts
5.   Required the licensing of pickets and union business agents
6.   Outlawed the closed and union shops and preferential hiring
7.   Prohibited political contributions by unions
8.   Established compulsory arbitration as the method of settling disputes in important industries
9.   Defined union unfair labor practices of various sorts
10. Prohibited mass or abusive picketing
11. Authorized seizure, injunctions, damage suits, discharge, fines, and imprisonment for various types of violation

Some of it, particularly the early legislation, went too far and was declared unconstitutional by the courts: compulsory union incorporation in Colorado; the embargo on jurisdictional strikes, hot cargo, and secondary boycotts in California; the licensing of union business agents in Florida and Texas; and even the requirement of union financial reports in Idaho. On the other hand, much of it stood and still stands, as a network of rules and regulations for union administrators to cope with in the conduct of their business. The most important limitation upon the effectiveness of the states in regulating union activity was their limited jurisdiction (to matters of intrastate concern) and the doctrine of the supremacy of Federal law. Whatever consolation this limitation might have been for union leaders, however, was soon dispelled by the Taft-Hartley Act, which contained a passage specifically giving state open-shop (right-to-work) laws precedence over the Federal statute.

By 1946, with strikes everywhere, Congress was also restive. Although it was an election year, the Federal legislature succeeded in passing a short law, the Lea Act,[16] designed to put a stop to featherbedding by musicians in the radio broadcasting industry, amended the Hobbs Antiracketeering Law,[17] and then enacted the Case bill, a major control measure with a number of the features later found in the Taft-Hartley Act. The Case bill was vetoed by President Truman, and Congress was unable

[16] U.S. Code 1946, Title 47, Sec. 506.
[17] U.S. Code 1946, Supp. III, Title 18, Sec. 1951.

to produce the two-thirds majority required to pass it over his disapproval. Part of the shock of the Taft-Hartley law the following year was due to its successful passage over the President's veto, until then regarded as a safe defense by organized labor.

1946 to 1947: The portal-to-portal pay controversy.   During 1946 and 1947, the portal-to-portal pay dispute blew up into a major issue with repercussions that probably helped to bring about passage of the Taft-Hartley Act. It was touched off by a Supreme Court decision, *Anderson v. Mt. Clemens Pottery Co.*,[18] in which the portal-to-portal doctrine previously in effect in mines and lumber camps was applied to manufacturing. The doctrine was that "travel time" (from the mine "portal" to the job and back again at the end of shift) should be considered "time worked" in computing pay and overtime, if the exertion (trip) was under the employer's control or for his benefit. At the Mt. Clemens (Michigan) Pottery Company, the exertion consisted of punching in on the time clock, cleaning up, walking to and from work locations in the factory, turning lights on and off, etc. The decision made possible an avalanche of overtime wage claims by unions under the Fair Labor Standards Act (many of them at a penalty rate of triple damages) which mounted up to between $5 and $6 *billion* in the spring of 1947. To remedy the situation, Congress passed the Portal-to-Portal Act of 1947,[19] with, among other things, a cutoff date for back claims of May 14, 1947, except where a written contract or custom already in effect supported the claim.[20]

1947: THE TAFT–HARTLEY ACT

The Labor Management Relations (Taft-Hartley) Act of 1947 was the answer to 12 years of demands for amendment of the "one-sided" Wagner Act; hence, its most important section, Title I, was (and is) a heavily amended National Labor Relations Act. But that is not all there is to the law. It was also an attempt to summarize the national labor policy in a single statute and to extend governmental regulation to several phases of labor-management relations previously left up to the parties themselves. In the Commons and Andrews sequence of "suppression—toleration—en-

[18] 328 U.S. 680 (1946).

[19] Public 49, 80th Cong., 1st sess.

[20] The portal-to-portal pay issue is an excellent research assignment involving as it does several Supreme Court cases: *Tennessee Coal, Iron & Railroad v. Muscoda Local 123* [321 U.S. 590 (1944)]; *Jewell Ridge Coal Corp. v. Local 6167, UMWA* [325 U.S. 161 (1945)]; and others, including the Mt. Clemens case, as well as two major laws and the administrative rulings under them, the Fair Labor Standards Act and the Portal-to-Portal Act. Details of the parties, arguments, settlements, etc., can be found in current volumes of the *Monthly Labor Review, New York Times,* and other news sources.

couragement—intervention," it represents the final step, taken a short 12 to 15 years after the government's attitude turned to encouragement. In the Taft-Hartley Act, the Congress set definite—and in some cases very restrictive—limits to union activities which might prejudice the rights of employers, employes, and the public. In doing so, it necessarily distinguished between *the union* (as a quasi-corporate official entity) and *its members,* by giving the latter rights against the union.

The purpose of the law is protection. It still protects unions against employer unfair labor practices, but it also protects employers and employes (including union members) against *union* unfair labor practices, and it protects the government, political parties, and the general public against specified undesirable acts by labor organizations.

The Taft-Hartley Act was violently opposed by labor leaders, was passed over the veto of President Truman, was labeled the "slave labor law" by union officials, and its repeal was a major political objective of organized labor for a number of years. Nevertheless, by the pragmatic tests of survival and its apparent effect on the labor movement, the law has hardly turned out to be a union-wrecking instrument as was predicted. Although unquestionably clumsy and unworkable in part (the anti-closed-shop provisions, for example), discriminatory (non-Communist affidavits for union officials, but not for employers), and vague, it stood practically unchanged for 12 years (with only one minor procedural amendment) while organized labor advanced steadily in membership, finances, contract coverage, wage increases, and fringe benefits. At the same time, the law did redress the balance in favor of the individual worker and the small employer who may be as much at the mercy of a million-member union as they are under the thumb of a big corporation as employer or competitor.

The primary intent of the Taft-Hartley Act was to indicate that unions had come of age and were responsible for their actions, just like any other big and powerful organizations. The actions of unions, it implied, might affect adversely employers, workers (whether union members or not), and others, including the public in general. Specific protections were written into the act in favor of all three.

For the benefit of *employers:* The closed shop was outlawed, the union shop permitted conditionally, and state right-to-work laws (outlawing compulsory union membership in any form) were given precedence over Federal legislation. Unions of foremen were left unprotected, and unions of plant guards were denied permission to affiliate with other unions. Featherbedding, jurisdictional strikes, secondary and hot-goods boycotts, refusal to bargain in good faith, coercion of employers to violate the law— all were made union unfair labor practices. Unions were made suable and labor agreements were defined as contracts at law. Government officials were authorized to ask for injunctions in some cases and were required to do so in others, to halt union violations of the law.

For the benefit of *workers:* Employes were given the right to reject union membership except under valid union-shop agreements, and union coercion to force them to join was made an unfair labor practice. Professional and craft employes were encouraged to organize independently. Secret-ballot elections were required for representation and union-shop elections.[21] Union members under union-shop agreements could not be put in bad standing for anything except failure to pay fees and dues; excessive or discriminatory fees were made an unfair labor practice. Checkoff of dues required the union member's written consent and was revocable within 1 year or earlier. Unions were required to make an annual financial report to each member to qualify for protection by the NLRB; the audit and regulation of union trust funds was prescribed.

For the benefit of *others:* A national-emergency strike procedure was set up: fact-finding board, delay (80 days), a secret ballot of employes, etc. To qualify for protection by the NLRB, unions had to make extensive annual reports containing general and financial information to the Secretary of Labor, and union officials were required to sign non-Communist affidavits. Union political contributions or expenditures were forbidden. Strikes against the Federal government were made illegal and striking employes were subject to immediate discharge and loss of any accrued rights.

The tests: Compliance, constitutionality, legislative review.   Every piece of major social legislation in this country must pass three tests before it is considered established as public policy. First, it must be upheld by the courts as to constitutionality and in the interpretation of its provisions. Second, it must get public approval; that is, it must be accepted by the general public, especially by the individuals to whom it applies. Third, it is certain to come before the legislative body which produced it, for extension, modification, or repeal. If the law is concerned with controversial subject matter and involves a considerable shift of policy, the hurdles are correspondingly higher and the pressure on judges, administrators, and legislators is increased. A period of several years is usually required before it can be assumed that the statute has been absorbed into the general body of administrative and judicial rulings and into institutional practice.

On the judicial front, the constitutionality of the Taft-Hartley Act was soon established, without the loss of a provision. Four years after the law was passed, on the motion of Senator Taft, Congress deleted the requirement of a secret-ballot election before negotiation of a union-shop agreement. Other than that, the law went 12 years without amendment—until 1959—when much more severe restrictions were written into it to restrain various kinds of picketing, tighten up on secondary and hot-goods boycotts, require extensive reports by all unions as a matter of law, and give

[21] The latter was eliminated in 1951. Public 189, 82d Cong.

states the right to handle labor disputes which the NLRB turns down on grounds of size.[22]

The administrative record is equally impressive. A simple—though perhaps not conclusive—test of compliance is the workload of the NLRB, the principal administrative agency responsible for enforcing the law. In a sample year (1963 to 1964), for instance, the NLRB received 27,403 complaints or petitions, from the following sources:

17,226 from unions
6,643 from individuals (employes, both union and nonunion)
3,534 from employers
——————
27,403 total

A majority of the petitions from unions (10,017, or 58 per cent) were requests for representation elections, the remainder being charges of unfair labor practices by employers. On the other hand, the overwhelming majority of complaints by individual employes (5,865, or 88 per cent) and most of those by employers (2,546, or 72 per cent) were charges of unfair labor practices. In the 5,865 cases where individual employes were the complainants, 3,685 of the accusations (slightly over 60 per cent) were aimed at employers, and in 2,180 situations a union was named as the offender. During the year, 98 union-shop deauthorization petitions were filed with the Board.

The Board, in turn, closed 26,715 cases during the year. It settled 15,074 unfair labor practice cases, conducted 7,529 representation elections involving more than 550,000 employes, certified 4,296 unions as collective bargaining representatives, and petitioned the courts for 270 injunctions, 256 of them to restrain union unfair labor practices, and the remaining 14 to put a stop to employer violations. It was involved in six Supreme Court decisions and 244 reviews by courts of appeal, with marked success at both levels.[23]

The issue.   The basic issue of the law was *voluntarism* versus *intervention.* That means that its passage was a move *away from* a governmental policy of "hands off" in industrial relations and a move *in the direction of* closer supervision of union-management affairs. The act was

[22] In the Labor-Management Reporting and Disclosure Act of 1959. See Appendix to Chap. 9 for text and commentary on the Taft-Hartley Act.

[23] 29th Annual Report of the National Labor Relations Board, for the Fiscal Year ended June 30, 1964, Appendix A, *passim.* The annual reports of the Board are important sources of information for the student of labor relations. The activities of the agency are recorded in considerable detail, both statistically and descriptively. A reading of the most recent annual review is strongly recommended to any student wishing to get a "feel" of the nature of labor-management controversy at the point where tension is highest.

considered by some to indicate abandonment of our previous governmental policy of encouraging the parties to labor disputes to reach decisions voluntarily by means of free collective bargaining, in favor of a
policy in which the government intervenes at every point of the proceeding, with rules covering all steps in the bargaining process and even some
of the terms of the contract itself.[24]

On the other side, the law's supporters replied: What free collective
bargaining? Is it "free" collective bargaining to tie the employer's hands
behind his back (the Wagner Act), deny the courts the right to issue injunctions (Norris–La Guardia Act), and turn organized labor loose to
kick, gouge, and slug in the clinches, without even any responsibility under
the antitrust laws (the Clayton Act and the Hutcheson decision)? The
former setup may have contributed to "equality" of bargaining power in
the days when unions were small and the labor movement numbered less
than 5 million members, but what now, with 17 million trade unionists
and some labor organizations bigger than the biggest corporations? If it is
"intervention" to have a few rules for unions to follow in their dealings
with individual workers and employers, say these spokesmen, then let's
have a little.

The union reply to this, of course, is that all the things that were
denied to the employer during the 12 years of the Wagner and Norris–La
Guardia Acts were inequitable and unfair and should have been made
illegal, that their elimination simply put the two organizations (union and
corporation) on an equal plane and permitted free and equal bargaining
without interference by labor spies, strikebreakers, blacklists, and discriminatory discharges. To which, management counters with the questions: Are unions and their leaders perfect? Are there not labor racketeers
(citing the reports of the McClellan committee)? Should not unions be
required to bargain in good faith? Is there not featherbedding? Should
employers be handcuffed while unions settle their private grudges in jurisdictional strikes? Should not an individual employe have the right to
decide for himself whether or not he wants to join a union? And so on.

The issue *is* voluntarism versus intervention, but, like everything else,
it is a question of degree. No responsible labor leader is on record as asking for complete hands off by the government, for a return to pre-Wagner
Act days; and employers have very definite ideas of how far and in what
direction intervention should proceed (short of compulsory arbitration,
for example). The Taft-Hartley Act was a long step in the general direction that employers wanted to go. The Labor-Management Reporting and
Disclosure Act of 1959 was another. It appears settled that Commons and

[24] For a carefully argued statement of this point of view, see George W. Taylor,
Government Regulation of Industrial Relations (Englewood Cliffs, N.J.: Prentice-Hall,
Inc., 1948) and his contrast of "government-sponsored" and "government-regulated"
collective bargaining.

Andrews were correct in their prognosis, and that government intervention, of greater or lesser degree, will be an important factor in the industrial relations of the future in this country. The character and extent of
the intervention, however, will be major issues for a long, long time.

1948 TO 1953: THE KOREAN CONFLICT

It has been the fate of America during the twentieth century to go to
war under Democratic Presidents. This has been fortunate for organized
labor. Although it may be argued that any President would have had to
follow an equally friendly policy toward unions in wartime (McKinley
really inaugurated the tradition in 1898 during the Spanish-American
War), the fact remains that the war Presidents since 1900 have all been
both Democrats (Wilson, FDR, and Truman) and noticeably well disposed to organized labor prior to the event. In the Korean conflict, as in
the First and Second World Wars, unions increased in membership, added
to their bank accounts, and registered gains in wages, hours, and conditions of work of members.

The 1948 election. The upset reelection of President Truman in
1948 was as much of a surprise to his supporters, which included organized labor almost to a man, as it was to his opponent, Governor Thomas
E. Dewey of New York. Since Truman carried into office with him a
Democratic majority in both houses of Congress and had campaigned
vigorously against the Taft-Hartley Act, it was confidently expected by
labor leaders that the "slave-labor" law would be repealed without delay.
They were promptly disabused. The new Congress, as solidly Democratic
as its predecessor had been Republican, considered numerous suggestions,
including a bill of amendments submitted by Senator Taft, listened to
labor leaders who demanded all-out repeal or nothing—and did nothing.
Before the issue could be revived in 1950, the Korean conflict was on.

1950 to 1952: The Wage Stabilization Board. The invasion of
South Korea by the North Korean Communists on June 24, 1950, brought
war, war brought inflation, and inflation eventually brought wage and
price controls. Like the war, which nobody wanted, the stabilization program was unsatisfactory to everyone concerned, including those who did
the stabilizing. It was late in starting, interrupted by controversy, dam-
aged by clumsy administration, and finally sunk in the whirlpool of presidential politics. Wage stabilization was authorized in the Defense
Production Act of Sept. 8, 1950 [25] which gave the President power to
freeze prices on either a selective or a general basis but required each
price freeze to be accompanied by a wage freeze of the same scope.

[25] Public 774, 81st Cong.

Growth and maturity: 1936 to date

Methods and procedures were left to the Executive. Late in November the President appointed a nine-member Wage Stabilization Board (three labor, three industry, and three public representatives) on the pattern of the War Labor Board of the Second World War. Then, on Jan. 26, 1951, a general price and wage freeze was announced. By this time, the Consumer Price Index had risen 8 per cent over the June, 1950, level. In February, the labor members withdrew from all Federal mobilization agencies, including the Wage Stabilization Board, demanding a larger share in policy determination of the war program. Two months later, the President reorganized the WSB into an 18-member body (6 each of labor, industry, and public), and by the fall of 1951, the Board's regional organization was complete and functioning. It was just about a year too late; on Nov. 15, 1951, the CPI stood at 188.6 or 11 per cent over June 15, 1950.

THE STEEL DISPUTE OF 1952.   Before 1951 was out, the WSB had become entangled in the steel dispute of 1951 to 1952, which led directly to its collapse. The problem was negotiation of a new contract, covering more than 500,000 employes, between the United Steelworkers of America (CIO) and the basic steel industry. After 3 weeks of stalemated discussions the union announced a strike date, whereupon the President certified the dispute to the Wage Stabilization Board and the union postponed its walkout. The WSB recommended a substantial wage increase, fringe benefits, and a union shop. The union endorsed the proposals; the companies flatly refused them. To forestall a strike (which would shut off the supply of steel during wartime), President Truman seized the industry.

The seizure was the signal for a series of legal moves and countermoves, a 3-day strike by the union, and agreement by the Supreme Court to review the case. On June 2 (1952) the Court, in a 6 to 3 decision, held that the President had exceeded his constitutional powers and directed the return of the steel plants to their private owners. A general walkout began the same day and lasted until July 26, when a settlement was reached. The steel dispute was the WSB's Waterloo. Congress amended the Defense Production Act, taking away the Board's authority to handle disputes. The chairman and several other members resigned, and a reconstituted Board limped along until December, when it was overruled by the President in a case involving the United Mine Workers of America. Its abolition by President Eisenhower in February, 1953, was anticlimactic.[26]

[26] See Clark Kerr's article on "Governmental Wage Restraints: Their Limits and Uses in a Mobilized Economy." *American Economic Review*, May, 1952, pp. 359–384, which is both a general analysis and a specific evaluation of the experience of the Wage Stabilization Board during the Korean conflict. Kerr's note would be a good starting point for a research assignment covering the performance and accomplishments of the Board. This topic could hardly be improved on as an illustration of the possible mixture of politics, economics, and administrative confusion during a short-lived crisis period.

1946 to 1953: Union growth.   Unions came out of the Second World War with fat treasuries, big memberships, and a set of jitters concerning a postwar depression and the future of collective bargaining. However, the expected depression did not show up, and management, with few exceptions, gave no evidence of aggressive opposition. The principal cloud on organized labor's horizon was the Taft-Hartley Act, regularly blamed for everything that went wrong in union-management relations. Yet the demands for its repeal were weakened by the necessity of explaining away the union prosperity which was evident on all sides.

The Korean invasion snapped production and employment back to record high levels and produced a bargaining climate of the most favorable sort for union representatives. By the middle of 1953, national income stood at $310 billion as compared to $178 billion in 1946. There were 63 million people at work, while unemployment was a negligible 1.5 million. Union membership was at its all-time high, union security widely extended, and union contracts full of fringes, such as regular paid vacations (up to 4 weeks after 20 years), 6 to 10 paid holidays, fat shift differentials and overtime bonuses (up to triple time and a half), automatic productivity increases, cost-of-living escalator clauses, increased pension and welfare benefits, and so on. There was a new administration in Washington—Republican, no less—and its attitude toward organized labor was still unknown. The future might not be quite so rosy, but of the present and

Table 7-3. American trade-union membership, 1946–1953

Year	Total	AFL Members	%	CIO Members	%	Independents Members	%
1946	14,974,000	7,152,000	48	6,000,000	40	1,822,000	12
1947	15,414,000	7,578,000	49	6,000,000	39	1,836,000	12
1948	15,019,800	8,094,700	54	4,450,800	30	2,474,300	16
1949	14,694,900	8,143,200	55	4,314,000	29	2,237,700	16
1950	14,822,900	8,494,000	57	3,712,800	25	2,616,100	18
1951	15,772,200	9,497,400	50	4,182,900	27	2,091,900	13
1952	16,309,800	9,977,400	61	4,261,400	26	2,071,000	13
1953	17,315,600	10,438,000	60	4,837,900	28	2,039,700	12

Sources: *Statistical Abstract of the United States, 1959*, p. 238, for years 1946 and 1947. From 1948 onward, the data are from Leo Troy, "Trade Union Membership, 1897–1962," *The Review of Economics and Statistics*, February, 1965, pp. 93–113. Troy's series diverges sharply from the BLS series, particularly during the years of the Second World War (*e.g.*, his figures for 1944 and 1945 are 12,628,000 and 12,562,100), but the two draw together at the war's end. His series is used above, since the BLS series has no figures for the CIO for several years and the total is a rather free estimate of 15 million for three years in a row.

[handwritten margin note: Murray & Green died-end of an era]

immediate past there was no doubt. It was on the record. Membership figures for the years 1946 to 1953 are shown in Table 7-3.

1953 TO 1957: ERA OF COMPLACENCY

The years 1953 through 1957, covering President Eisenhower's first term and reelection, were the "return to normalcy" after the Korean conflict. There was a brief postwar recession from 1953 to 1954, a Republican President, a probusiness administration, prosperity, and full employment. However, in contrast to the same period in the 1920s, trade unions prospered along with the rest of the country. Starting late in 1952, the labor movement reorganized under new management and proceeded with the merger of the AFL and the CIO, completing the job just 3 years later, in December, 1955. By the fall of 1957, some cracks had appeared in the economic structure: a stock market decline, rise in unemployment, etc. Then, on October 4, 1957, the Space Age began with the launching by Soviet scientists of the first man-made satellite, Sputnik I. The era of complacency ended with a shock, as the Soviet Union demonstrated conclusively that it had surpassed the United States in space engineering.

[handwritten margin notes: Prosperity / a crack / -l- / Decline]

1952: New labor leaders. If there is one thing that organized labor is suspicious of, it is the military. If there is another, it is the Republican party. The two were combined in 1952 in the person of General Eisenhower as the Republican presidential candidate. This produced organized labor's first formal support of a presidential nominee. The AFL, the CIO, and the United Mine Workers of America joined in a resolution of support for the Democratic candidate, Adlai Stevenson. The Eisenhower victory then brought union officials face to face with the first possibly unfriendly Federal administration in 20 years. The shock soon made itself felt.

Five days after the election, Philip Murray, president of the CIO, died of a heart attack at the age of 66. Less than 2 weeks later, President William Green of the AFL succumbed, also to a heart attack, at the age of 79. Green was promptly replaced by George Meany, secretary-treasurer of the AFL since 1939. Murray's death, on the other hand, left two jobs open, the presidencies of the CIO and the United Steelworkers of America. Walter P. Reuther, president of the UAW, was elected top man in the CIO, while David J. McDonald, secretary-treasurer of the Steelworkers, succeeded to the presidency of the union. This cleared the decks for disposal of a piece of unfinished business, the merger of the AFL and the CIO.

[handwritten margin notes: Murray died C.I.O / Green follow A-F-L.]

1952 to 1955: The AFL–CIO merger. The purpose of the AFL–CIO merger was to unite the "House of Labor" once more as in the days

of Samuel Gompers and to put an end to the rivalry, raiding, jurisdictional disputes, and dual unionism which had grown up during the 17-year
split. Organized labor has always been a "movement," with strong feelings of brotherhood across craft and jurisdictional lines. The idea was to
bring the formal organization back in line with the basic unity of the institution, to stop the fighting between trade unionists and concentrate on
organizing the unorganized.

When Murray and Green died within a few days of each other in
November, 1952, their passing removed from the scene two former close
associates (both had been officers of the United Mine Workers of America and had learned their trade unionism from John L. Lewis) who had
been on opposite sides of the AFL-versus-CIO dispute since 1935 and
whose personal antagonisms had interfered with efforts to reunite the
federations. The new presidents, George Meany of the AFL and Walter
Reuther of the CIO, had different ideas. With clean slates, no background
of personal antagonism, and with eyes on the future instead of the past,
they immediately put the machinery in motion to bring the AFL and the
CIO together. It was a big job, reflecting credit on the two leaders and the
principal officers of both federations, and it took just 3 years to accomplish.

The key steps in the merger sequence were the negotiation of a "no-
raiding agreement" in June, 1953, which committed the unions which
signed it to respect the jurisdiction of any bona fide union covered by a
collective agreement, followed a year later (June, 1954) by an agreement to "safeguard established collective bargaining relationships," which
meant a guarantee of the existing job territories (covered by contract)
of the 94 unions signatory to the no-raiding commitment. By February,
1955, there was an "agreement for the merger" by a Joint Unity Committee, followed by approval of the new AFL–CIO constitution at the
annual meetings of the two federations early in December. The founding
convention of the AFL–CIO met December 5, 1955, with approximately
1,500 delegates present, reflecting a voting strength of 10,600,000 members from former AFL unions and 4,600,000 members from unions formerly affiliated with the CIO. The combined membership of 15,200,000
was a satisfactory 89.5 per cent of total trade-union membership of
16,990,000 for that date.

Did the merger accomplish its objectives? It unquestionably unified the
labor movement, eliminating dual organization at the national, state, and
local level, and bringing about a few inconsequential union mergers. It
greatly reduced raiding and other interunion struggles. Were the energies thus released diverted to organizing the unorganized? Here the
answer is just as clearly no. There is no evidence that organizing staffs
were increased and more campaigns mounted; in fact, quite the contrary.
What evidence there is shows reduction in organization effort and expense,

both by the Federation and its principal member unions.[27] What may have been overlooked is that elimination of "rivalry, raiding, jurisdictional disputes, and dual unionism" also meant elimination of one of the greatest stimulants in any field of activity: competition. Freed of danger from competing unions, with job territories guaranteed, many union officials have become "sunk in bureaucratic torpor," lacking in vigor and new ideas and concerned mainly with internal administrative affairs and maintenance of the *status quo.*

1954 to 1957: Prosperity.   The brief postwar recession of 1953 to 1954 brought a drop in GNP from $365.4 billion to $363.1 billion, cut national income almost $4 billion, and raised unemployment from 2.9 per cent of the labor force in 1953 to 5.6 per cent in 1954. It was soon overcome, and Prof. Arthur F. Burns, chairman of the Council of Economic Advisers, told how in his little book, *Prosperity without Inflation.*[28] The economy then took off, with successive increases in the GNP to $397.5 billion in 1955 (up $34.4), $419.2 billion in 1956 (up $21.7), and $442.5 billion in 1957 (up $23.3). Unemployment was 4.4, 4.2, and 4.3 per cent, respectively, for the 3 years.

Union membership precisely reflected economic conditions. There

Table 7-4.   American trade-union membership, 1954–1957

Year	Total	AFL		CIO		Independents	
		Members	%	Members	%	Members	%
1954	16,612,000	10,258,000	62	4,494,400	27	1,859,600	11
1955	16,989,700	10,593,100	62	4,608,300	27	1,788,300	11
		AFL–CIO					
1956	17,383,200	15,638,800—90%				1,744,400	10
1957	17,686,900	16,078,400—91%				1,608,500	9

Source: Leo Troy, "Trade Union Membership, 1897–1962," *The Review of Economics and Statistics,* February, 1965, pp. 93–113.

[27] See, for example, official reports of the AFL–CIO for 1957 and 1963. For 1957, it was reported: "As a result of these and other staff changes as of the date of this report, the Organization Department consists of 23 regional directors, 18 assistant regional directors, 215 field representatives, and 7 members of the headquarters staff, *a net reduction of 76 since the merger.*" *Proceedings, Constitutional Convention of 1957,* vol. II, p. 311 (italics added). In *Proceedings of the 5th Constitutional Convention, 1963,* vol. II, p. 275, is the statement: "the field staff was comprised of 23 regional directors, 16 assistant regional directors, 115 field representatives, and" a headquarters staff of 4. This was a further reduction of 105. Carrying the arithmetic further, the organization staff had been more than cut in half between the date of the merger and 1963: from 339 to 158.

[28] Garden City, N.Y.: Economica Books, 1958.

was a drop from the postwar high of 1953, then successive increases in
the 3 following years to the all-time peak for 1957 of 17,686,900. After that
came a long decline. Membership figures for the years 1954 to 1957 and
the distribution between the AFL–CIO and independents is shown in
Table 7-4.

1957 TO DATE: THE DECLINE OF THE LABOR MOVEMENT [29]

Since 1957, the United States labor movement has steadily lost ground
in membership, reputation, and freedom of action. The only exception,
and it is a big one, is in collective bargaining. At the bargaining table,
unions have successfully negotiated wage increases and fringe benefits of
major proportions, consistently exceeding the President's "guideposts,"
and giving rise to the argument that one of the causes of the decline was
the unions' success in getting everything they asked for, leaving "no place
to go." Nevertheless, in the face of higher and higher wages, generous job
security provisions, and fringes reaching the proportions of 13-week vacations with pay every 5 years, the road has been downhill. Whatever the
reasons (and many have been offered: union fraud and corruption, a big-
business drive to "get" the unions, restrictive legislation, the steady erosion of blue-collar jobs by automation, excessive unemployment, tired and
aging leadership), the facts were undeniable. Over-all union membership
fell 4 out of 7 years and at the low point in 1961 was more than a million

Table 7-5. American trade-union membership, 1958–1964

Year	Total	AFL–CIO		Independents	
		Members	%	Members	%
1958	17,399,000	13,994,000	81	3,405,000	19
1959	17,569,000	14,144,000	81	3,425,000	19
1960	17,505,000	14,103,000	81	3,402,000	19
1961	16,656,000	13,582,000	82	3,074,000	18
1962	16,958,000	13,846,000	82	3,112,000	18
1963	16,798,000	13,726,000	82	3,072,000	18
1964	17,187,000	14,058,000	82	3,130,000	18

Sources: BLS Bulletins 1267 (1959), 1320 (1961), 1395 (1963), and 1493 (1965). The
figures reported by the BLS have been adjusted, by the addition of estimated members
in "unaffiliated local and single-employer unions," and the subtraction of members outside the United States. The former range from 450,000 to 600,000; the latter have run
slightly over a million.

[29] See the pamphlet, *The Decline of the Labor Movement,* by Solomon Barkin,
trade unionist researcher, spokesman, and philosopher, a report to the Center for the
Study of Democratic Institutions, Santa Barbara, California, 1961.

below the peak of 1957. By 1964, the labor movement had recovered half of the lost ground, to a total of 17,187,000 members. Figures for the years 1958 to 1964 are shown in Table 7-5.

1957 to 1958: Recession.   Although preceded by the start of the McClellan committee hearings early in 1957, the recession of 1957 to 1958 gave the labor movement its first downward push. The slump was brief but severe. Instead of the $23-billion rise of the year before, GNP took a $1-billion drop; unemployment rose from 4.3 per cent to 6.8 per cent, the highest figure since 1940; and the Consumer Price Index jumped 3.3 points. Union membership fell from 17,687,000 to 17,399,000, a loss of 288,000. The downswing was counteracted by accelerated Federal spending in 1958, mainly on defense items, which together with the "built-in" stabilizers of a steep reduction of tax revenues and an increase in unemployment compensation payments, produced a record peacetime Federal deficit of $12.9 billion. The recovery of 1959 to 1960 was only partial, and by 1961 unemployment was again above 6 per cent. In the meantime, the labor movement had other things to worry about, chief among them the McClellan committee.

1957 to 1959: The McClellan committee.   In January, 1957, the United States Senate authorized an eight-man "Select Committee on Improper Activities in the Labor or Management Field," under the chairmanship of Senator John L. McClellan of Arkansas. With official pledges of support from the AFL–CIO—the executive council of which resolved "that if a trade union official decides to invoke the fifth amendment for his personal protection and to avoid scrutiny by proper legislative committees, law enforcement agencies, or other public bodies into alleged corruption on his part, he has no right to continue to hold office in his union" [30] —the McClellan committee began hearings in February. It continued throughout 1957, 1958, and on into 1959 to expose corruption and malpractices on the part of union officials, employers, and their agents ("labor relations consultants") which were shocking in nature and which eventually sent a number of men to jail and produced the Labor Management Reporting and Disclosure Act of 1959.[31]

[30] "Taking the Fifth" became a favorite method of avoiding testifying to the committee, with some unsavory characters using it scores or hundreds of times at a single hearing. See the *Monthly Labor Review,* March, 1957, pp. 350–352, for text of the AFL–CIO's Codes of Ethical Practices on "Local Union Charters," "Health and Welfare Funds," "Racketeers, Crooks, Communists, and Fascists," etc.

[31] The Hon. Robert F. Kennedy, now United States Senator from New York and formerly (1961–1964) Attorney General of the United States, was counsel and chief investigator for the McClellan committee. See his book, *The Enemy Within* (New York: Harper & Row, Publishers, Incorporated, 1960), for a revealing summary of the tactics of corrupt union officials and the problems of investigating them.

No one, no matter how prounion his sentiments, has had the temerity to argue that the McClellan committee disclosures had no effect on the labor movement, and many have felt that the publicity given fraud and corruption on the part of labor leaders—especially Teamster officials— was a critical factor in the decline from 1957 onward. Although delicately omitting to mention either the committee or any of the principals by name, Solomon Barkin drew the following conclusions, in a section headed "The Sullied Image of Unions": [32]

Effect of McClellan Committee

The scandals that have engulfed some leaders of organized labor have alienated many one-time friendly elements in society. Widespread skepticism as to the sincerity and purposes of sections of the trade union movement has replaced the almost unqualified enchantment prevalent in the Thirties. Politicians have found it possible to build careers on exposures of union corruption. Middle-class protagonists of social reform tend to shy away from alliances with organized labor, whereas until recently they regarded such support as essential. . . .

The prime object of the McClellan committee's investigation was the Teamster union and especially some of its top officers—Vice-president Frank Brewster, President Dave Beck, and his successor, James Hoffa, who was elected while under charges of corruption from both the committee and the AFL–CIO. Along with the Teamsters, however, complaints were received and studies made of the Allied Industrial Workers, The Carpenters, the Operating Engineers, the Bakery and Confectionery Workers, the United Textile Workers, and the Amalgamated Meat Cutters and Butcher Workmen.[33] In March, 1958, the committee issued an interim report suggesting corrective legislation in five areas of labor-management and internal union relations. A second report was published in August, 1959, covering five specific areas of corruption and malpractice, with especial emphasis on "James R. Hoffa." [34] A month later, on Sept. 14, 1959, President Eisenhower signed into law the Labor-Management Reporting and Disclosure Act of 1959. It was a comprehensive statute, regulating in minute detail many aspects of union organization and operation and containing a number of severely restrictive amendments to the Taft-Hartley Act. The law was voted through by Congress and signed by the President in the midst of a historic work stoppage, the steel strike of 1959.

1st report

2nd report & James R. Hoffa

& LAW

1959: Steel strike.   The steel dispute of 1959 resulted from the clash of two rigidly held points of view which were developed through newspaper advertising and public statements into rallying points for employers in general and the labor movement as a whole. Management (in

---

[32] S. Barkin, *The Decline of the Labor Movement,* pp. 26–27.

[33] For a brief survey of developments, see the *Monthly Labor Review,* April, May, August, and December, 1957.

[34] See the *Monthly Labor Review,* May, 1958, pp. 518–520, and September, 1959, pp. 981–991, for text and summaries.

featherbedding ???

the person of a committee representing 12 major steel producers) led off
by requesting extension of the agreement then in effect for another 2 or 3
years without change as "noninflationary" or, as an alternative, the
countering of any increase in wages or benefits by a relaxation of restrictive work rules (featherbedding) in steel plants to permit more efficient
operation. The union refused even to discuss any modification of local
work rules (President McDonald of the United Steel Workers conceded
that 100,000 jobs, or about 1 in 5 in the steel industry depended on restrictive work rules) and demanded an extensive list of wage and fringe
improvements, which it held it was entitled to as a result of productivity
gains in the industry since the last contract was negotiated in 1956. On
July 15, 500,000 steelworkers struck. Three months later they were still
out, with secondary unemployment (layoffs in related industries) raising
total unemployment due to the strike to the neighborhood of 1 million.

why that
way aslike

On Nov. 7, after 116 days of shutdown, the government finally obtained a Taft-Hartley 80-day injunction on grounds of a national emergency. Before the 80-day period ended, the strike was settled. It was the
heaviest single work stoppage that the country had ever suffered in terms
of man-days lost (both primary and secondary) and raised once again the
question of the permissible limits of "free collective bargaining" in basic
industries. The strike was widely viewed as an irresponsible display of
stubbornness and disregard for the national welfare. It arose just as the
country was pulling out of the recession of 1958 and had as a background the McClellan committee's lurid picture of violence and fraud
within the Teamsters and other unions. It was a perfect setting for the
passage of a tough law and the Landrum-Griffin bill was just that.

Views

Exam

1959: Landrum-Griffin Act.   Twelve years seems to be the interval
between Federal labor laws of the first rank: the Wagner Act of 1935, the
Taft-Hartley Act of 1947, and the Labor-Management Reporting and Disclosure Act of 1959. The 1959 law was Congress's first full-scale attempt
to regulate the internal operations of unions, that is, their relations with
their members. In practical effect, this means the relations between union
officials and members. It was a long step. The statute outlined a detailed
and punitive list of things that unions, union officers, and union employes
(as well as employers and "labor relations consultants") must do or refrain from doing, with criminal penalties (fines and imprisonment) for
violation and several provisions for civil actions—lawsuits and injunctions
—as well as investigations by the Secretary of Labor. In addition, the act
substantially amended the Taft-Hartley Law, mostly in the direction of
greater restrictions upon unions.[35]

Do's
Don'ts
analysed b/q
Union

The net effect of the Labor Reform statute (apart from the amend-

[35] The law is discussed extensively in Chap. 11, and the text, with commentary,
is included in the Appendix thereto.

ments of the Taft-Hartley Act) is to remove unions from the category of private voluntary organizations and give them full status as quasi-public institutions, responsible at law to their members and to the Federal government, and under the obligation to conduct their affairs in the full light of publicity with respect to the most intimate details of financial and administrative practice.

1961 TO DATE: A FRIEND IN THE WHITE HOUSE AGAIN

1960: Labor backs Kennedy-Johnson.   The days of impartiality were over. If anything more were needed, the Landrum-Griffin Act of 1959, passed with the backing of President Eisenhower, was the clinching argument. Organized labor was now a full political partner of the Democratic party and no one knew better that the key to Federal favors lay with the occupant of the White House. On August 26, 1960, the general board of the AFL–CIO, meeting in Washington, endorsed the Democratic candidates, John F. Kennedy and Lyndon B. Johnson, for President and Vice-President respectively, and called on trade unionists everywhere to give them "full and unstinting" support. The subsequent Kennedy-Johnson victory, by a thin popular margin but a comfortable Electoral College majority, was nowhere received with greater enthusiasm than at AFL–CIO headquarters, across Lafayette Park from the President's mansion. The substantial nature of the victory soon became apparent in President Kennedy's labor-agency appointments.

1961: Secretary of Labor Goldberg.   In mid-December, 1960, President-elect Kennedy announced the impending nomination of Arthur J. Goldberg, for years General Counsel to the CIO and the United Steelworkers of America, as Secretary of Labor. Goldberg replaced James P. Mitchell, a former department store executive (Macy's and Bloomingdale's), who had served through most of Eisenhower's two terms. The significance of the shift became apparent as other key appointments were released: Frank W. McCulloch, former administrative assistant to Senator Paul H. Douglas of Illinois, as chairman of the National Labor Relations Board; William E. Simkin, an experienced arbitrator and expert on labor-management relations, as director of the Federal Mediation and Conciliation Service; and W. Willard Wirtz, labor lawyer, university law professor (Northwestern), and arbitrator, as Undersecretary of Labor. To organized labor, they were a refreshing change from the management-oriented policy-makers of the previous 8 years.

1961 and 1962: The Kennedy labor program.   President Eisenhower left office during a recession. The recovery of 1959 to 1960 had never been more than partial, and by the time inauguration day rolled around

in January, 1961, unemployment was a staggering 7.7 per cent (5,385,000 unemployed out of a civilian labor force of 69,837,000). The recession hit bottom in February (with 8 per cent unemployed) just as President Kennedy sent to Congress his first proposals to "get the country moving again." They consisted of temporary extension of unemployment compensation payments, up to 13 weeks (making their duration 39 weeks instead of 26); increasing the minimum wage from $1 to $1.25 per hour and increasing coverage by an additional 4,300,000 employes; raising minimum Social Security payments from $33 to $40 per month; and passage of the Area Redevelopment Act, which provided grants for retraining of unemployed workers. He also set up a Labor-Management Policy Committee, headed by Secretary Goldberg, to make recommendations for further action. In March, 1962, Congress passed the Manpower Development and Training Act,[36] which authorized a much broader retraining program than the Area Redevelopment Act.

The results were a substantial improvement over 1961. Gross national product, which had slowed to a rise of only $15.6 billion (3 per cent) between 1960 and 1961, moved up $36.7 billion, an increase of more than 7 per cent. With prices reasonably stable (the CPI was up 1.2), hours worked, weekly earnings, and total employment increased significantly.[37] Unemployment was 5.6 per cent as compared to 6.7 per cent in 1961. In September, 1962, Mr. Goldberg was appointed a Justice of the United States Supreme Court, and Willard Wirtz succeeded him as Secretary of Labor.

1962: Collective bargaining with the Federal government. On Jan. 17, 1962, President Kennedy signed Executive Order 10988, which laid down the rules for "orderly and constructive relationships . . . between employee organizations and management officials" in the executive branch of the government. Following the recommendations of a presidential task force headed by Secretary of Labor Goldberg, the order reiterated the right of government workers to join unions (or refrain from joining) without risk of coercion or reprisal, and denied recognition to unions asserting the right to strike against the government, advocating overthrow of the government by force or violence, or practicing racial, religious, or other forms of discrimination. Three types of recognition were specified: informal, the "right to be heard," to unions representing less than 10 per cent of the employes in a unit; formal recognition, with the right to be consulted, to units with 10 to 50 per cent of the employes organized; and exclusive recognition, with the right to negotiate agreements, if a majority were organized. The subject matter to be bargained was limited to

[36] Public Law 87–415.
[37] See "American Labor in 1962; A Retrospect," *Monthly Labor Review,* January, 1963, pp. 14–15, for details.

personnel policies and working conditions, with a restricted right to grievance arbitration; all budgetary matters, assignment of personnel, the mission of the agency, etc., were specifically proscribed.[38]

Notwithstanding the limited scope of the activity permitted, the order was a shot in the arm for unions of government employes. By the middle of 1965, an AP dispatch reported that the Post Office Department alone had 24,116 exclusive bargaining units and 328,500 postal employes had volunteered for the checkoff of dues. Union membership in the Federal departments was up by a third, to a total of more than 1 million.[39] The membership effects on some of the larger unions of government employes during the 4-year period, 1960 to 1964, is shown below: [40]

Union	Membership			
	1960	1964	Up	%
American Federation of State, County and Municipal Employees	210,000	235,000	25,000	12
American Federation of Government Employees	70,000	139,000	69,000	99
United Federation of Postal Clerks	135,000	139,000	4,000	3
National Association of Letter Carriers of the United States	138,000	168,000	30,000	18
National Postal Union	32,000	62,000	30,000	94
National Rural Letter Carriers Association	38,000	42,000	4,000	11
Total	623,000	785,000	162,000	26

1964 —: Labor and President Johnson.   The assassination of President Kennedy on November 22, 1963, brought to the presidency Lyndon B. Johnson, and Mr. Johnson in turn brought to the presidency the greatest vigor of presidential performance that the country had seen in generations. The new President's labor policy—much of it carried to completion during 1964, his first year in office—was essentially that of his predecessor, extended and expanded. It included an $11 billion tax cut for economic expansion, a strong protective Civil Rights Act which set up an Equal Employment Opportunity Commission to reduce job discrimination against Negroes, an Economic Opportunity Act to help poor communities and particularly their unemployed members, and best of all, a favorable attitude toward unions and collective bargaining.[41]

[38] See the *Monthly Labor Review,* February, 1962, pp. III–IV, for a summary of the order.

[39] *Los Angeles Times,* Sept. 6, 1965, I, p. 7.

[40] BLS Bulletins 1320 (1961), 1493 (1965), *passim.*

[41] For a brief summary of the year's developments, see "An Account of American Labor in 1964," *Monthly Labor Review,* December, 1964, pp. 1385–1392.

Organized labor's endorsement of President Johnson in the presidential election of 1964 was a formality. If some unionists had been cool to him before, his support of labor's objectives and the prompt enactment of a legislative program which had the approval of everyone in the labor movement quickly warmed them up. With the stimulus of the tax cut, the economic improvement which began in 1961 was carried forward and increased. By midsummer of 1964, GNP was running at a prosperity rate $40 billion (7 per cent) above the previous year ($618 billion versus $577 billion). Finally, the Republican nomination of Senator Goldwater, the most anti-union candidate since William Howard Taft, eliminated any defections. There is small doubt that solid trade-union backing contributed to the President's landslide victory on November 3, by a popular margin of 15,800,000 votes,[42] and labor leaders looked forward confidently to a long period of mutual respect and exchange of favors with the President.

THE RISE AND DECLINE OF ORGANIZED LABOR SINCE 1936   *Summary*

One conclusion stands out with respect to the years 1936 onward in American labor history. This relatively short interval has seen developments at least equal in importance for the labor movement to anything that had gone before. For one thing, organized labor grew up. The proof of this statement, if any were needed, would be the rise of union membership from 4.2 million in 1936 to 17.4 million 20 years later. With the growth came power; labor organizations found themselves in a position to influence the economic and political environment of the country. And with the power came responsibility, a shift in public sentiment of major proportions as reflected in the Taft-Hartley Act of 1947, numerous state right-to-work laws, the Landrum-Griffin Act of 1959, and eventually the penetrating and revealing investigations of the McClellan committee into union ethics and codes of conduct. And finally, as the pressure for responsibility reached a climax, the labor movement sustained an abrupt check: freedom of action was curtailed, membership dropped off, prestige declined.

What factors contributed to the rise of organized labor to its position of power and responsibility and then reversed the trend so sharply?

Support of the Federal government. A feature of most of the period—and especially its early portion—was a national government friendly to organized labor and its objectives. The Federal government is incomparably the most powerful single force in the country. In legislation, administration, and court decisions, it steadily underwrote the thesis that

[42] Senator Goldwater carried only six states in one of the most paradoxical elections on record. Five of the six were in the Deep South—Alabama, Georgia, Louisiana, Mississippi, and South Carolina—and they went Republican against the first Southern Democratic candidate for President since the Civil War.

organized labor and collective bargaining are desirable institutions and must be protected and encouraged. Even with the swing to regulation of unions in the Taft-Hartley Act and the Landrum-Griffin Act, the basic protections of the Wagner Act of 1935 were left untouched. It is hard to believe that trade unionism could have thrived as it did without this backing. Nevertheless, the shift toward "intervention" (Commons and Andrews's fourth stage of governmental response) inevitably applied the brakes. The downswing in union fortunes began and gained momentum during the last years of the Eisenhower administration, certainly the most neutral of all Federal administrations to organized labor since 1932.

Troubled times: Depression and war.

The depression psychosis was well fixed by 1936, and "security" was a national objective. To the laboring man security meant a job to which he had a right. This was also the union view, and where they could, unions fought for jobs for their members and for an equitable distribution of the existing work among them. The "new economics" was born that year, with its emphasis upon purchasing power and the maintenance of continuous full employment. It called for a more equal distribution of personal incomes and for government spending to correct for deficiencies in private investment. This was economics that unionists could understand and vote for. Trade-union objectives are higher wages, greater purchasing power, and more security for low-income groups. Deficit spending was a politically attractive doctrine, since it meant either higher appropriations or lower taxation or both. Unions supported it and the government supported the unions, with a high degree of mutuality of interest and purpose.

Two wars with only a 5-year interval between (1941–1945 to 1950–1952) eliminated depression but not the depression psychology. The need for uninterrupted production in wartime and later in postwar reconversion gave organized labor the lever it needed. Unions capitalized on the favorable attitudes of wartime agencies and on the security fixation of workers still fearful of a return to postwar mass unemployment. They recruited members, negotiated plant-wide and company-wide agreements, blanketed industries with standard contract clauses, and fought for and obtained closed- and union-shop provisions to maintain membership and stabilize contract administration. Long-term continuing prosperity did the rest, at least through 1957, the last year of low postwar unemployment. (The rate for 1957 was 4.3 per cent.) In 1958, unemployment averaged 6.8 per cent and it did not drop below 5 per cent again until 1965. However, while the specter of the 1930s was again being raised, union membership failed to respond. Why? One explanation has been the leadership pattern.

Leadership and the new challenge.

The rise of organized labor in the 1930s and 1940s coincided with the rise of a new set of leaders, whose vision and willingness to rebel forced the labor movement to accept a form of organization (industrial) appropriate to the times and whose energy and determination carried to success the shock tactics necessary to organize the automobile, steel, and other mass-production industries. The man most responsible was John L. Lewis, president of the United Mine Workers of America, and his principal lieutenants were Sidney Hillman, president of the Amalgamated Clothing Workers, and Philip Murray, at first chairman of the Steel Workers Organizing Committee and then President of the United Steelworkers of America. Now these leaders are gone and a new generation presides over the labor movement while once more a fundamental structural change in the pattern of employment in industry (automation) raises problems for unions. Where are the leaders who will have the courage and vision to break with the past as Lewis, Hillman, and Murray did in 1935? With one or two notable exceptions they are not in sight, and another major revolution (like the CIO in 1935) may be required to break out of the traditional pattern toward new objectives. One of these objectives must be the organization of clerical, sales, technical, and professional workers.

Organizing the white-collar workers.   The main effect of automation is to substitute white-collar (clerical, technical, professional) workers for blue-collar employes. In the expansionist days of the 1930s and 1940s, labor organizers paid little attention to office staff and concentrated on the P&M (production and maintenance) workers in the shops and factories across the nation. There were enough of the latter and to spare for all the organizers available and their success was reflected in the rising mass memberships of unions in the steel, auto, rubber, and electrical industries. Now the available blue-collar labor force in these and other mass-production industries is either stationary or growing very slowly; in some, it is actually declining while production moves steadily ahead. The balance of employment has shifted heavily in favor of white-collar and service occupations. For example, in July, 1965, a civilian labor force of 74,854,000 persons was distributed as follows: [43]

White-collar workers	32,271,000	(women: 14,012—43%)
Blue-collar workers	27,614,000	(women: 4,124—15%)
Service workers	9,712,000	(women: 6,254—64%)

Unions have never had much luck organizing the white-collar employe.[44] However, unless something can be done to make organization attractive to the clerical, sales, technical, and service occupations, with their high proportions of women workers, their generally higher educa-

[43] *Employment and Earnings,* August, 1965, p. 10.
[44] See, for a discussion of the problem, "Unionization of White-collar Employees: Extent, Potential, and Implications," by Benjamin Solomon and Robert K. Burns, in *The Journal of Business,* April, 1963, p. 141.

tional qualifications, their different environments and routines, the decline of the labor movement will continue and may be accelerated.

The merger of the AFL and the CIO.   One thing the present leaders of organized labor have done is to bring about "labor unity." In 1936, the labor movement was split into two segments headed up by the American Federation of Labor (AFL) and the Committee for Industrial Organization, later to become the Congress of Industrial Organizations (CIO).[45] Twenty years afterward, the break was repaired and the two came together in the AFL–CIO.[46] The key figures in the merger were George Meany and Walter Reuther, presidents respectively of the AFL and the CIO, and their announced purpose was to conserve energies being spent by trade unionists in fighting each other and to combine against recalcitrant employers for greater efficiency in organizing the unorganized.

Has the promise been realized? NO

The answer can only be no. From practically the effective date of the merger (which took several years to jell) the labor movement has been losing members rather than gaining them. While other factors have also been influential, there is no evidence whatever of an increase in organizing activity, unless it be by the Teamsters, who refused to sign the no-raiding agreement from the beginning and in 1957 were ejected from the new federation for unethical practices. The facts are that organizing staffs were cut back sharply by both the federation and a number of the more important member unions immediately after their jurisdictions were guaranteed and dual unionism forbidden (and the security of union officials thereby enhanced). It seemed never to occur to the members of the AFL–CIO Executive Council that in building fences around existing job territories they were also eliminating one of the greatest of all stimulants to achievement: competition. There may be more than coincidence in the rise of union membership from 1936 to 1956 with the labor movement divided into competing leagues and the subsequent decline of union membership from 1957 onward after competition between unions had been voted unfair.

Political action.   In its new mass memberships recruited during the 1930s and 1940s, organized labor discovered a potent political weapon. It was already organized—for economic action. Why not for political action too? All that was needed was a practical set of political techniques. The brain and energy of Sidney Hillman and his colleagues demonstrated that union structure (especially industrial union structure) was as well fitted for political campaigning as for strike action and picketing. Since

[45] The CIO was formed in October, 1935 as a committee of the AFL, but its members were suspended by the AFL Executive Council in 1936 for "dual unionism."

[46] See above, pp. 199–201 for details.

the techniques adopted (by the Political Action Committee—PAC—in 1943) call for alliance with the preferred political party (usually the Democratic party) at local, state, and national levels, organized labor's contribution to the result is always open to argument. Nevertheless, there were President Franklin D. Roosevelt's reelection to a fourth term in 1944, Truman's upset victory over Dewey in 1948, and Senator John F. Kennedy's win over Vice-President Richard Nixon in 1960, all of them with the unquestioned support of trade unionists of every persuasion. Also, in 1954, 1956, and 1958, there were Democratic majorities in both houses of Congress—in 1956, in the face of a popular majority for President Eisenhower of almost 10 million.

For the future the raw statistical facts were undeniable. With something like 17 million trade unionists in the United States, a candidate who could mobilize the union vote could count on at least double that many potential ballots to start with. If union organization and persuasion were applied to political activity with the same vigor that they had previously been applied to the attainment of improved wages, hours, and working conditions, could the labor bloc be defeated? From a number of quarters have come warnings of a Labor party if union representatives are overlooked in political planning. While the very suggestion would make Sam Gompers move restlessly in his grave, the 1960s are not 1886 nor even 1924. As a *potential* political power of the first order, organized labor has arrived.

READINGS

Joseph G. Rayback, *A History of American Labor* (New York: The Macmillan Company, 1966) brings the story of the labor movement up past the merger of the AFL–CIO. A crosscut analysis of organized labor, with most of the topics taken from the recent past, is Jack Barbash, *Unions and Union Leadership* (New York: Harper & Row, Publishers, Incorporated, 1960).

EIGHT

THEORIES OF
UNIONISM

The labor movement has come a long way in the United States since Sam Gompers was elected president of the American Federation of Labor in 1886. It has multiplied by a factor of 25 (from about 650,000 to 17,000,-000) while the total population grew by 3.5.[1] Collective bargaining—adopted formally as national policy in 1935—has revolutionized the status of wage and salary earners, strengthening and stabilizing the labor market through job-security devices, annual pay increases related to the rise in productivity, and the steady accrual of fringe benefits. In membership, economic power, and political influence, organized labor has supplanted such previously dominant groups as the farmer and the independent businessman. There are four times as many members of unions as there are people working on farms and three times as many as there are proprietors or partners running their own businesses. "Labor" nowadays means *organized* labor. And to a considerable degree, organized labor is a "movement," with a definite institutional pattern, a common philosophy, a core of dedicated constituents, and a goal.

But what is the goal?

Is it Sam Gompers's succinct and dramatic "More and ever more of the product of our labor"? Is such an objective enough to hold together a complex and differentiated group of 17 million men and women; to keep them paying dues, attending meetings, electing delegates, walking the picket line, doing without during strikes, and periodically putting in long hours electioneering after a full day's work? To some people, trade unionism seems almost a religion, to be propagandized and defended under any circumstances. To others, it appears to be a faith, adhered to quietly but no less firmly, although with due recognition of its faults and weaknesses.

What is the basis of this faith? What makes people join and support

[1] From 58 million in 1886 to 200 million in 1967.

214

trade unions? Why have unions appeared and prospered and become more and more powerful? What conditions in modern society make trade unions necessary? Are the conditions political, economic, psychological, or technological in nature?

These questions are not just academic exercises. The United States, for example, is thoroughly committed to a policy of protection and encouragement of labor organization. That would be a poor policy if the goals of trade unionism were incompatible with the more basic goals of our society. According to Marx and Engels, trade unions are only an intermediate step in the class struggle toward the overthrow of existing social and political institutions and the dictatorship of the proletariat. Do American trade unions fit this description? And if not, what description do they fit? The answer, if there is any, will be found in a study of the origins and objectives of the labor movement. It is the function of theory to try to supply such answers.

There will be no absolute agreement by students of the labor movement as to which theories should be studied, but there would probably be unanimity on some of them. No review of theory could afford to leave out Marx and Engels, the Webbs, Commons, Hoxie, and Perlman. From there, the selection becomes more difficult and is influenced by the writer's point of view and purpose. In this book, four other writers will be added, to give more complete representation in terms of background and theoretical coverage. The complete list includes one German, Karl Marx (and his coauthor Friedrich Engels); two Englishmen, Sidney Webb (and his wife and coauthor Beatrice Potter Webb), and G. D. H. Cole; and six Americans, John R. Commons, Robert F. Hoxie, John Mitchell, Selig Perlman, Frank Tannenbaum, and Henry C. Simons. In background, they range from active revolutionaries (Marx and Engels) through the academic ranks (Cole, Commons, Hoxie, Perlman, Simons and Tannenbaum) to high public office through politics and the civil service (Webb), and active labor leadership (Mitchell). In theory, they run the gamut from the revolutionary design of Marx to the influence of technology cited by Tannenbaum.

THE CLASS STRUGGLE: GERMAN, BRITISH, AMERICAN

The original Marxian theory: Bourgeois versus proletariat.   Karl Marx (1818–1883), along with his close friend and partner, Friedrich Engels, was the founder of "scientific" socialism, or present-day Communism. Marx was born in Treves, Prussia, went to high grammar school in Treves, and then studied law, history, and philosophy at the universities of Bonn and Berlin, taking his Ph.D. degree at the latter in 1841. He was strongly influenced by Hegel, with whom he subsequently disagreed, retaining the dialectical method of his master but arriving at different conclusions. Marx's deduction (the famous "dialectical materialism") was to the effect that social and political institutions could not be regarded as autonomous phenomena or as natural outgrowths of the human spirit, but were rather rooted in the *material* conditions of life. The anatomy of civic society, he decided, was to be found in economics. Since his radical views made an academic career impossible, Marx took up journalism, becoming the editor of the *Rheinische Zeitung*, which was suppressed in 1843.

Shortly afterward, Marx went to Paris, where the Socialist movement was extremely active, to study economics and to write. Before the year was out, he had formally announced the fundamental conclusion around which his life work was built, namely, the "class struggle" and the necessity of the emancipation of the proletariat through the dissolution of all constituted society and its replacement by the classless community. In Paris, Marx met Friedrich Engels, and from 1844 on, the two collaborated in perfect agreement and the closest friendship. From Paris, Marx moved to Brussels, where he and Engels wrote the *Manifest der Kommunisten* in 1847, on the eve of the French and German revolutions. Returning to Germany, Marx took an active part in the revolt, was tried for high treason and acquitted, but was expelled from Prussia and subsequently from France. He moved to London in the latter part of 1849 and lived there until his death, taking an active part in the International Working Men's Association, which was founded in 1864, and spending his days in the British Museum, where he did most of the research for *Das Kapital*.

Friedrich Engels (1820–1895) was born in Barmen of a prosperous commercial family and in 1842 was sent to work in a factory of his father's in Manchester, England, where he became interested in the Chartist and Owenite movements and studied laissez-faire economics. He met Marx in Paris 2 years later and spent the next 5 years in France, Germany, and Belgium organizing underground revolutionary groups and collaborating with his new friend in various publications, including the *Manifesto*. Engels turned back to business in 1850 and supported Marx while the latter wrote *Das Kapital*. Retiring in 1869, he busied himself with general revolutionary activity until his death. He was a member of the general council of the First International and influential in the Second. He edited Marx's posthumous works and wrote widely on problems of Socialist theory and practice.

THE POLITICO-REVOLUTIONARY THEORY OF THE LABOR MOVEMENT OF MARX AND ENGELS.   In the eyes of Marx and Engels the organized labor movement is an intermediate step in the class struggle, the fight for power by the proletarian (wage-worker) class to overthrow the *bourgeoisie* (capitalist businessmen). The short-run purpose is to eliminate competition among the workers, which keeps them disorganized and at the mercy of their employers: "Organization of the proletarians into a class, and consequently into a political party, is continually being upset again by the competition between the workers themselves. But it ever rises up again, stronger, firmer, mightier." [2] The villain of the piece is modern industry, which

. . . has converted the little workshop of the patriarchal master into the great factory of the industrial capitalist. Masses of laborers, crowded into the factory, are organized like soldiers. As privates of the industrial army they are placed under the command of a perfect hierarchy of officers and sergeants. Not only are they slaves of the bourgeois class, and of the bourgeois State, they are daily and hourly enslaved by the machine, by the over-looker, and above all, by the individual bourgeois manufacturer himself. [3]

But this situation has its own solution: the necessary conditions of industrial production carry the seeds of its own downfall. They result in the regimentation of workers, the obliteration of distinctions of rank and craft, the reduction of wages and the standard of living, irregular employment, and its corollary, insecurity. The disputes between labor and management take on more and more of the character of class conflict:

Thereupon the workers begin to form combinations (Trades' Unions) against the bourgeois; they club together in order to keep up the rate of wages; they found permanent associations in order to make provision beforehand for these occasional revolts. Here and there the contest breaks out into riots. [4]

But the formation of unions, even successful ones, is not the true aim. [5]

Now and then the workers are victorious, but only for a time. The real fruit of their battles lies, not in the immediate result, but in the ever expanding union of the worker. . . . Every class struggle is a political struggle. . . . Of all the classes that stand face to face with the bourgeoisie today, the proletariat alone is the really revolutionary class. The other classes decay and finally disappear in the face of modern industry; the proletariat is its special and essential product. . . . The advance of industry, whose involuntary promoter is the bourgeoisie, replaces the isolation of the laborers, due to competition, by their revolutionary combination, due to association. The development of Modern Industry, therefore, cuts from under its feet the very foundation on which the bourgeoisie produces and appropriates products. What the bourgeoisie therefore produces, above all, are its own grave-diggers. Its fall and the victory of the proletariat are equally inevitable.

Trade unions are not ends in themselves; they are not agencies for the protection of workers' rights in a permanent, equitable society. They are essentially political institutions, a means of consolidating and solidifying the workingman's position on a parity with, and eventually superior to, that of any other members of the community. The motives which drive men into them are economic insecurity, political exploitation, and social degradation. The labor movement is a *collective* movement, on an inter-

---

[2] *Communist Manifesto* (Chicago: Charles H. Kerr & Company, no date), p. 25.
[3] *Ibid.*, p. 22.
[4] *Ibid.*, p. 24.
[5] *Ibid.*, pp. 24–26, 29.

national scale, in which the interests of the workers are identical and always in opposition to those of their masters.

> The proletarians have nothing to lose but their chains.
> They have a world to win.
> Working men of all countries, unite! [6]

Collective bargaining in the Fabian Socialist system of the Webbs.
Sidney James Webb (Baron Passfield) and his wife, Beatrice Potter Webb, were scholars, reformers, politicians, and leading Fabian Socialists. Sidney was born in London, July 13, 1859, was well educated in private schools in England and on the Continent, and afterward held a succession of government jobs obtained through civil service competition. His career included a professorship at the London School of Economics, membership in Parliament from 1922 to 1929, the Secretaryship of State for Dominion Affairs and for the Colonies, and service on innumerable royal and departmental commissions for the study of various economic and social problems. He was the author of a large number of books and reports, and coauthor (with his wife) of many more.

THE WEBBS' THEORY OF INDIVIDUAL DEMOCRACY.   If any book is the bible of trade unionism, it is the Webbs' *Industrial Democracy*.[7] It is still the classic statement of the assumptions, purposes, and methods of organized labor. It consists of an exhaustive analysis of British trade unionism, based on 6 years of painstaking empirical investigation. Peculiarly enough, it was a by-product. As the Webbs have explained elsewhere,[8] the purpose of their 6-year research was to present a definitive history of the British labor movement, which was duly published in 1894. They then discovered that a rearrangement and reexamination of their notes, accumulated for historical purposes, permitted a crosscut analysis of the organized labor movement in terms of assumptions, politics, economic rationalizations, and effects. The result was *Industrial Democracy*.

The essence of the Webbs' position is indicated by the title of their book. Trade unionism is the extension of democracy from the political sphere to that of industry and the overcoming of managerial dictatorship. Unionism thus serves to strengthen the liberties of the individual worker by giving him representation in a bargaining situation, the outcome of which will determine his standard of living and his working environment. In the absence of such representation, all the dimensions of the employer-employe relationship are imposed upon the workingman from above, and he is forced to accept because he has no "reservation price"

---

[6] *Ibid.*, p. 58.

[7] Sidney Webb and Beatrice Webb, *Industrial Democracy* (New York: Longmans, Green & Co., Inc., 1920, first published in 1897).

[8] *Methods of Social Study* (New York: Longmans, Green & Co., Inc., 1932).

below which he may refuse to sell his services. He *must* work, and his bargaining power is nonexistent. The result is a servile condition incompatible with the precepts of a free society.

Men and women of the upper or middle classes are totally unable to realize what state of body and mind, what level of character and conduct, result from a life spent, from childhood to old age, amid the dirt, the smell, the noise, the ugliness, and the vitiated atmosphere of the workshop; under constant subjection to the peremptory, or, it may be, brutal orders of the foreman; kept continuously at laborious manual toil for sixty or seventy hours in every week of the year; and maintained by the food, clothing, house-accommodation, recreation, and family life which are implied by a precarious income of between ten shillings and two pounds a week [roughly $2.50 to $10, at the rate of exchange in effect in 1897]. If the democratic state is to attain its fullest and finest development, it is essential that the actual needs and desires of the human agents concerned should be the main considerations in determining the conditions of employment. Here, then, we find the special function of the Trade Union in the administration of industry.[9]

This function—of representing and protecting the interests of workingmen—is not just a temporary obligation, arising from the current state of modern industrial development, nor does it lead eventually to the all-embracing "dictatorship of the proletariat" of Marx and Engels. The Webbs agreed with Marx that the modern capitalist state was a transitional phase of political organization, but as Fabian Socialists they saw a different outcome in the evolution of political forms. They rejected emphatically the "classless society." The proper resting place of control in the modern industrial community was envisioned as democratic socialism, with a distribution of functions similar to that now in effect, but with a guarantee of a national minimum of security to all citizens and the direction of major industrial processes in public hands. In this type of society, organization of workers would continue to play an important role.

It is essential that each grade or section of producers should be at least so well organized that it can compel public opinion to listen to its claims, and so strongly combined that it could if need be, as a last resort against bureaucratic stupidity or official oppression, enforce its demands by a concerted abstention from work, against every authority short of a decision of the public tribunals, or a deliberate judgment of the Representative Assembly itself.[10]

In their analysis of the causes of trade unionism the Webbs placed the major emphasis upon the invidious effects of competition. In the "higgling" of the market, the ruthless struggle for commercial and industrial survival based on comparative prices, with its long chain of pressures extending from the consumer through the retailer to the wholesaler to the manufacturer, is to be found the explanation of the workers' misery. Trade unionism performs its greatest service in the capitalist, free enterprise

[9] Webb and Webb, *op. cit.*, p. 821.
[10] *Ibid.*, p. 825.

society by lifting from the individual employee the heavy pressure of competition over wage rates, hours, and conditions of work.[11]

In order to accomplish this, two major devices are used: (1) restriction of numbers and (2) the common rule. Restriction of numbers (limitations upon entry to the trade) is admittedly uneconomic, undemocratic, and undesirable. In the good society it will have to be abandoned in large part, except for the exclusion of children, the unqualified, and other undesirables. The common rule (uniform standards of wages, hours, and working conditions), on the other hand, is economically valid and politically desirable. It should be extended by law in the form of national minimum standards.

The Webbs ranged themselves on the side of the class struggle, "the long-drawn-out battle of interests between capitalist employers and manual working wage-earners." [12] Unlike Marx, however, they saw the resolution of the conflict in equality and collective negotiation, rather than the liquidation of the business class and worker dictation. Trade unions are working-class democracies.

The agitation for freedom of combination and factory legislation has been, in reality, a demand for a "constitution" in the industrial realm. The tardy recognition of Collective Bargaining and the gradual elaboration of a Labor Code signifies that this Magna Charta, will, as democracy triumphs, inevitably be conceded to the entire wage-earning class.[13]

G. D. H. Cole's industrial unionism and control of industry. George Douglas Howard Cole, Fellow of University and Nuffield Colleges, Oxford, was a British academic man of the pure type. He was educated at St. Paul's and Oxford and became a Fellow of Magdalen College upon graduation. A detective-story writer in his spare time (with his wife, Margaret Isabel Cole as coauthor), most of Cole's economic writing was on labor problems.

COLE'S THEORY OF UNION CONTROL OF INDUSTRY.   Cole's views of the proper function of organized labor and its role in the world of the future were most fully stated in his book *The World of Labour*, published in 1913.[14] Cole was a Socialist, who had written extensively for the (Socialist) Fabian Research Department. In the socialist state of the future he saw the goal of labor as something more than the Webbs' representation of the interests of workers and something less than the Marxian dictatorship of the proletariat. It was the "control of industry" by the true producers, the workers, in partnership with the state. The theory of producer

---

[11] See Chap. 15 for a detailed explanation of the Webbs' "bargain theory" of wages.

[12] Webb and Webb, *op. cit.*, p. xvi.

[13] *Ibid.*, p. 841.

[14] London: G. Bell & Sons, Ltd.

control, which Cole endorsed with some qualifications, was the "syndicalist" dogma of ownership and direction of the means of production. The principal union development necessary to this end, he said, is *industrial unionism*, of which he was one of the leading proponents.

Cole conceded that industrial unionism, with "all workers working under a single employer or group of employers . . . organized in a single Union," [15] is arguable only upon the assumption that trade unionism is regarded as a class movement based upon the class struggle. If that is not the meaning of the labor movement, then there is good reason for the skilled worker to hold aloof from those less advantageously situated than himself and so maintain his monopoly of jobs and pay. On the other hand, if the labor movement is a part of the class struggle, then mass formations of labor are needed to combat the mass formations of capital, and the requirements of unity deny sectional groupings based on class or craft.

Cole himself had no doubts about the assumption. "Trade Unionism exists today to carry on the class-struggle." He said:

> The class-struggle is preached, not on the ground that it is desirable, but on the ground that it is a monstrous and irrefutable fact. The class-struggle is established in our social institutions, and it is only by means of the class-struggle that we can escape from it. [16]

This in turn implies great power, which can be attained only through universal membership of the laboring classes in trade unions and improved organization. The intermediate and ultimate stages of the class struggle are succinctly outlined in the following passage:

> The "greater" Unions, as we have seen, will be in a far better position than the existing overlapping and rival unions for achieving the compulsory Trade Unionism which must come in time, if the control of industry is to be in any degree "syndicalised." At the same time, it will be realised that even the compulsory Trade Union of which "greater" Unionists dream is not the "Guild," the producing unit of which we are in search. . . . The position, however, will be changed when the State becomes the employer; for the State is not in the same sense a producer. The way will, then, be open, under nationalisation, for the evolution of the "Guild," the real "Industrial Union" embracing all the producers in any given industry.

Cole was pessimistic concerning union political action, even venturing the prediction that "the present Labour Party can never become a majority and would be sadly at a loss to know what to do if it did become one." (The first Labour Cabinet, under Prime Minister Ramsay MacDonald, took office in January, 1924.) His final observation on the political functions of organized labor were dogmatic and explicit:

> If Trade Unionism is to fit itself for the control of industry, it must stick to its last, and, if it is to meddle with politics at all, it must create for that purpose a

[15] *Ibid.*, pp. 212–213.
[16] *Ibid.*, p. 370.

special organ with a separate existence. The control of industry may be the future destiny of the Trade Unions; the direct control of the whole national life is most emphatically not for them.

The pragmatic approach of John R. Commons.   John R. Commons (1862–1944), professor of political economy at the University of Wisconsin, dean of American labor scholars, was the founder of the "Wisconsin school" of institutional economists. Commons studied at Oberlin College and Johns Hopkins University, where he came under the influence of Professor Richard T. Ely, himself one of the earliest students of the labor movement in this country. Following his graduation, Commons taught at Wesleyan, Oberlin, Indiana, Syracuse, and finally came to rest at Wisconsin, once more under the supervision of Ely, who had preceded him there as head of the department. It was a favorable environment. The University of Wisconsin is located at Madison, which is also the state capital. During most of Commons's term of service (1904 to 1932) the state government was dominated by the progressivism of "Fighting Bob" La Follette, and the tie-up between the two state institutions was close. Commons alternated in service between the campus and the capitol, with spells of outside investigation for the Federal government and private organizations. His researches produced a tremendous volume of writing of a miscellaneous character, primarily oriented to the condition of the workingman and the relationship between the state and private business organizations. John R. Commons was a born skeptic, an indefatigable investigator, a thoroughly unsystematic thinker, and one of the most inspirational teachers and supervisors in the history of higher education in America. His greatest contribution to the study of the American labor movement was to arouse the enthusiasm of gifted graduate students and set them to work, individually and in platoons, producing masterpieces of research. Commons's own views are typically to be found in fragmentary observations in his reports and journal articles, in his autobiography, or as introductory summaries to major works like the *History of Labor in the United States.*[17]

COMMONS'S "ENVIRONMENTAL" THEORY OF THE AMERICAN LABOR MOVEMENT.   A convinced institutionalist, Commons believed what he saw with his own eyes or found in the record. He was skeptical of generalizations, especially those of the armchair variety, and this skepticism kept him from indulging in long-range predictions or guesses as to fundamental aims. Nonetheless, Commons had a theory of the labor movement and this theory had a set of basic premises. The premises were Marxian, although the conclusions, being those of a careful observer and a restrained reporter, would hardly have satisfied the German philosopher. Commons regarded the labor movement as an aspect of the class struggle, and his

[17] Vol. I (New York: The Macmillan Company, 1919), pp. 3–21.

method of investigation indicated a firm belief in the influence of political and economic institutions upon the thoughts and actions of men.[18] He regarded the labor movement in America as *delayed and thwarted* by a number of factors, the first of which (in his catalog) was *free land.*

The condition which seems to distinguish most clearly the history of labour in America from its history in other countries is the wide expanse of free land. As long as the poor and industrious can escape from the conditions which render them subject to other classes, so long do they refrain from that aggression on the property rights or political power of others, which is the symptom of a "labour movement." [19]

The necessary precondition to free land was universal manhood suffrage, "which alone could make land a political issue." But the right to vote was not an unmixed blessing: it diverted the workingman from his proper business of organization and class unity into *visionary and unprofitable political ventures* where he was consistently outwitted:

The tragedy, the credulity, the fiasco, the lessons learned, forgotten, learned again, the defection of leaders, the desperate reaction to violence or anarchism, the disintegration of unions—these are the moving picture of eight decades of that universal suffrage, for which the laborer would give his life, but by which he has often followed a mirage.[20]

The trouble with political action was that in America it was not the voice of the people, but the province of professional politicians who used the parties as bulwarks of special interests. Nonetheless, it was political and economic action and not any benevolent assistance from on high that produced free land and the other gains of the workingman:

We are likely to ascribe to the bounty of nature what proceeds from the struggle of classes. Like the laissez-faire philosophers, we trace back to a benevolent physical nature what springs directly from our social nature, and shows itself in organization and political effort. . . . Free land was not a mere bounty of nature; it was won in the battle of labour against monopoly and slavery.[21]

Ranking next as a major influence upon the labor movement of the nineteenth century was the tremendous *expansion of markets,* which occurred as the country was opened up to trade without any handicap or barriers other than competition. The mere size of the market area "changed the character of competition, intensified its pressure, separated manufacturers from agriculture, introduced the middleman, produced new align-

---

[18] "The labour history of the country . . . is the story of how, in the course of three centuries, the wage-earner, as a distinct class, has been gradually, even violently, separating himself from the farmer, the merchant, and the employer [Commons's synonym for manufacturer]" (*ibid.,* p. 3).

[19] *Ibid.,* pp. 3–4.

[20] *Ibid.,* p. 5.

[21] *Ibid.,* p. 4.

ments of social classes, and obliterated the futile lines that distinguish the jurisdiction of States." [22] The chief products of this competitive melee were two: the *merchant-capitalist,* who acted as middleman between the manufacturer and the retailer and drove a hard bargain with each, and the *financier,* who aided the merchant in his extension of credits.

The effects of the new competition upon labor were much as described by the Webbs. It was the function of the manufacturer-employer to drive a hard wage bargain in order to satisfy the merchant-capitalist, who was the servant of the retailer and his customers. This produced a series of "sweated" trades and drove employes to their first conscious combination with others of their class in "trade" unions, and away from the guildlike associations of earlier days, which included masters as well as journeymen.

A fourth important influence was found in the organs of government. The confused pattern of state and Federal law made extensive legislative reforms impracticable, while the courts, "blocking the way of a new aggressive class with precedents created to protect a dominant class," were vetoing the laws which labor in its political struggles had been able to get passed. The final step in *judicial usurpation of power* came with the use of the injunction. The main effect of these obstacles was to turn labor away from political action to reliance upon organization and economic power. Additional influences of great importance have been *immigration,* with its influx of races, nationalities, and languages, thrown together in a single competitive area, and *cycles of prosperity and depression,* which Commons found to have a positive correlation with the rise and fall of union activity.

But what of the long-run aims and aspirations of the labor movement? On these, Commons was reticent. He discussed socialism and anarchism and found that neither properly described the American labor movement for long. Rather, the outcome had been opportunistic and nonrevolutionary and implied an acceptance of capitalism which fell considerably short of even the Webbs' expectations of political evolution:

As long as the wage-earning class accepts the existing order and merely attempts to secure better wage bargains, its goal must eventually be some form of the "trade agreement," which recognizes the equal bargaining rights of the organized employers. Its union is not "class conscious" in the revolutionary sense of socialism, but "wage-conscious" in the sense of separation from, but partnership with, the employing class.

Beyond that point Commons, the scholar, refused to go. If the labor movement was the class struggle, the classes had somehow made a deal. American unionism was not revolutionary or class conscious but was primarily "business" unionism, a term devised by Commons's contemporary and associate, Robert F. Hoxie.

[22] *Ibid.,* p. 6.

THE UNION AS A MONOPOLY: BENEFICIAL OR PERNICIOUS?

Mitchell's counter-monopoly theory of unionism.   John Mitchell (1870–1919) was an American labor leader. Orphaned at an early age, he started to work when he was 9, went into the mines at the age of 10, and joined the Knights of Labor when he was 15. Upon the subsequent collapse of that Order, he took out membership in the United Mine Workers of America, becoming president of the union in 1899. He retired from the presidency in 1908 on account of ill health and became a free-lance lecturer and writer on labor problems. In 1914 he was appointed Commissioner of Labor for the State of New York and later became chairman of the State Industrial Commission. Mitchell was active in the AFL, serving as vice-president from 1899 to 1914, and was second only to Gompers in his influence upon policy. He fought the craft principle as the exclusive basis of organization and established the right of the miners to organize on an industrial basis in 1901. Two years later, while still president of the union, he published *Organized Labor*. Mitchell was an advocate of "prudent business methods" and the "sacredness of contract" and proved outstandingly successful as a union official and tactician. He is probably the first labor leader whose fortune at the time of his death amounted to a quarter of a million dollars.

MITCHELL'S ECONOMIC PROTECTION THEORY OF TRADE UNIONISM.   The explanation of trade unionism, according to one of its most successful practitioners in this country, lies in the economic protection it affords to workingmen. The essence of organized labor is the collective bargain, which gives the worker economic equality with the employer, rids him of fear, raises his efficiency, and establishes his citizenship in the industrial order. A corollary of this proposition is the absolute rejection of the individual bargain:

The fundamental reason for the existence of the trade union is that by it and through it, workmen are enabled to deal collectively with their employers. . . . Trade unionism thus recognizes that the destruction of the workingman is the individual bargain, and the salvation of the workingman is the joint, united, or collective bargain.[23]

The reasons for preferring collective dealings over individual bargaining are the usual ones: the employer's advantageous situation with reference to finance, market information, and the like, and the individual workman's complete lack of means of putting pressure on the purchaser of his services. But it is a question of bargaining power, *within existing market institutions,* and not of the class struggle. As definitely as any writer, Mitchell denies the thesis of opposition of interests.

[23] *Organized Labor* (Philadelphia: American Book and Bible House, 1903), pp. 2–4.

Labor unions are *for* the workman, but *against* no one. They are not hostile to employers, not inimical to the interests of the general public. They are for a class, because that class exists and has class interests, but the unions did not create and do not perpetuate the class or its interests and do not seek to evoke a class conflict. There is no necessary hostility between labor and capital. Neither can do without the other; each has evolved from the other. Capital is labor saved and materialized; the power to labor is in itself a form of capital. There is not even a necessary, fundamental antagonism between the laborer and the capitalist. Both are men, with the virtues and vices of men, and each wishes at times more than his fair share. Yet, broadly considered, the interest of the one is the interest of the other, and the prosperity of the one is the prosperity of the other.[24]

Simons: Unions as strongholds of violence and special privilege. Henry C. Simons (1899–1946), professor of economics at the University of Chicago, was an economic theorist. His writings on trade unionism are mainly confined to a single short article, "Some Reflections on Syndicalism," which appeared in the *Journal of Political Economy*, March, 1944.[25] However, that article stands as the high-water mark of denunciation of organized labor in the English language. It is terse, vigorous, and unqualified. If Simons is right, trade unionism is wrong and has no place in a democratic, free society. He makes this clear in his second paragraph:

Advocates of trade-unionism are, I think, obligated morally and intellectually to present a clear picture of the total political-economic system toward which they would have us move. For my part, I simply cannot conceive of any tolerable or enduring order in which there exists widespread organization of workers along occupational, industrial, functional lines.

SIMONS'S THEORY OF MONOPOLISTIC, ANTIDEMOCRATIC TRADE UNIONISM. Trade unionism, according to Simons, is monopoly, founded on violence and hence antidemocratic, with the goal of restricting output to raise the price of the commodity it has for sale—labor. The fundamental conflict of interest in society is not between employer and employe but between "every large organized group of laborers and the community as a whole." In contrast, "we generally fail to see . . . the identity of interest between the whole community and enterprises seeking to keep down costs [*i.e.*, employers]. Where enterprise is competitive—and substantial, enduring restraint of competition in product markets is rare—enterprisers represent the community interest effectively."

That unions are monopolistic Simons takes for granted. "All bargaining power is monopoly power," and "monopoly power . . . has no use

[24] *Ibid.*, p. ix.

[25] The article has been reprinted in a collection of Simons's works, *Economic Policy for a Free Society* (Chicago: The University of Chicago Press, 1948), pp. 121–159.

"Syndicalism," from the French "syndicalisme" and "syndical," has a special meaning in connection with trade unionism. It refers to the radical program of the general strike and organized control of production. One of Simons's theses was that this was the ultimate goal (or necessary effect) of combinations of workingmen.

save abuse." While "enterprise monopoly . . . is always plagued by competition . . . and . . . a deeply hostile, if lethargic, attitude of courts, legislatures, and the public . . . labor monopolies are, now or potentially, a different kind of animal . . . they enjoy an access to violence which is unparalleled in other monopolies." The friends of unionism "have promoted the organization of innumerable industrial armies, with implicit sanction to employ force, coercion, and violence to the full extent of their power, at least to prevent competing sales of services at rates below their own offers."

What are the results? Wages forced above the "natural" rate (Simons was a confirmed marginal productivity theorist, with some backward leanings to the wages-fund doctrine of classical economics), unorganized workers driven out of employment or into lower-paid occupations, and a steadily increasing differential between the wages in organized occupations and the unorganized. In a vivid passage, he summed up the probabilities (or rather certainties, as he saw them):

Organization is a device by which privilege may be intrenched and consolidated. It is a device by which the strong may raise themselves higher by pressing down the weak. Unionism, barring entry into the most attractive employments, makes high wages higher and low wages lower. Universally applied, it gets nowhere save to create disorder. . . . We cannot all get rich by restricting production. Monopoly works when everyone does not try it or when few have effective power. . . . But the dictator will be installed long before monopoly or functional organization becomes universal. Must we leave it to the man on horseback, or to the popes of the future, to restore freedom of opportunity and freedom of occupational movement?

But to Simons the economic problem is secondary to the political. He recurs constantly to the theme of *power*, secured by violence and exercised against the community for the aggrandizement of the few:

We have never faced the kind of minority problem which widespread, aggressive, national and regional unions and their federations present. They are essentially occupational armies, born and reared amidst violence, led by fighters, and capable of becoming peaceful only as their power becomes irresistible. . . . Peaceful strikes, even in the absence of overt violence or intimidation, are a meaningless conception. . . . Where the power is small or insecurely possessed, it must be exercised overtly and extensively; large and unchallenged, it becomes like the power of strong government, confidently held, respectfully regarded, and rarely displayed conspicuously. But . . . this apparent peacefulness . . . is unsubstantial and deceptive. It marks a fundamental disintegration of the state's monopoly of coercion. Here, possibly, is an awful dilemma: democracy cannot live with tight occupational monopolies; and it cannot destroy them, once they attain great power, without destroying itself in the process.

Perlman's theory of job-rationing monopoly.   Selig Perlman (1888–1959), professor of economics at the University of Wisconsin, was born in Bialystok, Poland, and came to the United States in 1908. He was educated at the University of Wisconsin, joining the economics staff there in

1919, and was the chief disciple and eventually the inheritor of Commons's intellectual leadership in labor economics at that school. Perlman wrote extensively on the labor movement, being the author of *A History of Trade Unionism in the United States* (1922) and *A Theory of the Labor Movement* (1928), among others.

PERLMAN'S THEORY OF THE "SCARCITY CONSCIOUSNESS" OF MANUAL WORKERS.   This theory rests on a special form of class division, but without any long-run expectation of either control of industry or political reorganization through the means of trade unionism. The ultimate goal, whether in this country or abroad, under medieval or modern conditions, is "communism of opportunity." It is reached by solidarity and job control, through which there is a "rationing" of the existing job opportunities among the members of the group. To Perlman this is the fundamental axiom of working-class combination.

It is the author's contention that manual groups, whether peasants in Russia, modern wage earners, or medieval master workmen, have had their economic attitudes basically determined by a consciousness of scarcity of opportunity, which is characteristic of these groups, and stands out in contrast with the business men's "abundance consciousness," or consciousness of unlimited opportunity. Starting with this consciousness of scarcity, the "manualist" groups have been led to practising solidarity, to an insistence upon an "ownership" by the group as a whole of the totality of economic opportunity extant, to a "rationing" by the group of such opportunity among the individuals constituting it, to a control by the group over its members in relation to the conditions upon which they as individuals are permitted to occupy a portion of that opportunity—in brief, to a "communism of opportunity." This differs fundamentally from socialism or communism, which would "communize" not only "opportunity," but also production and distribution—just as it is far removed from "capitalism." . . . "Communism of opportunity" in the sense here employed existed in the medieval gilds before the merchant capitalists had subverted them to the purposes of a protected business men's oligarchy; in Russian peasant land communities with their periodic redivisions, among the several families, of the collectively owned land, the embodiment of the economic opportunity of a peasant group; and exists today in trade unions enforcing a "job control" through union "working rules." [26]

The rationale of "communism of opportunity" is described as follows:

If . . . opportunity is believed to be limited, as in the experience of the manual worker, it then becomes the duty of the group to prevent the individual from appropriating more than his rightful share, while at the same time protecting him against oppressive bargains. *The group then asserts its collective ownership over the whole amount of opportunity,* and, having determined who are entitled to claim a share in that opportunity, undertakes to parcel it out fairly, directly or indirectly, among its recognized members, permitting them to avail themselves of such opportunities, job or market, only on the basis of a "common rule." Free competition becomes a sin against one's fellows, anti-social, like a self-indulgent consumption

[26] *Theory of the Labor Movement* (New York: Augustus M. Kelley, 1949, reprint), pp. 6–7.

of the stores of a beleaguered city, and obviously detrimental to the individual as well. A collective disposal of opportunity, including the power to keep out undesirables, and a "common rule" in making bargains are as natural to the manual group as "laissez-faire" is to the business man.[27]

Perlman's theory, therefore, places heavy reliance upon the psychological reactions of workingmen. Some men are born risk takers, others are not.

The typical manualist is aware of his lack of native capacity for availing himself of economic opportunities [in the] . . . complex and ever shifting situations of modern business. . . . Added to this is his conviction that for him the world has been rendered one of scarcity by an institutional order of things, which purposely reserved the best opportunities for landlords, capitalists and other privileged groups.

His refuge is in a fair distribution of available work among the "legitimate" contenders, exclusion of "outsiders," presentation of a solid bargaining front to both employers and customers—in a word, in combination and collective unity.

GROUP THEORIES OF TRADE UNIONISM

Hoxie's business unionism.   Robert F. Hoxie (1868–1916), a professor of economics at the University of Chicago, was one of the group of institutionalists strongly influenced by Thorstein Veblen. Like his friend, Commons, he was a tireless investigator, tough-minded and skeptical, whose career was cut short by ill health and overwork. In 1915, he published *Scientific Management and Labor,* a summary of trade-unionist criticisms of the methods and philosophy of Frederick W. Taylor. His most important book, *Trade Unionism in the United States* (1917), was finished after his death, from notes he had collected over the years. It is one of the classics of labor literature.

HOXIE'S FUNCTIONAL CLASSIFICATION OF TRADE UNIONS.   Hoxie's greatest contribution to the theory of unionism was to establish the idea of *functional types* of labor organization and to identify the principal types to be found in this country. A "functional type" is the result of a "common interpretation of the social situation," [28] which produces agreement among the group as to the problem facing its members and the kind of remedial program which will solve it. The result is a set of agreed aims, policies, and methods which distinguish a union or a set of unions from others which diagnose the social situation differently. The main types of union-

[27] *Ibid.,* p. 242. Italics in the original.
[28] *Trade Unionism in the United States* (New York: Appleton-Century-Crofts, Inc., 1921), p. 58.

ism, according to Hoxie, were five: business, uplift, revolutionary, predatory, and dependent.[29]

1. *Business unionism,* by all odds the most prevalent and influential in the United States, meant a form of labor organization that was trade-conscious rather than class-conscious, that represented the viewpoint of the employes of a given craft or industry rather than of the working class as a whole, and whose principal aims were the improvement of wages, hours, and working conditions of the immediate group, regardless of other workers or the general social and economic situation. Business unionism looks upon itself as a bargaining institution, and its goal as an advantageous trade agreement. It tends to be exclusive, to limit membership, to be a high-fee, high-dues type of club, to emphasize discipline, and to develop autocratic leadership which can maintain itself as long as it can "deliver the goods" in the form of higher wages and greater security. In dealing with employers, business unions are generally temperate and cooperative, with an eye out for a profitable compromise, although noted for their blustering tactics at the conference table and their ability to hit and hit hard when conditions seem to call for direct action such as the strike or boycott.

A modern illustration of business unionism on the Hoxie pattern would be the Machinists or the IBEW. However, practically all American unions today are primarily "business" unions, with a greater or less degree of "welfare" flavoring. Hoxie emphasized that none of the functional types he described would ever be found in pure form but would always combine characteristics of other groups. The identifying symbol that he used merely pointed to the dominant trait of that section of the labor movement.

2. *Uplift unionism* was identified by its idealistic viewpoint. It placed emphasis upon the moral and social values of combination and their contribution to a better life in terms of personal dignity, leisure and culture, security, and better living standards. It could be found, according to Hoxie, in trade-conscious or class-conscious labor groups; and its most conspicuous marks were its techniques of action—welfare programs, mutual insurance, political action, producer and consumer cooperation, and the like. Unions in the garment trades, such as the Amalgamated Clothing Workers and the International Ladies' Garment Workers, have always been Exhibit A of this form of combination.

3. *Revolutionary unionism,* as its name implies, is the real Marxian brand. It is radical in theory and in action, strongly class-conscious, contemptuous of the existing social and economic order, and eager to replace it with a brand-new political setup. Revolutionary unionism has one central theme: the harmony of interests of all workers, regardless of differences in skills or living standards, and the opposition of these interests to

[29] R. F. Hoxie, "Trade Unionism in the United States, General Character and Types," *Journal of Political Economy,* vol. 22 (1914), pp. 203–216.

the interests of their employers. Its objective is to unite all workingmen into a single, unified, fighting organization; its methods, collective bargaining and political action (as intermediate steps), direct action (strike and boycott), sabotage, and violence. Past examples are the Western Federation of Miners, led by "Big Bill" Haywood, and the Industrial Workers of the World (IWW). Hoxie noted that revolutionary unionism had never represented more than a negligible fraction of the United States labor movement.

4. *Predatory unionism* is gangsterism in union form. Its chief characteristic is lack of principle (other than "look out for number one") and concentration on short-run objectives. It operates by means of bribes, extortion, the sale of "protection," and monopoly combinations with employers. It was prevalent in the building trades in the past. Recently, however, it is best illustrated by the fraud, collusion (sweetheart contracts), and violence employed by officers of the Teamsters union, as exposed by the McClellan committee in 1957 and 1958.

5. *Dependent unionism* is a parasitic form of labor organization which depends upon the support of other labor groups or of employers who gain advantages by being unionized. Unions of barbers, for example, have been encouraged by barbership proprietors in order to standardize hours of work and other matters, such as prices. Some employers encourage unions in order to put the union label on their products. Needless to say, dependent unionism is an unimportant segment of the labor movement in the United States.

To Hoxie, trade unionism was a pragmatic, shifting, grass-roots movement. He rejected implicitly the assignment of a fixed basic cause, economic or political or historic, as the explanation of worker combination. This amounted to a denial of the class-struggle theory of Marx or Cole and brought him close to Commons's environmental-adaptation theory, without the latter's underlying class commitment.

Tannenbaum's anti-technology theory.   Frank Tannenbaum, author and economist, was born in Austria in 1893, came to the United States in 1905, and was educated at Columbia, the New School for Social Research, and the Brookings Institution. He was a newspaper correspondent in Mexico for a number of years, worked on a number of commissions and surveys, mostly on Mexican problems, and since 1935 has been on the staff of Columbia University. His principal work on labor is *The Labor Movement* (1912).

TANNENBAUM'S THEORY OF "MAN VERSUS THE MACHINE."   The dominant influence in modern society, according to Tannenbaum, is "the machine," which is "the center of gravity in the present-day industrial community. . . . What land did for the noble in the days of feudalism and what the competitive market and free bank connections do for the

merchant, the factory does for the worker." [30] It focuses his energies, demands his constant attention, takes away his tools, destroys his skill, replaces craftsmanship with dull, monotonous, routine duties, regiments his
working day, and forces him to live in crowded, unkempt quarters with
little time or energy for personal interests. The result is insecurity.

If anyone undertakes to describe the last hundred years in terms of what it has
meant to the individual man and woman he will have to tell a story of worry, doubt,
hesitancy, sorrow and tribulation, centered around the fact of individual economic
insecurity. That is *the* fact in the life of the individual. It is true of practically
everyone, but it applies more generally and in its most trying form to the worker.[31]

As for the labor movement, it is "the result, and the machine is the
major cause." The main function of the labor movement is to overcome
insecurity. To do this, it must control the machine. This need is not entirely economic, it is in part psychological: "The complexity of the
machine, the noise, the dirt, the monotony, the consequent suppression of
creative impulses . . . explain the discontent, the bitterness and the insistence on greater control, as much as economic need itself." The thing
which keeps the labor movement from being purely constructive and
creative is the fact that it must fight for its existence, that it is opposed
and blocked by employers who reject a collective adjustment to the problems posed by mechanical industry in favor of unilateral determination
accomplished by themselves. The ultimate outcome, according to Tannenbaum, is inevitable: labor control of industry, complete security, elimination of the profit motive, and industrial democracy.

The labor movement which began as a defence against insecurity operates as a
means of stabilizing a dynamic world without destroying its dynamic character and
seems destined to achieve complete control of the industrial functions of the community by substituting service for profit in industrial enterprise—and with service,
introducing democracy into industry.

In thus seeing control of industry as the goal of trade unionism, and
industrial unionism as the principal means, Tannenbaum underwrites a
number of Cole's conclusions. The class struggle as such, however, is
absent from Tannenbaum's premises, as he specifically defines insecurity
to include everyone in the machine society.

Tannenbaum's conclusions have recently been underscored by Erich
Fromm, who describes today's worker as an "alienated mass man, headed
in the same direction of human automation as the whole society." Fromm's
prescription is very like Tannenbaum's of 40 years earlier:

This means, applied to the worker, that he must become a responsible and active
participant in the whole process of work. . . . Increased technical knowledge

[30] *The Labor Movement* (New York: G. P. Putnam's Sons, Knickerbocker Press,
1921), pp. 23, 28, 29.
[31] *Ibid.*, pp. 6–7. For subsequent quotes, see pp. 29, 42, 135–136, 137.

could make even routine work more interesting. Furthermore, the factory is more than a combination of machines—it is an economic and social entity. Even if the work itself is boring, each worker can participate actively in the economic planning, and the considerations preceding it, and in the organization and administration of the factory as a social unit where man spends the larger part of his life.[32]

Recent additions to union theory. The modern trend in union theorizing is to regard the union as a political organization, an entity apart from its membership (which is heterogeneous and constantly changing), with a sovereignty and survival value of its own, and to emphasize group advantage and particularity. Arthur M. Ross, commissioner of Labor Statistics and former director of the Institute of Industrial Relations at Berkeley, writes: "The trade union is a political institution which participates in the establishment of wage rates [among other things]." [33] Another who has stressed this point of view is E. Wight Bakke, director of the Labor and Management Center at Yale University.[34]

A political view of union function is also held by Professor Frederick H. Harbison, director of the Industrial Relations Section at Princeton University. In Harbison's terms the union-management relationship is a naked struggle for power, the control of industry being the prize. Harbison denies any unitary character of the labor movement, in the United States at least, and finds a common element only in the characteristic struggle with employers for employe support and the privilege of dictating the terms of the working agreement.[35]

SUMMARY

What should the student believe?

There is a wide variety of doctrines to choose from. Happily, however, not all of them are in conflict. Some support others. Trade unionism is a complex, many-sided institution. It is more than probable that there are social, psychological, political, and economic impulses constantly at work throughout the labor movement. It might therefore be possible to form an eclectic theory of the labor movement which would include the "higgling of the market," the influence of the machine upon society, the "scarcity consciousness" of the manual worker, the "business" function of Hoxie, Commons's historical stream of consciousness, and the class struggle into a single doctrine, without any one concept's being in direct con-

[32] "Freedom in the Work Situation," *Labor in a Free Society* (Berkeley, Calif.: University of California Press, 1959), pp. 10, 13.

[33] *Trade Union Wage Policy* (Berkeley, Calif.: University of California Press, 1948), p. 43.

[34] See his *Mutual Survival, the Goal of Unions and Management* (New Haven, Conn.: Yale Labor and Management Center, 1946).

[35] F. H. Harbison and R. Dubin, *Patterns of Union-Management Relations* (Chicago: Science Research Associates, Inc., 1947), p. 6.

flict with another. However, it would probably turn out to be a profitless performance. In theory, as in cooking, including everything often means coming up with nothing.

It is well to remember Harbison's caution against thinking of the labor movement as a homogeneous, unified whole:

> There is not now nor has there ever been a unified labor movement in this country. . . . There are jurisdictional disputes and ideological controversies. . . . In many respects the American union movement is a sort of competitive system within itself.[36]

These remarks could just as well be applied to British or Continental trade unionism. Hence, the assumptions, purposes, and policies of one union or set of unions may not be the same as those of another union or set of unions at the same time, or of themselves at an earlier or later date.

The theorists cited above have pointed to factors that they considered significant in the origin and growth of organized labor. Their observations have stood the test of time in that they are standard references for the study of the history and philosophy of the labor movement. No one of them, however, is regarded as so important as to make it unnecessary to be familiar with the contributions of others. In the final analysis, each student must decide for himself. If the problem is approached with an open mind and conclusions are based upon careful study and comparison, the result will be a better understanding of an important institution.

READINGS

In addition to the books and articles referred to in the text, the student might read Mark Perlman, *Labor Union Theories in America* (Evanston, Ill.: Row, Peterson & Company, 1958); Charles E. Lindblom, *Unions and Capitalism* (New Haven, Conn.: Yale University Press, 1949); and John K. Galbraith, *American Capitalism: The Concept of Countervailing Power* (Boston: Houghton Mifflin Company, 1952).

[36] *Ibid.*

NINE
COLLECTIVE
BARGAINING

"It is hereby declared to be the policy of the United States to . . . encourage
. . . the practice and procedure of collective bargaining."
TAFT–HARTLEY ACT

Since 1935, it has been the established policy of the United States to encourage "the practice and procedure of collective bargaining." What is
collective bargaining and why should it be encouraged? Both the "what"
and the "why" are spelled out in the National Labor Relations Act, which
is Title I of the Taft-Hartley Act of 1947. The "what" is found in Sec. 8d
of Title I. To bargain collectively is "the performance of the mutual obligation of the employer and the representative of the employees":
1.   To meet at reasonable times and confer in good faith with respect to
wages, hours, and other terms and conditions of employment.
2.   To negotiate an agreement, or any question arising under an agreement.
3.   The execution of a written contract if an agreement is reached, but
4.   Neither party has to agree to a proposal or make a concession.
     The above are the general rules. If there is already an agreement in
effect, that is, if the question is extension or renewal of the agreement
(and this of course is the case 99 per cent of the time), then neither party
may terminate or modify the contract unless it gives 60 days advance
notice of its intention. It must also offer to meet and confer about a new
or modified contract, notify the Federal Mediation and Conciliation Service and any state mediation agency of the dispute, and continue the existing agreement in full force and effect, without strike or lockout, during the
60-day period.
     These are the main procedural limits established by law for collective
bargaining where the parties are in interstate commerce and thus subject
to the Federal labor code. Violation of any of these rules is a refusal to
bargain collectively and an unfair labor practice and is subject to enforcement by the National Labor Relations Board.
     Why are employes protected in their right to organize and bargain
through union representatives? What is it supposed to get us? Two things,

235

according to the law. First, it helps to avoid "strikes and other forms of industrial strife and unrest, brought on by union demands for recognition"; second, it remedies a basic inequality of bargaining power between employers and employes:

The inequality of bargaining power between employes who do not possess full freedom of association or actual liberty of contract, and employers who are organized in the corporate or other forms of ownership association substantially burdens and affects the flow of commerce, and tends to aggravate recurrent business depressions, by depressing wage rates and the purchasing power of wage earners in industry and by preventing the stabilization of competitive wage rates and working conditions within and between industries [Title I, Sec. 1].[1]

THE PRACTICE AND PROCEDURE OF COLLECTIVE BARGAINING

The principal business of unions is collective bargaining. They have other activities: they take part in politics; they conduct welfare programs for their members—health, education, recreation, etc.; and they join in community drives for religious, charitable, and other purposes. But these latter are always marginal and secondary. In the United States, trade unionism is essentially "business" unionism, and the business is negotiation and administration of collective agreements covering wages, hours, and conditions of work.

This may sound simple but it is not. Collective bargaining is a very big and important activity. Thousands of people, in unions and in management, spend a large part of their time either negotiating agreements or "administering" them, which means translating their terms into paychecks, work assignments, shift privileges, seniority rights, fringe benefits, and disciplinary actions. There is a whole library of literature dealing with collective bargaining in all its phases: the various bargaining patterns found in different occupations and industries; [2] the legal limitations upon both the procedure of bargaining and the subjects covered by the contract,[3] the effects upon the labor market and business management; [4] and the variety of ways that the problems which arise have been worked out

[1] This is essentially John Mitchell's anti-monopoly theory of trade unionism. See Chap. 8, p. 225.

[2] See, for example, the series of monographs on collective bargaining in West Coast industries, by staff members of the Institute of Industrial Relations, University of California (Berkeley): *Industrial Relations in the Pacific Coast Longshore Industry,* by Betty V. H. Schneider and Abraham Siegel; *Labor Relations in the Hawaiian Sugar Industry,* by Curtis Aller; *Collective Bargaining in the Motion Picture Industry,* by Hugh Lovell and Tasile Carter; *Industrial Relations in the California Aircraft Industry,* by Arthur P. Allen and Betty V. H. Schneider; *Collective Bargaining in the Pacific Northwest Lumber Industry,* by Margaret S. Glock; and others.

[3] See, for example, *Labor Law Course,* 15th ed. (New York: Commerce Clearing House, Inc., 1965), Sec. 2002–3647.

[4] American Management Association, *Understanding Collective Bargaining: The Executive's Guide* (New York: The American Management Association, n.d.).

and resolved.[5] There are specialists in collective bargaining at all levels and in dozens of different industries. Probably no one knows or understands the whole picture. Nevertheless, the essentials are similar, in Seattle as in Florida, and in San Diego as in Boston. The aims of the agreements have much in common, in industries as different as building construction and automobile manufacturing. With knowledge of the essentials it is not hard to understand why collective bargaining has become the dominant institution in the American labor market.

Collective bargaining is essentially a system of "joint management" or "industrial self-government" based on a written contract. The written agreement reflects a joint understanding covering wages, hours, fringe benefits, work rules, and a number of "noneconomic" matters such as seniority, grievance procedure, or union representation. In actual operation, the range of matters jointly handled or discussed is often much broader than the agreement indicates, but unless abrogated by special understandings or long-standing practices, the agreement as written is controlling. At the same time, the agreements vary greatly—in length, coverage, detail, and emphasis—and the individual systems of industrial relations that they establish (or represent) are equally distinct. This is what is sometimes referred to as the "pattern" of collective bargaining. For example, there is one pattern of labor relations (organization, philosophy, methods of negotiation, and contract coverage) on the railroads and another quite different pattern in the steel industry. Both aim at much the same objects, but they go about it in very different ways. This is partly because of the different operating requirements in running trains and making steel, partly because of historical accident, partly a result of governmental regulation, and so on. The pattern (over-all) of collective bargaining in America is complex and constantly changing. However, some of its main outlines are quite stable, and the process itself is rather uniform, whether in metals mining, department stores, longshoring, or airframe manufacturing.

It is the process or "procedure" of collective bargaining that is established policy in the United States. This means the method of arriving at a joint agreement between the employer and the union and then "administering" it while it is in effect. This is the common, ordinary, "newspaper" understanding of the term, the side of it that gets attention (negotiations, strikes, wage demands, etc.) because it is often the dramatic side. Good procedure is fundamental to the system if the system is to work well, and there are three main steps in the process: recognition of the union by the employer; negotiation of the agreement (including of course, renegotiations); and "administration" of the agreement, either through the work rules or by grievance bargaining with or without arbitration.

[5] An excellent short introduction to recent developments is James J. Healy (ed.), *Creative Collective Bargaining* (Englewood Cliffs, N.J.: Prentice-Hall, Inc., 1965).

RECOGNITION

Recognition means that the employer accepts the union as the official representative of certain stipulated employes and agrees to deal with the union, instead of the employes individually, concerning matters of employment. With recognition, the union moves into the position of responsible economic agent in a contractual relationship. Nowadays, recognition usually comes about as a result of an NLRB election. If the union wins, it is "certified" as the representative of the employes in the "bargaining unit." The recognition clause is frequently the opening section of the agreement and identifies the parties to the contract, as in the following:

LOS ANGELES AREA DIVISIONS—North American Aviation, Inc., a corporation, located at International Airport, Los Angeles 45, hereinafter called "the Company," recognizes the International Union, United Automobile, Aircraft and Agricultural Implement Workers of America (UAW), and its unit, Local 887 (successor to Local 683, UAW–CIO), hereinafter called "the Union," as the sole and exclusive collective bargaining agency of those employees designated in the NLRB certification dated April 14, 1941, for the purpose of collective bargaining with respect to rates of pay, wages, hours of employment and other conditions of employment.

Sometimes the clause also defines the bargaining unit; that is, it says which employes are covered by the agreement and which are not, as in the following from a Steelworkers' agreement:

The Company recognizes the Union as the exclusive representative for the purpose of collective bargaining in respect to rates of pay, wages, hours of employment and other conditions of employment of the hourly paid production, transportation, construction and maintenance employees on the payroll of the Company at its Indiana Harbor Works and its Chicago Heights Works, excluding superintendents, assistant superintendents, foremen, assistant foremen, office employees, salaried employees, technical engineers, technicians, draftsmen, chemists, bricklayers, timekeepers, watchmen and nurses.

The issue.   Recognition interposes a third party (the union) between the employer and his employes and for that reason was, and still is, opposed by many employers. The issue which is raised is fundamental; an argument over recognition is really an argument over unionism itself. Both unions and management have realized this in the past, and disputes over recognition have been among the bloodiest and most uncompromising on record, including such famous battles as the Ludlow (Colorado Fuel and Iron), Homestead, Coronado, Herrin, and Republic Steel conflicts. The issue is now settled if the employer is in interstate commerce and the union can enroll a majority of the employes in the bargaining unit, since the employer is then required by law to recognize the union. If, as Justice Oliver Wendell Holmes said, "law is the crystallized moral sentiments of the people," then it is the ethical conclusion of the people of America that unions deserve to be recognized. However, not all employers are converted, and trade unionists are skeptical of the sincerity of some of those with whom they have contracts and negotiate regularly.

The union position in the matter is obvious. If trade unionism is worthwhile, then recognition is a fundamental right, since trade unionism without recognition is unimaginable. The issue is basic and unarbitrable. Employers who must be forced into recognizing the union or who advise employes against union membership or who criticize the law for requiring recognition are enemies of the union and of the workingman, untrustworthy, and bad citizens. They deny a privilege to others (organization) which they enjoy themselves (in the form of the corporation) and profess motives of brotherhood and concern for the workers whereas their real aim is exploitation and the maintenance of a preferred position.

The employer's argument is that union recognition separates the managerial staff from the rank and file, with resultant complications in the chain of command, and that there is a loss of morale due to the employe's being put into a position of divided loyalty or "opposition" to management, rather than of cooperation with him, which is the natural relationship. Recognition of the union means that the employer may no longer deal directly on a man-to-man basis with the employes so represented. The employer may contend that organized labor performs no useful function which is not already provided for in the managerial setup. When the union comes in, it lowers productivity, establishes inflexible working rules, produces endless dispute, and induces the employes to soldier (the slowdown), to haggle over imaginary dissatisfactions (grievances), and to engage in strikes and boycotts. The union is notoriously careless of the rights of the owners of the business (stockholders), to whom management is responsible, and of the public, which demands uninterrupted service and low prices. It is a troublemaking device, usually led by a group of "outside agitators."

It was the purpose of the Wagner Act in 1935 to put an end to the struggle between employers and unions over the issue of recognition, and it succeeded very well. Such disputes, if in interstate commerce, are now subject to compulsory arbitration by the NLRB and are decided by secret-ballot elections. If the union can get over half the votes, it is certified and the law then requires the employer to recognize it and bargain with it. There are similar agencies in a number of the larger industrial states, but not in all. In certain sections of the United States—the South especially—there is little or no state protection of the right to organize and bargain collectively.

NEGOTIATING THE AGREEMENT

Union contract negotiations get more attention nowadays than any other phase of collective bargaining for the simple reason that they are news.

They produce the big public disputes that may result in strikes, picketing, and boycotts. Even if a strike is avoided, the deadline of contract termination is a news item in itself, with employers speeding up production to anticipate a work stoppage, union committees meeting to frame demands, mediators hurrying back and forth to try to find a solution, and if the dispute affects a major industry, the President or Vice-President or Cabinet members taking a stand one way or another or urging the parties to settle.

As a matter of fact, the disputes which become front-page news tend to overemphasize the wrong thing—the failure of collective bargaining. It is the extent of peaceful union-management negotiations which is surprising. There are more than 125,000 union contracts in effect in the United States, covering some 18 million employes. Some of the larger unions have as many as 10,000 agreements with different employers. At least 90 per cent of these are amended or renewed regularly without a work stoppage or a serious threat of one. However, industrial peace is not news and industrial strife is. It is hardly to be expected that the sober exercise of "the mutual obligation of the employer and the representative of the employes" to meet, confer, resolve their points of view, and commit the result to writing, will be publicized widely. Yet that is exactly what happens in the overwhelming majority of the cases, to the benefit of all concerned.

The actual process of negotiations is as varied as the situations and parties involved. In many cases, it is highly informal and worked out casually in an atmosphere of mutual trust, with full agreement by both sides on the standards of reference (wages, fringes, work rules, etc.) on which agreement is to be based. In others, bargaining is on an "arm's length" basis, with very formal proceedings and careful control of such ground rules as the agenda, submissions, attendance of observers, publicity releases, etc. In still other cases, fortunately rare, few or no rules are observed other than the required legal steps and the parties compete for publicity, tactical advantage, and favorable governmental intervention in every way possible. The last *full-scale* example of this sort of deadlock was the steel dispute of 1959—the biggest single strike, in terms of lost man-hours of work, in the history of the country—when agreements were renegotiated covering more than 500,000 members of the United Steelworkers of America in 12 major steel-producing companies.[6]

The great steel strike.   The steel dispute of 1959 is a landmark among labor disputes. It was not only the biggest shutdown on record, a

[6] More recent illustrations are the New York City newspaper shutdown of 1962–1963; the railroad firemen's 4-year battle with the carriers, 1959–1963, ending in compulsory arbitration; and the New York City transit strike of January, 1966. Each is worthy of investigation and analysis in terms of issues, personalities, tactics, and (governmental) intervention.

true industry-wide walkout covering the entire basic steel industry; it was at the same time a monumental *failure* of collective bargaining, with both parties failing to live up to the requirement to "confer in good faith" in order to reach agreement. It produced Presidential, Vice-Presidential, and Cabinet-level intervention; was settled under the threat of compulsory arbitration; was a major factor in the passage of the Landrum-Griffin Act; and is widely credited with starting the economy on the downswing which became the recession of 1960. It is therefore worth examining in some detail.

The setting was a 3-year contract terminating June 30, 1959. Months before, the union's national wage policy committee met to frame demands and lay out union strategy. As early as March, the President of the United States requested that both the industry and the union exercise restraint in arriving at a settlement which would avoid an increase in steel prices and thus help to hold down inflation. Late in April, the union notified the companies of its desire to modify the agreement, negotiations began May 18 under the eyes of Federal mediators, and it was soon clear that neither the industry nor the union representatives were prepared to compromise their previously announced positions. The principal sticking point was the industry's demand for relaxation of "local work rules" that it claimed supported thousands of unnecessary jobs (featherbedding) in steel plants across the country. If this were done, management offered a wage and fringe "package" adding up to about 31 cents per hour over another 3-year period.

The union rejected any tampering with the "local work rules" clauses and demanded a wage and fringe package approximating 52 cents per hour. On June 25, the union president asked President Eisenhower to establish an "impartial fact-finding board" to investigate the issues involved. The President declined, on grounds of a policy of "nonintervention," but again called on the parties to "bargain responsibly" and proposed an extension of time before the work stoppage, then scheduled for July 1. The union set the strike date back 2 weeks, negotiations continued deadlocked as before, and the walkout began on July 15.

Bargaining sessions were resumed sporadically, but got nowhere. The Secretary of Labor set up fact-finding machinery of his own, while the Director of the FM & CS tried at least to get the parties to meet, and at most to budge from their positions. Both the steel companies and the union ran full-page advertisements in daily papers across the country, arguing their case with open letters to their opponents plus facts and figures of their own collection. The companies accused the union of "striking for inflation," and the union accused the companies of a basic intent to "destroy the union." In September, with the strike 2 months old, the President again called for "intensive, uninterrupted, good faith bargaining with a will to make a responsible settlement." The Secretary of

Labor announced that he would ask the President to invoke the Taft-Hartley national-emergency dispute machinery if the strike continued on into October. By this time, inventories in the hands of steel users, which had been built up to a very high level during the first 6 months of the year, were largely worked off and a number of construction jobs and automobile plants closed down for lack of steel. "Secondary" unemployment—on railroads and in plants closed by lack of steel—had risen to half or more of the primary figure of 530,000.

On Oct. 9, after a final appeal to the parties, the President turned to the emergency provisions of the Taft-Hartley Act and called in a fact-finding board as the preliminary step to getting an injunction stopping the strike for 80 days. The board began hearings on the twelfth and on the nineteenth told the President that it was unable "to point to any single issue of any consequence whatsoever upon which the parties are in agreement." Two days later, the Federal government was granted an 80-day injunction, but the union appealed the order on grounds that the national health or safety was not adversely affected by the strike, with the additional contention that the injunction provisions of the law were unconstitutional. Oct. 26, the Kaiser Steel Corporation defected from the industry group and settled for a 20-month wage and fringe package totaling $22\frac{1}{2}$ cents per hour, plus an innovation: two committees, one of which would resolve work-rules problems on a local basis, while the other, a tripartite body (management-union-public), would recommend a long-range plan for "equitable sharing between the stockholders, the employees, and the public of the fruits of the company's economic progress."

The day after the Kaiser settlement, the United States court of appeals upheld the government's injunction, and the union promptly appealed to the Supreme Court, which declined on Nov. 7 to reverse the lower court. The union immediately told the strikers to return to work, and within 10 days most of the half a million union members were back on the job. The strike, however, was not over but just suspended.

Negotiations between the union and the industry proved just as fruitless as before and early in December the President of the United States announced that "the government cannot just sit idly on its hands" if the dispute remained unsettled. Both the union and the employers conducted private polls to determine if the workers would go out on strike again late in January when the injunction period ended. The answer as reported by both sides seemed to be yes. At this point, the Vice-President and Secretary of Labor began private efforts at mediation, which eventually proved to be successful at a compromise package of 41 cents for the 30 months remaining of the 3-year contract period. Part of the persuasion was the probability that Congress would legislate promptly for compulsory arbitration or government seizure if the strike was renewed in January. The new agreement was signed just about a year after the union had begun preparing for negotiations.

This was an extreme example of the most complicated and cumbersome form of the collective-bargaining process, with all the formal governmental machinery in use and with final settlement brought about by extralegal mediation efforts of high officials. It is not typical but, being an extreme, is illustrative. What was lacking throughout was the basic requirement for bargaining and one that cannot be legislated into effect —the willingness to see the other party's point of view and to compromise and the intention to reach agreement in good faith and avoid or end a work stoppage. It is this fundamental of "voluntarism"—and not the required formal steps—which brings about agreement in 95 out of 100 contract negotiations each year and keeps the system working.

THE COLLECTIVE BARGAINING SYSTEM

The most important institutional change that unions have brought about in modern society is to formalize the employment agreement. In the absence of unions, few contracts of employment are even discussed at any length, and still fewer are reduced to writing. A typical hiring on an individual-bargaining basis consists of an employer's announcement of the wage rate and the authorization of an applicant to report to work. Sometimes even the wage rate is not mentioned. The employer may or may not subsequently tell the employe the firm's policies regarding work assignments, overtime, transfer, promotion, demotion, discharge, layoff, vacation, sick leave, seniority rights, and discipline. The employer may not even have any such policies, relying rather on *ad hoc* decisions as problems arise. For the new employe without union representation, the customary source of information on such matters is the grapevine, supplemented now and then (in the case of progressive firms) by a manual of instructions telling *him* what he should do and expect, but with little emphasis on the reciprocal obligations of the employer in the policy areas listed above.

These obligations come to light in successive stages as situations arise and as the employe is notified of management's decision. *In the customary case, under individual bargaining,* there is no consultation of the employe's wishes, no request for his opinion, no interest in his reaction, and no opportunity for him to protest. Both policy and administration in personnel matters are strictly unilateral, authoritative, and often arbitrary.

Unionization makes two big changes in this picture. First, there is a full and complete exploration of the employer's policies, conducted by an independent and suspicious third party (the union) representing the interests of the workmen. Second, the employer's personnel policies are made explicit, in writing, with emphasis on the *rights of the employes*—the subject matter which was formerly omitted in even the rare cases that employers furnished manuals of information.

The union contract.   The new employe who is hired under a "trade agreement"[7] nowadays is relatively well informed as to his rights and privileges on the job. Before he goes to work or even applies, he may look over the union's contract with the employer and get a detailed picture of the situation from the clauses covering wages; hours of work and scheduling; the treatment of tardiness, absenteeism, and other rule violations; the handling of overtime, holidays, call-outs, and vacations; his seniority rights; the reasons for suspension and discharge; how layoffs will be handled; the grievance procedure; and many special items such as lunch periods, insurance, medical service, and training programs. It is all down in black and white in a pocket-sized pamphlet which the union (and the employer) will urge him to study and which his union representative will be glad to explain to him if he has any questions.

Nor is the protection afforded by his contract a remote and nebulous affair to the union member. It is a dynamic, living set of principles governing every minute of his working time, with an official representative of the union (the business representative or shop steward) stationed close by to protest to management whenever the employer's obligations are not carried out. This is in sharp contrast to the positive, one-sided treatment of pre-union days, especially in the case of the relatively defenseless unskilled and semiskilled workmen of many large firms. To such men, it may well seem that they have acquired industrial citizenship for the first time. No understanding of the spirit of trade unionism or of the typical union man's regard for the "rules" is possible without an appreciation of this fundamental change in his position relative to management. It is unlikely that this status will be readily given up by anyone who has sampled both.

Union contracts are by no means uniform in size or content. Since they are collections of working rules, governing the relations of the employer, the union, and the union members, they necessarily vary according to the industries or occupations to which they apply. Since they deal with problems which arise in employment relations, they develop over time, and new provisions are negotiated as new problems appear. The typical industrial-union agreement is rather lengthy, detailed, and complicated. It has two aspects: reciprocal rights and obligations between management and the union *as an organization* (union-security clauses, no-strike obligations), and reciprocal rights and obligations between management and the employes covered by the agreement, *as individuals.*

---

[7] "Trade agreement" means the same thing as "union contract." There are a number of such terms—"labor agreement," "union-management agreement," "collective agreement," "working rules"—all of which stand for the written agreement reached through collective bargaining between management and a union.

What is a good contract?

A good union contract is one which (1) has an adequate coverage (sets up rules establishing the reciprocal obligations of management, the union, and the employes in all areas where controversy is most likely to arise), (2) provides security for the union and its members, (3) establishes high standards of employment (wages, hours, and working conditions), (4) outlines a judicial procedure for interpreting and applying the contract to actual work situations (the grievance procedure), and (5) provides for its own modification, renewal, or termination.

ADEQUATE COVERAGE.   What are the subjects that must be dealt with in a trade agreement to ensure coverage of the major issues arising between management and the workers? One way to find out is to see what representative and influential unions include in their contracts. For instance, a recent agreement between North American Aviation, Inc., and the United Auto Workers covers the following topics:

Appeal and arbitration (of unsettled grievances)
Bulletin boards (use by the union)
Discrimination (among workers, on any grounds)
Duration (of the agreement)
Foremen (to do supervisory work only)
Grievance procedure
   First step—second step—third step
   Sole duties, responsibilities, and limitations of union representatives
      Alternate committeemen
      Chairman of grievance committee
      District stewards
      Grievance committee
      Vice-chairman of grievance committee
      Zone committeemen
   General provisions (of the grievance procedure)

Discharge procedure	Payment for grievance time
Discipline procedure	Productivity standard
Employee request for steward	Time limits
Grievance investigation	
and processing	

Hours and special pay provisions

Excused absences for union business	Paydays
Holidays	Premium pay
Incomplete day's work	Rest periods
Jury examination and jury service	Shift differential
Lost time	Smoking on the job
Normal shift hours	Special hours and extra work
Illness and health	

Insurance
Leaves of absence
Management prerogatives
Military service
Notices (by registered mail, etc.)
Qualifications and enforcement (of the company and the union)
Recognition (of the union as representative of the workers)
Representation (division of plant into districts, zones, etc.)
Safety
Seniority (11 pages, covering layoff, recall, promotion, rights, etc.)
Strikes and lockouts (the no-strike and no-lockout pledge)
Union deductions (the checkoff and forms to be used)
Union security (maintenance of membership)
Vacation and sick leave allowance
Wages (includes job classification, escalator, deferred increases, etc.)

It will be seen immediately that information on even a few of the items listed above is a far cry from the almost total ignorance of the employe under individual bargaining as to his own status. It is of perhaps equal significance to the workingman that he has a *right to know* the terms of his employment and may at any time ask to have a provision clarified or explained. This, however, brings up one of the big issues of which employers have complained. The contract is down in writing, while working conditions in an industrial plant are a very fluid thing. Adjustment and interpretation of the meaning of contract provisions are required constantly. It is true in some cases—perhaps, as employers have argued, in many cases—that the practice of informing employes of their rights tends to produce a group of "shop lawyers," workmen who are more concerned over their privileges than their performance, to the detriment of the cooperation necessary to produce efficiently.

There is no doubt that operating under a union contract, with its explicit statement of the mutual rights and obligations of the employer and the employes, provides a natural forum for the troublemaker, or that troublemakers do exist. The alternative, however, as the union is quick to point out, is authoritarian direction by management and the assumption that employes cannot be trusted to know the terms under which they work. This is the real test of joint relations, and the answer is to be found in day-to-day administration of the agreement, which comes to a focus in the relations between first-line supervisors (foremen) and the union agents in the shop or on the job. If they can cooperate amicably and sensibly on a practical basis, there is little to fear from troublemakers, whether of the boss or the worker variety. It is a fact that such cooperation is in effect in literally thousands of industrial, commercial, and construction operations all the time.

UNION SECURITY

This is one of the biggest and liveliest issues in industrial relations today. Union security means a number of things, but the primary factor is *a stable and established membership.* It is achieved by contract clauses which make union membership a necessary condition of employment; persuasion (which sometimes reaches the proportions of coercion); and union services, such as good contracts and efficient grievance handling, which carry obvious advantages to the workers who pay the dues. Union security is sometimes threatened by other unions, which may claim jobs or employes that the first union has established a right to. This results in a "jurisdictional" dispute, which may prove as bitter and long-drawn-out as any struggle between labor and management.

The direct route to union security is "job control." The most reliable form of union security, in the eyes of trade unionists in this country, has always been some form of contract clause which gives members of the union the inside track on jobs. The ultimate in union security is the closed shop, under which the union supplies all candidates for employment. However, since 1947 the Taft-Hartley Act has prohibited the closed shop and substituted for it the "union shop" as the maximum union security legal in interstate commerce. There are many variations of the same principle. For example, the Bureau of Labor Statistics lists and describes several degrees of contractual security, as follows: [8]

1. Under the closed shop, all employees must be members of the union at the time of hiring and they must remain members in good standing during their period of employment. *[handwritten: illegal today]*

2. Workers employed under a *union-shop* agreement need not be union members when hired, but they must join the union within a specified time, usually 30 to 60 days, and remain members during the period of employment. . . . In some cases, the union shop is modified so that those who were employed before the union shop was established are not required to become union members.

3. *Maintenance of membership,* as a general rule, requires that all employees who are members of the union a specified time after the agreement is signed and all who later join the union must remain members in good standing for the duration of the agreement. Following the pattern of the maintenance-of-membership clause established by the National War Labor Board, most of the agreements with this type of union-security clause provide for a 15-day period during which members may withdraw from the union if they do not wish to remain members during the life of the agreement.

4. Under *preferential hiring* no union membership is required but union members must be hired, if available.

5. *Sole bargaining* means that the . . . union is the bargaining agent for all employees and negotiates the agreement covering all workers in the bargaining unit whether they are members of the union or not.

[8] U.S. Bureau of Labor Statistics, *Handbook of Labor Statistics,* 1947, p. 131, italics supplied.

After the Taft-Hartley Act was passed in 1947, another kind of union security appeared, called the "agency shop." It required that all employes in the bargaining unit pay the regular fees and dues, but they did not have to join the union. This meant that the union was "agent" for the employes, but not their "representative."

Extent of union security.   The next question is: How many unions and union members have some form of union security and what kinds? Is the union shop typical? The answer is yes. As of today, more than four out of five union members are covered by closed-shop, union-shop, or maintenance-of-membership agreements. A BLS survey of December, 1959, showed almost exactly three-quarters (74 per cent) of a sample of 7,500,000 workers employed under closed-shop or union-shop contracts, with an additional 7 per cent in maintenance-of-membership bargaining units.[9] Railroads and airlines were omitted from the survey, as coming under separate legislation—the Railway Labor Act. Since these industries have a high degree of union security, the proportion shown above would be increased, if anything. The high degree of union-security coverage is the more remarkable, as the BLS survey included right-to-work states, in which any form of compulsory membership is prohibited.

The issue of union security.   In its simplest form, union security means compulsory union membership. A man must have a union card to get or hold his job. Without it, he is barred from that portion of the labor market covered by the labor agreement. A great many people feel that it is unfair, discriminatory, and contrary to the basic principles of a free society to let a group of private organizations (unions) have the power to make such crucial decisions. Since 1943, an organized and determined legislative drive has produced 19 state right-to-work laws or constitutional amendments prohibiting any form of compulsory union membership. (A "right-to-work" law is one that says, in effect, that the right to work may not be abridged or denied because of membership or lack of membership in any labor organization.) Hardly a year passes without more right-to-work bills or petitions being introduced. The state laws and constitutional amendments are made much more effective by Sec. 14b of the Taft-Hartley Act, an "enabling provision" which makes the state law on this subject apply to agreements falling within interstate commerce, *if* the state law is more restrictive than the Federal statute. They thus take precedence over Federal legislation like the Taft-Hartley Act itself.

The closed shop.   What are the issues of union security? [10] There are a number of them, depending on the form the security takes. Historic-

[9] *Monthly Labor Review,* December, 1959, p. 1348.
[10] For a brief résumé, see O. W. Phelps, *Union Security* (Los Angeles, Calif.: Institute of Industrial Relations, University of California, 1953).

ally, the closed shop was demanded by unions as a guarantee that employers would make no attempt, either openly or behind the scenes, to "break"
the union. The closed shop persists today, as a form of job control, especially in the "casual" markets—building construction, longshoring, musicians, stage and screen crafts—where employment is typically for brief
periods with one employer and where it would be easiest for an open-shop
movement to take hold. The standard device of the closed-shop craft
unionist, today as in the cordwainers' dispute in Philadelphia in 1806, is to
refuse to work alongside the nonunion man. Unfortunately, the closed shop
has often been directly tied in with the "closed union," in which not even
qualified craftsmen can get a card at times of low employment and in
which apprenticeship (the only avenue to becoming a journeyman and
therefore a cardholder) may be limited to relatives and friends or to no
one at all.[11]

On the employer's side, the question of the closed shop is one of the
right of management to choose its personnel. If it must take them from a
union hiring hall, the choice is narrowed, and the right to pick and choose
may be restricted or eliminated completely. Some unions restrict their own
membership, keeping out qualified workmen by means of high initiation
fees or by a simple "closing of the books." In such cases, the employer
may be offered poorly qualified job applicants when well-qualified ones
are walking the streets in search of jobs.

There is a public-interest angle to the question, too. If a union has
closed-shop agreements with all the employers in a labor market and the
union itself is a "closed" organization, then what becomes of the workmen
who are denied membership in the union? The issue is this: Should membership in a labor organization be a prerequisite to the holding of a job if
the labor organization is to pass on who will and who will not be admitted
to membership? The Taft-Hartley Act recognized this difficulty by making
it an unfair labor practice for a union with a union-shop agreement to
charge "unreasonable" initiation fees or dues or to expel a member for
any reason other than his failure to pay his dues.

The union shop.   The more modern arguments for union-security
clauses play down the danger of union busting by employers and stress
positive reasons for requiring all employes to take out cards. One is the
elimination of "free riders," employes who get the benefits of union activity but refuse to help support the organization. There are many such,
because of the requirement in the National Labor Relations Act that a
union which has signed a majority of the employes in a given bargaining
unit must be recognized as the "sole bargaining" agent for all employes

---

[11] This is a large and important part of the organized labor force and often not
sufficiently recognized. For an excellent short treatise on the subject, see Van Dusen
Kennedy, *Nonfactory Unionism and Labor Relations* (Berkeley, Calif.: Institute of
Industrial Relations, University of California, 1955).

in the unit. It is the union view that free riders should be forced to shoulder their share of the costs, at least. Another argument is "union-management cooperation." Given a union shop, say union officials, the necessity of continuous recruitment and organizing effort will be greatly reduced, and the union will no longer have to call management names periodically and think up grievances, real or imaginary, to persuade employes to join. The union can then get down to brass tacks with management and throw its influence in the direction of greater efficiency, cost reduction, and other firm objectives. It can even side *with* management in some cases, if it thinks conditions warrant, an action that would be unthinkable if it were hustling for votes to win a representation election or trying to round up a few more members to strengthen its budget and bargaining position.

Management's reply is that the arguments are plausible but specious. Given a union shop, union officials are more likely to press every possible advantage in bargaining and grievance procedure, to become dogmatic and arbitrary in consultations, with a "take it or leave it" attitude, to increase progressively both entrance fees and dues to exorbitant heights, and to shut out qualified nonmembers upon one pretext or another. A union shop, says management, will have the same effect upon union leaders as upon anyone else. It will make them fat, lazy, careless of duty and service, and unreasonable to deal with. They should be kept on their toes, as most businessmen are, by competition and by the necessity of demonstrating that they deserve the support of members. "Free rider" is just another name for the unconvinced nonmember of a union. The free rider in a shop is just as desirable as the shopper who goes from store to store comparing price and quality. He keeps both union and management in line and makes them look to their policies and performance.

However, the union shop is a great improvement over the closed shop in two respects, from the viewpoint of management. First, it permits the employer to hunt up and hire his own employes, regardless of union affiliation at the time. This widens the employer's market and frees him of bureaucratic union restrictions in his selection of personnel. Second, it eliminates the "closed" union shop, since the union is committed to taking in men the employer hires and the devices of "closed books," high fees, etc., are at least forced into the open where they have a harder time flourishing. The union has something to say about this too. Letting the employer do the hiring makes him in effect the recruiting agent for the union. That is all right if the union is willing to take anybody and if it can be assumed that all those hired are ready and willing to become good union members. But can that be assumed? What if the employer hires stool pigeons and labor spies for the express purpose of weakening the union and eventually breaking it down? [12]

[12] A practice uncovered by the McClellan committee and prohibited in the Labor-Management Reporting and Disclosure Act of 1959.

It is perhaps incorrect to speak of a single attitude toward anything like the closed or union shop on the part of all organized labor. A union which has grown up in the tradition of exclusiveness, with the closed shop, high fees and dues, and a restricted membership, will fear and resent the requirement of an "open front door." Industrial unions, on the other hand, were much less critical of the statutory restrictions on admission and membership. Many of them, in fact, favor the union-shop agreement, coupled with the checkoff, as the ideal form of union security. This type of contract makes the employer the recruiting and fiscal agent of the union, with a consequent saving of time and energy on the part of union officials. The industrial union, in turn, feels much less reluctant to admit indiscriminately anyone the employer may hire, since its policy is to take in everyone, regardless of craft or class.

Maintenance of membership was a wartime compromise which satisfied neither union nor employers, a halfway point between the union shop and sole bargaining. Since successful maintenance of membership, from the union viewpoint, produces something hardly distinguishable from the union shop, labor's objective has been to get an outright union-shop contract. Management, for its part, has frequently been just as glad to get away from the constant union drive to enroll 100 per cent of the workers under its provisions. The result has been a steady decline in the number and coverage of maintenance-of-membership agreements.

The jurisdictional dispute. The union's security may be jeopardized by other unions, with or without the collusion of the employer, but the employer will always be involved, sometimes disastrously. The dispute may be over work jurisdiction—carpenters versus electricians over the right to install conduits, for example—or it may be over the right to organize the employes in a given occupation or firm. The real issue is the same in both cases, the control of a given class of jobs by a certain labor organization. The 20-year split between the AFL and the CIO greatly aggravated the problem of jurisdictions, since both federations frequently had member unions claiming jurisdiction over identical groups of employes—for example, the Retail Clerks (AFL) and the Retail, Wholesale & Department Store Union (CIO). The merger of the AFL and the CIO has done much to reduce and eliminate jurisdictional arguments.

No type of labor dispute has received less sympathy from employers and the public than the disagreement over jurisdiction. Since the union's only real weapon is the strike, the penalty is visited directly on the employer and his customers and only indirectly on the cause of it all, the other union. In 1947, the Taft-Hartley Act banned work stoppages as a result of jurisdictional disputes, making them an unfair labor practice.

The dispute over jurisdiction is directly associated with the principle of exclusive craft unionism, according to which the limits of a given labor organization are defined in terms of the kind of work done. In modern industrial society, these limits are more easily drawn between industries than between crafts or trades (although industrial jurisdictions are hazy enough), since the latter are undergoing constant revision due to technological advances and the substitution of machinery for manpower. Automation is a current case in point. The traditional locale of the jurisdictional fight is in the building trades, where bricklayers, carpenters, electricians, structural iron workers, lathers, painters, and others may be engaged on the same construction job and frequent opportunities arise for disagreement over the right to do a particular job. To the union actually involved, an encroachment or "invasion"by another union is just as serious a threat to its security as the union-breaking tactics of an employer and must be resisted at all costs. Such disputes will continue to arise as long as a large number of autonomous, sovereign trade unions compete for employes and jobs within an active industrial society. The principal policy question is how to settle them. On this score the case seems good for arbitration by a public body, to avoid subjecting employers and the public to stoppage of service.

The checkoff. Union security is founded upon a stable and established membership, the road to which is union job control. Membership means bargaining power and support. And support means money. It would be wrong to overemphasize the importance of financial support, as though that were all the union wanted from its members. There is no substitute for high morale, which shows itself in the solid backing of union policies, the disciplined execution of necessary but unpleasant duties such as strikes, and the willing performance of the many detailed and minor tasks incident to union operation, such as committee work and shop stewardship. Nonetheless, in the present advanced state of union organization, the treasury is a vital factor in success or failure.

The source of union funds is the membership, but the assumption that a given membership *automatically* produces the income expected of it is an error. Union dues are assessed like taxes, in small amounts from large numbers of people, to be paid periodically, month by month. Their collection is a job in itself, and union members, being much like anyone else, are negligent, forgetful, short of cash, and likely to fall in arrears. Once in arrears, the sum owed grows rapidly and may soon assume the proportions of a problem to the workingman who is trying to spread his pay over the current expenses of a family and payments on a car, a TV set, or a house. It does not improve his relations with his union to be dunned for the back payments. At the same time, it takes a great deal of time, energy, and tact on the part of local officials to keep all members in good standing and the treasury in the black. The obvious solution, just as in the case of income taxes, is a payroll deduction to be paid over to the union by the employer. This deduction is called "the checkoff."

One advantage of the checkoff, from the standpoint of the national union, is that the payment may be made to the international headquarters rather than to the local, with the national remitting the balance due the local union. This practice frees the national officers from what could be an embarrassing financial dependence upon the local chapters of the union. The United Steelworkers of America use this procedure. The more general practice, however, is for the employer to remit directly to the local union, as stipulated in the following clause taken from an agreement between the United Automobile Workers and the Chrysler Corporation:

Deductions for any calendar month shall be remitted to the designated financial officer of the Local Union as soon as possible after the tenth (10th) day of the following month. Local management shall furnish the designated financial officer of the Local Union, monthly, with a list of those for whom deductions have been made and the amounts of such deductions.

THE DUES PICKET LINE.   The main appeal of a checkoff provision in the contract is its elimination of the need for a "dues picket line." In these days of mass unionism, with local lodges running to memberships in the hundreds or even thousands, the simple mechanics of dues collection can be a major problem. At a minimum, members must be located, solicited, and the dues accepted and receipted for. Since many union members attend meetings only seldom and live miles apart from one another, the obvious point of contact is the workplace. The dues picket line results. Shop stewards or local financial officers periodically take positions at plant entrances and check off the arriving or departing workmen for unpaid dues, fees, and assessments.

The procedure is undignified, time-consuming, and productive of arguments and disputes. The man who has paid already may be delayed in line along with those who have not, until his card is checked. If the line is set up at the beginning of shift, it may throw some men late; if at the end of shift, it will come when everybody is tired and in a hurry to get home. Men come to work without money and must be caught again later. If the line is on payday, checks must be cashed and change made, and the delay is compounded. It is not surprising that the checkoff is widely used, especially in contracts without membership-security clauses. Here again, the Taft-Hartley Act establishes limits. Each worker individually must sign a checkoff agreement and his commitment has a maximum term of 1 year.

Checkoff coverage.   The checkoff, as a form of union security, has somewhat broader coverage than the union shop. The BLS study referred to above showed that dues were checked off in 77 per cent of the cases, initiation fees in 54 per cent, and assessments in 27 per cent. Checkoff provisions were most prevalent in sole-bargaining shops. To some degree, membership-security clauses and the checkoff are substitutes for one another: 96 per cent of all workers covered in the sample had one or both.

SECURITY FOR THE WORKER

The security of the union member is a more complicated proposition. In the casual (nonfactory) trades, the employe usually moves from job to job and his seniority with any one employer is therefore brief and unimportant. His security rests on the union's control of all jobs in the local labor market and on its control of who is eligible to apply for them. He has no special rights to any single particular job in the market, but he is one of a limited number of eligibles for any job of his classification (carpentering, stevedoring, etc.) which does show up. Within that group, he takes his chances, and if the group is restricted in size, he is seldom out of work long. Dismissal (discharge) from a job may be resisted now and then as unfair, but in general it is not considered too important. It merely shortens a work span that would be relatively brief anyway. His pay rates, hours of work, and privileges on the job are taken care of by the union work rules.[13]

In permanent employment ("factory" or "industrial" unionism), on the other hand, the worker's basic security is his position on the seniority roster. This settles his rights during layoff and rehiring after layoff, his prerogatives with respect to promotion, demotion, transfer, bidding for preferred shifts and work assignments, and many other privileges and considerations. For these reasons, seniority is always outlined in detail and the grounds for loss of seniority are specified precisely, as follows:

An employee shall lose all seniority rights if he or she:
1. Voluntarily quits the services of the Company;
2. Is discharged and the discharge is not reversed through the grievance procedure;
3. Fails to report within five (5) consecutive working days after notification by registered letter or telegram unless a satisfactory reason is given for not reporting;
4. Is absent for five (5) consecutive working days without properly notifying the Company unless a satisfactory reason is given;
5. Fails to report on the first day following the expiration of a leave of absence, unless a satisfactory reason is given;
6. Has been laid off for a continuous period of eighteen (18) months.

Seniority is still a very live issue between unions and management. To the union and the long-service workman, it represents security through job control. It rules out the elimination of older employes through the casual method of the general layoff and failure to rehire those above a cer-

[13] See Kennedy, *op. cit.*, on this.

tain age, and it forces recognition of the "service" factor, which is objective, measurable, and easily ascertainable, relative to the "efficiency" factor, which is (to employes, at least) often subjective, arbitrary, and whimsical in application. Above all, it establishes *certainty* of employe status, rather than the harassing fear of being "next" on management's list in time of retrenchment.

The employer's argument is equally valid, from the standpoint of managerial responsibility. Who can say what the shifts of consumer demand and technological improvement are going to bring? A machine, a process, a department, which yesterday was essential, may tomorrow be rendered obsolete. The employes affected may be well trained, efficient, with long service records. On the other hand, they may also be specialized and incapable of retraining into other work as valuable as what they have been doing. If they must be kept and converted to new jobs, while the occupiers of those jobs are let go, what happens to efficiency and output and cost and price? The first two go down and the last two go up.

The above agrument is even stronger on promotions. Promotional seniority implies that ability increases in direct ratio to experience, a thesis which even union officials do not try to defend. Yet many unions want an uncompromising seniority rule for promotions as well as layoffs and re-hiring. The result of the argument is very often a compromise, with management promising to give full consideration to length of service and to make seniority the basis of decision if other things are equal.

It will be noted in the list of reasons for loss (breaking) of seniority given above that five of the seven grounds are within the control of the union member. Only item 2 (discharge) and item 6 (layoff of 18 months) are initiated by management, and both are covered by the agreement. On layoff, the employe takes his turn in line with his seniority. If he is off for 18 months, the company is in a bad way or he has very low seniority. Nevertheless, he has that much time to find another place to work before his job rights terminate entirely. He is usually equally well protected against arbitrary discipline or discharge by a clause in the "management rights" section of the contract, like the following: "The right to hire, promote, discharge or discipline for cause, and to maintain discipline and efficiency of employes is the sole responsibility of the Company provided it does not conflict with other provisions of this Agreement. . . ."

It is the phrase "for cause" which makes the difference. This means that any discipline or discharge must be justifiable in terms of proper grounds, correct procedure, satisfactory proof, appropriateness of the punishment, and absence of extenuating circumstances.[14] If it fails on any of these, a grievance is in order, and if pushed to arbitration, it has a good

[14] See O. W. Phelps, *Discipline and Discharge in the Unionized Firm* (Berkeley, Calif.: University of California Press, 1959), for a review of the protections available to union members against arbitrary action by management.

chance of being upheld and the company reversed. This is discipline by "due process" as against the more authoritarian methods employed in the absence of a union. It is crucial to the employe's security as the final step in a system of tenure. It has the effect of changing the contract of employment from one in which either party has the option of terminating at any time to one in which the employe may terminate for any reason or no reason but the employer only for cause.

Still another type of security for the union member is a schedule of dismissal-pay allowances for the long-service worker who loses his job because of permanent curtailment of operations. For example (from a Steelworkers' agreement):

When, in the sole judgment of the Company, it decides to close permanently a plant or discontinue permanently a department of a plant or substantial portion thereof and terminate the employment of individuals, an employee whose employment is terminated either directly or indirectly as a result thereof because he was not entitled to other employment with the company . . . shall be entitled to a severance allowance in accordance with and subject to the following provision. . . .

An eligible individual shall receive severance allowance based upon the following weeks for the corresponding continuous Company service:

Continuous company service	Weeks of severance allowance
3 years but less than 5 years	4
5 years but less than 7 years	6
7 years but less than 10 years	7
10 years or more	8

The severence allowance is one form of attack upon a very fundamental form of employe insecurity—the inroads of machine technology upon jobs.[15] The issue of technological unemployment calls for different answers in the long and the short run, in times of full and of low employment, and in the case of industries with elastic demand for their products and those with inelastic demand. The union view on the substitution of machines for men is that the change will not be made if it does not improve the employer's earnings position and that, since the impact of the change is very severe on, typically, a small number of workmen, a part of the gain might well be shared with those employes through a security guarantee. The union may also point out that these changes take place most often in large establishments, which have a regular turnover. All the employer needs to do, then, is to stop hiring and rearrange his present staff until the slack is taken up and the displaced employes are comfortably settled in new jobs. The union argues that employes are not alone in put-

[15] There are many other approaches to the threat of automation, of course: retraining, early retirement, job guarantees, etc.

ting personal security above advancement of the race and that, if there is a gain in efficiency, some of its advantages may well be applied to the point of greatest cost, the loss of employment by displaced workmen.

WAGES, HOURS, AND FRINGE BENEFITS

These provisions are the heart of any collective agreement and the most common subjects of collective negotiation. A good contract calls for high wages, short hours (at basic rates), and a wide and generous range of fringe benefits. The wage provisions may be very simple—a single hourly rate for each job—or very complicated. Instead of single rates, there may be rate ranges, and the actual rate paid may be a function of the assignment of one of scores of job classifications to the appropriate labor grade. and the finding of the proper rate within the range. Rate ranges call for a progression system, by which workers move up within the range. This may be automatic (a 5 cent rise each 16 weeks until the top of the range is reached) or by merit on the judgment of management, or a combination of the two—say, automatic progression halfway up the range and by merit thereafter. There may also be an escalator clause, which calls for an increase in the base rate with each upward movement of the Consumer Price Index (and within limits, decreases when the CPI drops); and there may be a "productivity factor," which is essentially an annual deferred increase of a certain number of cents per hours or a percentage of the base rate.

However, base rates are only the beginning. They are supplemented by overtime—the standard is time and a half for any time worked over 8 hours in one day or 40 hours in one week—by premium rates (double or triple time for Sundays and holidays, in some agreements), and by shift differentials, which may be quite an addition on the third shift, with 8 hours pay for $6\frac{1}{2}$ (or 7 or $7\frac{1}{2}$) hours work. For example, the formula for hourly overtime pay on the third shift in one contract is:

$$\frac{1\frac{1}{2} \times 8 \text{ (hourly base rate plus shift differential)}}{6\frac{1}{2}}$$

(Figure it out, using a base rate of $2.50 and a shift differential of 10 cents per hour.) There are also special bonuses for difficult and dangerous work, such as "flight line" work, handling explosives, and so on.

A shorter basic work week now seems to be shaping up, as an adjustment to the greater productivity under automation and electronic control devices. Some of these are quite dramatic. For example:

A chemical company has recently opened a magnesium mill which is capable of producing more magnesium sheet and plate than the total previous national capacity. A musical record company has installed new automatic machines with which four men turn out eight times as many records as 250 men had previously produced. An automobile engine part which was once produced at the rate of 38 per hour by five men and two machines is now produced by 1 man at one machine at the rate of 750 per hour.[16]

Clark Kerr estimates that by 1975 we may be down to a 1,700-hour year from the present 2,000-hour year.[17] This would be a 32- to 33-hour week, perhaps in a 4-day work week. The AFL–CIO has had a 30-hour week as a basic policy objective for years.

The fringe on top.   The really startling change of the last 25 years in the economic area of the labor agreement has been the growing list of fringe benefits. A "fringe" is any kind of benefit having economic value to the employe, other than his basic wage and perhaps the standard overtime required by law: time and a half over 40 hours per week. It thus includes premium rates (for Sundays, holidays, sixth or seventh day of the week, and shift differentials); time paid for but not worked: "report" or "call-in" pay, for showing up when no work is available, vacation allowance ranging up to 13 weeks every 5 years, rest periods, time off for jury examination and service; protection against contingencies, such as unemployment benefits, compensation in case of accident or illness; deferred wage payments such as pensions; and many others.

The "fringe" drive started in the Second World War, really took hold during the Korean conflict, and since 1952 has steadily gained momentum. Depending on how "fringes" are classified, there are at least 40 different kinds of benefits in the group, ranging from a paid holiday on the employe's birthday to extensive hospital and surgical benefits paid for by the employer.[18]

The reason for the growth of fringes is easy to understand; they are popular with both employers and employes. For employers, by and large, a fringe concession of another paid holiday or an extra week's vacation is less expensive than a wage increase. The units of cost in most cases are smaller, and they are therefore used frequently as counters in the bargaining game. The more expensive fringes—pensions, medical and hospital insurance, and the like—are highly desirable in themselves and with some of them (pensions, for example), the cost may be deferrable for quite long periods.

Employes also like fringes, just as most people like the frosting on the cake better than the cake itself. Fringes add greatly to the employe's se-

[16] William A. Faunce, *Automation and Leisure,* 1959–60 Reprint Series (East Lansing, Mich.: Labor and Industrial Relations Center, Michigan State University).

[17] *The Prospect for Wages and Hours in 1975,* Reprint 122 (Berkeley, Calif.: Institute of Industrial Relations, University of California, 1959).

[18] See *Fringe Benefits—1965* (Washington: Chamber of Commerce of the United States, 1966).

curity, covering such tremendously important contingencies as sickness for himself and family, accidental disability, old age and unemployment, and such minor contingencies as required jury duty and military service. They also relax the stern discipline of industrial life by adding free time (with pay) on holidays and vacations, during weddings and deaths in the family, and on birthdays. Fringes also blunt the hardship of shift and overtime work by making it more remunerative and tend to reduce it in amount by making it too costly for the employer. Fringes add a number of new dimensions and much greater flexibility to the standard, three-dimensional "wages-hours-conditions of work" job combination.

At the same time, fringe benefits have been the source of some concern because of their permanent character. A fringe once embedded in a contract is rarely if ever removed. To the employe, it is a privilege in addition to being a contractual right, and giving it up would be resisted strenuously. Also, by now the total cost of fringes is by no means minor. It is estimated that for industry in general, this cost is more than 20 per cent of the total employment bill, and in some sectors of the economy it is as much as one-third.[19] Fringe-benefit costs have been rising rather rapidly, and the deferred payments—pensions, medical and surgical contingencies—may mount up forbiddingly in the future. Employers have been warned to look closely at the fringe picture and to exercise restraint in granting additional types of indirect economic benefits.

MAKING THE CONTRACT WORK: THE GRIEVANCE PROCEDURE

Union contracts are customarily printed up in pocket-sized pamphlets, approximately 4 by 6 inches in size, and every union member is urged to keep a copy with him at all times. They vary in length and number of provisions. However, even an average agreement, 50 or 60 pages in length, calls for considerable study and interpretation. It is one thing to set down rules for the guidance of employer-employe relations and often quite another thing to apply them to action situations. It is almost axiomatic that no union contract is complete without a clear statement of the method to be followed in settling disputes over the meaning of its clauses. This method is called the "grievance procedure."

"Grievances" are employe complaints, or "gripes." Since management is boss, management of necessity interprets the contract in the first place by making work assignments, scheduling operations, directing employes to do certain things, issuing pay checks, and the like. If it seems to a union member that managerial actions are running counter to the rules, he may

[19] In 1962, according to a BLS survey, "supplementary pay practices" (the BLS's delicate term for "fringes") in manufacturing amounted to 53.4¢ per hour for the United States as a whole, or 22 per cent of payroll. *Monthly Labor Review*, November, 1964, pp. 1273–1277.

report a grievance to his shop steward or his business agent, and if the latter agrees that it is a valid complaint, the grievance procedure is set in motion. The big difference between this and individual-bargaining procedure is that, in the absence of a union, the complaint is reported to the foreman, who is often the author of the orders or actions complained of. Probably no phase of employe relations has been more neglected, under individual bargaining, than the grievances of workers. Certainly no privilege is more highly prized by union men than the right to a full consideration of their grievances, with successive appeals to higher and higher ranks of authority in the company and a final decision by an impartial arbitrator selected by the two parties.

Grievances may or may not be restricted to interpretation of the existing contract. Most contract terminology is broad enough to cover any dispute over wages, hours, or working conditions which may arise and threaten to interrupt operations. However, the huge majority of complaints are with respect to interpretation, and this type of dispute is customarily so designated. The main idea is to keep operations going without interruption. A typical statement of purpose of the grievance procedure is the following (from a Steelworkers' contract):

Should any differences arise between the Company and the Union, or its members employed by the Company, as to the interpretation or application of, or compliance with, the provisions of this agreement regarding working conditions or other matters, or should any local trouble of any kind arise, there shall be no interruptions or impeding of the work, work stoppages, strikes or lockouts on account of such differences, but an earnest effort shall be made by the Company and the Union to settle such differences orderly and promptly in accordance with the procedure hereinafter set forth in this Section.

The steps in the grievance procedure are customarily laid out from start to finish in the agreement in explicit fashion in order to safeguard the rights of all parties—management, workers, and the union. Interpretation of the contract is the proof of the pudding. If the rules are considered the legal framework of employment relations, then the decisions over grievances are the final verdicts which determine the rights of parties. Hence, both management and the union keep a close watch on proceedings and are quick to challenge any act which is out of order.

One of the biggest issues in the grievance procedure arises in the very first step, the reporting of the complaint by the employe. The union would like to have every grievance reported in the first instance to the union representative (shop steward or business agent) and to him only. The union representative would then report the complaint to the first-line supervisor, as the first step in the process of settling the dispute. Management insists, with vehemence, that the employe have the right to take up any grievance directly with his supervisor, in the presence of the union representative or not, as he may choose, with the right to appeal to the union if not satisfied with the foreman's decision. The union's argument is that the shop committeeman is the employe representative on the grounds and that he should know all instances of contract violation if he is to render good service. Management answers that many so-called grievances are merely cases of misunderstanding and can be settled promptly and satisfactorily on an informal basis, without resort to the machinery of a union-management conference. Denying the employe the right to approach the foreman, it is claimed, would unnecessarily complicate the exchange of information between the two and make the coordination of work at the operating level difficult and inflexible.

What is really at stake is the loyalty of the individual worker, who is at one and the same time an employe of the company and a member of the union. What management is demanding is that supervisors be permitted to compete on an equal basis with union representatives for the respect of union members by having a chance to correct misunderstandings or errors without "going to court."

The heart of the procedure, however, is found in the clauses of the agreement which describe the successive "steps" toward dispute settlement. These steps establish the hierarchy of appeals, through bipartisan (union-management) committees to a final point of decision by an impartial umpire. There is considerable variation, both as to the number of steps and the manner of referral to an arbitrator for a final decision in different unions and different industries. The general pattern, however, is standard. The procedure described below, taken from a Textile Workers' contract, is typical of the settlement process.

Adjustment of grievances

Should any problems, differences or disputes arise with relation to rates of pay, hours of work or conditions of employment, an earnest effort shall be made to settle such differences in the steps provided. The procedure for adjustment of grievances is as follows:

Step 1. By adjustment between the Union Steward accompanied by the aggrieved employee and the general foreman of the department concerned.

Step 2. If the grievance is not adjusted in Step 1 it shall be reduced to writing and submitted to the Superintendent of the mill within three (3) working days by a member of the shop committee or business agent of the union.

Step 3. By adjustment between the Vice-President, the director of personnel or the mill superintendent of the company and the International Union representatives and shop committee. The company will not be obligated to pay for any time spent in grievances under this step in excess of eight (8) hours in any week.

Step 4. In the event the grievance is not satisfactorily settled in Step 3 within five working days, it may be referred to arbitration as hereinafter provided.

Arbitration. Any dispute, difference, disagreement or controversy of any nature or character, whether or not a grievance, between the Union and the Employer which has not been satisfactorily adjusted within fifteen working days after the initiation of conferences between representatives of the Union and the Employer, shall be promptly referred to arbitration by either party hereto as follows:

Within five working days after receipt of written notice of a demand for arbitration sent by either party to the other, the parties shall mutually agree upon a single arbitrator who shall hear and decide the dispute. If the parties shall fail to agree upon a single arbitrator within the aforesaid five day period, then and in that event the arbitrator shall be appointed by the American Arbitration Association in accordance with its rules. The Arbitrator shall hold hearings upon the issue, make such investigations as he shall deem necessary to a proper decision, and render his decision in writing, which shall be final and conclusively binding upon the parties hereto. The expense of the Arbitrator shall be shared equally by the Union and the Employer.

As will be seen from the above, the full grievance procedure is complicated, impressive, time-consuming, and expensive. Both the union and management think twice before taking positions which will force a dispute to the next higher level, and only matters of the utmost significance to the two parties are carried forward to arbitration. Nonetheless, it is there, available to every union member without cost, backed by the weight and prestige of the staff of the national union, if his contractual rights are violated by a careless management. It is a far cry from the tentative requests for hearings and the passive acceptance of one-way decisions which characterized the preunion shop. It unquestionably adds to costs. It also unquestionably adds to the dignity of the rank-and-file employe. The testimony of union men is emphatic on its importance: the grievance procedure is at the top of the list of cherished prerogatives under collective bargaining.

RENEGOTIATION

Union contracts may run to a certain date or continue indefinitely until one party or the other requests a change. Agreements between the carriers and the railway operating brotherhoods are of the latter kind, with no termination date specified and all provisions remaining in effect until changed by agreement of the parties. However, most contracts are for a definite term. They may or may not provide for automatic extension but usually contain explicit instructions as to the proper procedure for reopening and renegotiation. For example, the clauses below set the limits of a 3-year agreement between the Auto Workers and a parts manufacturing firm.

Termination

This Agreement dated as of December 1, 1965, shall continue in full force and effect without change until November 30, 1968. If neither party shall give notice to terminate this Agreement as provided above, or to modify this Agreement as hereinafter provided, the Agreement shall continue in effect from year to year after November 30, 1968, subject to termination by either party on sixty (60) days' written notice prior to November 30th of any subsequent year.

If either party desires to modify or change this Agreement it shall, sixty (60) days prior to November 30, 1968, or any subsequent November 30th date, give written notice to such effect. Within ten (10) days after receipt of said notice, a conference will be arranged to negotiate the proposals in which case this Agreement shall continue in full force and effect until terminated as provided hereinafter.

MANAGEMENT–UNION CONSULTATION

A union can have recognition, security, and a good contract and still not be a full partner in collective bargaining. Full partnership calls for union-management consultation on all issues which arise between the company and the employes, whether within or without the agreement. What the union wants is *acceptance,* in the full sense of the word, as the agent of the employes in the productive process. In a sense, that is what unions have been forcing on management over the years, but legal recognition is one thing, acceptance another. The latter implies *informal* acknowledgment of the importance of the union's function and consideration of its point of view in all appropriate situations, regardless of contractual stipulations. It implies regard for the feelings of union representatives, who are just as sensitive of their prerogatives as corporation vice-presidents and factory superintendents, and comprehension of the fact that the union has a definite place in the social system of the factory, shop, or job. Acceptance is the only possible basis for union-management cooperation, about which so much is said and written and so little done.

Notwithstanding their apparent similarity, union "acceptance" is a long, long jump from union "recognition and security." It means that management thinks of the union as an integral part of the total operating structure and calls upon the union in the solution of personnel problems as naturally as it would refer a legal problem to its general counsel. Since management, as a function, is primarily the management of men, this implies a theory of joint administrative responsibility. It is joint, because the union is not responsible to, and does not report to, management. The difficulty of arriving at any such state of mutual trust between two organizations, both of which tend to consider themselves sovereign in their respective spheres, should not be minimized, particularly when the joint relations must be the basis for many quick decisions affecting operations.

The issue here is the fundamental one of a division of union and management prerogatives and the effect of such assignment upon individual firms and the society as a whole. For one thing, the result will probably never be as *orderly* as operations upon the authoritarian basis, and the outcome may appear to be—and may be in fact—a reduction of efficiency. However, there are many intangibles involved, not least among which is the morale of the working force. Disorder—at least, surface disorder—is always a characteristic of democracy and recognition of the rights of individuals.[20] Is the result necessarily less efficient? If so, the performance of national economies is a surprising contradiction to the general rule. What authoritarian system has outproduced the United States?

Several subissues of great importance and very high controversial voltage are raised by the primary riddle of union-management prerogatives. One is the extent to which unions are willing to assume management *responsibilities* of the same order of magnitude as the *authority* they actually exercise in entering into contracts with employers and helping to interpret the contracts. An example of this is the question of union discipline and observance of contract commitments, particularly no-strike clauses, which prohibit work stoppages during the life of the agreement. Employers have repeatedly charged that unions are both unwilling and unable to impose adequate penalties upon their members to stop contract violations and have asked for legal authority to penalize breaches of the agreement. The Taft-Hartley Act met this complaint by establishing union agreements as contracts at law and by making both employers and unions legally responsible for their proper observance.

Another subissue raised by the question of union-management prerogatives is the extent to which union representatives are to be taken into the confidence of management. This comes close to the heart of the whole question of union acceptance and union-management cooperation. On the one hand, without some knowledge of company policies and problems, no union man can be expected to assume responsibility for making decisions which will advance the company's well-being. On the other hand, the union man has other loyalties than to the company, and the organization which he represents may have contractual relations with other, and perhaps competing, firms. Can management assume that data on prices, sales, costs, profits, and accounting practices will be kept confidential and not used as a bargaining lever for forcing concessions or even be disclosed to rivals? It is not an easy question to answer, and union spokesmen have not been able to clarify the situation much. Some have even indicated that they preferred to be excluded from managerial discussions and to stay in the role of outside "watchdog" over the interests of members.

The desire for acceptance, however, still stands. No matter what the decision on relative prerogatives, the existence of a union agreement implies the assignment of some area of authority to the bargaining representative of the employes. In this general area, the union feels that it

[20] It may, of course, be argued that trade unionism does not mean democracy in industry but rather that means regimentation of workers by "labor bosses" in mass organizations far larger than any employing units, where their individuality has even less chance for expression than in their dealings with management. However, this argument is almost sure to fail if a check is made of the individual worker's *opportunities* for expressing an opinion (casting a vote) on policies and leadership in both his union and his company.

should be taken into account as a natural and normal part of the operating organization and not treated as an outsider. In this area, decisions should not be unilateral and authoritative, whether covered by contract or not. They should be arrived at through consultation and conference, just as high policy judgments are processed through executive committees or boards of directors. Nor should the process be one of strict, legalistic fulfillment of contract obligations and nothing more. The proper basis of good union-management relations is a belief in mutual sincerity, fairness, and understanding. At this point, so the union contends, joint administration can be directed to the mutual advancement of common ends.

READINGS

For an excellent short survey of collective bargaining up to date, the reader is referred to: Jas. J. Healy (ed.), *Creative Collective Bargaining* (Englewood Cliffs, N.J.: Prentice-Hall, Inc., 1965). See also, a poorly named but very good book on union-management relations: Arthur Kornhauser, R. Dubin, and A. M. Ross, *Industrial Conflict* (New York: McGraw-Hill Book Company, 1954).

APPENDIX

THE TAFT–HARTLEY ACT (AS AMENDED)

The Taft-Hartley Act [1] (its real name, "Labor Management Relations Act, 1947" is seldom used) was passed in 1947 over President Truman's veto. It was then and has been since one of the most controversial pieces of legislation ever passed by Congress. Labor leaders resent it; businessmen are lined up solidly behind it; and it has been an issue in presidential campaigns and almost every session of Congress since 1947. After several unsuccessful attempts, it was finally amended in a number of important ways in the Labor-Management Reporting and Disclosure Act of 1959 (the Landrum-Griffin law). The changes in the law are almost entirely in the direction of making it more restrictive on unions.

The Taft-Hartley Act is a big, long, complicated law. It governs the rights of employers and unions in interstate commerce in their dealings with one another. This means that it sets the rules of industrial relations in most businesses of any importance. It also means that some grasp of the law is a must for students of labor relations. However, the statute in its original form (like most legislation) is hard to read and understand, some of its sections are now long out of date, and the various passages differ greatly in relative importance.

In this appendix, the text of the act, as amended by the Reporting and Disclosure Act of 1959, is given verbatim, except for certain passages which no longer have any effect. Then the sections are commented on briefly in a separate column on the right-hand side of each page. The idea is to give readers the feel of the statute as it stands in the United States Code and the opportunity to read and study it either as a unit or by sections, assisted by a minimum of interpretation to save time and speed up understanding.

An Act

To amend the National Labor Relations Act, to provide additional facilities for the mediation of labor disputes affecting commerce, to equalize legal responsibilities of labor organizations and employers, and for other purposes.
Be it enacted by the Senate and House of Representatives of the United States of America in Congress assembled,

Short title and declaration of policy

SECTION 1.   (a)   This Act may be cited as the "Labor Management Relations Act, 1947."

[1] 61 Stat. 136.

(b) Industrial strife which interferes with the normal flow of commerce and with the full production of articles and commodities for commerce, can be avoided or substantially minimized if employers, employees, and labor organizations each recognize under law one another's legitimate rights in their relations with each other, and above all recognize under law that neither party has any right in its relations with any other to engage in acts or practices which jeopardize the public health, safety, or interest.

It is the purpose and policy of this Act, in order to promote the full flow of commerce, and prescribe the legitimate rights of both employees and employers in their relations affecting commerce, to provide orderly and peaceful procedures for preventing the interference by either with the legitimate rights of the other, to protect the rights of individual employees in their relations with labor organizations whose activities affect commerce, to define and proscribe practices on the part of labor and management which affect commerce and are inimical to the general welfare, and to protect the rights of the public in connection with labor disputes affecting commerce.

Title I—Amendment of National Labor Relations Act

Sec. 101.   The National Labor Relations Act is hereby amended to read as follows:

Findings and policies

"Section 1. The denial by some employers of the right of employees to organize and the refusal by some employers to accept the procedure of collective bargaining lead to strikes and other forms of industrial strife or unrest, which have the intent or the necessary effect of burdening or obstructing commerce by (a) impairing the efficiency, safety, or operation of the instrumentalities of commerce; (b) occurring in the current of commerce; (c) materially affecting, restraining, or controlling the flow of raw materials or manufactured or processed goods from or into the channels of commerce, or the prices of such materials or goods in commerce; or (d) causing diminution of employment and wages in such volume as substantially to impair or disrupt the market for goods flowing from or into the channels of commerce.

"The inequality of bargaining power between

The Taft-Hartley Act contains five "titles," corresponding to chapters, by far the most important of which is Title I. The "National Labor Relations Act," of course, is the Wagner Act, passed in 1935 and in effect with practically no change until passage of the Taft-Hartley Act in 1947. It was a strictly unilateral (one-way) law, prohibiting unfair labor practices by employers and implying by its silence on the subject that unions did not commit any unfair labor practices. The biggest change in the amended National Labor Relations Act, on this and the following pages, is the prohibition of *union* unfair labor practices and the

employees who do not possess full freedom of association or actual liberty of contract, and employers who are organized in the corporate or other forms of ownership association substantially burdens and affects the flow of commerce, and tends to aggravate recurrent business depressions, by depressing wage rates and the purchasing power of wage earners in industry and by preventing the stabilization of competitive wage rates and working conditions within and between industries.

"Experience has proved that protection by law of the right of employees to organize and bargain collectively safeguards commerce from injury, impairment, or interruption, and promotes the flow of commerce by removing certain recognized sources of industrial strife and unrest, by encouraging practices fundamental to the friendly adjustment of industrial disputes arising out of differences as to wages, hours, or other working conditions, and by restoring equality of bargaining power between employers and employees.

"Experience has further demonstrated that certain practices by some labor organizations, their officers, and members have the intent or the necessary effect of burdening or obstructing commerce by preventing the free flow of goods in such commerce through strikes and other forms of industrial unrest or through concerted activities which impair the interest of the public in the free flow of such commerce. The elimination of such practices is a necessary condition to the assurance of the rights herein guranteed.

"It is hereby declared to be the policy of the United States to eliminate the causes of certain substantial obstructions to the free flow of commerce and to mitigate and eliminate these obstructions when they have occurred *by encouraging the practice and procedure of collective bargaining and by protecting the exercise by workers of full freedom of association, self-organization, and designation of representatives of their own choosing,* for the purpose of negotiating the terms and conditions of their employment or other mutual aid or protection.²

Definitions

"SEC. 2.   When used in this Act—
"(1)   The term 'person' includes one or more
² Italics added.

---

regulation of unions to keep them from interfering with the rights of employers, employes, and the public.

This paragraph was added in 1947 and reflects the purpose of "equalizing" the responsibilities of employers and unions by setting standards for the latter to observe.

This paragraph is the key passage in the "findings and policies," with its wording unchanged from what it was in the Wagner Act of 1935.

It is through "definitions" that persons or

individuals, labor organizations, partnerships, corporations, legal representatives, trustees, trustees in bankruptcy, or receivers.

"(2)   The term 'employer' includes any person acting as an agent of an employer, directly or indirectly, but shall not include the United States or any wholly owned Government corporation, or any Federal Reserve Bank, or any State or political subdivision thereof, or any corporation or association operating a hospital, if no part of the net earnings inures to the benefit of any private shareholder or individual, or any person subject to the Railway Labor Act, as amended from time to time, or any labor organization (other than when acting as an employer), or anyone acting in the capacity of officer or agent of such labor organization.

"(3)   The term 'employee' shall include any employee, and shall not be limited to the employees of a particular employer, unless the Act explicitly states otherwise, and shall include any individual whose work has ceased as a consequence of, or in connection with, any current labor dispute or because of any unfair labor practice, and who has not obtained any other regular and substantially equivalent employment, but shall not include any individual employed as an agricultural laborer, or in the domestic service of any family or person at his home, or any individual employed by his parent or spouse, or any individual having the status of an independent contractor, or any individual employed as a supervisor, or any individual employed by an employer subject to the Railway Labor Act, as amended from time to time, or by any other person who is not an employer as herein defined.

"(4)   The term 'representative' includes any individual or labor organization.

"(5)   The term 'labor organization' means any organization of any kind, or any agency or employee representation committee or plan, in which employees participate and which exists for the purpose, in whole or in part, of dealing with employers concerning grievances, labor disputes, wages, rates of pay, hours of employment, or conditions of work.

"(6)   The term 'commerce' means trade, traffic, commerce, transportation, or communication among the several States, or between the District of Columbia or any Territory of the United States and any State or other Territory, or between any foreign

---

organizations are exempted from the law and its jurisdiction clarified. The principal exemptions from the amended NLRA are governmental employers (Federal, state, and local), nonprofit hospitals, employers subject to the Railway Labor Act; and farm labor, domestic servants, family labor (children, wives, or husbands of employers), independent contractors, supervisors, and employes subject to the Railway Labor Act. In paragraph (3), workers on strike are defined as still employes, in the meaning of the act—which means acceptance of the union theory of the strike. Paragraph (9), defining "labor dispute," is an example of how the act's jurisdiction is extended. This is a broad definition, primarily because of the final clause, "regardless of whether the disputants stand in the proximate relation of employer and employee."

The exclusion of supervisors in Paragraph (3) was to kill off the Foreman's Association of America, which had a respectable 20,000 members by 1947, and was negotiating agreements with employers in the Detroit area. Denying them access to the NLRB was a deathblow. By 1959, the FAA had disappeared.

country and any State, Territory, or the District of Columbia, or within the District of Columbia or any Territory, or between points in the same State but through any other State or any Territory or the District of Columbia or any foreign country.

"(7) The term 'affecting commerce' means in commerce, or burdening or obstructing commerce or the free flow of commerce, or having led or tending to lead to a labor dispute burdening or obstructing commerce or the free flow of commerce.

"(8) The term 'unfair labor practice' means any unfair labor practice listed in section 8.

"(9) The term 'labor dispute' includes any controversy concerning terms, tenure or conditions of employment, or concerning the association or representation of persons in negotiating, fixing, maintaining, changing, or seeking to arrange terms or conditions of employment, regardless of whether the disputants stand in the proximate relation of employer and employee.

"(10) The term 'National Labor Relations Board' means the National Labor Relations Board provided for in section 3 of this Act.

"(11) The term 'supervisor' means any individual having authority, in the interest of the employer, to hire, transfer, suspend, lay off, recall, promote, discharge, assign, reward, or discipline other employees, or responsibly to direct them, or to adjust their grievances, or effectively to recommend such action, if in connection with the foregoing the exercise of such authority is not of a merely routine or clerical nature, but requires the use of independent judgment.

"(12) The term 'professional employee' means—

"(a) any employee engaged in work (i) predominantly intellectual and varied in character as opposed to routine mental, manual, mechanical, or physical work; (ii) involving the consistent exercise of discretion and judgment in its performance; (iii) of such a character that the output produced or the result accomplished cannot be standardized in relation to a given period of time; (iv) requiring knowledge of an advanced type in a field of science or learning customarily acquired by a prolonged course of specialized intellectual instruction and study in an institution of higher learning or a hospital, as distinguished from a general academic education or from an apprenticeship or from training in the performance of routine mental, manual, or physical processes; or

"(b)   any employee, who (i) has completed the courses of specialized intellectual instruction and study described in clause (iv) of paragraph (a), and (ii) is performing related work under the supervision of a professional person to qualify himself to become a professional employee as defined in paragraph (a).

"(13)   In determining whether any person is acting as an 'agent' of another person so as to make such other person responsible for his acts, the question of whether the specific acts performed were actually authorized or subsequently ratified shall not be controlling.

National Labor Relations Board

"SEC. 3.   (a)   The National Labor Relations Board (hereinafter called the 'Board') created by this Act prior to its amendment by the Labor Management Relations Act, 1947, is hereby continued as an agency of the United States, except that the Board shall consist of five instead of three members, appointed by the President by and with the advice and consent of the Senate. Of the two additional members so provided for, one shall be appointed for a term of five years and the other for a term of two years. Their successors, and the successors of the other members, shall be appointed for terms of five years each, excepting that any individual chosen to fill a vacancy shall be appointed only for the unexpired term of the member whom he shall succeed. The President shall designate one member to serve as Chairman of the Board. Any member of the Board may be removed by the President, upon notice and hearing, for neglect of duty or malfeasance in office, but for no other cause.

"(b) [3]   The Board is authorized to delegate to any group of three or more members any or all of the powers which it may itself exercise. The Board is also authorized to delegate to its regional directors its powers under section 9 to determine the unit ap-

(13) This definition is of especial interest. It is aimed at the difficult problem of connecting union members (and union officials) with the union as an organization, in order to show the responsibility of the latter for acts of the former. For example, in the case of an unauthorized strike—perhaps before the 60-day waiting period was up—would the union be responsible, or would the responsibility be that solely of the striking union members? The definition of agency given in paragraph (13) is intended to make it easier to trace responsibility to the union. "Authorization" in advance or "ratification" after the fact are standard legal tests of agency. Here they are specifically ruled out as "controlling," leaving the Board and the courts to decide from more circumstantial evidence whether or not the responsibility is that of the organization or its members as individuals. See Sec. 301(e) below for more on this subject.

The National Labor Relations Board (NLRB) was considerably modified in size, constitution, and duties in the Taft-Hartley Act. The

---

[3] Section 3(b) was enlarged and restated by amendment contained in the Landrum-Griffin Act of 1959, but the basic provisions were unchanged [Sec. 701(b) of the R & D Act].

propriate for the purpose of collective bargaining, to investigate and provide for hearings, and determine whether a question of representation exists, and to direct an election or take a secret ballot under subsection (c) or (e) of section 9 and certify the results thereof, except that upon the filing of a request therefor with the Board by any interested person, the Board may review any action of a regional director delegated to him under this paragraph, but such a review shall not, unless specifically ordered by the Board, operate as a stay of any action taken by the regional director. A vacancy in the Board shall not impair the right of the remaining members to exercise all of the powers of the Board, and three members of the Board shall, at all times, constitute a quorum of the Board, except that two members shall constitute a quorum of any group designated pursuant to the first sentence hereof. The Board shall have an official seal which shall be judicially noticed.

"(c)   The Board shall at the close of each fiscal year make a report in writing to Congress and to the President stating in detail the cases it has heard, the decisions it has rendered, the names, salaries, and duties of all employees and officers in the employ or under the supervision of the Board, and an account of all moneys it has disbursed.

"(d)   There shall be a General Counsel of the Board who shall be appointed by the President, by and with the advice and consent of the Senate, for a term of four years. The General Counsel of the Board shall exercise general supervision over all attorneys employed by the Board (other than trial examiners and legal assistants to Board members) and over the officers and employees in the regional offices. He shall have final authority, on behalf of the Board, in respect of the investigation of charges and issuance of complaints under section 10, and in respect of the prosecution of such complaints before the Board, and shall

main changes were the increase in size from a three-man to a five-man agency and the addition of a General Counsel, who in effect became the prosecuting attorney, with authority to decide on the "investigation of charges and issuance of complaints . . . and in respect of the prosecution of such complaints before the Board."

The general purpose of the enlargement of the personnel of the Board and the addition of a General Counsel was to make the prosecuting and judicial functions of the agency independent of one another and to provide enough "judges" to speed the handling of cases. In other words, the General Counsel and his staff were to prosecute and the Board was to judge. Later, it was proposed that the number of Board members be increased to seven, but the proposal failed.

(c) The annual reports of the NLRB are interesting and highly instructive as to the activities of the agency. They are to be found in practically all college and university libraries and are strongly recommended as suppementary reading for students who really want to understand the way the act works. A study of some of the Board's hearings and decisions is equally pertinent and beneficial.

have such other duties as the Board may prescribe or as may be provided by law. In case of a vacancy in the office of the General Counsel the President is authorized to designate the officer or employee who shall act as General Counsel during such vacancy, but no person or persons so designated shall so act (1) for more than forty days when the Congress is in session unless a nomination to fill such vacancy shall have been submitted to the Senate, or (2) after the adjournment sine die of the session of the Senate in which such nomination was submitted.

"SEC. 4. (a) Each member of the Board and the General Counsel of the Board shall receive a salary of $12,000 a year, shall be eligible for reappointment, and shall not engage in any other business, vocation, or employment. The Board shall appoint an executive secretary, and such attorneys, examiners, and regional directors, and such other employees as it may from time to time find necessary for the proper performance of its duties. The Board may not employ any attorneys for the purpose of reviewing transcripts of hearings or preparing drafts of opinions except that any attorney employed for assignment as a legal assistant to any Board member may for such Board member review such transcripts and prepare such drafts. No trial examiner's report shall be reviewed, either before or after its publication, by any person other than a member of the Board or his legal assistant, and no trial examiner shall advise or consult with the Board with respect to exceptions taken to his findings, rulings, or recommendations. The Board may establish or utilize such regional, local, or other agencies, and utilize such voluntary and uncompensated services, as may from time to time be needed. Attorneys appointed under this section may, at the direction of the Board, appear for and represent the Board in any case in court. Nothing in this Act shall be construed to authorize the Board to appoint individuals for the purpose of conciliation or mediation, or for economic analysis.

"(b) All of the expenses of the Board, including all necessary traveling and subsistence expenses outside the District of Columbia incurred by the members or employees of the Board under its orders, shall be allowed and paid on the presentation of itemized vouchers therefor approved by the Board or by any individual it designates for that purpose.

"SEC. 5. The principal office of the Board

The last sentence in Sec. 3(d) was added by the L–G act of 1959, Sec. 703. It stops the President from keeping someone in office as General Counsel for an indefinite period without the "advice and consent" of the Senate. (In 1959, the House and Senate were Democratic, the President a Republican.)

The last sentence in paragraph (a) is a piece of nonsense.

Everyone familiar with the work of the Board knows that a very large part of it is "conciliation" or "mediation," if these words are given their customary meaning. Less than 10 per cent of all complaints result in formal hearings and awards; the remainder are

shall be in the District of Columbia, but it may meet and exercise any or all of its powers at any other place. The Board may, by one or more of its members or by such agents or agencies as it may designate, prosecute any inquiry necessary to its functions in any part of the United States. A member who participates in such an inquiry shall not be disqualified from subsequently participating in a decision of the Board in the same case.

"Sec. 6.   The Board shall have authority from time to time to make, amend, and rescind, in the manner prescribed by the Administrative Procedure Act, such rules and regulations as may be necessary to carry out the provisions of this Act.

Rights of employees

"Sec. 7.   Employees shall have the right to self-organization, to form, join, or assist labor organizations, to bargain collectively through representatives of their own choosing, and to engage in other concerted activities for the purpose of collective bargaining or other mutual aid or protection, *and shall also have the right to refrain from any or all of such activities except to the extent that such right may be affected by an agreement requiring membership in a labor organization as a condition of employment as authorized in section 8(a)(3).*[4]

Unfair labor practices

"Sec. 8.   (a)   It shall be an unfair labor practice for an employer—

"(1)   to interfere with, restrain, or coerce employees in the exercise of the rights guaranteed in section 7;

"(2)   to dominate or interfere with the formation or administration of any labor organization or contribute financial or other support to it: *Provided,* That subject to rules and regulations made and published by the Board pursuant to section 6, an employer shall not be prohibited from permitting employees to confer with him during working hours without loss of time or pay;

"(3)   by discrimination in regard to hire or tenure of employment or any term or condition of

[4] Italics added.

compromised (mediated, or adjusted) in some fashion or other. See any annual report of the Board.

Sec. 7. This is the basic policy of the law; the italicized part was added in 1947; it was an important addition and much resented by unions, since it implied that individual employes might need protection from union pressure to join. The exception, of course, refers to situations where a legal union-shop agreement is in effect.

The prohibited unfair labor practices are the fundamental ground rules of industrial relations in the United States and everyone should learn what they are, not necessarily verbatim but in his own words. In more ordinary language, they are as follows:

Sec. 8(*a*). Employers must not (1) interfere with employes when they are organizing or bargaining collectively according to law; (2) engage in "company" unionism; (3) discriminate employment to encourage or discourage membership in any labor organization: *Provided,* That nothing in this Act, or in any other statute of the United States, shall preclude an employer from making an agreement with a labor organization (not established, maintained, or assisted by any action defined in section 8(a) of this Act as an unfair labor practice) to require as a condition of employment membership therein on or after the thirtieth day following the beginning of such employment or the effective date of such agreement, whichever is the later, (i) if such labor organization is the representative of the employes as provided in section 9(a), in the appropriate collective-bargaining unit covered by such agreement when made; and (ii) unless following an election held as provided in section 9(e) within one year preceding the effective date of such agreement, the Board shall have certified that at least a majority of the employees eligible to vote in such election have voted to rescind the authority of such labor organization to make such an agreement: *Provided further,* That no employer shall justify any discrimination against an employee for nonmembership in a labor organization (A) if he has reasonable grounds for believing that such membership was not available to the employee on the same terms and conditions generally applicable to other members, or (B) if he has reasonable grounds for believing that membership was denied or terminated for reasons other than the failure of the employee to tender the periodic dues and the initiation fees uniformly required as a condition of acquiring or retaining membership;

"(4) to discharge or otherwise discriminate against an employee because he has filed charges or given testimony under this Act;

"(5) to refuse to bargain collectively with the representatives of his employees, subject to the provisions of section 9(a).

"(b) It shall be an unfair labor practice for a labor organization or its agents—

"(1) to restrain or coerce (A) employees in the exercise of the rights guaranteed in section 7: *Provided,* That this paragraph shall not impair the right of a labor organization to prescribe its own rules with respect to the acquisition or retention of membership therein; or (B) an employer in the selection of his representatives for the purposes of collective bargaining or the adjustment of grievances;

in hiring, promotion, or discharge among employes to encourage or discourage union membership, other than to sign a union-shop agreement under the rules prescribed in the law; (4) discriminate against employes filing charges or giving evidence under the act; or (5) refuse to bargain collectively as required by law.

Sec. 8(*b*). Unions must not (1) restrain or coerce employes who refuse to join the union or cooperate with it, in the absence of a union-shop agreement; (2) bring pressure on an employer to force an employe to join a union, nor bar an employe from membership under a union-shop agreement for

"(2) to cause or attempt to cause an employer to discriminate against an employee in violation of subsection (a)(3) or to discriminate against an employee with respect to whom membership in such organization has been denied or terminated on some ground other than his failure to tender the periodic dues and the initiation fees uniformly required as a condition of acquiring or retaining membership;

"(3) to refuse to bargain collectively with an employer, provided it is the representative of his employees subject to the provisions of section 9(a);

"(4) (i) to engage in, or to induce or encourage any individual employed by any person engaged in commerce or in an industry affecting commerce to engage in, a strike or a refusal in the course of his employment to use, manufacture, process, transport, or otherwise handle or work on any goods, articles, materials, or commodities or to perform any services; or (ii) to threaten, coerce, or restrain any person engaged in commerce or in an industry affecting commerce, where in either case an object thereof is—

"(A) forcing or requiring any employer or self-employed person to join any labor or employer organization or to enter into any agreement which is prohibited by section 8(e);

"(B) forcing or requiring any person to cease using selling, handling, transporting, or otherwise dealing in the products of any other producer, processor, or manufacturer, or to cease doing business with any other person, or forcing or requiring any other employer to recognize or bargain with a labor organization as the representative of his employees unless such labor organization has been certified as the representative of such employees under the provisions of section 9: *Provided,* That nothing contained in this clause (B) shall be construed to make unlawful, where not otherwise unlawful, any primary strike or primary picketing;

"(C) forcing or requiring any employer to recognize or bargain with a particular labor organization as the representative of his employees if another organization has been certified as the representative of such employees under the provisions of section 9;

"(D) forcing or requiring any employer to assign particular work to employees in a particular labor organization or in a particular trade, anything other than the failure to "tender" (offer to pay) dues and fees; (3) refuse to bargain collectively with an employer, if certified as the representative of his employes; (4) call a strike, institute a hot-goods boycott, or threaten or coerce anyone, for the purpose of (A) forcing an employer (who is not in the building construction or apparel and clothing industries) to agree to quit or refrain from doing business with anyone; (B) forcing anyone to stop using any products or doing business with any other person, or forcing another employer to deal with a union when it is not certified as the representative of his employes, but this shall not make primary strikes or picketing unlawful; (C) forcing an employer to deal with a union when some other union is the certified representative of his employes; (D) settling a jurisdictional dispute, unless the employer is defying an order of the Board; *provided* (and this applies to the fourth union unfair labor practice in its entirety) that no one is required to cross a picket line in an authorized strike, and labor disputes may be publicized by any means other than picketing if the publicity is truthful and "does not have the effect of inducing any individual employed by any person other than the primary employer in the course of his employment *to refuse to pick up, deliver, or transport any goods, or not to perform any services, at the establishment of the employer*

craft, or class rather than to employees in another labor organization or in another trade, craft, or class, unless such employer is failing to conform to an order or certification of the Board determining the bargaining representative for employees performing such work: *Provided,* That nothing contained in this subsection (b) shall be construed to make unlawful a refusal by any person to enter upon the premises of any employer (other than his own employer), if the employees of such employer are engaged in a strike ratified or approved by a representative of such employees whom such employer is required to recognize under this Act: *Provided further,* That for the purposes of this paragraph (4) only, nothing contained in such paragraph shall be construed to prohibit publicity, other than picketing, for the purpose of truthfully advising the public, including consumers and members of a labor organization, that a product or products are produced by an employer with whom the labor organization has a primary dispute and are distributed by another employer, as long as such publicity does not have an effect of inducing any individual employed by any person other than the primary employer in the course of his employment to refuse to pick up, deliver, or transport any goods, or not to perform any services, at the establishment of the employer engaged in such distribution;

"(5) to require of employees covered by an agreement authorized under subsection (a)(3) the payment, as a condition precedent to becoming a member of such organization, of a fee in an amount which the Board finds excessive or discriminatory under all the circumstances. In making such a finding, the Board shall consider, among other relevant factors, the practices and customs of labor organizations in the particular industry, and the wages currently paid to the employees affected;

"(6) to cause or attempt to cause an employer to pay or deliver or agree to pay or deliver any money or other thing of value, in the nature of an exaction, for services which are not performed or not to be performed; and

"(7) to picket or cause to be picketed, or threaten to picket or cause to be picketed, any employer where an object thereof is forcing or requiring an employer to recognize or bargain with a labor organization as the representative of his employees, or

engaged in such distribution." (Italics added.) The final phrase is clearly aimed at the Teamsters union.

Section 8(b)(4) was enlarged and restated in Sec. 704(a) of the L–G act. The principal changes are found in subsections (ii) on threats and coercion, (A) forcing employers to enter into hot-goods agreements, (B) the forcing of "other" employers to deal with unions not certified as representatives of their employes —again probably aimed at the Teamsters, and the second proviso, on "truthful" publicity and the avoidance of its "secondary" effects.

Unions must not (5) charge excessive or discriminatory initiation fees; (6) engage in featherbedding or make-work practices; or (7) engage in "organizational" or "recognition" picketing if: (A) the employer has already recognized another union, (B) an NLRB election has been held during the preceding year, or (C) a petition for certification has not been filed with the Board within 30 days from the beginning of the picketing; again with the proviso of freedom to picket or publicize the dispute truthfully and without secondary effects.

The seventh union unfair labor practice was added by amendment in the L–G act, Sec. 704(c). Its purposes are clear: to stop raiding, provide

forcing or requiring the employees of an employer
to accept or select such labor organization as their
collective bargaining representative, unless such labor
organization is currently certified as the representative of such employees:

"(A) where the employer has lawfully recognized
in accordance with this Act any other labor
organization and a question concerning representation may not appropriately be raised
under section 9(c) of this Act,

"(B) where within the preceding twelve months a
valid election under section 9(c) of this Act
has been conducted, or

"(C) where such picketing has been conducted without a petition under section 9(c) being filed
within a reasonable period of time not to exceed thirty days from the commencement of
such picketing: *Provided,* That when such a
petition has been filed the Board shall forthwith, without regard to the provisions of section 9(c)(1) or the absence of a showing of
a substantial interest on the part of the labor
organization, direct an election in such unit as
the Board finds to be appropriate and shall
certify the results thereof: *Provided further,*
That nothing in this subparagraph (C) shall
be construed to prohibit any picketing or other
publicity for the purpose of truthfully advising
the public (including consumers) that an employer does not employ members of, or have a
contract with, a labor organization, unless an
effect of such picketing is to induce any individual employed by any other person in the
course of his employment, not to pick up, deliver or transport any goods or not to perform
any services.

"Nothing in this paragraph (7) shall be construed to permit any act which would otherwise be
an unfair labor practice under this section 8(b).

"(c)   The expressing of any views, argument,
or opinion, or the dissemination thereof, whether in
written, printed, graphic, or visual form, shall not
constitute or be evidence of an unfair labor practice
under any of the provisions of this Act, if such expression contains no threat of reprisal or force or
promise of benefit.

a breathing spell between
elections, and force a settlement of disputes over
organization, along with a
repeat of the warning to
the Teamsters.

(c) This is the "free
speech" clause, primarily
for the benefit of employers,
giving them the right to
express their views regarding
either a specific union or
unionism in general. Previously the NLRB had often
held such communications to
be unfair labor practices.

"(d) For the purposes of this section, to bargain collectively is the performance of the mutual obligation of the employer and the representative of the employees to meet at reasonable times and confer in good faith with respect to wages, hours, and other terms and conditions of employment, or the negotiation of an agreement, or any question arising thereunder, and the execution of a written contract incorporating any agreement reached if requested by either party, but such obligation does not compel either party to agree to a proposal or require the making of a concession: *Provided,* That where there is in effect a collective-bargaining contract covering employees in an industry affecting commerce, the duty to bargain collectively shall also mean that no party to such contract shall terminate or modify such contract, unless the party desiring such termination or modification—

"(1) serves a written notice upon the other party to the contract of the proposed termination or modification sixty days prior to the expiration date thereof, or in the event such contract contains no expiration date, sixty days prior to the time it is proposed to make such termination or modification;

"(2) offers to meet and confer with the other party for the purpose of negotiating a new contract or a contract containing the proposed modifications;

"(3) notifies the Federal Mediation and Conciliation Service within thirty days after such notice of the existence of a dispute, and simultaneously therewith notifies any State or Territorial agency established to mediate and conciliate disputes within the State or Territory where the dispute occurred, provided no agreement has been reached by that time; and

"(4) continues in full force and effect, without resorting to strike or lockout, all the terms and conditions of the existing contract for a period of sixty days after such notice is given or until the expiration date of such contract, whichever occurs later: The duties imposed upon employers, employees, and labor organizations by paragraphs (2), (3), and (4) shall become inapplicable upon an intervening certification of the Board, under which the labor organization or individual, which is a party to the contract, has been superseded as or ceased to be the representative of the employees subject to the provisions of section 9(a), and the duties so imposed

(d) One of the most difficult features of the NLR Act to administer is the question of what constitutes a refusal to bargain collectively as found in the fifth employer unfair labor practice. In the Taft-Hartley Act, the accumulated definitions of successive NLRB awards and court decisions were summed up for the benefit of those subject to the law. The essential elements are: to meet and confer in good faith; to execute a written contract if any agreement is reached; to give 60-days notice of intention to terminate or modify any agreement in effect (that is, no "quickies," either strike or lockout or change of conditions); to notify any Federal or state or territorial mediation agency of the existence of a dispute; and to continue any existing contract in full force or effect for the 60-day period.

shall not be construed as requiring either party to discuss or agree to any modification of the terms and conditions contained in a contract for a fixed period, if such modification is to become effective before such terms and conditions can be reopened under the provisions of the contract. Any employee who engages in a strike within the sixty-day period specified in this subsection shall lose his status as an employee of the employer engaged in the particular labor dispute, for the purposes of sections 8, 9, and 10 of this Act, as amended, but such loss of status for such employee shall terminate if and when he is reemployed by such employer.

"(e) It shall be an unfair labor practice for any labor organization and any employer to enter into any contract or agreement, express or implied, whereby such employer ceases or refrains or agrees to cease or refrain from handling, using, selling, transporting or otherwise dealing in any of the products of any other employer, or to cease doing business with any other person, and any contract or agreement entered into heretofore or hereafter containing such an agreement shall be to such extent unenforceable and void: *Provided,* That nothing in this subsection (e) shall apply to an agreement between a labor organization and an employer in the construction industry relating to the contracting or subcontracting of work to be done at the site of the construction, alteration, painting, or repair of a building, structure, or other work: *Provided further,* That for the purposes of this subsection (e) and section 8(b)(4)(B) the terms 'any employer', 'any person engaged in commerce or an industry affecting commerce', and 'any person' when used in relation to the terms 'any other producer, processor, or manufacturer', 'any other employer', or 'any other person' shall not include persons in the relation of a jobber, manufacturer, contractor, or subcontractor working on the goods or premises of the jobber or manufacturer or performing parts of an integrated process of production in the apparel and clothing industry: *Provided further,* That nothing in this Act shall prohibit the enforcement of any agreement which is within the foregoing exception.

"(f) It shall not be an unfair labor practice under subsections (a) and (b) of this section for an employer engaged primarily in the building and construction industry to make an agreement covering

(e) This section, added by the L–G act, Sec. 704(b), refers to the "hot goods" clauses negotiated in a number of labor agreements after passage of the Taft-Hartley Act in 1947. The "hot goods" clauses were a method of negotiating around the provisions of Sec. 8(4), which made hot-goods boycotts in and of themselves unfair labor practices.

The purpose of the exemption of the building construction and apparel and clothing industries, contained in the first two provisos of Sec. 8(e) was to water down union and union-supported political opposition to the amendments of the NLR Act contained in the 1959 law.

(f) This portion of the law, added by amendment in the L–G act, Sec. 705(a), is an attempt to make the employees engaged (or who, upon their employment, will be engaged) in the building and construction industry with a labor organization of which building and construction employees are members (not established, maintained, or assisted by any action defined in section 8(a) of this Act as an unfair labor practice) because (1) the majority status of such labor organization has not been established under the provisions of section 9 of this Act prior to the making of such agreement, or (2) such agreement requires as a condition of employment, membership in such labor organization after the seventh day following the beginning of such employment or the effective date of the agreement, whichever is later, or (3) such agreement requires the employer to notify such labor organization of opportunities for employment with such employer, or gives such labor organization an opportunity to refer qualified applicants for such employment, or (4) such agreement specifies minimum training or experience qualifications for employment or provides for priority in opportunities for employment based upon length of service with such employer, in the industry or in the particular geographical area: *Provided,* That nothing in this subsection shall set aside the final proviso to section 8(a)(3) of this Act: *Provided further,* That any agreement which would be invalid, but for clause (1) of this subsection, shall not be a bar to a petition filed pursuant to section 9(c) or 9(e).

(b) Nothing contained in the amendment made by subsection (a) [5] shall be construed as authorizing the execution or application of agreements requiring membership in a labor organization as a condition of employment in any State or Territory in which such execution or application is prohibited by State or Territorial law.

Representatives and elections

"SEC. 9.   (a) Representatives designated or selected for the purposes of collective bargaining by the majority of the employees in a unit appropriate

---

union-security (compulsory membership) provisions of the act workable when applied to building-trades unions. Building-trades unions are traditionally closed-shop organizations and as such would come under the ban of Sec. 8(a)(3). They have not been interfered with, primarily because the NLRB has stayed out of such disputes, recognizing that the NLR Act is designed to cover permanent employes and simply does not fit the "casual" trades, where employment is short-term, fluctuating, and the employe's security lies in the union's control of a geographical labor market rather than a "bargaining unit" such as a plant, firm, or collection of firms.

The main features of the modification are a 7-day union-shop provision without prior certification of majority status, plus union preference in hiring. The arrangement is clumsy and is not used. Closed-shop unions continue to be closed-shop, and operate as they have since 1947, when the Taft-Hartley Act was passed.

This is a reiteration of the "right to work" enabling provision of the act. See below, Sec. 14(b).

Sec. 9. The two main jobs of the NLRB are (1) the prevention of unfair labor

---

[5] Subsection (a) is Sec. 8(f) above. It was Sec. 705(a) of the Labor-Management Reporting and Disclosure Act.

for such purposes, shall be the exclusive representatives of all the employees in such unit for the purposes of collective bargaining in respect to rates of pay, wages, hours of employment, or other conditions of employment: *Provided,* That any individual employee or a group of employees shall have the right at any time to present grievances to their employer and to have such grievances adjusted, without the intervention of the bargaining representative, as long as the adjustment is not inconsistent with the terms of a collective-bargaining contract or agreement then in effect: *Provided further,* That the bargaining representative has been given opportunity to be present at such adjustment.

"(b) The Board shall decide in each case whether, in order to assure to employees the fullest freedom in exercising the rights guaranteed by this Act, the unit appropriate for the purposes of collective bargaining shall be the employer unit, craft unit, plant unit, or subdivision thereof: *Provided,* That the Board shall not (1) decide that any unit is appropriate for such purposes if such unit includes both professional employees and employees who are not professional employees unless a majority of such professional employees vote for inclusion in such unit; or (2) decide that any craft unit is inappropriate for such purposes on the ground that a different unit has been established by a prior Board determination, unless a majority of the employees in the proposed craft unit vote against separate representation or (3) decide that any unit is appropriate for such purposes if it includes, together with other employees, any individual employed as a guard to enforce against employees and other persons rules to protect property of the employer or to protect the safety of persons on the employer's premises; but no labor organization shall be certified as the representative of employees in a bargaining unit of guards if such organization admits to membership, or is affiliated directly or indirectly with an organization which admits to membership, employees other than guards.

"(c) (1) Whenever a petition shall have been filed, in accordance with such regulations as may be prescribed by the Board—

"(A) by an employee or group of employees or any individual or labor organization acting in their behalf alleging that a substantial number of employees (i) wish to be represented for collective bargain-

practices, and (2) certifying unions as the official representatives of employes for the purposes of collective bargaining. This section tells how the latter is done. The main procedural steps are as follows:

1. The filing of a petition with the NLRB by an employe, a union, or an employer, asking the Board to settle a question of representation.

2. An investigation by the Board, to see if a hearing is necessary.

3. A hearing (if the answer to number 2 is yes), after which the "appropriate bargaining unit" is decided.

4. A secret-ballot election, to decide whether or not the employes want to be represented and by whom.

5. Certification of the results to the parties (unions and employer).

This may sound rather simple, but there are a lot of prerequisites and provisos to be observed, along with one very critical fundamental decision. First, the Board has to decide what is the "appropriate bargaining unit." This means the group of employes eligible for membership in the union which is petitioning and may be (1) all the employes of the employer, minus probably the supervisors and usually the office force; (2) all the members of a given craft, such as machinists; (3) all the employes of one plant (production and maintenance workers, that is); or (4) the employes of one department or one shop or any other subdivision the Board may decide. This is obviously a

ing and that their employer declines to recognize their representative as the representative defined in section 9(a), or (ii) assert that the individual or labor organization, which has been certified or is being currently recognized by their employer as the bargaining representative, is no longer a representative as defined in section 9(a); or

"(B) by an employer, alleging that one or more individuals or labor organizations have presented to him a claim to be recognized as the representative defined in section 9(a); the Board shall investigate such petition and if it has reasonable cause to believe that a question of representation affecting commerce exists shall provide for an appropriate hearing upon due notice. Such hearing may be conducted by an officer or employee of the regional office, who shall not make any recommendations with respect thereto. If the Board finds upon the record of such hearing that such a question of representation exists, it shall direct an election by secret ballot and shall certify the results thereof.

"(2) In determining whether or not a question of representation affecting commerce exists, the same regulations and rules of decision shall apply irrespective of the identity of the persons filing the petition or the kind of relief sought and in no case shall the Board deny a labor organization a place on the ballot by reason of an order with respect to such labor organization or its predecessor not issued in conformity with section 10(c).

"(3) No election shall be directed in any bargaining unit or any subdivision within which, in the preceding twelve-month period, a valid election shall have been held. Employees engaged in an economic strike who are not entitled to reinstatement shall be eligible to vote under such regulations as the Board shall find are consistent with the purposes and provisions of this Act in any election conducted within twelve months after the commencement of the strike. In any election where none of the choices on the ballot receives a majority, a run-off shall be conducted, the ballot providing for a selection between the two choices receiving the largest and second largest number of valid votes cast in the election.

"(4) Nothing in this section shall be construed to prohibit the waiver of hearings by stipulation for the purpose of a consent election in conformity with regulations and rules of decision of the Board.

crucial decision, and many an election has been won or lost on the Board's decision to include or exclude certain employes.

In deciding upon the appropriate bargaining unit, the Board must observe certain rules set up in paragraph (b): give professional and craft employes a chance to vote for separate representation before including them with other employes, and keep guards in unions separate from other workers.

There are rules for elections too [see paragraph (c)(3)]. To begin with, a majority of the *votes cast* wins, just as in election to public office, even though the total voting may be only a small fraction of those eligible to vote. An election is good for 12 months and may not be repeated short of that time, no matter what change of heart has occurred in the meantime. Employes on an "economic" strike (for wages, hours, etc.) are not necessarily entitled to reinstatement, but may vote (by L–G act amendment, reversing the original provision); employes on strike against unfair labor practices also may vote in elections. A runoff election must be held if no one gets a full majority of the votes cast.

Certification works in reverse too [see Sec. 9(e)(1), below]. If 30 per cent of the employes in a bargaining unit

"(5)   In determining whether a unit is appropriate for the purposes specified in subsection (b) the extent to which the employees have organized shall not be controlling.

"(d)   Whenever an order of the Board made pursuant to section 10(c) is based in whole or in part upon facts certified following an investigation pursuant to subsection (c) of this section and there is a petition for the enforcement or review of such order, such certification and the record of such investigation shall be included in the transcript of the entire record required to be filed under section 10(e) or 10(f), and thereupon the decree of the court enforcing, modifying, or setting aside in whole or in part the order of the Board shall be made and entered upon the pleadings, testimony, and proceedings set forth in such transcript.

"(e)   (1) Upon the filing with the Board, by 30 per centum or more of the employees in a bargaining unit covered by an agreement between their employer and a labor organization made pursuant to section 8(a)(3), of a petition alleging they desire that such authority be rescinded, the Board shall take a secret ballot of the employees in such unit and certify the results thereof to such labor organization and to the employer.

"(2)   No election shall be conducted pursuant to this subsection in any bargaining unit or any subdivision within which, in the preceding twelve-month period, a valid election shall have been held.

Prevention of unfair labor practices

"SEC. 10.   (a)   The Board is empowered, as hereinafter provided, to prevent any person from engaging in any unfair labor practice (listed in section 8) affecting commerce. This power shall not be affected by any other means of adjustment or prevention that has been or may be established by agreement, law, or otherwise: *Provided,* That the Board is empowered by agreement with any agency of any State or Territory to cede to such agency jurisdiction over any cases in any industry (other than mining, manufacturing, communications, and transportation except where predominantly local in character) even though such cases may involve labor disputes affecting commerce, unless the provisions of the State or Territorial statute applicable to the de-

with a union-shop agreement so petition, the Board must hold a *de*certification election by secret ballot.

Sec. 10. The prevention of unfair labor practices is the main business of the National Labor Relations Board. The procedure is roughly as follows:
1. A "charge" of unfair labor practice is made by a union, or an employe, or an employer to the local office of the NLRB.
2. An investigation is made and the charges are adjusted, mediated, or dismissed as of no consequence.

termination of such cases by such agency is inconsistent with the corresponding provision of this Act or has received a construction inconsistent therewith.

"(b) Whenever it is charged that any person has engaged in or is engaging in any such unfair labor practice, the Board, or any agent or agency designated by the Board for such purposes, shall have power to issue and cause to be served upon such person a complaint stating the charges in that respect, and containing a notice of hearing before the Board or a member thereof, or before a designated agent or agency, at a place therein fixed, not less than five days after the serving of said complaint: *Provided,* That no complaint shall issue based upon any unfair labor practice occurring more than six months prior to the filing of the charge with the Board and the service of a copy thereof upon the person against whom such charge is made, unless the person aggrieved thereby was prevented from filing such charge by reason of service in the armed forces, in which event the six-month period shall be computed from the day of his discharge. Any such complaint may be amended by the member, agent, or agency conducting the hearing or the Board in its discretion at any time prior to the issuance of an order based thereon. The person so complained of shall have the right to file an answer to the original or amended complaint and to appear in person or otherwise and give testimony at the place and time fixed in the complaint. In the discretion of the member, agent, or agency conducting the hearing or the Board, any other person may be allowed to intervene in the said proceeding and to present testimony. Any such proceeding shall, so far as practicable, be conducted in accordance with the rules of evidence applicable in the district courts of the United States under the rules of civil procedure for the district courts of the United States, adopted by the Supreme Court of the United States pursuant to the Act of June 19, 1934. . . .

"(c) The testimony taken by such member, agent, or agency or the Board shall be reduced to writing and filed with the Board. Thereafter, in its discretion, the Board upon notice may take further testimony or hear argument. If upon the preponderance of the testimony taken the Board shall be of the opinion that any person named in the complaint has engaged in or is engaging in any such unfair

3. If the charge seems to be justified and is not settled to everyone's satisfaction, however, the Board serves a formal "complaint" upon the party charged (employer or union) and sets a date for a hearing.

4. The hearing is held, and the testimony given in it is put into writing.

5. The Board then renders a decision, issuing a cease-and-desist order to the offender, or dismissing the complaint as unsubstantiated, or doing something else which the violation calls for.

This section of the act has numerous limitations and special provisos. For example, there is a 6-month "statute of limitations" for unfair labor practices; that is, if not reported within 6 months, they cannot be prosecuted [paragraph (b)]. The Board not only may tell offenders to cease and desist (legal language for "stop"), it can also require "affirmative action," such as reinstatement of employes with or without back pay, the loss of which was due to illegal discharge or suspension. Reinstatement, however, is not available to employes fired "for cause," which presumably means for inefficiency or disciplinary reasons [paragraph (c)]. The Board can go to court to get its order enforced [paragraph (e)], or either party to the dispute may do the same to get the order reviewed and set aside [paragraph (f)]. Any time after a formal complaint has been served, the Board *may* go to court for a restraining order, or injunc-

labor practice, then the Board shall state its findings of fact and shall issue and cause to be served on such person an order requiring such person to cease and desist from such unfair labor practice, and to take such affirmative action including reinstatement of employees with or without back pay, as will effectuate the policies of this Act: *Provided,* That where an order directs reinstatement of an employee, back pay may be required of the employer or labor organization, as the case may be, responsible for the discrimination suffered by him: *And provided further,* That in determining whether a complaint shall issue alleging a violation of section 8(a)(1) or section 8(a)(2), and in deciding such cases, the same regulations and rules of decision shall apply irrespective of whether or not the labor organization affected is affiliated with a labor organization national or international in scope. Such order may further require such person to make reports from time to time showing the extent to which it has complied with the order. If upon the preponderance of the testimony taken the Board shall not be of the opinion that the person named in the complaint has engaged in or is engaging in any such unfair labor practice, then the Board shall state its findings of fact and shall issue an order dismissing the said complaint. No order of the Board shall require the reinstatement of any individual as an employee who has been suspended or discharged, or the payment to him of any back pay, if such individual was suspended or discharged for cause. In case the evidence is presented before a member of the Board, or before an examiner or examiners thereof, such member, or such examiner or examiners, as the case may be, shall issue and cause to be served on the parties to the proceeding a proposed report, together with a recommended order, which shall be filed with the Board, and if no exceptions are filed within twenty days after service thereof upon such parties, or within such further period as the Board may authorize, such recommended order shall become the order of the Board and become effective as therein prescribed.

"(d)   Until a transcript of the record in a case shall have been filed in a court, as hereinafter provided, the Board may at any time, upon reasonable notice and in such manner as it shall deem proper, modify or set aside, in whole or in part, any finding or order made or issued by it.

tion [paragraph (*j*)], and it *must* apply for injunctions to stop strikes and boycotts for the purposes stated in Sec. 8(*b*)(4)(*A–D*) above [paragraph (1)]. In cases where jurisdictional disputes are the subject of unfair labor practice complaints [Sec. 8(*b*)(4)(*D*)], the Board must hear and decide the dispute [paragraph (*k*)].

"(e)   The Board shall have power to petition any circuit court of appeals of the United States (including the United States Court of Appeals for the District of Columbia), or if all the circuit courts of appeals to which application may be made are in vacation, any district court of the United States (including the District Court of the United States for the District of Columbia), within any circuit or district, respectively, wherein the unfair labor practice in question occurred or wherein such person resides or transacts business, for the enforcement of such order and for appropriate temporary relief or restraining order, and shall certify and file in the court a transcript of the entire record in the proceedings, including the pleadings and testimony upon which such order was entered and the findings and order of the Board. Upon such filing, the court shall cause notice thereof to be served upon such person, and thereupon shall have jurisdiction of the proceeding and of the question determined therein, and shall have power to grant such temporary relief or restraining order as it deems just and proper, and to make and enter upon the pleadings, testimony, and proceedings set forth in such transcript a decree enforcing, modifying, and enforcing as so modified, or setting aside in whole or in part the order of the Board. No objection that has not been urged before the Board, its member, agent, or agency, shall be considered by the court, unless the failure or neglect to urge such objection shall be excused because of extraordinary circumstances. The findings of the Board with respect to questions of fact if supported by substantial evidence on the record considered as a whole shall be conclusive. If either party shall apply to the court for leave to adduce additional evidence and shall show to the satisfaction of the court that such additional evidence is material and that there were reasonable grounds for the failure to adduce such evidence in the hearing before the Board, its member, agent, or agency, the court may order such additional evidence to be taken before the Board, its members, agent, or agency, and to be made a part of the transcript. The Board may modify its findings as to the facts, or make new findings, by reason of additional evidence so taken and filed, and it shall file such modified or new findings, which findings with respect to questions of fact if supported by substantial evidence on the record considered as a

These are the ground rules for appeals to the courts by the Board for enforcement of its orders, including the issuance of injunctions.

whole shall be conclusive, and shall file its recommendations, if any, for the modification or setting aside of its original order. The jurisdiction of the court shall be exclusive and its judgment and decree shall be final, except that the same shall be subject to review by the appropriate circuit court of appeals if application was made to the district court as hereinabove provided, and by the Supreme Court of the United States upon writ of certiorari or certification as provided in sections 239 and 240 of the Judicial Code, as amended (U. S. C., title 28, secs. 346 and 347).

"(f) Any person aggrieved by a final order of the Board granting or denying in whole or in part the relief sought may obtain a review of such order in any circuit court of appeals of the United States in the circuit wherein the unfair labor practice in question was alleged to have been engaged in or wherein such person resides or transacts business, or in the United States Court of Appeals for the District of Columbia, by filing in such court a written petition praying that the order of the Board be modified or set aside. A copy of such petition shall be forthwith served upon the Board, and thereupon the aggrieved party shall file in the court a transcript of the entire record in the proceeding, certified by the Board, including the pleading and testimony upon which the order complained of was entered, and the findings and order of the Board. Upon such filing, the court shall proceed in the same manner as in the case of an application by the Board under subsection (e), and shall have the same exclusive jurisdiction to grant to the Board such temporary relief or restraining order as it deems just and proper, and in like manner to make and enter a decree enforcing, modifying, and enforcing as so modified, or setting aside in whole or in part the order of the Board; the findings of the Board with respect to questions of fact if supported by substantial evidence on the record considered as a whole shall in like manner be conclusive.

"(g) The commencement of proceedings under subsection (e) or (f) of this section shall not, unless specifically ordered by the court, operate as a stay of the Board's order.

"(h) When granting appropriate temporary relief or a restraining order, or making and entering a decree enforcing, modifying, and enforcing as so modified, or setting aside in whole or in part an

In this section, the right of appeal is extended to the parties subject to the Board's orders—employers and unions. It is exercised with great frequency. Appeal of the Board's rulings has produced a large volume of litigation, at both the CCA and Supreme Court level. See any annual report of the Board, or any current volume of Supreme Court decisions.

order on the Board, as provided in this section, the jurisdiction of courts sitting in equity shall not be limited by the Act entitled 'An Act to amend the Judicial Code and to define and limit the jurisdiction of courts sitting in equity, and for other purposes', approved March 23, 1932 (U. S. C., Supp. VII, title 29, secs. 101–115).

"(i)   Petitions filed under this Act shall be heard expeditiously, and if possible within ten days after they have been docketed.

"(j)   The Board shall have power, upon issuance of a complaint as provided in subsection (b) charging that any person has engaged in or is engaging in an unfair labor practice, to petition any district court of the United States (including the District Court of the United States for the District of Columbia), within any district wherein the unfair labor practice in question is alleged to have occurred or wherein such person resides or transacts business, for appropriate temporary relief or restraining order. Upon the filing of any such petition the court shall cause notice thereof to be served upon such person, and thereupon shall have jurisdiction to grant to the Board such temporary relief or restraining order as it deems just and proper.

This is the "injunction" provision, which broke open the Norris–La Guardia Act's practical suppression of the use of restraining orders in labor disputes. It is strengthened by paragraph (1) below, which makes a request for an injunction mandatory in every case where a formal complaint is filed under Section 8(b)(4)— the hot-goods and secondary-boycott unfair labor practices.

"(k)   Whenever it is charged that any person has engaged in an unfair labor practice within the meaning of paragraph (4)(D) of section 8(b), the Board is empowered and directed to hear and determine the dispute out of which such unfair labor practice shall have arisen, unless, within ten days after notice that such charge has been filed, the parties to such dispute submit to the Board satisfactory evidence that they have adjusted, or agreed upon methods for the voluntary adjustment of, the dispute. Upon compliance by the parties to the dispute with the decision of the Board or upon such voluntary adjustment of the dispute, such charge shall be dismissed.

"(1)   Whenever it is charged that any person has engaged in an unfair labor practice within the meaning of paragraph (4) (A), (B), or (C) of section 8(b), or section 8(e) or section 8(b)(7), the preliminary investigation of such charge shall be made forthwith and given priority over all other cases except cases of like character in the office where it is filed or to which it is referred. If, after such investigation, the officer or regional attorney to whom the matter may be referred has reasonable cause to believe such charge is true and that a complaint should issue, he shall, on behalf of the Board, petition any district court of the United States (including the District Court of the United States for the District of Columbia) within any district where the unfair labor practice in question has occurred, is alleged to have occurred, or wherein such person resides or transacts business, for appropriate injunctive relief pending the final adjudication of the Board with respect to such matter. Upon the filing of any such petition the district court shall have jurisdiction to grant such injunctive relief or temporary restraining order as it deems just and proper, notwithstanding any other provision of law: *Provided further,* That no temporary restraining order shall be issued without notice unless a petition alleges that substantial and irreparable injury to the charging party will be unavoidable and such temporary restraining order shall be effective for no longer than five days and will become void at the expiration of such period: *Provided further,* That such officer or regional attorney shall not apply for any restraining order under section 8(b)(7) if a charge against the employer under section 8(a)(2) has been filed and after the preliminary investigation, he has reasonable cause to believe that such charge is true and that a complaint should issue. Upon filing of any such petition the courts shall cause notice thereof to be served upon any person involved in the charge and such person, including the charging party, shall be given an opportunity to appear by counsel and present any relevant testimony: *Provided further,* That for the purposes of this subsection district courts shall be deemed to have jurisdiction of a labor organization (1) in the district in which such organization maintains its principal office, or (2) in any district in which its duly authorized officers or agents are engaged in promoting or protecting the interests of employee members. The service of legal process upon such officer or agent shall constitute service upon the labor organization and make such organization a party to the suit. In situations where such relief is appropriate the procedure specified herein shall apply to charges with respect to section 8(b)(4)(D).

"(m) Whenever it is charged that any person has engaged in an unfair labor practice within the meaning of subsection (a)(3) or (b)(2) of section

The limitations and provisos on the mandatory issuance of injunctions.

(Try condensing the injunction provisions of the Act in a brief statement in nonlegal language.)

8, such charge shall be given priority over all other cases except cases of like character in the office where it is filed or to which it is referred and cases given priority under subsection (1).

Investigatory powers

"SEC. 11.   For the purpose of all hearings and investigations, which, in the opinion of the Board are necessary and proper for the exercise of the powers vested in it by section 9 and section 10—

"(1)   The Board, or its duly authorized agents or agencies, shall at all reasonable times have access to, for the purpose of examination, and the right to copy any evidence of any person being investigated or proceeded against that relates to any matter under investigation or in question. The Board, or any member thereof, shall upon application of any party to such proceedings, forthwith issue to such party subpenas requiring the attendance and testimony of witnesses or the production of any evidence in such proceeding or investigation requested in such application. Within five days after the service of a subpena on any person requiring the production of any evidence in his possession or under his control, such person may petition the Board to revoke, and the Board shall revoke, such subpena if in its opinion the evidence whose production is required does not relate to any matter under investigation, or any matter in question in such proceedings, or if in its opinion such subpena does not describe with sufficient particularity the evidence whose production is required. Any member of the Board, or any agent or agency designated by the Board for such purposes, may administer oaths and affirmations, examine witnesses, and receive evidence. Such attendance of witnesses and the production of such evidence may be required from any place in the United States or any Territory or possession thereof, at any designated place of hearing.

"(2)   In case of contumacy or refusal to obey a subpena issued to any person, any district court of the United States or the United States courts of any Territory or possession, or the District Court of the United States for the District of Columbia, within the jurisdiction of which the inquiry is carried on or within the jurisdiction of which said person guilty of contumacy or refusal to obey is found or resides or transacts business, upon application by the Board shall have jurisdiction to issue to such person an order requiring such person to appear before the Board, its member, agent, or agency, there to produce evidence if so ordered, or there to give testimony touching the matter under investigation or in question; and any failure to obey such order of the court may be punished by said court as a contempt thereof.

"(3)   No person shall be excused from attending and testifying or from producing books, records, correspondence, documents, or other evidence in obedience to the subpena of the Board, on the ground that the testimony or evidence required of him may tend to incriminate him or subject him to a penalty or forfeiture; but no individual shall be prosecuted or subjected to any penalty or forfeiture for or on account of any transaction, matter, or thing concerning which he is compelled, after having claimed his privilege against self-incrimination, to testify or produce evidence, except that such individual so testifying shall not be exempt from prosecution and punishment for perjury committed in so testifying.

"(4)   Complaints, orders, and other process and papers of the Board, its member, agent, or agency, may be served either personally or by registered mail or by telegraph or by leaving a copy thereof at the principal office or place of business of the person required to be served. The verified return by the individual so serving the same setting forth the manner of such service shall be proof of the same, and the return post office receipt or telegraph receipt therefor when registered and mailed or telegraphed as aforesaid shall be proof of service of the same. Witnesses summoned before the Board, its member, agent, or agency, shall be paid the same fees and mileage that are paid witnesses in the courts of the United States, and witnesses whose depositions are taken and the persons taking the same shall severally be entitled to the same fees as are paid for like services in the courts of the United States.

"(5)   All process of any court to which application may be made under this Act may be served in the judicial district wherein the defendant or other person required to be served resides or may be found.

"(6)   The several departments and agencies of

the Government, when directed by the President, shall furnish the Board, upon its request, all records, papers, and information in their possession relating to any matter before the Board.

"SEC. 12.   Any person who shall willfully resist, prevent, impede, or interfere with any member of the Board or any of its agents or agencies in the performance of duties pursuant to this Act shall be punished by a fine of not more than $5,000 or by imprisonment for not more than one year, or both.

Limitations

"SEC. 13.   Nothing in this Act, except as specifically provided for herein, shall be construed so as either to interfere with or impede or diminish in any way the right to strike, or to affect the limitations or qualifications on that right.

"SEC. 14.   (a)   Nothing herein shall prohibit any individual employed as a supervisor from becoming or remaining a member of a labor organization, but no employer subject to this Act shall be compelled to deem individuals defined herein as supervisors as employees for the purpose of any law, either national or local, relating to collective bargaining.

"(b)   Nothing in this Act shall be construed as authorizing the execution or application of agreements requiring membership in a labor organization as a condition of employment in any State or Territory in which such execution or application is prohibited by State or Territorial law.

"(c)   (1) The Board, in its discretion, may, by rule of decision or by published rules adopted pursuant to the Administrative Procedure Act, decline to assert jurisdiction over any labor dispute involving any class or category of employers, where, in the opinion of the Board, the effect of such labor dispute on commerce is not sufficiently substantial to warrant the exercise of its jurisdiction: *Provided,* That the Board shall not decline to assert jurisdiction over any labor dispute over which it would assert jurisdiction under the standards prevailing upon August 1, 1959.

"(2)   Nothing in this Act shall be deemed to prevent or bar any agency or the courts of any State or Territory (including the Commonwealth of Puerto Rico, Guam, and the Virgin Islands), from assuming and asserting jurisdiction over labor disputes over

Sec. 14(*a*). This provision tells supervisors that they may join unions, but if they do, they will not have the protection of the act.

Section 14(*b*) is one of the more strongly resented sections of the law (by unions). What it does is rule out any form of union security (compulsory membership via closed shop, union shop, maintenance of membership, etc.) in states with "right to work" laws. Without this enabling provision, unions and firms in interstate commerce would be exempt from such local statutes, but with it they are under the jurisdiction of state legislatures on this one point.

Sec. 14(*c*) was added by amendment in the L–G act, Sec. 701(*a*). It eliminated the "no man's land" in labor law by assigning any labor disputes in interstate commerce that the NLRB declined to act on, to the jurisdiction of the appropriate state or

which the Board declines, pursuant to paragraph (1) of this subsection, to assert jurisdiction.

"SEC. 15.   Wherever the application of the provisions of section 272 of chapter 10 of the Act entitled 'An Act to establish a uniform system of bankruptcy throughout the United States,' approved July 1, 1898, and Acts amendatory thereof and supplementary thereto (U.S.C., title 11, sec. 672), conflicts with the application of the provisions of this Act, this Act shall prevail: *Provided,* That in any situation where the provisions of this Act cannot be validly enforced, the provisions of such other Acts shall remain in full force and effect.

"SEC. 16.   If any provision of this Act, or the application of such provision to any person or circumstances, shall be held invalid, the remainder of this Act, or the application of such provision to persons or circumstances other than those as to which it is held invalid, shall not be affected thereby.

"SEC. 17.   This Act may be cited as the 'National Labor Relations Act.'

territorial courts and agencies. It also took away the right of the NLRB to limit its own jurisdiction further than it had as of Aug. 1, 1959.

The "no man's land" came about because of the Supreme Court's doctrine of "pre-emption," which means that once the Federal Congress has legislated in a certain area, that area is "pre-empted" (appropriated to the exclusion of others) and controversies arising therein may not be referred to state courts or agencies even though the Federal agency declines to assert jurisdiction for any reason. This means, of course, that no court or mediating or arbitrating agency is then available to help settle the dispute, and the parties are in a legal "no man's land."

The NLRB has always limited its own jurisdiction by refusing to act in labor disputes occurring in small firms, since it does not have the staff or budget to accomplish the job. Nonetheless, many small firms are in interstate commerce. These firms and the unions representing their employes or trying to represent them may now apply to state courts and agencies for assistance.

Title II—Conciliation of Labor Disputes in Industries Affecting Commerce; National Emergencies

SEC. 201.   That it is the policy of the United States that—

(a)   sound and stable industrial peace and the advancement of the general welfare, health, and safety of the Nation and of the best interests of employers and employees can most satisfactorily be secured by the settlement of issues between employers and employees through the processes of conference and collective bargaining between employers and the representatives of their employees;

(b)   the settlement of issues between employers and employees through collective bargaining may be advanced by making available full and adequate governmental facilities for conciliation, mediation, and voluntary arbitration to aid and encourage employers and the representatives of their employees to reach and maintain agreements concerning rates of pay, hours, and working conditions, and to make all reasonable efforts to settle their differences by mutual agreement reached through conferences and collective bargaining or by such methods as may be provided for in any applicable agreement for the settlement of disputes; and

(c)   certain controversies which arise between parties to collective-bargaining agreements may be avoided or minimized by making available full and adequate governmental facilities for furnishing assistance to employers and the representatives of their employees in formulating for inclusion within such agreements provision for adequate notice of any proposed changes in the terms of such agreements, for the final adjustment of grievances or questions regarding the application or interpretation of such agreements, and other provisions designed to prevent the subsequent arising of such controversies.

Sec. 202.   (a)   There is hereby created an independent agency to be known as the Federal Mediation and Conciliation Service (herein referred to as the "Service," except that for sixty days after the date of the enactment of this Act such term shall refer to the Conciliation Service of the Department of Labor). The Service shall be under the direction of a Federal Mediation and Conciliation Director (hereafter referred to as the "Director"), who shall be appointed by the President by and with the advice and consent of the Senate. The Director shall receive compensation at the rate of $12,000 per annum. The Director shall not engage in any other business, vocation, or employment.

(b)   The Director is authorized, subject to the civil-service laws, to appoint such clerical and other personnel as may be necessary for the execution of the functions of the Service, and shall fix their compensation in accordance with the Classification Act of 1923, as amended, and may, without regard to the provisions of the civil-service laws and the Classifica-

Title II of the act does three things: (1) it creates a Federal Mediation and Conciliation Service and outlines its duties; (2) it sets up a procedure to be followed in the case of strikes which create national emergencies; and (3) it tells the Bureau of Labor Statistics to keep a file of union contracts on hand as a reference source in the settlement of disputes. The FM & CS was not a new agency, just the long-established United States Conciliation Service under a new name and new management. The purpose of the arrangement was to get the Conciliation Service out of the Department of Labor and make it an independent agency responsible directly to Congress—the theory being that an agency for the settlement of labor disputes should not be located in a department dedicated to the interests of one of the parties.

tion Act of 1923, as amended, appoint and fix the compensation of such conciliators and mediators as may be necessary to carry out the functions of the Service. The Director is authorized to make such expenditures for supplies, facilities, and services as he deems necessary. Such expenditures shall be allowed and paid upon presentation of itemized vouchers therefor approved by the Director or by any employee designated by him for that purpose.

(c) The principal office of the Service shall be in the District of Columbia, but the Director may establish regional offices convenient to localities in which labor controversies are likely to arise. The Director may by order, subject to revocation at any time, delegate any authority and discretion conferred upon him by this Act to any regional director, or other officer or employee of the Service. The Director may establish suitable procedures for cooperation with State and local mediation agencies. The Director shall make an annual report in writing to Congress at the end of the fiscal year.

(d) All mediation and conciliation functions of the Secretary of Labor or the United States Conciliation Service under section 8 of the Act entitled 'An Act to create a Department of Labor,' approved March 4, 1913 (U.S.C., title 29, sec. 51), and all functions of the United States Conciliation Service under any other law are hereby transferred to the Federal Mediation and Conciliation Service, together with the personnel and records of the United States Conciliation Service. Such transfer shall take effect upon the sixtieth day after the date of enactment of this Act. Such transfer shall not affect any proceedings pending before the United States Conciliation Service or any certification, order, rule, or regulation theretofore made by it or by the Secretary of Labor. The Director and the Service shall not be subject in any way to the jurisdiction or authority of the Secretary of Labor or any official or division of the Department of Labor.

Functions of the service

SEC. 203. (a) It shall be the duty of the Service, in order to prevent or minimize interruptions of the free flow of commerce growing out of labor disputes, to assist parties to labor disputes in industries

Read Sections 203 and 204 with care. This is really a very important agency, but mediators are essentially

affecting commerce to settle such disputes through conciliation and mediation.

(b)   The Service may proffer its services in any labor dispute in any industry affecting commerce, either upon its own motion or upon the request of one or more of the parties to the dispute, whenever in its judgment such dispute threatens to cause a substantial interruption of commerce. The Director and the Service are directed to avoid attempting to mediate disputes which would have only a minor effect on interstate commerce if State or other conciliation services are available to the parties. Whenever the Service does proffer its services in any dispute, it shall be the duty of the Service promptly to put itself in communication with the parties and to use its best efforts, by mediation and conciliation, to bring them to agreement.

(c)   If the Director is not able to bring the parties to agreement by conciliation within a reasonable time, he shall seek to induce the parties voluntarily to seek other means of settling the dispute without resort to strike, lock-out, or other coercion, including submission to the employees in the bargaining unit of the employer's last offer of settlement for approval or rejection in a secret ballot. The failure or refusal of either party to agree to any procedure suggested by the Director shall not be deemed a violation of any duty or obligation imposed by this Act.

(d)   Final adjustment by a method agreed upon by the parties is hereby declared to be the desirable method for settlement of grievance disputes arising over the application or interpretation of an existing collective-bargaining agreement. The Service is directed to make its conciliation and mediation services available in the settlement of such grievance disputes only as a last resort and in exceptional cases.

SEC. 204.   (a)   In order to prevent or minimize interruptions of the free flow of commerce growing out of labor disputes, employers and employees and their representatives, in any industry affecting commerce, shall—

(1)   exert every reasonable effort to make and maintain agreements concerning rates of pay, hours, and working conditions, including provision for adequate notice of any proposed change in the terms of such agreements;

(2)   whenever a dispute arises over the terms or application of a collective-bargaining agreement

without authority other than their ideas, integrity, or prestige with the parties. As a result, their functions must be very loosely defined.

and a conference is requested by a party or prospective party thereto, arrange promptly for such a conference to be held and endeavor in such conference to settle such dispute expeditiously; and

(3) in case such dispute is not settled by conference, participate fully and promptly in such meetings as may be undertaken by the Service under this Act for the purpose of aiding in a settlement of the dispute.

SEC. 205. (a) There is hereby created a National Labor-Management Panel which shall be composed of twelve members appointed by the President, six of whom shall be selected from among persons outstanding in the field of management and six of whom shall be selected from among persons outstanding in the field of labor. Each member shall hold office for a term of three years, except that any member appointed to fill a vacancy occurring prior to the expiration of the term for which his predecessor was appointed shall be appointed for the remainder of such term, and the terms of office of the members first taking office shall expire, as designated by the President at the time of appointment, four at the end of the first year, four at the end of the second year, and four at the end of the third year after the date of appointment. Members of the panel, when serving on business of the panel, shall be paid compensation at the rate of $25 per day, and shall also be entitled to receive an allowance for actual and necessary travel and subsistence expenses while so serving away from their places of residence.

(b) It shall be the duty of the panel, at the request of the Director, to advise in the avoidance of industrial controversies and the manner in which mediation and voluntary adjustment shall be administered, particularly with reference to controversies affecting the general welfare of the country.

This Panel has seldom been convened and when it has been convened, it has never accomplished much.

National emergencies

SEC. 206. Whenever in the opinion of the President of the United States, a threatened or actual strike or lock-out affecting an entire industry or a substantial part thereof engaged in trade, commerce, transportation, transmission, or communication among the several States or with foreign nations, or engaged in the production of goods for commerce, will, if permitted to occur or to continue, imperil the national

An important part of Title II is the national-emergency strike procedure, found in Secs. 206 to 210. The method, adapted from the Railway Labor Act, relies on publicity and delay. It is a six-step process, as follows:

health or safety, he may appoint a board of inquiry to inquire into the issues involved in the dispute and to make a written report to him within such time as he shall prescribe. Such report shall include a statement of the facts with respect to the dispute, including each party's statement of its position but shall not contain any recommendations. The President shall file a copy of such report with the Service and shall make its contents available to the public.

SEC. 207. (a) A board of inquiry shall be composed of a chairman and such other members as the President shall determine, and shall have power to sit and act in any place within the United States and to conduct such hearings either in public or private, as it may deem necessary or proper, to ascertain the facts with respect to the causes and circumstances of the dispute.

(b) Members of a board of inquiry shall receive compensation at the rate of $50 for each day actually spent by them in the work of the board, together with necessary travel and subsistence expenses.

(c) For the purpose of any hearing or inquiry conducted by any board appointed under this title, the provisions of sections 9 and 10 (relating to the attendance of witnesses and the production of books, papers, and documents) of the Federal Trade Commission Act of September 16, 1914, as amended (U.S.C. 19, title 15, secs. 49 and 50, as amended), are hereby made applicable to the powers and duties of such board.

SEC. 208. (a) Upon receiving a report from a board of inquiry the President may direct the Attorney General to petition any district court of the United States having jurisdiction of the parties to enjoin such strike or lock-out or the continuing thereof, and if the court finds that such threatened or actual strike or lock-out—

(i) affects an entire industry or a substantial part thereof engaged in trade, commerce, transportation, transmission, or communication among the several States or with foreign nations, or engaged in the production of goods for commerce; and

(ii) if permitted to occur or to continue, will imperil the national health or safety, it shall have jurisdiction to enjoin any such strike or lock-out, or the continuing thereof, and to make such other orders as may be appropriate.

1. The President decides that a strike or lockout (either threatened or actual) imperils "the national health or safety" and appoints a board of inquiry to investigate and report to him.

2. The President then may tell the Attorney General to petition a district court for an injunction stopping the strike or lockout.

3. If an injunction is granted, the board of inquiry is reconvened with a 60-day deadline to report on developments, especially "the employer's last offer of settlement."

4. The NLRB then has 15 days to take a secret ballot of the employes on the question of accepting the employer's last offer and is given 5 days more to certify the outcome to the Attorney General.

5. The Attorney General then must ask the court to discharge the injunction, and the court has no alternative but to comply.

6. The President makes a full report to Congress with recommendations for appropriate action.

The national-emergency strike procedure has been used a number of times, with fairly satisfactory results, if the test is the settlement of disputes (and that is certainly one of the more important standards). Nevertheless, many feel that the results are rather inconclusive, a judgment not too surprising since the procedure is pretty inconclusive itself. However, that may be its virtue. It is strictly a presidential tool, since the first and biggest decision

(b) In any case, the provisions of the Act of March 23, 1932, entitled "An Act to amend the Judicial Code and to define and limit the jurisdiction of courts sitting in equity, and for other purposes," shall not be applicable.

(c) The order or orders of the court shall be subject to review by the appropriate circuit court of appeals and by the Supreme Court upon writ of certiorari or certification as provided in sections 239 and 240 of the Judicial Code, as amended (U.S.C., title 29, secs. 346 and 347).

SEC. 209.   (a) Whenever a district court has issued an order under section 208 enjoining acts or practices which imperil or threaten to imperil the national health or safety, it shall be the duty of the parties to the labor dispute giving rise to such order to make every effort to adjust and settle their differences, with the assistance of the Service created by this Act. Neither party shall be under any duty to accept, in whole or in part, any proposal of settlement made by the Service.

(b) Upon the issuance of such order, the President shall reconvene the board of inquiry which has previously reported with respect to the dispute. At the end of a sixty-day period (unless the dispute has been settled by that time), the board of inquiry shall report to the President the current position of the parties and the efforts which have been made for settlement, and shall include a statement by each party of its position and a statement of the employer's last offer of settlement. The President shall make such report available to the public. The National Labor Relations Board, within the succeeding fifteen days, shall take a secret ballot of the employees of each employer involved in the dispute on the question of whether they wish to accept the final offer of settlement made by their employer as stated by him and shall certify the results thereof to the Attorney General within five days thereafter.

SEC. 210.   Upon the certification of the results of such ballot or upon a settlement being reached, whichever happens sooner, the Attorney General shall move the court to discharge the injunction, which motion shall then be granted and the injunction discharged. When such motion is granted, the President shall submit to the Congress a full and comprehensive report of the proceedings, including the findings of the board of inquiry and the ballot

of all, that a strike threatens to "imperil the national health or safety," is up to the Chief Executive. For as long as the procedure is law, it will probably be possible to work up an argument for or against this way of slowing down the big and important work stoppages.

taken by the National Labor Relations Board, together with such recommendations as he may see fit to make for consideration and appropriate action.

Compilation of collective bargaining agreements, etc.

SEC. 211. (a) For the guidance and information of interested representatives of employers, employees, and the general public, the Bureau of Labor Statistics of the Department of Labor shall maintain a file of copies of all available collective bargaining agreements and other available agreements and actions thereunder settling or adjusting labor disputes. Such file shall be open to inspection under appropriate conditions prescribed by the Secretary of Labor, except that no specific information submitted in confidence shall be disclosed.

(b) The Bureau of Labor Statistics in the Department of Labor is authorized to furnish upon request of the Service, or employers, employees, or their representatives, all available data and factual information which may aid in the settlement of any labor dispute, except that no specific information submitted in confidence shall be disclosed.

Exemption of Railway Labor Act

SEC. 212. The provisions of this title shall not be applicable with respect to any matter which is subject to the provisions of the Railway Labor Act, as amended from time to time.

Title III

Suits by and against labor organizations

SEC. 301. (a) Suits for violation of contracts between an employer and a labor organization representing employees in an industry affecting commerce as defined in this Act, or between any such labor organizations, may be brought in any district court of the United States having jurisdiction of the parties, without respect to the amount in controversy or without regard to the citizenship of the parties.

(b) Any labor organization which represents employees in an industry affecting commerce as defined in this Act and any employer whose activities

Title III is a set of *general* safeguards against the misuse of union power. (For example, it is the only operative portion of the act that applies to employes coming under the Railway Labor Act.) In summary, its five sections do the following: Section 301 makes unions suable and specifies that violation of a union contract is grounds for a suit for damages. Section 302 regulates the checkoff of union dues and payments

affect commerce as defined in this Act shall be bound by the acts of its agents. Any such labor organization may sue or be sued as an entity and in behalf of the employees whom it represents in the courts of the United States. Any money judgment against a labor organization in a district court of the United States shall be enforceable only against the organization as an entity and against its assets, and shall not be enforceable against any individual member or his assets.

(c) For the purposes of actions and proceedings by or against labor organizations in the district courts of the United States, district courts shall be deemed to have jurisdiction of a labor organization (1) in the district in which such organization maintains its principal office, or (2) in any district in which its duly authorized officers or agents are engaged in representing or acting for employee members.

(d) The service of summons, subpena, or other legal process of any court of the United States upon an officer or agent of a labor organization, in his capacity as such, shall constitute service upon the labor organization.

(e) For the purposes of this section, in determining whether any person is acting as an "agent" of another person so as to make such other person responsible for his acts, the question of whether the specific acts performed were actually authorized or subsequently ratified shall not be controlling.

into union-management trust funds. Section 303 cracks down a second time on the strikes, boycotts, and picketing outlined in Sec. 8(b)(4)(A–D). Here they are not only unfair labor practices but are "unlawful," and the stigma is again applied to employe organizations normally coming under the Railway Labor Act. Section 304 prohibits political contributions or expenditures by labor organizations and makes violation a misdemeanor punishable by fine or imprisonment or both. Section 305 prohibits strikes by employes of the Federal government, with penalties of immediate dismissal, loss of civil service status, and ineligibility for reemployment for 3 years. In the opinion of organized labor, Title III contains some of the most objectionable parts of the Taft-Hartley Act.

To begin with (Sec. 301), unions distinctly did not (and still do not) want to "sue and be sued as entities" or to be legally bound by the acts of their "agents," especially with the generous definition of the latter found in the act.

Section 301(e) reiterates the point made in the "Definitions," Sec. 2(13), of the National Labor Relations Act, thus expanding it to cover all employes (and unions) in interstate commerce. It is aimed at the difficult problem of connecting union members—and union officials—with the union for purposes of assigning responsibility to the latter. The definition in both places is intended to make it easier to trace responsibility to the union. "Authorization" in advance or "ratification" after the fact are standard legal tests of agency. Here they are ruled out as controlling, leaving the Board and the courts to decide from more circumstantial evidence the connection between personal acts and union responsibility.

Restrictions on payments to employee representatives

SEC. 302.   (a)   It shall be unlawful for any employer or association of employers or any person who acts as a labor relations expert, adviser, or consultant to an employer or who acts in the interest of an employer to pay, lend, or deliver, or agree to pay, lend, or deliver, any money or other thing of value—

(1) to any representative of any of his employees who are employed in an industry affecting commerce; or

(2) to any labor organization, or any officer or employee thereof, which represents, seeks to represent, or would admit to membership, any of the employees of such employer who are employed in an industry affecting commerce; or

(3) to any employee or group or committee of employees of such employer employed in an industry affecting commerce in excess of their normal compensation for the purpose of causing such employee or group or committee directly or indirectly to influence any other employees in the exercise of the right to organize and bargain collectively through representatives of their own choosing; or

(4) to any officer or employee of a labor organization engaged in an industry affecting commerce with intent to influence him in respect to any of his actions, decisions, or duties as a representative of employees or as such officer or employee of such labor organization.

(b)   (1) It shall be unlawful for any person to request, demand, receive, or accept, or agree to receive or accept, any payment, loan, or delivery of

Section 302(a), (b), (c) was expanded and restated by amendment in the L–G act, Sec. 505. To regulate the checkoff and payments into trust funds, Congress first prohibited every kind of payment by employers to unions or their representatives and then outlined the exceptions. Among these were payments for services rendered as employes, the checkoff of union dues, and payments into trust funds, the latter two only under specific conditions and limitations [see clauses (4) and (5)]. Very specifically *not* exempted from the prohibition were fees demanded from operators of motor vehicles "as a fee or charge for the unloading, or in connection with the unloading, of the cargo of such vehicle," unless compensation for services as employes. (This is clearly another restriction aimed at the Teamsters union.)

Both the checkoff and trust funds (pension and welfare benefits) have become big business, very big business, with the private financial rights of many in-any money or other thing of value prohibited by subsection (a).

(2) It shall be unlawful for any labor organization, or for any person acting as an officer, agent, representative, or employee of such labor organization, to demand or accept from the operator of any motor vehicle (as defined in part II of the Interstate Commerce Act) employed in the transportation of property in commerce, or the employer of any such operator, any money or other thing of value payable to such organization or to an officer, agent, representative or employee thereof as a fee or charge for the unloading, or in connection with the unloading, of the cargo of such vehicle: *Provided,* That nothing in this paragraph shall be construed to make unlawful any payment by employer to any of his employees as compensation for their services as employees.

(c) The provisions of this section shall not be applicable (1) in respect to any money or other thing of value payable by an employer to any of his employees whose established duties include acting openly for such employer in matters of labor relations or personnel administration or to any representative of his employees, or to any officer or employee of a labor organization, who is also an employee or former employee of such employer, as compensation for, or by reason of, his service as an employee of such employer; (2) with respect to the payment or delivery of any money or other thing of value in satisfaction of a judgment of any court or a decision or award of an arbitrator or impartial chairman or in compromise, adjustment, settlement, or release of any claim, complaint, grievance, or dispute in the absence of fraud or duress; (3) with respect to the sale or purchase of an article or commodity at the prevailing market price in the regular course of business; (4) with respect to money deducted from the wages of employees in payment of membership dues in a labor organization: *Provided,* That the employer has received from each employee, on whose account such deductions are made, a written assignment which shall not be irrevocable for a period of more than one year, or beyond the termination date of the applicable collective agreement, whichever occurrs sooner; (5) with respect to money or other thing of value paid to a trust fund established by such representative, for the sole and exclusive benefit of the employees of such employer, and their families and

dividual employes involved. A trust fund necessarily produces fiduciary responsibilities—a responsibility now assigned to all union officers and representatives by the L–G act, Sec. 501— which means that the trustee occupies a position of trust in the handling of other people's money. Responsibilities of this sort are seldom left unregulated for long in our type of society.

This whole section is an outstanding example of the "reverse order" of legal draftsmanship, in which everything is first prohibited and then the exceptions to be permitted are detailed. It is a tiresome, clumsy, and indirect method of making a point—"legalese" at its worst.

dependents (or of such employees, families, and dependents jointly with the employees of other employers making similar payments, and their families and dependents): *Provided,* That (A) such payments are held in trust for the purpose of paying, either from principal or income or both, for the benefit of employees, their families and dependents, for medical or hospital care, pensions on retirement or death of employees, compensation for injuries or illness resulting from occupational activity or insurance to provide any of the foregoing, or unemployment benefits or life insurance, disability and sickness insurance, or accident insurance; (B) the detailed basis on which such payments are to be made is specified in a written agreement with the employer, and employees and employers are equally represented in the administration of such fund, together with such neutral persons as the representatives of the employers and the representatives of employees may agree upon and in the event the employer and employee groups deadlock on the administration of such fund and there are no neutral persons empowered to break such deadlock, such agreement provides that the two groups shall agree on an impartial umpire to decide such dispute, or in event of their failure to agree within a reasonable length of time, an impartial umpire to decide such dispute shall, on petition of either group, be appointed by the district court of the United States for the district where the trust fund has its principal office, and shall also contain provisions for an annual audit of the trust fund, a statement of the results of which shall be available for inspection by interested persons at the principal office of the trust fund and at such other places as may be designated in such written agreement; and (C) such payments as are intended to be used for the purpose of providing pensions or annuities for employees are made to a separate trust which provides that the funds held therein cannot be used for any purpose other than paying such pensions or annuities; or (6) with respect to money or other thing of value paid by an employer to a trust fund established by such representative for the purpose of pooled vacation, holiday, severance or similar benefits, or defraying costs of apprenticeship or other training programs: *Provided,* That the requirements of clause (B) of the proviso to clause (5) of this subsection shall apply to such trust funds."

(d)   Any person who willfully violates any of

the provisions of this section shall, upon conviction thereof, be guilty of a misdemeanor and be subject to a fine of not more than $10,000 or to imprisonment for not more than one year, or both.

(e) The district courts of the United States and the United States courts of the Territories and possessions shall have jurisdiction, for cause shown, and subject to the provisions of section 17 (relating to notice to opposite party) of the Act entitled "An Act to supplement existing laws against unlawful restraints and monopolies, and for other purposes," approved October 15, 1914, as amended (U.S.C., title 28, sec. 381), to restrain violations of this section, without regard to the provisions of sections 6 and 20 of such Act of October 15, 1914, as amended (U.S.C., title 15, sec. 17, and title 29, sec. 52), and the provisions of the Act entitled "An Act to amend the Judicial Code and to define and limit the jurisdiction of courts sitting in equity, and for other purposes," approved March 23, 1932 (U.S.C., title 29, secs. 101–115).

(f) This section shall not apply to any contract in force on the date of enactment of this Act, until the expiration of such contract, or until July 1, 1948, whichever first occurs.

(g) Compliance with the restrictions contained in subsection (c)(5)(B) upon contribution to trust funds, otherwise lawful, shall not be applicable to contributions to such trust funds established by collective agreement prior to January 1, 1946, nor shall subsection (c)(5)(A) be construed as prohibiting contributions to such trust funds if prior to January 1, 1947, such funds contained provisions for pooled vacation benefits.

Boycotts and other unlawful combinations

SEC. 303. (a) It shall be unlawful, for the purpose of this section only, in an industry or activity affecting commerce, for any labor organization to engage in any activity or conduct defined as an unfair labor practice in section 8(b)(4) of the National Labor Relations Act, as amended.

(b) Whoever shall be injured in his business or property by reason of any violation of subsection (a) may sue therefor in any district court of the United States subject to the limitations and provisions of section 301 hereof without respect to the

Section 303 was, and is, intended as a crackdown on secondary and hot-goods boycotts. In Sec. 8(b)(4), they were made unfair labor practices; here they are defined as "unlawful." The difference is that an unfair labor practice must be reported to a certain agency (the NLRB) by a certain party and can be remedied only

amount in controversy, or in any other court having jurisdiction of the parties, and shall recover the damages by him sustained and the cost of the suit.

Restrictions on political contributions

SEC. 304.   Section 313 of the Federal Corrupt Practices Act, 1925 (U.S.C., 1940 edition, title 2, sec. 251; Supp. V, title 50, App., sec. 1509), as amended, is amended to read as follows:

"SEC. 313.   It is unlawful for any national bank, or any corporation organized by authority of any law of Congress, to make a contribution or expenditure in connection with any election to any political office, or in connection with any primary election or political convention or caucus held to select candidates for any political office, or for any corporation whatever, or any labor organization to make a contribution or expenditure in connection with any election at which Presidential and Vice Presidential electors or a Senator or Representative in, or a Delegate or Resident Commissioner to Congress are to be voted for, or in connection with any primary election or political convention or caucus held to select candidates for any of the foregoing offices, or for any candidate, political committee, or other person to accept or receive any contribution prohibited by this section. Every corporation or labor organization which makes any contribution or expenditure in violation of this section shall be fined not more than $5,000; and every officer or director of any corporation, or officer of any labor organization, who consents to any contribution or expenditure by the corporation or labor organization, as the case may be, in violation of this section shall be fined not more than $1,000 or imprisoned for not more than one year, or both. For the purposes of this section 'labor organization' means any organization of any kind, or any agency or employee representation committee or plan, in which employees participate and which exists for the purpose, in whole or in part, of dealing with employers, concerning grievances, labor disputes, wages, rates of pay, hours of employment, or conditions of work."

in certain ways: cease-and-desist orders, rehiring, a payment of back wages, etc. Something that is "unlawful" can be reported by anyone to a court having jurisdiction, and the law asserts that [Sec. 303(*b*)] "whoever shall be injured in his business or property by reason of any violation . . . may sue therefor in any district court of the United States. . . ." The extension of possible jeopardy is tremendous and adds to the specific limitations on use of secondary and hot-goods boycotts.

Section 304 reflected the fears of Congress, a political body, that labor unions or the AFL–CIO might become in effect political parties with slush funds and a concentrated vote that could swing important elections—for President, say, or congressman or senator. It therefore prohibited political "contributions or expenditures" by labor organizations as such, putting unions alongside of national banks and corporations in the Federal Corrupt Practices Act of 1925. This action left it open for officers and members to make such contributions but meant that the union's general funds could not be drawn on to finance a political campaign. Since it is not so easy to get union members to contribute separately for political purposes, this prohibition puts a considerable damper on the activities of COPE, the political affiliate of the AFL–CIO, as well as the political activities of individual unions.

Strikes by government employees

SEC. 305.   It shall be unlawful for any individual employed by the United States or any agency thereof including wholly owned Government corporations to participate in any strike. Any individual employed by the United States or by any such agency who strikes shall be discharged immediately from his employment, and shall forfeit his civil service status, if any, and shall not be eligible for reemployment for three years by the United States or any such agency.

Section 305 shows how the government feels about strikes on the part of its own employes.

Title IV

Creation of joint committee to study and report on basic problems affecting friendly labor relations and productivity

Title IV is now long out of date and is therefore omitted.

Title V

Definitions

SEC. 501.   When used in this Act—

(1)   The term "industry affecting commerce" means any industry or activity in commerce or in which a labor dispute would burden or obstruct commerce or tend to burden or obstruct commerce or the free flow of commerce.

(2)   The term "strike" includes any strike or other concerted stoppage of work by employees (including a stoppage by reason of the expiration of a collective-bargaining agreement) and any concerted slow-down or other concerted interruption of operations by employees.

(3)   The terms "commerce," "labor disputes," "employer," "employee," "labor organization," "representative," "person," and "supervisor" shall have the same meaning as when used in the National Labor Relations Act as amended by this Act.

The "Definitions" in Sec. 501 apply to the whole law (all five titles) and not just to the amended National Labor Relations Act, as did those in Sec. 2 of Title I.

The purpose of Sec. 502 is to prevent the act's being held unconstitutional in violation of the Fifteenth Amendment to the Constitution of the United States. This amendment prohibits forced labor or involuntary servitude except as a punishment for crime. What the "saving provision" means is that, even though organized work stoppages (strikes, slowdowns, boycotts) may be ruled out of order, it is still the privilege of anyone to quit his job as an individual. Remember strikers work on the theory that they are merely "suspending" work for the time being and have not actually given up their jobs.

Saving provision

SEC. 502.   Nothing in this Act shall be construed to require an individual employee to render labor or service without his consent, nor shall anything in this Act be construed to make the quitting of his labor by an individual employee an illegal act; nor shall any court issue any process to compel the performance by an individual employee of such labor

Students interested in this law might well look

or service, without his consent; nor shall the quitting of labor by an employee or employees in good faith because of abnormally dangerous conditions of work at the place of employment of such employee or employees be deemed a strike under this Act.

up President Truman's veto message, with which he returned the bill as unsatisfactory. (It is on file as H. Doc. 334, 80th Cong., 1st sess.)

Separability

SEC. 503.   If any provision of this Act, or the application of such provision to any person or circumstance, shall be held invalid, the remainder of this Act, or the application of such provision to persons or circumstances other than those as to which it is held invalid, shall not be affected thereby.

TEN

STRIKES AND OTHER KINDS OF DISPUTE SETTLEMENT

A warning. When union and management negotiators fail to reach agreement, a strike is the result. A strike is always news—often front-page news. It means conflict, disorder, shutdown of plant or work site, workers unemployed, picketing, recrimination by spokesmen for the union and the employer, public inconvenience and community tension, and the possibility of violence. Strikes are the only kind of union activity that a great many people ever read or hear about. Most of the 100,000 or more union contracts that are renegotiated every year, *without* a walkout or the threat of one, do not get into the record. They will not be found on even the back pages of a newspaper, while the 3 or 4 per cent that produce strikes are headlined on page 1. It is thus inevitable that the number of strikes, as well as their impact and severity, will be overemphasized and distorted. It is well to keep this in mind when studying the strike question.

Strikes, with their accompanying *picketing*, highlight conflict; along with the *boycott*—another weapon of organized labor, now used very sparingly—they appear when the *diversity* of interests of employers and employes produces a deadlock. They are countered by employer tactics of equal variety and determination, and the resulting struggle naturally draws the interest of bystanders. In a country where so much emphasis is put upon rivalry and competition, the annual round of union-management contests is big-league entertainment. It is overshadowed in public interest only by such superior diversions as a major election or a war. To the union, however, a resort to "direct action" is a very serious matter. The relationship between the use of economic force on the one hand, and collective bargaining on the other, is as follows:

1. Collective bargaining is the goal; it is what the union was created for and exists for, its reason for being.
2. Strikes, picketing, and boycotts are at times the only means by which the union feels that it can advance toward its goal—of security, a good

310

contract, and acceptance. In military terminology, collective bargaining is the campaign, whereas strikes and boycotts are the individual battles which collectively add up to winning or losing.

Direct action in collective bargaining. The essence of collective bargaining is dispute settlement—the resolution of conflicting views into a workable compromise. Such a brief definition, however, gives little hint of the tremendous range of methods which may be employed to persuade an opponent to agree. It is collective bargaining, for example, to win a point through tact and politeness at the conference table. It is also collective bargaining to close an employer's plant, bar the owner from the property, and threaten violence to nonunion workmen who try to return to their jobs. In between may come an infinite variety of tactics designed to impress, persuade, influence, bluff, startle, frighten, or force the other party into agreement. No current issue of employer-employe relations raises more questions of policy, public and private, than the permissible limits of union and employer action in the settlement of disputes.

The reason is, of course, that the effects of union-management conflict cannot be isolated to the parties themselves. Management and union members produce, between them, a large portion of the goods and services which are consumed by a modern society. It happens that the production of some of the most necessary products and crucial services in this country is dependent upon the efforts of unionized workmen (*e.g.,* railroad transportation, coal mining, trucking, the manufacturing of iron and steel). In any union-management struggle, there eventually comes a time when some third party is injured, either because he becomes involved at a moment of high tension or, more often, because he must do without something that he wants or needs because the dispute between labor and management has shut off the supply. This last can be pretty serious when the supply is all bus and subway service in New York City, as in the Transit Workers' strike of January, 1966. At such times, the excitement runs high and public officials—in this case, the newly elected Mayor Lindsay of New York City, Governor Rockefeller, and Federal representatives such as the Secretary of Labor—get apprehensive.

One of the big public-policy problems confronting the American people today, therefore, is a code of industrial relations which will provide a satisfactory method of dispute settlement—satisfactory, that is, not only to the parties themselves but also to the general public. One such solution, widely advocated at present but flatly rejected by both unions and management, is compulsory arbitration. Used extensively in wartime (Second World War and the Korean conflict), it has had one big peacetime application, the 1963 Railroad Arbitration Act, which required binding arbitration of two issues (the use of firemen in freight and yard service, and the size of train crews) in order to avoid a strike by 200,000 operating employes in five unions.[1] However, before a policy decision is arrived at, there should be some understanding of the ways in which unions and management try to gain an advantage over each other. Some very ill-advised labor legislation has sprung from ignorance of the nature of employer-employe disputes or the need for methods to resolve them. A prime example is New York's Condon-Wadlin law which was openly violated in the Transit strike of 1966, but which was never invoked by the authorities because of its obvious failings.[2]

STRIKES IN THEORY AND IN PRACTICE

Theory of the strike.   The ultimate union reliance in dealing with employers is upon the strike. A strike, according to the Bureau of Labor Statistics, is a "temporary stoppage of work by a group of employees in order to express a grievance or to enforce a demand."[3] This definition of a strike, however, raises an important issue, since it is not acceptable to many people, especially employers. It implies that the employes have not quit (given up) their jobs but have merely temporarily suspended working at them. According to this theory, therefore, the employe on strike is still in full possession of all job rights, including his seniority, the privilege of voting on questions of union representation, and so forth. But what if the employer has replaced the striking employes with nonstrikers who are willing to accept the rates of pay, hours, and conditions of work which are in dispute? What, if any, are the rights of the new employes?

The union answer, of course, is that the newcomers are "scabs" (strike-breakers), with no rights to consideration of any kind. This is the traditional and universal view of organized labor, but hardly one on which there is universal agreement outside trade unions. The employer's position is that, if he can fill the jobs with qualified men willing to work on the terms rejected by the union and its members, he should be permitted to go ahead and operate and the new employes to hold their jobs, exactly as he (or anyone else) is permitted to buy and sell in the best markets he can find.

Which is right?

[1] Public Law 88–108, Aug. 28, 1963. For a summary of the provisions of the act, see the *Monthly Labor Review,* October, 1963, pp. 1187–88.

[2] The law's main inadequacy was its failure to provide a substitute method of dispute settlement in place of strikes, which were prohibited.

[3] *Handbook of Labor Statistics, 1947,* p. 134. The counterpart to the right to strike is the right to lock out, which is correspondingly defined as "a temporary withholding of work from a group of employees by an employer (or group of employers) in order to coerce them into accepting the employer's terms." The employer, of course, has much less need of the lockout, since he is ordinarily the more passive party in collective bargaining and also is actively in charge of the business and so may put policies into effect without consulting the union if they do not violate the agreement.

It is doubtful that any categorical reply can be given to the question. For a number of years the National Labor Relations Board interpreted strikes according to the union definition (that used by the BLS), permitting strikers to vote on questions of representation and denying that privilege to the employes hired to replace them. The policy was changed in 1947 by the Taft-Hartley Act, with job rights given to the newcomers and exclusion from voting of workers engaged in an "economic" strike (one over wages, hours, etc.). It was changed back again in the Reporting and Disclosure Act of 1959, as follows: "Employees engaged in an economic strike who are not entitled to reinstatement shall be eligible to vote . . . in any election conducted within twelve months after the commencement of the strike." [4]

The really fundamental issue in the case is the right of employes who refrain from joining labor unions to have access to jobs which unions have laid claim to. This issue was decided in favor of the individual worker by the Taft-Hartley Act—except under valid union-shop agreements—in a shift away from the preference that unions enjoyed under the Wagner Act. The new decision was and is unacceptable to unions, and it may be expected that there will be dispute over the issue for some time to come.

The right to strike.   There is another issue raised by the way "strike" is defined that goes even deeper than the job rights of nonstrikers. It is the accusation, made now and then by representatives of organized labor, that any limitation of the right to strike is a move in the direction of involuntary servitude and therefore contrary to the Thirteenth Amendment to the Constitution of the United States.[5] This charge clearly rests on a misunderstanding of the law, which makes a sharp distinction between that which can be done individually and that which can be done in concert. A strike is a concerted action by a group of employes. A complete prohibition of the right to strike would still not bar employes from giving up their jobs individually and so would hardly constitute involuntary servitude.

Since the strike is the union's major weapon, organized labor has been extremely jealous of its protection and sensitive to any attempt to curtail its use on any grounds whatever. A typical statement of view is the following, taken from an editorial in the *American Federationist*, official journal of the AFL:

Strikes are never welcomed by the public and seldom desired by industry or labor. But they may be necessary to promote the general welfare and to establish justice for workers. *The right to strike is inseparable from human freedom.* No genuine de-

[4] Sec. 702.
[5] "Neither slavery nor involuntary servitude, except as a punishment for crime whereof the party shall have been duly convicted, shall exist within the United States, or any place subject to their jurisdiction."

mocracy will consider outlawing strikes, but ample facilities for helping to adjust issues and problems that cause strikes should be provided.[6]

This viewpoint is very widely held, and not only by members of trade unions. It has been impressed upon legislators, for example, to the point where guarantees of the right to strike are frequently included in legislation regulating union-management relations. For example, the Taft-Hartley Act still contains the following assurance:

Nothing in this Act, except as specifically provided for herein, shall be construed so as either to interfere with or impede or diminish in any way the right to strike, or to affect the limitations or qualifications on that right.

Nonetheless, the "right to strike" is itself a fundamental issue, which has been flatly denied by spokesmen for both industry and government, who contend that concerted action by employes is not a right at all but a privilege, which may be limited, modified, or taken away if abused. Under the Taft-Hartley Act, for instance, employes of the Federal government do not have the right to strike at all and if they do so are subject to immediate dismissal and the loss of seniority and reemployment rights for 3 years.[7]

The facts of the matter are, of course, that there are very few absolute rights, and certainly the "right to strike" is not one of them. There have been legislative, administrative, or judicial limitations upon strikes at all periods of the country's history, and the casebooks are full of decisions which distinguish between "legal" and "illegal" walkouts. What the trade unionist is probably asking for is no limitation of the right to strike in favor of any *private* interest, and he looks with suspicion upon all restrictions, since sad experience in the past has taught him that this may be the outcome of moves nominally made for protection of the public. In view of the fact that corporate bodies and trade unions are now of such size that a single contest (as in steel, railways, or airlines) may disrupt large sections of the economy, the line between public and private interests becomes increasingly harder to draw.

Congress took cognizance of the problem first in a series of laws dealing with labor relations on the railways, and in the Taft-Hartley Act it set up a complicated procedure for the handling of "national emergency" strikes, which includes the use of fact-finding boards, injunctions, cooling-off periods, and polls of the employes. This procedure has been used a number of times, but the issue is still far from settled. Limitations upon the right to strike, even in walkouts that appear to "imperil the national health or safety," are strongly opposed by union leaders and just as strongly supported by representatives of management and the general

---

[6] February, 1946. Italics supplied.

[7] This was copied after New York's Condon-Wadlin law and is of course equally deficient, as no substitute method of settling disputes is provided in the act.

public. At the level of national health and safety, the argument for limitation seems unanswerable, but the level is hard to define, and a method satisfactory to everyone has yet to be worked out.

The size of the problem.   The next question is: Are strikes really such a problem? Are there enough of them, and are they big enough, really to threaten to interfere with the national welfare? Earlier the point was made that most employer-employe bargaining was carried on peacefully, without any interruption of work. Can there be a serious strike problem consistent with such a fact? Union spokesmen say no, that interruptions of service are minor and inconsequential compared with the total volume of man-hours of work performed and that the inconvenience caused by a work stoppage now and then is a small price to pay for the preservation of labor's fundamental right to strike. The basic figures which labor relies on to support this argument are found in Table 10-1, which shows the volume of work stoppages in the United States from 1936 to 1965, as measured by several different standards.

According to the table, it looks as though organized labor has a pretty good case. The volume of strikes has not increased appreciably in 30 years.[8] There were 4,740 of them in 1937 and over 3,000 a year every year from 1943 onwards, with one exception: 2,468 in 1954. At the other extreme, there were 5,117 in 1952, the top year since and the top year of all. The average length of strikes, measured in calendar days, has also not increased; the 23 to 24 days of recent years just about equals the average time loss of the later 1930s. Nor has there been a noticeable increase in the number or percentage of workers involved. There were 1,860,000 men out in 1937 and 1,640,000 in 1964. If one considers the increase in the size of the labor force and in the total number of trade-union members, this is a very conservative rise, especially when one considers the *drop* in percentage figures of workers involved—from 7.2 per cent of the employed labor force in 1937 to 3.4 per cent in 1964.

Only when we get to the volume of man-days lost as a result of work stoppages is there statistical evidence of any increasing seriousness of the problem, and here the data fluctuate. In 1946, an all-time record was set, with a loss of 116 million man-days of working time. This was more than three times the loss of the highest preceding year, 1945, during which 38 million working days were missed, and almost double the biggest year

---

[8] Most work stoppages are from strikes. The BLS does not separate strikes and lockouts in its statistics, nor does the Federal Mediation and Conciliation Service. The main reason is to avoid arguments over causation and charges that the record is being loaded in favor of one or another of the parties. It is common practice for both unions and management to charge the other party with responsibility for shutdowns, and in many cases it is actually difficult to tell whether the stoppage was caused by a union or a management decision. However, there is little doubt that strikes are the immediate cause of 90 per cent or more of the total.

Table 10-1. Work stoppages in the United States, 1936–1965

Year	Stoppages		Workers involved		Man-days of idleness	
	Number	Average length (days)	Number (000's)	Per cent of all employed	Number (000's)	Per cent of all working time
1936	2,172	23.3	789	3.1	13,900	0.21
1937	4,740	20.3	1,860	7.2	28,400	0.43
1938	2,772	23.6	688	2.8	9,150	0.15
1939	2,613	23.4	1,170	4.7	17,800	0.28
1940	2,508	20.9	577	2.3	6,700	0.10
1941	4,288	18.3	2,360	8.4	23,000	0.32
1942	2,968	11.7	840	2.8	4,180	0.05
1943	3,752	5.0	1,980	6.9	13,500	0.15
1944	4,956	5.6	2,120	7.0	8,720	0.09
1945	4,750	9.9	3,470	12.2	38,000	0.47
1946	4,985	24.2	4,600	14.5	116,000	1.43
1947	3,693	25.6	2,170	6.5	34,600	0.41
1948	3,419	21.8	1,960	5.5	34,100	0.37
1949	3,606	22.5	3,030	9.0	50,500	0.59
1950	4,843	19.2	2,410	6.9	38,800	0.44
1951	4,737	17.4	2,220	5.5	22,900	0.23
1952	5,117	19.6	3,540	8.8	59,100	0.57
1953	5,091	20.3	2,400	5.6	28,300	0.26
1954	2,468	22.5	1,530	3.7	22,600	0.21
1955	4,320	18.5	2,650	6.2	28,200	0.26
1956	3,825	18.9	1,900	4.3	33,100	0.29
1957	3,673	19.2	1,390	3.1	16,500	0.14
1958	3,694	19.7	2,060	4.8	23,900	0.22
1959	3,708	24.6	1,880	4.3	69,000	0.61
1960	3,333	23.4	1,320	3.0	19,100	0.17
1961	3,367	23.7	1,450	3.2	16,300	0.14
1962	3,614	24.6	1,230	2.7	18,600	0.16
1963	3,362	23.0	941	2.0	16,100	0.13
1964	3,655	22.9	1,640	3.4	22,900	0.18
1965	3,770	n.a.	1,464	3.2	22,930	0.18

Sources: *Handbook of Labor Statistics, 1950*, p. 142; *Statistical Abstract of the United States, 1959*, p. 239; *1965*, p. 249; *Monthly Labor Review*, May, 1966, p. 596.

since—1959, with 69.0 million man-days lost. Yet even in 1946 the total loss was less than 1.5 per cent of all available working time, and in recent years there has been a decrease in this column: from 0.27 per cent for 1936 to 1939 to 0.16 per cent for 1961 to 1965.[9] This reduction becomes significant when one takes into account the relatively tremendous increase

[9] These statistics are in line with the "withering away of the strike" conclusions of Arthur M. Ross and Paul Hartman, in *Changing Patterns of Industrial Conflict*, Chap. 4 (New York: John Wiley & Sons, Inc., 1960).

in union membership; strikes are an *organized* activity, not spontaneous uprisings.

Then why all the worry? Why does Congress pass laws which limit the right to strike, and public opinion apparently support such legislation? Is it, as some labor leaders insist, a conspiracy to reduce the American workingman to a condition of servitude by weakening his union and taking away its most potent weapon? The answer, which comes impartially from a number of sources, is no. Strike regulation is called for, according to these observers, because the actual burden of work stoppages is inadequately reflected in the statistics, being more a question of size and "impact" (concentration and industrial location) than of averages. According to this view, the burden has to be measured qualitatively rather than quantitatively, although the argument is backed up with figures. It is a matter of shock, or concentrated interference with the economy, rather than over-all total. This means big strikes, strikes of long duration, and strikes in basic industries that affect other economic activity adversely.

There has been an increase in the number of big strikes—over 10,000 workers involved—since 1945. More big strikes are lasting longer, and the dislocations caused by the biggest walkouts (secondary unemployment and shutdowns in related industries) get steadily more serious. For example, in 1964, a low-count strike year, analysis shows that 18 *major stoppages* (10,000 or more workers each) produced about half of the total idleness. From the standpoint of *duration*, strikes lasting a month or more were responsible for over three-quarters (76 per cent) of all mandays lost.[10] Among the major shutdowns of the year were a walkout of 265,000 workers at General Motors for 45 days, a strike by 25,000 employes of the Ford Motor Company, and an industry-wide longshore work stoppage on the Atlantic and Gulf Coasts in which the national-emergency provisions of the Taft-Hartley Act were invoked and in which the strike was resumed 3 weeks *after* the expiration of the 80-day injunction. The biggest strike of all was in 1959, when a walkout of 530,000 members of the United Steelworkers of America shut down the basic steel industry for 116 days—from July 15 to Nov. 7—with a direct loss of 40 million to 50 million man-days of working time and secondary unemployment estimated at half as much again. This one strike produced a larger total of man-days lost than had been expended by all strikers in any single year for which there are records except 1946.

The strike as a weapon: Strikes and strike substitutes. There is another reason why the strike problem is more important than the statistics seem to indicate. There are more strikes (and near strikes) than are put down as such. In other words, the statistics are inadequate. The primary reason is the difficulty of defining the word "strike" so as to catch

[10] *Monthly Labor Review*, June, 1965, pp. 661–63.

all cases of "temporary stoppage of work by a group of employes", for the purpose of expressing a grievance or enforcing a demand. An organized slowdown of work is such a case, as is the calling of union business meetings during working hours.[11] As a result, in recent years many strikes and strike substitutes have been ruled out of bounds by no-strike clauses in labor agreements.

NO-STRIKE CLAUSES.   The purpose of a no-strike clause in a union contract is to ensure that work will not be interrupted by walkouts over grievances. In return, the union ordinarily gets a full grievance procedure ending with arbitration, which is a guarantee that stalemated grievances (denied by management) will not pile up and become a source of irritation. A simple no-strike clause, from a recent Steelworkers agreement is as follows:

There shall be no strikes, work stoppages or interruptions or impeding of work. No officers or representatives of the Union shall authorize, instigate, aid or condone any such activity. No employee shall participate in any such activities.
The applicable procedures of this Agreement will be followed for the settlement of all grievances. [Step 5 of the procedure calls for submission of unsettled grievances to an impartial umpire.]
There shall be no lockouts.

The no-strike clause has practically eliminated strikes over grievances in industrial (factory) unionism. They still occur in casual employment, especially building construction, and some of the service trades (hotels, restaurants, etc.), but by and large, the work stoppage "for the purpose of expressing a grievance" is becoming rare.

The strike has also been practically eliminated as an organizing device, since it is the function of the NLRB and state labor relations agencies to settle disputes over recognition. Very few union organizers prefer to risk a strike for recognition when they can get a decision by calling in an official of the NLRB. If they do call a walkout to aid in organization, the employer will promptly invoke the National Labor Relations Act himself to get the dispute settled by a vote. For all practical purposes, therefore, the strike is now confined to the settlement of "economic" disputes, which means the renegotiation of expiring agreements. It is nonetheless still a very flexible and powerful weapon and may at times be accomplished in fact without incurring the burdens which go with a formal walkout: the unemployment of workers, replacement of strikers by the employer, prosecution for illegality of purpose, etc. One of the evidences of union generalship is the ability to employ the various kinds of strikes and strike substitutes when necessary so as to get the most return for the least cost.

[11] A suggested class assignment is to have students read *Intl. Union, UAWA, Local 232 v. Wisconsin Employment Relations Board,* 336 U.S. 249 (1949) and evaluate the opinions of the majority and the minority of the United States Supreme Court with respect to the legality of the union's tactics.

How many varieties of strikes (and near strikes) are there?

There are several which have been used at one time or another in the past and which will probably be employed again in the future, for example, *the slowdown*. This is, as its name implies, a concerted reduction of the rate of output for the purpose of bringing pressure on the employer. It is not necessarily a protest against the speed of work demanded by management, although it may be. It is a temporary device and will be abandoned as soon as the purpose is gained or the grievance disappears. And it is a violation of contract if the agreement contains a no-strike clause. Nevertheless, it is used in cases where a grievance may have no contractual basis or is too intangible (resentment of supervision, for example) for formal presentation. If successful, it is relatively cost-free, and a subtle and powerful method of bringing pressure on management, especially where output rates cannot be controlled by piece rates or mechanical speeds as on an assembly line.[12]

Another type of strike substitute is the *strike vote*, or threat of walkout. It is standard practice to arm the representatives of the union with a strike vote before they start bargaining with management, as an indication that the union means business. Union members know that there will be many more affirmative votes than there will be strikes. It is thus one of the counters in the bargaining game, short of a work stoppage, like an *extra load of grievances* put into the hopper or individual or *group absences* within the termination-of-seniority limit to harass supervisors and make operations difficult. Another form of work interruption which may be sanctioned in the agreement is a *union business meeting* or series of meetings called during working hours. Still another is a *protest stoppage* for a definite period of time (a day, half a day, or perhaps only an hour or two), after which work is resumed as usual.

The *strike itself* is subject to a number of legal limitations—correct purpose, advance notice, exhaustion of other procedures for dispute settlement, conformity with contract provisions (no-strike clauses, etc.). It is also carefully hemmed in by the internal regulations of most unions, requiring advance authorization from the national headquarters or from a joint city central committee before a local may stage a walkout. The final expression of organized labor's dissatisfaction with conditions in the community is the *general strike*, a work stoppage by all union members in a given area. The object of the general strike is to coerce the government, and its result is a shutdown of all essential services. These are both extremes, and the general strike is therefore surrounded with great risk. The British General Strike of 1926 was directly responsible for the highly restrictive Trade Disputes and Trade Unions Act of 1927, which pro-

---

[12] As late as February, 1960, the United States Supreme Court ruled such "harassing tactics" within the law and not a refusal to bargain, as held by the NLRB. See *Monthly Labor Review*, April, 1960, p. 392.

hibited any kind of strike against the government, direct or indirect, and also denied the use of sympathetic strikes, mass or residential picketing, or the political use of trade-union funds. There have been limited examples of the general strike in the United States (in the San Francisco Bay Area in 1934 and again in 1936, each time over police support of nonstrikers) but the circumstances and the action were exceptional and by no means in line with regular union strike policy.

STRIKE POLICY, STRATEGY, TACTICS

Strike issues.   Very few people, labor leaders and union members included, enjoy strikes. For the labor leader, a strike is always a risk. If it is lost, he will take a cut in prestige and may lose his job and even his union. The general record of strike success since 1937 has tended to obscure the historical fact that strikes can be lost and that the results can be disastrous for the unions involved. For union members, strikes mean loss of pay, which may or may not be made up by what is won from employers, and there is the additional risk of being replaced by nonstrikers with the consequent permanent loss of jobs. Unions are therefore rather cautious about decisions to strike, and union leaders weigh the issues carefully before recommending such extreme action. It is a widely known fact in union circles, but not so well known elsewhere, that many official recommendations of a strike vote are turned down by the membership. It takes a very important issue to bring out the declaration of war (which is what a strike call amounts to), and all parties concerned mull it over fully before deciding to walk out.

What are the issues that unions and their members feel are worth a strike?

For a number of years the BLS has collected information on strike issues, and the statistics reflect clearly the shift of attention from one type of issue to another as union organization progressed, business conditions rose and fell, and the economic scene was successively dominated by depression, war, and postwar prosperity. From 1935 to 1941 was the great organizing period in the history of the American labor movement. In all those years, the issue of "union organization" (which means union recognition and security) produced more work stoppages than any other type of dispute with management. In 6 of the 7 years, it produced as many shutdowns as all the other issues combined. With the virtual settlement of the recognition question in 1941, disputes over union organization declined to insignificance. In terms of lost working time, the drop was even more noticeable. Work stoppages over questions of union organization and related matters produced only eight per cent of all man-days of idleness in 1964. See Table 10-2.

Table 10-2.   Major issues involved in work stoppages, 1964

Major issues	Stoppages		Workers, %	Man-days idle, %
	Number	%		
Wages, hours, and supplementary benefits (fringes)	1,700	47.2	42.9	46.8
Plant administration (discharge and discipline, work loads, local plant work rules, safety, etc.)	596	16.3	35.1	36.4
Organization and union security (recognition, union shop, etc.)	556	15.2	5.3	7.7
Interunion (jurisdiction, sympathy strikes, etc.)	454	12.4	4.0	1.3
Job security (seniority, subcontracting, and similar issues)	213	5.8	10.6	6.4
Other issues (grievances, contract duration and termination)	112	3.1	2.1	1.4
Totals	3,655	100.0	100.0	100.0

Source: *Monthly Labor Review,* June, 1965, p. 665.

Just as in the sample year, 1964, the primary strike issue over the years since the Second World War has always been the economic one of "wages, hours, and supplementary benefits (fringes)."

This is the "package" demand which may be relied upon to appear in almost any serious dispute, either as the basic request or as a support for other demands. The components of the wage and fringe package are now extremely complicated. They almost always include a change in the basic rates, either a flat increase in cents per hour or a percentage rise, and there is frequently added a provision for correcting inequities, which means either spreading the gap between individual job rates or ranges, or closing them. Then there may be an escalator clause, to provide for automatic increases or decreases in the basic rates in line with changes in the Consumer Price Index (the cost of living); and there may or may not be a request for a deferred rate increase (if the agreement is to be long-term, that is, run for more than a year) called at times a "productivity factor." Fringe demands may run to a score or more of premium, penalty, or overtime rates; time off with pay (holidays, vacation, birthdays, and sick leaves); medical, hospital, surgical, and pension benefits; and many others. It is little wonder that after settlement of the dispute and signing of the agreement, management and the union often disagree widely as to the actual cost to the company and benefits to the members, even when both are talking in terms of cents per hour.

The next three categories—plant administration, union security, and jurisdictional disputes—have about the same weight in terms of number of work stoppages, but quite different importance when columns 3 and 4 of Table 10-2 are examined. The big strikes, involving many workers and in consequence many man-days lost, grow out of issues of plant administration. A high proportion of these, in turn, are over disputes about discharge and discipline, and work loads.

Factors influencing strike policy. It is difficult to generalize about union strike policy, except to say that almost any conclusions concerning it have to be qualified so many times as to be practically useless. The use of strikes by unions ranges all the way from policies of complete self-denial (some unions of government employes) to an attitude of extreme aggressiveness, in which the slightest grievance becomes a pretext for a walkout. Some unions have carried on collective bargaining for years without a shutdown; others open every bargaining conference with an implied threat of strike, manipulate the strike weapon with imagination and abandon, and almost seem to enjoy breaking off relations with management.

However, without attempting to establish rules which will apply in all cases, it is possible to point to some of the factors which will influence the strategic use of strikes. Some of the leading ones are (1) general economic conditions, (2) union leadership and morale, (3) the personnel policies of employers, (4) statutory and legal limitations upon strike action, (5) policies and identification of local law-enforcement officials, and (6) the over-all political and social environment. It is not possible to say in advance which of the above is more and which is less important. At different times and in different situations, first one and then another may prove controlling. However, it is a fair bet that attention to these half-dozen factors will contribute to an understanding of the strike policy of a given union or group of unions.

1. *General economic conditions* are important to unions in two ways. They have a significant effect on the volume of employment available, and they influence the cost of living. Trade unionists may not call them that, but they know what "real wages" are. Few issues produce a more reliable strike temper than the sight of a paycheck standing still while prices rise. An examination of Table 10-1 will reveal that without exception the years of rising prices (1937, 1941 to 1946, and 1950 to 1952) were the years of lots of strikes. This generalization does not hold for *prosperity,* as such. The 1960s have been prosperous, but from 1960 to 1965 the price level held reasonably steady. Strikes were at a low level for the whole period, most of which was also characterized by a rising level of employment.

On the employment side, both union leaders and union members are realists. They are well aware that a walkout at a time when the employer is contemplating a reduction in force or a possible shutdown for lack of orders will carry little punch. Likewise, the possibility that striking union men will find other part-time jobs (a standard practice) is much less. And finally, in most states a striker is not eligible for unemployment insurance, whereas a man laid off by the employer is. It takes a tough issue to make a group of men jeopardize their job insurance rights at a time when a little negotiation might persuade the employer to issue layoff slips which carry compensation privileges up to 6 months in duration.

On the prosperity side of the cycle, an employer with orders, potential profits, and a high or expanding payroll is an employer in a vulnerable position for a shutdown or threat of one. He is likely to listen to reason, see his way clear to compromise, and think up concessions of his own to present to the union's strike committee. The union, in turn, is apt to be in good financial condition, with a well-filled war chest, ready to back up its demands with action. A shutdown is not inevitable, but it is easier in such circumstances for a strike to occur.

2. The *morale* of the union is as important as the morale of an army. It is primarily the union members who risk their jobs, lose their pay,[13] and man the picket line. Very few strikes are called without a vote of ratification by the members who will be affected, and many are called off when the vote cannot be rounded up, or proves indecisive. Strike morale depends in large part upon two things: the attitudes of union members toward the immediate issue and the long-run indoctrination of the union. The big issues for most trade unionists are union security; wages, hours, and conditions of work; and grievances against management. Show most union members that a real issue exists in one of these categories, and a strike vote will issue as a matter of course. It is not unusual for membership sentiment to run ahead of the official view in strike matters, and many a union officer has tried to damp down strike talk which he did not want to see snowball into a walkout.

One reason why union officials try to avoid strikes is that they distrust their members' conviction and staying power. It is one thing to get heated up over an alleged injustice, and another to dig in and stay out on strike when bills are unpaid and management is offering inducements to start a "back to work" movement. Strikes called in haste invite defection, retreat, failure, and loss of prestige for the union. Hence, labor leaders try to hold walkouts to a minimum, use them only on the most important occasions, and see to it that the treasury is in shape to stand the strain and that the members are fully aware of their responsibilities before being called on to make the sacrifice.

It would be unrealistic to deny the influence of *union leadership* in strike decisions. It is the job of a leader to make decisions, and official recommendations are always listened to with respect. Like others in posi-

---

[13] A number of unions also shut off the pay of union officials and staff during strikes, as a gesture of comradely self-sacrifice.

tions of power, the union head is also in control of key information and the channels of communication needed to put his ideas over. It is even arguable that union members rely more on their leaders than do the members of other kinds of organizations (because of ignorance of issues, strategic necessity, etc.), although this would be hotly debated by many union officers who have to stand for reelection year after year. Particularly if the leadership has been successful in a series of disputes with management, its influence may become enormous, and any opposition treated as disloyalty.

On the other hand, it is equally possible to overstress the weight of union leadership. Union leaders canvass membership sentiment and count votes as carefully as any municipal political boss, and their recommendations as often as not are tailored to their findings. The public conception of the domineering, dictatorial, decisive labor leader, in the image of John L. Lewis or Jimmy Hoffa, is only partially correct even for those men. It is strictly inaccurate for many leaders of very large and powerful unions, in which both the spirit and the letter of democratic procedure are observed with scrupulous regard for due process.

3. Strikes are called by unions, but not for fun. A strike is always a protest against something, either an existing practice or a refusal of a request (demand) which the union feels is justified. Naturally, most protests are directed at management (the exceptions are jurisdictional and general strikes), so the *personnel policies of employers* are always a factor in the strike situation. The tip-off on *what* policies to look for is found in the catalog of principal strike issues. First on the list comes any threat to the union's security, in the form of a refusal to bargain, a proposal to weaken the union-security clause in the contract, an indication of preference for another union, discharge of a union official, the use of strike-breakers (scabs), or even management criticism of the union. Any one or any combination of these is likely to bring all good union men up on the alert, ready for counteraction. What they spell is insecurity, nonacceptance of the union, the threat of withdrawal of recognition. And, if persisted in, they will probably spell strike.

There is less likelihood of a union's resorting to a strike over contract terms than over protection of its own security, and still less likelihood of a walkout over grievances. Nonetheless, both are significant sources of work stoppages, the former especially so. In each case, it may be the attitude of management, as much as the position it takes on the issues, that brings on the shutdown. An employer may be a tough negotiator and drive a hard bargain and still have the respect of the union and its members and run small risk of a strike, *provided* he demonstrates sincerity and good faith in all his dealings. An employer and his representatives may also watch the grievance procedure with an eagle eye and insist on fair treatment for the company, without any loss of union cooperation and with small risk of strike, *provided* there is no stalling, delay, buck passing, or dodging of issues. Good personnel administration starts with *attitudes* (of fairness, tolerance, cooperation) and is rounded out by *policies* (on recruitment, training, seniority, job classification and pay, and discipline). Very few firms with a reputation for good personnel administration have a long strike record.

4. There are plenty of *statutory and legal limitations* upon strikes at all levels of government, and unions are very respectful of them. When the community, through its legislatures and courts, turns thumbs down on certain kinds of work stoppages, there may be a roar of disapproval from labor leaders, but most of them observe the rule. Some kinds of strikes are prohibited: against the Federal government, over grievances on the railroads, in support of secondary boycotts and jurisdictional disputes, and the like. Others are held up for a time after the dispute is made public, by one device or another: cooling-off periods, emergency-board investigations, mediation, and offers of arbitration. Still others may be ruled in violation of contract and bring an award of damages to the employer (if there is a no-strike clause in the agreement, etc.). Every restriction is a hindrance of sorts and tends to reduce the use of strikes. That is their purpose. The volume of "red tape" has grown steadily over the years, and there is no apparent reason to expect a reversal of the trend.

5. Strike management often calls for breaches of the peace, mainly in the form of picket-line brawls. In such cases, it makes a lot of difference if the local police are with you or against you. The policing of industrial disputes is not the proudest chapter in the history of American government. It is not too much to say that the *attitudes of local law-enforcement officers* have decided the issue in a very large number of disputes. Prior to 1930, it was common practice for sheriffs and chiefs of police to deputize plant guards and strikebreakers. It was rare for a strike to be won under such circumstances, since the pickets and their supporters found themselves lined up against the law. After 1937, it was more common for police to turn their backs while strikers engaged in mass picketing, trespassing and sabotage, and threats of violence against nonstrikers. For a long time after 1937, very few strikes were lost.

Local law enforcement is not the sole, perhaps not the primary, reason for the change in fortune of trade unions, but no seasoned union organizer would put it last on the list of important factors. It must be calculated as carefully as union morale and finances in the planning of strike strategy.

6. Finally, there is the *over-all political and social environment*. This may seem distant and intangible, and some outstanding labor leaders have disregarded it to their cost and the cost of the labor movement as a whole. Nevertheless, most successful union officials keep carefully abreast of public opinion at the grass roots and in Congress. There are years when the public is almost automatically back of strikes (1937), years when it is

sick and tired of work stoppages and employer-employe recrimination (1947), and years when it is shocked by revelations of union fraud and corruption (1958–59—the McClellan committee). Only the most aggressive and recalcitrant officials try to swim against the stream, for reasons of probable immediate benefit or disregard of the effect on public policy.

Strike management. Strike management can be separated from strike policy for purposes of study, but not in actuality. They represent different stages of policy decision by the union, which are conveniently marked off by the actual walkout but which are closely tied together in performance. Some elements of strike management, for instance, may be in operation before the actual shutdown occurs. They may or may not continue to be employed throughout the duration of the dispute. These include the boycott, the presentation of demands, publicity releases and propaganda charges against employers, requests for governmental intervention, and operations designed to strengthen the morale of members. One important tactic in strike management, however, must wait until the workers have laid down their tools. It is picketing.

PICKETING

Picketing is a reflection of the union theory of the strike, the theory that the employes on strike retain their jobs and job rights during a temporary suspension of work. The function of picketing is to protect those job rights from nonstrikers and to ensure that the suspension of work is reflected in a corresponding suspension of activity by the employer. In other words, it is to make sure that the employer's place of business is shut down tight and that the production of goods and services and their delivery to customers is stopped.

Picketing used to be the key to strike success. If the picketing was effective, the odds were that a strike would be won. If the picketing was unsuccessful, it was a good bet that the strike would be lost. There always have been some unions (Locomotive Engineers, Musicians, International Longshoremen and Warehousemen) with such an inclusive membership among the qualified personnel for a given type of work that they could walk off the job with assurance that they could not be replaced.[14] In most cases, however, substitutes were available, new employes could be trained in a hurry, or the duties of nonstriking workers (especially managerial staff) could be expanded to keep up a portion of production, so that there was no complete shutdown and operations could be brought slowly back to normal. It was the purpose of picketing to prevent this and also to advertise the strike to other unionists and sympathizing customers and bystanders.

[14] Nevertheless, they used pickets too when on strike.

Nowadays picketing is less crucial. The rules of the labor-management game have become better established; "quickie" strikes are prohibited by law (Taft-Hartley Act) and no-strike clauses in agreements; the parties (employers and unions) are better acquainted with each other and relations have matured; tricks and short cuts are viewed skeptically on both sides as possibly more damaging in the long run than straightforward, businesslike dealings, even if the result must be a work stoppage and test of economic strength. In this kind of situation, picketing is more a matter of form than of resistance to strikebreaking replacements. The function of picketing is to advertise the dispute, check on the employer's observance of the shutdown, and maintain the tradition of vigilance that organized labor has found necessary to its existence.

Picketing, of course, serves purposes other than the winning of strikes. The Landrum-Griffin Act of 1959 bore down heavily on several types of picketing, distinguished by *purpose*. For example, the law made it a felony (penalties: fines up to $10,000 and imprisonment up to 20 years) for anyone to engage in "extortionate" picketing, with the object of forcing an employer to "pay off" for protection—*i.e.*, withdrawal of the pickets. The act also regulated "recognition" or "organizational" picketing, in which a union sets up a picket line around a business it is trying to organize, although it may have no representation among the employes. Recognition picketing was made an unfair labor practice for longer than 30 days in any case, unless by the end of that time an NLRB election had been petitioned for, and also (1) if the employer had already lawfully recognized another union, or (2) if an NLRB election had been held during the preceding year.

The R & D Act then reiterated the basic right to picket (for the purpose of truthfully advising the public—including consumers—that an employer does not employ members of, or have a contract with, a labor organization) but made another important exception aimed directly at the Teamsters union: "unless an effect of such picketing is to induce any individual employed by any other person in the course of his employment, not to pick up, deliver or transport any goods or not to perform any services." [15] Since "respecting a picket line" is one way of showing sympathy for another union in difficulties, the last-named exception was a major blow aimed at union solidarity. Many labor disputes have been won because union members not directly parties to the dispute—and especially the powerful and strategically located Teamsters—refused to cross a picket line "to pick up, deliver or transport goods or perform services."

The picketing issue.   The primary issue of picketing is what is peaceful and what is not. There is a wide difference of opinion on the subject. At one extreme is the view that picketing by its very nature cannot be

[15] Sec. 704, Title VII, amending the Taft-Hartley Act.

peaceful, as both the word (with its military connotation) and the practice carry an implied threat which will influence the actions of others.[16] This argument is supported by the numberless instances of actual violence known to be associated with picketing and the clear proof of intimidation by threat and otherwise in cases of mass picketing and obstruction.

The classic limitation of the right to picket was given in the case of *Vegelahn v. Guntner*,[17] in which a sidewalk patrol of two men who had been accosting employes was ruled out of bounds as intimidating. At even that early date (1896), however, there was dissent, from Justice Oliver Wendell Holmes, then a member of the supreme judicial court of Massachusetts. As in so many similar cases, Mr. Justice Holmes's position is now the law. The leading case is *Thornhill v. Alabama*,[18] in which a state law forbidding "loitering or picketing" was held unconstitutional as a violation of the constitutional protection of free speech. The Court's argument is summarized in the following passages:

In the circumstances of our times the dissemination of information concerning the facts of a labor dispute must be regarded as within that area of free discussion that is guaranteed by the Constitution. . . . The range of activities proscribed by Section 3448 [of the Alabama State Code], whether characterized as picketing or loitering or otherwise, embraces nearly every practicable, effective means whereby those interested—including the employees directly affected—may enlighten the public on the nature and causes of a labor dispute. . . . It may be that effective exercise of the means of advancing public knowledge may persuade some of those reached to refrain from entering into advantageous relations with the business establishment which is the scene of the dispute. Every expression of opinion on matters that are important has the potentiality of inducing action in the interests of one rather than another group in society. But the group in power at any moment may not impose penal sanctions on peaceful and truthful discussion of matters of public interest merely on a showing that others may thereby be persuaded to take action inconsistent with its interests.

But what of more forceful means than "peaceful and truthful discussion" of matters in dispute? In the Thornhill decision the Court expressly ruled out one kind of excess by saying: "We are not now concerned with picketing *en masse* or otherwise conducted which might occasion such imminent and aggravated danger . . . as to justify a statute narrowly drawn to cover the precise situation giving rise to the danger." The issue is still undecided; it awaits further definition and the creation of sanctions appropriate to the modern conception of the job rights and responsibilities of organized labor.

[16] H. Cooper, "The Fiction of Peaceful Picketing," *Michigan Law Review*, vol. 35 (1932), p. 73.
[17] 167 Mass. 92, 44 N.E. 1077 (1896).
[18] 310 U.S. 88 (1940).

THE BOYCOTT

Trade unionism's major weapon is the "refusal to deal," the withdrawal of contractual relations. Its principal form is the strike, which is the refusal to *sell* the services of its members; the complement of the strike is the boycott, which is the refusal to *buy* from firms or *handle* or *work on* materials of which it disapproves. Picketing is used to support both the strike and the boycott. It is the attempt to extend the union's refusal to deal to third parties, through either force or persuasion.

The ordinary boycott is customarily supported by strolling pickets, who carry "We don't patronize" signs and advertise that the place of business is "unfair" to organized labor. This tactic often seems innocuous, but it may prove so efficient as to be disastrous to the employer. An example is the situation in which the boycott is supported by sympathetic customers who take their business elsewhere or by other trade unionists, whose services are indispensable to the picketed firm. If building-trades craftsmen refuse to cross a picket line set up by a single union (as they invariably do), all work comes to a stop. Like the sympathetic strike, the refusal to cross a picket line or the refusal to patronize a struck business firm has long been a tactic common to the labor movement as a whole. Although used infrequently nowadays, the boycott can be a powerful weapon. As a result, it is carefully limited and circumscribed by law in the Taft-Hartley Act, especially the *secondary* boycott, which extends a labor dispute to those who would ordinarily be noninvolved third parties.

The boycott has a long and checkered history, and its use is not confined to organized labor. It is a standard business weapon, used to kill off competition. Professional associations rely upon it to enforce their criteria of good conduct upon administrators, colleagues, and the community. In its quarterly *Bulletin,* for instance, the American Association of University Professors regularly blacklists any college or university administration that violates its standards of academic freedom and tenure; and the American Medical Association and its related College of Physicians and Surgeons use the same device to exclude unacceptable practitioners from hospitals and other medical facilities. The trade-union boycott was countered for many years by employers through the blacklist of workmen who were active in union affairs, a practice that is now illegal under the National Labor Relations Act.

Types of boycott.   As practiced by organized labor, two stages of the boycott should be clearly distinguished: primary and secondary. The *primary boycott* is the withdrawal of patronage from the firm with which there is a labor dispute. It means that a union asks its own members and the members of other labor organizations and all friends and sympathizers to refrain from dealing with (buying from) an employer of whom it does not approve. The disapproval may stem from any kind of antiunion activities, but the issue is the same. In the union's eyes the employer is engaging in an unfair practice and should be passed over in favor of his competitors whose policies are more acceptable.

The primary boycott has seldom been held illegal; [19] on the other hand, it is often completely ineffective. This is particularly true when the employer is a manufacturer and his customers are business firms and not individuals. A trade-union boycott against the General Motors Corporation, for instance, would not reduce the company's sales by much, since it sells almost exclusively to dealers. The boycott, to be effective, would have to be applied to the latter.

However, a boycott of sales agents of General Motors products would be a *secondary boycott,* which means bringing pressure to bear against third persons, not parties to the labor dispute, to force them to discontinue dealing with the employer who is guilty of the unfair practices. A special type of secondary boycott, and one much deplored by employers, is the "hot goods" boycott. This is the refusal of union men to work on materials produced with nonunion labor. It is "secondary" in that it is directed at an employer with whom there is no dispute and constitutes an interference with his business operations which may be substantial.

The secondary boycott has always been under suspicion in this country and has frequently been held illegal. The stated grounds of the decisions have varied, but the underlying idea seems to be that it is wrong to force innocent bystanders to take sides in a dispute between an employer and his employes. The leading decision for many years was *Loewe v. Lawlor,* in which an employer was granted triple damages under the Sherman Act for loss of business resulting from a secondary boycott. This view seemed controlling until the Hutcheson decision, in 1940, finally removed union action from the jurisdiction of the Sherman Act. For a time the secondary boycott enjoyed an uneasy respectability, which came to an end with the passage of the Taft-Hartley Act, in 1947, with its powerful restrictions upon work stoppages in support of either "secondary" or "hot goods" boycotts.

The Landrum-Griffin Act of 1959 extended and tightened the Taft-Hartley restrictions on secondary boycotts and especially hot-goods boycotts. As the law now stands, it is an unfair labor practice for anyone to

[19] An exception was the decision of the United States Supreme Court in *Gompers v. Bucks Stove & Range Co.,* 221 U.S. 418 (1911), in which a blacklist of "unfair" employers, published in the AFL's journal, the *American Federationist,* was held to be an actionable conspiracy under the Sherman Act. Gompers received a suspended jail sentence, and the blacklist was immediately discontinued, never to be revived.

engage in or to get anyone else to engage in "a refusal in the course of his employment" to use, handle, or work on any materials with the idea of forcing *anyone* to cease using such materials or to cease doing business with another (nonunion) producer. It is not only an unfair labor practice, it is also "unlawful," [20] which means that anyone whose business is hurt by such a practice may sue the person or organization (union) that is responsible. The law also made "hot cargo" contracts illegal, except in the building construction and garment industries. A hot-cargo contract is an understanding between a union and an employer whereby the latter agrees to "cease or refrain from handling, using, selling, transporting or otherwise dealing in any of the products of any other employer." Such understandings are incorporated in union contracts and applied against the nonunion producers of materials or finished goods. (Exemption of building construction [limited to work done on the construction site] and the garment industry was a political maneuver to water down opposition to the Landrum-Griffin bill.) Under the L-G act, except as noted, such agreements are unenforceable and void.

The issue of the boycott.   The real issue raised by the boycott is the same as that of the sympathetic strike and the general strike, to wit, the allowable range of a labor dispute. Behind that is the deeper issue of the nature of the labor problem, whether group advantage or class struggle. The question is: Should members of trade unions, without respect to affiliation or immediate interest in disputes, be permitted to spread the area of a disagreement by striking or boycotting ("refusing to deal" with) any or all employers indiscriminately, or should they be restricted to taking punitive action only when they can demonstrate an immediate beneficial interest in the question at issue?

The answer to the question will depend upon the premises from which one starts. If the working class is seen as a single, cohesive unit, with interests which are identical and largely opposed to those of their employers, the reply will be in favor of a broad interpretation of "labor dispute," as found in the Act of 1959.

The term "labor dispute" includes any controversy concerning terms, tenure, or conditions of employment, or concerning the association or representation of persons in negotiating, fixing, maintaining, changing, or seeking to arrange terms or conditions of employment, *regardless of whether the disputants stand in the proximate relation of employer and employee.*[21]

Under this kind of interpretation, a labor dispute is not a private fight, and anybody can get in. It was well established under the Norris–La

[20] Secs. 704a and e.
[21] Sec. 3g, italics added.

Guardia Act of 1932 (which had a similarly broad definition of "labor dispute") that injunctions could not be used to stop sympathetic strikes or secondary boycotts. The Taft-Hartley Act reversed this policy with respect to the secondary boycott and reinstituted the injunction, along with cease-and-desist orders and suits for damages as control mechanisms.

Which was right?

Organized labor insists upon the right to use the secondary boycott, especially the refusal to work on nonunion goods. Employers declare that such actions are intolerable interferences with freedom to purchase in the best market and will, if permitted, result in union dictation of purchasing policies (an encroachment upon managerial prerogatives), higher costs, competitive disadvantage, and the enforcement of union membership upon employes who do not so choose of their own free will and accord. The policy of the United States in recent years with respect to *specific* regulations of strikes, picketing, and boycotts, is clearly one of limiting disputes as much as possible to the primary parties. An important question of public policy is raised, and the issue is by no means clear to all observers. The conscientious student of labor problems should familiarize himself with the premises involved and the implications of a decision either way, in order to determine what his own position is.

COMPULSORY ARBITRATION

The power tactics of labor unions are the strike, supported always by picketing and sometimes by the boycott. It should not be forgotten that the resort to economic force is always in the background. The union which neglects its "preparedness" invites the same sort of treatment as a nation that lets its military potential run low. Union-management negotiations are a species of diplomacy (labor agreements are sometimes compared with treaties between sovereign nations), and it is still unduly optimistic to assume that strength at the bargaining table is unrelated to power on the picket line. In the foreseeable future, at least, the relative grasp of strike tactics and strategy by labor and management are important elements in the industrial relations picture.

Nevertheless, during the decade of the 1960s, direct action has been used more and more sparingly, its place taken by the more peaceful and rational methods of collective bargaining: negotiation, argument, fact finding, mediation, and arbitration. In the great majority of cases nowadays, union strategy is to avoid the test of a strike—which is as it should be. Maturity in labor relations, as in most fields of conflict of interest, means the substitution of compromise, negotiation, and adjudication in place of settlements dictated by force. There are gains on two levels: resources otherwise expended in strikes and boycotts (lost wages, production, and profits) are saved; and the settlements themselves should eventually be more acceptable and reflect a more thoughtful balancing of interests than those brought about by conflict.

Alternative methods of dispute settlement.   If the parties to a labor dispute are unable to agree upon a settlement, there is only one feasible alternative to a strike and that is *arbitration.* "Arbitration" means just one thing: a final and binding settlement by an impartial (disinterested) third party. The third party may be called an arbitrator, a judge, a board, a commission, a trial examiner, or a referee, but regardless of title, he (or "it," if it is a board) does just one thing: within the area of his instructions, he hears the arguments of the parties, listens to testimony and cross-examination, analyzes the exhibits, and finally renders an *award,* which the parties are bound to accept, either by prior agreement on their part or because they are required to do so by law.

It is important to recognize that there is really no other alternative. Given the failure of the parties to come to agreement, it is either strike or arbitration. *Mediation* is no solution; it is advisory only, is presently in effect in every labor dispute of any consequence (by command of the Taft-Hartley Act and of the laws of most states), and may be disregarded entirely by either or both the union or the employer. *Conciliation* is a milder form of mediation, practiced by the parties themselves upon each other—if they are still in disagreement, it too has failed. *Seizure of the industry,* as has been done in wartime, leaves the dispute itself unresolved, and any settlement of the controversy is by government fiat and still farther from either the interests or control of the parties. *Prohibition* of strikes, as in the New York State Condon-Wadlin law and Sec. 305 of the Taft-Hartley Act, leaves labor without a weapon but provides no alternative method of settling the dispute. The parties may be helped toward a solution—by mediation, fact-finding and delay (as in the national-emergency strike procedure of the Taft-Hartley Act), Presidential intervention, and/or the appointment of special panels of experts—but if they still cannot agree, two methods remain: force (a strike) or argument (arbitration).

It follows that if, for any reason, a work stoppage is held to be so clearly against the public interest (*e.g.,* a nationwide railroad shutdown, a national trucking strike) as to rule out a settlement by force, then recourse must be had to *compulsory arbitration* of the issues. This is what happened in the railway firemen's dispute that ran from 1959 to 1963 and culminated in the Railroad Arbitration Act of the latter year.

The compulsory arbitration issue.   Compulsory arbitration is the bugaboo of both management and organized labor; both are loudly and authoritatively on record as opposed to it. Along with most labor commentators, they favor continued free collective bargaining and the private settlement of disputes through negotiation, strikes, and lockouts.[22] What this really means, of course, is that both organized labor and management groups (the National Association of Manufacturers and the Chamber of Commerce of the United States) deny the proposition that *any* peacetime work stoppage is sufficiently damaging to the public interest to justify insistence upon continued service or production. Neither has offered any alternative solution other than direct action. This is the more surprising since both unions and employers are well aware of the advantages of arbitration and have long since adopted it as *compulsory* in the settlement of grievances arising under labor-management agreements. Strikes over deadlocked grievance procedures are now almost unheard of; the disputes go automatically to arbitrators who hear and decide the issues.

Grievances are not the only kind of labor dispute subject to compulsory arbitration.[23] For 30 years now, disputes over organization (to enforce recognition of the union), along with claims of unfair labor practices, have gone to the National Labor Relations Board instead of being settled by strike and lockout.[24] The National Labor Relations Act (now "Title I" of the Taft-Hartley Act) is a classic example of compulsory arbitration. The decisions and awards of the NLRB are authoritatively binding third-party decisions over issues which may be brought to the tribunal at the option of either party, but from which the responding party may not abstain or abstains at his peril. The NLRB is a labor court of limited jurisdiction, handling the kinds of disputes mentioned above. It does not have absolute jurisdiction over even those. Instead, the parties may settle their disputes over recognition themselves, if they wish to and are able to do so.

Some of the major objections to compulsory arbitration arise from two mistaken beliefs: (1) that it is the same everywhere and (2) that it would have to be (or would be) applied immediately on a broad scale to industry generally. Neither view is correct. Arbitration can be compulsory in every case, as was true of wage settlements under the Wage Stabilization Board during the Korean conflict, but it does not have to be so. It may also be at the option of either party (as in cases coming before the NLRB), or of a public authority (the President, a governor, an administrator). It may be restricted to certain industries (utilities, transportation systems, public employes) or to certain types of disputes, as in the case of

---

[22] See, *e.g.*, Harry Bernstein (labor editor of the *Los Angeles Times*), "Ban on Strikes Going Too Far," in the *Times* of February 13, 1966, Section G, p. 1, for the standard presentation of this viewpoint.

[23] See O. W. Phelps, "Compulsory Arbitration: Some Perspectives," *Industrial and Labor Relations Review,* October, 1964, pp. 81–91.

[24] For the past 20 years—since passage of the Taft-Hartley Act—the Board has also had the responsibility for settling jurisdictional disputes, along with controversies over certain types of work assignments, secondary boycotts, featherbedding, and other prohibited grounds for work stoppage.

grievances. The compulsion may be absolute or partial—that is, recommendatory, as in the case of a fact-finding board's proposals. The arbitrators themselves may be *ad hoc* (selected individually for each case that arises) or permanent (as in the umpire systems at General Motors and North American Aviation, Inc.), the board may be tripartite (with labor, management, and the public represented, as in the National War Labor Board of the Second World War) or public member only—for example, the National Mediation Board of the Railway Labor Act. The arbitrators may be selected by the parties themselves from a panel, either through agreement or by a strike-out method,[25] or they may be appointed by a governmental authority (President, governor, a judge, the Federal Mediation and Conciliation Service) or a private agency—*e.g.,* the American Arbitration Association. The arbitration may be conducted under strict statutory (legal) guidelines, as are found in the National Labor Relations Act, as amended, and the issues put to the tribunal may be either inclusive or selective. Various kinds of review and appeal procedures may be made available.

The key objection to compulsory arbitration of contract disputes is that here the parties' interests are at stake, and the arbitrators would be in effect telling management and labor how the former would run their business and the latter under what conditions they were going to work. To use a governmental analogy, a decision on contract terms is a "legislative" act, whereas arbitration is fundamentally a "judicial" process. What would the arbitrator use to guide him, comparable to the terms of the existing contract in grievance arbitration or the terms of the National Labor Relations Act in disputes coming before the NLRB? As a matter of fact, there are several such guidelines. First, and most important of all, there are *the terms of submission,* which may and often do set very precise limits to both the issues to be ruled on and the range of the arbitrators' decision.[26]

A second safeguard would be the *composition of the tribunal,* which would normally be tripartite in a contract dispute, with members representing both the union and the employer in addition to the public commissioners. The labor and management representatives would know the issues well and would keep the board from making errors due to ignorance. Third, there is *the existing agreement* (practically all contract negotiations are now *re*negotiations), with transcripts of past negotiations, review of contract development through the years, and the test of con-

[25] After flipping a coin to see who goes first, the parties (representatives of the union and the management) in turn strike names off a list until only one is left. The remaining "least undesirable" choice is the arbitrator.

[26] The Railroad Arbitration Act of 1963 put before the board just two issues: the elimination of unneeded firemen, and the "crew consist" dispute. The remaining issues were remanded to the parties for further bargaining and were promptly settled.

formity to related agreements in the same or other industries. For any experienced arbitrator these would set practical limits to the range of his decision. Fourth, would be *the proposals of the parties,* with their arguments and exhibits; and fifth, the *standard criteria used in bargaining sessions,* over the years—interfirm and interindustry comparisons, cost of living, conditions of the industry, national wage guidelines, etc.[27] Finally, there are literally scores of highly experienced arbitrators in all sections of the country, with extensive backgrounds in labor relations in every type of industry.[28] A five-man board, with three public members drawn from this group, plus a representative each from the employer and union involved, might not produce a fully satisfactory substitute for a bargained decision, but it would be unlikely to make any serious errors.

It is always to be preferred if the parties to a labor dispute can work out a settlement between themselves. If arbitration is optional—which it can be and still be compulsory [29]—this course is still open to the disputants.[30] The main arguments for a bargained settlement are (1) the desirability of reserving the largest possible area to private decision-making, and (2) acceptability, which is almost always enhanced if the decision is arrived at by the parties themselves.[31] On the other hand, it is usually overlooked that there may be some inherent advantages to be derived from arbitration, other than just continuous production and employment. One is the greater likelihood of equity—meaning, a fair settlement. There is no reason to assume that a decision based on economic power is necessarily fairer than one based on argument, rather the contrary. Certainly the issues will be more sharply defined in a controlled adversary process, with its orderly presentation of positions, rebuttal, and cross-examination, and without the bluffs, threats, misstatements of fact, and interplay of personalities frequently observed in bargaining.

In the final analysis, however, the question of dispute settlement will turn on the public interest. If there is *never* a case where the public benefit from labor peace outweighs the benefits to the parties accruing from resort to a work stoppage, then strikes, lockouts, picketing, and boycotts are the logical means of deciding issues. If, however, there is such a

[27] These criteria and their use in the limited arbitration of new contracts up to 1953 are fully set forth in Irving Bernstein, *The Arbitration of Wages* (Berkeley, Calif.: University of California Press, 1954).

[28] See, for example, *National Academy of Arbitrators, Membership Directory 1965–66* (Detroit, Michigan—1130 First National Building).

[29] That is, as an alternative to a strike.

[30] See Carl M. Stevens, "Is Compulsory Arbitration Compatible with Bargaining?" *Industrial Relations,* February, 1966, p. 38, for a discussion of the effects of the *availability* of arbitration to the parties on their bargaining posture.

[31] Neither of these, of course, is absolute. It is perfectly possible for a union and employer to conspire to the disadvantage of the public, and in some cases (face-saving, for example) a third-party settlement of a dispute will enhance acceptability.

thing as a national (or even local or regional) emergency which will result from a walkout, then alternative methods of dispute settlement should be considered.

This country already has fact-finding and delay procedures incorporated in both the Railway Labor Act and the Taft-Hartley Act. However, in these laws, once the statutory delays are past, a strike is again legal, and has occurred in a few cases. It would seem to be only a wise precaution to add to the President's authority in each case the option of calling for arbitration at the end of the delay period if, in his opinion, a renewal of the work stoppage would damage the national (local, regional) health or safety. This would be a minimal addition to the President's powers, with the optional feature allowing for administrative flexibility and judgment. At the same time, it would permit conclusive action without the necessity of referring the matter to Congress as at present.[32]

READINGS

A wide range of contributors on these subjects may be found in Arthur Kornhauser, Robert Dubin, and Arthur M. Ross (eds.), *Industrial Conflict* (New York: McGraw-Hill Book Company, 1954). A recent definitive study of the strike as a tactical weapon of unionism is Arthur M. Ross and Paul Hartman, *Changing Patterns of Industrial Conflict* (Berkeley, Calif.: Institute of Industrial Relations, University of California, 1960). For elaboration of some of the points made in this chapter, see O. W. Phelps, "Compulsory Arbitration: Some Perspectives," *Industrial and Labor Relations Review*, October, 1964, pp. 81–91. For a sociologist's analysis of the strike, see Robert Dubin, *Working Union-Management Relations: The Sociology of Industrial Relations* (Englewood Cliffs, N.J.: Prentice-Hall, Inc., 1961), Chaps. 8 and 9.

[32] This feature would have saved years of time and a huge expenditure of both money and official attention in the railway dispute ending with arbitration in 1963, and would have arrived at precisely the same decision.

ELEVEN

UNION MANAGEMENT AND THE LANDRUM-GRIFFIN ACT [1]

The job of managing a union is somewhat like that of running a political party. Unions are nonprofit organizations like political parties, and their officers get and hold their jobs by election, in which each union member has one vote, no more, no less.[2] At the same time, unions are permanent associations with regular sources of income and a managerial structure set up to perform definite functions. In this respect they resemble legal firms or corporations more than political parties, and the resemblance becomes more definite when they bargain, negotiate, make contracts, and handle grievances with employers. They have all the problems of finance, personnel, policy, and operations commonly associated with any nonprofit institution—government agency, church, or community relief organization. In addition, unions conduct periodic elections in which the contest may be as bitterly fought as the struggle for municipal control in Chicago or New Orleans. The labor leader has two imperatives for survival: he must hold his job (that is, keep on being elected) and he must have an organization to represent, which means hang on to his membership. It is the latter imperative which makes "union security"—the closed shop, the union shop, the checkoff, etc.—such a high-priority item in collective bargaining.

Since September, 1959, when the Landrum-Griffin Act was passed and approved, many union officers feel that their job, which they considered tough enough already, has been mined and boobytrapped to an un-

---

[1] The full text of Titles I to VI of the Landrum-Griffin Act, with commentary, is in the Appendix to this chapter.

[2] A union is fundamentally a political organization, not an economic one. The primary distinction, aside from purpose (nonprofit versus profit-making), between a "political" and an "economic" organization is the basis of control. If voting control is based on the membership at one vote apiece, the organization is political in character; if votes are based on the amount of investment or property holdings—number of shares of stock, capital supplied, partnership agreement—that is, if control may be *legally* monopolized by one or a few members, the organization is essentially economic.

338

conscionable degree and that they themselves are subject to ambush at any time. For instance, the L-G act imposes 12 specific criminal penalties of fine and imprisonment (ranging up to $10,000 fine and 20 years in jail), plus half a dozen or so authorizations of "civil actions" (suits for damages, pleas for injunctions, etc.) and official investigations for violation of its myriad regulations. It requires *all* union officials (and employes too, other than clerical, if they handle funds or property), clear down to the steward in the shop, to assume *fiduciary* responsibility for union funds,[3] to be bonded, and to be subject to suit by members for allegedly falling short.

And the concluding Title VI contains the following invitation:

Sec. 601. (*a*) The Secretary [of Labor] shall have power when he believes it necessary in order to determine whether any person has violated *or is about to violate* any provision of this Act (except title I . . .) to make an investigation and in connection therewith he may enter such places and inspect such records and accounts and question such persons as he may deem necessary . . . [with the right to subpoena witnesses and documents specifically added].

The above is a considerable grant of discretionary power and there is no certainty that it will not be abused. Union management can no longer be considered apart from the web of Federal rules now spun about the simplest details of operation (*e.g.*, holding vouchers, worksheets, and receipts for 5 years after their use in the required reports).

Variable union structure.   Labor unions are "adaptive" organizations. This means that they fit their form of organization to their needs. The different types of union structure are bewilderingly complicated. They include local unions ranging in size from 20 or 30 members or less to the huge Ford Motor Company Rouge plant local of the United Auto Workers, with its 30 to 40,000 members; there are national or international unions with a size range from several hundred to more than a million members; national and international federations, state federations, city federations; district organizations headed by "district representatives"; city central bodies composed of representatives of all or most unions in the locality; specialized local committees (of the building trades, for example, or one union such as the Building Service Employees' International Union); joint negotiating committees (the railway brotherhoods, the UAW and the Machinists, etc.); and many others.

A local of the National Federation of Post Office Clerks, for example, bears little resemblance to a local of the UAW, and neither of them has

---

[3] For the meaning of "fiduciary" see the careful and explicit wording of Sec. 501 of the act in the Appendix which follows. In business, fiduciary responsibility is customarily held to apply only to strictly financial officers: treasurers, comptrollers, etc., or to financial firms: banks, building and loan associations, brokerage houses, and the like.

much similarity in numbers, organization, or operating procedure to a local of the Brotherhood of Painters, Decorators and Paperhangers of America. The first is a local of government employes, with no right to strike and no binding contract with its employer; its activities and those of the national of which it is a part are mainly lobbying and grievance handling. An Auto Workers local, on the other hand, is an industrial unit, with an average membership of 1,000 skilled, semiskilled, and unskilled plant workers. The members are probably concentrated in a single industrial establishment and covered by a detailed agreement with the employer, which is policed by a complicated hierarchy of union plant officials supervised by a nearby district representative of the international union. The Painters local is typically a much smaller group (average membership around 150) than that of the UAW, composed of skilled craftsmen only, who work in a local labor market, but few of whom work for the same employer or work for any employer for a long time, whose agreement is a much briefer affair detailing principally rates of pay and work rules, and whose membership is stable and closely controlled under a closed shop and tight admission regulations. None of the above three would admit any relationship to the many locals of "company" unions around the country, which are associations of employes of a single employer, unaffiliated with any national or international union or the AFL–CIO. Although perfectly legal, if organized and administered by the employes without assistance or interference by the employer, these are not bona fide unions in the eyes of a Carpenter, a Teamster, or a Steelworker.

The same or even greater variations in structure are found in national or international unions (for example, contrast the International Union of Journeymen Horseshoers of the United States and Canada, with 20 locals and a membership of 285, with the complex organization of the International Association of Machinists and Aerospace Workers—membership about 800,000; a skyscraper headquarters at 1300 Connecticut Avenue, N.W., in Washington, D.C.; around 2,000 locals spread from Miami to Seattle and from San Diego to Portland, Maine—some of them craft, some industrial, and some a combination of the two; a highly structured district organization, etc.). Extremely varied and complicated organization patterns are also to be found within some of the larger units, such as the AFL–CIO, and in many of the joint committees of the larger cities: New York, San Francisco, St. Louis, etc.

It is wise to keep in mind the extreme complexity of the world of trade unionism. Nevertheless, there is a distinct pattern to union organization, and many of the contrasts are variations on a basic theme. The primary elements of organization for most of the labor movement in this country are three: the local, the national (or international), and the federation. These are the fundamentals; if they are understood thoroughly, the remainder of the picture can be filled in without much trouble.

THE LOCAL UNION: RIGHTS OF MEMBERS

The local is the basic unit of trade unionism. It is where the union member has his membership, attends meetings, pays his dues, votes for officers or representatives who go to the district or national conventions, and expects attention to be paid to his grievances against his employer or other workers. The local is ordinarily the unit that has the contract with the employer. It is, in short, the unionist's home. He may identify himself by the national label—as a Machinist, a Bricklayer, or a Teamster; his contract may be negotiated by a representative of the national union; and some of his more important benefits (strike funds, supplemental unemployment payments, pensions, etc.) may be administered by the national. Nevertheless, his citizenship in the union and his standing with fellow members are functions of local decision. If he is to move up in the union, the action is initiated at the local level. If he is to be disciplined for violation of rules, it is by the local. And if there should be any mishandling or violation of his rights as a member, the manipulation will be conducted at the local level, either by local officials or by the device of trusteeship, in which the national supersedes the authority of the local officers and either suspends or discharges them.

Local unions are organized in various ways, depending on the distribution of the membership geographically and on the method prescribed in the constitution of the national organization. However, it is practically universal for the officers—a president, secretary-treasurer, and sometimes additional functionaries such as vice-presidents—to be elected by majority vote of the membership at meetings announced for that purpose. In the past, such meetings were often conducted with little formality and perhaps with little opportunity for anyone who disagreed with the incumbent officers to express an opinion, nominate an opposition candidate, or even to vote freely. The national or local union with a full-fledged opposition party was an extreme rarity, the International Typographers Union being the most widely publicized example in this country. Elections were held at irregular intervals and in some cases so infrequently as to make the tenure of officeholders practically permanent.

Elections.   The Labor-Management Reporting and Disclosure Act of 1959 (hereafter referred to as either the Landrum-Griffin [L-G] or the R & D Act) changed things. In the "Bill of Rights," Title I of the law, every union member is assured of equal rights with other members in nominating candidates, voting in elections, and attending and participating in membership meetings, subject only to "reasonable" rules, which must be in the constitution and bylaws of the union. Full freedom of speech and assembly in union meetings is guaranteed, along with the right to "express . . . views upon candidates in an election. . . ." Any interference with these or any other rights found in the law, by means of violence or the threat of such, to restrain or intimidate a union member makes the violator subject to fines up to $1,000 or imprisonment for up to 1 year, or both.

The foregoing are merely the general rules. In Title IV of the act, elections are dealt with in detail. For local unions, they must be held at least once every 3 years. (The maximum period is 4 years for "intermediate bodies"—general committees, system boards, etc.—and 5 years for national or international unions.) Election must be by secret ballot for both officers and delegates to conventions. Opportunity must be given for the nomination of candidates, and every member in good standing is eligible to be a candidate and to hold office.

"Good standing," however, has certain limitations. In the contest for union office, convicted criminals are ruled out of bounds.[4] They may not serve as "officer, director, trustee, member of any executive board or similar governing body, business agent, manager, organizer, or other employee (other than . . . clerical or custodial)" of any union unless a 5-year period has elapsed since the date of conviction or the end of imprisonment for crime. The felonies which are a bar to union office include robbery, bribery, extortion, embezzlement, grand larceny, burglary, arson, murder, rape, assault with intent to kill or injure, narcotics violations, etc.[5]

Extensive safeguards are prescribed to ensure fair elections. For example, every union man has the right to vote for and support the candidate of his choice "without being subject to penalty, discipline, or . . . reprisal of any kind by such organization or any member thereof." Election notices must be mailed individually to each union member at his home address not less than 15 days prior to the meeting. The votes must be counted and the results published separately for each local union (in national or district elections), and the ballots and records must be saved for at least 1 year. The election must be conducted in accordance with the constitution and bylaws of the union, and if the latter are inconsistent with the law, they must be changed to conform.

Nor is this all. No dues money or employer contributions may be

---

[4] The exclusion originally included Communists, but the United States Supreme Court ruled in June, 1965, that Sec. 504 of the act making it a crime for a Communist to hold union office was unconstitutional, on grounds that the provision failed to specify rules of general applicability and was thus a bill of attainder. See *U.S. v. Brown,* 381 U.S. 437.

[5] The legislative technique of *listing* the proscribed criminal actions instead of using a generally inclusive term such as "any felony" raises an interesting question. Hoffa was convicted of jury tampering, a crime not included in the list. Could he then legally continue as president of the Teamster's union while serving his sentence in the penitentiary?

spent to promote the candidacy of anyone (presumably the incumbents) for union office, and the union must "comply with all reasonable requests of any candidate to distribute by mail or otherwise at the candidate's expense" any campaign literature and must refrain from discrimination in favor of one candidate over another. If campaign advertising is sent out by the union in favor of one person, "similar distribution at the request of any other bona fide candidate shall be made," with equal treatment in the matter of expense. Every candidate has the right to inspect membership lists and to have observers at the polls and at the counting of the ballots. If a union member believes that some of the above rules have been violated, he may notify the Secretary of Labor, who will investigate, and if the complaint is a valid one, the Secretary will bring suit to have the election set aside and another held.

This is quite a change from the old happy, catch-as-catch-can days of running unions as though they were private clubs. The idea is to make unions democratic, responsible, and representative of the will of the members, to ensure the citizenship rights of minorities, and to permit protests to arise within the organization as a normal process. Too often in the past, the law implies, protests by members were treated as antiunion disloyalty and were smothered either by threats and intimidation or by election manipulation.

The right to sue and to testify. Union members are guaranteed the right to sue their union or any of its officers or to bring charges against the union before an administrative agency (the NLRB, for example). They may also "appear as a witness in any judicial, administrative, or legislative proceeding, or . . . petition any legislature or legislator." The only limitation upon any of these rights is that the member must exhaust reasonable hearing procedures within the union (if they do not exceed a 4-month period) before taking action against it or its officers. No interested employer or employer association may finance or encourage the union member's action, unless it is a formal party to the proceedings.

The member's right to sue the union takes on more significance when coupled with the following guarantees, found in the law:
1. The right to receive and examine a copy of any collective bargaining agreement affecting the member
2. The right to be informed by the union of the provisions of the act
3. Full access to the detailed procedural and financial information which the union must report to the Secretary of Labor annually
4. The right to sue in a Federal court to recover misappropriated union funds or property
5. The right to sue for violation of the trusteeship provisions of the act
6. The right to be protected against disciplinary action brought by the union, its officers, or its employes, for exercising his membership privileges

Unions have as many disaffected members as any other type of organization. It would be naïve to think that some of them will not take advantage of the act's invitation to correct what they consider bad management, disregard of their personal rights or privileges, or undue attempts to persuade them to conform to union policy. There is no question but that the long history of unionism contains many cases of clear violation of members' rights through trickery, violence, or the threat of violence. There is also no question but that the long history of unionism in this country contains many instances of company spies, stool pigeons, treachery, disloyalty, "boring from within," and just plain disagreement over fundamentals of strategy and tactics. The issue raised by these provisions of the act is whether the means provided for protection of the bona fide complainant may not offer as much opportunity for harassment by malcontents as for placing hobbles on the limited number of unprincipled union officials who will always be with us. Time alone will tell. Meanwhile, a considerable proportion of the time of bona fide, hardworking union officers will be applied to giving strict attention to the new rules in order to avoid being cited or sued for violation of the law.

LOCAL GOVERNMENT AND ADMINISTRATION

Three essentials of the democratic process are as consistently relied on in union government as anywhere else in American political or economic life: (1) election of leaders, (2) the referendum, and (3) committee organization. The Landrum-Griffin Act requires local elections at least once every 3 years. Actually, most locals elect every year. The union official can never afford to forget his constituency because he is certain to have to go before the members shortly to justify his performance. This has both good and bad effects. The period is rather short for some kinds of policy decisions, and it may be that the necessity of standing for reelection will force the adoption of policies that are immediately popular but seem unwise over the longer run. Just as in municipal politics, more of the official's time may be given to electioneering than to doing his job.

On the other side of the picture, frequent submission to the electorate *is* democratic. Criticism of it implies criticism of democracy as a mode of operation. To many workers, trade unionism means industrial democracy, and democracy means participation in the affairs in which they are materially interested. An official who has to stand for reelection once a year is, in their eyes, an official who must consider their opinions and defer to them if they are in the majority. The union is then run by the membership, not by a managerial group insulated from rank-and-file opinion, which is the very thing the union was organized to change.

The same criticism and defense are applied to the process of referendum. Few organizations of any kind submit as many policy decisions to the membership for ratification as trade unions. It is standard practice to require a majority vote of ratification before any contract is signed with an employer, and there are plenty of instances on record where the membership has sent its officials back to demand specific changes, after first rejecting the recommendations of its representatives that the proposals be accepted. Nor are trade agreements the only subjects for review. Membership policies, dues changes, assessments, grievance decisions, and many other choices are regularly put before local meetings for a majority vote before adoption. Some of them must be. The R & D Act says that any change in the rate of local dues or initiation fees, or any general or special assessment, has to be voted into effect either "by majority vote by secret ballot of the members in good standing . . . or . . . by majority vote of the members . . . voting in a membership referendum conducted by secret ballot."

The resolution of issues is frequently simplified by referral to committees. The committee form of organization, with a variety of viewpoints represented, is a standard method of reducing controversies to manageable form or presenting partly digested proposals for approval, amendment, or rejection. It is used regularly at the local level, but particularly in district, regional, and national conventions.

Administration.   The government of a union is one thing, administration of its affairs another. Government is the province of the membership: their constitutional rights of selection of leaders, choice of basic policies, etc. It is the main concern of the Labor Reform Act. Administration, on the other hand, is the responsibility of the elected union officers. It is bargaining, negotiations, organization, paying bills, and day-to-day adjustment and interpretation of a complicated contract or an equally complicated set of work rules, which must be made to relate to a constantly changing operating situation. The purpose of administration of a labor agreement is the meeting of minds and uninterrupted operation. In spite of some impressions to the contrary, neither unions nor their members like to lose time through argument, strikes, or lockouts. The essence of administration is compromise and cooperation; its essential qualifications are tact, responsibility, and a reputation for accuracy and fairness. The shop steward or business agent of a local who is constantly in hot water with the employers the union has agreements with is just as much of a problem to the union as he is to the plant officials. On numerous occasions this type of local officer has been persuaded to relinquish his job in favor of someone who can get along with management.[6]

The actual job of the local administrator (whether steward, presi-

[6] See Clinton S. Golden and Harold J. Ruttenberg, *The Dynamics of Industrial Democracy,* Chap. III, "Development of Leadership" (New York: Harper & Row, Publishers, Incorporated, 1942), for comments on this problem.

dent, or business representative) is often worthy of a good salary. It is he
who must turn a complicated, formal agreement into a mutually satisfactory working relationship between his own membership and a managerial staff of foremen, superintendents, and legal experts, some of whom
may be thoroughly hostile to the idea of submitting to outside dictation in
running the affairs of the company. The bargaining experts from national
headquarters, if there were any, are long since gone. The agreed statement of principles which they left behind looks fine on paper. But what
does it mean, when applied to the constantly changing panorama of production operations? Here, in contract interpretation, is where the test of
collective bargaining takes place. And that test calls for conference after
conference, explanation after explanation, and hours of plain hard study.

To begin with, the local officers must be thoroughly familiar with the
agreement itself, which may be anything from a one-page declaration of
principles to a complete covenant of more than a hundred pages of fine
print. Local leaders inevitably become experts in "industrial jurisprudence," [7] or the application of principles to cases to produce workable
decisions. But no one becomes even competent at such a job without long
hours of careful concentration and a familiarity with existing precedents.
Then, both as a supplement to the handling of grievances and for the conduct of union meetings, the local officials must also know the constitution
and bylaws of the national union, especially the sections which bear on
the rights, privileges, and responsibilities of the local chapters. This is no
small chore in itself. For example, the *Constitution of the Grand Lodge,
District and Local Lodges of the International Association of Machinists*
consists of 117 pages of small print in a pocket-sized pamphlet, and 11
articles and 36 pages in the section on local lodges alone.

The above is just the homework. Knowing the contract provisions is
one thing, applying them quite a different matter. What happens when a
union member is disciplined for smoking in the washroom or reporting
late for work and protests to his steward? How will a man's seniority be
affected by his transfer from one department to another? What is the
proper way of figuring overtime through the lunch hour? What does
"insubordination," a standard ground for discharge, consist of? What is
an "apprentice," a "part-time employe," or an "experienced employe," and
how do the stated provisions apply to them? What evidence is required
to prove that an employe is "called out" and therefore eligible for reporting pay? How does the discontinuance of a department or a job affect
the rights of the employe or employes?

There is plenty of work for the grievance committee, no matter how
explicit the agreement is on every possible contingency. The shop steward
(at the foreman's level) and the committeeman (at the next level above

[7] A term used by Sumner H. Slichter, in his *Union Policies and Industrial Management,* Chap. I (Washington, D.C.: The Brookings Institution, 1941).

in the grievance procedure) must not only know the working rules (union terminology for the "agreement"), but must also know the exigencies of plant operation and the individual peculiarities of their members and the managerial staff. All will enter into the decisions they make. In view of the multiplicity of problems and the formality of the agreements, disputes are not surprising. The surprising thing is that so many agreements work so well, with so little actual hindrance to the output of goods and services.

In all this work the local official is the advocate of the union member, but he cannot afford to be an unreasoning defender of all causes brought to him. Much of his time will be spent in explaining why he must reject complaints as unjustified, and in outlining the meaning of the contract terms to employes who are unable or who have not troubled to learn the provisions of the compact. If he goes too far in this, he will lose the respect and support of his associates. If he swings too much the other way, management will distrust his judgment and a heavy load of grievances will be carried beyond him to the higher officials and arbitration. It is harassing, time-consuming, exacting work, and he does much of it for nothing or for very little, other than as a contribution to his union.

In addition to their regular dealings with management, local union officials must also keep in mind recruitment, the handling of finances, the conduct of meetings, cooperation with other locals in matters of common concern, district and national conventions with their accompanying election of officers and ratification of policy proposals, and, nowadays, a regular program of political action. It is no job for the unconvinced, the short of wind, or the slow of mind or action. Throughout the country there are thousands of persons maintaining, on a consistent schedule, a program of activities like that described above, often in addition to a regular job at the bench or on the assembly line.

THE PATTERN OF UNION ORGANIZATION

Most local unions are fully integrated administrative units of national or international unions. The relationship is often indicated by the local's title, e.g., "Local Union 1501, International Union of Electrical, Radio & Machine Workers—AFL–CIO." This may be because the local was organized in the first place by the national, or if not, the members elected to affiliate with it.

National affiliation means prestige, services (literature, speakers, funds, strike assistance, advice, etc.), career openings, and the subtle but powerful stimulation of identification with important and far-reaching causes. National affiliation usually means affiliation with the AFL–CIO too, which also has state and local services, and still more prestige. The typical union organization in this country is the local, affiliated with a national or international union, which in turn is affiliated with the big federation, the American Federation of Labor and Congress of Industrial Organizations. This typical form of organization may be pictured as a three-level affair (as shown in Fig. 11-1). About 85 per cent (15 million) of all union members in the United States are so organized. Most of the

Fig. 11-1.   *Typical trade-union organ-ization in the United States*

remainder are in locals affiliated with national unions which are inde-pendent of any federation, like the United Mine Workers of America or the Teamsters. This two-level form of organization is shown in Fig. 11-2a. Something over 15 per cent (2.5 million) trade unionists are so organized. A third type of organization is the local union affiliated directly with the AFL–CIO without intervening membership in any national or interna-

Fig. 11-2.

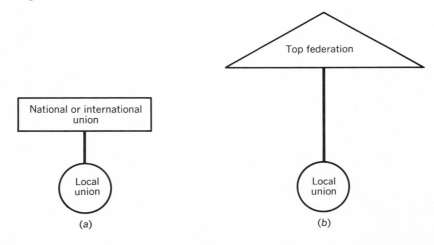

tional union, as illustrated in Fig. 11-2*b*. This is a transitional form of organization and its total membership varies, depending on the current level and success of AFL–CIO organizing activity. In 1965, there were about 50,000 members in 255 directly affiliated locals of the AFL–CIO.[8] Finally, there are the single-level, independent, "company" unions at the local stage of organization; they are illustrated in Fig. 11-3. There are probably more than 500 such single-firm independent unions in the country, with a total membership of around 500,000.

This does not by any means exhaust all the possibilities of "affiliation," an overworked word in labor matters. If the local is a member of a big national union, there may be a joint council of all the locals in that union in a particular city for purposes of common action and support. Then there will be "regional" and "district" councils, organized for the same

Fig. 11-3.   Independent local company union

reason. There will also be local "trades" or "industrial" councils, "city" and "county" councils, composed of locals from different unions in the same industry, such as building construction, the metal trades, or maritime affairs. They have the same purpose, to present a unified front to employers and to support each other in common undertakings.

THE NATIONAL (INTERNATIONAL) UNION

A "national" union is not necessarily national in its scope and coverage, any more than an "international" is necessarily a world-wide organization. A union customarily becomes a national when it consists of more than one local; the term "national" is a convention denoting a secondary stage in organization involving the delegating of authority beyond the limits of the local officials. When a union calls itself a national or international, it is in effect laying claim to all the employes in the country or the world who come within the jurisdiction it has laid out for itself. This claim is often disputed. Many nationals are actually district or regional organizations, like the National Maritime Union, which controls the Gulf and East Coasts and the Great Lakes, but has practically no members on the Pacific Coast, where the Seafarers' International Union of North America and its principal subsidiary, the Sailors' Union of the Pacific, represent most sailors.

Unions tend to add "international" to their names when they establish

[8] The comparable figures for 1963 were 52,000 and 299; for 1961, 71,000 and 360; for 1959, 108,000 and 507. Another clue to the direction of the trend in organizing activity by the AFL–CIO. See above, Chap. 6.

a branch or branches in Canada. No American internationals have branches outside North America and few of them anywhere else but across the northern border.

Notwithstanding the limitations mentioned above, many national unions are truly nationwide in scope, with locals and members in all or most states, or at least in those states where there are industries employing workmen who come within the union's jurisdiction. The United Mine Workers of America blankets the coal mining areas in the United States from Alabama to Colorado to Pennsylvania and West Virginia. The railway operating brotherhoods go anywhere the railroads go. The big building-trades unions (the Carpenters, the Plumbers, the Bricklayers, the Plasterers) have local lodges from the Atlantic to the Pacific and from the Mexican to the Canadian borders and on north. The Teamsters will be found anywhere nonrail land transportation is used. The term "national" may be, and often is, a convention denoting hardly more than two levels of organization, but the genuinely *national* union, with a perspective and organization and membership of equivalent scope, is an established fact in American economic life. Economically and politically, the national union is the dominant unit in the labor movement today.[9]

Relations between the local and the national (international) union. If the local union is a member of a national, what is the relationship between the two? Is it a sovereign unit, federated with other locals to form a larger body, but ready to secede at any time that it disagrees with the policies of the headquarters group? Or is it just a branch outpost of the international, acting mainly as income collector and local contract representative with the employer or employers?

There may be some difference if the local was organized entirely through the efforts of local employes or if the work of recruitment and the like was done by an outside organizer sent in by an interested national union or the AFL–CIO. However, no matter what the assistance from the outside, local union affairs are largely left in the hands of local personnel. What matters are decided at the local level, and which ones are decided upstairs?

There is no hard and fast rule regarding this relationship which will hold in all cases. In general, relations between locals and their "parent" national or international bodies are very close. Trade unionists tend to think of themselves as members of the national (as a Carpenter, or Teamster, or Steelworker), although their legal membership is in a numbered local chapter rather than in the bigger organization, and it is not uncommon for one local to refuse to accept new members transferring from another local because of a change of residence. In regard to policies set by

[9] See Lloyd Ulman, *The Rise of the National Union* (Cambridge, Mass.: Harvard University Press, 1956), for an illuminating analysis of this trend.

the international union, however, there is considerable variation in the degree of autonomy exercised by local lodges.

The main factor is the character of the market for the goods or services the union members produce. If the market for the product is local, the local union will have considerable autonomy. An example is the building trades, where the local "building trades council" is the genuine repository of decisions of policy, rather than the national headquarters of the various craft unions. If the market is national in scope, as in the case of automobiles, the local union's area of decision is much more limited, and the national union makes the important policy decisions, which the local has little choice but to follow.

The reasons are fairly obvious. A local of the United Steelworkers can do little to influence the supply of steel as a whole, or to its own market area, no matter how powerful it may be with the employer or employers in that area. If it shuts down the output of the local branch manufacturer, steel is shipped in from the outside. On the other hand, a local or group of locals of bricklayers (or carpenters or plasterers) may completely control the supply of such services in a single area and can (and often do) shut off the production of new buildings in that locality until their demands are met or they decide to compromise. No substitute supply of buildings is available from the outside, as in the case of steel or automobiles. Hence, a local union in the building trades may carry on a very efficient strike without outside assistance, whereas the same action on the part of a local of automobile workers or rubber workers or steel workers would be unrealistic in the extreme. It would probably catch only branch plants of large employers and not seriously interfere with the operations of the major corporations in the industry.

The nature of industrial organization reinforces the point. Unions bargain with employers. The employers in the steel, rubber, and automobile industries are corporations with nationwide (in fact, international) production and distribution patterns. The key bargaining must be with the top corporate officers in charge of industrial relations. Building contractors, even the biggest ones, are generally local or regional firms—much smaller than the corporate giants in mass production or distribution. The bargaining is therefore on the local or regional level and the employers band together in regional units, like the Southern California chapter of the Associated General Contractors of America.

Since a majority of trade unionists are employed in industries with more than local markets, a majority of local unions look to the nationals for policy decisions and assistance in dealing with employers. Local unions handle the day-to-day details of recruitment, membership, finance, bargaining, and grievance procedure, but their decisions tend to be standardized by definite national policies in all these matters. They are signatories to agreements with employers which are noticeably uniform in content, with standard clauses worked out by bargaining specialists on the staff of the national union, and they are usually limited by strict rules as to the calling of strikes or other forms of direct action which will require national assistance for success. In addition, they are often supervised closely and given advice and assistance by a district representative of the national union, located nearby.

However, the cooperation between locals and nationals is not by any means a one-way affair. Strong locals are an absolute prerequisite for a strong national union, and any local has the ultimate right of secession, a right that has been exercised enough times to keep national officers concerned about morale on the grass-roots level. Nor is the income which locals pay into the national treasury a case of "taxation without representation." Local officers are invariably delegates to district, regional, and national conventions and have a voice in arriving at the policy decisions which will govern their subsequent operations. Having had a hand in the formation of policy, and being familiar with the reasons for its adoption, they have a more proprietary attitude toward it and present it with conviction to their membership at the local level.

Trusteeships.   A local union is the custodian of the name, reputation, and goodwill of the national or international union. There are many locals; in some of the big nationals and internationals they run into the thousands—for example: Maintenance of Way Employees—1,331; Steelworkers—3,100; Machinists—1,971; IBEW—1,735.[10] If a local union gets out of line, it can do great damage to the national by bringing the organization and all its members into disrepute. For this reason, most nationals try to keep a tight check on strike authorizations, financial practices, and the like. Nevertheless, the wide range of local autonomy in the past has permitted some local officers to rig elections, raise fees and dues, manipulate the books and records, negotiate "sweetheart" contracts, collect bribes and kickbacks, and divert union business to friends and relatives. To eliminate such practices, national and international unions resort to the device known as "trusteeship." They send one or more authorized "trustees" from national headquarters to take over the office, books, and records of the local union, conduct an audit of its affairs, check up on its officers, and correct any bad practices they find. When the situation is straightened out and the local is once more in condition to conduct its own affairs democratically and responsibly, the trusteeship is brought to an end

Unfortunately, the trusteeship can be used in reverse. A set of corrupt national officers may take over a local union in order to accomplish the precise purposes the trusteeship is supposed to put an end to. The corrupt "trustees" may remove from office the honest local officials, hold phony elections, intimidate the members by violence or threat of violence, milk the local treasury, and so on. Such fraudulent trusteeships may be

[10] As of 1963.

continued indefinitely, especially if profitable. The McClellan committee of the United States Senate found incontrovertible evidence of such use of trusteeships, and a whole section of the Landrum-Griffin Act of 1959 was devoted to regulating the device.

Under the terms of Title III of the law, a trusteeship may be imposed only in accordance with the union's constitution and bylaws and for such proper reasons as eliminating corruption or financial skulduggery, assuring the performance of collective-bargaining agreements, restoring democratic procedures, etc. While the trusteeship is in operation, any selection of delegates or officers must be by secret ballot in a full and fair election, and no funds of the local except the regular per capita tax or assessments paid by all local members everywhere may be transferred to the national. To assure compliance with these mandates, any trusteeship imposed must be reported within 30 days to the Secretary of Labor with a full roundup of reasons for the action and a complete financial statement of the local's condition at the time the trusteeship began. This report must be repeated every 6 months, except that financial matters may be detailed once a year in the regular report required of all unions. The reports are public information, just like all other reports required by law, which means that anyone may see or get copies of them. They must be signed by the president and treasurer (or other principal officers) of the national, who then become personally responsible for both their filing and any false statements known to be in them. Criminal penalties ($10,000 fine/1 year imprisonment, or both) are stipulated for any form of violation or misrepresentation in reporting (false entry, withholding, concealment, destruction of records, etc.), as well as in the holding of elections and transfer of funds.

If a union member feels that a trusteeship is being violated, he can complain to the Secretary of Labor who *must* investigate and, if he finds the complaint valid, take the matter to court, asking damages or an injunction. (The name of the informing union member need not be disclosed.) If they so choose, the members of the local union may sue the national direct. In the absence of complaints, trusteeships are "presumed valid" for the first 18 months, but after that time they are "presumed invalid" and the national union must show by "clear and convincing proof" that the continuation of the trusteeship is necessary if it is challenged by a member, the local union, or the Secretary of Labor. Under these rules, fewer trusteeships will be instituted and those that are will be conducted very carefully by the officers assigned to such duty.

Finances.　　A union cannot operate without money, any more than a business, a family, or a church. The union's income is mainly from the regular monthly dues paid by members; these are supplemented by initiation fees and now and then by general or special assessments voted by the membership.

There is a wide range of fees and dues charged by different union locals and great variety in the way in which the amounts collected are split between the local and the national, and in some cases, the district organization. The charges reflect the differing policies of unions as to membership, organization, and services. For example, unions of skilled mechanics organized on the craft theory, being generally older and having a more complete line of member benefits (sickness, death, unemployment, and the like), have a consistently higher schedule of fees and dues than the newer industrial unions, with their inclusive, mass, lower-paid memberships. Members of industrial unions cannot afford as high dues as skilled craftsmen, and the large memberships of industrial locals make them less necessary. The discrepancy is especially noticeable in the entrance fees, which, in the skilled trades, represent the price of admission to an exclusive society, while in the industrial unions they are more in the nature of registration payments for the exercise of a basic right.

By the end of the Second World War standard AFL initiation fees in 300 local unions ranged from $5 to $300, with the great majority of locals charging from $25 to $100 for the privilege of admission. Some went much higher; AFL initiation fees ranging from $500 to $3,000 have been reported. In contrast, the range of entrance fees to CIO unions in 1946 was from $1 to $50, with only two unions above the $25 figure. By 1953, the range was $1.50 to $100, with five unions charging $25 or more for the privilege of admission. The majority of unions still charge relatively small amounts, with fees of $5 and $10 common as initial payments; some of them describe the initiation fee as the "first month's dues for new members."

By June, 1960, the range of initiation fees in a sample of 38,000 local unions showed 63 out of 100 at $10 or less, 23 per cent between $10 and $50, and only 2 per cent over $200: [11]

Initiation fee	Number of unions	Per cent
No initiation fee	1,905*	5
Less than $5	5,432†	14
$5.00 to $10	16,855‡	44
$10.01 to $50	8,684	23
$50.01 to $200	4,498	12
$200.01 to $1,400	605§	2
Total	37,979	100

* In most of these cases, the initiation fee would be the first month's dues.
† A nominal charge only; over 60 per cent for $2.00 or less.
‡ 9,625 @ $5.00; 5,372 @ $10.00.
§ Only 17 locals charged more than $500.

[11] *Monthly Labor Review*, January, 1961, p. 33.

The picture is similar in the matter of dues. The range of AFL (mostly craft) union dues in 250 locals in 1945 was from 50 cents to $7 a month, with the heaviest concentration in the range from $1.50 to $4.[12] The customary range for CIO dues at the same time was from $1 to $3 a month, with the majority at or near the bottom of the range. By 1953, most CIO dues were $2 or $3 a month, with several at $4 or $5. Since then, union dues have risen along with other kinds of dues, fees, and service charges. A monthly dues payment of $5 is collected by the locals of several of the larger national unions and is probably a fair approximation of the current cost of membership. However, the trend is up. If the price level continues to rise, and along with it, the fees for medical, legal, and other types of services, union dues will follow. One type of dues policy of some national unions is to set a minimum that may be charged by the local and along with it either a flat fee or a percentage of the total that must be paid to the national as its per capita share. The local is then permitted to decide on the actual amount the members will pay.

For June 30, 1960, a survey of 36,817 local unions showed the following distribution of monthly dues requirements: [13]

Prevailing rate of dues, June 30, 1960	Local unions	Per cent
No dues required	847	2
Less than $3	7,108	19
$3 to $5.99	25,866*	71
$6 to $9.99	2,547	7
$10 to $24.99	444	1
$25 to $35	5	
Total	36,817	100

* There were 11,004 at less than $4.00 and only 5,705 at $5.00 or more.

Local unions are the sources of income, since they are usually the collecting agencies and the custodians of membership. (Not always, however. In the checkoff of Steelworkers' dues, the money is sent direct to the national headquarters and the local's share is returned to it by the national treasurer.) The income of the national union is derived from a split of the member's dues, part of which is sent to headquarters as the "per capita tax." The size of the tax varies. At its general convention in 1959, for example, the UAW increased its basic dues from $3 to $5 a month, with a distribution as follows: $1.25 for a general strike fund, $1.75 to the international union, and $2 to the local. At the same time, it reported a mem-

[12] Philip Taft, "Dues and Initiation Fees in Labor Unions," *Quarterly Journal of Economics,* February, 1946, p. 221.
[13] *Monthly Labor Review,* January, 1961, p. 32.

bership of 1,144,000. If these figures held stable, it would mean an annual income to the international union of $24,024,000 from dues alone, exclusive of initiation fees and other income, plus an addition of $17,160,000 per year to the strike fund.[14]

Local income is a simple function of the size of the membership and the share of the dues retained, plus such fringe items as initiation fees (also shared with the national organization in many cases), reinstatement fees, fines, and now and then, in exceptional cases, income from rental or other property. Locals of the UAW average more than 1,000 members each. An average local therefore would have a basic income of at least $24,000 a year to pay its paid officials and office help, and to cover rent, stationery, supplies, and miscellaneous costs such as travel. Most locals are much smaller than the UAW average and have correspondingly smaller income, even if the dues are higher.

A report from the U.S. Department of Labor in June, 1962, placed total income of all unions in the country at approximately $1.4 billion, with $923 million coming from dues and fees and $506 million from the return on investments. Of this sum, the local unions kept $831 million, or 59 per cent; $492 million went to the nationals; and $105 million went as per capita taxes to the AFL–CIO or state and regional federations. The annual income of the top half dozen unions was listed as:

International Brotherhood of Electrical Workers (IBEW)	$65,300,000
United Steelworkers of America (USW)	62,100,000
United Auto Workers (UAW)	42,100,000
International Typographical Union (ITU)	22,700,000
International Ladies' Garment Workers Union (ILGWU)	21,700,000
United Mine Workers of America (UMWA)	20,500,000

At the local level, unions are like churches in that they rely heavily on the unpaid services of members. There are customarily two elected officials: a president and a secretary, who may also be treasurer or business manager. The latter is usually paid something for his work in keeping the books and records of the organization, and the president may get a token salary as a mark of respect or to cover his out-of-pocket expenses and reimburse him in part for the long hours he will surely put in, but it is a big and well-financed local that can afford either of these officers on full time. In addition the union appoints department or shop stewards to act as its representatives on the job and to handle grievances. These positions carry prestige, allow more freedom of movement, embody top seniority, and give the holder the right to handle union business on company time, but they ordinarily pay no salary. Union work on the local plane is a labor of love, unremunerative in itself but indispensable training for ad-

[14] The total, of $41,184,000, is borne out by the reported income for 1961 of $42,100,000. See above.

vancement to positions of greater responsibility at the district or national level.

In June, 1962, John L. Holcombe of the Bureau of Labor-Management Reports of the U.S. Department of Labor announced that "half of all the nation's union locals are worth less than $2,276 each and pay their officers a total of less than $767 a year." [15]

UNION OFFICERS

Being an officer of a union became much less fun with the passage of the Landrum-Griffin Act. Some of the functions of union officials are the same as those of any other nonprofit organization. They must set up and administer an organization (personnel), raise the money to pay the bills and carry on necessary operations (finance), and decide on long-run, intermediate, and immediate objectives (policy), giving priority to the most important problems and trying to find time for secondary matters. The special functions of union managers are those related to the major purposes of unionism—collective bargaining, political action, and miscellaneous activities among the membership and in the community: welfare work, education, philanthropy, recreation, etc. The general effect of the Landrum-Griffin Act was to decree that union officers will hereafter operate in a "goldfish bowl," under a spotlight of publicity equal to or exceeding that required of almost any other form of organization in modern society. This is accomplished through the medium of required reports.

Reports on union administrative policies.   Every union must keep on file with the Secretary of Labor a copy of its constitution and bylaws and a detailed report—kept up to date by annual notices of any changes—of the matters listed below. "Every union" includes, of course, nationals and internationals, and also local unions, where the information is pertinent to local conditions or varies from one local to another. The data requested are:

1.   Name, mailing address, and location of the principal office where records are kept
2.   Name and title of each of its officers
3.   Initiation fees and fees for work permits where used
4.   Regular dues or fees or any other periodic payments required of members
5.   Detailed statements or references to documents showing "provision made and procedures followed with respect to each of the following:"
   a.   Qualifications or restrictions on membership
   b.   The levying of assessments

[15] *Newsweek*, June 25, 1962, p. 66.

c. Participation in insurance or other benefit plans
d. Authorization for disbursements of funds
e. Audits of financial transactions
f. The calling of regular and special meetings
g. The selection of officers and stewards and of any other union representatives, and the manner in which each one is elected, appointed, or otherwise chosen
h. Discipline or removal of officers or agents for breaches of trust
i. The imposition of fines, suspensions, and expulsions of members, including grounds for action and the provision for notice, hearing, judgments, and appeals
j. The authorization of bargaining demands
k. The ratification of contract terms
l. The authorization for strikes
m. The issuance of work permits

Financial reports. In addition to a report on its administrative policies and procedures, every union must file annually with the Secretary of Labor a financial report containing the following information "in such detail as may be necessary accurately to disclose its financial condition *and operations* for its preceding fiscal year:" [16]

1. Assets and liabilities at the beginning and end of the fiscal year
2. Receipts of any kind and the sources thereof
3. Salary, allowances, and any other direct or indirect payments (including reimbursed expenses) to any officer or employe who during the year received more than $10,000 from the union or any other union affiliated with it directly or indirectly
4. Direct and indirect loans made to any officer, employe, or member, which total more than $250 during the year, with a statement of purpose, security if any, and arrangements for repayment
5. Direct and indirect loans to any business firm—their purpose, security if any, and arrangements for repayment
6. Any other disbursements made by it (with the purposes of same) in such categories as the Secretary of Labor may direct

All the information described above (both administrative and financial) must be made available to all of the union's members, and any member may sue in a Federal district court to force the union to permit him (for just cause) to examine any books, records, or accounts of the union as may be necessary to verify the reports. If the suit is successful, the court may at its discretion charge the costs of the action as well as a reasonable attorney's fee to the defendant (union).

The above reports, both administrative and financial, are general institutional (union) information which must be supplied regularly to the

[16] Italics added.

Secretary of Labor. They do not, however, completely satisfy the curiosity of Congress and are supplemented by required reports from union officers as individuals, from employers, and from "labor relations consultants."

Reports of union officers. Every union officer and employe (other than clerical or custodial) must file an annual report with the Secretary of Labor covering any sort of "conflict-of-interest" transaction with an employer that the union represents or is trying to represent, from which arrangement the union official or a member of his family might conceivably benefit in a financial way. Such transaction could be a money payment, transfer of stock, a loan, a purchase or a sale, or a "business arrangement"—anything, in fact, except the payment of wages for his services as an employe. In addition, he must report any current acquisition of stock or existing stockholding or other form of "legal or equitable interest" in any company the union has organized or is trying to organize. As a check, the same kind of reports are required of employers in reverse, especially if the payments are made for the purpose of "causing such employe or . . . employes to persuade other employes to exercise or not to exercise . . . the right to organize and bargain collectively." A third category of report, and in some cases a still further check, is that by "labor relations consultants," who have agreed to try to influence employes with respect to how they use their bargaining rights or to supply an employer with information about union activities. Any such agreement must be reported within 30 days and payments made under it must be announced to the Secretary of Labor annually. The only persons exempt from this requirement are lawyers who have an attorney-client relationship with one of the parties.

REPORTS AS PUBLIC INFORMATION. All of the reports, including the general administrative and financial reports of unions, are "public" information. This means that anyone who wishes to can get a copy of any report from the Secretary of Labor, at cost. What is more costly to the unions is the requirement that the records from which the reports are made, including "vouchers, worksheets, receipts, and applicable resolutions," must be saved for at least 5 years. The signers of the reports—the chief officers of the union—are personally responsible for their filing and the information contained in them and are subject to criminal penalties of fine and/or imprisonment if there is any sort of willful violation: failure to file, false statements, incomplete disclosure, false entry, destruction of records, etc.

Query: What other type of organization—business, nonprofit, governmental—must disclose in such detail to the general public its policies, practices, and finances? Query: Is this invasion of privacy justified, on the record, when comparison is made with other kinds of organizations?

Fiduciary responsibilities of union officials. The Landrum-Griffin Act added an extra dimension to the normal hazards of being a union officer by assigning him full fiduciary responsibility. What this means is clearly stated in the law itself:

The officers, agents, shop stewards, and other representatives of a labor organization occupy positions of trust in relation to such labor organization and its members as a group. It is, therefore, the duty of each such person . . . to hold its money and property solely for the benefit of the organization and its members and to manage, invest, and expend the same in accordance with its constitution and bylaws and . . . resolutions of the governing bodies . . . to refrain from dealing with [the union] as an adverse party or in behalf of an adverse party in any matter connected with his duties and from holding or acquiring any pecuniary or personal interest which conflicts with the interests of such organization. . . . A general exculpatory provision in the constitution and bylaws of [a union] . . . purporting to relieve any such person of liability for breach of the duties declared by this section shall be void as against public policy [Sec. 501].

It should be pointed out that this goes beyond the legal or statutory responsibility of corporation officers in general or of most government officials or of the official family of most nonprofit institutions. There is no doubt of the moral desirability of such a mandate—for any official in any type of organization—but fiduciary responsibility has a special legal implication. It implies a standard of performance above the average in care and prudence—like that expected of a trust officer of a financial institution. This should be considered in connection with the section of the act which follows, to wit: When any union officer "is alleged to have violated" the duties described above and the union or its governing board "refuse or fail to sue or recover damages or secure an accounting or other appropriate relief" after being asked to do so, any member may sue for the same purpose.

The act makes it a Federal crime for an officer of a union to embezzle or steal or convert union funds to his own use. It also requires the bonding of any union official who handles funds or property, prohibits unions from lending to any of their officers or employes in excess of $2,000, and directs that neither the union nor an employer may pay the fine of an officer or employe convicted under the act. The law expressly prohibits unions or any of their representatives from disciplining any member for exercising his rights under the act and makes it a criminal offense for anyone through force or violence or the threat of such to do so.

Official pay and perquisites. The good jobs in trade unionism are on the national and federation levels. The highest reported pay is that of the president of the Teamsters, with the salary of $100,000 per year; the next highest that of the chief executive of the Railway Clerks, at $80,000. George Meany now gets $70,000 as president of the AFL–CIO, while William F. Schnitzler, secretary-treasurer, receives $45,000, less than the

$50,000 salary paid to the presidents of the Miners and the Steelworkers. However, these are the top figures; the heads of some very large and powerful unions get by on half these amounts or less. The great majority of union presidencies pay less than $25,000 a year, most of them much less.

The salary of the president is not the whole picture. Career opportunities in the larger trade unions include such additional jobs as secretary-treasurer (who may be paid as much as the president and who at times outranks him in authority), vice-president (one or more), and from a dozen to a score of regional directors on salaries ranging from $7,500 to $15,000 per year. Union officers customarily have generous expense allowances for travel, entertainment, and the like. The big international unions and the AFL–CIO also have extensive staffs of professional and technical employes: lawyers, economists, statisticians, research experts, publicists, etc. All these come high, and the unions do not hesitate to pay for top-grade service, which they expect to match the quality of performance of corporation experts.

The job of the union officer.   What do union officials at the national level do? Like corporation executives, they must concentrate on policy, promotion (extension of organization), finances, and publicity. Unlike corporation managers, union officers must also keep in mind their political responsibilities, both internal and external. The internal political responsibilities are considerable in a union the size of the International Brotherhood of Electrical Workers, with its 800,000 members distributed across the country in more than 1,700 local unions.

POLICY.   The principal recurring problems of union policy are *wage demands* and *union security*, and the methods to be used in realizing them. It is an exceptional union nowadays that does not have a wage policy, formulated in convention after extensive study and recommendations by officials and technical experts from the home office. This policy may or may not be binding on the local unions, depending on the degree of autonomy the latter enjoy. In some cases, as, for example, the Steelworkers and Autoworkers, the pattern of increase (or decrease) is set nationally by bargaining between the national union officials and one or more major firms, and the entire industry falls into line with only minor variations here and there. In other cases, like the building-trades unions, a national policy is a guide and nothing more, to be used as an indication of what the leaders think is proper but which may be departed from in local situations with some freedom.[17]

The advantage of a national policy is obvious. It is only from the vantage point of national perspective that over-all conditions in the country and the industry can be appraised and the favorable and unfavor-

[17] The authoritative study of this subject is Arthur M. Ross, *Trade Union Wage Policy* (Berkeley, Calif.: University of California Press, 1948).

able factors balanced against one another. Some recent examples of very inclusive national wage policy were the first-, second-, and third-round "patterns" of wage increase after the end of the Second World War, each of which was set after a period of prolonged negotiation, including strikes, between the national union officers and representatives of some of the leading firms in the country's biggest industries. Another example was the shift from emphasis on basic wage rates to emphasis on pension and welfare funds in 1949. Still more recent are the job-guarantee and early retirement features negotiated between 1960 and 1964 in Pacific Coast longshoring, automobile manufacture, and the steel industry. The standard union objective is at least maintenance and if possible improvement of the wage position of its members, but there are many roads to the one end: basic rates, "fringe items," reduction of hours, welfare funds, etc. It is the job of the national officers to estimate a feasible target, devise an appropriate wage "package" to be asked for, put into its members' hands the arguments (cost of living, rise in labor productivity, profits of the employer, comparable wages in other industries) which will have the most telling effect at the bargaining table, and provide expert advice and assistance in important local negotiations.

Union security is a question of getting and keeping members. The union has two great enemies in its struggle for survival. One is the employer, who competes for the loyalty of members and potential members. The other is apathy, the tendency for members to take the union and its benefits for granted and to backslide in attendance and dues. Outright "union busting" by the employer has been prohibited for firms in interstate commerce since 1935 by the Wagner Act and subsequent legislation, but employers still have the right to point out to employes which side their bread is buttered on and to present reasons why, in their opinion, a union is unnecessary.[18] Since the employers pay the wages and control the future of employes through work assignments and promotion, they have some heavy artillery in the duel for worker loyalties. If the union is careless, the employer's natural strategic position may be reinforced by the members' boredom and the steady drain of dues.

To counteract backsliding, the union uses persuasion, coercion (now and then), and formal agreements which make union membership necessary or advantageous in holding a job: closed- and union-shop contracts, preference agreements, and maintenance-of-membership clauses. Combined with these, where possible, is the checkoff of union dues, to make the monthly payment as painless as possible. The type of union-security agreement to be sought, the argument in its favor, and the actual bargaining to get it are considered by all national unions as a major responsibility, and no local issue excites their support more readily. Regular con-

[18] They have this right only if their arguments are not coupled with threats, expressed or implied.

tact with local chapters to keep up morale and emphasize the benefits of membership are also on every national officer's schedule. A threat to security at any point is a threat to the union itself and is met with every weapon that the union can lay hands on.

PROMOTION. One phase of the problem of security is *extension of organization*. A union is like other organisms; it either goes ahead or goes backward. A union standing still is a union on the decline. It is a prime job of the national officers to see to it, first, that all or most of the workers in the industry or craft are enrolled and, second, that organizing efforts are extended to workers in related fields who are eligible for inclusion in the union's jurisdiction. This calls for a permanent program of increase of membership through the creation of new locals and the addition of new members to existing locals. The major fields for the extension of membership today are the South, which is still only partially organized, the white-collar workers in clerical and sales employment, and the growing body of technicians in automated industries.

FINANCE. Collective bargaining (especially if work stoppages are involved), extension of organization, and regular day-to-day administration, all call for personnel and financial support. Finding the men and the money is a constant responsibility. The organizing and administrative staff of the national union is the customary career route for promising local workers, and well-established unions usually have as many candidates as they can use. The financial picture, in these days of high wages and full employment, is generally satisfactory. The basic income figure for a national union is a function of the monthly "per capita tax" (the national union's share of the regular monthly dues), which usually ranges from $1 to $2, times the membership. If a union has 300,000 members and the tax is $1.50 ($18 a year), the union's annual revenue from this source will be $5,400,000.

The level of dues is important to members and dues increases have been connected with political revolts, strong protests from the members, and dropouts from the union.[19] Dues, fees, and assessments were considered important enough by Congress to be protected in the "Bill of Rights" of the L-G act by detailed requirements of majority vote for an increase of the first two (dues and initiation fees) or levying of the latter.[20] Dues income is the union's primary source of revenue, although it is supplemented by initiation and reinstatement fees, assessments voted by the membership, gifts, and earnings from property and investments, some of which are quite sizable.

Assets and annual income running in the millions (or even the hun-

---

[19] See, for example, the protests raised against the increase of per capita taxes of directly affiliated local unions of the AFL–CIO, from $1 to $1.50 per month in the 1959 convention. *Proceedings*, vol. I, pp. 335–347.

[20] Title I, Sec. 101(a)(3).

dreds of thousands) call for financial management a good deal above the level of the corner grocery store. They involve collection and disbursement procedures, a program of accounting and auditing of funds, banking and investment practices, protective devices (bonding), and responsibility. All these are among the functions of union officials at the national level. In addition, they elect, or are asked to assume, a number of fiscal duties for their district and local organizations, such as auditing the books and reporting to the membership. The administration of large welfare and pension funds is a recent and growing activity, which adds to the fiduciary responsibilities of union officers.[21]

PUBLICITY.   Few kinds of organizations have more compelling reasons for good publicity than trade unions. Relations with members call for a strong and persistent selling program. Relations with employers in many cases demand a powerful propaganda line. Relations with the general public and governmental agencies may affect the outcome of bargaining negotiations, disputes with management, and membership drives. Direct political action has added another publicity job to the many already assumed. Publicity is therefore a major function of the big national unions and the federation.

The principal organ of publicity is the union journal, a must with the larger unions. Many of the union magazines are full-scale weekly and monthly periodicals, containing news, official reports, technical articles, propaganda, cartoons, and comic strips of interest to members. Subsidiary items on the printed publicity schedule are pamphlets and releases on special problems like housing, the cost of living, and legislation, and the standard union output of instructions and exhortation to new members. Publicity also includes platform speeches by union leaders, radio programs, mass meetings, appearances before congressional and state legislative committees, and appeals to governmental executives from the President of the United States down.

UNION POLITICS.   Union officers cannot afford to forget that they are constantly running for office. One of their functions is, therefore, to build a personal political machine within the union. This is the time-honored method of ensuring continuance in elective office where there is competition for the job, and the jobholder who neglects his political fences may find himself on the outside looking in while others fashion organization policy and direct its affairs. Machine building is accomplished by the standardized methods of distribution of patronage (appointment of friends and political supporters to influential positions), campaigning for programs and policies associated with official sponsorship, and monopoly

[21] For a detailed example of how *not* to administer such a fund, see R. and E. James, *Hoffa and the Teamsters* (Princeton, N.J.: D. Van Nostrand Company, Inc., 1965), Part IV, "Hoffa's Financial Sources of Power," pp. 213–320.

of the organs of publicity to promote personal reputations and the myth of indispensability.

Sometimes more direct methods have been used, such as the personal appointment (in lieu of election) of a workable minority of the representatives to the national convention, control of the vote-counting apparatus, and the packing of election meetings with supporters to the exclusion of opponents. It was normal procedure in some conventions to permit no opposition measures or criticism of the current union administration to arise from the floor, even to the point of physical violence against the critics. The "Bill of Rights" and "Elections" provisions of the Landrum-Griffin Act were designed to eliminate these practices.

The extent to which real democracy, in terms of convention discussion and voting, is relied upon varies among unions, but the patronage and publicity aspects of machine politics are almost never absent. Their success is obvious in the long and uninterrupted terms of office of national and federation leaders. The American Federation of Labor had two presidents in 66 years—Gompers and Green—if the 1 year that Gompers was out of office in 1894 is excluded. Lewis was president of the UMWA from 1920 to 1960, and the terms of office of Harrison of the Railway Clerks, Dubinsky of the Ladies' Garment Workers, Curran of the NMU, Bridges of the ILWU, Moreschi of the Hod Carriers, Bates of the Bricklayers, and many others are plain evidence of the security of union presidents. The service records of top union officers compare favorably with those of corporation executives and far exceed the average time in office of chief executives in public jurisdictions.

ORGANIZATION AND FUNCTIONS OF THE AFL–CIO

Still another career level open to trade unionists is working for the AFL–CIO.[22] Salaries and prerequisites are on a par with those in the big national and international unions, sometimes exceeding the latter. Some of the jobs in the Federation are filled by officers of the member nationals without additional salary, whereas others are full-time positions in which the incumbent is paid from the Federation's budget. President Meany and Secretary-Treasurer Schnitzler, for example, have no union responsibilities outside the Federation, although of course they retain their cards in the Plumbers and Bakery Workers, respectively. Other top jobs in the Federation are director of organization (Wm. L. Kircher), the presi-

[22] There are other federations of unions in this country—the principal one being the National Federation of Independent Unions (almost a contradiction in terms)—but in size or influence they are negligible compared to the AFL–CIO. As in the classic illustration of different orders of magnitude, they would not even be in the ratio of the flea to the cow, but more like the flea-on-the-flea to the cow.

dencies of the departments, general counsel (J. Albert Woll), director of political education (Al Barkan), director of publications (Saul Miller), director of legislation (Andrew J. Biemiller), and so on.

Organization of the AFL–CIO.   The AFL–CIO has a complex and intricate form of organization, to enable it to perform its various functions, the main outlines of which are shown in Fig. 11–4. The Federation setup still reflects the political necessities of the merger of 1955. The basic political fact at that time was that the AFL outweighed the CIO in membership, 2 to 1. This was taken into account in the merger agreement of February, 1955, with respect to the selection of officers, the composition of the principal policy-making units, and the addition of the Industrial Union Department.[23] The impress of this balance-of-power arrangement is plain in the Federation structure.

The supreme authority in the AFL–CIO, as in the previous federations, resides in the general convention, which meets every 2 years. From the convention, authority flows to the executive council, which is to meet at least three times a year on call of the president. The council is composed of the president and secretary-treasurer and 27 vice-presidents of the Federation, 17 of whom are from former AFL unions and 10 from unions formerly in the CIO. To advise the executive council, there is a general board, meeting at least once a year, composed of the members of the council and a principal officer of each affiliated union and each department. From the executive council authority extends to the president and secretary-treasurer, who are the executive officers of the organization, handling its day-to-day business. George Meany and William F. Schnitzler, president and secretary-treasurer respectively of the AFL, were elected to the same jobs in the new combined organization. Advising the executive officers is an Executive Committee, which meets twice a month. It is composed of the two executive officers and six vice-presidents, three of whom are former AFL vice-presidents and three former CIO officers. To advise the president, there are 15 standing committees, dealing with such matters as:

Economic policy: Walter P. Reuther, chairman
International affairs: George M. Harrison, chairman
Legislative: George Meany, chairman
Research: William F. Schnitzler, chairman

THE DEPARTMENT.   "Department" is an overworked word in the AFL–CIO. There are three kinds of departments: staff, organization, and trade and industrial. The 13 staff departments, headed mostly by directors,

[23] A brief summary of the steps to merger, the structure and leadership of the AFL–CIO, and comments on problems and goals, is found in the *Monthly Labor Review,* February, 1956, pp. 141–149.

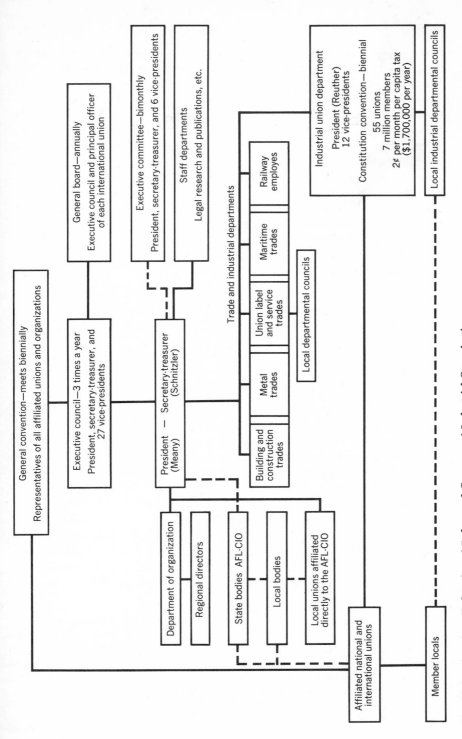

Fig. 114. *American Federation of Labor and Congress of Industrial Organizations*

General convention—meets biennially
Representatives of all affiliated unions and organizations

Executive council—3 times a year
President, secretary-treasurer, and 27 vice-presidents

President — Secretary-treasurer
(Meany)   (Schnitzler)

General board—annually
Executive council and principal officer of each international union

Executive committee—bimonthly
President, secretary-treasurer, and 6 vice-presidents

Staff departments

Legal research and publications, etc.

Trade and industrial departments

Building and construction trades

Metal trades

Union label and service trades

Maritime trades

Railway employes

Local departmental councils

Industrial union department

President (Reuther)
12 vice-presidents

Constitution convention—biennial
55 unions
7 million members
2¢ per month per capita tax
($1,700,000 per year)

Local industrial departmental councils

Department of organization

Regional directors

State bodies AFL-CIO

Local bodies

Local unions affiliated directly to the AFL-CIO

Affiliated national and international unions

Member locals

cover a wide variety of functions. In some cases, as in education, legislation, and research, they complement the activities of a standing committee. In others, they handle or advise on operating problems such as accounting, legal, library, purchasing and supplies. The Department of Organization, on the other hand, is an executive division, reporting to the president. It has a number of assistants to the director as well as representatives in 23 regions throughout the United States and in Puerto Rico. Its job is to assist member unions in extending or strengthening their organization or to organize the unorganized on its own account.

What are usually thought of as the departments of the AFL–CIO, however, are its trade and industrial departments. These are committee-type organizations composed of representatives of the unions found in a single industrial group, or, as in the case of the Industrial Union Department, unions with a common form of organization. The departments and the men heading them are: [24]

Building and Construction Trades Department: C. J. Haggerty, president
Industrial Union Department: Walter P. Reuther, president
Maritime Trades Department: Paul Hall, president
Metal Trades Department: B. A. Gritta, president
Railway Employes' Department: Michael Fox, president
Union Label and Service Trades Department: Richard F. Walsh, president
Government Employes Council: E. C. Hallbeck, chairman

The functions of the departments are to solve problems of jurisdiction, organization, and cooperation, in which some or all members of each department have a common interest. Each has a president (or chairman) and a secretary-treasurer, holds its own convention, and maintains one or more publications. Most of them have been divisions of the AFL for many years.

The Industrial Union Department (IUD). The new face in the gallery is the Industrial Union Department and it belongs to the biggest member there. With a total membership of around 7 million in 55 affiliated unions, the IUD has about half the membership and slightly less than half the unions in the AFL–CIO. The announced purposes of the department are to:

. . . promote the interests of industrial unions, assist in collective bargaining, engage in legislative activity with respect to matters of interest to industrial

[24] Some of the men named above are full-time officers (Haggerty, Gritta, Fox), paid by the Federation like Meany and Schnitzler and with no outside union duties. The others are primarily heads of important unions and give only part-time supervision to the department: Reuther, president of the UAW; Hall, president of the Seafarers' International Union; Walsh, president of the Stage Employes and Moving Picture Machine Operators; and Hallbeck, president of the United Federation of Postal Clerks. The latter receive their pay from the union they head and give unsalaried service to the department.

unions, act as a clearinghouse of information, engage in research and related activities, and administer the CIO organizational disputes agreement.

The Industrial Union Department is in fact a subfederation within the AFL–CIO. It is the old CIO, enlarged slightly to admit a number of former AFL unions organized in whole or in part on an industrial basis. The IUD reflects the fact that the merger was originally a "marriage of convenience," imposed from the top down and entered into with reservations by some very important unions in both the AFL and the CIO. The marriage (merger) has thus far shown few signs of breaking up and every year that passes without serious division increases the chances of permanence. The hyphenated character of the Federation remains, nevertheless, in both title and structure.

Powers of the AFL–CIO.   The AFL–CIO has very little constitutional power and depends largely upon the voluntary cooperation of its member unions. Like the AFL and the CIO before it, it is a rather loose federation of independent and autonomous unions. A member union may leave the AFL–CIO at any time and for any reason, and there is no power in the Federation's constitution to stop it. What power the AFL–CIO does have is negative. It can expel a union for practices or policies of which it disapproves, as it did the Teamsters, the Bakers, and the Laundry Workers at its second biennial convention in 1957; or it can insist that a union meet satisfactory standards of performance if it wants to stay in, that is, put it on probation, as was done with the Distillery Workers at the same time; or it can refuse admission or readmission until its standards are met, as it was still doing with the Teamsters in 1967, 10 years after expulsion.[25] It can go further. If it sees fit, the Federation can charter a competing union to try to take the membership away from an expelled union. This has been done in the past, both successfully and unsuccessfully. The CIO expelled the United Electrical Workers (UE) in 1949 for Communist domination and chartered the International Union of Electrical, Radio and Machine Workers (IUE) in its place, with Jim Carey, former president of the UE, as its head. After 10 years, the IUE had around 400,000 members and more than 450 locals, while the UE reported a membership of 100,000 and 115 locals.[26] The AFL's experiment in dual unionism was less successful. In September, 1953, the AFL expelled the International Longshoremen's Association (ILA) on grounds of domination by corrupt influences and simultaneously chartered the International Brotherhood of Longshoremen, presumably to succeed it. However, the Brotherhood was defeated by the ILA in a series of representation elections, and the latter retained a majority of the membership.

[25] The Teamsters had filed no formal request for readmission, but the matter had come informally before the Executive Council at every convention from 1959 on, being raised by the many friends of the Teamsters within the AFL–CIO.

[26] The 1964 figures were IUE—265,000, UE—164,000.

In 1959, the ILA, judged to be purged of its corrupt influences, was re-admitted to the AFL–CIO. Thus, chartering a successor union to take the place of one expelled has its risks. No such action has been taken by the AFL–CIO to compete with the Teamsters, expelled in 1957.

Functions of the AFL–CIO.   The AFL–CIO is a service organization. Its main jobs are defense and assistance: to guarantee the autonomy of its members and to perform general services which will help its member nationals or which the latter cannot conveniently do for themselves. The Federation can and does set policies which tend to be followed by its members, but it cannot enforce conformity on them, and it is extremely rare for the AFL–CIO as such to mix into the internal affairs of any union, no matter how far it strays off the path of righteousness.[27] The slightest indication of any such intent usually results in the union's withdrawal from the Federation; secession—like that of the Carpenters and Miners and Machinists in the past—may occur simply from dissatisfaction with a policy adopted in convention.

Nevertheless, the activities of the big federation are extremely important and with the growing political consciousness of the labor movement in this country can hardly fail to become more so. This results from the fact that trade unionism is a movement; the Federation and its officers are the only spokesmen that can represent organized labor as a whole or in large blocs. Hence, no labor representative can go before a congressional committee with more authority than the president of the AFL–CIO. The AFL–CIO's legislative activities (on Federal, state, and local levels) have long been among its foremost responsibilities, and the recent added emphasis on direct political action has one principal channel: the Committee on Political Education (COPE). The location of Federation headquarters in Washington, D.C., is a clue to the importance of this function. A catalog of Federation activities would therefore have to give an important place to *representation,* but it would not stop there; the AFL–CIO also gives a great deal of attention to *interunion relations* (mainly through the biennial convention), the *extension of organization, publicity,* and *research.*

REPRESENTATION.   The AFL–CIO employs legislative representatives (lobbyists), whose job it is to follow the work of Congress and bring pressure to bear in favor of bills that the Federation favors, while opposing antilabor measures. They are reinforced regularly by personal appearances of top Federal officials, as well as by important leaders of national and international unions, especially members of the Federation's executive

---

[27] The "Codes of Ethical Practices," adopted shortly after the merger (and during the McClellan committee's most active period), seemed to indicate some abandonment of this tradition. However, the Codes have been very little in evidence since the 1957 convention.

council. The Federation introduces witnesses at hearings, produces factual information for congressmen, organizes mass invasions of Washington during the consideration of critical measures, fills its own papers with arguments, and provides handouts for the press. The Federation buys radio time and provides platform speakers to present labor's side of the case on important issues. This work is duplicated at the level of the state and municipal legislative bodies by state and local councils or branches of the AFL–CIO.

Labor leaders call on the President of the United States, governors, and mayors, to support their program, and through Federal and state departments of labor are often enlisted to help draft bills and write vetoes. The "labor lobby" is an active and powerful force among the organized special interests in America. It is directed primarily from the offices of the AFL–CIO, at 815 Sixteenth Street NW, Washington 6, D.C.

Representation does not stop with lobbying. It has at least two other important techniques: legal action and politics. For more than half a century it has been the job of the top labor organizations to support labor causes in court, wherever they may arise, and to institute test actions to question the constitutionality of legislation inimical to the interests of trade unions. From the time of the Danbury Hatters Case (*Loewe v. Lawlor,* 1908), there has been hardly a term of the Supreme Court without one or more appearances by the Federation's general counsel attacking what labor considered bad laws or defending labor's constitutional rights. Political activity is an even more positive extension of the representation function of the Federation. The AFL–CIO now has a permanent political branch, with a director in charge, a budget ($973,000 in fiscal year 1965), a general staff, an elaborate network of organization on a national basis, and a continuing program of publicity and electioneering. The Committee on Political Education endorses candidates, supports measures, assists in campaigns, and in many respects matches the work of the formal political parties.

THE BIENNIAL CONVENTION.   The oldest regular activity of the Federation is the holding of conventions, formerly annual, now biennial, meeting in the odd-numbered years. These are organized labor's top legislative sessions, comparable to the meetings of the United States Congress. They are matched by state, regional, and local conventions for the same purpose.

On the face of things, little of a tangible nature is accomplished at the convention. Elected delegates from the affiliated national unions and a variety of miscellaneous organizations (state and local federations, city central bodies, trade councils, federal labor unions) meet for a number of days, elect officers, listen to speeches of officers and guest celebrities, argue issues from the floor, adopt policy recommendations, renew acquaintances, and discuss problems informally among themselves. Much of what goes on is cut and dried. The officers are almost invariably re-elected. The policy proposals of the executive council (the main policy committee) are usually adopted with slight protest. The speeches are the usual time-consuming, tiresome orations. It is seldom that a real division of opinion appears, and it often seems that the expense of the meeting could have been saved and the time of the delegates put to better advantage at their regular duties.

The conviction of experienced observers of the labor movement, however, is to the contrary. Just as in the legislative sessions of public bodies, a nucleus of leaders works around the clock to hammer out organized labor's "line" for the coming year. Policy recommendations *are* promptly ratified on the floor as a usual thing, but it is because the members of the council have carefully weighed competing suggestions and worked out compromises acceptable to the great majority of the delegates. The convention is an important sounding board. Its deliberations and the record of its proceedings are studied carefully by labor leaders throughout the country, by management groups, and by public officials. The policies it adopts are likely to be guides to action for labor groups from one end of the country to the other, in bargaining with employers, in support of political candidates and measures, and in promotion and extension of organization.

The convention brings together many leaders of diverse union groups, right wing, left wing, and middle of the road. These men are normally immersed in their own affairs, forced to concentrate on immediate issues of concern principally to them and their unions. In the convention they find that their own problems are in some cases common to all, in some cases exceptional and limited to their own trade or industry. They find how others have met and solved problems, what the trends are in organization, bargaining, and legislation in other parts of the country, and what developments constitute threats or cause for gratification. And they find out in a way which would be impossible through reliance upon correspondence or printed reports. Organized labor has its trade secrets, like commercial and business operations, which are not ventilated in print. In the privacy of conversation, however, ideas are exchanged freely, and often agreement is reached on issues which would create powerful dissension in an open forum or in printed form. The convention is a great leveler and unifier. It was rightly regarded by Gompers and his associates as indispensable to an effective labor movement.

The convention also brings to the surface leadership and potential leadership. The essence of leadership in union affairs, as in other forms of activity, is the ability to influence others in face-to-face negotiations, to contribute new ideas which catch the imagination of associates, and to show the conviction and drive necessary to carry through programs. These qualities are demonstrated in group activities, of which the annual convention is an important example and the only one on a national and at the same time a multiunion basis. Election to an important position in the Federation is a high honor for the man and his union, a testimonial to his standing among his colleagues. It may lead to national recognition and is almost certain to strengthen the recipient within his own union.

FEDERATION FINANCES.   The Federation, like the national unions, is financed mainly by a per capita tax, levied on the affiliated member unions according to the membership they claim as a voting base in the convention. The per capita tax is a monthly charge of 7 cents per head. Thus, with a "paid" membership [28] of approximately 11 million in 1965, the AFL–CIO received $10,825,483 from this source. On the other hand, the directly affiliated local unions of the Federation pay $1.50 per month ($18 per year) per member instead of 7 cents. With about 49,700 such members in 1965, the additional dues revenue was $812,371. There are other sources of revenue too: a split of initiation fees charged by its directly affiliated locals; assessments both of the latter and of the general membership; income from distribution of the weekly newspaper, the AFL–CIO News; and income from rental property and investments. The total for 1965 was $11,963,546.[29]

As is obvious, income from the 7-cent tax on the general membership is the main source of revenue. A union like the United Brotherhood of Carpenters and Joiners of America, reporting 700,000 members, pays $588,000 for the privilege of affiliation. The bill for the Auto Workers and the Steelworkers, reporting 1,150,000 and 876,000 members respectively, was $965,735 and $750,508. The expulsion of the Teamsters—with a membership in excess of 1,500,000—means a loss of more than $1,250,000 a year in dues revenue.

It should be noted that the total income of the AFL–CIO is considerably below that of its more important member unions individually. (This is one reason, among others, for the prominence of the national and international unions in the world of organized labor.) Nonetheless, a gross nontaxable income of $10 million to $12 million a year is a fair-sized sum. It will support a wide variety of activities. These include, for 1965: headquarters administrative expenses of $966,389; promotion of membership drives into unorganized territory—$152,457; public relations, carried on by means of speakers, radio and television programs, recordings, film and projectors, etc.—$984,448; publications—the AFL–CIO News, the American Federationist, pamphlets, and reprints—$607,411; research—$220,303; legislative activity, or lobbying—$282,453; international affairs—the International Confederation of Free Trade Unions, the Inter-American Regional Organization, etc.—$818,941; political activity—

[28] The "paid" membership may differ from the actual membership, as some unions report less than their full strength in order to lessen the tax bill.

[29] Proceedings, vol. II, pp. 11, 16.

the Committee on Political Education—$973,194; civil rights—$125,008; and so on.

ORGANIZATION.   The organizing work of the AFL–CIO is carried on in conjunction with drives by the individual member nationals or internationals, or, in spots where the latter are inhibited by jurisdictional rules or restricted for some other reason, the Federation goes it alone. The Federation can openly approach any unorganized group in the name of an existing union or in the name of no national union but with affiliation direct to the AFL–CIO itself. If there are not enough recruits to support a local chapter of an existing national union, the new members are put in a directly affiliated local of the AFL–CIO. When the group becomes large enough it is then assigned to the union with appropriate jurisdiction.

RESEARCH AND PUBLICITY.   The AFL–CIO has many small unions as members, far more in fact than the large and powerful ones most frequently mentioned here and elsewhere. A tiny labor organization like The Granite Cutters' International Association of America, with 1,200 members in 12 locals, or even a "small" one like the United Hatters, Cap and Millinery Workers International Union, with 32,000 members in about 90 locals, is not in a position to support a research staff or carry on extensive publicity, any more than it is in a good position to employ lobbyists or finance a fight with employers. The services of the Federation are far more vital to its small- and medium-sized unions than to the huge organizations with hundreds of thousands of members and revenues exceeding those of the Federation itself. It carries the brunt of the battle for them, in the form of general and special services that they cannot afford on their own.

And, however matter-of-factly the struggle between management and labor is described by businessmen and union leaders, it is at bottom a contest of ideas. The side which neglects its arguments, its public relations, its diplomatic connections, or its facts is very likely to come out second best, whether the issue be a grievance, a bargaining conference, a strike, or the passage of legislation. Hence, there has been a steady growth of emphasis on research and publicity by the Federation and the big unions. This emphasis has taken the form of employment of complete staffs of technical specialists: economists, statisticians, public relations specialists, and lawyers; demands for extension of labor education; the assignment of union men to university training programs in labor economics; the development of programs of "worker education" by both the Federation and individual unions; the support of Federation and union journals and newspapers; and a multitude of publicity activities both inside and outside the membership to influence attitudes on the labor question.

READINGS

It is often useful at this point for the student to spend some time with official documents: union constitutions and convention proceedings. At least, he should examine the latest *Proceedings of the AFL–CIO: Constitutional Convention,* vol. I, "Daily Proceedings," and vol. II, "Executive Council Reports." A good written exercise is to summarize a union constitution in a short (10-page) essay. Do this, for example, with the *Constitution of the International Union, United Automobile, Aircraft and Agricultural Implement Workers of America (AFL–CIO)* or with the *Book of Laws of the International Typographical Union* or with other similar charters.

General books on the subject of union operations are Jack Barbash, *The Practice of Unionism* (New York: Harper & Row, Publishers, Incorporated, 1956); Philip Taft, *The Structure and Government of Labor Unions* (Cambridge, Mass.: Harvard University Press, 1954); Florence Peterson, *American Labor Unions,* 2d rev. ed. (New York: Harper & Row, Publishers, Incorporated, 1963); Lloyd Ulman, *The Rise of the National Union* (Cambridge: Harvard University Press, 1956).

APPENDIX

To chapter eleven

THE LANDRUM–GRIFFIN ACT

The Labor-Management Reporting and Disclosure Act of 1959 [1] was the direct outcome of the investigations of the Senate Select Committee on Improper Activities in the Labor or Management Field (the "McClellan committee"), and its main outlines followed closely the legislative recommendations of that committee in its report of Mar. 28, 1958. [2] Since the committee spent a majority of its time scrutinizing the affairs of the Teamsters union and especially its then president, James R. Hoffa, [3] and its former president, Dave Beck, the act reflects to a considerable degree the practices of Teamster officials which Congress deemed improper.

The statute is a broad and inclusive regulative measure, designed to (1) guarantee the "citizenship" rights of union members, (2) require fiscal responsibility of union officials and representatives, and (3) force the full disclosure by unions, employers, and "labor relations consultants" of any kind of action which might prejudice the rights of employes to organize and bargain collectively. The act is full of teeth, with numerous specified criminal penalties for infringement or violation.

In this appendix, the full text of the law is given verbatim, with the exception of Title VII and one or two other portions, which are amendments of the Taft-Hartley Act and have been included in that law in the Appendix to Chap. 9. Along with the text is a limited commentary, to assist the reader who is not familiar with legal language.

An Act

To provide for the reporting and disclosure of certain financial transactions and administrative practices of

The short title of the law has been settled by

[1] 73 Stat. 519 (Public Law 86-257, September 14, 1959).
[2] See *Monthly Labor Review*, May, 1958, p. 518.
[3] The committee's report on Hoffa is summarized in the *Monthly Labor Review* September, 1959, p. 981.

labor organizations and employers, to prevent abuses in the administration of trusteeships by labor organizations, to provide standards with respect to the election of officers of labor organizations, and for other purposes.

Be it enacted by the Senate and House of Representatives of the United States of America in Congress assembled,

Short title

SECTION 1.   This Act may be cited as the "Labor-Management Reporting and Disclosure Act of 1959."

Declaration of findings, purposes, and policy

SEC. 2.   (a)   The Congress finds that, in the public interest, it continues to be the responsibility of the Federal Government to protect employees' rights to organize, choose their own representatives, bargain collectively, and otherwise engage in concerted activities for their mutual aid or protection; that the relations between employers and labor organizations and the millions of workers they represent have a substantial impact on the commerce of the Nation; and that in order to accomplish the objective of a free flow of commerce it is essential that labor organizations, employers, and their officials adhere to the highest standards of responsibility and ethical conduct in administering the affairs of their organizations, particularly as they affect labor-management relations.

(b)   The Congress further finds, from recent investigations in the labor and management fields, that there have been a number of instances of breach of trust, corruption, disregard of the rights of individual employees, and other failures to observe high standards of responsibility and ethical conduct which require further and supplementary legislation that will afford necessary protection of the rights and interests of employees and the public generally as they relate to the activities of labor organizations, employers, labor relations consultants, and their officers and representatives.

(c)   The Congress, therefore, further finds and declares that the enactment of this Act is necessary

---

public usage, as the "Landrum-Griffin Act." This is in line with the past practice of identifying Federal labor laws by the names of their authors: Wagner, Taft-Hartley, etc.

(*b*) These are the McClellan committee investigations, referred to previously in several places.

to eliminate or prevent improper practices on the part of labor organizations, employers, labor relations consultants, and their officers and representatives which distort and defeat the policies of the Labor Management Relations Act, 1947, as amended, and the Railway Labor Act, as amended, and have the tendency or necessary effect of burdening or obstructing commerce by (1) impairing the efficiency, safety, or operation of the instrumentalities of commerce; (2) occurring in the current of commerce; (3) materially affecting, restraining, or controlling the flow of raw materials or manufactured or processed goods into or from the channels of commerce, or the prices of such materials or goods in commerce; or (4) causing diminution of employment and wages in such volume as substantially to impair or disrupt the market for goods flowing into or from the channels of commerce.

Definitions

SEC. 3.   For the purposes of titles I, II, III, IV, V (except section 505), and VI of this Act—

(a) "Commerce" means trade, traffic, commerce, transportation, transmission, or communication among the several States or between any State and any place outside thereof.

(b) "State" includes any State of the United States, the District of Columbia, Puerto Rico, the Virgin Islands, American Samoa, Guam, Wake Island, the Canal Zone, and Outer Continental Shelf lands defined in the Outer Continental Shelf Lands Act (43 U.S.C. 1331–1343).

(c) "Industry affecting commerce" means any activity, business, or industry in commerce or in which a labor dispute would hinder or obstruct commerce or the free flow of commerce and includes any activity or industry "affecting commerce" within the meaning of the Labor Management Relations Act, 1947, as amended, or the Railway Labor Act, as amended.

(d) "Person" includes one or more individuals, labor organizations, partnerships, associations, corporations, legal representatives, mutual companies, joint-stock companies, trusts, unincorporated organizations, trustees, trustees in bankruptcy, or receivers.

(e) "Employer" means any employer or any

Note that the definitions in Sec. 3 affect only Titles I, II, III, IV, V (except Sec. 505), and VI of the act. Section 505 and Title VII are the amendments of the Taft-Hartley Act. The two laws have different purposes: in general, the Taft-Hartley law is to regulate labor-management relations, and the Reporting and Disclosure Act is to regulate internal union affairs. Thus, words in customary use in industrial relations may have different meanings in the two statutes.

group or association of employers engaged in an industry affecting commerce (1) which is, with respect to employees engaged in an industry affecting commerce, an employer within the meaning of any law of the United States relating to the employment of any employees or (2) which may deal with any labor organization concerning grievances, labor disputes, wages, rates of pay, hours of employment, or conditions of work, and includes any person acting directly or indirectly as an employer or as an agent of an employer in relation to an employee but does not include the United States or any corporation wholly owned by the Government of the United States or any State or political subdivision thereof.

(f) "Employee" means any individual employed by an employer, and includes any individual whose work has ceased as a consequence of, or in connection with, any current labor dispute or because of any unfair labor practice or because of exclusion or expulsion from a labor organization in any manner or for any reason inconsistent with the requirements of this Act.

(g) "Labor dispute" includes any controversy concerning terms, tenure, or conditions of employment, or concerning the association or representation of persons in negotiating, fixing, maintaining, changing, or seeking to arrange terms or conditions of employment, regardless of whether the disputants stand in the proximate relation of employer and employee.

(h) "Trusteeship" means any receivership, trusteeship, or other method of supervision or control whereby a labor organization suspends the autonomy otherwise available to a subordinate body under its constitution or bylaws.

(i) "Labor organization" means a labor organization engaged in an industry affecting commerce and includes any organization of any kind, any agency, or employee representation committee, group, association, or plan so engaged in which employees participate and which exists for the purpose, in whole or in part, of dealing with employers concerning grievances, labor disputes, wages, rates of pay, hours, or other terms or conditions of employment, and any conference, general committee, joint or system board, or joint council so engaged which is subordinate to a national or international labor organization, other than a State or local central body.

For example, in Paragraph (i) compare this definition of "labor organization" with that in the Taft-Hartley Act; or in (j) check this against No. 7 (Sec. 2) of the Taft-Hartley Act, on the meaning of "affecting commerce."

(j)   A labor organization shall be deemed to be engaged in an industry affecting commerce if it—

(1)   is the certified representative of employees under the provisions of the National Labor Relations Act, as amended, or the Railway Labor Act, as amended; or

(2)   although not certified, is a national or international labor organization or a local labor organization recognized or acting as the representative of employees of an employer or employers engaged in an industry affecting commerce; or

(3)   has chartered a local labor organization or subsidiary body which is representing or actively seeking to represent employees of employers within the meaning of paragraph (1) or (2); or

(4)   has been chartered by a labor organization representing or actively seeking to represent employees within the meaning of paragraph (1) or (2) as the local or subordinate body through which such employees may enjoy membership or become affiliated with such labor organization; or

(5)   is a conference, general committee, joint or system board, or joint council, subordinate to a national or international labor organization, which includes a labor organization engaged in an industry affecting commerce within the meaning of any of the preceding paragraphs of this subsection, other than a State or local central body.

(k)   "Secret ballot" means the expression by ballot, voting machine, or otherwise, but in no event by proxy, of a choice with respect to any election or vote taken upon any matter, which is cast in such a manner that the person expressing such choice cannot be identified with the choice expressed.

(l)   "Trust in which a labor organization is interested" means a trust or other fund or organization (1) which was created or established by a labor organization, or one or more of the trustees or one or more members of the governing body of which is selected or appointed by a labor organization, and (2) a primary purpose of which is to provide benefits for the members of such labor organization or their beneficiaries.

(m)   "Labor relations consultant" means any person who, for compensation, advises or represents

(m) The addition of "labor relations consultant"

an employer, employer organization, or labor organization concerning employee organizing, concerted activities, or collective bargaining activities.

(n) "Officer" means any constitutional officer, any person authorized to perform the functions of president, vice president, secretary, treasurer, or other executive functions of a labor organization, and any member of its executive board or similar governing body.

(o) "Member" or "member in good standing," when used in reference to a labor organization, includes any person who has fulfilled the requirements for membership in such organization, and who neither has voluntarily withdrawn from membership nor has been expelled or suspended from membership after appropriate proceedings consistent with lawful provisions of the constitution and bylaws of such organization.

(p) "Secretary" means the Secretary of Labor.

(q) "Officer, agent, shop steward, or other representative," when used with respect to a labor organization, includes elected officials and key administrative personnel, whether elected or appointed (such as business agents, heads of departments or major units, and organizers who exercise substantial independent authority), but does not include salaried nonsupervisory professional staff, stenographic, and service personnel.

(r) "District court of the United States" means a United States district court and a United States court of any place subject to the jurisdiction of the United States.

Title I—Bill of Rights of Members of Labor Organizations

Bill of Rights

SEC. 101.   (a)   (1) EQUAL RIGHTS.—Every member of a labor organization shall have equal rights and privileges within such organization to nominate candidates, to vote in elections or referendums of the labor organization, to attend membership meetings, and to participate in the deliberations and voting upon the business of such meetings, subject to reasonable rules and regulations in such organization's constitution and bylaws.

(2) FREEDOM OF SPEECH AND ASSEMBLY.— Every member of any labor organization shall have

to those regulated by the Labor Reform Act may be regarded as either rounding out the trilogy or continuing the tradition of adding another party in each piece of major labor legislation, to wit: Wagner Act (employers), Taft-Hartley (unions), and Landrum-Griffin (third parties).

Summarized, the "Bill of Rights" means that a union member has the right to (1) nominate candidates; (2) vote in elections; (3) attend and take part in membership meetings; (4) vote on increases in dues, initiation fees, or assessments; (5) sue or testify against the union or any of its officers;

the right to meet and assemble freely with other members; and to express any views, arguments, or opinions; and to express at meetings of the labor organization his views, upon candidates in an election of the labor organization or upon any business properly before the meeting, subject to the organization's established and reasonable rules pertaining to the conduct of meetings: *Provided*, That nothing herein shall be construed to impair the right of a labor organization to adopt and enforce reasonable rules as to the responsibility of every member toward the organization as an institution and to his refraining from conduct that would interfere with its performance of its legal or contractual obligations.

(3)   DUES, INITIATION FEES, AND ASSESSMENTS. —Except in the case of a federation of national or international labor organizations, the rates of dues and initiation fees payable by members of any labor organization in effect on the date of enactment of this Act shall not be increased, and no general or special assessment shall be levied upon such members, except—

(A)   in the case of a local labor organization, (i) by majority vote by secret ballot of the members in good standing voting at a general or special membership meeting, after reasonable notice of the intention to vote upon such question, or (ii) by majority vote of the members in good standing voting in a membership referendum conducted by secret ballot; or

(B)   in the case of a labor organization, other than a local labor organization or a federation of national or international labor organizations, (i) by majority vote of the delegates voting at a regular convention, or at a special convention of such labor organization held upon not less than thirty days' written notice to the principal office of each local or constituent labor organization entitled to such notice, or (ii) by majority vote of the members in good standing of such labor organization voting in a membership referendum conducted by secret ballot, or (iii) by majority vote of the members of the executive board or similar governing body of such labor organization, pursuant to express authority contained in the constitution and bylaws of such labor organization: *Provided*, That such action on the part of the executive board or similar

(6) *not* be disciplined in any way or for any reason except nonpayment of dues, without (a) written charges, (b) time to prepare a defense, and (c) a full and fair hearing; (7) receive a copy of any labor agreement affecting him; (8) be told about this law by the union; and (9) sue the union for appropriate relief (including an injunction) if any of the above rights are violated.

governing body shall be effective only until the next regular convention of such labor organization.

(4) PROTECTION OF THE RIGHT TO SUE.—No labor organization shall limit the right of any member thereof to institute an action in any court, or in a proceeding before any administrative agency, irrespective of whether or not the labor organization or its officers are named as defendants or respondents in such action or proceeding, or the right of any member of a labor organization to appear as a witness in any judicial, administrative, or legislative proceeding, or to petition any legislature or to communicate with any legislator: *Provided,* That any such member may be required to exhaust reasonable hearing procedures (but not to exceed a four-month lapse of time) within such organization, before instituting legal or administrative proceedings against such organizations or any officer thereof: *And provided further,* That no interested employer or employer association shall directly or indirectly finance, encourage, or participate in, except as a party, any such action, proceeding, appearance, or petition.

(5) SAFEGUARDS AGAINST IMPROPER DISCIPLINARY ACTION.—No member of any labor organization may be fined, suspended, expelled, or otherwise disciplined except for nonpayment of dues by such organization or by any officer thereof unless such member has been (A) served with written specific charges; (B) given a reasonable time to prepare his defense; (C) afforded a full and fair hearing.

(b) Any provision of the constitution and bylaws of any labor organization which is inconsistent with the provisions of this section shall be of no force or effect.

Civil enforcement

SEC. 102.   Any person whose rights secured by the provisions of this title have been infringed by any violation of this title may bring a civil action in a district court of the United States for such relief (including injunctions) as may be appropriate. Any such action against a labor organization shall be brought in the district court of the United States for the district where the alleged violation occurred, or where the principal office of such labor organization is located.

Retention of existing rights

Sec. 103.   Nothing contained in this title shall limit the rights and remedies of any member of a labor organization under any State or Federal law or before any court or other tribunal, or under the constitution and bylaws of any labor organization.

Right to copies of collective bargaining agreements

Sec. 104.   It shall be the duty of the secretary or corresponding principal officer of each labor organization, in the case of a local labor organization, to forward a copy of each collective bargaining agreement made by such labor organization with any employer to any employee who requests such a copy and whose rights as such employee are directly affected by such agreement, and in the case of a labor organization other than a local labor organization, to forward a copy of any such agreement to each constituent unit which has members directly affected by such agreement; and such officers shall maintain at the principal office of the labor organization of which he is an officer copies of any such agreement made or received by such labor organization, which copies shall be available for inspection by any member or by any employee whose rights are affected by such agreement. The provisions of section 210 shall be applicable in the enforcement of this section.

Information as to act

Sec. 105.   Every labor organization shall inform its members concerning the provisions of this Act.

Title II—Reporting by Labor Organizations, Officers and Employees of Labor Organizations, and Employers

Report of labor organizations

Sec. 201.   (a) Every labor organization shall adopt a constitution and bylaws and shall file a copy thereof with the Secretary, together with a report, signed by its president and secretary or corresponding principal officers, containing the following information—

Title II is a substitute for (and a tremendous expansion of) the optional reporting requirements of the Taft-Hartley Act. However, where the latter could be (and were, in some

(1) the name of the labor organization, its mailing address, and any other address at which it maintains its principal office or at which it keeps the records referred to in this title;

(2) the name and title of each of its officers;

(3) the initiation fee or fees required from a new or transferred member and fees for work permits required by the reporting labor organization;

(4) the regular dues or fees or other periodic payments required to remain a member of the reporting labor organization; and

(5) detailed statements, or references to specific provisions of documents filed under this subsection which contain such statements, showing the provision made and procedures followed with respect to each of the following: (A) qualifications for or restrictions on membership, (B) levying of assessments, (C) participation in insurance or other benefit plans, (D) authorization for disbursement of funds of the labor organization, (E) audit of financial transactions of the labor organization, (F) the calling of regular and special meetings, (G) the selection of officers and stewards and of any representatives to other bodies composed of labor organizations' representatives, with a specific statement of the manner in which each officer was elected, appointed, or otherwise selected, (H) discipline or removal of officers or agents for breaches of their trust, (I) imposition of fines, suspensions, and expulsions of members, including the grounds for such action and any provision made for notice, hearing, judgment on the evidence, and appeal procedures, (J) authorization for bargaining demands, (K) ratification of contract terms, (L) authorization for strikes, and (M) issuance of work permits. Any change in the information required by this subsection shall be reported to the Secretary at the time the reporting labor organization files with the Secretary the annual financial report required by subsection (b).

(b) Every labor organization shall file annually with the Secretary a financial report signed by its president and treasurer or corresponding principal officers containing the following information in such detail as may be necessary accurately to disclose its

instances) sidestepped if the union elected to do without the services of the NLRB, the requirements of Title II are obligatory on all labor organizations in interstate commerce and *in addition*, where the circumstances require them, are obligatory on union officers and staff members, on employers, and on certain independent contracting third parties [see Sec. 203 (*b*)] or "labor relations consultants" of employers.

financial condition and operations for its preceding
fiscal year—

(1) assets and liabilities at the beginning and end
of the fiscal year;

(2) receipts of any kind and the sources thereof;

(3) salary, allowances, and other direct or indirect
disbursements (including reimbursed expenses)
to each officer and also to each employee who,
during such fiscal year, received more than
$10,000 in the aggregate from such labor organ-
ization and any other labor organization affiliated with it or with which it is affiliated, or
which is affiliated with the same national or international labor organization;

(4) direct and indirect loans made to any officer,
employee, or member, which aggregated more
than $250 during the fiscal year, together with
a statement of the purpose, security, if any, and
arrangements for repayment;

(5) direct and indirect loans to any business enterprise, together with a statement of the purpose,
security, if any, and arrangements for repayment; and

(6) other disbursements made by it including the
purposes thereof;

all in such categories as the Secretary may prescribe.

(c) Every labor organization required to submit a report under this title shall make available the
information required to be contained in such report
to all of its members, and every such labor organization and its officers shall be under a duty enforceable
at the suit of any member of such organization in any
State court of competent jurisdiction or in the district
court of the United States for the district in which
such labor organization maintains its principal office,
to permit such member for just cause to examine any
books, records, and accounts necessary to verify such
report. The court in such action may, in its discretion,
in addition to any judgment awarded to the plaintiff
or plaintiffs, allow a reasonable attorney's fee to be
paid by the defendant, and costs of the action.

(d) Subsections (f), (g), and (h) of section 9
of the National Labor Relations Act, as amended, are
hereby repealed.

(e) Clause (i) of section 8(a) (3) of the National Labor Relations Act, as amended, is amended
by striking out the following: "and has at the time
the agreement was made or within the preceding

(c) Read this paragraph
with care. What would be
"just cause" for a union
member to ask to examine
the books, records, and
accounts of the union?
Does this sound like an
invitation to sue?

Secs. 9(f), (g) of the
NLRA were the reporting
requirements of the Taft-
Hartley Act, made obsolete
by Sec. 201 of this law. Sec.
9(h) was the non-Communist-
affidavit requirement.

twelve months received from the Board a notice of compliance with sections 9 (f), (g), (h)."

Report of officers and emloyees of labor organizations

SEC. 202.   (a)   Every officer of a labor organization and every employee of a labor organization (other than an employee performing exclusively clerical or custodial services) shall file with the Secretary a signed report listing and describing for his preceding fiscal year—

(1) any stock, bond, security, or other interest, legal or equitable, which he or his spouse or minor child directly or indirectly held in, and any income or any other benefit with monetary value (including reimbursed expenses) which he or his spouse or minor child derived directly or indirectly from, an employer whose employees such labor organization represents or is actively seeking to represent, except payments and other benefits received as a bona fide employee of such employer;

(2) any transaction in which he or his spouse or minor child engaged, directly or indirectly, involving any stock, bond, security, or loan to or from, or other legal or equitable interest in the business of an employer whose employees such labor organization represents or is actively seeking to represent;

(3) any stock, bond, security, or other interest, legal or equitable, which he or his spouse or minor child directly or indirectly held in, and any income or any other benefit with monetary value (including reimbursed expenses) which he or his spouse or minor child directly or indirectly derived from, any business a substantial part of which consists of buying from, selling or leasing to, or otherwise dealing with, the business of an employer whose employees such labor organization represents or is actively seeking to represent;

(4) any stock, bond, security, or other interest, legal or equitable, which he or his spouse or minor child directly or indirectly held in, and any income or any other benefit with monetary value (including reimbursed expenses) which he or his spouse or minor child directly or indirectly derived from, a business any part of which con-

Sec. 202. Divested of its laborious wording, what this section tried to accomplish is the disclosure of any form of payment or benefit which might have suspicious implications (say, as a bribe) from an employer or a labor relations consultant to a union representative. The general idea was to reveal any conflicts of interests on the part of union representatives or employes.

sists of buying from, or selling or leasing directly or indirectly to, or otherwise dealing with such labor organization;

(5) any direct or indirect business transaction or arrangement between him or his spouse or minor child and any employer whose employees his organization represents or is actively seeking to represent, except work performed and payments and benefits received as a bona fide employee of such employer and except purchases and sales of goods or services in the regular course of business at prices generally available to any employee of such employer; and

(6) any payment of money or other thing of value (including reimbursed expenses) which he or his spouse or minor child received directly or indirectly from any employer or any person who acts as a labor relations consultant to an employer, except payments of the kinds referred to in section 302(c) of the Labor Management Relations Act, 1947, as amended.

(b) The provisions of paragraphs (1), (2), (3), (4), and (5) of subsection (a) shall not be construed to require any such officer or employee to report his bona fide investments in securities traded on a securities exchange registered as a national securities exchange under the Securities Exchange Act of 1934, in shares in an investment company registered under the Investment Company Act of 1940, or in securities of a public utility holding company registered under the Public Utility Holding Company Act of 1935, or to report any income derived therefrom.

(c) Nothing contained in this section shall be construed to require any officer or employee of a labor organization to file a report under subsection (a) unless he or his spouse or minor child holds or has held an interest, has received income or any other benefit with monetary value or a loan, or has engaged in a transaction described therein.

Report of employers

SEC. 203.   (a)   Every employer who in any fiscal year made—

(1) any payment or loan, direct or indirect, of money or other thing of value (including reimbursed expenses), or any promise or agreement there-

Sec. 203 clarifies the preceding section somewhat, by indicating the possible purpose of the payments or benefits, as "persuasion,"

for, to any labor organization or officer, agent, shop steward, or other representative of a labor organization, or employee of any labor organization, except (A) payments or loans made by any national or State bank, credit union, insurance company, savings and loan association or other credit institution and (B) payments of the kind referred to in section 302(c) of the Labor Management Relations Act, 1947, as amended;

(2) any payment (including reimbursed expenses) to any of his employees, or any group or committee of such employees, for the purpose of causing such employee or group or committee of employees to persuade other employees to exercise or not to exercise, or as to the manner of exercising, the right to organize and bargain collectively through representatives of their own choosing unless such payments were contemporaneously or previously disclosed to such other employees;

(3) any expenditure, during the fiscal year, where an object thereof, directly or indirectly, is to interfere with, restrain, or coerce employees in the exercise of the right to organize and bargain collectively through representatives of their own choosing, or is to obtain information concerning the activities of employees or a labor organization in connection with a labor dispute involving such employer, except for use solely in conjunction with an administrative or arbitral proceeding or a criminal or civil judicial proceeding;

(4) any agreement or arrangement with a labor relations consultant or other independent contractor or organization pursuant to which such person undertakes activities where an object thereof, directly or indirectly, is to persuade employees to exercise or not to exercise, or persuade employees as to the manner of exercising, the right to organize and bargain collectively through representatives of their own choosing, or undertakes to supply such employer with information concerning the activities of employees or a labor organization in connection with a labor dispute involving such employer, except information for use solely in conjunction with an administrative or arbitral proceeding or a criminal or civil judicial proceeding; or

"interference," "restraint," or "coercion" of employes in the exercise of their rights to organize and bargain collectively.

This section ties up the disclosure obligation pretty tightly by making it incumbent on employers and labor relations consultants as well as on union representatives. Thus, if the law is complied with, any such agreement or payment would be reported by at least two and possibly three parties to the arrangement.

(5) any payment (including reimbursed expenses) pursuant to an agreement or arrangement described in subdivision (4);

shall file with the Secretary a report, in a form prescribed by him, signed by its president and treasurer or corresponding principal officers showing in detail the date and amount of each such payment, loan, promise, agreement, or arrangement and the name, address, and position, if any, in any firm or labor organization of the person to whom it was made and a full explanation of the circumstances of all such payments, including the terms of any agreement or understanding pursuant to which they were made.

(b) Every person who pursuant to any agreement or arrangement with an employer undertakes activities where an object thereof is, directly or indirectly—

This is the labor relations consultant section.

(1) to persuade employees to exercise or not to exercise, or persuade employees as to the manner of exercising, the right to organize and bargain collectively through representatives of their own choosing; or

(2) to supply an employer with information concerning the activities of employees or a labor organization in connection with a labor dispute involving such employer, except information for use solely in conjunction with an administrative or arbitral proceeding or a criminal or civil judicial proceeding;

Sec. 203(b)(2) and (c). This is an interesting problem in distinguishing between information about improper, or at least suspicious, activities and bona fide information service which is protected and may be kept confidential. The purpose of the act of course is to get the improper information gathering reported but to let the rest pass. See also (d) to (g).

shall file within thirty days after entering into such agreement or arrangement a report with the Secretary, signed by its president and treasurer or corresponding principal officers, containing the name under which such person is engaged in doing business and the address of its principal office, and a detailed statement of the terms and conditions of such agreement or arrangement. Every such person shall file annually, with respect to each fiscal year during which payments were made as a result of such an agreement or arrangement, a report with the Secretary, signed by its president and treasurer or corresponding principal officers, containing a statement (A) of its receipts of any kind from employers on account of labor relations advice or services, designating the sources thereof, and (B) of its disbursements of any kind, in connection with such services and the purposes thereof. In each such case information shall be set forth in such categories as the Secretary may prescribe.

(c)   Nothing in this section shall be construed to require any employer or other person to file a report covering the services of such person by reason of his giving or agreeing to give advice to such employer or representing or agreeing to represent such employer before any court, administrative agency, or tribunal of arbitration or engaging or agreeing to engage in collective bargaining on behalf of such employer with respect to wages, hours, or other terms or conditions of employment or the negotiation of an agreement or any question arising thereunder.

(d)   Nothing contained in this section shall be construed to require an employer to file a report under subsection (a) unless he has made an expenditure, payment, loan, agreement, or arrangement of the kind described therein. Nothing contained in this section shall be construed to require any other person to file a report under subsection (b) unless he was party to an agreement or arrangement of the kind described therein.

(e)   Nothing contained in this section shall be construed to require any regular officer, supervisor, or employee of an employer to file a report in connection with services rendered to such employer nor shall any employer be required to file a report covering expenditures made to any regular officer, supervisor, or employee of an employer as compensation for service as a regular officer, supervisor, or employee of such employer.

(f)   Nothing contained in this section shall be construed as an amendment to, or modification of the rights protected by, section 8(c) of the National Labor Relations Act, as amended.

(g)   The term "interfere with, restrain, or coerce" as used in this section means interference, restraint, and coercion which, if done with respect to the exercise of rights guaranteed in section 7 of the National Labor Relations Act, as amended, would, under section 8(a) of such Act, constitute an unfair labor practice.

Attorney-Client communications exempted

Sec. 204.   Nothing contained in this Act shall be construed to require an attorney who is a member in good standing of the bar of any State, to include in any report required to be filed pursuant to the provisions of this Act any information which was

Sec. 204. A majority of congressmen, both House and Senate, are attorneys, some no longer active and some still practicing. No

lawfully communicated to such attorney by any of his clients in the course of a legitimate attorney-client relationship.

Reports made public information

SEC. 205.   (a)   The contents of the reports and documents filed with the Secretary pursuant to sections 201, 202, and 203 shall be public information, and the Secretary may publish any information and data which he obtains pursuant to the provisions of this title. The Secretary may use the information and data for statistical and research purposes, and compile and publish such studies, analyses, reports, and surveys based thereon as he may deem appropriate.

(b)   The Secretary shall by regulation make reasonable provision for the inspection and examination, on the request of any person, of the information and data contained in any report or other document filed with him pursuant to section 201, 202, or 203.

(c)   The Secretary shall by regulation provide for the furnishing by the Department of Labor of copies of reports or other documents filed with the Secretary pursuant to this title, upon payment of a charge based upon the cost of the service. The Secretary shall make available without payment of a charge, or require any person to furnish, to such State agency as is designated by law or by the Governor of the State in which such person has his principal place of business or headquarters, upon request of the Governor of such State, copies of any reports and documents filed by such person with the Secretary pursuant to section 201, 202, or 203, or of information and data contained therein. No person shall be required by reason of any law of any State to furnish to any officer or agency of such State any information included in a report filed by such person with the Secretary pursuant to the provisions of this title, if a copy of such report, or of the portion thereof containing such information, is furnished to such officer or agency. All moneys received in payment of such charges fixed by the Secretary pursuant to this subsection shall be deposited in the general fund of the Treasury.

Sec. 205. This section means that any of the reports the law calls for —from unions, union representatives, employers, or labor relations consultants—are available to *anybody* and either they may be examined in the files of the Department of Labor [see paragraph (*b*), "on the request of any person"] or a copy will be furnished at cost [paragraph (*c*), first sentence]. This is real "gold-fish bowl" publicity; no private organizations and very few public agencies —certainly not Congress (*e.g.*, expense accounts of members)—are under any such obligation to expose themselves to the idle or interested curiosity of reporters, researchers, labor-contract negotiators, public prosecutors, or other potential critics.

Retention of records

SEC. 206.   Every person required to file any report under this title shall maintain records on the matters required to be reported which will provide in sufficient detail the necessary basic information and data from which the documents filed with the Secretary may be verified, explained or clarified, and checked for accuracy and completeness, and shall include vouchers, worksheets, receipts, and applicable resolutions, and shall keep such records available for examination for a period of not less than five years after the filing of the documents based on the information which they contain.

Sec. 206. This provision, while perhaps necessary, might well have been suggested by the National Association of Filing Case Manufacturers.

Effective date

SEC. 207.   (a)   Each labor organization shall file the initial report required under section 201(a) within ninety days after the date on which it first becomes subject to this Act.

(b)   Each person required to file a report under section 201(b), 202, 203(a), or the second sentence of 203(b) shall file such report within ninety days after the end of each of its fiscal years; except that where such person is subject to section 201(b), 202, 203(a), or the second sentence of 203(b), as the case may be, for only a portion of such a fiscal year (because the date of enactment of this Act occurs during such person's fiscal year or such person becomes subject to this Act during its fiscal year) such person may consider that portion as the entire fiscal year in making such report.

Rules and regulations

SEC. 208.   The Secretary shall have authority to issue, amend, and rescind rules and regulations prescribing the form and publication of reports required to be filed under this title and such other reasonable rules and regulations (including rules prescribing reports concerning trusts in which a labor organization is interested) as he may find necessary to prevent the circumvention or evasion of such reporting requirements. In exercising his power under this section the Secretary shall prescribe by general rule simplified reports for labor organizations or employers for whom he finds that by virtue of their size a detailed report would be unduly burdensome, but the Secretary may revoke such provision for simplified forms of any labor organization or employer if he determines, after such investigation as he deems proper and due notice and opportunity for a hearing, that the purposes of this section would be served thereby.

Criminal provisions

SEC. 209.   (a) Any person who willfully violates this title shall be fined not more than $10,000 or imprisoned for not more than one year, or both.

(b)   Any person who makes a false statement or representation of a material fact, knowing it to be false, or who knowingly fails to disclose a material fact, in any document, report, or other information required under the provisions of this title shall be fined not more than $10,000 or imprisoned for not more than one year, or both.

(c)   Any person who willfully makes a false entry in or willfully conceals, withholds, or destroys any books, records, reports, or statements required to be kept by any provision of this title shall be fined not more than $10,000 or imprisoned for not more than one year, or both.

(d)   Each individual required to sign reports under sections 201 and 203 shall be personally responsible for the filing of such reports and for any statement contained therein which he knows to be false.

Sec. 209. Criminal penalty: a year in jail or $10,000 fine or both, for (a) any form of willful violation; (b) willful false statement or other form of misrepresentation; or (c) willful error, concealment, or destruction of records. (d) The responsibility is personal to the signer. He pays the fine or goes to jail.

Civil enforcement

SEC. 210.   Wherever it shall appear that any person has violated or is about to violate any of the provisions of this title, the Secretary may bring a civil action for such relief (including injunctions) as may be appropriate. Any such action may be brought in the district court of the United States where the violation occurred or, at the option of the parties, in the United States District Court for the District of Columbia.

Sec. 210. If the sheriff doesn't get the violator, then an action for damages or a request for an injunction may be used. These, incidentally, are available before the violation occurs ("or is about to violate any of the provisions . . .").

Title III—Trusteeships

Reports

SEC. 301.   (a) Every labor organization which has or assumes trusteeship over any subordinate labor organization shall file with the Secretary within thirty days after the date of the enactment of this Act or the imposition of any such trusteeship, and semiannually thereafter, a report, signed by its president and treasurer or corresponding principal officers, as well as by the trustees of such subordinate labor organization, containing the following information: (1) the name and address of the subordinate organization; (2) the date of establishing the trusteeship; (3) a detailed statement of the reason or reasons for establishing or continuing the trusteeship; and (4) the nature and extent of participation by the membership of the subordinate organization in the selection of delegates to represent such organization in regular or special conventions or other policy-determining bodies and in the election of officers of the labor organization which has assumed trusteeship over such subordinate organization. The initial report shall also include a full and complete account of the financial condition of such subordinate organization as of the time trusteeship was assumed over it. During the continuance of a trusteeship the labor organization which has assumed trusteeship over a subordinate labor organization shall file on behalf of the subordinate labor organization the annual financial report required by section 201(b) signed by the president and treasurer or corresponding principal officers of the labor organization which has assumed such trusteeship and the trustees of the subordinate labor organization.

(b) The provisions of sections 201(c), 205, 206, 208, and 210 shall be applicable to reports filed under this title.

(c) Any person who willfully violates this section shall be fined not more than $10,000 or imprisoned for not more than one year, or both.

(d) Any person who makes a false statement or representation of a material fact, knowing it to be false, or who knowingly fails to disclose a material fact, in any report required under the provisions of

Title III. The McClellan committee found that trusteeships had been used, in a few instances, to take away the rights of members of local unions, milk the local's treasury, and to further the private purposes of officers of the national union. This title sets up detailed reporting requirements, defines the lawful purposes of trusteeships, protects the citizenship rights of the local union members, and arranges for time limits to the trusteeship and enforcement of the regulations.

Paragraphs (c), (d), (e). Criminal penalties for violations of reporting requirements and personal responsibility.

this section or willfully makes any false entry in or willfully withholds, conceals, or destroys any documents, books, records, reports, or statements upon which such report is based, shall be fined not more than $10,000 or imprisoned for not more than one year, or both.

(e)   Each individual required to sign a report under this section shall be personally responsible for the filing of such report and for any statement contained therein which he knows to be false.

Purposes for which a trusteeship may be established

SEC. 302.   Trusteeships shall be established and administered by a labor organization over a subordinate body only in accordance with the constitution and bylaws of the organization which has assumed trusteeship over the subordinate body and for the purpose of correcting corruption or financial malpractice, assuring the performance of collective bargaining agreements or other duties of a bargaining representative, restoring democratic procedures, or otherwise carrying out the legitimate objects of such labor organization.

Unlawful acts relating to labor organization under trusteeship

SEC. 303.   (a)   During any period when a subordinate body of a labor organization is in trusteeship, it shall be unlawful (1) to count the vote of delegates from such body in any convention or election of officers of the labor organization unless the delegates have been chosen by secret ballot in an election in which all the members in good standing of such subordinate body were eligible to participate, or (2) to transfer to such organization any current receipts or other funds of the subordinate body except the normal per capita tax and assessments payable by subordinate bodies not in trusteeship: *Provided,* That nothing herein contained shall prevent the distribution of the assets of a labor organization in accordance with its constitution and bylaws upon the bona fide dissolution thereof.

(b)   Any person who willfully violates this section shall be fined not more than $10,000 or imprisoned for not more than one year, or both.

Sec. 303. This section protects the voting rights of members and the funds of local unions under trusteeship. Paragraph (*b*) provides for the usual criminal penalty for violation: $10,000 fine/a year in jail, or both.

Enforcement

Sec. 304. (a) Upon the written complaint of any member or subordinate body of a labor organization alleging that such organization has violated the provisions of this title (except section 301) the Secretary shall investigate the complaint and if the Secretary finds probable cause to believe that such violation has occurred and has not been remedied he shall, without disclosing the identity of the complainant, bring a civil action in any district court of the United States having jurisdiction of the labor organization for such relief (including injunctions) as may be appropriate. Any member or subordinate body of a labor organization affected by any violation of this title (except section 301) may bring a civil action in any district court of the United States having jurisdiction of the labor organization for such relief (including injunctions) as may be appropriate.

(b) For the purpose of actions under this section, district courts of the United States shall be deemed to have jurisdiction of a labor organization (1) in the district in which the principal office of such labor organization is located, or (2) in any district in which its duly authorized officers or agents are engaged in conducting the affairs of the trusteeship.

(c) In any proceeding pursuant to this section a trusteeship established by a labor organization in conformity with the procedural requirements of its constitution and bylaws and authorized or ratified after a fair hearing either before the executive board or before such other body as may be provided in accordance with its constitution or bylaws shall be presumed valid for a period of eighteen months from the date of its establishment and shall not be subject to attack during such period except upon clear and convincing proof that the trusteeship was not established or maintained in good faith for a purpose allowable under section 302. After the expiration of eighteen months the trusteeship shall be presumed invalid in any such proceeding and its discontinuance shall be decreed unless the labor organization shall show by clear and convincing proof that the continuation of the trusteeship is necessary for a purpose allowable under section 302. In the latter event the

Section 304 permits anonymous complaints to the Secretary of Labor as a basis for investigation and civil suits for relief of violations, or union members may sue on their own. Paragraph (c) sets the time limits: a trusteeship established on proper grounds is "presumed valid" for 18 months, although it may be overthrown by "clear and convincing proof" of bad faith; after 18 months, the trusteeship is "presumed invalid" and the "clear and convincing proof" must be offered by the national union in order to continue it.

court may dismiss the complaint or retain jurisdiction of the cause on such conditions and for such period as it deems appropriate.

Report to Congress

SEC. 305.   The Secretary shall submit to the Congress at the expiration of three years from the date of enactment of this Act a report upon the operation of this title.

Complaint by Secretary

SEC. 306.   The rights and remedies provided by this title shall be in addition to any and all other rights and remedies at law or in equity: *Provided,* That upon the filing of a complaint by the Secretary the jurisdiction of the district court over such trusteeship shall be exclusive and the final judgment shall be res judicata.

Title IV—Elections

Terms of office; election procedures

SEC. 401.   (a) Every national or international labor organization, except a federation of national or international labor organizations, shall elect its officers not less often than once every five years either by secret ballot among the members in good standing or at a convention of delegates chosen by secret ballot.

(b) Every local labor organization shall elect its officers not less often than once every three years by secret ballot among the members in good standing.

(c) Every national or international labor organization, except a federation of national or international labor organizations, and every local labor organization, and its officers, shall be under a duty, enforceable at the suit of any bona fide candidate for office in such labor organization in the district court of the United States in which such labor organization maintains its principal office, to comply with all reasonable requests of any candidate to distribute by mail or otherwise at the candidate's expense campaign literature in aid of such person's candidacy to all members in good standing of such labor organization and to refrain from discrimina-

Title IV is a detailed set of rules for enforcing democratic procedure in union elections. The main elements consist of minimum time limits for elections (5 years for nationals or internationals, 4 years for intermediate bodies such as joint boards, 3 years for local unions); protection of the rights of opposition (nonadministration) candidates; protection of members' voting rights; prohibition of the partisan use of union funds; removal of local union officers guilty of "serious misconduct"; and a procedure for setting aside invalid elections and superseding them with elections supervised by the Secretary of Labor.

Paragraph (c) of Sec. 401 covers the "equal treatment" of candidates, with respect to the distribution of literature,

tion in favor of or against any candidate with respect to the use of lists of members, and whenever such labor organizations or its officers authorize the distribution by mail or otherwise to members of campaign literature on behalf of any candidate or of the labor organization itself with reference to such election, similar distribution at the request of any other bona fide candidate shall be made by such labor organization and its officers, with equal treatment as to the expense of such distribution. Every bona fide candidate shall have the right, once within 30 days prior to an election of a labor organization in which he is a candidate, to inspect a list containing the names and last known addresses of all members of the labor organization who are subject to a collective bargaining agreement requiring membership therein as a condition of employment, which list shall be maintained and kept at the principal office of such labor organization by a designated official thereof. Adequate safeguards to insure a fair election shall be provided, including the right of any candidate to have an observer at the polls and at the counting of the ballots.

(d) Officers of intermediate bodies, such as general committees, system boards, joint boards, or joint councils, shall be elected not less often than once every four years by secret ballot among the members in good standing or by labor organization officers representative of such members who have been elected by secret ballot.

(e) In any election required by this section which is to be held by secret ballot a reasonable opportunity shall be given for the nomination of candidates and every member in good standing shall be eligible to be a candidate and to hold office (subject to section 504 and to reasonable qualifications uniformly imposed) and shall have the right to vote for or otherwise support the candidate or candidates of his choice, without being subject to penalty, discipline, or improper interference or reprisal of any kind by such organization or any member thereof. Not less than fifteen days prior to the election notice thereof shall be mailed to each member at his last known home address. Each member in good standing shall be entitled to one vote. No member whose dues have been withheld by his employer for payment to such organization pursuant to his voluntary authorization provided for in a collective bargaining agree-

nondiscrimination by the union, the inspection of membership lists, etc.

(e) Fair elections mean equal opportunity to nominate candidates, to run for office, and to vote without being disqualified on technical grounds or "being subject to penalty, discipline, or improper interference or reprisal of any kind" by the union or any union member. It means that the members have adequate (15 days) notice of any election coming up. It also means that any candidate may have his own observer at the polls and the counting of ballots, that election results must be announced for each local

ment shall be declared ineligible to vote or be a candidate for office in such organization by reason of alleged delay or default in the payment of dues. The votes cast by members of each local labor organization shall be counted, and the results published, separately. The election officials designated in the constitution and bylaws or the secretary, if no other official is designated, shall preserve for one year the ballots and all other records pertaining to the election. The election shall be conducted in accordance with the constitution and bylaws of such organization insofar as they are not inconsistent with the provisions of this title.

(f) When officers are chosen by a convention of delegates elected by secret ballot, the convention shall be conducted in accordance with the constitution and bylaws of the labor organization insofar as they are not inconsistent with the provisions of this title. The officials designated in the constitution and bylaws or the secretary, if no other is designated, shall preserve for one year the credentials of the delegates and all minutes and other records of the convention pertaining to the election of officers.

(g) No moneys received by any labor organization by way of dues, assessment, or similar levy, and no moneys of an employer shall be contributed or applied to promote the candidacy of any person in an election subject to the provisions of this title. Such moneys of a labor organization may be utilized for notices, factual statements of issues not involving candidates, and other expenses necessary for the holding of an election.

(h) If the Secretary, upon application of any member of a local labor organization, finds after hearing in accordance with the Administrative Procedure Act that the constitution and bylaws of such labor organization do not provide an adequate procedure for the removal of an elected officer guilty of serious misconduct, such officer may be removed, for cause shown and after notice and hearing, by the members in good standing voting in a secret ballot conducted by the officers of such labor organization in accordance with its constitution and bylaws insofar as they are not inconsistent with the provisions of this title.

(i) The Secretary shall promulgate rules and regulations prescribing minimum standards and procedures for determining the adequacy of the removal

union separately, and that the ballots and records must be saved for 1 year.

procedures to which reference is made in subsection (h).

Enforcement

SEC. 402.   (a)   A member of a labor organization—

(1) who has exhausted the remedies available under the constitution and bylaws of such organization and of any parent body, or

(2) who has invoked such available remedies without obtaining a final decision within three calendar months after their invocation,

may file a complaint with the Secretary within one calendar month thereafter alleging the violation of any provision of section 401 (including violation of the constitution and bylaws of the labor organization pertaining to the election and removal of officers). The challenged election shall be presumed valid pending a final decision thereon (as hereinafter provided) and in the interim the affairs of the organization shall be conducted by the officers elected or in such other manner as its constitution and bylaws may provide.

(b)   The Secretary shall investigate such complaint and, if he finds probable cause to believe that a violation of this title has occurred and has not been remedied, he shall, within sixty days after the filing of such complaint, bring a civil action against the labor organization as an entity in the district court of the United States in which such labor organization maintains its principal office to set aside the invalid election, if any, and to direct the conduct of an election or hearing and vote upon the removal of officers under the supervision of the Secretary and in accordance with the provisions of this title and such rules and regulations as the Secretary may prescribe. The court shall have power to take such action as it deems proper to preserve the assets of the labor organization.

(c)   If, upon a preponderance of the evidence after a trial upon the merits, the court finds—

(1) that an election has not been held within the time prescribed by section 401, or

(2) that the violation of section 401 may have affected the outcome of an election,

the court shall declare the election, if any, to be void and direct the conduct of a new election under super-

Section 402 is the procedure for filing a complaint regarding a union election, its investigation by the Secretary of Labor, and (if the latter finds "probable cause" of a violation), a civil action against the union to have the election set aside. If the court finds for the complainant, the election is declared void and the Secretary is told to conduct another in conformity with the constitution and bylaws of the union (which must be in conformity with this act) and certify the results to the court; whereupon the court will enter a decree naming the officers of the union.

For a succinct account of such an investigation and its outcome, see "Interim Report on the IUE Election," *Monthly Labor Review,* May, 1965, pp. 562–565. The "fair election" requirements of the Act have contributed to a notable turnover of union presidents during the 1960s.

vision of the Secretary and, so far as lawful and practicable, in conformity with the constitution and bylaws of the labor organization. The Secretary shall promptly certify to the court the names of the persons elected, and the court shall thereupon enter a decree declaring such persons to be the officers of the labor organization. If the proceeding is for the removal of officers pursuant to subsection (h) of section 401, the Secretary shall certify the results of the vote and the court shall enter a decree declaring whether such persons have been removed as officers of the labor organization.

(d)   An order directing an election, dismissing a complaint, or designating elected officers of a labor organization shall be appealable in the same manner as the final judgment in a civil action, but an order directing an election shall not be stayed pending appeal.

Application of other laws

SEC. 403.   No labor organization shall be required by law to conduct elections of officers with greater frequency or in a different form or manner than is required by its own constitution or bylaws, except as otherwise provided by this title. Existing rights and remedies to enforce the constitution and bylaws of a labor organization with respect to elections prior to the conduct thereof shall not be affected by the provisions of this title. The remedy provided by this title for challenging an election already conducted shall be exclusive.

Effective date

(Sec. 404 set a maximum time limit of one year for amendment of a union's constitution and bylaws to comply with the requirements of Title IV. The year was up September 14, 1960.)

Title V—Safeguards for Labor Organizations

Fiduciary responsibility of officers of labor organizations

SEC. 501.   (a)   The officers, agents, shop stewards, and other representatives of a labor organization occupy positions of trust in relation to such organization and its members as a group. It is, there-

The safeguards in Title V are primarily financial but include also some character qualifications for

fore, the duty of each such person, taking into account the special problems and functions of a labor organization, to hold its money and property solely for the benefit of the organization and its members and to manage, invest, and expend the same in accordance with its constitution and bylaws and any resolutions of the governing bodies adopted thereunder, to refrain from dealing with such organization as an adverse party or in behalf of an adverse party in any matter connected with his duties and from holding or acquiring any pecuniary or personal interest which conflicts with the interests of such organization, and to account to the organization for any profit received by him in whatever capacity in connection with transactions conducted by him or under his direction on behalf of the organization. A general exculpatory provision in the constitution and bylaws of such a labor organization or a general exculpatory resolution of a governing body purporting to relieve any such person of liability for breach of the duties declared by this section shall be void as against public policy.

(b)   When any officer, agent, shop steward, or representative of any labor organization is alleged to have violated the duties declared in subsection (a) and the labor organization or its governing board or officers refuse or fail to sue or recover damages or secure an accounting or other appropriate relief within a reasonable time after being requested to do so by any member of the labor organization, such member may sue such officer, agent, shop steward, or representative in any district court of the United States or in any State court of competent jurisdiction to recover damages or secure an accounting or other appropriate relief for the benefit of the labor organization. No such proceeding shall be brought except upon leave of the court obtained upon verified application and for good cause shown, which application may be made ex parte. The trial judge may allot a reasonable part of the recovery in any action under this subsection to pay the fees of counsel prosecuting the suit at the instance of the member of the labor organization and to compensate such member for any expenses necessarily paid or incurred by him in connection with the litigation.

(c)   Any person who embezzles, steals, or unlawfully and willfully abstracts or converts to his own use, or the use of another, any of the moneys, funds,

union officeholding. The financial side is taken care of by assigning "fiduciary" responsibility to union officers and representatives, insisting that they be bonded, and limiting the amount a union can loan to any of its officers or employes.

Section 501(a) is about as good a definition of fiduciary responsibility as could be asked for; it is worth reading in its own right. The meaning of "exculpatory" may be inferred from the text, but if that is not sufficient, Webster's definition is "tending to clear from alleged fault or guilt."

(b) If a union member thinks a violation has occurred and the union will not or does not take action, he can bring suit on his own for damages (or "other appropriate relief") plus costs and attorney's fees.

(c) Embezzlement or theft by a union officer or employe may bring a

securities, property, or other assets of a labor organization of which he is an officer, or by which he is employed, directly or indirectly, shall be fined not more than $10,000 or imprisoned for not more than five years, or both.

$10,000 fine or 5 years in jail or both.

Bonding

SEC. 502. (a) Every officer, agent, shop steward, or other representative or employee of any labor organization (other than a labor organization whose property and annual financial receipts do not exceed $5,000 in value), or of a trust in which a labor organization is interested, who handles funds or other property thereof shall be bonded for the faithful discharge of his duties. The bond of each such person shall be fixed at the beginning of the organization's fiscal year and shall be in an amount not less than 10 per centum of the funds handled by him and his predecessor or predecessors, if any, during the preceding fiscal year, but in no case more than $500,000. If the labor organization or the trust in which a labor organization is interested does not have a preceding fiscal year, the amount of the bond shall be, in the case of a local labor organization, not less than $1,000, and in the case of any other labor organization or of a trust in which a labor organization is interested, not less than $10,000. Such bonds shall be individual or schedule in form, and shall have a corporate surety company as surety thereon. Any person who is not covered by such bonds shall not be permitted to receive, handle, disburse, or otherwise exercise custody or control of the funds or other property of a labor organization or of a trust in which a labor organization is interested. No such bonds shall be placed through an agent or broker or with a surety company in which any labor organization or any officer, agent, shop steward, or other representative of a labor organization has any direct or indirect interest. Such surety company shall be a corporate surety which holds a grant of authority from the Secretary of the Treasury under the Act of July 30, 1947 (6 U.S.C. 6–13), as an acceptable surety on Federal bonds.

Section 502 is a very extensive bonding requirement, both in its inclusion and exclusion aspects. It specifies "every officer, agent, shop steward, or other representative or employee" of any union, and then further on says that any person who is *not* covered by such bonds may not "receive, handle, disburse, or otherwise exercise custody or control" over funds or property. The bonds must be obtained from American companies approved by the Secretary of the Treasury [last sentence of paragraph (a)], and may not be placed through a broker or company in which a union or union representative has an interest.

One authority states that "the net effect of these requirements . . . is to place great power over unions in the hands of bonding companies and greatly to increase the costs of bonding." [4] He illustrates by citing a report of the Teamsters union, which formerly paid Lloyds of London 35 cents per $1,000 on a policy covering all officers. Under this law, as many as 8,000 of the union's officers may have to be

---

[4] Benjamin Aaron, "The New Labor Bill," *The Nation*, Nov. 21, 1959, p. 373, Reprint No. 91 of the Institute of Industrial Relations, University of California (Los Angeles).

(b) Any person who willfully violates this section shall be fined not more than $10,000 or imprisoned for not more than one year, or both.

individually bonded at costs up to $11.75 per $1,000.
(*b*) Violation may be punished by $10,000 fine or a year in jail, or both.

Making of loans; payment of fines

SEC. 503. (a) No labor organization shall make directly or indirectly any loan or loans to any officer or employee of such organization which results in a total indebtedness on the part of such officer or employee to the labor organization in excess of $2,000.

(b) No labor organization or employer shall directly or indirectly pay the fine of any officer or employee convicted of any willful violation of this Act.

(c) Any person who willfully violates this section shall be fined not more than $5,000 or imprisoned for not more than one year, or both.

Section 503 limits the loan indebtedness of any officer or employe of a union to $2,000 from the union and prohibits unions from paying any fines for violation of this law.
(*c*) For violations: $5,000/1 year in jail, or both.

Prohibition against certain persons holding office

SEC. 504. (a) No person who has been convicted of, or served any part of a prison term resulting from his conviction of, robbery, bribery, extortion, embezzlement, grand larceny, burglary, arson, violation of narcotics laws, murder, rape, assault with intent to kill, assault which inflicts grievous bodily injury, or a violation of title II or III of this Act, or conspiracy to commit any such crimes, shall serve—

(1) as an officer, director, trustee, member of any executive board or similar governing body, business agent, manager, organizer, or other employee (other than as an employee performing exclusively clerical or custodial duties) of any labor organization, or

(2) as a labor relations consultant to a person engaged in an industry or activity affecting commerce, or as an officer, director, agent, or employee (other than as an employee performing exclusively clerical or custodial duties) of any group or association of employers dealing with any labor organization,

for five years after such conviction or after the end of such imprisonment, unless prior to the end of such

Sec. 504. Persons convicted of any of the 14 specified crimes or of "conspiracy to commit any such crimes" may not lawfully hold responsible positions in unions, employer associations, or act as labor relations consultants. The right to serve is restored 5 years after conviction or the end of imprisonment for such. A union officer (but not an officer of an employer association or an employer directly) violates the act if he knowingly permits anyone to assume or hold office contrary to the above.
Sec. 504 originally included membership in the Communist party along with conviction of crime as a bar to holding office in a union or employer association, etc. The Communist-

five-year period, in the case of a person so convicted or imprisoned, (A) his citizenship rights, having been revoked as a result of such conviction, have been fully restored, or (B) the Board of Parole of the United States Department of Justice determines that such person's service in any capacity referred to in clause (1) or (2) would not be contrary to the purposes of this Act. Prior to making any such determination the Board shall hold an administrative hearing and shall give notice of such proceeding by certified mail to the State, county, and Federal prosecuting officials in the jurisdiction or jurisdictions in which such person was convicted. The Board's determination in any such proceeding shall be final. No labor organization or officer thereof shall knowingly permit any person to assume or hold any office or paid position in violation of this subsection.

(b)   Any person who willfully violates this section shall be fined not more than $10,000 or imprisoned for not more than one year, or both.

(c)   For the purposes of this section, any person shall be deemed to have been "convicted" and under the disability of "conviction" from the date of the judgment of the trial court or the date of the final sustaining of such judgment or appeal, whichever is the later event, regardless of whether such conviction occurred before or after the date of enactment of this Act.

Amendment to Section 302,
Labor Management Relations Act, 1947
(SEC. 505)
[See Sec. 302 of the Taft-Hartley Act, Appendix to Chap. 9, for text of this section.]

Title VI—Miscellaneous Provisions

Investigations

SEC. 601.   (a)   The Secretary shall have power when he believes it necessary in order to determine whether any person has violated or is about to violate any provision of this Act (except title I or amendments made by this Act to other statutes) to make an investigation and in connection therewith he may enter such places and inspect such records and accounts and question such persons as he may deem necessary to enable him to determine the facts relative thereto. The Secretary may report to inter-

party membership exclusion, however, was held unconstitutional by the United States Supreme Court, in *United States v. Brown* (June 7, 1965), on grounds that the provision was a bill of attainder: as a legislative action, it inflicted punishment on a particular group without a judicial trial. The decision was 5 to 4, with Justices White, Harlan, Clark, and Stewart dissenting. A brief summary of the opinions is in the *Monthly Labor Review,* September, 1965, pp. 1108–1109.

(*b*) Violation: $10,000/1 year, or both.

Title VI lives up to its name; it is extremely miscellaneous in character. Section 601 gives the Secretary of Labor very broad powers to "enter, inspect, question, report, and subpoena persons and papers." Only Title I (the Bill of Rights) and amendments to other laws (such as

ested persons or officials concerning the facts required to be shown in any report required by this Act and concerning the reasons for failure or refusal to file such a report or any other matter which he deems to be appropriate as a result of such an investigation.

(b)   For the purpose of any investigation provided for in this Act, the provisions of sections 9 and 10 (relating to the attendance of witnesses and the production of books, papers, and documents) of the Federal Trade Commission Act of September 16, 1914, as amended (15 U.S.C. 49, 50), are hereby made applicable to the jurisdiction, powers, and duties of the Secretary or any officers designated by him.

the Taft-Hartley Act) are exempt from the Secretary's right to investigate, and Title I has its own enforcement provision in Sec. 102.

Extortionate picketing

SEC. 602.   (a)   It shall be unlawful to carry on picketing on or about the premises of any employer for the purpose of, or as part of any conspiracy or in furtherance of any plan or purpose for, the personal profit or enrichment of any individual (except a bona fide increase in wages or other employee benefits) by taking or obtaining any money or other thing of value from such employer against his will or with his consent.

(b)   Any person who willfully violates this section shall be fined not more than $10,000 or imprisoned not more than twenty years, or both.

Section 602 is another exercise in definition: to distinguish "extortionate" from other picketing. Note the last phrase in paragraph (a). Does it add anything to the meaning of the sentence? Here the penalty for violation gets really rough: $10,000/20 years, or both.

Retention of rights under other Federal and state laws

SEC. 603.   (a)   Except as explicitly provided to the contrary, nothing in this Act shall reduce or limit the responsibilities of any labor organization or any officer, agent, shop steward, or other representative of a labor organization, or of any trust in which a labor organization is interested, under any other Federal law or under the laws of any State, and, except as explicitly provided to the contrary, nothing in this Act shall take away any right or bar any remedy to which members of a labor organization are entitled under such other Federal law or law of any State.

(b)   Nothing contained in titles I, II, III, IV, V, or VI of this Act shall be construed to supersede or impair or otherwise affect the provisions of the Railway Labor Act, as amended, or any of the obliga-

Sections, 603, 604, and 607 are concerned with Federal-state relations (both statutory and administrative) and attempt to avoid a possible conflict of laws. Sections 605 and 606 are procedural. None of these five sections adds to or subtracts anything from the substantive content of the act.

Quite the contrary is true of Secs. 609 and 610, however. The first of the two says that if a union or a union representative by

tions, rights, benefits, privileges, or immunities of any carrier, employee, organization, representative, or person subject thereto; nor shall anything contained in said titles (except section 505) of this Act be construed to confer any rights, privileges, immunities, or defenses upon employers, or to impair or otherwise affect the rights of any person under the National Labor Relations Act, as amended.

Effect on state laws

Sec. 604.   Nothing in this Act shall be construed to impair or diminish the authority of any State to enact and enforce general criminal laws with respect to robbery, bribery, extortion, embezzlement, grand larceny, burglary, arson, violation of narcotics laws, murder, rape, assault with intent to kill, or assault which inflicts grievous bodily injury, or conspiracy to commit any of such crimes.

Service of process

Sec. 605.   For the purposes of this Act, service of summons, subpena, or other legal process of a court of the United States upon an officer or agent of a labor organization in his capacity as such shall constitute service upon the labor organization.

Administrative Procedure Act

Sec. 606.   The provisions of the Administrative Procedure Act shall be applicable to the issuance, amendment, or rescission of any rules or regulations, or any adjudication, authorized or required pursuant to the provisions of this Act.

Other agencies and departments

Sec. 607.   In order to avoid unnecessary expense and duplication of functions among Government agencies, the Secretary may make such arrangements or agreements for cooperation or mutual assistance in the performance of his functions under this Act and the functions of any such agency as he may find to be practicable and consistent with law. The Secretary may utilize the facilities or services of any department, agency, or establishment of the United States or of any State or political subdivision

disciplinary action discriminates against a union member for exercising his rights under the act, the member may sue the union and/or its representative, or go to court for an injunction. If, however (Sec. 610), the interference with the member's rights is through force or violence or the threat of such, the offense becomes a criminal one and the penalty is $1,000/1 year, or both.

of a State, including the services of any of its employees, with the lawful consent of such department, agency, or establishment; and each department, agency, or establishment of the United States is authorized and directed to cooperate with the Secretary and, to the extent permitted by law, to provide such information and facilities as he may request for his assistance in the performance of his functions under this Act. The Attorney General or his representative shall receive from the Secretary for appropriate action such evidence developed in the performance of his functions under this Act as may be found to warrant consideration for criminal prosecution under the provisions of this Act or other Federal law.

Criminal contempt

SEC. 608.   No person shall be punished for any criminal contempt allegedly committed outside the immediate presence of the court in connection with any civil action prosecuted by the Secretary or any other person in any court of the United States under the provisions of this Act unless the facts constituting such criminal contempt are established by the verdict of the jury in a proceeding in the district court of the United States, which jury shall be chosen and empaneled in the manner prescribed by the law governing trial juries in criminal prosecutions in the district courts of the United States.

Section 608 is a protection from "injunction judges." Criminal contempt is the penalty for violation of an injunction, technically an offense against the authority of the court. If the alleged contempt is committed away from the courtroom, the fact of the action charged must be proved before a jury and not be left up to the judge to decide.

Prohibition on certain discipline by labor organization

SEC. 609.   It shall be unlawful for any labor organization, or any officer, agent, shop steward, or other representative of a labor organization, or any employee thereof to fine, suspend, expel, or otherwise discipline any of its members for exercising any right to which he is entitled under the provisions of this Act. The provisions of section 102 shall be applicable in the enforcement of this section.

Deprivation of rights under act by violence

SEC. 610.   It shall be unlawful for any person through the use of force or violence, or threat of the use of force or violence, to restrain, coerce, or intimidate, or attempt to restrain, coerce, or intimidate any member of a labor organization for the purpose of interfering with or preventing the exercise of any right to which he is entitled under the provisions of this Act. Any person who willfully violates this section shall be fined not more than $1,000 or imprisoned for not more than one year, or both.

Separability provisions

SEC. 611.   If any provision of this Act, or the application of such provision to any person or circumstances, shall be held invalid, the remainder of this Act or the application of such provision to persons or circumstances other than those as to which it is held invalid, shall not be affected thereby.

Title VII—Amendments to the Labor Management Relations Act, 1947, as Amended

[Sections 701 to 706 omitted. See explanation in opposite column.]

SEC. 707.   The amendments made by this title shall take effect sixty days after the date of the enactment of this Act and no provision of this title shall be deemed to make an unfair labor practice, any act which is performed prior to such effective date which did not constitute an unfair labor practice prior thereto.

Approved September 14, 1959.

Sections 701 to 706 of Title VII are substantive amendments of the Taft-Hartley Act and have been incorporated in the text of that law in Appendix II.

PART THREE
FULL EMPLOYMENT

TWELVE

THE MENACE
OF UNEMPLOYMENT

Unemployment is the greatest risk of the wage earner and the most serious domestic problem of the twentieth century. Billions of dollars have been spent to overcome it, governments have fallen because of it, books and articles by the score have been written about it. Nevertheless, a quarter of a century after the disappearance of true mass unemployment with the onset of the Second World War, the fear of layoff still haunts the minds of employes, employers, and public officials. Unemployment is extremely complex, in type and effects, as well as in theories of causation. It is uniquely the labor problem of modern times, the major cause of destitution among working people. Prior to 1900 that distinction went to low wages.

The fear of unemployment has a solid basis in the country's memory. For 12 years—1930 through 1941—mass unemployment was a way of life in the United States, and many now working remember the experience. The unemployed worker is typically a man without property who is cut off from income and status. For him and his family the successive steps of a protracted layoff are (1) loss of job, (2) loss of savings, (3) loss of home, car, and other property carrying indebtedness, (4) application for relief, (5) loss of skills, (6) loss of friends, and (7) loss of self-respect. The demoralizing effect of lack of work upon family after family has been documented many times and is beyond dispute.[1]

Widespread unemployment is a depression phenomenon with equally serious effects upon business, both public and private. It is accompanied by abandonment of plans, contraction of operations, forced sales, liquidation, bankruptcy, and failure of tax collections. Confidence vanishes, credit

---

[1] For a graphic picture of the impact of layoff on individual workers and their families, with emphasis on technology (automation) as the cause, see Ben H. Bagdidian, "I'm Out of a Job, I'm All Through," *Saturday Evening Post,* Dec. 18, 1965, p. 32.

413

weakens, and values decline. The whole structure of economic life, so much of it based on optimistic anticipations, tends to sag under the weight of prolonged deflation.

✗ THE DEFINITION AND MEASUREMENT OF UNEMPLOYMENT

Definition.   Unemployment is hardly the exact thing which the precise reports in the newspapers seem to imply. Behind the figures which are released once a month by the U.S. Bureau of the Census lies many a difficult question of definition as to just what an unemployed person is. The basic definition was revised January 1, 1967, to "anyone over 16 years of age not working but looking for a job." However, before this description can be put to use, it must be refined considerably. The way the Census Bureau does this is as follows. Persons are excluded as "employed" if they are: [2]

1.   "At work"—those who did any work for pay or profit, or worked without pay for 15 hours a week or more on a family farm or business;

2.   "With a job but not at work"—those who did not work and were not looking for work but had a job or business from which they were temporarily absent because of vacation, illness, industrial dispute, bad weather, or were taking time off for personal reasons. The remainder are unemployed if they are looking for work.

There is one important gap in the above definitions. They still leave the meaning of "looking for work" up in the air. And it is the size of this group which sets the limits to the labor force.

What does a person have to do to be "looking for work"? Does reading the want ads suffice? Or must he make some formal applications to possible employers or register with an employment agency? And if so, how often and how regularly should he maintain his contacts? Still more to the point, what kind of work must he be looking for? If he is offered one kind of work (say, as a filling station attendant) and turns it down because he wants another kind (say, as a clerk in an office), is he still unemployed? The essence of the definition of unemployment is that it is *involuntary*. At what point of insistence upon definite terms and conditions of work does the searcher's unemployment become self-chosen and therefore voluntary?

These are all questions which state unemployment compensation offices are called upon to answer daily as they pass upon the validity of claims for unemployment insurance. Like so many other legal and social questions, they turn upon the matter of *intent*. Is a man who is offered a

---

[2] *Employment and Earnings*, any issue, "Labor Force Data," p. 2-E. There is another limitation in the monthly survey of the labor force. "Inmates of institutions" are not covered. Hence, the strict definition of the eligible labor force is: "anyone over 16 years of age and not an inmate of an institution (penitentiary, reformatory, mental hospital, etc.)."

job at $1.50 an hour but who refuses, in order to look further for one at $1.75 an hour, still involuntarily unemployed? What about the problem of location? Probably no one would insist that a workman should accept a job that was 2 or 3 hours away from his home by the most convenient form of transportation. Is a refusal justified if an hour's trip is involved, and is the refuser still involuntarily unemployed? But suppose it is a 50-minute, a 40-minute, a 30-minute trip? Where is the line to be drawn? Is a member of a trade union involuntarily unemployed if he refuses a job in an open-shop plant? And vice versa, is a nonunion man justified in refusing to take a job which calls for compulsory union membership? There are always a number of people on the fringes of the labor market who are looking for a job that exactly suits their tastes. Are they "unemployed" until they find it?

A definition of involuntary unemployment based on acceptance of "any job, anywhere, at any rate of pay, under any conditions of work" would reduce the *figures* on unemployment considerably. Thirty years ago it was the actual definition which society used to distinguish working-men from those not in the market. However, it would be considered harsh and unrealistic under present-day conditions of specialization and flux in the labor market. It represents simply one extreme on the scale of unemployment definition. The question for the statisticians is how far to go in the opposite direction and still present a meaningful picture.

The range of unemployment.   The problems of definition described above do not invalidate current estimates of unemployment, but they justify some skepticism of their precision. Comparisons of past and present quantities of unemployment are open to still more question. Rough as the present measurements are, it is well to remember that statistical techniques, methods of definition and measurement, and the availability of data on unemployment have all improved very markedly during the last 3 decades. Any estimates of unemployment in the United States prior to 1930 are largely guesses, no matter how much care is taken in their compilation. The raw data are not available for accurate analysis, and very wide margins of tolerance must be allowed for the results. It is only since 1929 that the major statistical agencies of the Federal government have made serious attempts to estimate regularly the amount of unemployment in the country.

In any case, the absolute amounts of unemployment do not reveal the problem. It is the *ratio*, or percentage of the labor force affected by lack of work, that is important. Table 12-1 shows the proportion of the civilian labor force without jobs in 1900, 1910, and from 1920 onward. The right-hand column reveals clearly the depression year of 1921, followed by the prosperity of the later 1920s, the discouraging decade of the 1930s, the war boom begun in 1942, and the four minor postwar recessions of 1949 to 1950, 1953 to 1954, 1957 to 1958, and 1960 to 1961.

Table 12-1.   Unemployment in the United States, 1900–1965
(In thousands)

Year	Unemployed	Per cent civilian labor force out of work	Year	Unemployed	Per cent civilian labor force out of work
1900	1,647	6	1942	2,660	4.7
			1943	1,070	1.9
1910	553	1	1944	670	1.2
			1945	1,040	1.9
1920	558	1	1946	2,270	3.9
1921	4,754	11	1947	2,356	3.9
1922	2,917	7	1948	2,325	3.8
1923	749	2	1949	3,682	5.9
1924	2,034	5			
1925	817	2	1950	3,351	5.3
1926	464	1	1951	2,099	3.3
1927	1,620	4	1952	1,932	3.1
1928	1,857	4	1953	1,870	2.9
1929	1,550	3.2	1954	3,578	5.6
			1955	2,904	4.4
1930	4,340	8.7	1956	2,822	4.2
1931	8,020	15.9	1957	2,936	4.3
1932	12,060	23.6	1958	4,681	6.8
1933	12,830	24.9	1959	3,813	5.5
1934	11,340	21.7			
1935	10,610	20.1	1960	3,931	5.6
1936	9,030	16.9	1961	4,806	6.7
1937	7,700	14.3	1962	4,007	5.6
1938	10,390	19.0	1963	4,166	5.7
1939	9,480	17.2	1964	3,876	5.2
			1965	3,456	4.6
1940	8,120	14.6	1966 (Apr.)	2,802	3.7
1941	5,560	9.9			

Sources: Figures from 1900 to 1928 from *Economic Almanac for 1946–47* (New York: National Industrial Conference Board, Inc., 1947), p. 269; for 1929 to 1965, from *Employment and Earnings,* January, 1966, p. 1; May, 1966, p. 25.

It is important to point out that *some* unemployment is normal and inevitable at the best of times in any large labor market, reflecting simply the mobility of workers in their readjustment to a constantly changing industrial and commercial pattern. A complete absence of unemployment would indicate a static condition which would be thoroughly undesirable. There are many good reasons for changing jobs—personal difficulties, technological displacement, structural change in industry or job patterns, and so on. In order to get the best allocation of human resources, it is necessary for people to move about, from job to job and from region to region, and in the process they are unemployed for varying periods of time. What the proper level of "normal" unemployment should be is another question. It has been variously estimated at 3 per cent (Sir William Beveridge, Great Britain), 4 per cent (the President's Council of Economic Advisers), and 5 per cent (the Committee for Economic Development).

Table 12-1 should be interpreted in light of the above. If 5 per cent is taken as "normal," for example, how many of the 46 years from 1920 to 1965 were problem years in terms of unemployment? Quite a few, certainly (and some of them—1931 to 1940, for example, really catastrophic in amount) but not all, and in fact not even a majority. On the other hand, if the target is set at a *maximum of 4 per cent,* as proposed by the President's Council of Economic Advisers, the picture changes markedly. For 12 straight years, from 1954 to 1965, the country failed to meet this test, and sometimes by wide margins. In particular, the apparently chronic high levels of recent years have caused alarm. Finally, if the allowable limit is Beveridge's 3 per cent, the performance of the American economy has been satisfactory only seven times in the 45 years from 1921 to 1965, and four of the seven were in wartime.

Normal unemployment. The purpose of a study of unemployment is to do something about it. However, policies of relief or prevention should be related to causes, and not everyone is out of work for the same reason. The nature of an industrial society makes some kinds of unemployment inevitable at all times. The major questions are: What kinds and how much? There may be no precise, quantitative answers to such inquiries, but the issues will be clarified by a glance at the principal sources of idleness and a consideration of their relative importance. There is no absolutely standardized classification of "kinds" of unemployment, but the five groupings used below are regarded as primary causes of workers being out of jobs. They are (1) technological, (2) seasonal, (3) frictional, (4) discriminatory, and (5) recession unemployment.

Number 1 is the big question mark today. The current name for it is "automation" and the question runs: Does (Will) automation produce cumulative, constantly rising unemployment? The agency which supports this point of view with tracts, conferences, and publicity is the Center for the Study of Democratic Institutions, at Santa Barbara, California, and the high priest of the movement is Robert Theobald, author of *Free Men and Free Markets,*[3] *The Challenge of Abundance,*[4] and other titles. His predictions are challenged just as firmly by other economists, as, for example, Professor Yale Brozen, of the University of Chicago,[5] who contend

[3] Garden City, N.Y.: Anchor Books, Doubleday & Company, Inc., 1965.
[4] New York: New American Library of World Literature, Inc., 1961.
[5] *Automation and Jobs,* Selected Papers No. 18, Graduate School of Business, University of Chicago.

that *technological* dislocations, along with *seasonal* and *frictional* unemployment, are thoroughly normal by-products of a progressive, high-speed, industrial economy, and policies are already in force which are designed to keep them (or their effects) within manageable limits. Whether normal or not, the three mentioned above are aggravated by the fourth, a major cause (perhaps "the" major cause) of *chronic* unemployment—discrimination, based on color, creed, age, sex, and union affiliation or the lack of it. Finally, there is recession, or "depression," unemployment, one of the great social problems of modern times.

AUTOMATION

Automation is the end point of technological development, the purpose of which is to replace manpower with machinery which will produce more smoothly, more efficiently, more accurately, and more economically than human beings. The key factor in automation is the computer and "feedback," by means of EDP, or "electronic data processing." The computers are actuated by cards or magnetic tapes which contain information that regulates machine operation. An automated machine can start, stop, accelerate, slow down, count, inspect, test, remember, compare and measure such dimensions as space, time, sound, temperature, etc. With feedback all the above can be accomplished automatically.

The machine can now be designed so that it will not only load itself and complete all operations without any human control but it will adjust itself for tool wear or even change its own tools when necessary and inspect its own work for quality and conformance to specifications.[6]

What are the results in terms of productivity? One example is the production of an engine block from a rough casting at the Ford Motor Company: time reduced from 24 hours to $14\frac{1}{2}$ minutes. In the assembly of radios, two men operate equipment that produces 1000 units a day in place of the 200 men required previously. An electrical manufacturing company uses a computer to process a payroll for 26,000 employes in 25 minutes of calculations per week, including regular pay, overtime, absences, late-to-work adjustments, withholding tax, union dues, social security, bond purchases, pension deductions, local charities, etc. Automatic dispatching equipment used by railroads makes up freight and passenger trains with no direct labor whatever—only a yardmaster operating controls in a tower.[7] And so on.

[6] *Automation and Major Technological Change* (Washington: IUD, AFL–CIO, 1958), p. 28.

[7] See W. Buckingham, *Automation,* Chap. 2, "Automation Today" (New York: New American Library of World Literature, Inc., 1963), for dozens of illustrations of the dramatic impact of technology on output.

Automation is essentially the displacement of men by machines, and machines have been replacing men as far back as history goes. However, the process has been speeded up dramatically during the last century, and especially during the last quarter of a century. True automation, which means the addition of feedback controls to computers which then dictate adjustments or corrections of the production process is still in its teens, but like some teen-agers it is growing so rapidly that even solid businessmen have become alarmed. In 1950, there were probably not a dozen computerized plants in operation in the United States. Five years later, the number was still less than a hundred, but by 1960, more than 11,000 computers were in use—not all or even a majority of them in production; many were programmed for scientific and engineering problems, some for clerical and administrative work—and another 5,000 were on order. By 1970, it has been variously estimated that the computer population will range from 40,000 to 75,000, with a large increase in the number of fully automatic production organizations; that is, new plants built from the ground up around a computerized control system.[8] Whether in the plant, the office, the executive suite, or the library, the purpose of automation is the same: laborsaving. The question is: How much unemployment does it create? The problem divides into two parts, long-run effects and short-run effects.

Taking the long period first, it may be observed that there has been a good deal of technological progress in the world's history: in transportation, from pack animals to jet propulsion; in prime movers, from manpower to electricity; in communication, from smoke signals to radio; and in tools, from stone axes to automatic screw machines. If technological unemployment actually does accumulate over the long run, it would seem inevitable that everyone should be unemployed today. On the contrary, the world's population has increased most noticeably during the period of greatest technological advance and with the exception of a few depression years has been busily employed in mines, mills, factories, fields, and stores. Long-run technological unemployment is a myth; there is no such thing. Nevertheless, myths survive and some myths tend to grow. In February, 1966, with unemployment at the lowest level in 8 years (around 4 per cent), *Time* highlighted the following prediction for the year 2000 A.D.:

In automated industry, not only manual workers, but also secretaries and most middle-level managers will have been replaced by computers. The remaining executives will be responsible for major decisions and long-range policy. Thus, society

[8] See Charles C. Killingsworth, *Automation, Jobs and Manpower*, Michigan State University, School of Labor and Industrial Relations, Reprint Series No. 62; Buckingham, *loc. cit.;* Jno. T. Dunlop, *Automation and Technological Change* (Englewood Cliffs, N.J.: Spectrum Books, Prentice-Hall, Inc., 1963), for estimates of rates of introduction of the new technology.

will seem idle, by present standards. According to one estimate, only 10% of the population will be working, and the rest will, in effect, have to be paid to be idle.[9]

This prophecy came in the midst of the computer explosion of the mid-1960s, following several years of dire alarms about the elimination of job opportunities by automation.

The short-run problem has two dimensions: mobility of labor and the demand for the products of the industry affected by automation. Techno-logical progress, brought about by improved mechanical equipment like mechanical cotton pickers and sugar-cane harvesters in the past (during the Second World War) or by automated factories today, produces off-setting employment to counterbalance the work lost by field hands and production workers. Someone has to make the machines and the tools which are used to produce them, and the factories with their complicated servomechanisms and electronic computing devices. This creates a transfer problem, the solution of which depends on the degree of substitution and the occupational mobility of the laborers involved. Where reductions of employment are severe, the direct transfer of production workers from plant operations to the manufacture of the equipment which replaces them is highly unlikely. In these cases, the most important factor is the general condition of the labor market. If the demand for employes of all kinds is high, the absorption of the displaced men into other jobs will be relatively easy and frictionless. If it is low, unemployment will be aggra-vated by layoffs due to automation.

There is also the question of costs, prices, and competition in the automated industry. The analysis runs something as follows: A firm sub-stitutes machines for men in order to reduce costs. If costs are reduced, what happens then? The answer depends on the state of competition, which is just another way of saying that it depends on the elasticity of de-mand for the company's products. If demand is elastic, it will pay the com-pany to pass on the cost reduction in the form of reduced prices to the tune of greater sales and larger net revenue. If the proportionate increase in physical volume of sales is equal to the proportionate decrease in the number of employes required in production, there will be no unemploy-ment. The gain in physical volume may be greater, in which case there will be a net gain in employment.

On the other hand, the proportionate increase in sales may be less than the percentage reduction of working force. Cost reduction may not show up in lower prices, and the output may be held at the same or only slightly higher levels, in which cases there will be reduced employment. If the company managers act rationally and the elasticity of demand for their product is less than unity, this will be the case. It is particularly likely to occur in depressed times, with low purchasing power, limited

[9] *Time*, Feb. 25, 1966, p. 29.

demand, and many internal problems of company financing. The unemployment thus produced will be aggravated by lowered mobility of labor, both regionally and jobwise.

Trade unionists have been particularly aware of the short-run hardships brought on by technological innovation. The policies of unions have included (1) opposition to mechanization (the linotype, "canned" music, etc.) which will throw union members out of work, (2) featherbedding and make-work policies ("local work rules" in the steel industry), (3) payment of dismissal wages based on length of service, and (4) negotiating agreements to retrain and use present employes on the new equipment. Union leaders like Walter Reuther have also called for governmental attention to special hardship areas (the auto industry in and around Detroit) where the effects of automation have been concentrated.

Seasonal unemployment.   Seasonal layoffs have two main sources: weather and style. Weather affects the work load at different times of the year in agriculture, fishing, forestry, food processing, building construction, sports, travel, etc. Much of this is taken care of by part-time additions to the labor force. (The summer bulge in employment is always several millions; in June, 1965, employment was almost 5 million above the January figure.) Fashion and trade customs are the second principal cause of seasonal layoff, as new models are brought out in clothing, automobiles, radio and television sets, etc. These are aggravated by the Christmas and Easter rushes, which concentrate a large proportion of certain kinds of buying into a few weeks of the year.

There is no way of knowing just how much unemployment comes about as a result of seasonal factors, but the nature of the idleness makes it a less serious threat to stability than other kinds. For one thing, the psychological burden is reduced; the employe may be cut off temporarily from income, but his status as a wage earner is less impaired. He expects to be and usually is reemployed when the season comes round again. Another peculiarity of seasonal idleness is that it is recurring and therefore predictable. The *risk* is thus greatly reduced, since the burden may be eliminated or moderated by planning. The principal planners have been employes themselves, who arrange for fill-in jobs, and private employers, who have tried to avoid the costs of irregular operations through new marketing policies (shifting of new-model automobile announcements from spring to fall), more regular production, and storage of the produce during slack selling periods (Procter and Gamble, soap manufacturers), etc. If the general demand for labor is strong, seasonal idleness is a minor factor in the employment problem.

Frictional unemployment.   Frictional unemployment is the irreducible minimum of people out of work because of the necessity (or desirability) of transferring from one job to another in a broad, dynamic, rapidly changing labor market. (Automation is a case directly in point; it changes both the structure of industry and the "job mix," requiring readjustment of the factors of production.) Such job shifts are to be encouraged, since they result in better allocation of human resources. "Frictional" unemployment, in turn, can be broken down into a number of subclasses.

One is "structural," which means unemployment caused by a change in the "structure" of industry. Even in good times, some industries decline in importance and perhaps in absolute volume of production. The reason may be a shift of taste on the part of consumers, who begin to spend their money elsewhere, or it may arise from exhaustion of resources, as in mining; or it may come about as a result of automation and its effects on the relative efficiency of competing firms. Whatever the reason, the demand for labor falls off, either relatively or absolutely or perhaps both, and the inflow of workers into firms in the industry must be diverted to other firms in different industries. This takes time, and the lesson is often learned only after prolonged unemployment among the workmen in the declining industry, many of whom may prefer to wait for a chance to go back to work with their old company rather than try to learn a new trade in a new kind of business, even though it seems to be prospering.

Structural unemployment has another dimension: occupational. There will be structural unemployment if the members of the labor force are highly specialized (and they are, in this country) either by preference or training and if the job skills offered in the market do not match the openings for personnel. Since people select their own vocations and often engage in long periods of education or apprenticeship before becoming eligible for regular employment, it is not surprising that the skill offerings now and then get out of line with the demand. The current shortage of teachers, a result in part at least of the expansion of population in the last couple of decades, is one example. Another is the effect of automation (in the strict sense) on the labor market. The demand for production workers falls and the need for technical and supervisory personnel increases. For example, a study of the automobile industry showed that in the 6-year period from 1947–1948 to 1953–1954, the total of production workers increased 8 per cent, while the total of nonproduction workers (technical, supervisory, clerical) increased 20 per cent, and output rose 69 per cent.[10] The author reported that "a majority of management representatives as well as of workers and union leadership in the . . . industry . . . expressed the opinion that automation would result in at least some short term displacement of workers."

Professional education or the training of a highly skilled mechanic is a matter of years and thousands of dollars of investment. Indoctrina-

[10] *Automation and Leisure*, 1959–60 Reprint Series, Michigan State University, Labor and Industrial Relations Center.

tion is equally strong. Ministers do not transfer easily into industrial or commercial work, after taking the vows of ordination, which is one of the reasons why ministers as a class are economically underprivileged. Professional people, skilled mechanics, and many other occupational groups (for example, officeworkers, salespeople, and farmers) find it hard to give up an occupation which through familiarity, specialization, and indoctrination has become a way of life for them. If the occupation is specialized to an industry (as in the case of farming, teaching, medical and legal service, etc.) and the industry becomes depressed, there is very likely to be structural unemployment.

Another kind of frictional unemployment is that known as "personal." It arises from the necessity of close cooperation between people in the great majority of jobs and the importance of personality in the social environment thus created. The dislocations caused by social incompatibility on the job have become the subject of extensive investigations into "human relations in industry." There is little doubt that personality difficulties produce considerable unemployment in the form of job shifting, but within limits the results are good. The man who is "unemployable" by one firm, or who finds a given job unbearable because of associates, working conditions, or a boss with whom he does not get along, may turn out to be a valuable and contented member of another organization.

CHRONIC UNEMPLOYMENT—DISCRIMINATION

Probably the most distressing form which unemployment takes in this country is job discrimination—the refusal to hire people because they belong to some sort of "undesirable" minority group. It goes further than the refusal to hire; it also means limitation of career opportunities, like refusing to upgrade Negroes into supervisory positions. The unemployment created by discrimination is chronic, deep-seated, and persistent. Although most noticeable during recessions, it shows through the statistics of employment at all times. Any current issue of *Employment and Earnings* will reveal the pattern. For example, the January, 1966 report on the labor force showed the following contrasts for the preceding month: [11]

	December, 1965	
	Per cent of civilian labor force	Per cent of the unemployed
Nonwhite	11	22
Women	36	41
Men, age 45 and over	25	32
Operatives and laborers	24	34
Beginners (no previous experience)	1	10

[11] Pp. 5, 6.

Discrimination is primarily an abuse of minorities, although in exceptional cases (as with Negroes in some parts of the South) it may be used to keep a numerically larger group in subordination. Nonwhites (especially Negroes), some unassimilated national groups (Mexicans), beginners, the unskilled, women, and "old people," are commonly subject to employment bias. So also are trade unionists and nonunion workers, each of which has been at times protected by law from the discriminatory practices of the other. Employes subject to discrimination are not hired at all, or are hired for only the poorest and dirtiest work, or are hired at substantially lower rates than is customarily paid for the jobs. The particular form that employment prejudice takes will usually depend on the state of the labor market and the employer's need for personnel, but it may be modified by local custom or law.

No labor problem is more subtle, has deeper roots, or is harder to attack than discrimination. Employment must necessarily be a cooperative situation, and freedom of choice in arriving at a decision has long been considered fundamental for both employer and employe. No one would suggest forcing a workman to take a job he did not want (with the exception of conscription into the armed services), and his right to reject an offer of employment is embedded in the Constitution of the United States. However, here again the basic issue is the essential inequality of position of the employer and the employe. In some places steps have already been taken to reduce the arbitrariness of decisions which may be marginal or incidental to the employer but are vital to the employe.

Job discrimination is practiced by both employers and employes, sometimes together and sometimes separately. One important form that employe discrimination takes is the union member's refusal to tolerate the employment of nonunion men, expressed through closed and union shops, union preference, maintenance-of-membership agreements, and the like. Where the union man is the victim of discrimination, the active agent is usually the employer rather than the other employes, and for many years the blacklist and yellow-dog contracts were employed to keep union sympathizers out of employment and union membership at a low point. Corrective legislation (the Norris–La Guardia Anti-injunction Act of 1932 and the Wagner Act of 1935) finally eliminated the blacklist and other forms of employer discrimination against union members in interstate commerce, just as later legislation—the Taft-Hartley Act of 1947 —was aimed in part at the most serious form of union discrimination, the closed shop. The right-to-work laws and state constitutional amendments now in effect in 19 states are expressly designed to remove prounion discrimination of any form from the job market: closed shops, union shops, preferential hiring, maintenance-of-membership agreements, etc.

Employes and their representatives have often been responsible for the application of job discrimination to Negroes, Orientals, Mexicans, convicts, women, and children. The forms that the discrimination takes are to exclude the members of the minority groups from employment where possible, and, where this cannot be done, to see to it that they get the most undesirable jobs, with the poorest working conditions and the lowest pay.

Trade unions campaigned for Oriental exclusion and Western unions have refused admission to Chinese and Japanese workers, as well as Mexicans. Trade unions also led in the campaign to exclude convict-made goods from local and interstate markets. Some unions, especially Southern locals, refuse admission to Negroes or consign colored members to lower-ranking jobs without the right to advance under seniority rules. The same policies may be applied to women and underage workers. The worst exclusion practices are the property of the older craft unions; by and large, industrial unions are liberal in their admission policies and active in promoting the civil rights of minority groups.

How discrimination works. The results of discrimination show up in the distribution of jobs. Nonwhites (read "Negroes") are concentrated in the competitive, unorganized, poorly paid occupations of laborer and service worker, especially domestic servants. In December, 1965, although 49 per cent of the white civilian labor force was in white-collar jobs, only 20 per cent of nonwhites were so employed. At the other end of the scale, only 11 per cent of white workers were found in service occupations, whereas 33 per cent of nonwhites were janitors, domestics, charwomen, and so on. Eleven white workers out of every hundred were either a manager, a proprietor, or an official; only 3 per cent of nonwhites had this status. One out of every six nonwhites is an unskilled laborer, as compared to one out of twenty whites.[12] Members of the discriminated minorities are the last to be hired, the first to be let go, and the slowest up the promotion ladder. In the job market, as in other areas of society, they are second-class citizens. The economic effects of discrimination are those of monopoly everywhere: poor allocation of human resources, monopoly gains for the fortunate majority groups, inferior earnings in overcrowded low-grade occupations open to minorities, a reduction in gross output, and a lowered standard of living for everyone.

Complexity of the problem. The attack upon employment discrimination would be easier if the issue were less subtle. The heart of the problem lies in the fact that employment is a *social* as well as a functional activity. At times, the essence of the work situation is found in the personal relationships of the working group, mainly (1) cooperation between employes and (2) submission to the authority of supervisors. The elements of effective cooperation and subordination (the acceptance of leadership)

[12] *Employment and Earnings,* January, 1966, p. 10.

are understanding, appreciation, and respect. If these are lacking, individual skills may be rendered useless.

It is argued that it may not be possible for two employes to work together if they have a basic antagonism which springs from deeply embedded social prejudices originating outside of the workplace. They may not even be able to talk to each other or stay in close physical proximity. With our current social mores, it may be impossible to require rank-and-file workers to accept supervision from a member of another racial group (a Negro, say) or from the opposite sex, if the workers are men. Adult employes often resent being asked to work alongside children, especially if the youngsters are precocious, as they often are, and prove to be faster and more efficient than their elders. Like members of different races and sexes, teen-age children and adults are on different social levels, with a different language, different interests, and different points of view. The equality of employment may be irksome to grown persons who are accustomed to the respectful deference of children at home.

However, on the opposite side of the issue are ranged practically all psychologists, sociologists, and anthropologists, as well as the great majority of the evidence where integration has been tried. Individual personality clashes are unquestionably a fact, and must be recognized and adjusted to, but wholesale or group antipathies so great as to make cooperation impossible tend to melt away once exclusionary policies are eliminated. In employment, particularly, even in the South, it has proved to be possible to grant Negroes equal treatment without disrupting operations if management and unions adhere steadily to a commitment of equal opportunity. This is the assumption upon which all fair-employment legislation is based, and no substantial body of evidence is available to indicate the assumption is incorrect. The primary difficulty in correcting discriminatory employment practices in matters of race is to find qualified Negro applicants, because of the disadvantages suffered by the colored race in education, standard of living, home environment, and community ostracism.

The drive for fair employment.   On the public-policy level, the drive for fair employment has two main prongs: equal-pay laws protecting women workers and anti-discrimination measures aimed at overcoming employment prejudice based on "race, color, religion, sex, or national origin." "Women's rates" substantially lower than the wages paid men for the same kind of work have long been commonplace in American industry, on grounds of more rapid turnover, less flexibility in assignment, higher rates of tardiness and absenteeism, shorter hours of work required by law, etc. In many cases, the arguments were obviously specious, but the lower rates persisted. Since equal-pay-for-equal-work is a basic premise of wage and salary administration, it was inevitable that the matter would come up for regulation. By 1963, there were 23 states with equal-pay laws applying to various named industries, and in that year the Federal government adopted legislation requiring that women get pay equal to men if their jobs call for "equal skill, effort, and responsibility, and . . . are performed under similar working conditions." [13] The states with equal-pay acts include all the heavily populated industrial areas: New York, California, Pennsylvania, Illinois, Ohio, Michigan, Massachusetts, etc., but with only one Southern state represented: Arkansas.[14]

The Federal Equal Pay Act of 1963 was an amendment to the Fair Labor Standards Act of 1938 (as amended). It went into effect June 11, 1964, and provided that:

For purposes of administration and enforcement, any amounts owing to any employee which have been withheld in violation of this subsection shall be deemed to be unpaid minimum wages or unpaid overtime compensation under this act.

The law will undoubtedly be a powerful influence towards equalization. Where combined with state codes, it will have a potent impact.

Fair employment practice (FEP) legislation. The main attack upon discrimination has come through state and Federal laws setting up standards of nondiscriminatory hiring and employment enforced by administrative commissions. It is not an easy thing to do. All hiring and many employment practices—for example, promotion—call for discrimination, discrimination in favor of the better-qualified applicant or worker. What the FEP commission has to do is to satisfy itself that an employer is using an improper basis for selection or upgrading and attempt to bring about a change by persuasion and agreement, and if that fails, to take the offender to court for punitive action of some sort. Twenty-two states and a number of the larger cities have FEP commissions with full powers of enforcement. Three other states make discrimination on grounds of race, color, etc., a misdemeanor punishable by fine or imprisonment, but there is no administrative board or commission to enforce the law.[15]

The big new factor in the picture is the Federal Civil Rights Act of 1964,[16] Title VII of which is devoted to "Equal Employment Opportunity." The key section is Number 703, which provides that:

It shall be an unlawful employment practice for an employer:
(1) to fail or refuse to hire or to discharge any individual, or otherwise discriminate against any individual with respect to his compensation, terms, condi-

[13] Public Law 88-38.
[14] See *Economic Indicators Relating to Equal Pay, 1963,* pamphlet 9, Women's Bureau, U.S. Department of Labor, 1963.
[15] See Paul H. Norgren and Samuel E. Hill, *Toward Fair Employment* (New York: Columbia University Press, 1964), Chaps. 5, 6.
[16] 78 Stat. 241.

tions, or privileges of employment, because of such individual's race, color, religion, sex, or national origin; or

(2) to limit, segregate, or classify his employees in any way that would deprive or tend to deprive any individual of employment opportunities or otherwise adversely affect his status as an employee, because of such individual's race, color, religion, sex, or national origin.

The same restrictions are applied to employment agencies with respect to applications, listings, and referrals, and to trade unions with respect to admission to membership and to "causing or attempting to cause an employer to discriminate" against a worker in violation of the guarantees listed above.

To administer and enforce the law, Sec. 705 creates an Equal Employment Opportunity Commission (EEOC) of five members with staggered 5-year terms of office. The EEOC is instructed to investigate and endeavor to eliminate any violations by "informal methods of conference, conciliation, and persuasion," with the records of such proceedings kept confidential. If unsuccessful, however, the EEOC may file charges and institute civil actions in Federal district courts, which are expressly empowered to enjoin further violations and to order affirmative action of a corrective nature: reinstatement, back pay, etc. The EEOC is given full investigative powers and may subpoena witnesses and require the submission of records and documents as needed.

The "equal employment opportunity" provisions of the Civil Rights Act of 1964 are of course a tremendous step forward in the drive for fair treatment of Negroes in the labor market. The act blankets interstate commerce in all 50 states, including the South where no state fair employment law has a chance of passage. The prohibitions are explicit, the powers of investigation and enforcement are adequate, and the accompanying guarantees in the other titles of the statute—nondiscriminatory access to public accommodations, for example—have a reinforcing effect. Regarded simply as a statement of national policy, its influence would be extensive, but the law of course goes much further.

How much further, only time will tell. The EEOC must be staffed, financed, organized, its employes trained, policies set and tested, and its judgments reviewed by the courts. Much will depend on the cooperation it receives from employers (and employment agencies and unions) and from state agencies where FEP laws are in effect. In all probability, its progress will fail to satisfy the most ardent civil-rights leaders while at the same time appearing unduly interventionist to employers. There is little doubt that the correction of discriminatory practices reaching back over generations will take a long time. The primary reason for this is that racial discrimination extends far beyond employment into a comprehensive social pattern of inferior education, broken homes, delinquency, segregated and inadequate housing, apathy, and despair. One of the first things that FEP investigators discover is a shortage of qualified Negro applicants, especially for jobs requiring skills, training, and responsibility.

On the other hand, the power of encouragement and protection must not be discounted too much. The widening of the area of job opportunity through the elimination of formal discrimination, and the active recruitment of hitherto excluded men and women, can only have a beneficial impact. When combined with improved education and equal treatment in other sectors of the community, the Federal guarantee of equal employment opportunity will prove to be a powerful stimulant to the ambitions of Negroes everywhere.

Other kinds of discrimination.   There are, of course, many varieties of job discrimination which are not touched by a fair employment practices commission, some of which are written into law. Union and anti-union discrimination are examples. Another is veterans' preference. There is hardly a civil service law in the country which does not contain a veterans' preference clause, giving first or sole claim upon some classes of public jobs to former members of the armed services. The motivation for these favors has usually been an appeal to the veteran vote, and the effect, of course, is strictly uneconomic and inequitable, since there are no grounds for believing that ex-soldiers make better public employes than civilians, either individually or as members of groups. The same laws usually contain a prohibition of selection of employes on the basis of racial, religious, or political affiliation, the last-named of which is violated regularly for patronage purposes.

Another form of employment discrimination which has worked many hardships in the past has been the refusal of employers to hire new employes (or to rehire those laid off) after they pass a certain age level: 50, 45, 40, or even 35 in some instances. This form of prejudice is particularly noticeable during depressed periods. It is rationalized on many grounds: difficulty of retraining for new jobs, greater susceptibility to accident and sickness, lack of indoctrination, higher insurance and pension costs. "Industrial superannuation," at an early age, is a genuine risk of the industrial worker, especially in the high-speed, mechanized, closely integrated, mass-production industries of modern times.

A number of ways have been proposed for combating it. One is education. It has been demonstrated that older employes are *not* more accident-prone than their younger colleagues, or at least that accidents are not a function of age. Nor is it proved that older men are harder to deal with, lacking in versatility, or harder to train. Evidence and opinion to the contrary may be found in industrial as well as academic circles. Another attack upon the problem is reliance upon seniority as a basis for layoff and rehiring and for job assignment. Seniority is traditional on the railroads, in trade-union circles everywhere, and in many other classes of employment, notably the officer corps of the armed services, among school-teachers, and in the classified civil service. Its rapid spread in recent years is further evidence of the growth of interest in employe security at the expense, if need be, of the ultimate in efficiency.

The problem of employment discrimination, whatever its form, is as complicated and vexing as any to be found in industrial relations. Discrimination is of all types of unemployment the one where caution, gradualness, and experimentation are to be recommended with respect to policies of correction.

There is one additional and significant point to be made about job discrimination in all its forms. It flourishes in bad times and melts away where there is a strong demand in the labor market. Nothing does more to reduce employment bias than good business, a steady demand for the output of industry, and a general feeling of security on the part of both employers and employes. This is one more powerful argument for accepting the economic objective of "continuous full employment" and for taking direct, positive steps to avoid the unemployment of depression, with its end products of fear, suspicion, and group prejudice.

TAKING CARE OF NORMAL UNEMPLOYMENT

Technological, seasonal, and frictional unemployment may be "normal," in the sense of being unavoidable in an industrial civilization and by-products of otherwise useful and desirable kinds of change—scientific progress, shifts of production to accommodate new consumer tastes, reallocation of human resources, etc. They are nevertheless a heavy burden to those thrown out of work, even temporarily. Unemployment due to discrimination is also "normal," in the sense that it is always present. To soften the effects of these forms of involuntary idleness, preventive steps have been taken as a matter of public policy. The two most important types of policy relied on in recent years have been (1) improvement of the mechanics of the labor market, and (2) unemployment insurance.

The United States Employment Service. The United States Employment Service has been the answer to the demand for a system of cost-free public labor exchanges which would centralize the function of placement in the principal markets of the country and (presumably) reduce the necessity of reliance upon the expensive private employment agencies. The present network of offices dates from the passage of the Wagner-Peyser Act of 1933, although a number of states and cities had public placement agencies before that time, and there was an earlier, short-lived United States Employment Service set up during the First World War.

The present Employment Service has operated under two distinct handicaps from the beginning. In the first place, the offices were originally set up as adjuncts to the payment of job insurance during the Depression of the 1930s, and the function of placement was subordinated to that of registration of applicants for out-of-work benefits. The service was housed with unemployment-compensation staffs, dominated by officials more concerned with the payment of claims than with finding jobs for applicants, and limited in funds and personnel to such innocuous activities as keeping records and interviewing. The second handicap was the form of organization, which was by states rather than nationally. Since employment was considered a local matter and the payment of unemployment compensation was made a state function by the complicated provisions of the Social Security Act, the placement offices were also under state direction and subject to state personnel and administrative practices. This made for very uneven performance from state to state, with the general level of efficiency below average. It is common knowledge that in many states the employment service is a patronage province, with a high proportion of payrollers. The United States Employment Service and Affiliated State Employment Services, as it is called, is really a federation of state employment offices, with a head office at Washington and a journal, *The Labor Market and Employment Security.*

The state employment services today are undeniably more efficient and have more self-respect than before. From 1942 to 1946, they were nationalized and put under central direction with adequate funds to implement the government's manpower policies. This raised salaries (staff members went on the Federal payroll, which has a scale considerably above the state average), enhanced prestige, improved the quality of personnel, and, what was most important, changed the point of view to emphasis upon recruitment and placement. A vigorous program of employer visits, counseling, testing, and publication of job information was put into effect, and the number of referrals (sending applicants out to apply for jobs) and placements multiplied several times over. These functions continued to be emphasized after the return of the services to the states. Nevertheless, the state employment offices are seldom relied on by business firms for recruitment of personnel above the unskilled level, or for anything but transient labor.

Unemployment insurance. Unemployment insurance (UI) is intended mainly for those irregularly out of work, like the victims of technological and frictional unemployment and the seasonally unemployed. However, people do not come to state unemployment-compensation offices wearing tags which classify them as seasonally or technologically unemployed, and many times it would be impossible to identify the cause. So the laws governing the payment of insurance set up instead the requirement of a given number of weeks of employment during some previous work period (usually the preceding year) which makes it hard for those regularly unemployed for a large portion of each year to qualify.

This creates problems of interpretation which have been hinted at already. The requirements and procedures were summarized a number of years ago in an article in the U.S. Labor Department's *Labor Information Bulletin*. They are still standard practice.

A worker in covered [insured] employment does not automatically draw benefits when he becomes unemployed. He must have earned a certain amount in wages or worked a certain number of weeks in a "covered" job during a certain period of time before becoming unemployed. He must also be able to work, available for work, and willing to accept a suitable job. He must register for work at a public employment office and file a claim for benefits. He may be disqualified for benefits if he left his job without good cause, was discharged for misconduct in connection with his work, or if he was directly engaged in a labor dispute resulting in a stoppage of work. Both employers and workers have the right to appeal if they are not satisfied with the decision of the State employment security agency.

A worker may not be disqualified for benefits if [he refuses to take a job which] is vacant because of a lock-out or labor dispute; if the wages, hours, and conditions of work are substantially less favorable than those available for similar work in the locality; or if he would be required to join a company union or to resign from or refrain from joining, a bona fide labor organization.[17]

Unemployment compensation became a national policy in the United States with the passage of the Social Security Act in 1935, although one state (Wisconsin) had set up a job insurance system a few years earlier. Employment being considered a local matter, a Federal-state system was devised, and the states were "persuaded" to cooperate.

The Social Security Act furnished the incentive to . . . States to establish their own unemployment insurance systems by levying a uniform payroll tax of 3 per cent on employers of eight or more workers in at least 20 weeks during a calendar year. In those States which establish their own . . . system . . . employers were allowed a 90-percent credit against the Federal tax for the contributions paid to their State provided the State law met certain specified Federal standards. In addition to offering reduction in Federal tax to employers, the act provided that the entire cost of administering the State laws would be paid out of Federal funds.[18]

The "incentive" was state control of funds and personnel, since it was expected that most states would prefer to run the show at home rather than have it administered from Washington. The incentive worked, and by 1938, when payments began, there were unemployment-compensation laws in all the states.

Unemployment insurance is financed by payroll taxes paid by employers. There are over 60 million workers with "wage credits" (which means that some of their past wages were covered by the payroll tax and they have been issued a social security card and number), and upward of

[17] *Labor Information Bulletin,* August, 1948, p. 6.
[18] *Ibid.,* p. 5.

46 million with "insured status," that is, those who are eligible for payments if laid off. This is approximately three-quarters of all employes and over four-fifths of all nonagricultural employes in the country. About $3 billion is paid into the Federal unemployment trust fund each year by more than 1 million employers covered by the Social Security Act.[19] The balance in the fund varies, ranging from around $8 billion, for example, in 1955, to $6 billion at the end of 1961, and $7 billion in 1964.

The level of the trust fund depends on both employers' contributions and the rate of benefit payments during the year. In years of high employment, such as 1964, more will be taken in through payroll taxes than is paid out to unemployed workers. In that year, employer contributions were $3,048,000,000, while payments to those out of work were $2,522,000,000. In recession years, outgo exceeds income. In 1961, for example, employers paid in $2,450,000,000, but benefits totaled $3,423,-000,000. Thus, with total unemployment averaging 4,806,000, or 6.7 per cent of the civilian labor force, the *insured* unemployment averaged 2,101,000 throughout the year—less than half. These, of course, were not the same people all the time; a total of 7,066,000 unemployed persons received benefits during 1961. The average benefit was $33.80 per week (up to $36 by 1964), and the average duration of payments was 15 weeks.[20]

Unemployment insurance is not an issue any more. In an industrial society, people are constantly thrown out of work through no fault of their own, and ordinarily they have little savings to fall back on. Out-of-work benefits help to tide them and their families over while readjustment takes place. It reduces apprehension over the possible loss of a job, contributes to the maintenance of purchasing power (thus acting as one of the "built-in stabilizers" of the economy), and, being taken for granted, produces no loss of self-respect. A modern nation must have some kind of provision for short-term unemployment. If job insurance is not available, many of the unemployed will promptly become public charges through other channels. The current questions are those of amount and duration, rather than the idea itself.

The proper level of unemployment benfits.   The amount and duration of unemployment insurance benefits vary from state to state since their statutory basis is joint Federal-state legislation, and it is the state law which sets the maximum weekly amounts which a qualified claimant may receive and the maximum time limit for the payment of benefits. These range from 20 weeks at $25 per week in Louisiana, to 26 weeks at $65 per week in California. Only one state has a straight maximum duration

[19] Many small employers are exempt under state laws and there are a number of exempt categories in the Social Security Act, *e.g.,* farm labor.
[20] Data from the *Statistical Abstract of the United States, 1965,* p. 300.

above 26 weeks—Pennsylvania, with 30—but several others have automatic extension up to 50 per cent (13 more weeks, usually) when insured unemployment rises to "excessive" levels: 6 per cent in California, Connecticut, Idaho, etc. The average maximum allowance is $35 to $41 per week, found in about a dozen states, but several also have flexible maximums based on a percentage of the state's average weekly wage. However, these are *maximums*, not averages. In 1964, as noted above, the average payment nationwide was $35.98 per week (with the average in the low-benefit states much lower still, of course) and the average length of time payments were made, 15 weeks. (This may be compared to average weekly earnings in manufacturing for 1964 of $103.) Duration depends on the time worked during the qualifying period (the preceding year, usually) as well as on the length of layoff. Payments also depend on the level of the worker's wage as well as the maximum set by law.

The question, stated simply, is: Should the level of benefits be raised and the permissible duration of benefits be extended? As things stand now, the maximum payment permitted by law is considerably less than half of average weekly earnings in most states; for the country as a whole, it has been estimated at about 40 per cent. The *actual* payments are still smaller, amounting to approximately 33 per cent of customary earnings. Is this enough?

It is certainly smaller than the percentage returns when the law first went into effect in 1939. At that time, the average maximum payment permissible, countrywide, was closer to 65 per cent of weekly earnings. Since then, the actual cost of payroll taxes to employers has declined until today it is in the neighborhood of 2 per cent as compared to 2.7 per cent in 1938. This has come about as a result of what is called "experience rating," under which the tax rate is reduced when the state's unemployment trust fund reaches a certain level, due to an excess of employer contributions over benefit payments.

The above is clearly unfair, and especially so since it has resulted in considerable part from the technicality of experience rating. A reasonable target would be that the majority of the unemployed should get *actual* weekly benefit payments of at least half their wages. As to duration of payments, it is on record that during every recession, large numbers of unemployed exhaust their benefits before finding work. During 1961, for example, over 2 million claimants had their insurance cut off while they were still unemployed. It seems clear that under modern conditions, 26 weeks is not long enough to carry unemployed workers through the fluctuations which still affect the labor market. If cut off from job insurance, the man out of work is still a public responsibility, which merely means shifting the burden to another department—relief—and placing an often undeserved stigma upon the recipient. The answer would seem to be (1) a uniform Federal standard of benefits, with specified minimums and ceilings (maximums) in the range of $30 to $60 weekly (based on 1965 average weekly earnings), with a maximum duration of at least 39 weeks (9 months) and perhaps 1 year; (2) elimination of experience rating and an increase of payroll taxes to at least 3 per cent (which would raise present annual employer contributions about $1.5 billion).

Supplemental unemployment benefits (SUB). The problem of more adequate unemployment insurance has been attacked by some unions, especially the United Auto Workers and the Steelworkers, through collective bargaining. The result has been provision for "supplemental unemployment benefits." These are cash payments to laid-off workers *in addition to* their regular state unemployment insurance. They are designed to bring the weekly benefits up to 60 or 65 per cent of basic weekly take-home (after tax) pay for a period of 26 weeks (auto contracts). The plan is financed through a trust fund, into which the employer pays a certain sum for every man-hour worked: 5 cents in the original agreement of the Auto Workers with the Ford Motor Company. The fund is built up to an agreed maximum ($55 million in the original case), after which no further contributions are made by the employer until the total falls. If the fund is paid down to 13 per cent of the maximum, payments to laid-off employes are reduced; if it falls below 4 per cent, benefit payments cease altogether.

A hypothetical example was described as follows:

Assume a Detroit area employee with wife and one child, with a base wage rate plus cost-of-living allowance for a 40-hour week of $100 before taxes and $87.02 after taxes. If laid off, he is eligible for $42 a week from the Michigan State unemployment fund. During the first week of layoff, the worker would receive no benefits [supplemental]. For the next 4 weeks he would receive $14.56 from the SUB trust fund in addition to the $42 from the state, making a total of $56.56 in benefits, or 65 percent of his "take-home" pay. If unemployed during the next 22 weeks, he would receive $10.21 from SUB, which, plus the $42 from the state, would bring his benefits total to $52.21, or 60 percent of take-home pay.[21]

Is this the way to do it?

It is one way, and certainly an intelligent and courageous attempt to compensate for inadequate state benefits; however, it is capable of only limited extension (to large firms), imposes a heavy administrative and records-keeping burden on the union and the employer, and is in effect a forced transfer of income from high-seniority employes, who are less likely to be affected by layoff, to low-seniority employes. The plan is also unworkable in states where the supplemental benefits are ruled to be wages, thus denying workers their regular state unemployment payments. It has one important indirect advantage. The raising of state unemployment insurance benefits will automatically reduce the load on the SUB trust

[21] *Monthly Labor Review*, August, 1955, p. 878.

fund; if raised high enough, payments from the private fund would cease. This should enlist the sympathies of employers toward the raising of state unemployment benefits, as the latter action would result in a direct financial saving.

UNEMPLOYMENT DUE TO OLD AGE

People may be made idle by inability to work, just as much as by inability to get a job. They are not technically "unemployed," since they are outside the labor force—that is, neither working nor looking for work—but the economic effect is much the same, and the size of the principal group in this category, the elderly, is large enough to constitute a major problem. The manner of providing for the aged, a large proportion of whom are without income, is a domestic issue that has been with us since the Townsend plan (a proposal to pay a flat $200 a month to everyone over 65 years of age) appeared in the 1930s. One thing that elderly people can do is vote. At one time in the 1930s, more than 50 congressmen were pledged to the Townsend plan. It may be expected that this question will be a public issue for many years to come.

   The problem.   In 1965, there were more than 18 million persons 65 years old and over in the United States; they were 9 per cent of the total population. By 1985, it is estimated that there will be 25 million past their sixty-fifth birthday—10 per cent of the population. It is important to note, however, that the increased life expectancy of the average American has not carried with it anything like an equivalent extension of his term of employment; perhaps even the contrary. Old age is a form of employment disability which more and more people must face as time goes on.

   The problem of disability due to age is one of cost. Most old people are simply outside the labor force in an industrial society. In 1965, for example, 14,500,000 of the "oldsters" who had passed 65 were not in the labor force—that is, did not have a job and were not looking for one. The "labor-force participation rate" of this age group was only 17 per cent as compared to 55 per cent for those 60 to 64 years of age. Nevertheless, the elderly must be cared for, either by themselves (through savings), relatives, or by the government, and their support will be a steadily increasing burden on the economy during the lifetime of anyone who reads this book. The main issues are the source and character of the support: whether it should be through private savings and retirement plans, contributory public pension systems, or old-age benefits paid for by direct taxation; whether it should be in money or in kind; and how much it should be.

There will, of course, be plenty of arguments over how much old people should get and how it should be collected and paid. The Townsend plan, which in original form called for pensions of $200 a month for everyone 65 years of age and over, to be financed by a general "transactions tax," is one of the more liberal examples. At the other end of the scale in terms of generosity there are the public charity and pension plans in actual operation. They vary in kind from minimum subsistence in county poorhouses, through county and state pensions, to the old-age and survivors' insurance programs of the Federal government under the Social Security Act. These are supplemented by a bewildering variety of public and private retirement programs for specific groups of employes—the armed services, police, firemen, corporation executives, union members, schoolteachers, and many others. Pension business is very big business in the United States today, and it is getting bigger every year.

Under the federally administered old-age, survivors', and disability insurance (OASDI) system, some 62 million civilian jobs were covered, as of 1963—80 per cent of all workers, self-employed and otherwise. Another 8 million (11 per cent) were members of retirement plans of state and local governments, the Federal civil service, and special programs of the armed services. Supplementing the public system were more than 15,000 private retirement plans, most of them negotiated through collective bargaining, which covered more than 25 million beneficiaries, or 40 per cent of the persons already under OASDI. The approximately 6 million persons who were not earning retirement protection under any plan were mostly farmers, employes of nonprofit religious and charitable institutions, and domestic and farm workers who could not meet the test of regular employment required for eligibility.

The OASDI program.   The size of the old-age section of the population in this country, its current growth, and the anticipated cost of its support, seem to make it inevitable that the main reliance will be on the Federal government. By 1965, more than 20 million persons were receiving regular monthly payments under Federal old-age, survivors', and disability insurance. About three-quarters of these (14 million) were past 65 and on pensions, of which 11 million were retired workers and 3 million were wives or husbands of retired or disabled employes. The remaining 6 million consisted of widows (and widowers), children, and parents under the survivorship program. Benefit payments during 1965 amounted to $1,400 million a month, or $16.8 billion a year.[22] Both the number of recipients and the total of payments has been growing steadily and will

[22] This was just double the total 7 years earlier, in 1958. Data on public and private pension systems from the *Statistical Abstract of the United States, 1965*, Sec. 10, *passim*.

continue to grow steadily for some time in the future. The rise is as follows:

Year	Recipients (thousands)	Monthly payments (thousands)	Yearly payments (millions)
1940	222	$ 4,070	$ 48
1950	3,477	126,857	1,510
1955	7,960	411,613	4,930
1958	12,430	697,529	8,360
1961	16,495	1,071,693	12,860
1964	19,800	1,325,445	15,905

By contrast, private pension plans pay out around $2.5 billion to some 2.3 million recipients each year.

OASDI is paid for by a $4\frac{1}{8}$ per cent tax on wages up to $4,800 a year and a similar tax on the employer's payroll, making $8\frac{1}{4}$ per cent in all. The tax is supposed to increase by 1968 to an eventual $4\frac{5}{8}$ per cent each, or $9\frac{1}{4}$ per cent in all. A $9\frac{1}{4}$ per cent levy on payrolls will be a heavy tax, especially when added to unemployment insurance taxes on the same source, but it will still probably do little more than cover the costs of the program. By 1985, there will be 25 million people 65 years of age and older in the United States and probably a corresponding increase in the number of eligible "survivors": widows, children, and parents. The taxed payrolls will have to total $486 billion a year (they were $263 billion in 1964) to produce $45 billion in payments—or $150 a month for 25 million pensioners, not counting other types of survivorship.

This is the issue, then: How many old people can the country support, at what level of subsistence, and how should the program be paid for and administered? In less than 20 years, around twenty-five million persons will be past 65 years of age, and very few of them will be self-supporting, even in part. There is less and less room for employment of the elderly in a modern, high-speed mechanized industrial society; in fact, the maximum age of employment may fall far below 65 in some industries. Some very considerable increases in productivity will be necessary to support such a burden of disability without a reduction in the average standard of living.

READINGS

The Labor Market and Employment Security, monthly journal of the U.S. Employment Service; *Employment and Earnings,* monthly journal of the Bureau of Labor Statistics of the U.S. Department of Labor. The latter periodical contains the "Monthly Report on the Labor Force," and an Annual Supplement Issue in May has the equivalent of the previous "Annual Report on the Labor Force."

The classic study of unemployment from a labor-market point of view is Paul H. Douglas and Aaron Director, *The Problem of Unemployment* (New York: The Macmillan Company, 1931). On technological unemployment, see Walter Buckingham, *Automation: Its Impact on Business and People* (New York: Mentor Executive Library Books, 1963). An excellent book of readings on the various issues raised by unemployment is Arthur M. Okun, *The Battle against Unemployment* (New York: W. W. Norton & Company, Inc., 1965). Seymour L. Wolfbein, *Employment, Unemployment, and Public Policy* (New York: Random House, Inc., 1965) goes into the measurement problems in addition to policy problems. All three of the above are in paperback. *Unemployment in a Prosperous Economy* is a report of the Princeton manpower symposium of May, 1965, edited by Wm. G. Bowen and Frederick H. Harbison.

THIRTEEN
FULL EMPLOYMENT
AND ITS PROBLEMS

RECESSION UNEMPLOYMENT

Recession unemployment is unemployment which occurs during the recession (depression) phase of the business cycle. The immediate cause is obvious to everyone: a general lack of demand for labor. However, the demand for labor is a "derived" demand, meaning that it is dependent upon the demand for something else—in this case, the goods and services which labor is hired to produce. The marks of a recession are (1) reduced sales of goods and services, (2) a falling price level, (3) restriction of output of consumers' goods, (4) a slowing down of the heavy (producers' goods) industries, (5) credit contraction, and (6) spreading unemployment.

Recession unemployment is irregular in occurrence, hard to predict, and extremely variable as to duration and intensity. It ranges in depth from the 7 per cent of 1958 and 1961 to the 25 per cent of the labor force out of work in 1933 (Table 12-1) and in duration from the 1 year of 1957 to 1958 to the 12 years, 1930 to 1941. To eliminate recession unemployment, it is of course necessary to avoid recessions, and particularly to keep them from developing into depressions.

As the most important single peacetime source of misery and destitution, recession unemployment is one of the major social problems of modern times. It has also been the focal point of the most violent controversy over economic policy to arise during the twentieth century. The dispute has been over control of the business cycle, and the disputants are, on the one hand, orthodox economists and businessmen who believe that a free-market society is inherently stable and who therefore propose that the government follow a policy of *laissez faire,* and, on the other hand, the full-employment theorists, whose advice seems to lead inevitably to some form of "managed economy." As a matter of public policy, the controversy now seems settled in favor of the latter; the managed economy is with us, for better or for worse. The questions now are not "whether," but "how," "when," and "how much." However, the dispute continues with respect to matters of effect: on prices, economic growth, the national debt, etc.

THE KEYNESIAN REVOLUTION

The modern theory of employment is an outgrowth of the "Keynesian revolution" in economics, which dates from the publication of *The General Theory of Employment, Interest and Money*, in 1936.[1] The author apparently intended the book to be a denial of existing orthodox theory, and in order to avoid misunderstanding he made the repudiation clear in his opening chapter, which also set some sort of record for brevity. Chapter 1, entitled "The General Theory," is given below *in toto:*

I have called this book the *General Theory of Employment, Interest and Money*, placing the emphasis on the prefix *general*. The object of such a title is to contrast the character of my arguments and conclusions with those of the *classical* * theory of the subject, upon which I was brought up and which dominates the economic thought, both practical and theoretical, of the governing and academic classes of this generation, as it has for a hundred years past. I shall argue that the postulates of the classical theory are applicable to a special case only and not to the general case, the situation which it assumes being a limiting point of the possible positions of equilibrium. Moreover, the characteristics of the special case assumed by the classical theory happen not to be those of the economic society in which we actually live, with the result that its teaching is misleading and disastrous if we attempt to apply it to the facts of experience.

   * The "classical economists" was a name invented by Marx to cover Ricardo and James Mill and their *predecessors,* that is to say for the founders of the theory which culminated in the Ricardian economics. I have become accustomed, perhaps perpetrating a solecism, to include in "the classical school" the followers of Ricardo, those, that is to say, who adopted and perfected the theory of the Ricardian economics, including (for example) J. S. Mill, Marshall, Edgeworth and Prof. Pigou.

Keynes's subject was "depression and how to avoid it." Notwithstanding his insistence that emphasis be placed on the word "general" in the title, most readers agree that the stress is upon "employment" and how to maintain it. The answer, in a nutshell, is management of the economy, by means of fiscal and monetary policy. The primary contribution of *The General Theory* was to identify the significant factors and set measurable standards by which the "management" should be conducted.

The dissenters.   It was hardly to be expected that "the governing and academic classes" who had been brought up on the (orthodox) classical economics, would unanimously embrace the new point of view. There was and still is much in *The General Theory* that is hard to swallow, even if it is so. As is always the case after a shift in basic premises, many of the

[1] J. M. Keynes, *The General Theory of Employment, Interest and Money* (New York: Harcourt, Brace & World, Inc., 1936).

policy implications seem radical and foreign. Even if it is true that the characteristics assumed by the classical theory "happen not to be those of the economic society in which we actually live," much of the social, economic, and legal framework of that society is founded upon the belief that they present an accurate picture. There are many who will insist that by the pragmatic test the present system has worked with far more efficiency than any other yet tried. The new doctrine has therefore been denounced as socialistic, collectivistic, and unsound, and the intensity of the reaction has been proportional to the degree of prosperity of the times.

Part of the dissent from national-income policy is certainly psychological. National-income economics was identified as depression economics. *The General Theory* was conceived during depression, published during depression, and dealt mainly with deflation and unemployment. It argued that orthodox economic policy would inevitably lead to more frequent and more serious depressions and presented a theoretical defense of extensive government management of tax revenues and spending, the volume of credit, and rates of interest, in order to support national income and with it, full employment. It is only natural that businessmen, with optimistic and expansionist viewpoints, and economists who grew up in the tradition of Ricardo, Mill, and Marshall, should look with suspicion upon a program that denied their most fundamental convictions, to wit, that free markets, free enterprise, and competition will by themselves produce full employment and a steadily rising standard of living. More than 3 decades of prosperity since the beginning of the Second World War have steadily reinforced these convictions—notwithstanding the obvious use of Federal government deficit financing which accompanied the result. All economists and many businessmen are now "Keynesians," but many decline the title with asperity.

Nor are the suspicions of the orthodox group without foundation. There is much of a noneconomic nature which underlies the classical economic theory, and some fundamental and long-cherished values are bound to suffer if economic policy is oriented to the new approach. An example is freedom—the right of the individual to do as he wishes with his own private property, whether it be capital or labor services. No orthodox economist would deny that such freedom has been greatly (and necessarily) abridged, in this country as well as others, during the last century, but the idea of free choice remains as a postulate of our economic system. That idea will be weakened if reliance upon free enterprise as the central motivating and equilibrating force in the economy is abandoned. In the minds of many, free choice is a value for which there are few substitutes.

On the economic and administrative side, it has been pointed out that the "managed economy" may well raise as many problems as it solves. Chief among these will be the quality of the "management." It will be politically chosen, of course, and the manner of selection will influence both the character and the objectives of the administration. The direction of public enterprises, either here or abroad, has not yet been proved so clearly superior to private management as to dispel all doubts about the results. At the same time, the scope and complexity of the problems to be solved are far beyond anything yet attempted in time of peace. Finally, the detailed models of the fully employed society, as drawn by some of the chief disciples—Beveridge,[2] Wootton,[3] and Hansen,[4] among others— have done little to reassure the skeptics.

Full employment. The central issue in national income analysis is how to get and keep "continuous full employment," but one of the consequences of the shift of viewpoint has been to change the meaning of the words. In orthodox terminology "full employment" meant the full employment of *resources*—all kinds of resources, including capital and raw materials as well as labor. It was reached when there was maximum output of goods and services, regardless of whether all persons wanting to work had jobs or not. The new meaning is the more popular one of full employment of the labor force. It has been variously defined, but a widely accepted version is that of Beveridge:

Full employment . . . means always having more vacant jobs than unemployed men. . . . It means that the jobs are at fair wages, of such a kind, and so located that the unemployed men can reasonably be expected to take them; it means, by consequence, that the normal lag between losing one job and finding another will be very short. The proposition . . . means that the labour market should always be a seller's market rather than a buyer's market.[5]

It may be argued that the definitions are interchangeable, that full employment of resources will inevitably mean the employment of all qualified workers in the market, and vice versa. Nonetheless, there is a difference in emphasis. The full employment of *people* implies a broader distribution of income than might occur in a more productive but less equalitarian society, placing the emphasis upon the allocation of income instead of its amount. The stress is upon security rather than productivity, an accent which is maintained throughout the analysis. Adoption of the program means accepting "continuous full employment" of the labor force as the major economic objective of modern society. However, there are still quite different beliefs as to the proper road to travel to get there and stay there.

[2] W. H. Beveridge, *Full Employment in a Free Society* (New York: W. W. Norton & Company, Inc., 1945).

[3] Barbara Wootton, *Full Employment* (London: Victor Gollancz, Ltd., 1943), and *Freedom under Planning* (Chapel Hill, N.C.: University of North Carolina Press, 1945).

[4] Alvin H. Hansen, *Economic Policy and Full Employment* (New York: McGraw-Hill Book Company, 1947).

[5] Beveridge, *op. cit.*, p. 18.

In the orthodox view one of the main causes of unemployment is the rigidity of prices, especially the prices of factors of production which enter into costs. Where such prices are kept above their "natural" level, either by monopoly, combination, or government support, the result is a distortion of cost-price relationships which will restrict output and employment, reduce incomes, and which may start a "downward spiral" of deflation, leading to depression. Among prices which are the most inflexible, especially on the downward side, are wages. For the economy as a whole, they also constitute the largest single item of production costs. Flexible wage rates are often therefore a prime objective of businessmen and economists, along with flexible prices for raw materials, capital, and consumers' goods. If these prices adjust rapidly and easily to changes in demand, so the analysis goes, no resources will be held off the market, unemployment will be at a minimum, and a high level of output of goods and services will be maintained.

This opinion was flatly rejected by Keynes in the dictum that "there is . . . no ground for the belief that a flexible wage policy is capable of maintaining a state of continuous full employment. . . . The economic system cannot be made self-adjusting along these lines." His reasons for thinking so are outlined below (Chap. 15) and, with them, his proposal of a national wage policy based on a stable money wage level in the short run and a slowly rising money wage level in the long run. It is apparent, however, that the solution thus offered has a price. The problems of *administering* a national wage program with a controlled general pay level were disregarded in the analysis, but they could not be overlooked if the theories were made the basis of public policy. On this subject the critics have had as much of a field day as Keynes did in dissecting the operations of a free labor market.

THE THEORY OF EMPLOYMENT

The theory of employment is simple, definite, and easy to understand. It rests upon a single, well-defined, measurable standard: national income. Employment is a function of income. As long as national income is high, employment will be high; when national income drops, employment falls with it. To maintain "full employment," find the level of national income which will produce the level of employment desired and see to it that the level of national income is maintained. The level of national income can be controlled by the Federal government through its fiscal and monetary policies. By far the more powerful and more important of these is the former. The key to full employment therefore is the proper use and application of a "compensatory fiscal policy," that is, a fiscal policy which provides a counterbalance to the "natural" fluctuations of national income or gross national product (GNP).

Compensatory fiscal policy.   Fiscal policy is the management of government finance. It consists of two principal operations: taxation (to produce revenue) and appropriations (spending). A "compensatory" fiscal policy is one designed to help the national income stay in balance by managing taxation and appropriations so that their effects on business investment and consumer spending are stabilizing rather than unsettling. For example, if the rates of business investment and consumer spending show evidence of declining, the Federal government may reduce income taxes (which will increase the take-home pay in the hands of consumers) and increase its spending on missiles, roads, public buildings, and the like (which will raise the total of its purchases from private businesses). Thus, the government's fiscal policy will tend to counterbalance ("compensate for") the decline of private spending. If the action is timely and the amounts involved (tax reductions and/or increased appropriations) large enough, a decline in national income with its accompanying increase in unemployment may be arrested or avoided. Full employment will be maintained. Precisely the same action may be taken in reverse (tax increases and/or reduced appropriations) to slow down overexpansion and inflation.

Stated technically, national income (Y) is a function of consumption (C), investment (I), and government finance (G).

$$C \text{ plus } I \text{ plus } G \text{ equals } Y$$

Consumption is private spending by individuals on final products—goods and services. Investment is private business expenditure for purposes of *expansion* (not maintenance or replacement) of plant, equipment, or inventory, or any combination of the three. Government finance is Federal fiscal operations, either appropriations (whether for investment—expansion—or consumption is immaterial) or taxation or both. The level of consumption spending (C) is determined by the amount of consumer income and the consumption function, that is, the different propensities to consume of the different income classes. Since the income classes do not change rapidly, the principal characteristic of consumer spending as a component of national income is its *stability*. Private investment (I), on the other hand, is determined by the "marginal efficiency of capital," which simply means the apparent profitability of any new (additional) investment. The prospect for profits can change rapidly. As a total, therefore, the level of private investment spending is highly variable and *unstable*. The principal characteristic of government finance (G) is that it is *controllable*.

For purposes of control, C is of lesser importance in the short run. Both theoretically and practically, it has proved to be highly stable; consumers do not change their spending habits radically except in emergencies. The I is another matter. It reflects the investment climate and may shift up or down very rapidly in short periods of time, carrying Y with it. The answer to control is to manipulate G to counterbalance I and thus keep Y at a level which will maintain full employment.

G in turn may be modified in a variety of ways. It consists of a combination of taxation and appropriations, but this is seldom a 1 to 1 relationship. If an increase of G is called for, it may be obtained by holding the level of taxation unchanged and increasing appropriations, or the same effect (so far as fiscal policy is concerned) may be produced by holding appropriations steady and reducing taxes. Either way will produce a deficit and put more money in the hands of private individuals: in the first case, of businessmen directly; in the second, of consumers. If radical action is called for, both may be employed at the same time. In reverse, if a decrease of G is in order, either (1) appropriations may be reduced while taxes are held unchanged, or (2) taxes may be increased while the level of appropriations is left as is. Either will produce a fiscal surplus, the additional sum being withheld from the incomes of private parties, either wage earners or businessmen. The use of a compensatory fiscal policy implies both deficit *and* surplus financing—not just the former —when conditions call for them.

However, this is just where one of the major criticisms arises, and on the practical level it is powerful indictment. Deficit financing calls for lowering taxes and/or increasing appropriations, both of which are politically profitable at all times. They are popular with the general public and with the business community. Surplus financing, on the other hand, means either raising taxes or cutting appropriations or both, and neither action has ever been considered the sure way to be reelected to Congress. No one likes to have his taxes raised, and reduced appropriations mean loss of contracts for roads or buildings or goods and services of some other kind and along with them the loss of jobs and income by people employed on the projects. There is no denying that the direction of political pressure will be towards deficits, which means towards expansion and inflation. To many people, a compensatory fiscal policy is synonymous with deficit financing; as a practical political matter, they may not be far wrong.

The relationship of saving and investment. In theory, the national-income equation may be stated two ways. The income-formation equation is:

$$C \text{ plus } I \text{ equals } Y \ (G \text{ included in } I)$$

The income-disposal equation, however, is:

$$C \text{ plus } S \text{ equals } Y$$

What the latter means is that all income produced is allocable to individuals, who either receive it as wages, dividends, or rent, or else own the factors of production to which it is credited. Individuals receiving income either consume it (C) or save it (S). Saving is simply income not spent or consumed during the time period under consideration. Putting the two equations together, we get:

$$C \text{ plus } I \text{ equals } Y$$
$$C \text{ plus } S \text{ equals } Y$$
$$\text{Therefore, } I \text{ equals } S$$

Thus, during any given time period (say, a year), making allowances for lags and leakages, the total of investment spending by private businesses will equal the total of savings by individual income receivers.

On its face, this is a surprising conclusion. The total of savings is the result of (non)consumption decisions by more than 100 million consumers, whereas the total of investment is almost entirely the result of decisions to expand plant, equipment, and inventory, made by a much smaller number of businessmen. How can the totals possibly even approximate each other in size? The answer is that the equalization comes about through the effect of changes in I on the level of Y. For example, if consumers in the United States receive $600 billion in income during a 12-month period and spend $420 billion on consumers' goods and services, the average propensity to consume is 0.7. The balance, $180 billion, is saved (literally, not spent or consumed). Now, if an amount equal to this $180 billion is "invested," then a total of $600 billion is "spent," and the national-income total will remain unchanged. However, the $180 billion rate of savings may not be matched by a similar rate of investment. If only $150 billion is spent for investment purposes while $180 billion remains unspent by consumers, then the national-income total will fall at least $30 billion unless made up from other sources. On the other hand, if investment totals $200 billion for the same period, the national-income total will rise $20 billion at least. Such inequality in the *rates* of saving and investment is not only possible, it is highly probable, considering the multitude of spending decisions that make up the totals.

This is the major source of fluctuations in national income and employment, the basic cause of business cycles, according to Keynes. If the rate of investment (including G) tends to exceed the rate of saving, national income will rise; if the rate of I tends to fall below the rate of S, national income will decline. It is the function of a compensatory fiscal policy to keep such fluctuations within narrow limits, on the one hand to avoid inflation and overexpansion, and on the other, to maintain full employment and a steady rate of economic growth.

It is of course obvious that a drop in investment spending might be made up by a rise in consumer spending, or, in technical language, by an increase in the average propensity to consume. In the illustration above, if investment were only $150 billion but consumption rose to $450 billion (an increase in the average propensity to consume from 0.7 to 0.75), the national-income total would stand unchanged at $600 billion. And it is the total that counts. The government's capacity to increase the propensity to consume rests on its power to transfer income from one group in the country to another through taxation and subsidy. The lower-income groups' propensity to consume is very high. Policies which increase their incomes at the expense of upper-income classes will raise the average propensity to consume.

There is little doubt that the propensity to consume of lower-income groups is high, since this is only another way of saying that they spend most of what they make. The conclusion is obvious, since it takes everything that lower-paid workers earn to provide for themselves and their families. If the incomes of lower-paid employes are increased relatively to those of the better-paid workers and owners of property, the over-all rate of consumption will rise, and the economy will become more stable, since consumption is a more stable factor than investment. There will be a drop in the proportion of national income that is saved (unspent) and hence less of a tendency toward *over*saving relative to investment, which is the most powerful deflationary element in the economic system.[6]

The tendency for saving to exceed investment and bring on deflation, especially in prosperous times, is due to two influences. One is the increasing proportion of national income which goes to higher-income groups, and the consequent rise in both the absolute and relative amounts of saving. The other is the tendency for the marginal efficiency of capital to fall, which reduces the stimulus to invest. If the marginal efficiency of capital is high, there will be a rush to take advantage of the opportunities for profit; if it is low, investors will be wary, cautious, and hesitant about risking their money. In the short run, prosperity itself brings about conditions that reduce the probability of profit; high prices and restricted markets, increased costs, inefficiencies of organization, etc. If these factors slow down the expansion of investment at the same time that savings are increasing, there is very likely to be more saving than investment, a reduction in total spending (national income), and deflation leading to depression.

[6] This was not a doctrine calculated to make Keynes popular with the rich. However, he was fully alive to its implications and did not dodge the issue. On p. 373 of *The General Theory* he concluded: "Thus our argument leads towards the conclusion that in contemporary conditions the growth of wealth so far from being dependent on the abstinence (savings) of the rich as is commonly supposed, is more likely to be impeded by it. One of the chief social justifications of great inequality of wealth is therefore removed."

However, if the increased savings can be directed into genuine investment channels (expansion of business plant or operations), their deflationary effect will be overcome. This can be encouraged by keeping the interest rate consistently below the earning value (marginal efficiency) of capital, so that savers (especially businessmen) will seek an active outlet for their funds rather than the relatively riskless return from government bonds or seasoned industrial securities.

The decline in the marginal efficiency of capital has both short-run and long-run implications. For the long run, Keynes implied a steadily declining rate of return on invested capital. This might be due to reduction in the rate of population growth, exhaustion of known resources, slowing down of the rate of discovery of new resources, the difficulty of capital transfers from old to new industries, the institutionalization of business procedures, or public policies reducing both risks and opportunities with respect to investment. The result of such a downtrend in the marginal efficiency of capital could only be to slow down business expansion and with it the opportunities for investment. The policy conclusions follow from the analysis: a reduction in the proportion of national income which is saved (not spent) in order to avoid a chronic case of underinvestment and deflation; a declining rate of interest—to close to zero, eventually; or a permanent increase in government spending to compensate for the drop of investment.[7]

MANAGING FULL EMPLOYMENT

The modern theory of employment is simple, definite, and (on paper, at least) administratively feasible; that is to say, the factors dealt with are measurable quantities, amenable to administrative controls. They are economic magnitudes within the business and governmental system and are buttressed by a wide variety of monetary regulations—increase or decrease of bank reserves, variations in the rediscount rate at Federal Reserve banks, open-market operations, etc.—which add to their effectiveness.[8] That portion of national income most directly involved in fiscal management—public spending—is a customary public-policy function. National income, consumption, private investment, savings, and government outlays are all items which are capable of statistical definition, and the

[7] This is the "mature economy" or "stagnation" thesis, meaning that there is a limit to economic expansion and that every country must some day cope with the problems of a contracting economy (Great Britain, for example). It was at the time of publication and is today highly controversial, and it is vehemently denied by many writers on both theoretical and historical grounds. However, defenders of the thesis have some strong arguments on their side.

[8] See Arthur F. Burns, *Prosperity without Inflation* (Buffalo, N.Y.: Smith, Keynes and Marshall, 1958), especially Chap. 2, "Dealing with Recession and Inflation," for a brief explanation of the use of these devices in combination with fiscal policy.

rates at which they occur are now reported regularly by the Federal government in several of its publications. They are thus available for policy decisions if the policy makers wish to use them.

The United States has been committed to a "high" employment policy since passage of the Employment Act of 1946, and the President receives periodic reports from his Council of Economic Advisers created by the act. In 1947, the Federal government switched to a new set of national-income statistical categories, in line with modern national-income accounting.[9] From that time onward, detailed reports on the state of the economy have been available to all, and "full employment" has been a primary objective of domestic policy. However, the steps described above did not settle all the arguments. Much debate continues over the manner of carrying out the policy and its effects upon the economy.

Problems of fiscal management.   A compensatory fiscal policy for the maintenance of continuous full employment means the variation of public spending and/or taxation to keep national income constant or to keep it rising at some agreed rate of "economic growth." Ideally, this should be accomplished along with a stable price level (no inflation), a budget that balances out over the years so that there is no increase in the public debt, and a minimum of governmental intervention in economic affairs. This is a fairly tall order, especially when one considers the size of the job to be done, that is, the economic magnitudes dealt with, the number of choices or policy decisions to be made, and the governmental agencies involved and their methods of decision making.

The mere matter of increase in size is almost staggering. Table 13-1 shows the variations in gross national expenditure in the United States, by main classes of spending in selected years, for a 20-year stretch, from

Table 13-1.   **United States gross national product, by major components, selected years, 1945–1965 (In billions of $)**

Spending component	1945	1946	1952	1957	1958	1960	1961	1963	1965
Gross national product	215	211	348	443	442	503	518	589	676
Personal consumption	123	147	218	285	293	328	337	374	428
Private domestic investment	11	29	53	67	55	72	69	87	106
Net foreign investment	−2	4	0	5	1	3	4	6	7
Government purchases	83	31	77	86	93	100	108	122	135

Source: *Survey of Current Business,* various dates, "General Business Indicators," p. S-1.

[9] The changeover was described in detail in the July, 1947, *Supplement to the Survey of Current Business.*

1946 to 1965. As a measure of expansion, it might be observed that the dollar volume of GNP in 1965 was more than three times what it was in 1946—only 2 decades earlier—and more than 12 times the level of spending in the depression year of 1933, when GNP was $55.8 billion.

Looking backward, we see that it took only 4 years, from 1929 to 1933, for the spending total in the country to drop from $104 billion to $56 billion. Twelve years later (1945) it had risen to $215 billion, mainly under pressure of the Second World War. Without pause, it then rose to $348 billion in 1952, $443 billion in 1957, and 8 years later, in 1965, passed two-thirds of a trillion, or $676 billion. It was an unstable 30 years, going from a major depression through one major and one minor war, to the beginning of another shooting war in Vietnam, but who can say that the future will be less so? The relevant economic magnitudes have been increasing steadily in size, and one thing appears to be certain. Stabilization in the future, by whatever method it is accomplished, will call for measures which will seem pretty heroic compared to earlier experiments in that direction.

As an example, private investment (domestic and foreign) rose from $9 billion in 1945 to $33 billion in 1946, with an accompanying *fall* of $4 billion in gross national product, mainly because government purchases were dropping (due to cancellation of war contracts) from $83 billion to $31 billion annually. By 1957, government buying was back up to $86 billion, and 8 years later (1965), under the impetus of President Johnson's "Great Society" plus defense spending for the fighting in Vietnam, it reached $135 billion. In the latter year it was accompanied by a net investment input (domestic and foreign) of $113 billion. The end result, in gross national product, was a 220 per cent rise in 20 years (1946 to 1965) —from $211 billion to $676 billion. Query: How much of a job will it be to raise public outlay the appropriate amount if private investment should fall off $20 billion to $30 billion at some later date—especially when no one is certain just how much of an increase in public spending will be needed to compensate for a $25 billion loss in the private sector?[10]

The problem is now modified to a degree by the operation of what are known as "built-in stabilizers." These are fiscal mechanisms which go into effect automatically, without the necessity of major policy decisions. The two most important are income taxes and unemployment insurance. With

[10] There are differences of opinion on this point, depending upon whether one is pessimistic about the effects of government deficits on business confidence, and upon estimates of the "multiplier" effect of the different kinds of spending. The changes in gross national product during wartime seem to support the view that a more than equal ratio of public spending to private business investment will be required to keep total outlay unchanged. But if only dollar-for-dollar "compensation" is assumed, deficit spending in amounts of $20 billion to $30 billion a year—and these are conservative figures in some full-employment analysis—may seem pretty large to many people in a peacetime United States.

a steeply progressive individual income tax schedule, a drop in national income is reflected with great severity in tax returns. Since government spending is a function of appropriations and may be maintained or even increased regardless of income, the reduction of tax revenues produces an automatic deficit. This deficit is expanded in turn by increased payments of unemployment insurance to those laid off from work and also by a rise in total benefits of other kinds—relief, old-age assistance, etc.[11]

The "built-in stabilizers" will not do the job alone, however, even when supported by monetary policies to ease credit. In the 1957 to 1958 recession, the drop in GNP was less than $1 billion, because of the counterbalancing effect of steadily rising consumer expenditures (from $285 billion to $293 billion) and an increase of government purchases of $6.4 billion (see Table 13-1). These were almost enough to offset the decline in investment from $71.5 billion to $56.1 billion, but they did not stop the business downturn or the fall of employment. In order to take up the slack, the Federal government sustained a deficit of $12.4 billion in fiscal 1958 to 1959, the largest peacetime deficit on record at the time. (As a matter of comparison, the deficit alone in 1959 was almost one and a half times the total Federal budget of approximately $9 billion in 1940, less than 20 years before.)

The mere getting used to spending large sums is probably only a minor obstacle in the way of a fully employed economy. Two more difficult questions are when and how to spend the money. The "when" side of the problem is partly a matter of prediction and partly one of policy. In other words, how does one know that a recession is under way? [12] And if that part of it is settled, what schedule of spending is to be applied? Then, with the time and volume and rate of outlay decided, what vehicle will be used to get the cash into circulation? These are questions on which there is more than a little disagreement, even among professionals, but they have to be decided before any stabilizing action can be taken.

One phase of the problem is the fact that there are rather sizable fluctuations in total national outlay from season to season in a single year. For example, the gross national product in the last 3 months of 1957 was at the rate of $439 billion a year. By the first quarter of 1958 it had fallen to a rate of $426 billion. How much, if at all, should public spending have

---

[11] Unemployment insurance payments rose from $1,819 million in 1957 to $3,656 million in 1958. Since collections of payroll taxes into the unemployment insurance trust fund dropped from $1,544 million to $1,471 million, the addition to the deficit from this source was $1,910 million. Federal grants to state and local governments went up almost $1 billion at the same time.

[12] The debates recorded in the *Congressional Record* during the summer and fall of 1957 and the early months of 1958 will illustrate this issue in detail. They are recommended reading for anyone concerned with the general problem of maintaining full employment.

been increased (or taxes decreased)? Or, if there had been a rise of $13 billion instead, should it have been the signal for lowering the total of government expenditures?

The question is really one of what is to be considered a normal fluctuation about the mean decided upon as a full-employment rate of outlay. If the amplitude of permissible fluctuation were, say, $35 billion (about 5 per cent of GNP), then there might easily be a $50 billion to $70 billion decline to be made up before any action was taken at all. (The drop in GNP from the *summer* of 1957 to the first quarter of 1958 [a 6-month period] was $20 billion.) These amounts are approximately the size of the total Federal defense budget in recent years. Public spending on the scale indicated will require more than just the pulling of a switch.

When, where, and how much?   The rate of spending may be as hard for the professionals to agree upon as the time. Assuming that all the mechanics of the process for raising the level of government spending are set up and ready to go, is it better policy to start with the first sign of slackening business activity and gradually increase public spending as private demand and investment drop, or should the authorities wait until there is a marked recession from peak expenditure to allow for readjustment of the price level and overstimulation of the factor markets? In either case, the *quantity* of public money to be thrown into the market will have to be decided. For the sake of illustration, assume that GNP has been running at the rate of $700 billion a year. In two successive 3-month periods it drops $35 billion, to a level of $630 billion, and stabilization measures are considered imperative, as they unquestionably would be. How should fiscal policy be employed (more appropriations, reduced taxes, or both?), and in what volume, to arrest the decline and return the over-all total to a rate of at least $700 billion? For the fun of it, ask five different economists, bankers, or fiscal-policy experts for their opinions independently and then compare them.

There will have to be decisions, whether they are by consensus (unlikely) or majority vote in some policy body, like Congress, or the responsibility of the elected Chief Executive. One problem is the amount of time which may be taken up in simply arriving at the successive verdicts (1) that a recession is here, (2) that now is the time to spend, and (3) that this is the right amount and the right way. It would be much faster, and probably more efficient, to have the decisions made in advance, with certain policies to be carried out by strictly administrative personnel as successive statistical indicators were reached. This, however, implies agreement, certainty, and advance planning of a high order for a country as large as the United States, with popular political institutions.

Should the problem arise in the United States, it remains to be seen whether Congress would decide in advance to leave the establishment of a spending schedule in the hands of an administrative agency with power to act. The sums of money will be very large, there may be powerful opposition to the program from some quarters, and the *channels* of expenditure will have important repercussions for particular groups of both producers and consumers. These factors seem more likely to retard than speed up the process of reaching agreement so that action can be taken.

The essence of a compensatory spending program is *timing*. Even if all policy decisions were made in advance, there might be a problem of getting the mechanics of spending under way in time to do some good.

Public works. If, as was indicated previously, there is a possibility of declines of the range $50 billion or more within less than a year, how does one spend enough money quickly in peacetime to offset their effects? One answer has been public works, but public works have a serious weakness: their clumsiness as a means of spending money. They are hard to decide upon, require detailed advance planning and preparation (surveying, site acquisition, blueprinting, and contract letting), are slow to get under way and practically impossible to stop short of completion.

If reliance is placed upon public works to counteract rapid changes in gross national expenditure, it is reasonable to expect "too little, too late" in the early stages of recession and a huge program of partially completed construction projects on hand when recovery gets under way. Since a compensatory spending policy visualizes reductions in public outlay as private investment and consumption are restored to the full-employment level, there would then be the problem of disengaging the public treasury on something of the scale seen in 1945 to 1947, when public spending dropped $55 billion in 2 years. Then all that was required was the termination of munitions contracts, most of which had cancellation clauses in them at the start. Would it be possible to include such clauses in construction agreements running into the tens of billions? And would the communities and the politicians who represented them permit the abandonment of half-completed post offices, highways, bridges, docks, parks, or school buildings? Public works are a very clumsy method of getting money rapidly into the community on a large scale, and even clumsier when it comes to shutting off the flow.

There are other arguments against public works, too. The *need* for them is greater in good times than bad, so they tend to rise with the cycle rather than against it. It may be clearly contrary to the public interest to postpone the construction of highways, public buildings, and defense projects until depression. Reliance upon public works would also benefit one industry (construction) and one class of workers (building-trades craftsmen and laborers) far more than it would anyone else in the economy. And they are an industry and a class of workmen who are famed for inefficiency, monopolistic practices, featherbedding, and high prices. To use the relatively small construction industry as the funnel by which tens of billions of dollars are poured into the community would be to invite fraud, waste, and obstruction almost at the source of spending. Demands would probably soon be heard for the subsidization of other, more competitive industries: agriculture, manufacturing, the service trades, and the nonprofit activities of medical attention, social service, and education.

Tax reduction.   But if public works are not the answer, what is? There are many other industries and public services available for subsidy. In recent years, the military budget has provided a convenient outlet for the expansion of government contracts, and future space exploration and public uses of atomic energy offer opportunities for almost unlimited spending. Large amounts of money can easily be spent on public health, education, and welfare projects. However, an excellent case, both theoretical and technical, can be made for a quite different form of subsidy: the remission of taxes. If anyone is to be subsidized, why not the consumer or businessman directly? Tax remission can be carried as far as desired, up to and including "negative taxation," which means mailing checks to taxpayers in the lower brackets rather than collecting payments from them. It is deficit spending, just like borrowing for public works; in the case of tax reduction, however, public outlay is held constant and revenues are cut. All the administrative machinery that is needed is set up and operating and can be put in motion within a short time, with no delay for planning, preparation, or accumulation of men and equipment. And the actual spending would be on the basis of consumption and business investment choices, rather than bureaucratic decisions concerning public needs.

True, there would still have to be policy decisions with respect to prediction and the time and amount of spending. And there might be the necessity of varying the scale of income tax progression for remission purposes in order to ensure a high marginal propensity to consume (by raising the share of the lower-income groups). But it would be infinitely fairer to consumers and would avoid the necessity of industrial favoritism which would accompany any other form of subsidy. If a compensatory fiscal policy is to be adopted, tax remission is probably the most efficient method of putting it into operation.

FULL EMPLOYMENT, INFLATION, AND ECONOMIC GROWTH

There are plenty of problems to be ironed out in merely maintaining full employment, regardless of other economic objectives. However, other objectives must also be considered. Some of them are quite important. The basic question is: Does full employment have a price? And if so, is the price too high? The issue may be stated something as follows. We want:

1. Full employment
2. Economic growth
3. A stable price level
4. A balanced budget (no increase in the public debt)
5. Minimum government intervention in economic affairs
     Can we have all of them all the time?

The answer is probably no. If economics teaches anything at all, it teaches that we must learn to choose among available alternatives, and that having one thing often means going without something else. On the face of it, five such important and desirable outcomes are unlikely of achievement simultaneously, at least as currently defined. The more practical question is probably: Which of the five run parallel and which, if any, are in conflict? In all probability, the first two are pretty closely linked, as it is generally assumed that the road to economic growth is paved with full employment of the working population, along with the other factors of production. However, the *rates* at which these are to be maintained are something else again. In fact, the real argument turns on the permissible rates of various kinds of activity: rates of increase in prices and in the public debt, rates of unemployment, rates of increase in wage levels and in productivity, and rates of economic growth.

Economic growth.   "Economic growth" is the increase in volume of goods and services available to the consuming public, plus the increase in plant and equipment (public and private) for producing or processing them or transporting them from one place to another. Economic growth, in other words, is the increase in the real net national product. It may be stated in terms of physical things, as the additional volume of goods, services, factories, machinery, highways, airfields, public buildings, etc. More commonly it is summarized in monetary terms, in which case the figures must be corrected for changes in the price level. A rise in NNP figures does not necessarily mean more goods and services; it may mean only a rise in prices of the same volume of economic goods.

The rate of economic growth in the United States has varied from time to time. From 1947 to 1953, for example, with generally high employment and the Korean conflict, it was a strong 4.6 per cent; in the 6 peacetime years following (1953 to 1959) it dropped to 2.5 per cent annually; during the first 3 or 4 years of the 1960s, it was back up to 3.9 per cent.[13] Over the long pull, for the last 75 to 100 years, it is estimated to have been around 2.5 to 3 per cent. Which rate should be aimed at: a conservative $2\frac{1}{2}$ to 3 per cent, or a more rapidly expansionist 4 to 5 per cent, as argued by some? There is of course no way of saying offhand. As various authorities have pointed out, any answers to this kind of problem must be "it all

[13] *Hearings before the Joint Economic Committee,* 86th Cong., 1st sess., 1959, part 9B, p. 3094; *Economic Report of the President 1964,* p. 53.

depends." [14] Certainly the minimum to be attempted should be an increase in real national product of sufficient size to keep up with the increase of population, which is currently at a rate of about 1.4 per cent a year. Anything less than this will mean a drop in real per capita income. Anything beyond it depends on a number of factors: the level of employment considered to be "full," increases in labor productivity, effects on prices, the volume of government spending required, etc.

Full employment and inflation.   In the 13 years 1946 to 1958, the rates of unemployment were distributed as follows:

Number of years	Per cent	Dates
3	3	1951, 1952, 1953
6	4	1946, 1947, 1948, 1955, 1956, 1957
1	5	1950
2	6	1949, 1954
1	7	1958

The average for the period was 4.4 per cent. During the same 13 years, the Consumer Price Index rose from 83 to 124, or about 3 points per year. From 1958 to 1964, on the other hand, there were 3 years with 5 per cent unemployment, 3 with 6 per cent, and 1 with 7 per cent, an average for the period of 5.7 per cent. The rise in the CPI for this stretch was from 101 to 108, or 7 points, an average of 1 point per year. Is there a moral to be found in the comparison? Some think so, holding that if unemployment is kept below 5 per cent, money wages tend to rise faster than productivity, thus contributing to inflation.

The shift to a full employment economy is a most fundamental change, and one result of it is a tendency for money wages to run ahead of productivity. This shift is the dominant turning point in the history of money wages in the United States.

Wages and prices can be set by large unions and large corporations without close regard to either labor market or product market conditions. Wages can be raised despite some unemployment, and prices also can be increased more or less artificially. . . . This phenomenon has occurred within the context of an economy in which full employment is guaranteed by government, almost regardless of the conduct of the private wage and price-setting authorities. "Administered inflation" is a possibility.[15]

[14] See John T. Dunlop, *The Secular Outlook: Wages and Prices* (Berkeley, Calif.: Inst. of Industrial Relations, University of Calif., 1957).

[15] Clark Kerr, in "The Prospect for Wages and Hours in 1975," reprint of the Institute of Industrial Relations, University of California; from J. Stieber (ed.), *U.S. Industrial Relations: the Next Twenty Years* (East Lansing, Mich.: Michigan State University Press, 1958); citing Joseph W. Garbarino, "Unionism and the General Wage Level," *American Economic Review*, December, 1950, p. 893.

Wages, prices, and productivity.   Of course, a key factor in the outcome is labor productivity. If the rise of productivity is equal to the rise in money wages, then the output of goods and services will increase in practically direct ratio to the rise in purchasing power of consumers and the increased output will be taken off the market with little or no change in prices. However, labor productivity is one of the most difficult of statistical concepts to measure, and even more difficult to control or predict. Estimates of average increases in *general* productivity are in the range of 2 to 3 per cent but vary widely from industry to industry. What the future holds in the way of money-wage increases and upward movements of productivity has been guessed at by several well-qualified authorities, and the guesses may now be tested!

For example, Clark Kerr has suggested a possible 4 per cent per annum advance in money wages offset by a 2.5 per cent rise in productivity, to produce a 33 per cent increase in prices over an 18-year period—from 1957 to 1975.[16] For the same period, Lloyd Reynolds has hazarded a 3 per cent annual rise in wages offset by a productivity increase of 2 per cent, with prices going up 1 per cent a year, or a total of 19.6 per cent in the 18 years.[17] John Dunlop has offered a full range of possibilities, to wit:

Average annual rate of increase in productivity, %	Average annual rate of increase in wages, compensation per hour, %	Average annual increase in prices, %	Cumulative price increase 1957–1975, %
2.5	2.5	0	0
2.5	3.0	0.5	9.4
2.5	4.0	1.5	30.7
2.5	5.0	2.5	56.0
2.5	6.0	3.5	85.7
3.0	4.0	1.0	19.6
3.0	5.0	2.0	42.8
3.0	6.0	3.0	70.2

His judgment of the outcome was:

If by 1975 price increases over current levels are confined to 30 per cent, I believe the record should be marked as excellent. If price levels are more than 70 per cent higher than at present, I would now regard that record as quite unsatisfactory. . . . What can be done to raise average rates of increase in productivity to 3.0 per cent per year, and what can be done to keep increases in compensation per hour within 5 per cent per year? These figures would yield a 42.8 per cent price rise in 18 years, or 2.0 per cent a year.[18]

[16] *Op. cit.*, pp. 189–190.
[17] G. W. Taylor and F. C. Pierson (eds.), *New Concepts in Wage Determination* (New York: McGraw-Hill Book Co., 1958); see "The General Level of Wages."
[18] *Op. cit.*, pp. 13–14.

Well, how have the "three wise men" checked out? [19] Remarkably well, at the halfway mark. From 1957 to 1966, the Consumer Price Index rose 14 points (from 98 to 112), or 14.3 per cent. The productivity increase over the 9-year stretch was higher than any of the three allowed for, even Dunlop, with the maximum of his range—something over 3 per cent annually. The average increase in (bargained) money wages and fringes was on the order of 4 per cent per annum: Kerr right on the button, more generous than Reynolds predicted, and included in Dunlop's schedule (but less than his anticipation of 5 per cent or more). For a spot guesser, Kerr comes off best. The 14 per cent increase in consumer prices is a very reasonable halfway position towards his forecast of 33 per cent in 18 years; the higher increase of productivity was the difference. Reynolds' down-East Yale conservatism fell short of the trend in both wages and productivity; his estimate of 19.6 per cent increase in prices by 1975 will clearly be short of actuality. Dunlop's 2 per cent a year to a 43 per cent total by 1975 is at the other extreme. Nevertheless, with corrections for the productivity differential, he is well on target too.

At any rate, the case for three-quarters of the Phillips-curve relationship seems well established, to wit: wage increases minus productivity increases equal related price increases.

The relationship of wages and productivity, however, may be affected by a number of other factors in the situation. One is the distribution of the additional productivity between income and leisure. If workers choose shorter hours at higher wages to maintain take-home pay, then inflationary pressures will probably rise. Another factor is the level of full employment. There is little doubt that acceptance of a higher level of "normal" unemployment, say 6 or 7 per cent, on average, rather than the 4 to 5 per cent of recent years, would reduce inflationary pressures, both through the effects on wages and the lessened need of governmental expenditures to stimulate the economy. Is the price—an additional 1,500,000 unemployed —too high? Another factor to be considered is the matter of labor peace. If employers are to resist wage demands and hold out for moderate increases there will probably be more strikes. Strikes inconvenience the community and often more than inconvenience the employer shut down. How much of a price of this sort will be tolerated by employers, customers, and the government?

Finally, how much intervention by government in the form of direct

---

[19] It is hardly fair, of course, to review the predictions after a passage of years. It is almost one of the rules of the game that economic prophecies are promptly forgotten and never held against the predictors. In fact, they should not, as one prominent economist has ingeniously explained: "An economist deals in probabilities. If things turn out differently than predicted, he is not necessarily in error. It is merely that the improbable has happened." However, *ex post* review is a hazard of forecasting, as the three men quoted above well know.

controls (wage and price ceilings), regulation (emergency boards, crop quotas, compulsory arbitration), and special restraints (selective credit curbs) will be acceptable in addition to ordinary monetary and fiscal management? There is little doubt of the Federal government's ability to influence almost any sector of the economy it chooses to focus on: wages, prices, credit, new investment, consumption, research and technology, etc. It already intervenes in great depth in some of the above areas, *e.g.*, agriculture, collective bargaining. Should it work out additional stimuli and restraints, selectively, industry by industry or sector by sector, in order to try to achieve all the major economic objectives simultaneously?

The balanced budget and the national debt.   Full employment and economic growth, as presently defined, probably have their costs. One of these, in all likelihood, is a gradually rising price level.[20] Another may well be an unbalanced budget and a corresponding rise of the national debt. For the period 1954 to 1965, the Federal budget showed a surplus in 3 years and a deficit in 9 years. The years and the totals are shown in Table 13-2.

What does the net deficit of $49 billion, an average of more than $4 billion a year, signify? (For the 12 years, from 1948 to 1959, the net deficit

Table 13-2.   Federal government surpluses and deficits, 1954–1965 (In millions of dollars)

Year	Surplus	Deficit
1954		3,117
1955		4,180
1956	1,626	
1957	1,596	
1958		2,819
1959		12,410
1960	1,224	
1961		3,856
1962		6,378
1963		6,266
1964		8,226
1965		6,281
Total	4,446	53,533
Net		49,087
Yearly average		4,091

Source: *Statistical Abstract of the United States, 1965*, p. 392.

[20] See the Kerr-Reynolds-Dunlop comparisons above, and also the "Final Report" in *Wages, Prices, Profits and Productivity* (Arden House: American Assembly of Columbia University, June, 1959), p. 183.

was $25,774 million, the annual average $2,160 million.) Is it fair to extrapolate this $4-billion-a-year deficit into the future? Or is the period too short or too abnormal to provide a basis for comparison? It starts with the first full peacetime year after the end of the Korean conflict (1951 to 1953), reflects the recessions of 1957 to 1958 and 1960 to 1961, and towards the end shows the impact of the tax cut of 1964 and the rapidly escalating fighting in Vietnam.[21] An extension *backward* is not reassuring; there were 16 straight years of deficit financing, 1931 through 1946, and then a 7-year sabbatical with three surpluses and four deficits. Over-all, in the 35 years from 1931 to 1965, there have been 6 years with a balanced budget and 29 years in red ink. During that time, the Federal budget grew from $3.6 billion to $100 billion; fiscal operations today are of a different order of magnitude entirely from those of a generation earlier.

The concept of a "balanced budget" is much more than a matter of simple bookkeeping and living within one's income, as often seems to be implied in newspaper articles and the statements of public officials. The businessman's argument that "if I ran my business the same way the government does, I'd go broke," is simply irrelevant. Private and public finance operate from different premises and require very different methods. There is just enough similarity to be misleading—for example, both raise revenue, spend money, keep books, and report surpluses or deficits (profits or losses); but to carry out their most important functions, they must be operated in reverse.

The curious thing about the Federal government's budget is that once it is out of balance in either direction, the standard "businesslike" method of bringing it into balance is practically certain to unbalance it still further. For example, if the country is more prosperous than anticipated and tax revenues exceed estimates by a substantial amount, the natural way to bring the two figures into balance would seem to be either a tax reduction or an increase in governmental expenditure. However, most people know by now that the effects of either (or both) of these actions upon the economy is stimulating. The result is likely to be a still higher level of economic activity, increased tax revenues, and a larger surplus. If *stability* is the objective, the way to achieve it is to raise taxes and/or reduce governmental spending, thus reducing the spendable income of private consumers and the volume of orders of government contractors, and slowing down the rate of increase in gross national product.

When the Federal budget failed to balance in fiscal year 1958 by $2,819 million, there were few demands for a "balanced budget" of the simple, raise-revenues-and-decrease-expenditures variety. Instead, there was wide agreement (after a period of debate) that the proper action was just the reverse—a program of increased Federal expenditure, with tax

[21] The Federal government's fiscal year runs from July 1 to June 30; fiscal year 1965 therefore means the last half of 1964 and the first 6 months of 1965.

rates held constant, amounting to approximately $9 billion (from $72 billion in 1958 to $81 billion in 1959). This, combined with the effects of the "built-in stabilizers," produced a deficit of $12.4 billion. Business recovery was prompt and by fiscal 1960, the budget was in balance again, with unemployment back down to 5 per cent.

The basic issue of the balanced budget is not whether it should be or can be balanced from year to year, but whether, over the long pull, the surpluses will balance off the deficits, leaving the total of the national debt unchanged. It is a real issue, for hidden away far down underneath and out of sight, is the question of the "mature" economy and "economic stagnation." *A mature economy is one in which private consumption and private business investment will not of themselves produce a sufficient volume of economic activity to maintain full employment and economic growth.* It would be evidence of a maturing economy if it appeared that the government must play an ever-increasing role in economic life, either through budgetary increases more than proportional to the growth of national income, or, and more especially, through regular supplements to the gross national product through deficit financing.

During the 35 years from 1931 to 1965, the Federal budget multiplied approximately 28 times (from $3.6 billion to $100 billion) while the GNP grew from $76 billion to $676 billion, or nine times. During 29 of the 35 years, the Federal government operated at a deficit, adding $300 billion to the national debt (from $16.8 billion to $316.9 billion). It was anything but a "normal" generation, if there is such a thing any more, with a major depression and one major and one minor war, followed by the unprecedented tensions of the "Cold War," the "revolution of anticipations" in underdeveloped countries, and the uncertainties associated with scientific development in an age of nuclear physics. Nevertheless, the issue remains. Supposing it were possible, in the light of the Federal government's responsibilities at home and abroad, for the budget to be reduced in substantial amount (disarmament) with accompanying reductions in taxes. Would the private economy pick up the slack to the desired level of full employment and rate of economic growth? In other words, what would happen if "peace broke out" and the necessity of spending tens of billions annually on the military establishment dropped off sharply?

Of course, nobody knows the answer, and the multiple pressures of providing for national defense, foreign aid, debt service, and the special-interest needs of public health, education, agriculture, veterans, and whatnot, will certainly obscure the issue and may not permit experimentation with a reduced level of spending, whatever the foreign-relations picture. Nevertheless, the question should still be asked. Full employment in the periods when no wars were actually being fought has been accomplished in the United States at substantially increased levels of Federal budgeting ($3 billion in 1930, $9 billion in 1940, $40 billion in 1950, $77 billion in

1960, $108 billion in 1966) [22] and with deficits far exceeding the budgetary surpluses, both in total amount and number of years. Can full employment and economic growth be achieved in the future at relatively *decreased* levels of expenditure, with surpluses exceeding deficits? If they cannot, then another cost must be added to the probability of inflation as a part of the price to be paid for a fully employed society and a rising standard of living.

COLLECTIVE BARGAINING UNDER FULL EMPLOYMENT

There is a high degree of unanimity on the part of economists that the combination of free collective bargaining and guaranteed full employment is incompatible with stable prices.[23] The outcome is more likely to be an upward pressure on wage rates resulting in increases exceeding the rise in productivity and a resulting upward creep of prices. But what is to take the place of union-management negotiations as now practiced, if price stability is regarded as a major objective? The current approach to this problem—since 1962—is the official recommendation that wage increases be limited to the increases in man-hour productivity, or an estimated 3.2 per cent, according to the Council of Economic Advisers.

How have unions and their members reacted to the wage-price guidelines? They have uniformly denounced them as discriminatory and unfair, pointing out that the limitations apply only to bargained wage increases, leaving nonunion occupations, especially executive positions with their generous salary-and-bonus-plus-stock-option combinations entirely without any form of control, even of the "jawbone" variety. Also, how about the profits of corporations passed on as dividends to stockholders, the increased incomes of professional men such as doctors, lawyers, dentists, accountants, and the like, and the rising rates of return from rental properties and interest-bearing securities? Are these to move upward without restraint as union members are clamped under a 3.2 per cent ceiling?

Individual unions have therefore disregarded the guidelines or rejected them outright. Many important negotiations have exceeded the 3.2 per cent limit.[24] Nevertheless, the impact of a stated public policy, an-

[22] *Statistical Abstract of the U.S., 1965*, p. 392, Table No. 526. These are Federal administrative budget totals only; Federal cash payments were: for 1950, $43 billion; for 1960, $94 billion; for 1966, an estimated $150 billion.

[23] For example, Kerr, Reynolds, and Dunlop, quoted above. See also Wm. H. Beveridge, *Full Employment in a Free Society* (New York: W. W. Norton & Company, 1945), pp. 198–201.

[24] See, for example, the boilermakers' settlement in eight Western states for October, 1965, with a package increase of $1.15 an hour over a 3-year period, raising hourly scales in Washington-Oregon-Idaho-Utah to $5.50, in California-Arizona-Nevada to $6, and in Alaska to $7, with increases in pension-fund payments of 10 cents and 5 cents, in welfare-fund payments of 10 cents, and vacation-fund payments of 10 cents and 5 cents. *Monthly Labor Review*, January, 1966, p. 69.

nounced by the President and based on a logical connection (wages—productivity—prices) drawn by as respected a body as the Council of Economic Advisers is in process of becoming, may be considerable. At a minimum, it strengthens the employer's position in negotiations, by its precise limits and by its identification of unions as the primary cause of inflation. And there is substantial evidence that it has been successful. For example, a summary of "Developments under Major Bargaining Agreements, 1964," in the *Monthly Labor Review* of October, 1965,[25] covering 4,300,000 workers in the automobile, farm equipment, railroad, trucking, and coal mining industries, reported a *median general wage increase of 3.2 per cent* of straight-time average hourly earnings! The study included every negotiation affecting 1,000 or more workers in all manufacturing and nonmanufacturing industries except building construction, the service trades, finance, and government.[26]

What is likely to be the union position of the future?

With full employment their bargaining positions will be excellent, their treasuries full, their needs at least as great as before, and their officials confident and aggressive. Will wage demands be restricted to the relatively small percentages represented by increases in productivity? If they are, it will be contrary to anything discoverable so far in union history or policy. No union leader has ever set a finite limit to the long-run wage expectations of his membership, and the answer of Samuel Gompers to that question has stood through the years. "More," said Gompers, "more and ever more of the product of our labor."

If wage limitation is to be accomplished, there are three principal sources of regulation: (1) union self-restraint, (2) stiffer bargaining by employers, or (3) governmental compulsion by means of forced arbitration, wage setting, etc. Union self-regulation can mean but one thing: general union acceptance of a national wage policy, whatever it may be, and adjustment of competing union demands within the framework of a general labor organization so that the average wage level is advanced no more than is permitted by public decision. It means the end of competition for the largest wage increases between union leader and union leader, between union and union, and between union group and union group. Under union self-regulation, any violation of the general understanding by individual unions would be punishable by the other unions. It should hardly be necessary to point out that such a picture violates the most fundamental conceptions of union autonomy and assumes a unified and disciplined labor movement which is no more true of organized labor today than at any other time in the last 75 years.

Stiffer bargaining by employers means more strikes, lockouts, picket-

[25] P. 1190.
[26] The comparable negotiated wage increase for 1963 was 3.4 per cent. *Monthly Labor Review*, December, 1964, p. 1394.

ing, and other forms of interference with business activity and the general life of the community. It means a heightening of tensions between employers and their organized employes, a handicap to better human relations. It means extra sacrifices by the pattern-setting employers who take a stand and bear the brunt of the shutdowns, while other employers or industries enjoy continuous operations and perhaps increased sales and profits. Can employers put up a stiff front against wage increases beyond the rise in productivity, while at the same time perhaps reporting steady sales and good profits? The facts are that guaranteed full employment and the accompanying prosperity make it possible to pass on most wage increases (in excess of productivity increases) to the consumer in the form of price increases, make it more than ordinarily costly to suffer a strike, and make employers—like anyone else—amenable to friendly compromise and adjustment. To ask employers to hold down wage increases to the limit of productivity increases is to ask individual employers to sacrifice themselves and their stockholders for the general welfare and give their less socially minded competitors an opportunity to gain on them. If all (or most) employers agreed on a definite wage policy, it might have some effect, but such an agreement would probably require revision of the antitrust laws.

The third alternative is compulsory arbitration, which is uniformly rejected at present by both labor leaders and businessmen. The main problem here, as in self-regulation, is that of compulsion. There are always dissenters, who honestly and sincerely believe that they have been dealt with unjustly or that policies are wrong. Union dissent is customarily expressed in the form of a strike. What will happen to the "right to strike" under a national wage policy? Will it still be demanded as almost the equivalent of a constitutional liberty by trade unionists, and will it still be protected as zealously by courts, legislatures, and public opinion?

The answer, of course, is no. A national wage policy would be a national policy, just as any other, and it would have to be protected from those who refuse to accept the majority decision. However, enforcement by the government might prove to be a ticklish problem. The right to quit work *is* a constitutional liberty of the individual, and strikes are basically the collective exercise of such liberties. This country has had almost no experience of the suppression of strikes by the government, and where the latter has occurred, even on clear grounds of the public welfare, it has seldom proved popular. The New York City transit strike of the first two weeks of 1966 is an example. Under the state's Condon-Wadlin law, the 33,000 strikers were subject to immediate dismissal, loss of seniority and perquisites, and would be ineligible for rehiring for 3 years. Instead, eight union officials were imprisoned for the duration of the walkout and immediately released when the men went back to work.[27]

[27] *New York Times,* January 1–15, 1966, *passim.*

There are other angles to collective bargaining than wages. Job control, by means of seniority procedures, union shops, and hiring halls, is another major objective of organized labor. It, too, is protected in the last analysis by the right to strike. Will strikes for these ends, or to extend organization, be permitted, even though strikes for higher wages are banned? If so, there will be some delicate questions of definition for someone. It is possible, in fact common, for strikes and slowdowns to be actually for one purpose while the ostensible reason is something quite different. But any strike, slowdown, or lockout is an interference with full employment. How far and under what circumstances will "direct action" by unions be permitted with a national wage policy in effect? The answer is not immediately clear, but it may be guessed that it will be less than at present.

Organized labor is solidly on record in favor of guaranteed full employment as a responsibility of the Federal government. Unions are quick to point out a softening of the labor market, either locally or generally, and to demand corrective action. In the short run, of course, there is strong argument for union support of a full-employment program. It means, in effect, a request that the bargaining environment be kept favorable to organized labor. For the longer period, it may be that union leaders doubt the probability of any really serious attempts to hamper the right to strike, to bargain collectively, or to maintain job controls which interfere with labor mobility. Such doubts apparently are also in the minds of most writers on the subject, who find it difficult to reconcile free collective bargaining with all the needs of a fully employed economy but find it even more difficult to describe the kinds of controls to which organized labor must submit.

READINGS

J. M. Keynes, *The General Theory of Employment, Interest and Money*, Chap. 2, "The Postulates of the Classical Economics," Chap. 19, "Changes in Money-Wages," and Chap. 24, "Concluding Notes on the Social Philosophy towards Which the General Theory Might Lead" (New York: Harcourt, Brace & World, Inc., 1936).

W. H. Beveridge, *Full Employment in a Free Society*, Part IV, "A Full Employment Policy for Peace," and Part V, "Internal Implications of Full Employment" (New York: W. W. Norton & Company, Inc., 1945).

Arthur M. Okun (ed.), *The Battle against Unemployment* (New York: W. W. Norton & Company, Inc., 1965). William G. Bowen (ed.), *Labor and the National Economy* (New York: W. W. Norton & Company, Inc., 1965). Both of these are Norton paperbacks.

PART FOUR
WAGES AND EARNINGS

FOURTEEN
THE SIZE
OF THE
PAYCHECK

WAGE AND EARNINGS DIFFERENTIALS

What is a man-hour of labor worth?

Industry differentials.   It is worth more (on average) in one industry than in another. In November, 1965, the average hourly earnings
of production workers in five industries were:

Motion picture filming and distributing	$3.96
Motor vehicle manufacturing	3.44
Telephone communications	2.76
Retail trade	1.86
Laundries	1.54

Source: These and the following figures are taken from the *Monthly Labor Review,* January, 1966, pp. 23–37, and February, 1966, Table C-1.

Regional differentials.   It is worth more in one place than in another. In May, 1965, for instance, the average hourly earnings of maintenance electricians in five labor markets were as follows:

San Francisco–Oakland	$3.97
Chicago	3.46
New York City	3.15
Baltimore	2.95
Dallas	2.67

Job differentials.   And everybody knows that it is worth more in
one job than in another. The average hourly earnings in five plant occupations in the Los Angeles area had the following spread in May, 1965:

Tool- and diemakers	$3.63
Maintenance electricians	3.26
Assemblers, class A	2.98
Laborers, materials handling	2.52
Janitors	2.17

Of course, if managerial and professional employes had been included, the spread would have been many times greater.

What causes these differences? Why should a maintenance electrician in San Francisco earn 51 cents an hour more than one doing the same kind of work in Chicago, and the one in Chicago get 79 cents more than the one in Dallas? Why should a Ford plant worker get paid more than twice as much as a laundry worker? What sets the earnings of a tool- and diemaker at $3.63 per hour and those of a janitor at $2.17 per hour? These are just a few details picked at random from the complicated wage pattern that blankets the country. They illustrate the problem of *wage differentials,* one of the most important individual economic problems in the modern world. In our society, most people work for a wage or a salary; wage differentials set the level of individual pay and earnings, and therefore, to a considerable degree, the *comparative* living standards of families and individuals.

The term "wage differentials" means simply relative differences in rates of pay. As indicated above, there are job differentials, regional differentials, and industry differentials. These are the most prominent and best known, but they are not all. There are also well-established "firm" differentials (different rates of pay by different business firms for the same job in the same labor market), sex differentials (men getting more pay than women doing the same kind of work), racial differentials (Negro versus Caucasian, etc.), and age differentials (the very old and the very young receiving lower pay than the middle age groups).[1] The problem of differentials is one of the two big issues which are tied up with the paycheck; the other is the general level of wages, or the *average* standard of living.

The classic explanation of occupational wage differentials was offered almost 200 years ago by Adam Smith. He proposed five "principal circumstances which . . . make up for a small pecuniary gain in some employments, and counterbalance a great one in others":

First, The wages of labour vary with the ease or hardship, the cleanliness or dirtiness, the honourableness or dishonourableness of the employment. "Thus, in most places, take the year round, a journeyman taylor earns less than a journeyman weaver. His work is much easier. A journeyman weaver earns less than a journeyman smith. His work is not always easier, but it is much cleaner. . . .

Secondly, The wages of labour vary with the easiness and cheapness, or the difficulty and expense of learning the business. "Education in the ingenious arts and in the liberal professions, is . . . tedious and expensive. The pecuniary recompence, therefore, of painters and sculptors, of lawyers and physicians, ought to be much more liberal: and it is so accordingly."

Thirdly, The wages of labour in different occupations vary with the constancy

[1] See W. S. Woytinsky and Associates, *Employment and Wages in the United States,* Chaps. 37–41 (New York: The Twentieth Century Fund, Inc., 1953) for a detailed discussion and statistical analysis of earnings differentials by age, sex, race, industry, occupation, and region.

or inconstancy of employment. [The lower wages in manufacturing are compared with higher rates in the building trades.]

Fourthly, The wages of labour vary according to the small or great trust which must be reposed in the workmen. "The wages of goldsmiths and jewellers are every-where superior to those of many other workmen . . . on account of the precious materials with which they are intrusted."

Fifthly, The wages of labour in different employments vary according to the probability or improbability of success in them. [Where success is practically certain—as in shoemaking—the reward is low; where it is questionable, as in the legal profession, the reward of those ultimately successful is in proportion to the losses of all those who fail.] [2]

Smith did not explain why these circumstances would move employers to raise the wage of the workman, or improve the latter's bargaining position. However, put in the form of supply-and-demand analysis, they might make a respectable showing: *e.g.*, excessive hardship, dirtiness, or dishonorableness of employment will tend to discourage candidates, and the reduced supplies will bring about an increase in the rate relative to those occupations into which the surplus was drawn off. And so on, through difficulty and expense of learning, inconstancy of work, improbability of success, and the like. It at least sounds more logical.

The main difficulty with Smith's argument, of course, is simply that it isn't so—at least, not regularly enough to stand up. The dirtiest and hardest jobs are not the best paid, they are usually about the worst. Some of the hardest jobs to learn, with the longest and most expensive training periods, are among the more poorly paid: ministers, teachers, librarians, and researchers. Bank tellers handle the most valuable commodity of all, money, but are anything but highly paid for it. There are, of course, an equal number of good examples on the other side, but that doesn't add up to a valid theory. On the other hand, modern wage and salary classification experts regularly incorporate data very similar to Smith's in job descriptions to justify their schedules of wage differentials.

There are no quick answers to the questions raised by wage and salary differentials, but generations of employers, employes, labor leaders, and economists have argued over them. Employers and employes are interested in specific wage rates, the ones that apply to their plants and their jobs; they give only incidental attention to the general pay level. Union officials are interested in both. They must negotiate actual contracts which set specific rates, but their jurisdictions are often broader than the single employer and may cover an entire industry or a number of them. Hence, they cannot afford to ignore what is happening elsewhere. Students of labor problems are still less concerned with specific rates, except as they outline job and skill differentials, regional trends, comparative increases and decreases in different industries, and the theories which are put forth to explain or justify them.

[2] *Wealth of Nations* (New York: Modern Library, Inc., 1937), pp. 100–109.

Measuring and comparing the pay.   Very few economic concepts in regular daily use have more dimensions, and therefore give more opportunities for misunderstanding, than the pay received by employes. A good example is found in the brief tables used above (p. 469). They compare "average hourly earnings" in different occupations, regions, and industries. However, "average hourly earnings" is strictly a statistician's device; it is not the actual rate of pay per hour at which any employe is hired, unless by accident. It is arrived at by taking the employe's total pay per week and dividing it by the number of hours he worked. If the man worked overtime at a premium rate, or was "on shift" and had a shift differential added, his average hourly earnings will be higher than his basic rate. "Earnings" are made up of basic pay rates times hours worked, plus premium rates and bonuses, and minus any deductions for fines, scrap, breakage, etc. On the other hand, earnings are a far cry from *take-home pay,* which is what the employe receives after deductions for income tax, social security taxes, checkoff of union dues (if authorized), payments on bond purchases, etc.

There are three main levels to the total income picture for workers, and a fourth which falls partly in one and partly in another of the three. The three levels are (1) *basic rates,* by the hour or the piece (for wage workers) or by the week or month for salaried employes; (2) *earnings,* as described above; and (3) *income,* which is earnings plus any return from other sources, such as rent or dividends or profits from a business. Obviously, total income may be either more or less than earnings, as the return from sources other than work may be negative—losses instead of profits from a business conducted on the side, for example. The fourth dimension of income is the rapidly growing package of *fringe benefits,* or "supplementary wage provisions," as they are sometimes called. In some cases, fringes are premium rates for Sunday or holiday work, late shifts, or especially difficult or dangerous work. As such, they enter directly into earnings. Other kinds of fringes, however, like pensions and medical benefits, are either deferred until old age or are contingent upon illness or accident and therefore enter into lifetime income but can only be "imputed" (estimated) to current compensation. At times—when employe contributions are involved—they may even reduce current earnings and income. Still another form of fringe is pay for time not worked: holidays, vacations, sick leaves, etc. This undoubtedly produces "psychic" income and raises the hourly earnings figure if averaged in, but it does not add to the dollar volume of earnings or total income.

Real wages and earnings.   The confusion which may arise from comparing changes in wage rates with changes in earnings and vice versa is still further complicated by the important distinction between *money* wages and *real* wages, money earnings and real earnings, and so on. Real wages are money wages measured in terms of purchasing power, or "constant dollars." They are what money wages will buy. If prices are stable and money wages rise, then real wages rise. If, on the other hand, both prices and wages rise but prices rise more rapidly, as happened in the "buyers' panic" of 1950, brought on by the Korean conflict, real wages fall. Real wages or earnings are figured by dividing the current money figures by an index of the cost of living, such as the Consumer Price Index released each month by the U.S. Bureau of Labor Statistics.[3]

For example, average weekly earnings in the manufacture of household appliances rose from $112.88 to $122.11 between December, 1964, and December, 1965. During the same period, the Consumer Price Index went up from 108.8 to 111.[4] If the index was correct and reflected accurately the things household-appliance-manufacturing workers and their families bought, this means that real earnings rose 6 per cent. It is worked out in the following way—a process called *wage deflation,* or *earnings deflation.*

First, the average weekly earnings figures are deflated, to wit:

1. The purchasing power of $112.88 in December, 1964, was $103.75 in dollars of 1957 to 1959 value ($112.88 divided by 108.8).

2. The purchasing power of $122.11 in December, 1965, was $110.01 in dollars of 1957 to 1959 value ($122.11 divided by 111.0).

3. Thus, the *real* average weekly earnings—that is, purchasing power in dollars of equal value—rose $6.26 (from $103.75 to $110.01).

4. Finally—and the process should not stop short of this step—the rise in real earnings was 6 per cent ($6.26 divided by $103.75).

Many different figures appear in arguments over rates of pay, earnings,[5] income, etc., and a great deal of misunderstanding can be avoided if it is made clear just which level of income is being dealt with. It is perfectly possible for wage rates to rise while earnings fall (shorter hours of work), for income to move in the opposite direction from either earnings or wage rates, and vice versa. An example occurred during the Sec-

---

[3] This index "measures the average change in prices of goods and services purchased by urban wage-earner and clerical-worker families." The data are for 50 "cities," which means "the entire urban portion of the Standard Metropolitan Statistical Areas, as defined for the 1960 Census of Population; except that the Standard Consolidated Area is used for New York and Chicago." *Monthly Labor Review,* February, 1966, fn. 1, Table D-1.

[4] The base years of the CPI in effect in 1964 and 1965 were: 1957 to 1959 equals 100.

[5] It should be noted that the BLS avoids the use of the term "cost-of-living index" with reference to the Consumer Price Index, and also publishes regularly (in Table D-2 of the *Monthly Labor Review*) consumer price indexes for "selected areas" which vary by several points among themselves. Nevertheless, the CPI for the United States is the nearest thing to a general cost-of-living index available and is regularly used by economists, labor negotiators, and government officials as a measure of changes in the purchasing power of workers' incomes.

ond World War when labor leaders criticized the National War Labor Board for refusing certain pay increases, arguing that the wages in question had lagged behind the rise of the cost of living. The Board, in turn, contended that the workers' standard of living had not suffered. It turned out that the union critics were referring to basic rates, which *had* lagged behind the rise in living costs, whereas the Board had in mind earnings, which had outstripped the rise in prices, due to steady work, long hours, and overtime rates.

Psychic wages, earnings, and income. Still another dimension of the compensation problem is the "psychic" return to the worker. Although probably incapable of measurement, psychic income is a fact which should not be overlooked in the work situation. A job which the worker enjoys doing provides an added return over and above any real or money earnings; a job which is boring or distasteful, on the other hand, reduces the net satisfaction obtainable from the purchasing power it represents. In certain lines of work, especially the "callings"—the ministry, teaching, nursing—the psychic income is such a known factor that people can be induced to enter the occupations at rates considerably below those ordinarily paid employes with similar training and qualifications. Psychic returns may arise from various sources: a sense of service (missionaries, nurses, social service workers); stimulating and challenging routines of work (the professions and many of the skilled trades); the feeling of authority and responsibility (executive and supervisory positions); security and high assurance of career advancement (the civil service); leisure time (paid vacations, holidays, special leaves); preferred work environments and associates (union shops, specialized occupations and industries: farming, entertainment, the maritime trades); economic progress (pay raises, merit increases); and so on. Manipulation of psychic inducements, or the "economy of incentives," as Barnard puts it,[6] is one of the arts of management. In many cases, it may be the key factor in making the net compensation satisfactory to either individuals or groups of employes. At the same time, it does nothing to make the wage-differential picture more orderly or systematic.

The market for labor. A labor market is one of the hardest kinds of general market to describe in terms of conventional price theory, because of the number and degree of "imperfections" encountered. This shows up particularly in the most fundamental test of all. According to Marshall, a market is the area within which the price of a good (or service) tends toward equality quickly and easily.[7] However, everyone knows

[6] Chester I. Barnard, *The Functions of the Executive,* Chap. XI (Cambridge, Mass.: Harvard University Press, 1942).

[7] Alfred Marshall, *Principles of Economics* (New York: The Macmillan Company, 1936), p. 324.

of cases where different wages are paid for exactly the same kind of personal services by companies which are obviously in the same labor market, since they may be next-door neighbors or face each other across the street. In fact, it often turns out that a single company pays different rates to employes doing precisely the same kind of work in the same location; such cases are practically certain to turn up during wage and salary surveys. Since it may be assumed that one plant is in a single market for one particular kind of employe, the only conclusion possible is that the market is very imperfect.

There is little doubt that most labor markets are highly imperfect and that the effects of competition are therefore indirect and slow, leaving a wide range of indeterminacy. This judgment is further borne out by a study of the usual criteria of a good market: (1) homogeneity of the product, (2) mobility of the product, (3) large numbers of buyers and sellers, and (4) full knowledge of market conditions on the part of the participants.

HOMOGENEITY.   It would be difficult to think of anything regularly exchanged for money which is less homogeneous (uniform) than labor services. No matter how highly specialized and carefully classified, employes are never as equal in productivity as machines or as predictable in quality or reliability as commodities. The fact that they are human beings and that employment is inevitably a cooperative situation makes it certain that no two employes will prove to be exactly alike and probable that no one employe will be precisely the same on successive days or even in successive hours of the same day. Fatigue, anger, disgust, fear, pain, sorrow, and boredom are all capable of changing the workingman's productivity, with little or no outward sign. The extensive recent researches into human relations in industry are an attempt to measure the strength of some of these intangibles and discover ways of neutralizing their effects.[8]

MOBILITY.   Nor are workingmen highly mobile in search of jobs. It is a considerable decision for an employe, especially if head of a family, to give up his home and friends and neighborhood contacts, including schools, churches, and clubs, in search of a better position. The out-of-pocket expense is large, and the uncertainty of recovering it through the *marginal* addition to his wages is a strong deterrent. Labor mobility is concentrated heavily in the young, unmarried, unattached persons just entering the labor market. And many of them have strong aversions to leaving their home communities and friends in the absence of good proof of the wisdom of the move. What this means is not that mobility is lacking—merely that relative to the responses of capital and goods to price changes, the response of labor will be sluggish and imprecise.

[8] See, among others, F. J. Roethlisberger and W. J. Dickson, *Management and the Workers* (Cambridge, Mass.: Harvard University Press, 1939); John B. Knox, *The Sociology of Industrial Relations* (New York: Random House, Inc., 1955); Mason Haire, *Psychology in Management* (New York: McGraw-Hill Book Company, 1956).

KNOWLEDGE OF THE MARKET.   The "proof" referred to above is frequently lacking. In no other kind of market is information concerning prices and offers so difficult to get. Many employers treat news of job openings as highly confidential, and both employers and employes tend to consider wage and salary information as personal and confidential data, a factor which undeniably contributes to the lack of standardization of wage rates. Both buyers and sellers of labor services often move in complete ignorance of available supplies, competitive prices, and the intentions of potential bargainers. Although this situation has been improved somewhat by the equalizing effects of trade unionism and by the attempts of the United States Employment Service to publicize employment conditions, the labor market is still an area of opaque mystery to many who work for a living.

COMPETITION ON THE PART OF BUYERS AND SELLERS.   Finally, another important element of a truly competitive market is often lacking. There is seldom a large number of buyers (employers) actively competing for the services of a group of sellers (employes), and only in the most unusual situations do workingmen bid competitively against each other for jobs. The mechanics of employment make competitive bidding almost impossible, and the efforts of both organized employers and organized employes have been pointed in the opposite direction—that of increasing the monopoly positions of the two parties.

The points raised above make it clear that the standard supply-and-demand economic analysis must be used with great care and with extensive qualifications if it is to be applied to the determination of wage rates. It is nevertheless a fact that personal services are bought and sold daily in tremendous quantity in some kind of market. There *are* "going rates" for certain kinds of jobs, and while individual wage rates may differ, they often vary within a moderate range, indicating that some equilibrating force sets in when the extremes are reached. The relative potency of institutional and competitive forces is a matter of argument. Here it is sufficient to note that the imperfections of the market undoubtedly contribute to the many inexplicable differentials which exist.

Wages as costs and as income.   The wage problem originated when the first employer furnished materials, tools, or workplace, or some combination of the three, and paid people to do certain things at his direction. Specialization of tasks (division of labor), with its great contribution to efficiency of production, practically eliminated the possibility of telling what each individual employe's work was worth. In the nature of things, no one can say how much value is contributed by a tool- and diemaker, a maintenance electrician, an assembler A, a laborer handling materials, or a janitor, all of whom work in the same plant and combine their services to turn out one or a variety of products. Management, including fore-

men and accountants and market research specialists, must also be paid
from the revenue derived from the sale of the factory's output, to say
nothing of guards, watchmen, and investors who put up the money.

Yet however the determination is arrived at, the wages paid are *incomes* to the employes. This means that for all employes, from management down, the rate of pay will determine the scale of living. Since we are
all alive to the advantages of a higher living standard and since we know
and our employers know that there is no way of estimating precisely what
we are worth in our jobs, and since there is no reason to consider ourselves
overpaid rather than underpaid, we all spend a good deal of time figuring
how to "put the bite" on our employers for a raise. We use personal pressure (a baby in the family), organization pressure (union demands), economic pressure (threat of leaving), arguments, entreaties, cajolery, and
threats. Some of us, being more strategically situated or perhaps better
tacticians, succeed, while others do not. The results do not always make
the wage pattern more orderly.

Employers, meanwhile, are on the other side of the fence. Wages are
costs to them, and they cannot possibly pay all employes all they want. In
fact, with the best intentions in the world, two manufacturers of the same
product, located side by side, might not have anything like the same ability to pay for work done, since one of them might be going bankrupt while
the other was prospering. The success of a firm is a complex of general
prosperity, demand for the product or service, sales outlets and contacts,
efficiency of operations, and good capital structure. And while employers
may reject "ability to pay" as a principle of wage negotiations, it is a constant factor in their decisions. Prosperous times are times of rising wages,
high-profit industries are high-wage industries, and no one rejects a wage
demand more quickly than an employer who is losing money. So employers meet the pressures devised by their employes to extract pay raises and
react to them in various ways, depending upon the state of business, their
estimates of individual employes and the validity of their requests, the employes' group-bargaining power, and the importance of labor costs to
operations.

Wages as administered prices.   What the foregoing argument adds
up to is the conclusion that, by and large, wages must be considered as
"administered" prices rather than as rates set competitively in the market.
That is, wages may be (probably often are) set in the short run without
close or direct reference to existing market conditions: the current supply
of workers, the volume of unemployment, the rates paid by other employers in the market, the volume and character of turnover, etc. Since each
employer is subject to a different complex of pressures, the result is a
broad area of indeterminacy, with a considerable dispersion of rates for
individual jobs in the same market.

For example, in August, 1965, the average straight-time hourly earnings of janitors, porters, and cleaners in the Scranton, Pennsylvania, metropolitan area labor market was $1.79. However, the full range of earnings for this job classification was as follows:

Number of workers	Range of earnings
1	.70– .80
10	.80– .90
2	1.00–1.10
3	1.10–1.20
15	1.20–1.30
10	1.30–1.40
18	1.40–1.50
20	1.50–1.60
14	1.60–1.70
36	1.70–1.80
2	1.80–1.90
19	1.90–2.00
37	2.00–2.10
26	2.10–2.20
10	2.20–2.30
10	2.40–2.50
3	2.50–2.60
9	2.60–2.80
Total 245	

Source: *Area Wage Survey: The Scranton, Pennsylvania, Metropolitan Area, August, 1965,* BLS Bulletin 1465-3.

Query: In which 10-cent bracket would you say the "going rate" fell? Very similar dispersions of rates of earnings existed in the same labor market for office occupations such as secretaries (from $45 to $130 per week and over) and other plant, maintenance, and service occupations such as laborers handling materials (from $1.20 to $3.20 per hour), truck drivers (from $1.30 to $3.40 per hour), and so on. It is well established that an *uncontrolled* labor market will display a wide range of rates for the same job; a narrow range or a single rate for a given occupation throughout a labor market is prima-facie evidence of some form of regulation or control. However, such an outcome is hardly compatible with competitive pricing theory, in the usual sense; it is more in line with "administered" rate setting, as described above.

The competitive aspect of the labor market is still further clouded by the existence of competing, noncompeting, and partially competing groups. Marshall's description of wages as "quasi-rents" is derived from the second of these types of situations.[9] An occupational choice is often a

[9] *Op. cit.,* pp. 577–579.

long-run commitment, involving education, apprenticeship, training, and experience of various kinds. An extensive investment in education for a profession or training for a skilled trade is not lightly cast aside; in fact, it is often observed that employes accustomed to a certain form of much more ordinary occupation (truck driving, office work, mining, farming) hesitate to shift to a different kind of career, even if the alternative opportunities seem most promising. To a degree, they are "specialized" factors of production, and to that degree, the return for their work will vary with the advantages or prosperity of the industry or portion of it to which they are committed, and with their own rare or unusual capacities for the line of work chosen—or their lack of such. Marshall observed that the return for personal services of this type met the definition of an economic "rent" more nearly than it did that of a competitive price.

A worker committed for life to his particular type of job is in competition only with other workers in the same job. A carpenter is not in competition with a bookkeeper, a clothing salesman, or an automobile mechanic. A carpenter, in fact, is not even in competition with a lather, a glazier, or a painter, all of whom work alongside carpenters on construction jobs, and all of them doing jobs which most carpenters can do. When large numbers of skilled tradesmen work on a single job, as in building construction, and each trade is a monopoly of skills (closed shop, limited union membership) and its members are not in competition for jobs with the members of any other trade, the maximum upward pressure is exerted upon wages. To a degree, each trade is indispensable; the job cannot be completed without its contribution. Each trade also represents only a small fraction of the labor cost, so that concessions to individual work groups raise total costs only slightly. The result, as is well known, has been some of the highest rates of pay and earnings to be found anywhere, particularly during the postwar building boom. This is illustrated by figures on comparative average hourly earnings of production workers in December, 1965, for selected industries:

Contract construction		$3.76
Electrical contracting	$4.44	
Plumbing and heating	4.01	
Painting and decorating	3.86	
Petroleum refining		3.56
Blast furnace and basic steel products		3.44
Printing and publishing		3.12
Newspaper publishing	$3.39	
Motor freight transportation and storage		3.11
Wholesale trade		2.65
Finance, insurance, real estate		2.43
Laundries, cleaning and dyeing plants		1.55

Source: *Employment and Earnings,* February, 1966, Table C-2.

The absence of competition between groups of workers may be a function of physical limitations (sex, age); expensive preliminary education (doctors); unusual natural skills or abilities (entertainers, professional athletes); long periods of training (skilled craftsmen); arbitrary limitations upon entry to a trade (nepotism, examinations, apprenticeships, union membership restrictions, seniority, degree and licensing requirements); etc. Most workers are noncompetitive with some large groups of employes, partially competitive with others, and directly competitive with still others. A female stenographer in an office is simply not in competition with a building construction laborer. Women are not employed in the latter kind of work. She may be partially competitive with the bookkeepers or other office machine operators in the office where she works or elsewhere; this is a matter of opportunity, preference, acquisition of skill, etc. And she is probably directly in competition with any number of private secretaries, whose work she can do and whose generally higher rates of pay are attractive. In factory work, much the same sort of situation holds: there are promotional ladders, there are dead-end jobs, and there are many varieties of posting-and-bid arrangements, often with preferences extended to senior employes. On the other hand, transfers to another department may require going back to the foot of the departmental seniority roster, so that competition across departmental lines is at least minimized.

"Labor," or "personal services," is not an abstract, general commodity, but a highly specific performance in a given place at a given time. The hindrances to mobility mentioned above do not invalidate the competitive analysis entirely, but they complicate it, requiring numerous qualifications and exceptions to explain existing rates and differentials. The problem of wage differentials is one of competition among individuals (personal rates) and groups: rates or rate ranges for different job classifications, whether set unilaterally by wage and salary administrators or bargained for by unions. They are important; just how important will become apparent to most college graduates when they get jobs and start supporting families on their salaries and begin to figure what they could buy with the extra earnings of someone they know who enjoys a favorable wage differential. The relative earning positions of one employe versus another are matters of central importance to both.

Then how is the general pattern of wage differentials to be explained? Nobody knows for sure, although there are several explanations available. The answer must come in the form of a theory of wages which fits the facts and resists the efforts of those who disagree with it to discredit it. There may be no such single theory, at least to satisfy everyone, in a labor market as large, as varied, and as structured as that in the United States.

For example, if you are a college student expecting to be employed at a salary after graduation, the chances are better than one out of five that you will work for some government agency—Federal, state, or local.

In January, 1966, there were 13,318,000 persons on government salary (including the military services)—or 21 per cent of a total of 63,896,000 nonagricultural employes in the country.[10] They were distributed as follows: Armed Forces—2,890,000, Federal civilian—2,393,000, state and local —8,035,000. Government employment is not immune to competition from private industry, but here again there are important hindrances to mobility back and forth: terms of service (Armed Forces, elective officials); specialized training (postal service, schoolteaching); civil service requirements as well as accrued tenure, seniority, etc.; low-cost pensions and long leaves and medical benefits, and so on. In the matter of wage determination, government pay rates are definitely "administered," not determined competitively. They are set, for the most part, by legislative action, are rigid and strictly classified, and tend to lag behind other rates in adjustment upward. Another very large segment of the United States labor force is employed at rates set by negotiation between unions and employers. Here again, the rates are administered and may or may not reflect the "normal" rate that would be arrived at competitively.

The modern controversy over the usefulness of the marginal productivity theory, the bargain theory, and other wage doctrines in explaining wage levels and differentials is an outcome of the differing views as to which aspect of the market process should be emphasized. If there is to be some understanding of the problem of differentials or of the other questions arising under the heading of wage policy—living standards, the labor-capital ratio, the guaranteed annual wage, minimum-wages and maximum-hours legislation, etc.—it will be made possible by an explanation which points to the main forces in wage determination and leads to the adoption of policies which will maximize the general welfare. This is one of the functions of a study of wage theory. First, however, there is the problem of the general wage level.

LABOR'S SHARE OF THE NATIONAL INCOME

Wage differentials are a short-run problem. That is to say, there is constant shift, change, and readjustment in comparative wage levels, even in very short periods where many of the important factors of production— land use, capital investment, buildings, machinery, and even labor skills and job preferences themselves—are fixed and relatively unchangeable. The other side of the wage question is a longer-run proposition and raises issues of at least equal importance, economically and socially. One of

---

[10] *Employment and Earnings*, February, 1966, pp. 33, 47, 54. In fact, your chances of receiving a government paycheck are much better than one in five, since the government gets more than its share of college graduates. *E.g.*, about half of state and local governmental employment is in education, with a college degree as prerequisite to 90 per cent of the jobs.

**Table 14-1.   National income by distributive shares, selected years
(In billions of dollars)**

	1929	1933	1940	1947	1955	1965
National income	$87.8	$40.2	$81.6	$198.2	$330.2	$554.7
Shares:						
Compensation of employes	51.1	29.5	52.1	128.8	223.9	392.0
Unincorporated business						
income (farms, stores)	14.8	5.6	13.1	35.5	42.1	54.5
Corporate profits	10.1	−2.0	9.1	23.6	43.1	73.1
Rental income of persons	5.4	2.0	2.9	6.5	10.7	18.6
Net interest	6.4	5.0	4.5	3.8	10.4	16.5

Source: *Statistical Abstract of the United States, 1961*, p. 303; *Survey of Current Business*, March, 1966, p. S-2.

them is: How do workingmen come off in relation to the people whose income is mainly from property, that is, from private businesses, corporate earnings, rent, and interest? Do workers get their fair share of the national output? This is the question asked (and answered) with such emphasis by Karl Marx in his exploitation theory of wages.

Labor's share.   What is labor's share of the national income? Tables 14-1 and 14-2 show how the national income went down and back from 1929 to 1965 and how it was split among employes, proprietors, corporate earnings, rents, and interest. Table 14-1 gives the amounts in billions of dollars, while Table 14-2 shows the split-up by percentages. Both the amounts and the percentages going to wages and salaries should be increased considerably, since the wages of farmers, proprietors, self-employed business and professional men (that is, the return for their personal services), and unpaid family labor, are included in the totals of

Table 14-2.   National income by percentage shares, selected years

	1929	1933	1940	1947	1955	1965
National income	100	100	100	100	100	100
Shares:						
Compensation of employes	58	73	64	65	68	71
Unincorporated business income	16	14	16	18	13	10
Corporate profits	11	−5	11	12	13	13
Rental income of persons	7	5	4	3	3	3
Net interest	8	13	5	2	3	3

Source: Adapted from Table 14-1.

Table 14-3. Labor-Capital income ratio for selected years

	1929	1933	1940	1947	1955	1965
Labor	68	83	74	75	78	81
Capital	32	17	26	25	22	19

Source: Adapted from Table 14-2.

the unincorporated income account (number 2 in the tables). A very conservative estimate of the amount of the transfer required to correct for this omission in the statistics would be 10 per cent of the national income. (The self-employed and unpaid family labor comprised about 13 per cent of all persons with a job in January, 1966—9,086,000 out of 71,229,000. The one year [1933] when there was probably no net balance in the unincorporated business account, it still got 13 per cent of the national income. The $5.6 billion reported that year undoubtedly went in its entirety to repay proprietors and their unpaid family workers for their services in family enterprises.) Adding 10 per cent to the wage and salary account would give a labor-capital income ratio for the 6 selected years as shown in Table 14.3.

Of course, to say that "labor" gets $3 out of every $4, or $4 out of every $5 of national income, is to say very little, as it gives no clue to whether the proportion is too much, just right, or not enough. This is a very controversial point in arguments over wage theory and policy. We cannot even be certain about the trend, although in recent years it certainly appears to be up—see Table 14-3 for the stretch 1947 to 1965. Much of this could be simply different bookkeeping arrangements (like the man who marries his cook and reduces the national income by the amount of her former salary): group professional practice with payments in salary instead of division of receipts, incorporation of proprietorship and partnership firms, etc. Statistics of national income and its detailed breakdown into distributive shares go back only to 1929, and it is therefore not possible to say whether the lower labor-capital income ratio of 1929 was typical of the boom years of the 1920s or whether it was as much out of line as presumably the 1933 figures are, since they reflect the bottom trough of the Depression of the 1930s. However, there is some information on trends in income shares which seems to support the belief that the labor side of the income ratio has been growing.

The detailed information is for the 35-year period, 1913 to 1948, and the comparison is of changes in the income shares of the top 1 per cent of income receivers and the remaining 99 per cent of individuals receiving income in the United States. The basic data are shown in Table 14-4.

**Table 14-4.   Changes in income shares, upper 1 per cent
and lower 99 per cent of income receivers, 1913–1948**

	1913–1920	1920–1929	1929–1939	1939–1948
Top 1%	Up 55%	Up 32%	Down 39%	Up 78%
Bottom 99%	Up 90%	Up 1%	Down 18%	Up 174%

Year	Per cent of nation's income going to	
	Top 1% income group	Bottom 99% income group
1913	16	84
1920	14	86
1929	17	83
1939	13	87
1948	9	91

Source: Geoffrey H. Moore, "Secular Changes in the Distribution of Income," *American Economic Review,* May, 1952, p. 530.

What the data disclosed is indicated by the author in the following:

The end of the twenties marked a turning point in the structure of the income distribution. At that time relative income *inequality* was about as great as at any earlier time for which we have adequate records. During the first few years of the Great Depression [of the 1930's], a complex set of changes apparently diminished income inequality sharply at the upper end of the scale of income but increased it at the lower end. Hence we cannot give an unequivocal answer to the question whether the late twenties or the early thirties marked the all-time peak in income inequality. But it is clear that since then income inequality has diminished to previously unrecorded levels. One of the heritages of the Great Depression and especially of World War II is an altogether new distribution of income by size.[11]

From 1913 to 1920, the average income of the top 1 per cent of income receivers in the United States rose 55 per cent, from $5,679 to $8,803. During the same period, the average income of persons in the remaining 99 per cent (of income receivers) rose 90 per cent, from $296 to $563. The main event of this period was the First World War. In the United States labor market, this meant expansion of employment, high wartime wages, and a trade-union boom, with membership going to 5 million in 1920. Property incomes rose significantly, but workers' incomes almost doubled. The legacy of this increase in purchasing power was the prosperity of the 1920s.

It is in the 10-year period from 1920 to 1929 that the really shocking

[11] Geoffrey H. Moore, "Secular Changes in the Distribution of Income," *American Economic Review,* May, 1952, pp. 527–544, italics added. This study is an analysis of Simon Kuznets's findings in his *Shares of Upper Income Groups in Income and Savings,* done for the National Bureau of Economic Research.

discrepancy appears. During this decade of almost uninterrupted prosperity, the incomes of the top 1 per cent in the country rose on the average 32 per cent, from $8,803 to $11,625. By contrast, the average income of the remaining 99 per cent practically stood still, rising only 1 per cent—from $563 to $567. In these statistics are reflected the results of the "open-shop" American plan, the smashing of the trade-union movement, the antilabor decisions of the United States Supreme Court and lesser courts around the country, and the "return to normalcy" under Presidents Harding, Coolidge, and Hoover.[12] The rise in the incomes of the well-to-do is shown in the second part of Table 14-4; in 1929, the top 1 per cent of the population got 17 per cent of the national income. This, of course, was the group with the lowest marginal propensity to consume. The legacy of the 1920s was the Depression of the 1930s.

From 1929 to 1939, all classes of income dropped, but property incomes dropped harder than others. Average returns to the top 1 per cent of income receivers fell from $11,625 to $7,052, or 39 per cent. Incomes of the lower 99 per cent, on the other hand, dropped only 18 per cent, from $567 to $465. The last 6 years of this period included all of the first and part of the second administration of President Franklin D. Roosevelt—the heart of the New Deal. The emphasis was on relief, welfare, and recovery. In the labor market, the Federal government was prounion, for higher wages, shorter hours, and restrictions on child labor. Legal minimum wages, statutory overtime payments, unemployment insurance, old-age pensions, were added to the government's protection of the right to organize and bargain collectively. The labor market was structured heavily to protect the wage earner, both then and in the future. The legacy of the 1930s showed up in the income shares of the next period, 1939 to 1948.

The feature of the period of 1939 to 1948 was the Second World War, for which the United States began to prepare in 1940 and from which reconversion was not completed until at least 3 years after the shooting stopped in Japan in August, 1945. As usual, war brought prosperity; in the American labor market, it produced maximum employment, high wages, and a trade-union membership boom. It also brought with it, from the preceding decade, overtime rates after 40 hours of work and unemployment compensation. Property incomes rose rapidly; by 1948, the average income of a member of the top 1 per cent of the population (incomewise) was up from $7,052 to $12,531, or 78 per cent. However, this gain was far surpassed proportionately by the rise of the average worker's income to almost three times its former level, from $465 to $1,272, or up 174 per cent. This mushrooming of mass purchasing power, which seems (from Table 14-3) to have been maintained during the Korean conflict and afterward, provided the legacy of the 1950s: full employment and

[12] Moore says: "It is somewhat surprising to find that the mass of the population did not participate to a greater extent in the boom of the twenties."

rising national income, interrupted by a couple of minor recessions which were easily controlled.

The purchasing power test: Real wages and earnings.   Yet there is many a slip between a rise in money wages and a higher standard of living. If the cost of living goes up as fast as wages, there is no gain in purchasing power; if it goes up faster, there is a loss, although take-home pay may appear to be rising at the time. And if wages do not rise, in today's inflationary world, the worker inevitably loses. For example, from December, 1964, to December, 1965, the average hourly earnings of production workers in the "miscellaneous plastic products" industry rose only from $2.21 to $2.22. This means that wage *rates* must have been practically stationary, since average weekly hours were up correspondingly, from 41.7 to 41.8. During the same 12-month period, the CPI rose from 108.8 to 111, or 2 per cent. The *real* value of the average hourly earnings therefore *fell* 1.5 per cent, from $2.03 ($2.21 divided by 108.8) to $2 ($2.22 divided by 111).[13] This was the exception, of course; most earnings rose during 1965, and by more than enough to cover the rise in the cost of living. However, many individual workers, many job classes, and (as shown) even some whole industrial classifications failed to keep pace with the rising price index.

Another weakness in the formula, "Higher pay = better living standard," is the hours-of-work factor. Earnings equal the rate of pay times the hours worked. A gain in wage rates may be more than offset by a reduction in the hours worked. For example, production workers in the "periodical publishing and printing" industry had average *weekly* earnings of $127 in December, 1964, but only $121.13 in December, 1965. The average work week fell from 41.1 hours to 38.7 hours, with overtime down from 4.3 hours per week to 3 hours.[14] Another common experience in the mass-production industries is layoff. It may be caused by a seasonal drop in sales, shutdown for retooling (as in automobile manufacturing), a bottleneck on the final assembly line, or any one of a dozen other reasons. It may be a disguised discharge—if the reduction is permanent and the worker is not called back, at some point his seniority is broken. Whatever the explanation, it means short time, smaller paychecks or none for a while, and reduced annual earnings. It is the uncertainty and bad previous record for regularity of employment in some of the larger manufacturing industries which has been responsible for the drive for wage guarantees and supplementary unemployment benefits.

The standard of living.   One clue to the state of prosperity and average living standard is the per capita real income of the population

[13] *Employment and Earnings,* February, 1966, pp. 84–85; *Monthly Labor Review,* February, 1966, Table D-1, p. 238.
[14] *Employment and Earnings,* February, 1966, *loc. cit.*

Table 14-5. Per capita disposable personal income, selected years, 1950–1964

Year	Current dollars	Constant (1954) dollars
1950	$1,369	$1,523
1955	1,661	1,654
1959	1,904	1,755
1960	1,936	1,758
1961	1,985	1,788
1962	2,060	1,839
1963	2,125	1,874
1964	2,248	1,957

Source: *Statistical Abstract of the United States, 1965,* p. 327, adjusted.

as a whole. Table 14-5 shows the changes in per capita money and real income for selected years, 1950 to 1964.

In 1964, the spendable, after-tax money income of a typical American household, composed of a husband and wife and 1.3 children, amounted to $7,418.40. (There were 58,218,000 households in the United States in 1964.) Its buying power in 1954 dollars was $6,458.10, an increase of $1,432.20 (28 per cent) from 1950. Per capita *real* income of $1,957 (in dollars of 1954 value) was up 12 per cent in 5 years (from 1959) and 18 per cent in 9 years (from 1955).

By whatever standard that may be applied, this is a picture of unprecedented, high-level, material prosperity. It explains the tens of millions of automobiles, TV sets, refrigerators, washing machines, and telephones in millions of new American homes; the unprecedented demand for such homes at high prices and interest costs; the high per capita consumption of meats and other expensive foods; the heavy vacation and tourist traffic; and the crowded classrooms in colleges, universities, and private schools. The one big question mark in the table is a weakness of all averages; they do not reveal the distribution. However, there is plenty of additional evidence to confirm the widespread nature of the rise in living standards. In 1965, employe compensation accounted for 71 per cent of the national income; if wage and salary withdrawals of the self-employed and family labor were added, at least $4 out of every $5 of national income went for personal services, which means in general the low- and middle-income groups. Increases in average hourly earnings since 1940 were over 300 per cent in all industries reporting and ran as high as 500 to 600 per cent in some. A major factor in the wage bill of the last decade is the group of benefits known as "fringes," which are inadequately reflected in reports of employe earnings. Unemployment, as a national problem, had been insignificant for 18 years. Unlike the 1920s, it was a workingman's, not a rich man's, boom.

What caused it?

Obviously, no single explanation would be considered sufficient. Too many factors—economic, political, technological—are embodied in the complex which determines the gross national product. However, there would be certain major emphases in the replies to the question, and the redistribution of income noted by Moore (table, p. 484) would certainly get primary attention. A convinced trade unionist (committed to the bargain theory of wages) would insist that the improved bargaining position of the organized labor movement, grown from a feeble 3 million members in 1933 to around 18 million by 1957, should not be overlooked. A businessman, who is more likely to be a marginal productivity theorist (without knowing it), might point to the improved capital-labor ratio brought about by the rapid wartime and postwar expansion of plants and facilities, and to the competition by employers for key classes of employes such as engineers and scientists. Many economists would ascribe the steady increase since 1933 to the increased propensity to consume arising from the shift of national income to lower-income groups, combined with the huge increase of government outlay (the rise in the Federal budget from $4 billion in 1933 to $120 billion in 1967), much of it deficit spending.

The problem here is not individual or class wage differentials, but the *general* level of earnings and income. This is a major public policy question, to wit, the proper relationship of the general wage level to prices, productivity, profits, and economic growth. From Adam Smith to modern times, economists have considered the general welfare paramount, and it has been the standard claimed for each competing wage doctrine in turn. For almost two centuries, theorists have argued over what *does* or what *ought to* determine the wage pattern, and governments have legislated freely on the subject. A glance at some of the earlier doctrines will give perspective to the debate. Wage theory and policy have been a much disputed problem, and some of the older explanations are still influential, even in modern times.

SOME EARLY WAGE THEORIES

The purpose of this summary is to lead up to an examination of current wage theory. No one is in a good position to analyze or criticize modern social theories without some historical perspective. There is an evolutionary process in both social thought and social action, although it must be distinguished from the slow mutations of biology. Social evolution is very rapid and the rate of change seems to be increasing. Also, social change is Lamarckian in character. The transmission of acquired characteristics is an obvious factor in both social thought and organization. Many remnants of earlier philosophies and vestiges of discarded institutions may be found in modern society, some good and some bad. A knowledge of their origins is often useful in evaluating them.

Wage theory has gone through three stages of development since the Middle Ages. The first, and longest, historically, was the medieval period of church domination, with its doctrine of the "just price," which meant in reality a just wage. The second began with Adam Smith's publication of the *Wealth of Nations* in 1776 and carried through the nineteenth century. It was the period of British classical economics, and the wage theories of Smith, Ricardo, Mill, Senior, and Marx are all in the classical, Malthusian tradition. It remained for Karl Marx, the last of the true classicists, to carry Smith's labor theory of value to its logical conclusion in his exploitation theory.

The modern period in wage theory began with the development of neoclassical economic doctrine and its emphasis upon marginalism. The marginal productivity theory of wages was a direct outgrowth of this intellectual movement and dominated "sound" economic thought from the beginning of the twentieth century to the present day. It has met strong competition, however, from trade-unionist supporters of the "bargaining" theory of wages, led by Sidney Webb in England and John R. Commons and his disciples in America, and since 1936 it has been challenged even more violently by John Maynard Keynes, in *The General Theory of Employment, Interest and Money.*

The "just wage" of the Middle Ages.   The "just price" of medieval times was really a wage concept. Whether for the trader or the craftsman, it was that price for his wares which would enable him to maintain himself and his family according to their established position in the community. The just price was concocted by churchmen and given a moral flavor to support the *status quo*. It is a relic of a static society, from which both intellectual and material progress were absent, and it might seem to be of merely historical interest. Nevertheless, there are vestigial remnants of the just wage in some of the more advanced societies of modern times.

Adam Smith's wage theories.   When the Industrial Revolution got under way around the middle of the eighteenth century, a new set of economic ideas with more flexibility than those of the church fathers became a necessity. The need was answered eventually by Adam Smith, the father of political economy. Smith had much to say on the subject of labor: (1) He formulated the labor theory of value. (2) He pointed out the bargaining advantage enjoyed by masters over workmen, thereby foreshadowing the bargain theory of wages of a century later. (3) He anticipated Ricardo's subsistence theory. (4) He developed a theory to account for wage differentials.[15]

The labor theory of value, which Smith stated as a doctrine and then

[15] *Wealth of Nations* (New York: Modern Library, Inc., 1937), pp. 30, 66–68, 101–109. See above, pp. 470–471, for Smith's account of the basis for wage differentials.

conveniently disregarded or qualified out of existence, is as follows in the words of the author:

The full value of any commodity . . . to the person who possesses it, and who means not to use or consume it himself, but to exchange it for other commodities, is equal to the quantity of labour which it enables him to purchase or command. Labour, therefore, is the real measure of the exchangeable value of all commodities.

The real price of every thing, what every thing really costs to the man who wants to acquire it, is the toil and trouble of acquiring it. What every thing is really worth to the man who has acquired it, and who wants to dispose of it or exchange it for something else, is the toil and trouble which it can save to himself, and which it can impose upon other people. What is bought with money or with goods is purchased by labour, as much as what we acquire by the toil of our own body. That money or those goods indeed save us this toil. They contain the value of a certain quantity of labour which we exchange for what is supposed at the time to contain the value of an equal quantity. Labour was the first price, the original purchase-money that was paid for all things.

This peculiar idea has long been defunct as a principle of economics, but its influence is far from dead. Seventy years after Smith wrote, Karl Marx seized upon his theory of value and made it the central point in the most explosive social doctrine of modern times—the labor exploitation and class-struggle dogmas of nineteenth-century socialism and the communism of today.

In his chapter on the "Wages of Labour," Smith gave an early argument for labor organization, in terms which have a very modern ring:

What are the common wages of labour, depends every-where upon the contract usually made between those two parties (masters and workmen), whose interests are by no means the same. The workmen desire to get as much, the masters to give as little as possible. The former are disposed to combine in order to raise, the latter in order to lower the wages of labour.

It is not, however, difficult to foresee which of the two parties must, upon all ordinary occasions, have the advantage in the dispute, and force the other into compliance with their terms. The masters being fewer in number, can combine much more easily. . . . In all such disputes the masters can hold out much longer.

At the same time, he observed that there was a level below which wages could not go, in spite of the master's advantage, and this was the minimum amount necessary to maintain the laborer, his wife, and family. Smith's principal contribution to wage theory, however, was his analysis of the causes of wage differentials by occupation (see page 470).

Ricardo's "iron law" of wages.   Where Smith was concerned with wage differentials in the short run, Ricardo, a more confirmed theorist, took notice mainly of the general wage level in the long run. His theory was simply a restatement of Malthus in wage terms, to the effect that any short-period increase in wages above the level of subsistence would be canceled out within a generation or so by the increase in the population, so that the wage would forever remain a bare sufficiency to support life.

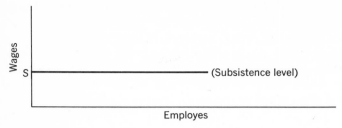

Fig. 14-1.

In diagrammatic form, Ricardo's theory would take the shape of Fig. 14-1. In a long-run schedule, each point on a line represents a period great enough for all factors to adjust, so that no elements are invariable. The wage would then be represented by a horizontal line at the subsistence level. The supply of labor would be whatever could be supported at this rate. It was a depressing view. Probably more than any other one thing, nineteenth-century wage theory earned for economics the title of "the dismal science."

If Malthus is correct, Ricardo is right; and if Malthus is wrong, Ricardo's "iron law" is invalid. There is a modern tendency for the *Essay on Population* of the reverend doctor to be considered as thoroughly discredited as the theory that the earth is flat. However, some recent writers of distinction have dissented from this conclusion,[16] and, since the end of the Second World War, practically all population theorists and conservationists have begun to be alarmed.

The Malthusian-Ricardian theory is an issue upon which the evidence of a single country may be misleading. America is the shining example of an economy with a rapidly increasing population, a constantly rising standard of living, and a decreasing fraction of the population at the subsistence level. Malthus was writing for the world, and the world picture is something else again. There has probably never been a time when more than a half of the population of the world (by projection approximately 1,460 million people in 1960) has been above what would be called a subsistence minimum in the United States, and it is at least doubtful that the proportion is rising.

From 1950 to 1964, the world's population rose 822 million, most of the increase coming in subsistence areas such as South and Central America, India, China, Japan, and the Netherlands Indies. At the same time, according to the practically unanimous conclusion of conservationists, the carrying capacity of the world's arable land is rapidly falling, as a result

[16] See, for example, Harrison S. Brown, *et al.*, *The Next Hundred Years* (New York: The Viking Press, Inc., 1957).

of erosion, soil exhaustion, deforestation, and the like. The two curves cannot continue indefinitely to swing in opposite directions. As Professor Joseph J. Spengler concluded, in his presidential address to the American Economic Association in New York City, December 29, 1965: "As matters stand, the longer-run prospect is definitely Malthusian, with man sitting on a demographic time bomb into which legislators, and others, here and abroad, continue to shovel combustibles." [17]

The exploitation theory of Karl Marx.   Marx took Smith at his word. The value of a commodity, Smith had said, was determined by the amount of labor used in its production. If this was the case (and Marx agreed that it was), then any part of the return withheld (profits, for example) was a surplus appropriated by the capitalist, and the result was exploitation of the workingman. Marx denied any productive contribution on the part of capital, holding that it was simply labor value withheld from its rightful owners. Land and other natural resources were as much the property of the working population as of those who held title to them. Also, they were useless without labor. The solution he proposed has received as much publicity as any social reform of modern times: Abolish the capitalist class and let laborers take over the means of production. Then everyone would contribute in line with his capacity and receive back a just share of the product. "From each according to his ability, to each according to his need."

There were, of course, several holes in the argument. What about the productive contribution of management (which Alfred Marshall later included among the factors of production along with land, labor, and capital)? And where would the savings and capital accumulations, which are undeniably a necessity, come from? How would "need" be determined, and by whom? Also, who would settle the really fundamental economic issue of resource allocation, and on what basis would industry be organized and its product divided among the workers? These are fundamental questions, which it is the job of any system of economic organization to answer. How they are answered will also have a significant effect upon efficiency.

In Marx's case, the technical inaccuracy of his theorizing has proved to be of secondary importance. One of the astounding events of the twentieth century has been the mass appeal of his theory of the exploitation of the working class and the rapid spread of Marxist socialist doctrines among large populations, especially those at or near the subsistence level.

---

[17] Joseph J. Spengler, "The Economist and the Population Question," *The American Economic Review*, March, 1966, pp. 1–24. This is one of the great presidential addresses to the association. It is a thorough and thoroughly depressing summary of the magnitudes and time factors involved in world population growth, two-thirds of the way through the twentieth century—indispensable reading for any student.

The residual claimant theory.   Karl Marx's exploitation theory was matched by an equally absurd but for a while popular theory of wages developed on this side of the Atlantic about the time of the great revolutionary's death (1883). It was the "residual claimant" theory of Francis A. Walker—an explanation of wages that would satisfy the most ardent capitalist. Walker argued that the amount of wages in the fund available for the payment of workers was determined by the product of industry, not the quantity of capital on hand (thereby distinguishing it from the wages-fund theory proper of J. S. Mill and his followers). However, what infuriated labor spokesmen and their sympathizers (and correspondingly delighted conservatives) was the order in which the employer was presumed to divide up said product. First, he deducted a portion for rent. Next, he set aside the necessary return of capital (interest). A third deduction was his own remuneration, profits. And lastly, the remainder became a wages fund for the hiring of labor. This position of the workingman as the "residual claimant" in the production process was rejected as harsh and unfair. Also, it was manifestly inaccurate in fact, as laborers were employed, then as now, and wages paid just as they are today, during the production period, in advance of sales, and often before it was known whether there would be a margin of profit or not.

As indicated, Walker's theory was an outgrowth of the wages-fund theory which dominated classical economic thought during the middle 50 years of the nineteenth century. For a long time thereafter, the wages-fund explanation was considered superseded by the marginal productivity theory. However, the former has now returned in a somewhat different guise to provide proof that sectional (group) wage increases have only a distorting effect and cannot contribute to an increase in the general wage level. It must therefore be dealt with in the following chapter.

READINGS

For the most complete treatment of the wages question in a single volume, see W. S. Woytinsky and Associates, *Employment and Wages in the United States* (New York: The Twentieth Century Fund, Inc., 1953). At the other end of the scale, an introductory primer for beginning students is: H. M. Douty, *Wages: An Introduction* (Los Angeles: Institute of Industrial Relations, University of California, 1951). For the managerial approach, try D. W. Belcher, *Wage and Salary Administration*, 2d ed. (Englewood Cliffs, N.J.: Prentice-Hall, Inc., 1962) or Jno. A. Patton, C. L. Littlefield, and S. A. Self, *Job Evaluation*, 3d ed. (Homewood, Ill.: Richard D. Irwin, Inc., 1964).

FIFTEEN

WAGE THEORY

THE ISSUES

Wage theory is not just an academic problem, of interest only to professors and students. It is a matter of day-to-day practical importance and of long-run security to every wage earner in the country (and there are almost 65 million of them) whether he believes the size of his paycheck is *primarily* affected by (1) the value of the marginal addition he makes to production, or (2) his bargaining power relative to that of his employer, or (3) a governmental wage policy based on full employment and wage supports.

Wage policy is based on theory. The policy may be that of an employer or group of employers, faced with the highly practical necessity of recruiting and maintaining a work force, or it may be the policy developed by a trade union or a group of unions and put in effect through collective bargaining procedures and negotiations. A third major source of wage policy is the government. Every modern industrialized nation has some kind of wage policy—probably several of them. If the theory employed is correct, a policy in line with it will be appropriate and helpful; if the theory is wrong, a policy based on it may well do more harm than good.[1]

If a wage earner thinks that competition for labor will force employers to pay him the full marginal return for his class of work, it will be rational for him to conclude that the time lost due to strikes and the money spent on union dues are wasted, since no employer is going to pay him more than he is worth and unions are simply another obstacle to the

[1] For samples of Federal wage policies in the United States, consult the "Findings and Policy" of the National Labor Relations Act, now "Title I" of the Labor Management Relations (Taft-Hartley) Act (see Appendix to Chap. 9); the Employment Act of 1946 (Public 304, 79th Cong.); or the Fair Labor Standards Act of 1938 (52 Stat. 1060), as amended, sections on minimum wages and maximum hours. The hearings and congressional debates on these measures are excellent sources of study for anyone interested in the issues raised.

494

efficient functioning of supply and demand in the labor market. Governmental intervention in the form of minimum-wage laws, a national wage policy, or otherwise will be equally undesirable. It can only create inflexibility and red tape, which will hamper labor mobility and the free adjustments necessary to keep the market in equilibrium, whereby each unit of the factors of production (of which every employe is one) is assured the maximum return in its employment.

On the other hand, if experience or argument makes him doubt that competition is effective in the labor market, then his bargaining position relative to that of his employer becomes more important. If competition does not force him to it, why should an employer pay a workman the full value of his productivity? It is good business to buy below the market if one can. The employe probably has not read Adam Smith, but many others since 1776 have suspected that "the workmen desire to get as much, the masters to give as little as possible." To the extent that the market does not function efficiently, the wage to be paid becomes a bargaining proposition. How does he, the employe, stack up against his employer for purposes of trading? The answer to this question may make the price of union membership seem less a cost than a necessity to an industrial employe. He is also likely to favor government action supporting the right to organize. A national policy of wage controls which may imply limiting the right to strike and other forms of organized action, however, is another thing. It limits his bargaining power and that of his union, and he will probably oppose it.

But suppose the employe we are considering was a wage earner from 1930 to 1965. Whether a believer in a competitive labor market or a union member in a solidly organized industry (like coal mining or the railroads), he may well have had 10 years (1930 to 1940) of lowered wages, along with unemployment, layoff, and short time. The employer could hardly be blamed; he was obviously losing money and may have gone broke or into receivership. The union could not save its members' jobs, although it could insist on a share-the-work policy and protect the older men through seniority rules. The wage level (and with it, regularity of work) did not improve markedly until 1941, when the government began to spend heavily on rearmament. After that, earnings rose steadily, until by 1948 they were more than double what they had been in 1939. By 1965 the factory employe who was earning only 66 cents an hour in 1940 was up to $2.67 an hour, or more than four times the pay of 25 years earlier. His real wages (standard of living) were up 80 per cent—from $1.10 to $1.98 (on the basis of 1947 to 1949 prices)—and his annual earnings more still, since his employment was far more regular and included many fringe benefits unknown in 1939.

If this employe were of a thoughtful turn of mind, he might look backward over the 35 years of experience and try to put his finger on what was responsible for the hard time he had in the 1930s and the relative prosperity of the 1940s, 1950s, and 1960s. He might conclude that a large volume of spending (high national income) meant full employment, with steady work and rising real wages. And who could make certain that there was a large volume of spending? Not private employers or their customers, whose demand for goods and services fell more than 50 per cent between 1929 and 1932, nor trade unions, which were equally helpless. Only the Federal government, which had demonstrated its purchasing strength from 1941 onward, seemed to be in a position to keep business going at a high level. To such an employe, a national policy setting a floor under wages, combined with a guarantee of continued full employment might make sense as a supplement to his reliance upon either a free labor market or his union.

The three points of view presented in the preceding paragraphs are merely very brief examples of the influences held to be most important by proponents of the marginal productivity theory of wages, the bargain theory, and the national-income explanation of wages and employment. They are by no means mutually exclusive, reflecting in many cases merely a difference of emphasis. There are probably few persons who find it possible to restrict themselves to the premises and implications of any one particular doctrine. Nevertheless, wage policy is an issue and as such it can be traced to differences in basic premises and the analysis stemming from the latter. Also, to a considerable degree it is possible to identify the groups associated with differing theories. Two such are employers and labor leaders.

Employers, including the general group known as "management," endorse the supply-and-demand assumptions of the marginal productivity theory as a part of their general approval of competition and a free market and their general disapproval of labor organization (monopoly) and public intervention. Endorsement, however, does not necessarily mean full personal agreement. It would be a rare employer who would deny the importance of bargaining power in the settling of individual or group wage rates. On the other side of the wage bargain, the fact that two-thirds of the country's employes are outside of trade unions does not necessarily imply their unconditional vote for competition in the labor market. It may simply mean that these workers find "individual bargaining" less hazardous than others do and the requirements of organization too burdensome or simply unavailable.[2]

The bargain theory of wages is, of course, a basic faith of organized

[2] It might be well to recall that the right to organize and bargain collectively is only partially protected, even within the jurisdiction of the National Labor Relations Board. Minorities in representation elections where the vote goes "No union" are denied protection, as are many employes in local (intrastate) commerce in states having no comparable protection of organization rights. It should also be remembered that many unorganized employes are the indirect beneficiaries of collective bargaining in related, contiguous, or competitive firms, industries, and occupations.

labor, but few trade unionists are under the illusion that it is a complete solution to the wages problem. The AFL–CIO is officially on record as favoring a full-employment program, higher minimum wages, and exclusion of women and boys from many occupations. Unions recognize the fact of competition in the labor market, both through policies restricting membership when their own members are out of work and in their wage negotiations with depressed industries and firms.

It is public policy in the United States to support the right to organize and bargain collectively as a means of raising the earnings of lower-income groups, but this is combined with severe restrictions upon various kinds of union tactics used in their organizing and in negotiations with employers; at times (*e.g.*, during a war) governmental restrictions may even be extended to direct wage controls. Governmental policy also embraces legal minimum wages, payments of time and a half for work beyond 40 hours a week, and a commitment to maintain "high" employment. It also includes support of public employment offices which are designed to improve the mechanism of the labor market, thus making competition more effective. Public wage policy is a practical affair and calls for a compromise of doctrines, with emphasis upon the elements which seem most important at the time. However, the policy proposals and the measures taken should be analyzed in terms of the related wage theories, their underlying premises, their strong points, and their weaknesses.

THE MARGINAL PRODUCTIVITY THEORY OF WAGES

The marginal productivity theory is the "orthodox" theory of wages. It is the oldest, the best known, and the most widely taught of the dominant wage theories of the twentieth century. It is thus somewhat paradoxical that during the past 30 years, the marginal productivity theory has so seldom been used as a basis for policy, either public or private, whether related to the setting of individual rates (differentials) or the maintenance of full employment and economic development—a rising standard of living. Like many other social theories, it seems to have been finally perfected and become most widely understood just as the conditions implied in its premises were being brought more and more into question.

The long-standing popularity of the theory is not hard to understand. It is the competitive theory, and in a society where belief in competition is an article of faith, it bolsters the emphasis upon production for a free market. In relating wages to workers' productivity as measured by market demand, it satisfies ethical as well as logical requirements. Men are paid what they are *worth*, rather than according to their social positions (just price), job characteristics (Smith), subsistence requirements (Ricardo), the available working capital (wages fund), what is left over (residual claimant), need (Marx), or bargaining power (Webbs). From the standpoint of the teacher and scholar, the marginal productivity theory is an integral portion of a beautifully symmetrical total theory of price and distribution which explains the workings of an economic system that is always tending toward equilibrium and the full use of all factors of production. On the practical side, the theory leaves employers in full charge of the pricing mechanism, on the assumption that the employers' interests are, if not invariably, at least usually parallel to those of society in general.[3] With so many arguments in its favor, even the critics of the theory have been tempted to say that if it is not valid, it ought to be, and perhaps the environment should be modified, not the theory.

In the short run: Wage differentials under competition.   The marginal productivity theory is deceptively named. It should have been called the "competitive" theory, since it is the assumption of competition in the labor market which distinguishes it from other wage doctrines. Under competition, there is a tendency for each factor of production (employe) to be paid an amount (a wage) equal to the value of the marginal addition to production of the last factor in the class to be employed—hence, the "marginal productivity" theory. The one fundamental underlying assumption is *competition for the factors of production and a free labor market,* with all that implies: large numbers of buyers and sellers, homogeneity of product (or service), mobility of the factors, full knowledge of market conditions by both buyers and sellers, free entrance to and exit from the market, and flexible prices.

How is it supposed to work in the short run?

A competitive market is an impersonal market, in which price is the guide and regulator. No single buyer or seller or any organized group of either is able to influence the market significantly. The value of anything offered for sale will correspond to the quantity of it that is offered. If the quantity is large relative to demand, the price at which all can be sold will tend to fall; if the supply is scarce, the price will tend to rise. Labor, being perishable and mobile, will shift from those occupations in which the supply is excessive to those in which there is a relative shortage until wage rates within each class are uniform for all employers (buyers),[4] and differ-

---

[3] For an unusually explicit statement of this assumption, see Henry C. Simons, "Some Reflections on Syndicalism," *Journal of Political Economy,* March, 1944, p. 2: "What we generally fail to see is the identity of interest between the whole community and enterprises seeking to keep down costs. Where enterprise is competitive —and substantial, enduring restraint of competition in product markets is rare— enterprisers represent the community interest effectively; indeed, they are merely intermediaries between consumers of goods and sellers of service."

[4] Note that this does not imply equal wage rates for the various classes or unlimited mobility. Some classes of labor are more productive than others and will receive higher prices; the class ratios will be determined by the kind of business the employer is in and the form of organization adopted. It is the marginal substitution of the employer's wage dollar which is equalized. Mobility would be high within the major classes—semiskilled or unskilled, for instance—but would need be only marginal between these classifications.

ences between classes reflect the productivity differentials of different skills
modified by the available supplies of qualified workmen for each occupational class.

Within the firm, the effects of this shifting are registered on the employer's cost curve. According to the law of diminishing productivity,
when other factors are held constant, each unit of a given type of labor
added by an employer results in a smaller increment of production than
its predecessor. The value increment is lower still, since it is ordinarily
true that larger output can only be sold at a lower price. Hence, the employer's cost function for each class of labor will be the reciprocal of a
downward-sloping curve of diminishing value increments of his product.
It will be to the employer's advantage to expand the number of employes
of each class until the additional wages he is required to pay just equal
the final value increment of production assignable to the last employe
added. This will be where Marginal Labor Cost (MLC) equals Marginal
Revenue Product (MRP).

The wage rate paid cannot be above or below that of another employer in the same market, since employes with knowledge of the differential will leave the low-wage firms and underbid their more highly paid
competitors. This shifts the high-wage employer's cost curve downward
and to the right, making it to his advantage to hire more workmen *at a
lower wage*. The process is shown graphically in Fig. 15-1. The employer's
demand curve for labor is the marginal revenue function of his product.
Under supply conditions S, equilibrium will be reached with A employes
at wage C. Competitive underbidding by employes attracted away from
lower-wage firms will move the labor-cost curve downward and to the
right, whereupon employment is expanded to a new equilibrium position,
with B employes at wage F. Final equilibrium is reached when the rate
of pay is uniform for each class of employe in the market area and there

Fig. 15-1. *Shift of employer's labor-supply (cost) curve due to influx of low-wage
employes*

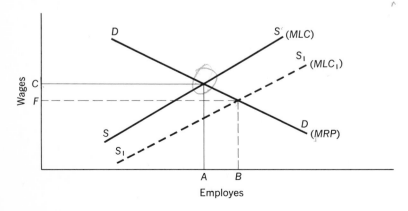

is no inducement for workers to transfer from one occupation or one employer to another.

For the labor market as a whole the situation is similar. Demand functions for different classes of labor are simply the sums of the demand curves of individual employers, and supply curves are totals of potential employes available at given wage rates. The market is in equilibrium at the point of intersection of the curves, as at A in Fig. 15-2, when the quantities demanded by employers just equal the offerings of employes at wage B.

Changes in either the demand or supply functions may come about quite naturally through an increase in the population of the area, expansion or contraction of firms in size or number, withdrawal of people from employment, or for other reasons. As the curves shift in response to changing conditions, wage rates adjust themselves flexibly, and employes transfer from one employer or occupation to another, with full employment and maximum return to each employe the outcome of each new equilibrium position.

The question of wage differentials is therefore answered as follows, according to marginal productivity theory: (1) Short-run regional differentials are possible, since most labor markets are local in character; these would be cured through time, however, as new entrants to the labor market, unattached and mobile, would search out the locations with the maximum pay levels. (2) Job differentials will reflect two things: (a) the relative productiveness of different classes of work and (b) the supply of qualified workmen in each grade or class. (3) Employer or firm differentials will be of short duration, since the combined pressures of employers in search of lower costs and employes looking for increased incomes will soon wipe them out.

Fig. 15-2. Equilibrium in the labor market

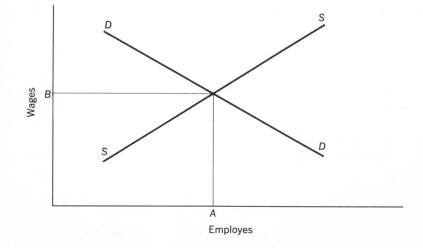

The marginal productivity theory in the long run.   If it is to be a complete theory, the marginal productivity doctrine must have something to say about wages in the long run. It does, as follows: The general level of wages in the long period is determined by the capital-labor ratio. According to this view, the productivity of labor varies directly with the tools it has to work with. Capital investment provides the tools. If capital investment is high, relative to the number employed, the wage will be high; if capital investment is low, there will be limited equipment for workers to use, productivity will be low, and the wage, which comes out of the product, can only be small. A simple illustration will be sufficient. A man digging a trench with his bare hands would make slow progress. If he is furnished with a pick and shovel, his productivity will be multiplied several times. But equip the digger with a caterpillar tractor bucket-type trench digger, and he will do the work of a hundred men with hand tools.

Industrial progress is technological progress, the harnessing of mechanical inventions to a succession of prime movers which give control over hundreds and thousands of horsepower: steam, electricity, internal combustion, and perhaps in the future, atomic energy. Prime movers and mechanical equipment require tremendous capital outlays. If this form of outlay is continued, expanded, and extended to new areas, labor productivity, which rose at an average rate of 3 per cent a year between 1850 and 1940,[5] may well continue to rise and perhaps at an increasing rate. But it will only do so if the capital investment is forthcoming.

The capital-labor ratio is also subject to an equilibrating process. Employers try to equalize the rate of marginal substitution in all the factor markets, capital as well as labor. If the price of labor is low, there is little incentive to substitute capital equipment for manpower. But if wages are high, there is rapid introduction of laborsaving devices through mechanical development and the use of forms of energy other than manpower. An economy with a high capital-labor ratio tends to be a high-wage economy, which in turn exerts a pressure toward increasing capital outlays.

Is the labor market "competitive" or "administered"?   Do wages in general reflect with reasonable promptness the shifts in supply occasioned, for example, by the influx of new entrants—with their various aptitudes and training—into the job market, or the changes in employers' demand functions due to shifts in consumer tastes, the rise of new industries, or technological change? In other words, to what extent is the price paid for labor competitively determined and to what extent is it "administered," which means that the price may be set in the short run without relation to quantities available or the state of demand.

There is of course no quick and easy answer to such a question. There

[5] *America's Needs and Resources* (New York: The Twentieth Century Fund, Inc., 1947), p. 23.

are many labor markets and highly individual variations exist within even small market patterns. In the United States as a whole, there are approximately 11 million employers (11,383,000 in the tax year 1961 to 1962 [6]) —ranging from the single-family farm with its use of hired help a few weeks out of a year to the Federal government, with its staff of more than 2 million—and around 65 million employes working at thousands of different kinds of jobs in a wide variety of industries. Some labor markets are clearly quite competitive—for example, the unstructured markets for casual labor in agriculture, domestic service, fruit and vegetable harvesting, and the like. However, in other equally casual (short-term employment) markets, the price is just as clearly insulated from the short-run effects of over- and undersupply, through union contracts that set the scale for a term of from 1 to 3 years. This is true of building construction, longshoring, the needle trades, and others.

A bargained wage rate may or may not be the "normal" rate, that is, the rate which, assuming competition, would have been set competitively by market forces in the absence of the union. The result has been argued both ways, Simons (and most others) holding that the outcome will be a rate above the normal, providing a monopoly advantage to the organized workers to the detriment of those unorganized,[7] and Friedman professing just the opposite, that unions have held wage rates below the level to which they would have risen if left exposed to competitive bidding.[8] Whichever is correct, one thing is certain. The rate arrived at through collective bargaining is a negotiated amount and not the same thing as a price fixed by competitive bidding, as, for example, the price of wheat or of a stock on the New York Stock Exchange.

There is of course no doubt whatever that the employer's position in collective bargaining negotiations is strongly affected by the extent to which labor costs enter into his total costs, thus affecting his price and his position vis-à-vis his competitors. However, it may well be that the employer's product price is an "administered" price, due to a monopoly or oligopoly situation in the industry. If such is the case, the employer's opposition to a wage (and cost) increase may well be less rigid than it otherwise would be. A price adjustment upward immediately following a wage increase (as is customary in the steel industry) may take much of the pain out of the new rate.

Nobody knows the actual extent of "administered" prices in the economy, but there is no doubt of their existence, and it is widely assumed that their range and importance is increasing rather than decreasing. The

[6] *Statistical Abstract of the U.S., 1965*, p. 490.

[7] Simons, *op. cit.*

[8] See his essay in D. McCord Wright (ed.), *The Impact of the Union* (New York: Harcourt, Brace & World, Inc., 1951).

Economic Research Department of the Chamber of Commerce of the United States says that:

With the exception of a few markets, mostly staples, administered pricing extends throughout the economy. It is typical in retailing and widespread in wholesaling; it is found throughout the service industries and manufacturing. . . . Administered pricing is so widespread that there is no method to render pricing in general more promptly responsive to changing supply and demand, without drastically changing our economy. Not only would economic concentration have to be greatly reduced, and methods of buying and selling completely changed, but the American consumer would have to learn to do without product differentiation.[9]

If the above is correct, it means that the pressure of price competition in the setting of the wage is at least made imprecise and blurred.

There are now in the neighborhood of 18 million employes in the United States working under labor-management agreements, all of them *negotiated* on one basis or another: interfirm, interunion, or interindustry comparisons, changes in the cost of living, the employer's ability to pay, or, where argument is not sufficient, a test of relative economic strength. The agreements covering these employes affect directly several million more employes, such as the unorganized clerical and supervisory workers in unionized firms and the unorganized firms in otherwise heavily organized industries or communities. Union organization is one of the primary elements of "structure" in the modern labor market. A structured labor market is one in which the manner and conditions of employment, including pay, are controlled through special market mechanisms: labor law, union contracts and work rules, civil service regulations, etc. These market mechanisms lay down the rules for the recruitment and hiring of workers, the administration of wages and salaries, opportunities for advancement to other jobs in higher labor grades, job rights during layoff and recall, and the tenure of employment.[10]

A structured labor market is not necessarily noncompetitive. However, a great many specific structural elements in the modern labor market are intended to and will certainly inhibit or dull the effects of competition. Examples are (1) the restrictions upon entry to large groups of occupations—the professions, the skilled trades, the civil service; (2) seniority limitations upon job assignment on the basis of skill or merit; (3) uniform pay rates, either by single rates or by automatic progression through rate ranges; (4) tenure rights, which make dismissal difficult; and especially (5) the accumulation of vested interests in employment with one firm or nonprofit agency (governmental or otherwise) such as: pension rights, fringe benefits that increase with seniority, and group welfare plans.

[9] *Economic Intelligence,* July, 1958, p. 2.
[10] O. W. Phelps, "A Structural Model of the U.S. Labor Market," *Industrial and Labor Relations Review,* April, 1957, p. 402.

A prime feature of the general labor market in the United States in recent years is the high and rising level of *nonprofit* employment. A very conservative estimate of its extent is 25 per cent of all nonfarm employes. Most of it, of course, is governmental. In February, 1966, for example, of a total of 65,328,000 nonagricultural employes, 13,376,000—or 20 per cent —were government workers, either civilian or military.[11] However, a very significant portion is "private" nonprofit—in schools, colleges, hospitals, foundations, research groups, churches, unions, etc. A noticeable characteristic of such employment is its stability, its failure to be influenced by fluctuations in the GNP or by community conditions. (During the 45 years from 1921 to 1966, government employment in this country—military and civilian—recorded an increase every year except five: 1929 to 1930, 1930 to 1931, 1931 to 1932, 1945 to 1946, and 1946 to 1947.) To a considerable degree, nonprofit employment seems to be regarded as national or community overhead. The labor costs involved are not prime costs, and the services provided are regarded as relatively indispensable, regardless of fluctuations in the demand for them.

Are the wages paid in the nonprofit industries competitive or administered? The actual rates are set by means of a number of involved and intricate procedures: wage and salary legislation, classification board regulations, rulings by boards of trustees, union negotiations, etc. As types, many of these institutions are notorious for their low scales of pay, often running far below the "going rates" in comparable occupations in the same locality. Internally, the test of marginal substitution, difficult enough in a commercial enterprise, is clouded by peculiarities of institutional accounting and the lack of a cost-and-revenue standard. (What is the marginal revenue product of a Treasury clerk?) Externally, there is unquestionably the competition provided by the existence of available jobs in private industry. However, even in the face of outside favorable differentials in wage scales and in "tight" labor markets, the nonprofit institutions are still able to staff their positions.[12]

It is hard to escape the conclusion that in the short run institutional wage scales are set and administered with little regard to either the existing labor supply or the demand for workers derived from the demand for the services produced by the organization. As in the case of negotiated wage scales and rates set in industries with an administered price structure (for products), this seems most likely to result in a blurring of the analysis, resulting in a considerable area of uncertainty within which the

[11] *Employment and Earnings,* March, 1966, *passim.*

[12] Even at such unbelievable rates as $35 to $40 a week for orderlies, porters, dietary workers, and nurses' aides in private nonprofit hospitals in New York City as late as the spring of 1959. See the *Wall Street Journal,* Pacific Coast Edition, Apr. 2, 1959, p. 11.

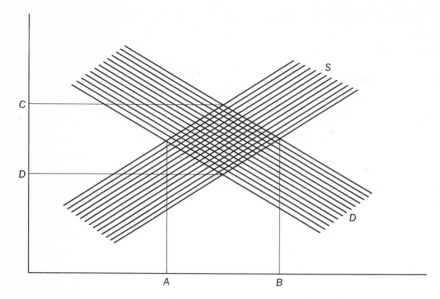

Fig. 15-3. Supply of and demand for labor in an administered market

actual rates are set in terms of bargaining, administrative policy, or political pressure. The outcome might be illustrated as in Fig. 15-3.

Under conditions of uncertainty, either the supply of labor or the demand for it or both may be represented by a band instead of a line. The
intersection of the functions will then be a zone instead of a point, with
both the actual rates and/or the actual numbers employed determined by
chance, by administrative decision, by bargaining, or by any other of a
number of influences. In Fig. 15-3, the range of possible employment
would be from A to B and the range of rates from C to D. The marginal
analysis is still applicable as an explication of underlying forces, but
reliance upon the competitive mechanism of bids and offers as a method
of making the day-to-day decisions of the market place seems quite likely
to produce major inequities.[13]

There is no question but that businessmen must estimate and cover
costs, that they must be aware of the prices and quantities available of the
productive factors they use, and that a high-wage policy is traditional in
the American economy. The only issue is whether the labor-market mechanism is sufficiently precise and responsive for competition to provide

[13] Of the sort, for example, which the National War Labor Board discovered in
the steel industry during the Second World War and which resulted in its order to
the industry and the union to work out a standard job-classification system with
appropriate differentials based on "equal pay for equal work."

the right answers within reasonable limits of tolerance. To the extent that the market is heavily structured and "administered," the answer seems to be in the negative. In addition, there must be added the evidence of the inherent lack of homogeneity, mobility, knowledge, and price equality reviewed earlier. The pricing mechanism of the labor market, even in "individual bargaining," in which long-term contracts of indefinite tenure, subject to interruption by either party upon short notice, are established orally and the terms worked out as conditions arise, is quite different from that ordinarily assumed by economic theorists. The latter is best illustrated by the bourse-type system of bids and offers for the exchange of commodities of an even quality which may be graded and classed for distribution to anonymous buyers. Personal services are not fungible (interchangeable one for another) and are hard to depersonalize.

The shape of the labor-supply curve.   The standard assumption with respect to the shape of the labor-supply curve is that it is positively inclined, as shown in Fig. 15-4*a* and not negatively inclined as pictured in 15-4*b*. This means simply that workers act competitively and acquisitively in the sale of labor services, increasing the quantities offered as the price rises. But in fact do they? As wages rise, do workers put in longer hours, and those who hesitated before apply for jobs? There is some prima-facie evidence to the contrary.

Who is there who does not know of the *withdrawal* of a wife or child from regular employment as a consequence of an increase in earning power of the head of the family? And, conversely, how many times has the layoff of a workingman sent two or three people in search of jobs, as other members of the family attempted to retrieve the loss of income? Increased leisure is one of the marks of a high standard of living. If these illustrations are typical, the supply curve of labor may be negatively in-

Fig. 15-4.   Positively and negatively inclined labor-supply curves

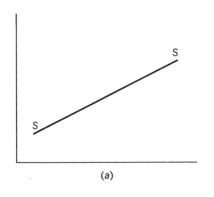

(a)

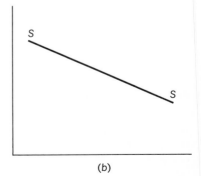

(b)

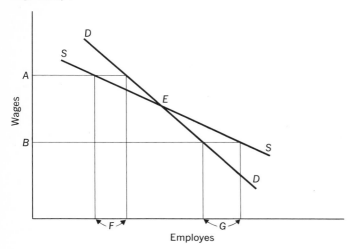

Fig. 15-5.   The negatively inclined labor-supply curve and instability

clined, at least at certain times and in certain markets. Such a possibility
has in fact been suggested by several writers.[14]

A negatively inclined labor-supply curve could easily result in the unstable situation shown in Fig. 15-5, where competitive bidding for jobs
and personnel merely drives the wage farther away from the point of
intersection of the curves and increases the gap between the quantity
demanded and that supplied. Below the spurious equilibrium point *E*,
competitive bidding by employes will only drive the wage down and increase the unemployment gap *F*. Above *E*, competitive recruitment by
employers will raise the wage level but merely widen the gap *G*, leaving
personnel needs unsatisfied.[15]

Negative inclination of the labor-supply curve creates other possibilities, two of which are illustrated in Fig. 15-6a and b.

According to 15-6a, the supply-and-demand curves for labor are con-
gruent throughout a considerable range. Equilibrium may be reached at
any wage between *A* and *B* or any range of employment from *G* to *F*.
With the situation as described in 15-6b, there is no possible point of
equilibrium, as the supply-and-demand curves do not intersect at any

[14] R. A. Lester, *Economics of Labor*, Chap. 5, "The Labor Market" (New York:
The Macmillan Company, 1941); Paul H. Douglas, *The Theory of Wages* (New
York: The Macmillan Company, 1933), pp. 269–314; Sumner H. Slichter, *Modern
Economic Society* (New York: Holt, Rinehart and Winston, Inc., 1931), pp. 620–627;
Clarence D. Long, *The Labor Force under Changing Income and Employment*
(Princeton, N.J.: Princeton University Press, 1958).

[15] This occurs only when the supply curve is negatively inclined *but more elastic
than* the demand curve.

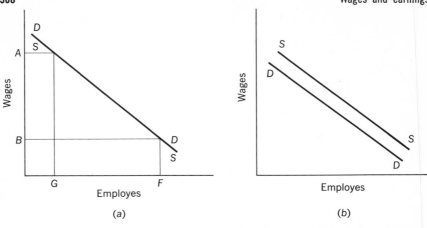

Fig. 15-6. Labor-market possibilities with a negatively inclined labor-supply curve

point. There will always be unemployed labor resources in the market. Any experienced observer will recall apparent examples of both: either constant unemployed labor reserves (15-6*b*) or the matching of demand and supply at various levels of wages (15-6*a*).

THE BARGAIN THEORY OF WAGES

If the labor market is an administered market, the wages paid in it will be "administered," and not set competitively. What explanation is there of the forces or pressures brought to bear in a market of this type? The most widely accepted hypothesis of this sort is the "bargain," or "bargaining" theory of wages, first developed by the Webbs and since then a fundamental of trade-union doctrine. It has none of the extensive technical apparatus of the marginal productivity theory. Simply stated, it is:

That wages, hours, and working conditions are largely a matter of the relative bargaining strength of the two sides; that without organization and concerted action there will be a tendency toward undesirable, if not the worst possible, conditions for the workers; that no adequate safeguard is found in the operation of the factors at work in the unorganized trade [competition]; that there is a flexible, changeable situation and that by means of organized effort positive improvement can be secured in wages, hours, and other important details of the labor contract and in their administration.[16]

In recent years, especially since 1933, the bargain theory has gained steadily as an explanation of the significant forces determining wage rates and differentials in the short run. Every "Area Wage Survey" published by the Bureau of Labor Statistics confirms the wide dispersion of rates

[16] H. A. Millis and R. A. Montgomery, *Organized Labor* (New York: McGraw-Hill Book Company, 1945), p. 356.

for individual jobs indicated above in Figure 15-3.[17] If the intersection of demand and supply curves is a *zone*, as has been proved time and again, then the following propositions are valid:

1. Within the given zone (from C to D, in Fig. 15-3), any rate will work.
2. Where the rate will be set will depend on the interests of the administering party or parties.
3. If the rate is set unilaterally by employers, it will tend toward the bottom of the zone: agriculture, domestic service, etc.
4. If the rate is set jointly (bargained) it will tend toward the top of the zone: building trades, steelworkers, autoworkers, etc.

The classic statement of the helplessness of the individual workman in dealings with his employer and the competitive pressure on wage rates is found in the Webbs' bible of trade unionism, *Industrial Democracy*.[18] In their chapter on "The Higgling of the Market" they outlined the chain of transactions which would force every employer, no matter how intelligent, farsighted, and public spirited, to take as much advantage of his workpeople as the most grasping and shortsighted of his rivals.

The first link in the chain is the bargaining (higgling) advantage of the capitalist employer over the individual applicant for work. On the score of inconvenience, waiting power, knowledge of the market, and awareness of the economic strength of his opponent, the employer is in a position to outgeneral and outmaneuver the workingman, who is typically a novice in the art of bargaining. And this he will be forced to do in self-defense, notwithstanding his sentiments of fair play. Why?

Paradoxical as it may appear, in the highly developed commercial system of . . . today the capitalist manufacturer stands at as great a relative disadvantage to the wholesale trader as the isolated workman does to the capitalist manufacturer. In the higgling of the market with the wholesale trader who takes his product, the capitalist manufacturer exibits the same inferiority of strategic position with regard to the alternative, with regard to knowledge of the circumstances, and with regard to bargaining capacity.

But it would be a mistake to consider that the pressure originates with the wholesaler. "Just as the manufacturer is conscious of his weakness in face of the wholesale trader, so the wholesale trader feels himself helpless before the retail shopkeeper to whom he sells his stock." This feeling arises from the retailer's closer contact with the ultimate market, the consumer. Retailers, therefore, must be courted by the wholesaler and induced to push the particular lines that he is interested in.

We come now to the last link in the chain, the competition between retail shopkeepers to secure customers. Here the superiority in knowledge and technical skill

[17] See BLS Bulletins 1465-11, 12, 13, 14, *et seq.*, for Wichita, Kansas, Boston, Omaha, Washington, and others, for October, 1965.

[18] Sidney and Beatrice Webb, *Industrial Democracy* (New York: Longmans, Green & Co., Inc., 1911), pp. 654–671.

is on the side of the seller, but this is tar outweighed by the exceptional freedom of the buyer. We thus arrive at the consumer as the ultimate source of that persistent pressure on sellers, which, transmitted through the long chain of bargainings, finally crushes the isolated workman at the base of the pyramid.

The conclusion is obvious from the analysis. Workmen should combine and resist the downward pressure on wages with a united front of their own. Equality of bargaining power through collective action is the only practical way to offset the harsh effects of competition.

The essential difference between the Webbs' theory and orthodox economic analysis was in the former's refusal to admit that there was competition in the factor markets. Employers of all classes competed bitterly and ruthlessly in the sale of their products, but not for employes or (by implication) for capital. Whether this was because of a continual labor surplus or by tacit agreement of employers not to "break the market" and bid up wages is not clear, but the analysis would dissolve if it were assumed that employers were scrambling for workers, as they unquestionably do in prosperous times. The Webbs' analysis would hardly fit the facts in the 1920s or the 1960s; on the other hand, it would not be out of line for the 1930s. In depressed periods, there is little competition for factors of production, and the numbers of unemployed during the 1930s indicate that labor is no exception. If, as is arguable from national-income theory, a general equilibrium is possible at a level of industrial stagnation and unemployment, the Webbs' premises seem less improbable.

Additional theoretical support for the bargain thesis came in 1936 with the publication of *The General Theory of Employment, Interest and Money*, with its flat denial that flexible wage rates will lead to full employment.[19] When combined with the argument for transfer of income to lower-income groups in order to increase consumption, the criticism of orthodox wage theory proved a powerful stimulant to collective bargaining. The wage policy proposed in *The General Theory* is in its essentials consistent with the bargaining theory and has been at least partially in effect in most modern economies in recent decades.

Criticisms of the bargain theory. The bargain theory of wages is as vulnerable to criticism as the marginal productivity theory. It has been questioned both as to its accuracy and its desirability; that is, whether it *is* or *should be* the most important influence in wage determination.[20]

[19] John Maynard Keynes, *The General Theory of Employment, Interest and Money* (New York: Harcourt, Brace & World, Inc., 1936), pp. 262–264.

[20] Strictly speaking, the second criterion (desirability) is irrelevant to the judgment of a theory. However, there is little doubt of the part played by qualitative judgments in the popularizing of theoretical systems. This is certainly one of the strengths of the marginal productivity theory. What better basis is there for settling the question of pay than what a man is worth? Consider also, Ricardo's "iron law" of wages and many others.

Employers, for instance, would be the first to attack the Webbs' assumption of lack of competition in the factor markets, including and perhaps especially labor. The current and long-standing drive to recruit scientific, engineering, and other technical personnel, even to the point of "pirating" (hiring away another employer's workers), is liberally illustrated in the want-ad columns of every large daily newspaper. The tight labor market of the postwar years and the rising wage and salary levels in both organized and unorganized areas are hard to reconcile with the Webbs' "downward pressure" of the higgling of the market.

Another fundamental charge against the theory is the contention that collective bargaining is not effective, that it does not actually raise wages as rapidly or as certainly as individual bargaining (where, presumably, competition is unhindered).[21] The natural reaction might be to dismiss this view as absurd, the product of employer propaganda. In the public mind, trade unions are indissolubly connected with wage demands and wage increases. However, there is contrary evidence to be considered. One set of wages that has risen most rapidly percentagewise since 1939 is that of one of the most completely unorganized large groups of workers in the country—farm laborers. From a daily rate of $1.60 in 1940, average farm pay in the United States rose to $7.30 in 1965,[22] an increase of 356 per cent. This was considerably more than the proportionate rise in earnings of manufacturing production workers (who are about 70 per cent unionized), which was 294 per cent for the same period—from 66 cents to $2.60 per hour. Nor were farm wage increases stimulated by any threat of organization; with a few minor exceptions, agricultural employes have been bypassed by union organizers. There is also strong informal evidence of equally significant pay increases for another very large group of individual bargainers, domestic servants. In Chicago, a 1939 rate of 30 cents an hour had by 1960 become $1.50 to $1.75 an hour plus carfare, and reports from other cities contain news of pay raises of the same order of magnitude. Domestic servants are not a small, isolated, or strategic group. There are more than 2 million of them in the United States, as many as there are employes of the railroads, coal mines, and the automobile industry combined.

On the other hand, using the same data, the argument may be turned the other way around. Under the bargain theory, both farm and domestic workers would be found at the bottom of the scales of pay for comparable work, since they are exposed with the least protection to the superior bargaining power of their employers. This is exactly their location. A glance at the rates of domestic servants in private homes as compared with those of custodial employes represented by the Building Service Employees

[21] See Friedman, *op. cit.* For a contrary view, cf. Arthur M. Ross, *Trade Union Wage Policy* (Berkeley, Calif.: University of California Press, 1948), pp. 113–133.

[22] *Statistical Abstract of the United States, 1966*, pp. 237, 243.

International Union, or the rates of farm laborers' pay vis-à-vis those of
members of the Hod Carriers and Building Construction Laborers Union
(from $3 to $3.85 per hour for helpers and laborers by 1965) is sufficient
to show the different orders of magnitude. Which comparison is controlling: comparable levels or proportionate increase?

The wages-fund theory in modern form.   One of the most powerful arguments against the bargain theory of wages has been the modern
revival of the wages-fund theory and its application specifically to trade
unionism. Whether stated in its most naïve and vulgar form [23] or dressed
up in more sophisticated supply-and-demand terms, it still harks back to
the proposition as stated by J. R. McCulloch: "The rate of wages in any
given country, at any specified period, depends on the ratio between the
portion of its capital appropriated to the payment of wages, and the
number of its labourers." [24] As applied to collective bargaining, the reasoning runs something like this: If the total to be paid in wages is fixed—that
is, is practically unalterable—then a pay raise negotiated by any unionized
group of workers can only mean that those outside the group (nonunion
workers, especially) will get less.

The most prominent advocate of this "teeter-totter" theory (if my
wage goes up, yours will go down) in recent years was Professor Henry
Simons of the University of Chicago. In his celebrated journal article,
"Some Reflections on Syndicalism," published in 1944, he argued:

Unionism implies ability of established workers in high-wage areas and occupations
to insulate themselves from competition, excluding inexperienced new workers and
qualitatively inferior labor from their markets. It enables an aristocracy of labor
to build fences around its occupations, restricting entry, raising arbitrarily the
costs and prices of its products, *and lowering the wages and incomes of those outside,* and of the poor especially. [25]

and, a few pages later on:

Organization is a device by which privilege may be intrenched and consolidated. It is a device by which the strong may raise themselves higher by pressing

[23] See, *e.g.,* A. L. Perry, *Elements of Political Economy* (1875), p. 154, quoted
in H. A. Millis and R. E. Montgomery, *Organized Labor* (New York: McGraw-Hill
Book Co., 1945), p. 361: "There is no use in arguing against any one of the four
fundamental rules of arithmetic. The question of wages is a question of division. It is
complained that the quotient (the wage) is too small. Well, then, how many ways
are there to make a quotient larger? Two ways. Enlarge your dividend, the divisor
remaining the same, and the quotient will be larger; lessen your divisor, the dividend
remaining the same, and the quotient will be larger."

[24] *A Treatise on the Circumstances Which Determine the Rate of Wages,* cited
in Millis and Montgomery, *op. cit.,* p. 360.

[25] Henry Simons, "Some Reflections on Syndicalism," *Journal of Political Economy,* March, 1944, reprinted in *Economic Policy for a Free Society,* p. 138, italics
added.

down the weak. *Unionism, barring entry into the most attractive employments, makes high wages higher and low wages lower.*[26]

The wages-fund theory is a deceptively simple and attractive theory, especially useful to those who want to discredit the bargain theory of wages. At first glance, its logic appears to be flawless. The major premise is almost a truism:

I.   At any given moment in time, or even for short periods of time, the amount budgeted for wages (and salaries) by a specific firm, in a given industry, or in a labor market, is a fixed sum. That is, it is a *total* which can be stated in dollars and cents, down to the last penny.

The minor premise is also a fact, to wit:

II.   All wage increases occur in the short run, the very short run, in fact. They go into effect on a certain date and apply to certain specified workers in very specific amounts.

The conclusion seems foregone:

III.   An increase for one group will mean a decrease for the rest. Funds drawn from the fixed total (Premise I) to pay the increase to the more fortunate workers (Premise II) leave a reduced balance to be spread over "those outside," to use Simons's terminology.

Is it true? Of course not, as everyone who has ever had anything to do with the labor market knows. The facts of life are totally and completely opposite. Try imagining a company manager, returning from a bargaining session with a plant union, in which the union has negotiated an increase of 10 cents per hour. The manager pats the clerical employes (unorganized) on the back and says: "Sorry, the boys in the plant are going to get 10 cents more, so you have to take a cut." Does it sound probable? Unfortunately for the theory, plenty of information is available on the subject. The most likely outcome is that the clerical employes, as well as lower line supervisors and most rank-and-file staff personnel, will get precisely the same pro rata increase on the exact date that it goes into effect in the plant.

In the local labor market and in the industry, the same effect is noticeable, and has been recorded time and again in the *Monthly Labor Review*, industry journals, and association publications. Wage increases, whether in rates or fringe benefits or both, tend to spread rapidly, in both organized and unorganized work groups, as the outcome of what may be called *invidious comparison*. The effect on organized labor has been clearly outlined by Arthur M. Ross, in his designation of "orbits of coercive comparison" among and between unions and labor negotiators.[27] What has not been sufficiently noticed is that the same effect is clearly apparent in the unorganized work force: clerical, technical, and supervisory employes

[26] *Ibid.*, p. 142, italics added.

[27] *Trade Union Wage Policy* (Berkeley, Calif.: University of California Press, 1948), pp. 53–64.

in the same plant and company; unorganized firms in the same labor markets and the same industry in either adjoining or distant labor markets; and finally, in unorganized industries, nonprofit employment, and government agencies.

The flaw in the reasoning outlined above is found in the major premise (Number I). The amount *budgeted for* wages and the *amount available* to pay wages are not the same thing. The amount available is never fixed. In fact, it is not an amount; it is a flow of income. And it may be increased or decreased at any time by diverting funds from reserves, reducing profit totals, searching out sources of additional revenue, borrowing, or what have you. Very few employes have ever had the experience of taking a wage cut simultaneously with (because of) a wage increase elsewhere in the same organization. Since the end of the Second World War, and especially in the last 20 years, literally millions of employes have had the experience of receiving unsolicited pay raises due to the successful collective bargaining of organized groups in the same or nearby plants. The annual pay raise which is an almost universal feature of American life today is an outgrowth of two major influences: (1) the continuous round of collective bargaining negotiations by unions from one end of the country to the other, and (2) the invidious comparisons which employers know that their unorganized employes will draw—as unjustly discriminated against— if their own incomes do not rise proportionately.[28]

Another indictment of the bargain theory consists of a series of objections to the basis for the settlements. For one thing, the comparative bargaining strengths of the two parties assure neither a just nor an economically appropriate outcome—the wage structure arrived at (either interfirm, interindustry, or interoccupational) may still be out of line, whether the test be efficient allocation of resources, price stability, or equal pay for equal work. The test of economic strength is not a standard universally accepted as consistent with either group or the general welfare, and an analysis of bargaining tactics discloses the varieties of pressures brought to bear in reaching settlements. In addition, there are the obvious social and economic costs of wage-dispute settlements under collective bargaining—strikes, lockouts, boycotts, mediation, arbitration—which must be added into the social accounting. At times, industry-wide bargaining may result in uneconomic simplification and standardization of wage structures, where local variation would be more in line with market conditions.

However, the most impressive weakness of the bargain theory is probably its opportunistic character. It is not a complete theory, since it has no long-run postulates. Wages are determined by the relative bargaining power of employers and employes, it says, and employes should organize in order to match the employer or overpower him. And for the future,

[28] The dictionary defines "invidious" as: Tending to excite odium, ill will, or envy; likely to give offense; esp., unjustly discriminating.

what do employes and their trade unions want? "More," said Samuel Gompers, long-time head of the AFL. However, this runs head on into the long-run argument of the marginal productivity theorists. If labor gets a steadily increasing share of the national product, can the capital-labor ratio be increased, or even maintained? Wages come out of the product of industry, and even trade unionists do not contend that they can be raised indefinitely without an increase in the output of goods and services. However, gains in output are a function of improved tools and equipment, not of harder work. And tools and equipment require capital. Where is it coming from? One answer came from Keynes, who rejected the competitive labor market as the Webbs and the trade unionists since them had done, and proposed a national wage policy coupled to a guarantee of continuous full employment at steadily rising levels of earnings for the lower-income groups.

KEYNES ON WAGES

Failure of the flexible wage policy.   Nowhere in *The General Theory* did Keynes make his rejection of the classical theory more definite than in his dictum on wages: "There is . . . no ground for the belief that a flexible wage policy is capable of maintaining a state of continuous full employment. . . . The economic system cannot be made self-adjusting along these lines." [29] He gave several reasons for coming to this conclusion, and the step-by-step argument recalls the Webbs' indictment of the "higgling of the market." Only this time, the prime factors are national income and the price level:

1. A reduction of wages will mean some reduction in prices, with its main effect a redistribution of real income from wage-earners to other members of the community who enjoy more stable earnings. This is more than likely to diminish the "propensity to consume" and therefore total purchasing power.
2. A wage reduction leads to the expectation of further wage cuts and results in the postponement of both investment and consumption, with consequent reduction of total spending.
3. There will be general resistance to wage cuts by workers, since it is always to the interest of workingmen in each individual case to try to maintain their own rates. The outcome will be unemployment from strikes and lockouts.
4. Widespread wage reductions imply a falling price level, which hastens the insolvency of business operating on borrowed money and increases the burden of the national debt and taxation, with adverse effects on business confidence. [30]

The criticism of free-market wage adjustments is summed up concisely, as follows:

It follows, therefore, that if labour were to respond to conditions of gradually diminishing employment by offering its services at a gradually diminishing money-

[29] Keynes, *op. cit.*, p. 267.
[30] *Ibid.*, pp. 262–264.

wage, this would not, as a rule, have the effect of reducing real wages and might even have the effect of increasing them, through its adverse influence on the volume of output. The chief result of this policy would be to cause a great instability of prices, so violent perhaps as to make business calculations futile in an economic society functioning after the manner of that in which we live. To suppose that a flexible wage policy is a right and proper adjunct of a system which on the whole is one of *laissez-faire*, is the opposite of the truth.[31]

The Keynesian wage policy: Inflexibility.   The solution, however, while leaving some room for collective bargaining and competitive individual wage adjustments, emphasized the importance of nationwide regulation to stabilize earnings. Said Keynes:

I am now of the opinion that the maintenance of a stable general level of money-wages is, on a balance of consideration, the most advisable policy for a closed system; whilst the same conclusion will hold good for an open system, provided that equilibrium with the rest of the world can be secured by means of fluctuating exchanges. There are advantages in some degree of flexibility in the wages of particular industries so as to expedite transfers from those which are relatively declining to those which are relatively expanding. But the money-wage level as a whole should be maintained as stable as possible, at any rate in the short period. . . .

Thus with a rigid wage policy the stability of prices will be bound up in the short period with the avoidance of fluctuations in employment. In the long period, on the other hand, we are still left with the choice between a policy of allowing prices to fall slowly with the progress of technique and equipment whilst keeping wages stable, or of allowing wages to rise slowly whilst keeping prices stable. On the whole my preference is for the latter alternative, on account of the fact that it is easier with an expectation of higher wages in future to keep the actual level of employment within a given range of full employment than with an expectation of lower wages in future, and on account also of the social advantages of gradually diminishing the burden of debt, the greater ease of adjustment from decaying to growing industries, and the psychological encouragement likely to be felt from a moderate tendency for money-wages to increase.[32]

There are three essential ideas in the Keynesian wage program, one of them a newcomer to a free-wage society, the second and third already in operation. They are:
1. A national wage policy
2. A stable money wage level in the short run
3. A rising money wage level in the long run

Proposition 1 is a relative novelty, propositions 2 and 3 established facts of American economic life.

A national wage policy might originate in either of two ways: cooperation or supervision. Supervision would mean an "administered" wage policy, and there is only one agency with the power or resources to attempt the job: the Federal government. An administered national wage policy

[31] *Ibid.*, p. 269.
[32] *Ibid.*, pp. 270, 271.

would be a novelty only in peacetime; we had one from 1941 to 1946, with the "Little Steel formula" as the policy and the National War Labor Board as the administrative agency. We had another during the Korean conflict of 1951 to 1953, administered by the Wage Stabilization Board. Opinions differ both as to the wartime efficiency and results, and the peacetime possibilities of this method of wage determination. In a sense, Australia and New Zealand have had the mechanism without the policy for a generation. To date, there are few strong advocates of an administered national wage policy in peacetime for the United States.

What about a national wage policy through the interaction of employers and unions? Professor Dunlop sees it as a possibility, but at the risk of jeopardizing the stability of wages in the short run:

We have reached the stage where a limited number of key bargains effectively influence the whole wage structure of the American economy. . . . The number of really key bargains may be placed in the neighborhood of twenty-five to fifty. . . . It would be a mistake to presume that labor organizations alone had brought us from a condition of isolated and independent labor markets to the present condition in which a few bargains are decisive to the whole wage level. Frequently the fact and location of price leadership determines the key wage bargain. The traditions of industries and localities or dominant personalities frequently establish the order in which firms wish to make any wage changes. Individual business firms are reluctant to make wage changes until recognized leaders have made their decisions.

There are thus a limited number of strategic and decisive points of wage determination in our system which effectively condition, within narrow limits, the whole structure and level of wage and salary rates. I believe this fact is not likely to be altered in the years ahead for it is deeply intrenched in our whole wage-price fabric. *This fact creates the possibility that labor and management in this country in the years ahead may develop a national wage policy.* It creates the danger that these key bargains may contribute to unwarranted and inflationary wage increases throughout the system.[33]

In the 20 years since Dunlop made the above appraisal, we have moved much closer to a national wage policy. Exactly 15 years after he gave his paper, the President's Council of Economic Advisers announced the "wage-price guideposts," which recommended holding wage increases to the rate at which man-hour productivity was increasing in the country as a whole.[34] If wages (representing purchasing power) rose at the same rate as productivity, it was reasoned that the increased buying power would be just sufficient to take the increased output of goods and services off the market, without any increase in prices. There were many gaps in this formula, but it has stood as the Federal government's policy for several years and is unlikely to be discontinued. The arguments pro and con will be reviewed in the next chapter.

[33] John T. Dunlop, "American Wage Determination: The Trend and Its Significance," Economic Institute on Wage Determination, Jan. 11, 1947. Italics supplied.

[34] See "Annual Report of the Council of Economic Advisers, 1962," in *Economic Report of the President, 1962* (Washington: U.S. Government Printing Office, 1962).

The inflation bugaboo has plagued the dreams of most national-income theorists. Even with an administered program (the managed economy), the problem of a stable wage level in the short run has been regarded with apprehension. Sir William H. Beveridge, one of the foremost British authorities on labor, dumped the problem squarely into the lap of organized labor. Brusquely he said:

So long as freedom of collective bargaining is maintained, the primary responsibility of preventing a full employment policy from coming to grief . . . will rest on those who conduct the bargaining on behalf of labour . . . there is no inherent mechanism in our present system, which can with certainty prevent competitive sectional bargaining for wages from setting up a vicious spiral of rising prices under full employment.[35]

He had two proposals: (1) that the central labor organizations (the British Trades Union Congress and the AFL–CIO in the United States) work out a unified wage policy which will ensure "that the demands of individual unions will be judged with reference to the economic situation as a whole," or (2) arbitration of wage demands.

Neither of these suggestions is ripe for adoption in the United States. The central labor organizations in the United States were created for and have followed a policy directly opposite to the one he asks for, namely, a guarantee of the autonomy and sovereignty of their members and consistent refusal to interfere in their affairs. To date there is no evidence of any intention to modify their purposes. The arbitration which he recommended is contrary to the emphatic preferences of most unions and employers, who consider third-party settlement of contract terms incompatible with their responsibilities. Furthermore, although Beveridge's description of the arbitration arrangements makes them sound suspiciously compulsory, he was unable to bring himself to describe the sanctions which would be used to force them on a recalcitrant minority. Unless something gives, the Beveridge proposals seem destined to founder on the rocks of free collective bargaining.

An equally distinguished theorist on this side of the Atlantic, Professor Alvin H. Hansen, has also been concerned with the problem of wage adjustment under full employment. In his book on *Economic Policy and Full Employment* he starts from the premise that wage policy involves not only the *level*, but also the *structure* of wage rates:

We cannot achieve full employment and a balanced development, if we allow building trades wage rates, for example, to rise far out of line with the general wage structure. If this should happen, wage earners could not afford with their relatively low incomes (low in comparison with the building trades) to buy houses that are priced out of the market by reason of high labor cost.

A full-employment wage policy thus involves (1) control of the level of wage

[35] *Full Employment in a Free Society* (New York: W. W. Norton & Company, Inc., 1945), pp. 199, 200.

rates, as aggregate demand is expanded, so as to promote an equilibrium ratio of wages to profits, on the one side, and prevent increases in unit costs and prices on the other; (2) a balanced wage structure so as to prevent important products (construction, for example) from being priced out of the market; (3) cost reductions, involving both advances in techniques and removal of monopolistic and restrictive practices.[36]

What does he suggest? A number of things, including guaranteed annual wages; more and better statistics on wages, prices, productivity, and costs; a permanent system of Federal mediation and arbitration of wage disputes (without a single detail on how it is to be used or when); a peacetime office of price research and administered prices on major products such as steel and automobiles; and industry-wide collective bargaining, with full facts on the total economic situation made a part of each negotiation.

The most intriguing feature of Professor Hansen's analysis is his reliance upon collective bargaining to bring about the delicate balance by which "wages in general . . . rise in accordance with *average* over-all gains in productivity." [37] The pessimism of Beveridge and Dunlop (and many others who share their doubts about independent trade-union negotiations under full employment) is shelved. No unified labor policy, no bargaining compulsions, no third-party interferences are specified. Instead, Hansen states his conviction that "under a policy of full employment there is reason to believe that labor's sense of responsibility will increase." The argument is as follows:

Under full employment, arbitrary advances in wages, out of line with productivity and a balanced wage structure, will clearly be at the expense of consumers—in other words at the expense of labor as a whole. . . . With the over-all facts available, the labor movement as a whole may be counted upon to resist such distortion. . . . During the war, in all the democracies, labor has demonstrated a sense of social responsibility. When society as a whole, through the government, undertakes responsibility for full employment and social welfare, labor may be expected, on past experience, to respond by living up to its social responsibilities. A positive program, policies openly arrived at based on all the available facts, protection from exploitation by unscrupulous groups, active participation by labor in policy formation—these are among the most important measures that may be counted upon to foster within the ranks of labor a high sense of social responsibility.[38]

Some questions. The Keynesian wage doctrine is part of a general program for the preservation of continuous full employment. The quotations from Beveridge and Hansen have been used to illustrate the variety of methods which may be proposed to reach practically identical objectives of a national wage policy and short-run wage stability. It is now

---

[36] Alvin H. Hansen, *Economic Policy and Full Employment* (New York: McGraw-Hill Book Company, 1947), pp. 157–158.

[37] *Ibid.*, p. 244.

[38] *Ibid.*, p. 246.

possible to view the suggestions with some perspective, as a number of years have elapsed since the authors attempted to visualize the problems arising from the juxtaposition of full employment and relatively uninhibited collective bargaining. One thing seems settled; they were correct in their apprehensions with respect to price stability. Negotiated wage increases (the "patterns") unquestionably exceeded the rise in productivity for a number of years, and coincided with a 77 per cent rise in the Consumer Price Index since the end of the Second World War—from an average of 76.9 in 1945 to 136.2 in January, 1966 (based on 1947 to 1949 prices). The extent to which wage increases were responsible has been a matter of argument. Nevertheless, although economists differ widely, most of them agree that general wage increases exceeding the rise of productivity will be inflationary. Judged on this basis, unions have been held responsible for from 20 to 50 per cent of the rise in the price level during the last 15, 20, or 25 years.[39]

Still, several questions remain to be answered.

1.   With our current collective bargaining practices, is the experience of 1945 to 1966 (a 77 per cent increase in the CPI) likely to be repeated? Is there a danger, in fact, that such "creeping" inflation will get out of hand and become, first, a "trotting" and finally a "galloping" inflation? Or will unions display Hansen's "high sense of social responsibility"?[40]

2.   One brake upon union wage demands is a "soft" labor market. Are inflation and unemployment alternatives? Must we have more of one to have less of the other, and how much?

3.   What other control devices are available to keep negotiated wage increases within the range of rising productivity during full employment: more information on industry, prices, costs, etc.; extension of Federal and state mediation and conciliation services; compulsory arbitration (government wage boards); a national wage policy laid down by Congress, setting limits to wage increases?

4.   How are interfirm, interindustry, and interregional differentials in prices, costs, productivity, and profits to be treated: on the basis of national averages, or individually, or by some compromise of the two?

5.   How will interunion and intraunion wage differentials be treated: preserved, compressed, or expanded, and if the first or second, by what standards or formulas?

6.   What controls will be applied to nonunion wage rates, either within

---

[39] Cf. Kerr, Dunlop, and others, cited previously. The Economic Research Department of the United States Chamber of Commerce assigns unions practically full responsibility. See *Inflation, Unions and Wage Policy* (Washington, D.C.: United States Chamber of Commerce, 1960). The AFL–CIO, on the other hand, points to the pricing policies of big business, restriction of output, and tight money policies of the government.

[40] See Ross, *op. cit.,* Chap. IV, "What Is Responsible Wage Policy?" on this.

the firm (clerical, technical, supervisory, and executive compensation) or otherwise, and how will such rates be related to negotiated increases? What sort of additional regulatory mechanism will this call for?

7. What productivity measures will be considered relevant: national, regional, industry, firm, or occupational? If other than broad averages, how will they be devised for, say, government, banking, insurance, entertainment—the service industries generally?

8. If negotiated or general wage increases are restricted to the proportionate rise of productivity, will this in turn affect the rise of productivity and which way: favorably or adversely?

9. Can wages be limited or restricted without similar checks upon profits and the earnings of the self-employed? If not, what kinds of controls will fit these cases?

These are not all the questions that can be raised, but they are a sample. None of them are easy to answer, and probably few economists or public administrators would welcome the responsibility for either setting policy or working out the mechanism for putting any given policy into effect. The overriding question is the extent and nature of public (official) involvement in the "private" wage policies of employers and unions. When this has been extensive and detailed in the past, as in the Second World War and the Korean conflict, both the general policies laid down and the manner in which they were implemented have come under heavy criticism. Governmental controls in peacetime over either wages or prices or both are anathema to the parties involved and are widely regarded as something to be avoided at almost any cost. Nevertheless, the government's acceptance of its implicit obligation to maintain high (full) employment does much to weaken the a priori case for nonintervention. If the government takes fiscal and monetary steps to maintain spending, production, and employment, can it overlook private irresponsibility in the form of administered prices, production, and wages which may endanger price stability and/or economic growth? The answer seems to be no, but the practicable measures to cope with such "irresponsibility" without doing serious inequity to the parties or injuring the general welfare are elusive.

READINGS

GENERAL: George W. Taylor and Frank C. Pierson, *New Concepts in Wage Determination* (New York: McGraw-Hill Book Company, 1958); Melvin W. Reder, "Wage Determination in Theory and Practice," *A Decade of Industrial Relations Research* (New York: Harper & Row, Publishers, Incorporated, 1958), pp. 64–97.

UNION WAGE POLICY: Arthur M. Ross, *Trade Union Wage Policy* (Berkeley, Calif.: University of California Press, 1948); John T. Dunlop, *Wage*

Determination under Trade Unions (New York: The Macmillan Company, 1944); James S. Youtsler, *Labor's Wage Policies in the Twentieth Century* (New York: Twayne Publishers, 1956).

WAGES AND EMPLOYMENT: Allan M. Cartter, *Theory of Wages and Employment* (Homewood, Ill.: Richard D. Irwin, Inc., 1959); Wm. G. Bowen (ed.), *Labor and the National Economy* (New York: W. W. Norton & Company, Incorporated, 1965).

SIXTEEN

NATIONAL
WAGE
POLICY

The United States has two basic wage policies—a minimum and a maximum—but they are quite different. The legal minimum wage in interstate commerce is a stated amount—for example, $1.40 an hour in most jobs. The "maximum" wage is not a stated amount, but a permissible *annual percentage increase*—3.2 per cent in 1966—and it has no legal standing as a limit, but is merely a recommendation of the Council of Economic Advisers.[1] Nevertheless, the "wage-price guideposts," with their percentage wage-increase limitations, are national policy—good or bad, enforceable or unenforceable, as the case may be—so long as the President of the United States endorses them and uses the power of his office to persuade unions and business firms to stay within them.

THE WAGE–PRICE GUIDEPOSTS

The wage-price guideposts (or "guidelines," as they are often called) first appeared in 1962 in the *Economic Report of the President,* as the Council of Economic Advisers' "Guideposts for Noninflationary Wage and Price Behavior."[2] They were appropriately general, were carefully qualified, and were limited both in application and expectation. The key statements were:

There are important segments of the economy where firms are large or employees well-organized, or both. In these sectors, private parties may exercise considerable discretion over the terms of wage bargains and price decisions. . . .

To wit: in such cases, wages and prices are administered, not market-determined.

[1] See *Economic Report of the President, 1966,* pp. 92–93. The applicable portion is reprinted in the *Monthly Labor Review,* March, 1966, pp. 278–282.

[2] Pp. 185–190, with the key sections reprinted in the *Monthly Labor Review,* March, 1962, pp. 286–287.

Individual wage and price decisions assume national importance when they involve large numbers of workers and large amounts of output directly, or when they are regarded by large segments of the economy as setting a pattern. Because such decisions affect the progress of the whole economy, there is legitimate reason for public interest in their content and consequences. . . .

Wages, prices, and productivity. If all prices remain stable, all hourly labor costs may increase as fast as economy-wide productivity without, for that reason alone, changing the relative share of labor and nonlabor incomes in total output. . . . If hourly labor costs increase at a slower rate than productivity, the share of nonlabor incomes will grow or prices will fall, or both. Conversely, if hourly labor costs increase more rapidly than productivity, the share of labor incomes in the total product will increase or prices will rise, or both. It is this relationship among long-run economy-wide productivity, wages, and prices which makes the rate of productivity change an important benchmark for noninflationary wage and price behavior.

Using unemployment as the third variable, the above paragraph may be illustrated by the Phillips curve as a graphical presentation of wage-price relationships. For example, with a productivity-increase factor of 3 per cent, and an assumed lowering of unemployment with rising wages and prices, the Phillips curve could be drawn as follows:

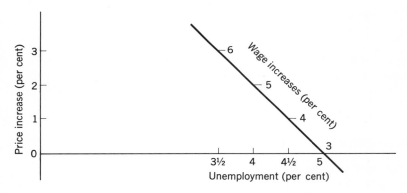

Fig. 16-1. The (American) Phillips curve

Restated, the productivity-price-wage propositions are:

1.   With a 3 per cent increase in man-hour productivity, there will be a 3 per cent increase in the output of goods and services.

2.   If consumer income (purchasing power) rises an equivalent amount, the additional output can (will) be sold without pressure on prices, one way or another.

3.   Most consumer income comes from wage-earner incomes, which are either set directly by union-management agreements or are influenced by changes in such.

4.   Therefore, if collective-bargaining negotiators, who "exercise considerable discretion over the terms of wage bargains . . ." hold wage in-

creases to the limits of productivity increase, there should be no inflation, and the relative shares of workingmen—that is, wage-earners—and
investors (nonlabor incomes) should remain about the same.

In the Annual Report of the CEA for January, 1964, the figure of 3.2
per cent appeared as the "annual average percentage change in output
per man-hour during [the] latest 5 years," [3]—in other words, the trend rate
of productivity increase. The magic number of *3.2 per cent* then became
the national standard by which negotiated union-management wage settlements were appraised as "inflationary" or "noninflationary." This was no
misinterpretation—the Council was very explicit, to wit:

> The guideposts contain two key propositions. The first—the general guidepost for
> wages—says that, in a particular firm or industry, the appropriate noninflationary
> standard for annual percentage increases in total employee compensation per man-
> hour (not just in straight-time hourly rates) is the annual increase in *national trend*
> [sic] output per man-hour. The standard *is not the productivity trend in the particular
> firm or industry* in question. *Nor is it the particular year's productivity change,* which
> can be influenced by short-run transitory factors.[4]

Two years later—by the end of 1965—the Council had changed its mind
about the length of the time-period for estimating the trend of productivity. Its argument was as follows:

> Now that the economy is at the end of its fifth year of uninterrupted expansion, a
> 5-year average no longer gives a reasonable approximation of the true productivity
> trend. The last recession year [1960] drops out of the average, yet the unsustain-
> able productivity gains of a year of recovery and 4 years of improving utilization
> are retained. If use of the 5-year average were continued this year and in coming
> years, the figure yielded by the 5-year moving average would rise at this time to
> 3.6 per cent and would undoubtedly fall substantially thereafter.[5]
>
> An analysis of recent productivity movements was presented earlier in this
> chapter. It is clear from this analysis that 3.6 per cent would not be an accurate
> measure of the true trend of productivity. Rather, it appears that the long-term
> trend, independent of cyclical swings, is slightly over 3 per cent.[6]
>
> For 1966, the Council specifically recommends that the general guidepost for
> wages of 3.2 per cent a year be continued.

To further support its position, the Council pointed to (1) the impact
of approaching full employment, (2) the probability of future productivity
gains not exceeding past trend values, (3) the consistency in the past of

---

[3] To wit, the years 1959 to 1963, inclusive; *Economic Report of the President,
1964,* Table 20, p. 114.

[4] *Ibid.,* p. 118, italics added except as noted.

[5] *Economic Report of the President, 1966,* pp. 92–93.

[6] "The . . . average of 2½ per cent for the longer period from 1919 to 1965 is
subject to the suspicion that it seriously understates the higher trend in the depression-
free postwar period. The productivity trend can also be estimated from data for the
shorter postwar period. . . . While these different methods do not yield identical
estimates, for the private sector they fall within the range of 3.0 to 3.3 per cent a
year." P. 80.

the 3.2 per cent increase with stability of wholesale prices, and (4) the coming increases in labor costs due to higher payroll taxes to finance social security and Medicare. To cap it all off, the Council dropped the productivity-trend table from its report and left open the number of years to be used as a basis for the trend estimate.

CRITICISMS OF THE WAGE–PRICE GUIDEPOSTS

The AFL–CIO, which had been openly critical of the guideposts all along, reacted violently to the new "open-end" method of estimating productivity trend. President George Meany led the attack: "By changing the rules for the formulation of the wage guidelines, in a deliberate effort to reduce them, the Council of Economic Advisers undermines their very credibility." [7] He then went on to pledge the "complete, wholehearted support of the labor movement" if a national emergency truly warranted over-all stabilization measures, but stressed that such a program would have to mean that "all costs, prices, profits, corporate executive salaries, dividends and wages" were equally restrained. The country would then, he said, be sharing equally the burdens and sacrifices of a national crisis. "But rigid 'guidelines' based on shifting methods are not the way to do it."

The wage-price guideposts are relatively new and may be only a temporary expedient in the search for a price-stabilization formula, but the probabilities are otherwise. In a fully employed, administered-wage-and-price economy, with inflation a constant threat, some form of official wage-price policy seems almost a certainty. Thus far, the "guideposts" are the only answer.

How satisfactory are they?

At first glance, on the theoretical level, they are persuasive—almost convincing.[8] There is no question but that the productivity of the labor force does increase from year to year, due primarily to capital investment in new technological devices (automation) but assisted also by better organization, the discovery of new and better ways of doing old tasks, increased demand (the opening up of mass markets), etc. Although the methods of measurement are complicated and there are wide variations as between industries and occupations, the annual rate of productivity increase can be measured and expressed as a percentage. If, at the same time, the general level of purchasing power in the country rises at the same percentage rate, the additional goods and services should be taken

---

[7] "Wage Guide Shift Scored . . . ," *AFL–CIO News*, January 29, 1966, pp. 1, 5.

[8] And remember what Keynes said: "the ideas of economists and political philosophers, both when they are right and when they are wrong, are more powerful than is commonly understood . . . soon or late, it is ideas, not vested interests, which are dangerous for good or evil." *The General Theory* . . . (New York: Harcourt, Brace & World, Inc., 1936), pp. 383–384.

off the market at stable prices. There will, of course, be individual variations—by industries and occupations and firms and product sales (some up,
some down)—but the general averages should hold reasonably steady.
Real consumer incomes (that is, in terms of goods and services enjoyed),
both labor and nonlabor, will rise by the amount of the increase in productivity, but the general level of prices should neither rise nor fall.

That is the theory; how does *the policy* stand up?

Obviously, not nearly as well as the general statement. There have
been a few limited attempts at price control—in steel, aluminum, copper—
on the part of the President and his Cabinet-level advisers, practically all
of it of the "jawbone" variety: exhortations, threats, persuasion, appeals
to patriotism and the general welfare. But the great and overwhelming
majority of prices—at consumer, wholesale, and industrial levels—are
totally without restraints and may (and do) move upward at will.[9] Of
course, if all prices were market-determined, no controls would be needed.
The price level would adjust automatically to restraints upon incomes.
However, not even the most conservative spokesman for big business contends that prices are set in such an impersonal manner. The fact is, as is
freely admitted, that prices are as widely "administered" as wages, perhaps more so. In which case, the question arises: Are not price restraints
as necessary as the limits on wage increases?

And how about corporate profits, and the earnings of partnerships, individual proprietors, and self-employed professional men (*e.g.*, doctors,
dentists, lawyers, accountants)? They seem to have been overlooked on
the policy level, as are the men who run the corporations, and own the
smaller business firms, who set their own level of compensation with no
public reference to any guideposts. In 1965, the profits, after taxes, of all
corporations in the United States rose 20 per cent over 1964, from $37.2
billion to $44.5 billion. Dividends were up 10 per cent and undistributed
profits 29 per cent. The income of proprietors rose 6.7 per cent; interest
income was up 8.6 per cent.[10] Is it reasonable to suppose that these increases in nonlabor incomes were completely unrelated to the rise of the
Consumer Price Index from 108.9 to 111 and of the Wholesale Price Index
from 101 to 104.6, between January, 1965, and January, 1966? Can a price
policy be only a *wage*-price policy, or must it not be an *incomes*-price
policy?

Next, how comprehensive are the guideposts as a wage policy?

No one, in government or out, has suggested a method of applying
them to the approximately 45 million nonagricultural wage and salary

[9] For example, between March, 1965, and March, 1966, the Consumer Price
Index for "Food" went up from 106.9 to 113.9, or 7 points (6.5 per cent). The sub-
component of "Meats, poultry, and fish" rose 17.3 points, from 99.6 to 116.9, a 17
per cent increase. *Monthly Labor Review*, May, 1966, p. 589.

[10] *Survey of Current Business*, April, 1966, p. S-2.

earners in the country who are neither union members nor work in organized bargaining units. These include managerial, technical, professional, sales, and clerical people, in addition to plant and service workers still unorganized. Many—perhaps most of them—now get annual increases in pay, a benefit for which they can thank organized labor, since it was the unions that taught the country the virtues of the annual pay review and upward adjustment. And it is ironic that such salary increases often exceed the wage-price guidelines, whereas unions are expected to observe these limits in their bargaining. For example, the American Association of University Professors reported in June, 1965, that average compensation (salary plus benefits) for all academic ranks in 683 reporting colleges and universities rose 6 per cent in 1964 to 1965, 5 per cent in 1963 to 1964, 5.8 per cent in 1962 to 1963, and 6.5 per cent in 1961 to 1962. The Association's "target" is 7.2 per cent a year.[11] Should college and university administrators observe the guideposts, or are academic wage-earners exempt?

Finally, how equitable is it, within the unionized area, to focus attention (controls?) only upon those "segments of the economy where firms are large or employees well-organized, or both"? The CEA's argument is that "individual wage and price decisions assume national importance when they involve large numbers of workers and large amounts of output directly, or when they are regarded by large segments of the economy as setting a pattern . . . there is legitimate reason for public interest in their content and consequences." [12]

How many "individual wage . . . decisions" (negotiations) have national importance justifying "public interest in their content and consequences"? Basic steel—519,600 production workers in March, 1966? Motor vehicles and equipment (customarily an interrelated three-step negotiation with General Motors, Ford, and Chrysler)—698,000 production workers in February, 1966, perhaps 75 to 80 per cent of them in the "Big Three" companies? What else? No other negotiation covers as many as 100,000 employes in a single contract, very few as many as 50,000. Are the individual negotiations with the aluminum and can industries, with Boeing, International Harvester, Lockheed, North American, of sufficient importance to justify singling them out for wage-increase limitations while tens of thousands of other agreements are bargained out in relative privacy?

Building construction is a good example, and the 1966 report of the Council of Economic Advisers devoted a section to prices and wages in the industry.[13] Pointing out that construction is one of our largest industries, with more than 4 million workers in 1965, the CEA observed that

[11] See the *AAUP Bulletin*, June, 1965, p. 25.

[12] From the 1962 *Report*, see above, p. 524.

[13] *Economic Report of the President, 1966*, pp. 85–86, with supplementary comments on pp. 55, 76, 78.

between 1960 and 1965 prices rose 2.2 per cent annually while average hourly earnings and union wage rates (exclusive of fringe benefits, which also rose) went up 3.8 per cent a year. For 1965 alone, the increase in prices was 2.9 per cent, of union wage rates 4.1 per cent, and average hourly earnings 4.5 per cent, with large deferred wage increases written into many contracts for 1966 and 1967. "Construction," the CEA concluded, "is clearly an industry that raises serious problems for wage-price stability."

The explanation, as everyone knows, is that the building trades bargain sectionally and locally and not industry-wide or nationally. Some unions bargain individually, some in groups, with local chapters of the Associated General Contractors or specialty contractors of one type or another. The market for the product is local and each trade's contribution to cost is small, which adds to its leverage in bargaining. Very few of the individual negotiations are large enough to attract the attention of the President or his advisers. And the results often bear little relationship to the wage-price guideposts. For example:

Early in February [1966] a strike in Chicago was settled by an agreement between the Builders Association and Local 150 of the Operating Engineers, on a package increase of $1.30-an-hour spread over a 4-year period for some 1,500 workers. Pay scales in the fourth year of the contract will range from $5.15 to $6.05 (compared with scales under the previous contract of $4.15 to $5.05), with a 20-cent increase retroactive to January 1, 1966, another on January 1, 1967, and 30-cent increases on January 1 of 1968 and 1969. Contributions were increased to 20 cents (from 10 cents) for welfare and to 15 cents in the first year and 20 cents in the second for pensions (from 10 cents); a vacation fund of 10 cents was to be established in 1967.[14]

As matters now stand, the wage-price guideposts are strictly pragmatic. The rule is: Put pressure where it is feasible to put pressure, and leave the rest. Unfortunately, a great deal is left out: all management salaries, bonuses, stock options, or other special forms of compensation; practically all professional, technical, supervisory, clerical, and sales salaries with any bonuses or special pay options; all self-employed professional men; all proprietor-owners of farms, stores, shops, and service establishments; all dividends from corporations, or gains from stockholdings or real estate sales or other private investments; all rises in rental or interest income; and a very large portion of negotiated wage increases under labor-management agreements—where the firms are medium-sized or small, the number of workers limited, and/or the new agreement is not regarded as pattern-setting.

It is hard to resist the conclusion that the omissions outweigh the inclusions—certainly a major flaw in any price-control scheme. The result is a dilemma: with so many sources of income omitted entirely, it is

[14] *Monthly Labor Review*, March, 1966, p. 308.

doubtful that the guideposts will work; if they can be made to work, the result will be highly inequitable. The 1966 rules change (from a 5-year moving average to an open-end estimate of productivity increase) did nothing to increase the credibility of the 3.2 per cent figure,[15] or of the CEA's objectivity. A major overhaul seems to be in order if a general price stabilization policy is to be a part of the national economic picture.

MINIMUM WAGES

The wage-price guideposts are just the latest addition to a long list of rules that employers must take account of in order to enjoy the privilege of hiring people and paying them wages. From one end of the country to the other, the United States is crisscrossed by a solid pattern of regulations—Federal, state, local—set up for the protection of the wage earner. For the employer, they set limits as to whom he can hire, how much he must pay, how long his employes can work, the kind of equipment they must have, how they are to be insured against accidents and disease and unemployment, his right to speak his mind on union matters, whether he can discipline them or not, and whom he can fire. A major and controversial portion of this protective network is minimum-wage legislation, and its associated maximum-hours and child-labor limitations.

For more than a quarter of a century the United States has been blanketed by a broad and inclusive Federal law, plus scores of state statutes and municipal ordinances, which have the purposes of setting "floors" under wages, "ceilings" over working hours, and reducing or eliminating child labor. The principal Federal statute is known officially as the Fair Labor Standards Act of 1938,[16] and unofficially as the Wage and Hour Law. It is supported by the Walsh-Healey Public Contracts Act,[17] which authorizes the government to regulate the wages, hours, and working conditions of employes on government contracts of $10,000 or over, and the Bacon-Davis prevailing wage law,[18] which sets wage standards to be included in the advertised specifications of contracts above $2,000, for the construction, alteration, or repair of public buildings. There are literally hundreds of state and local regulations limiting hours of work in hazardous trades, setting a maximum 8-hour day and 48-hour week for women, requiring compulsory school attendance for children below a certain age, prescribing minimum wages that may be paid, or otherwise regulating the terms of the employment contract.

[15] It should be noted that the CEA moved from an estimate based on a measured trend to an open forecast: "If use of the 5-year average were continued this year and in coming years, the figure yielded by the 5-year moving average would rise at this time to 3.6 per cent *and would undoubtedly fall substantially thereafter.*" See above, p. 525.

[16] 52 Stat. 1060.

[17] 49 Stat. 2036 (1936).

[18] 46 Stat. 1494 (1931), as amended.

The movement to regulate wages, hours, and child labor passed through a number of stages and reached a climax in the passage of the Fair Labor Standards Act of 1938. That law summed up the three different lines of regulation which had been in process for a century or more in an omnibus statute:

1. Its coverage was all employes in interstate commerce, with certain stated exceptions.

2. The original objective (in 1938) was a universal minimum wage of 40 cents an hour, to be approached gradually, as follows:

   a. A legal minimum rate of 25 cents an hour the first year (1939)

   b. A legal minimum rate of 30 cents an hour the next 5 years (1945)

   c. A legal minimum rate of 40 cents an hour thereafter

3. The second major objective of the Fair Labor Standards Act was a universal maximum work week of 40 hours at regular rates of pay, also to be approached gradually, as follows:

   a. A legal maximum work week of 44 hours the first year (1939)

   b. A legal maximum work week of 42 hours the second year (1940)

   c. A legal maximum work week of 40 hours thereafter

   d. Any hours worked in excess of these limits to be paid for at not less than one and a half times the regular rate

The AFL–CIO has pushed vigorously for amendment of the Act to shorten the legal work week to 35 hours (or even 30 hours) and to make the penalty overtime payment double time instead of time and a half,[19] but with no success. On the official level, the 40-hour, 5-day week seems to be an established standard of industrial employment, thus interrupting a downward trend of working hours from far back in the nineteenth century. Where hours reductions have occurred during the past 2 decades, they were made voluntarily or were negotiated by unions and incorporated in agreements with employers.

4. The third major objective of the Act, which was achieved outright, was prohibition of the employment of children under 16 years of age by anyone not a parent or guardian, or the employment of children under 18 in hazardous trades.

The minimum-wage section of the Fair Labor Standards Act has been amended several times, bringing the original rate of 40 cents per hour up to $1.60 by 1968. In 1949 the rate was raised to 75 cents, and in 1955 it was upped to $1. The next increase came in 1961, and it was more complicated.[20] Coverage was extended to about 8.5 million workers previously exempted and separate schedules of increase were set up for the newcomers. The minimum for workers already covered went to $1.15 in September, 1961, and 2 years later—in September, 1963—it rose to $1.25 per hour. For the 8.5 million newly covered workers, the increase was de-

[19] See vol. II, *Proceedings of the AFL–CIO, 6th Constitutional Convention* (1965), "Fair Labor Standards," pp. 193–195.

[20] Public Law 87-30.

layed to September, 1965. The latter were also brought gradually under the overtime provisions of the Act (see below) until by September, 1965, they were to receive time and a half for all hours worked over 40 in 1 week.[21]

In 1966, the minimum wage was raised again to $1.40 per hour by February, 1967, and 1 year later to $1.60, and coverage was extended to an additional 7 million workers: half a million farm employes (minimum of $1, rising in two annual installments of 15 cents each to $1.30), workers at retail and service firms (minimum of $1 an hour to rise in 4 annual installments of 15 cents to $1.60 in 1971), and blue-collar Federal workers not previously covered ($1.40 in 1967 and $1.60 in 1968). The big increase of coverage was in the second category, with the repeal of previous exemptions for laundry and dry cleaning, hotel, motel, restaurant, hospital, and automobile-aircraft-farm implement sales firms.[22]

This type of regulatory law presents a whole series of issues in a single package, some of which have been decided for the time being, while others are still in process. While the problems lie in the general areas of constitutional law, economics, and administration, their solutions have had a terrific practical impact upon employers and employes throughout the country. In the early months of 1947, for example, American employers were being sued for several *billion* dollars in back wages held to be due them under the overtime pay provisions of the law. In more ways than one, the Federal Wage and Hour Law has been a proving ground for the central direction of wage policy in the United States.

The judicial barricade. For a long time, the most important question was not whether wage and hour regulation was a good thing but whether or not the judges would permit it. The legislative and executive branches of government, being closer to the people and more representative, have been easier to influence, but there is a long line of state and Federal supreme court decisions declaring such acts unconstitutional. At the same time, the courts exercised their prerogative of inconsistency by alternating now and then with favorable rulings. A brief catalog of notable court cases on these issues follows:

Maximum hours

Ritchie v. People, 155 Ill. 98 (1895). Eight-hour law for women employed in factories and workshops declared unconstitutional by the Illinois supreme court.

Holden v. Hardy, 169 U.S. 366 (1898). A maximum 8-hour day for workmen in mines and smelters in the state of Utah upheld by the United States Supreme Court.

[21] *Monthly Labor Review,* July, 1961, p. 770.
[22] *Washington Post,* September 15, 1966, p. 1.

Lochner v. New York, 198 U.S. 45 (1905). A New York law limiting bakers to 10 hours a day held unconstitutional by the United States Supreme Court.

Muller v. Oregon, 208 U.S. 412 (1908). Oregon's maximum 10-hour-day law for women in factories or laundries upheld by the United States Supreme Court. The case for the state of Oregon (and regulation) was successfully argued by Louis D. Brandeis, later Associate Justice of the top Federal Court, and his voluminous brief for the defense, containing reams of social and economic data and a few paragraphs of legal precedent, gave rise to the term, a "Brandeis brief."

Bunting v. Oregon, 243 U.S. 426 (1917). An Oregon law limiting factory workers to 10 hours a day at regular rates of pay, plus 3 hours at time and a half, held constitutional by the United States Supreme Court.

Wilson v. New, 243 U.S. 332 (1917). A Federal law establishing a basic 8-hour day on the railroads without reduction in pay held constitutional by the United States Supreme Court.

Child labor

Hammer v. Dagenhart, 247 U.S. 251 (1918). A Federal law making it illegal to ship in interstate commerce goods produced with the aid of child labor held unconstitutional by the United States Supreme Court.

Bailey v. Drexel Furniture, 259 U.S. 20 (1922). A Federal law taxing firms 10 per cent of their net profits if they ship in interstate commerce goods produced with the aid of child labor held unconstitutional by the United States Supreme Court.

Minimum wages

Stettler v. O'Hara, 243 U.S. 629 (1917). An Oregon minimum-wage law for women held constitutional by the United States Supreme Court.

Adkins v. Children's Hospital, 261 U.S. 525 (1923). A Federal minimum-wage law for women in the District of Columbia held unconstitutional by the United States Supreme Court.

Schechter v. United States, 295 U.S. 495 (1935). The National Industrial Recovery Act of 1933, which contained in Sec. 7a the authority for the President to prescribe labor codes with minimum wages, maximum hours, and other conditions of employment, held unconstitutional by the United States Supreme Court.

Morehead v. People ex rel. Tipaldo, 298 U.S. 597 (1936). A New York minimum-wage law for women and children held unconstitutional by the United States Supreme Court.

West Coast Hotel v. Parrish, 300 U.S. 391 (1937). A Washington state minimum-wage law for women and children held constitutional by the United States Supreme Court.

United States v. Darby Lumber Co., 312 U.S. 100 (1941). The Federal Fair Labor Standards Act of 1938, regulating minimum wages, maximum hours of work, and child labor, held constitutional by the United States Supreme Court.

It is now a well-settled ruling of constitutional law that Congress and the state legislatures may regulate wages, hours of work, and the labor of women and children within their respective jurisdictions, without interference by the courts. It has been a long uphill fight to establish this right, and the detailed legal arguments in the cases listed above are much too complex for examination here. The main ground for nullification when statutes were held invalid was usually the due process clause of either the Fifth or the Fourteenth Amendment to the Federal Constitution, and the reasoning went something as follows:

1. The due process clauses read: "No person shall be . . . deprived of life, liberty, or property, without due process of law" (Fifth); "nor shall any State deprive any person of life, liberty, or property, without due process of law" (Fourteenth).
2. Freedom of contract is a property right.
3. Regulatory laws of this kind limit both the employe's and the employer's freedom of contract, thereby depriving both parties of property.
4. Hence, the laws are unconstitutional.

Where state laws were upheld, the explanation was that the regulation was a "reasonable" exercise of the state's police power. Federal regulations tend to be sustained on the basis of the commerce clause of the Constitution of the United States. ("The Congress shall have power to regulate commerce with foreign nations, and among the several States, and with the Indian tribes.")

No one has ever been able to find the thread of consistency running through the United States Supreme Court's decisions on regulatory questions, although scores of legal scholars have tried their hand at it. The big shift in judicial attitudes came in the spring and summer of 1937, following the court reorganization plan which President Franklin D. Roosevelt proposed earlier that year. It was reflected most dramatically in the change of view on minimum-wage legislation, whereby the Court, by a 5 to 4 decision, upheld the Washington state law (West Coast Hotel case), after turning down the New York law (Morehead case) by a 5 to 4 decision the year before. Since 1936, no major Federal regulatory law has been held unconstitutional.

Interstate commerce.   Under a federal form of government, one of the main problems of regulation is to decide who has jurisdiction. If employment is local (intrastate), the state government is responsible. If the employment is in an activity which crosses state lines (interstate), the national government is boss. Where there is uncertainty, it is up to the courts to decide, and the decisions have often been crucial for programs of regulation. For example, the first Federal child labor law was declared unconstitutional (in *Hammer v. Dagenhart*), largely on the grounds that it was an attempt by Congress to regulate activities which were essentially local in character, the employment of children in factories.

However, as conditions have changed and businesses have grown larger and the economy more interdependent, the judicial view of interstate commerce has expanded, with the greatest expansion occurring since the court reform of 1937. In 1937 the Supreme Court held, in *National Labor Relations Board v. Jones and Laughlin Steel Corp.*,[23] that manufacturing was in interstate commerce, after 150 years of ruling just the opposite. The basis for this and subsequent decisions of the same type was that some portion of the employer's business was conducted across state lines. In passing on the coverage of the Fair Labor Standards Act of 1938, the courts have given this principle its most extreme application to date.

They have held, for example, that a company doing less than 1 per cent of its business in interstate commerce was covered by the act.[24] They have also ruled that the law applied to employes of a fertilizer company which sold its product to farmers who used it to grow sugar cane, which was sold to sugar mills, processed into sugar and molasses, and then exported.[25] Neither the fertilizer nor the sugar cane moved in interstate commerce. However, it was reasoned that the occupations were necessary to the production of an ingredient of an article moving in commerce and were therefore equivalent to being engaged in interstate commerce itself.

The Supreme Court's more generous view of the jurisdiction of Congress relative to the states is approved by those who favor regulation and deplored by those who oppose it. For one thing, the Court has never returned any authority to the states after once assigning it to Washington; the traffic is all one-way, from state to Federal levels. For another, the Federal government is a much more powerful regulator than state and local agencies. It is not unknown for businesses to move out of states that attempted to control their activities, into a more friendly territory, or to extend their business across state lines in order to be classed as interstate and therefore out of reach of the local authorities. These excursions are checkmated by Federal controls, which are uniform throughout the states, and there is much less likelihood of transfer to foreign territory, since the out-of-pocket costs and subsequent risks would be much greater.

Although no one knows exactly where the line is drawn between interstate and intrastate commerce, there is little doubt that the former has superseded the latter as a basis for governmental controls in many lines of activity previously regarded as local. The trend in all fields of regulation,

[23] 301 U.S. 1 (1937).
[24] *Muldowney v. Seaberg Elevator Co.*, 39 F. Supp. 275 (1941).
[25] *McComb v. Super-A-Fertilizer Works, Inc.*, U.S.C.C.A. 1st Jan. 27, 1948.

but most noticeably with respect to employment, is transfer of responsibility from state to Federal levels. The new interpretation of the commerce clause gives Congress a basis for exploring practically any form of economic activity and indicates that the courts are not likely to be a barrier to further extension of Federal controls over wages and employment.

The child labor amendment.   There has never been much public defense of child labor in this country, although there has been powerful unorganized opposition to Federal attempts to prohibit it. After the Supreme Court stopped Congress's first two moves in that direction (in *Hammer v. Dagenhart* and *Bailey v. Drexel Furniture*), the House and Senate passed a joint resolution proposing an amendment to the Federal Constitution which would permit Congress "to limit, regulate, and prohibit the labor of persons under 18 years of age." [26] Considering the ease and promptness with which Congress had legislated on the subject, the child labor amendment had a curious history.

Following a heated conflict in Massachusetts, where ratification was defeated by popular vote, state legislatures throughout the country turned almost solidly against the idea. Within two years there were only four affirmatives, although practically every state body considered the question. (The proposal was voted on by one or both legislative bodies of 31 states during the first year after action by Congress.) In 1927, Montana ratified, and Colorado voted "Yes" in 1931. The situation stood unchanged until 1933, when a sudden shift in sentiment brought 14 ratifications. Four more appeared in 1935 and another four in 1937 bringing the total up to 28 states as against a needed 36. [27]

With the passage of the Fair Labor Standards Act and its subsequent approval by the Supreme Court, the amendment passed out of the picture.

No one has been able to explain fully the difficulty the amendment encountered. There was always opposition in the farm states, where there was fear of interference with the use of unpaid family labor, but even the industrial states with good previous records of support for liberal legislation (like Massachusetts) voted it down. Probably as good a guess as any is to blame it on the times. The latter half of the 1920s was not a period of either demand or support for public regulation of any kind. The Harding-Coolidge-Hoover era was a period of "normalcy" and revival of belief in *laissez faire*. A sharp change in public thinking is reflected in the 14 ratifications which showed up in 1933 and the subsequent successful legislative moves by the Roosevelt administration.

Child labor is unpopular in the United States because it runs counter to the American belief in education. The real issue is work versus school, and the verdict, for the record at any rate, has never been in doubt. Every

[26] 43 Stat. 670 (1924).
[27] O. W. Phelps, *Legislative Background of the Fair Labor Standards Act* (Chicago: University of Chicago Press, 1939), p. 13.

state has a compulsory school-attendance law (the most efficient means of controlling the work of minors), and an equal number regulate the conditions of employment of young people. The customary school-leaving age in the state statutes was 14 (which would normally be at the end of grade school), but quite a few states now set it at 16 (end of the sophomore year in high school), like the Federal law. There are also rules concerning hazardous occupations (age 18, usually), 8-hour days, 40-hour weeks, night work, and the use of special permits.

Since the issue is work versus school and since free public education is provided through high school everywhere, with almost enough junior college facilities for everybody in some states (California, for example) and more than two-thirds of all boys and girls finishing high school now, a move to raise the legal minimum age of employment to 18 would not be surprising. It would be supported by educators everywhere, trade unionists (who would prefer to have the competition of minors removed from the labor market), and public sentiment in bad times, when employed children and unmarried women are accused of taking jobs away from the heads of families. Extensive regulation of child labor may be expected to continue and increase, as another step in the process of structuring the labor market, a development which has been proceeding rapidly in this country since 1930.

The shorter-hours movement.   There has been a good deal of confusion concerning the drive for shorter working hours in this country, especially in recent years. In the United States today and for the past quarter century, the hours question has been almost entirely a *wages* question. What employes want, by and large, is not shorter hours of work but shorter hours at basic rates of pay and more hours at time and a half or double time. Raising the wage rate has been an objective of the shorter-hours movement ever since Ira Steward started the agitation for an 8-hour day back in 1860. Even in those days, the philosophy of the reform was expressed in the widely quoted verse:

> Whether you work by the piece or the day,
> Decreasing the hours increases the pay.

Ninety years ago, or even twenty-five years ago, however, there were other important purposes to be secured. Industrial work prior to 1900 approximated the sunup-to-sundown routine of farm life, and work weeks of 60, 72, and 84 hours were common in mines, mills, factories, and on the railroads. Emergency stretches of 18 to 24 hours, or longer, like the swing shifts in steel mills, were commonplace, and outright physical exhaustion of workmen at the end of the day was taken for granted. Remnants of this treadmill discipline carried well into the twentieth century. At the beginning of the First World War, the normal work week for over a third of all manufacturing employes in the country was 60 hours or more; the steel industry did not abandon the 12-hour day and the 7-day week until 1923.[28]

The early legislation limiting hours of work had the aim of cutting down fatigue and exhaustion. It therefore applied only to women, children, or men in heavy or hazardous trades like mining, railroading, and manufacturing. The 16-hour-day law on the railroads, which required any train crew with 16 consecutive hours of work to tie up for 8 hours of rest, is an example. These laws set limits to the working day and are quite different from modern legislation, like the Federal wage and hour law, which limits only the number of hours which may be paid for at the regular rate.

The hours provisions of the Fair Labor Standards Act have increased the earnings of American workmen far more than its wage provisions. The great majority of working people were well above the 25-, 30-, and 40-cent minimums at the time they went into effect, and likewise with the $1 and $1.25 minimums, which succeeded them in 1956 and 1963. With full employment, however, the only practicable method of increasing the labor force may be through an increase of working hours. The Second World War was an example; large numbers of employes, especially in government and war industries, worked a regular 48-hour week, the last 8 hours of which was at time and a half.

The Fair Labor Standards Act was passed in 1938, and its provisions were based on the depression experience of the 1930s. Average working hours and wages had both fallen to very low levels. Five years after the law was passed, the country was in the middle of the Second World War and both wage and hour provisions were thoroughly unrealistic by comparison with standard practice throughout the country. This revealed one major weakness of the act from the standpoint of administration: the inflexibility of standards written into the law itself for the regulation of a dynamic, changing economy.

The important things to keep in mind with respect to any further suggestions for reduction of working hours (the AFL–CIO, for example, is on record as favoring a basic 30-hour week) is that it is a *wage* question which is being raised. The issue is: Should earnings be increased by public action and is that the way to do it, to wit, by reducing the length of the standard, straight-time workday? The essential feature of this method of wage control is its "spread-the-work" tendency. By raising the employer's labor costs for hours worked beyond the standard, the law encourages the introduction of additional shifts with additional employes. As a matter of fact, this was one of the primary aims of the Fair Labor Standards Act when it was passed in 1938. With 10 million unemployed, "spread-the-work" was a popular objective. Is it an appropriate wage-raising device

[28] "Hours of Work in Manufacturing, 1914–43," *Monthly Labor Review*, April, 1944.

in the 1960s, with a national policy of government-guaranteed full employment at high wages?

The economics of minimum-wage laws.   This is a subject on which there are vigorous and divergent views. In addition to the hazards of unconstitutionality and the problem of jurisdiction, proponents of minimum-wage legislation have also had to contend with economists who told them that what they were trying to do was all wrong. A typical denunciation is that of Professor George J. Stigler, who argues that the guaranteed minimum wage must fail to achieve its major objective of reducing poverty and can do little if anything to reduce the employers' control of wages.[29] Instead, he finds that the principal results will be (1) misallocation of resources, (2) reduction of aggregate employment, and (3) distortion of family incomes plus reduction of total earnings.

Starting with the proposition that "each worker receives the value of his marginal product under competition," he disposes of point 1 as follows:

If a minimum wage is effective, it must therefore have one of two effects: first, workers whose services are worth less than the minimum wages are discharged (and thus forced into unregulated fields of employment, or into unemployment or retirement from the labor force); or, second, the productivity of low-efficiency workers is increased. . . . The discharged workers will, at best, move to unregulated jobs where they will secure lower returns. Unless inefficient workers' productivity rises, therefore, the minimum wage reduces aggregate output, perhaps raises the earnings of those previously a trifle below the minimum, and reduces the earnings of those substantially below the minimum. These are undoubtedly the main allocational effects of a minimum wage in a competitive industry.

The effects on aggregate employment seem equally certain.

The higher the minimum wage, the greater will be the number of covered workers who are discharged. . . . Whatever the number [which no one knows], the direct unemployment is substantial and certain; and it fairly establishes the presumption that the net effects of the minimum wage on aggregate employment are adverse.

And finally: "One cannot expect a close relationship between the level of hourly wage rates and the amount of family income. Yet family income and needs are the fundamental factors in the problem of poverty." Stigler then catalogs four significant discrepancies: (1) Hourly rates are effective only if received, and minimum-wage laws force the least productive into unemployment. (2) Hourly and annual earnings are not closely related, and it is the annual total which must be improved. (3) Family earnings are a group total, with many households having one or more supplementary workers contributing to the joint income. (4) Individual wage rates are still less related to family needs, for which family income is the best criterion.

[29] "The Economics of Minimum Wage Legislation," *American Economic Review,* vol. 36, pp. 358–365.

Warning that low incomes cannot be increased without impairing incentives, Stigler recommends a program of "assistance to the poor with regard to their need [measured by family composition] but without regard to their occupation." As between grants of money and grants in kind, he suggests that the former is much simpler administratively but will probably fall short of its goal, while the latter, though complicated, might conceivably do away with malnutrition, bad housing, and illiteracy, at a much lower money cost. Employer domination of the labor market he ascribes to labor immobility, which "would be reduced substantially by public provision of comprehensive information on employment conditions in various areas and industries" and by vocational training and loans to cover moving costs.

Stigler's presentation is a classic example of the classic argument against interference with free exchange, based on the assumption of competition in the factor markets. It is a vigorous and imaginative restatement of the same arguments that Professor John B. Clark used in objecting to the first American minimum-wage law, enacted in Massachusetts in 1912.[30] Since that time, Clark, Taussig, Stigler, and others of like view have been steadily and progressively and consistently overruled by the force of public opinion acting through Congress and state legislatures. Why have such cogent arguments been disregarded? Why have such certain evils been visited on the wage-earning public?

Perhaps one explanation is that there have been two schools of thought on minimum wages. An apostle of the favorable approach was Sidney Webb, who wrote the following, more than a generation ago, in defense of the Massachusetts law:

If the employer cannot go below a common minimum rate, and is unable to grade the other conditions of employment down to the level of the lowest and most necessitous wage earner in his establishment, he is economically impelled to do his utmost to raise the level of efficiency of his workers, so as to get the best possible return for the fixed conditions.

The minimum wage tends steadily to drive business into those establishments which are most favorably situated, best equipped, and managed with the greatest ability, and to eliminate the incompetent or old-fashioned employer. It perpetually stimulates the selection of the most efficient workmen, the best equipped employers, and the most advantageous forms of industry. And these results are permanent and cumulative.[31]

Employers who do not pay a living wage, who drive their workers for long hours without rest under dangerous or unsanitary conditions so as to actu-

[30] "The Minimum Wage," *Atlantic Monthly*, 1913, pp. 289–294, cited in Paul H. Douglas, C. N. Hitchcock, and W. E. Atkins, *The Worker in Modern Economic Society* (Chicago: University of Chicago Press, 1923), p. 842.

[31] "The Economic Theory of a Legal Minimum Wage," *Journal of Political Economy*, December, 1912, pp. 977–978, 984–990, cited in Douglas, Hitchcock, and Atkins, *op. cit.*, pp. 842–843.

ally shorten their lives, are parasites. They are obtaining a supply of labor
for which they do not pay:

If workers thus used up were horses, the employers would have to provide, in addition to the daily modicum of food, shelter, and rest, the whole cost of breeding and
training the successive relays necessary to keep up their establishments. In the
case of free human beings . . . this capital value of the new generation of workers is placed gratuitously at his disposal, on payment merely of subsistence from
day to day. In thus deteriorating the physique, intelligence, and character of their
operatives, such trades are drawing on the capital stock of the nation.

Webb, it will be remembered, was an early exponent of the bargaining theory of wages. His argument rejects Stigler's preliminary statement
on the effect of competition in the labor market:

The mere fact that employers are at present paying lower wages than the proposed
minimum is no proof that the labor is not "worth" more to them and to the customers; for the wages of the lowest grade of labor are fixed, not by the "worth," in any
sense, but largely by the urgent necessities of the "marginal" man, or, rather, the
"marginal" woman. It may well be that, rather than go without the particular commodity produced, the community would willingly pay much more for it, and yet
consume as much or nearly as much of it, as it now does. Nevertheless, so long as
the wage earner can be squeezed down to a subsistence wage, or more correctly, a
parasitic wage, the pressure of competition will compel the employer so to squeeze
him, whether the consumer desires it or not.

Who is right, Stigler or Webb?

A conclusion on minimum-wage policy depends on the wage theory
underlying it. Stigler is a marginal productivity theorist. He assumes competition on the part of employers and employes in the labor market, and
if his assumption is correct, his conclusions follow logically from the premises. Webb, on the other hand, specifically denies the conclusions of the
marginalists (notwithstanding his unorthodox use of the word "marginal")
and argues that competition has quite different effects from those claimed
for it by the classicists, to wit, that "each worker receives the value of his
marginal product under competition."

Like many others, Stigler solves the problem by assuming it away.
The real issue is very simply stated: *Is* the labor market competitive, in
the sense required by customary price theory? The thing which is sold, the
terms of sale, the institutions of exchange, the character of the parties to
the transaction, all indicate a high degree of individuality with a broad
dispersion of prices (wage rates), except where the bargain is collective.
In the latter case there may be a uniformity of price and service equal to
that of a high competitive exchange. However, it is a spurious uniformity
and would probably not satisfy price theorists, when embodied in a collective agreement negotiated by a powerful labor monopoly (which as
often as not is dealing with an equally tightly knit and powerful group of
employers).

Labor, which must be delivered in person and is sold in a free society in the form of continuously renewed long-term contracts of indefinite tenure, can only by the grossest fiction be reduced to the impersonality demanded by the classical free-market analysis. Mobility and full knowledge alone would not satisfy the requirements of competition, even if Stigler's suggestions for increasing them were successful. The basic fact with respect to both employers and employes is that they organize, both formally and informally, and refuse to underbid their rivals.

It may be convenient, but it is hardly realistic, to disregard the 25 million trade unionists, civil servants, and members of professional associations like the American Association of University Professors, the Engineers and Architects Association, and the multitude of local and regional groupings of governmental, technical, and scientific employes, who are busy adding to the market structure in order to limit entry to their own trade, standardize pay and services to be performed, guarantee tenure, and resist dismissal for incompetence or for other reasons. The explanation of wage rates and earnings differentials in a situation where "a limited number of key bargains effectively influence the whole wage structure" [32] is not found in the intersection of supply-and-demand curves, but in the complex of political and economic pressures brought to bear by unions in negotiations, by the equally complicated pattern of employer resistance to wage increases and additional fringe benefits, and by the less tangible but sometimes overwhelmingly important noneconomic factors such as union security or local work rules. Both unions and employer associations are facts of life in the labor market. Minimum-wage laws are the equivalent of organization of the lowest-paid workers. What have been the results?

One study, made in 1950, of the effects of the new 75-cent minimum upon wages and employment in Southern sawmills, a notoriously low-pay industry, reported the following changes in average hourly earnings: [33]

Average hourly earnings	Per cent of all workers	
	Fall, 1949	March, 1950
Under 75 cents	69.2	8.2
75–79.9 cents	11.0	66.3
80–99.9 cents	11.4	16.0
$1 or more	8.4	9.5
	100.0	100.0

What happened to employment? It dropped 2 per cent, from 180,000 in the fall of 1949 to 176,000 in March, 1950. (Total United States employment fell $2\frac{1}{2}$ per cent at the same time.) What else happened? All wage

[32] Dunlop, *op. cit.*, for the wording, but the idea is now commonplace.
[33] *Monthly Labor Review*, September, 1950, p. 313.

scales moved upward, with the occupational differentials at the bottom of the list compressed. A substantial number of firms that had been operating more than 40 hours a week cut back to a 40-hour standard. A move towards mechanization of the industry was speeded up; laborsaving devices were installed in a number of mills. Some mills closed down, but still more new ones started up. The most prevalent hourly rates of pay in the fall of 1949 were 50 cents (16 per cent of total), 60 cents (20 per cent), and 65 cents (15 per cent). Six months later they were 75 cents (66 per cent of total) and 80 cents (7 per cent).

In August, 1955, Congress raised the legal minimum wage from 75 cents to $1, the new rate to take effect Mar. 1, 1956. Once more, a study was made of the effects in the Southern sawmill industry, as part of a national survey in preparation for a report to Congress. In the Southern sawmills, the average hourly earnings of production workers rose from 88 cents in October–December, 1955, to $1.06 in April, 1956, or an increase of 20 per cent. (The comparable rise in average hourly earnings in all manufacturing was from $1.92 to $1.96, or 2 per cent.) Employment in sawmills fell 4 per cent, while employment nationwide dropped 1 per cent. Average hours worked per week in sawmills decreased from 44 in the fall of 1955 to 41 in April, 1956, whereas hours worked for all manufacturing dropped from an average of 41.2 per week to 40.3 per week. The Bureau of Labor Statistics (which made the study) reported that: "About one-third of the employers interviewed by field agents . . . regarding changes in operations reported important adjustments at about the time of the minimum wage change. Such adjustments included major changes in production, plant layout, production standards, and substantial curtailment of operations." [34] If there was "substantial curtailment of operations," it did not show up in the statistics. "In the first six months of 1956 Southern sawmills produced 4,314 million board feet of southern pine as compared with 4,400 million in the corresponding period of 1955. Production of southern hardwood was 1,974 million board feet during the 1956 period as compared with 1,954 million in 1955." [35]

The general conclusions of the report were equally serene:

First, the minimum wage increase had not, by December 1956, resulted in any substantial changes in the economic situation of the nation as a whole, as measured in terms of trends in employment, unemployment, price levels, and other economic indicators. Second, it had not resulted in an increase in hourly earnings of high paid employees proportionate to the increase of earnings of workers previously paid less than $1.00 an hour. [Nevertheless] . . . in the short run . . . the $1.00 minimum wage apparently resulted in some increases in earnings of workers previously paid the minimum rate or more. [36]

[34] *Studies of the Economic Effects of the $1.00 Minimum Wage,* Wage and Hour and Public Contracts Division, U.S. Department of Labor, March, 1957, pp. 48–49.
[35] *Ibid.*
[36] *Ibid.,* pp. 4–5.

The 75-cent minimum wage was introduced in January, 1950, in the trough of the first postwar recession; the $1 minimum went into effect in March, 1956, during a period of unbroken high prosperity. Two swallows do not make a summer, nor do two studies prove a case. Nevertheless, the evidence developed in these investigations seems to fit the Webb model better than that of Stigler. The student should read the full 1957 report, which isolates several low-wage industries, contrasts national effects with regional (Southern) effects, and compares the results in low-wage with those in high-wage industries.

For what it is worth, he might consider the position of organized labor, argued as follows:

Organized labor and the Wage and Hour Law stand together on the same platform —decent pay and reasonable hours of work.

Organized labor fought to place the law on the statute books. It has helped to make it successful. It has protected it from those opponents who would destroy it with amendments or starve it with meagre appropriations.

For organized labor, the law has performed one important service. It has made safe from the competition of sweated labor the high American wage and hour standards which the working man has won after decades of united effort.

Every union man is in competition with every other worker in the country who is able to do his work. He is in competition, not only with those workers who happen to live in his community, but also with those who live in communities with lower labor standards. For it is to those places where men are willing to work for a pittance that unscrupulous employers swarm like flies around honey.

The Wage and Hour Law has hammered into the permanent structure of America a floor below which wages cannot fall and a ceiling above which the hours of the working man should not go without payment of overtime rates. These standards are country-wide. The sewing machine operator in New York need no longer fear that his job will vanish because his employer can no longer compete with the man who has run away to another State where he can work his labor 60 hours a week. . . .[37]

If the labor market is not competitive, or competition is blurred, as indicated in Fig. 15-3, then what conclusions may be drawn? Some are as follows:

1. The employer will have a range of rates that he may pay in each occupational classification and his decision as to the actual rate will be an "administrative" decision, which may be influenced only slightly, if at all, by the supply of labor available or by his own need for it. He may (many employers do) raise rates during substantial unemployment, or on the other hand, he may decline to increase them when employes are scarce (*i.e.*, refuse to "break the market").

2. The employer, uncertain about his marginal-cost situation, will naturally attempt to protect himself against loss by a safe margin.

[37] *Organized Labor and the Wage and Hour Law* (Washington: U.S. Government Printing Office, 1941).

3.   The figure arrived at will be strongly influenced by nonrational and non-labor-market pressures: a "united front" of employers, current profitability of the firm, changes in living costs, background and character of the employes (for example, farm labor versus skilled craftsmen), regional tradition (Negro employment in the South), extent and type of labor organization, etc.

4.   One of the more powerful nonrational influences will be the bargaining positions of the two parties, which are usually very unequal in the case of the individual (unorganized) employe.

5.   An employer-administered wage schedule is an open invitation to exploitation and unfair advantage. It is the line of least resistance and, as Webb argued, discourages emphasis upon other avenues to business profits: operating efficiency, aggressive salesmanship, technological improvements. A minimum wage, set well below the market average, may be a deterrent to some of the worst forms of "sweating" and may increase the earnings of the covered employes without any noticeable decrease in their numbers. The evidence with respect to the operation of the Fair Labor Standards Act is substantially of this nature.

At the same time, it would be well to keep in mind the warnings. Employers cannot pay more for workers than they are worth in terms of the market demand for what they produce. It follows that at some level a required minimum rate will result in considerable unemployment. It is also true that certain classes of employes and many individual workers have very low productivity and earning power, but that is no good reason for their exclusion from employment. These exceptions to the general rule are recognized in the usual statutory provisions for substandard wage permits for learners, apprentices, and handicapped workers. Unfortunately, there are many employes who are substandard in productivity who are not easily identified as belonging to these three groups. It is important to keep the guaranteed minimum wage low enough to be sure that it does not bar large groups of workers from the market.

MINIMUM–WAGE ENFORCEMENT

Federal wage-hour and child-labor enforcement is the responsibility of the Wage and Hour and Public Contracts Divisions of the U.S. Department of Labor. This is no place for a review of the many technicalities which arise in the enforcement of a comprehensive public law. However, no student of labor problems should fail to comprehend some of the dimensions of the problem of applying standards of employment to close to 1 million firms employing 28 million workers. In its day-to-day application, the Fair Labor Standards Act is one of the most sweeping regulatory laws in the United States Code. The figures on enforcement activities of the Wage and Hour and Public Contracts Divisions at least give a brief

Table 16-1. Minimum-wage and overtime pay enforcement, 1955–1964
(dollar totals rounded)

Fiscal year		Number of firms investigated	Employes underpaid (less than the minimum and less than the legal overtime)	Back wages owed (000's)	Restitution made	
					Amount (000's)	Employes
75¢ mini- mum	1955	39,330	144,900	$ 12,151	$ 6,165	81,330
	1956	33,148	124,699	11,086	6,052	74,762
$1.00 mini- mum	1957	48,482	216,266	18,834	9,211	110,379
	1958	53,796	194,141	19,655	10,954	116,797
	1959	54,916	208,107	22,403	12,886	124,046
	1960	45,729	217,999	28,033	13,895	119,373
	1961	44,268	239,809	30,943	14,478	121,924
$1.15 mini- mum	1962	44,115	251,701	34,004	16,175	136,558
	1963	54,331	376,119	49,111	20,170	176,260
$1.25	1964	56,370	440,693	59,709	22,734	189,048
	Total	474,485	2,414,434	$285,920	$132,720 (46%)	1,250,477 (52%)

Source: *52nd Annual Report of the U.S. Department of Labor* (1964), p. 193.

profile of what minimum wage standards, overtime work regulations, and limitation of child labor mean in fact.

The first thing to understand is that the Divisions' work must be selective, a sampling process; they can never check up on all the companies that the law applies to. For example, the annual report for 1964 explains that a total of 56,370 "investigations" were made during the year,[38] or about 1 in 16 of the firms with covered employes. The Divisions therefore rely on the basic principle of British-American law enforcement which is that the great majority of the population will obey the rules voluntarily and that compulsion need be used against only a marginal fringe of violators. Unquestionably this assumption is correct as regards labor-market regulations. However, the fringe is there and the violations were numerous enough, even in the high-wage, full-employment decade of 1955 to 1964, to justify the supervision provided by the Divisions. A summary of 10 years of minimum-wage and overtime violations with back-pay restitution is given above in Table 16-1.

Summarized, the table shows that in 10 years of enforcement, the Wage and Hour and Public Contracts Divisions checked up on 474,485 firms and discovered that 2,414,434 of the employes had been underpaid, either in basic rates below the legal minimum in effect at the time or by failure to receive overtime after 40 hours of work per week. The total amount of the underpayment was $285,920,000—more than a quarter of a

[38] *52nd Annual Report of the U.S. Department of Labor,* fiscal year 1964, p. 186.

billion dollars. By explanation, negotiation, threat of prosecution, and prosecution itself, the Divisions were able to persuade employers to make restitution to 1,250,477 employes (52 per cent of those with valid claims), totaling $132,720,000, or 46 per cent of the wages due. Infractions were discovered in every section of the country, but were more frequent in the South and Southwest, which in 1963 to 1964 accounted for 46 per cent of the violations, as compared to 25 per cent of nonagricultural employment and 29 per cent of the population.[39]

Recent child labor violations. Many people are under the impression that children are no longer illegally employed in industry in the United States. That this impression is erroneous is illustrated by some of the child labor findings to determine compliance with the Fair Labor Standards Act. Some of the data:

1. During the year 1963 to 1964, there were 21,006 minors discovered to be illegally employed, 7,972 of them on farms and 13,034 in business firms.

2. On farms, 71 per cent were under 14 years of age; off the farm, 57 per cent were under 16 years of age and 43 per cent were 16 or 17 years old but employed in hazardous occupations.

3. Sample occupations in the underage group as disclosed in past reports: a 9-year-old boy turning logs in a lumber mill, a 13-year-old girl peeling tomatoes in a cannery, youngsters 8 and 11 cleaning bricks for a construction firm, a 12-year-old girl cutting peaches in a commercial dry yard, and a 13-year-old boy hanging chickens on a conveyor for a poultry-processing plant.

4. Examples of employment of 16- and 17-year-olds in hazardous occupations: hoist operator for a cotton gin, chain-saw operator in a logging operation, helper on a killing floor of a meat-packing house, operator of a 20-ton punch press in a tool and die factory.

5. Underage employes killed or seriously injured: a 16-year-old truck driver killed when a load of pulpwood crushed the cab of his truck, a 14-year-old boy whose arm had to be amputated after his hand had been caught in a meat grinder in a slaughterhouse, a 16-year-old boy struck by a falling tree in a logging camp, his skull fractured and unconscious for 6 weeks, amputation of the right arm of a 17-year-old boy whose hand got caught in a power-driven cutting machine he was operating in a wood-box manufacturing plant.

From the humanitarian standpoint, if from no other, it is hardly to be doubted that minimum-wage, maximum-hour, and child labor regulation in the United States has been a great assistance to many of the lowest-paid (some of them clearly exploited) employes in America. It should be re-

[39] *Ibid.,* p. 194. The 15 states included in the South and Southwest are: Virginia, West Virginia, Kentucky, Tennessee, North Carolina, South Carolina, Georgia, Florida, Alabama, Mississippi, Louisiana, Texas, Arkansas, Oklahoma, and New Mexico.

membered that the number of firms and employes and the amount of restitution shown above in Table 16-1 are a very inadequate measure of the over-all effects of the legislation. Unquestionably, the great majority of employers affected complied promptly upon passage of the act, and many more were brought into line by knowledge of inspections and enforcement activities. No investigation conducted since the law went into effect has supplied convincing proof of undue hardship, bankruptcy, or flight of capital. In the absence of such proof, the principal effect of the policy was to add several hundred millions of dollars to the incomes of very low-paid wage earners through the minimum-wage provisions and to increase the earnings of employes at all levels of pay by some incalculable amount through the overtime pay regulations.

All this took place during a period of generally full employment accompanied by a rising standard of living. At a different time and under different conditions the results might not have been the same. With a falling wage and price level the law might have added to unemployment and lowered total earnings. However, there are two schools of thought and two lines of argument on this subject too, and the trend in public policy, at least, is more in line with the wage-support point of view.

READINGS

Annual Reports of the Wage and Hour and Public Contracts Divisions of the U.S. Department of Labor for the last few years included as a section of the Department's report. These are brief, pithy, and interesting. A useful written exercise is to summarize one of these reports in a three-page or five-page essay.

Congressional debates on the Fair Labor Standards bill of 1937 (not passed), on the Fair Labor Standards Act of 1938, and on each of the minimum-wage increases: to 75 cents in 1949, to $1 in 1955, to $1.15–$1.25 in 1961.

Studies of the Economic Effects of the $1.00 Minimum Wage, March, 1957, by the Wage and Hour and Public Contracts Divisions of the U.S. Department of Labor.

For background material on these and other forms of pay regulation: J. R. Commons and J. B. Andrews, *Principles of Labor Legislation*, 4th rev. ed. (New York: Harper & Row, Publishers, Incorporated, 1936). This was the last edition; it is still the best single background source up to 1936.

O. W. Phelps, *The Legislative Background of the Fair Labor Standards Act* (Chicago: University of Chicago Press, 1939), for the growth of national sentiment in the form of statutes, constitutional amendments, and court decisions, which led up to the 1938 law.

One or more of the big court decisions of the past in each area: wages, hours, and child labor. For example: *Lochner v. New York* (hours), *Hammer v. Dagenhart* (child labor), and *Adkins v. Children's Hospital* (wages). See p. 523 for citations. For further study, compare two diverse opinions, such as *Ritchie v. People* and *Holden v. Hardy*, which take opposite sides on the question of maximum hours of work.

INDEX